7

Exploring Creation

with

General Science
2nd Edition

by Dr. Jay L. Wile

Exploring Creation With General Science, 2nd Edition

Published by
Apologia Educational Ministries, Inc.
1106 Meridian Plaza, Suite 220
Anderson, IN 46016
www.apologia.com

Manufactured in the United States of America
Sixth Printing, April 2013

ISBN: 978-1-932012-86-6

Printed by Courier, Inc., Kendallville, IN

All Biblical quotations are from the New American Standard Bible (NASB) unless otherwise stated

Full copyright statement for all images marked "© Lippincott, Williams, and Wilkins":
© 2007 Wolters Kluwer Health | Lippincott Williams and Wilkins

Any photo not credited in the text was done by the author.

Cover photos © Stockbyte (boy with test tube), © Mirka Moksha (crystals),
© Bryan Brazil (Grand Canyon), © Sascha Burkard (petrified wood), © Linda Bucklin (muscle man)

[Agency for all except Stockbyte: shutterstock.com, Agency for Stockbyte: Getty Images]

Cover design by Kim Williams

Need Help?

Apologia Educational Ministries, Inc., Curriculum Support

If you have any questions while using Apologia curriculum,
feel free to contact us in any of the following ways:

 By Mail: Curriculum Help
Apologia Educational Ministries, Inc.
1106 Meridian Plaza, Suite 220/340
Anderson, IN 46016

 By E-MAIL: help@apologia.com

 On the Web: http://www.apologia.com

 By FAX: (765) 608 - 3290

 By Phone: (765) 608 - 3280

Science.... what images does that word conjure up in your head? Is science dull and boring? Is it too hard for most people? Is it something that only nerds like? Well, in this course, you will begin to find out the answers to those questions. You will learn about the history of science, how to do science, the history of life, how your body works, and some of the amazing living creatures that exist in God's Creation. Like anything worth doing, this course will be hard work, but in the end, you will find it interesting and (hopefully) enjoyable. More than anything else, however, be prepared to be awed and amazed with what the Creator has made for **you!**

Pedagogy of the Text

This text contains 16 modules. Each module should take you about two weeks to complete, as long as you devote 30 to 45 minutes of every school day to studying science. At this pace, you will complete the course in 32 weeks. Since most people have school years that are longer than 32 weeks, there is some built-in "flex time." You should not rush through a module just to make sure you complete it in two weeks. Set that as a goal, but be flexible. Some of the modules might come harder to you than others. On those modules, take more time on the subject matter.

How will you know how much time per day to spend studying science? Well, start out working 30 minutes per day on the course. At the end of two weeks, see where you are. If you are done with the first module, you know 30 minutes per day is the right amount of time. If you aren't done with the module, you know you need to spend more time per day. Continue to change the amount of time per day until you find what it takes to cover a module in two weeks.

To help you guide your study, there are two sets of student exercises you should complete:

> The "On Your Own" questions should be answered as you read the text. The act of answering these questions will cement in your mind the concepts you are trying to learn. Answers to these questions appear at the end of the module. Once you have answered an "On Your Own" question, turn to the end of the module and check your work. If you did not get the correct answer, study the answer to learn why.

> You should answer the questions in the Study Guide at the end of the module *after* you have completed the module. This will allow you to review the important concepts from the module and help you prepare for the test.

Answers for the Study Guide questions, the tests, and test solutions for this course can be found in the Solutions and Tests for Exploring Creation with General Science manual.

Any information you should understand is centered in the text and put in boldface type. In addition, all definitions presented in the text should be memorized. Words that appear in boldface type (centered or not) in the text are important terms you should know. Some of the information in the course is presented in the form of tables or figures. Whether or not you will be given such information on the test depends on the information itself. If the study guide says you can use a particular figure or table, you will also be able to use that figure or table on the test. If a study guide question requires you to know the information in a table or figure and the study guide does not say you can use it, you will not be able to use it on the test.

Learning Aids

Multimedia Companion CD: This graphic throughout the book indicates that there is additional material on the CD relating to the current subject that you are studying. This CD contains videos of many things that you have probably not seen before, such as microscopic organisms. These videos will help you better understand concepts in the course. It has animated white board solutions of example problems, such as the mechanical advantage problems you must solve in Module 4. The CD also contains audio pronunciations of the technical words used in this book.

Course Website: In addition to the multimedia companion CD, there is a special website for this course that you can visit. The website contains links to web-based materials related to the course. These links are arranged by module, so if you are having trouble with a particular subject in the course, you can go to the website and look at the links for that module. Most likely, you will find help there. Finally, if you are enjoying a particular module in the course and would like to learn more about it, there are links to interesting websites that will allow you to learn more about the subject matter being discussed. To visit the website, go to the following address:

http://www.apologia.com/bookextras

When you get to the address, you will be asked for a password. Type the following into the password box:

Godisthecreator

Be sure that you do not put spaces between any of the letters and that the first letter is capitalized. When you click on the button labeled "Log In," you will see a link that will send you to the course website.

Student Notebook: You can purchase a Student Notebook to aid you in your studies. This notebook contains a daily student schedule and space for your personal notes. It has the questions and space for your answers to the On Your Own, Study Guide, and Summary questions. It has additional exercises for you to do to help you "dig deeper" into a subject, and it includes Scriptural materials to help you appreciate all of God's creation in your studies. The notebook also has lab report pages for each experiment found in the text.

Back of your textbook: There are also several items at the end of the book that you will find useful in your studies. There is a **glossary** that defines many of the terms used in the course and an **index** that will tell you where topics can be found in the course. In addition, there are three appendices in the course. **Appendix A** compiles some of the tables and figures that are found throughout the reading. **Appendix B** contains a Summary of each module in the course. These Summaries are presented as fill-in-the-blank exercises and practice problems. If you are having trouble studying for the tests, these Summaries might help you. Answers for the Summary questions for this course can be found in the Solutions and Tests for Exploring Creation with General Science manual. **Appendix C** contains a complete list of all the supplies you need to perform the experiments in this course.

Helpline: The beginning of your textbook lists ways for you to contact us directly if you have any questions while using Apologia curriculum.

Experiments

The experiments in this course are to be completed as you are reading the text. You need to keep a notebook that documents these experiments. As you write about each experiment in your notebook, you will be forced to think through all of the concepts explored in that experiment. This will help you cement these concepts into your mind. There is a recommended Student Notebook for this course. The lab report pages found in this notebook will help you understand the proper use of the scientific method. You should perform the experiments in the following way:

➢ When you get to an experiment, read through it in its entirety. This will allow you to gain a quick understanding of what you are to do.

➢ Following the scientific method, document your experiment as follows:

- o Objective or Purpose: In paragraph form, describe the purpose of the experiment. Why are you doing this experiment? What do you hope to discover or learn?

- o Hypothesis: After you have thought about the purpose of the experiment (and do a little research if necessary), you should be able to make an educated guess about what will happen.

- o Materials: List all of the materials you actually used to perform the experiment.

- o Procedure: In your own words, and in complete sentences, write a paragraph explaining what you actually did to complete the experiment.

- o Data and Observations – Record all of the data that you collect during the experiment in a data table.

- o Results: This should be a sentence or two that explains what your data show.

- o Discussion and Conclusions: This is the most important section of your report. Write a good paragraph or two explaining why you think you got the results that you did.

The experiments are designed to use household items. To give you the ability to prepare for the experiments, Appendix C lists the items you will need to perform the experiments in each module. Before you begin a module, then, look at Appendix C to make sure you have everything you will need.

PLEASE OBSERVE COMMON SENSE SAFETY PRECAUTIONS!
The experiments in this course are no more dangerous than most normal, household activity. Remember, however, that the vast majority of accidents do happen in the home. Chemicals used in the experiments should never be ingested; hot items and flames should be regarded with care; and all experiments should be performed while wearing eye protection such as safety glasses or goggles.

Exploring Creation With General Science
Table of Contents

MODULE #1: A Brief History of Science

Introduction

This course will take you on a tour of what I consider to be the most interesting of all human endeavors: **science**. Now, of course, I am well aware that many people (perhaps even you) do not think science is interesting. Nevertheless, I do believe that most people's dislike of science comes from bad curriculum and/or bad teachers, not the subject itself. Hopefully, as you go through this course, you will see why I find science so incredibly interesting, and if nothing else, you will at least develop an appreciation for this fascinating field of study.

So what is science, anyway? Well, the word "science" comes from the Latin word "scientia" (sye en' tee uh), which means "to have knowledge." It can be generally defined as follows:

Science – An endeavor dedicated to the accumulation and classification of observable facts in order to formulate general laws about the natural world

That's a nice definition, but what does it mean? It means that the *purpose* of science is to develop general laws that explain how the world around us works and why things happen the way they do. How do we accomplish such a feat? That's where the "accumulation and classification of observable facts" comes in. The *practice* of science involves experimentation and observation. Scientists observe the world around them and collect facts. They also design experiments that alter the circumstances they are observing, which in turn leads to the collection of more facts. These facts might eventually allow scientists to learn enough about the world around them so they can develop ideas that help us understand how the natural world works.

As is the case with any other field, the only way to truly understand where we are in science today is to look at what happened in the past. The history of science can teach us many lessons about how science should and should not be practiced. It can also help us understand the direction in which science is heading today. In the end, then, no one should undertake a serious study of science without first taking a look at its history. That's where we will start in the course. This module will provide you with a brief history of human scientific inquiry. If you do not like history, please stick with this module. You will start to sink your teeth into science in the next module. Without a historical perspective, however, you will not fully appreciate what science is.

The First Inklings of Science (From Ancient Times to 600 B.C.)

Some of the earliest records from history indicate that 3,000 years before Christ, the ancient Egyptians already had reasonably sophisticated medical practices. Sometime around 2650 B.C., for example, a man named **Imhotep** (eem' oh tep) was renowned for his knowledge of medicine. People traveled from all over the Middle East to visit Imhotep, hoping he would cure their illnesses.

Most historians agree that the heart of Egyptian medicine was trial and error. Egyptian doctors would try one remedy, and if it worked, they would continue to use it. If a remedy they tried didn't work, the patient might die, but at least the doctors learned that next time they should try a different remedy. Despite the fact that such practices sound primitive, the results were, sometimes, surprisingly effective. For example, Egyptian doctors learned that if you covered an open wound with moldy bread, the wound would heal quickly and cleanly. As a result, most Egyptian doctors applied moldy bread to their patients' wounds. Modern science tells us that certain bread molds produce **penicillin**, a chemical that kills germs that infect wounds! Thus, even though the Egyptian doctors knew *nothing* about germs, they were able to treat wounds in a way that helped avoid infections!

Another example of the surprisingly effective art of ancient Egyptian medicine can be seen in the way they treated pain. In order to relieve a patient who was in pain, Egyptian doctors would feed the patient seeds from a flowering plant called the **poppy**. Eating these **poppy seeds** seemed to relieve the patient's pain. Modern science tells us *why* this worked. Poppy seeds contain both **morphine** and **codeine**, which are excellent pain-relieving drugs still used today!

Mold photo © Iconex
Agency: www.shutterstock.com

FIGURE 1.1
Natural Remedies Used By Ancient Egyptians

Poppy photo © Tihis
Agency: www.shutterstock.com

Since some bread molds produce germ-fighting chemicals, they can aid in healing wounds.

Poppy seeds (and other parts of the plant) contain chemicals that help relieve pain.

Why was Egyptian medicine advanced compared to the medicine of other ancient nations? Well, at least one reason was the Egyptian invention of **papyrus** (puh pye' rus).

Papyrus – An ancient form of paper, made from a plant of the same name

As early as 3,000 years before Christ, Egyptians took thin slices of the stem of the papyrus plant, laid them crosswise on top of each other, moistened them, and then pressed and dried them. The result was a form of paper that was reasonably easy to write on and store.

The invention of this ancient form of paper revolutionized the way information was transmitted from person to person and generation to generation. Before papyrus, Egyptians, Sumerians, and other races wrote on clay tablets or smooth rocks. This was a time-consuming process, and the products were not easy to store or transport. When Egyptians began writing on papyrus, all of that changed.

Papyrus was easy to roll into scrolls. Thus, Egyptian writings became easy to store and transport. As a result, the knowledge of one scholar could be easily transferred to other scholars. As this accumulated knowledge was passed down from generation to generation, Egyptian medicine became the most respected form of medicine in the known world!

Although the Egyptians were renowned for their medicine and for papyrus, other cultures had impressive inventions of their own. Around the time that papyrus was first being used in Egypt, the Mesopotamians were making pottery using the first known potter's wheel. Not long after, horse-drawn chariots were being used. As early as 1,000 years before Christ, the Chinese were using compasses to aid themselves in their travels. The ancient world, then, was filled with inventions that, although they sound commonplace today, revolutionized life during those times. These inventions are history's first inklings of science.

As you progress through this course, you will see that it is divided into sections. Usually, at the end of each section, you will find one or two "On Your Own" questions. You should answer these questions as soon as you come to them in the reading. They are designed to make you think about what you have just read. These questions are often not very easy to answer, because you cannot simply look back over the reading and find the answer. You must *think* about what you have learned and make some conclusions in order to answer the question. You will find your first such question below. Answer it on a separate sheet of paper and then check your answer against the solution provided at the end of this module.

ON YOUR OWN

1.1 Although the ancient Egyptians had reasonably advanced medical practices for their times, and although there were many inventions that revolutionized life in the ancient world, most historians of science do not think of Egyptian doctors and ancient inventors as scientists. Why? (Hint: Look at the entire definition of science.)

True Science Begins to Emerge (600 B.C. to 500 A.D.)

As far as historians can tell, the first true scientists were the ancient Greeks. Remember, science consists of collecting facts and observations and then using those observations to explain the natural world. Although many cultures like the ancient Egyptians, Mesopotamians, and Chinese had collected observations and facts, they had not tried to use those facts to develop explanations of the world around them. As near as historians can tell, that didn't happen until the 6th century B.C., with three individuals known as **Thales**, **Anaximander** (an axe' uh man der), and **Anaximenes** (an axe' uh me' neez). Many historians view these three individuals as humanity's first real scientists.

Thales studied the heavens and tried to develop a unifying theme that would explain the movement of the heavenly bodies (the planets and stars). He was at least partially successful, as history tells us he used his ideas to predict certain planetary events. For example, he gained a great reputation throughout the known world when he correctly predicted the "short-term disappearance of the sun." What he predicted, of course, was a solar eclipse, an event in which the moon moves between the earth and the sun, mostly blocking the sun from view.

Anaximander was probably a pupil of Thales. He was much more interested in the study of life, however. As far as we know, he was the first scientist who tried to explain the origin of the human race without reference to a creator. He believed that all life began in the sea, and at one time, humans were actually some sort of fish. This idea was later resurrected by other scientists, most notably Charles Darwin, and is today called evolution. Later on in this course, I will discuss evolution, showing how the data we currently have do not support it.

Anaximenes was probably an associate of Anaximander. He believed that air was the most basic substance in nature. In fact, he believed all things were constructed of air. When air is thinned out, he thought, it grows warm and becomes fire. When air is thickened, he thought, it condenses into liquid and solid matter. We know, of course, that these ideas are wrong. Nevertheless, his attempts to explain all things in nature as being made of a single substance led to one of the most important scientific ideas introduced by the Greeks: the concept of **atoms**.

Leucippus (loo sip' us) was a Greek scientist who lived perhaps 100 to 150 years after Anaximenes. Although little is known about him, historians believe that he built on the concepts of Anaximenes and proposed that all matter is composed of little units called "atoms." As a result, Leucippus is known as the father of atomic theory. The works of his student **Democritus** (duh mah' crit us) are much better preserved.

Democritus used the following illustration to communicate his ideas about atoms: Think about walking towards a sandy beach. When you are a long way from the beach, the sand looks like a smooth, yellow blanket. As you get closer to the beach, you might notice that there are bumps and valleys in the sand, but the sand still looks solid. When you reach the beach and actually kneel down and examine the sand, you find that it is not solid at all. Instead, it is composed of tiny particles called "grains."

Democritus believed that all matter was similar to sand. Even though a piece of wood appears to be solid, it is, in fact, made up of little individual particles that Democritus and his teacher called atoms. Perform the following experiment to see the kind of observation best explained using the concept of atoms.

EXPERIMENT 1.1
Density in Nature

Supplies

- Vegetable oil
- Water
- Maple or corn syrup
- A grape
- A piece of cork
- An ice cube
- A small rock
- A tall glass
- Eye protection such as goggles or safety glasses

Introduction: Observations such as the ones you will make in this experiment are easy to explain when you assume the existence of atoms.

Procedure:

1. Take the glass and fill it about ¼ of the way with the vegetable oil.
2. Add an equal amount of water to the glass.
3. Add an equal amount of maple syrup to the glass.
4. Now look at the glass from the side. What do you see? In your laboratory notebook, make a sketch of what you see.
5. Drop the rock, the grape, the ice cube, and the piece of cork into the glass. Now what do you see? Add the rock, grape, ice cube, and cork to the sketch you made in step 4.
6. Clean up your mess and put everything away.

What did you see in the experiment? If everything went well, you should have seen that the liquids formed layers in the glass. The vegetable oil formed a layer on top, the water layer was in the middle, and the syrup layer was at the bottom. In addition, the cork should have floated on top of the vegetable oil; the ice cube should have floated on top of the water layer; the grape should have floated on top of the syrup layer, and the rock should have sunk to the bottom of the glass.

How in the world is this experiment evidence for the existence of atoms? Well, according to Democritus, the water, vegetable oil, and syrup are all made of individual particles called atoms. The way those atoms are packed together will determine each object's characteristics. For example, assuming that the atoms in water are packed more closely than those in vegetable oil, the water will be able to pass between the atoms in the vegetable oil, sinking to the bottom of the glass. In the same way, the atoms in the syrup are more tightly packed than those in water or vegetable oil, so the syrup's atoms were able to fall in between the atoms of both the vegetable oil and the water to land at the bottom of the glass.

Even solid objects are made up of atoms. Thus, the cork's atoms are packed together very loosely. As a result, the cork doesn't have much weight and cannot push its way through the atoms in the vegetable oil. That's why it floats on top of the vegetable oil. The atoms in the ice cube, however, are more tightly packed and make the ice cube heavy enough to push the atoms in vegetable oil out of the way. This allows it to sink through the vegetable oil. However, they are not tightly packed enough to allow the ice cube to push through the atoms in the water.

If substances were not composed of smaller particles (like atoms), it would be hard to understand how one substance could pass through another substance. However, if you imagine every substance to be made up of little grains (like sand), then passing through a substance would just be a matter of fitting between the grains or pushing the grains out of the way. Thus, if you assume the existence of atoms, results of experiments like the one you just did are easy to understand.

At this point, I am done discussing the experiment. Now that you know what the experiment shows, you can write a summary of it in your laboratory notebook. Write a brief description of what you did, followed by a discussion of what you learned. The goal you should have in mind is that someone who has never read this book should be able to read your laboratory notebook and understand what you did and what you learned. You should do this for *every* experiment.

Democritus was not well received in his time, but later scientists picked up on his ideas and refined them. Today, we know that all matter is made up of atoms. Indeed, today we can actually calculate how atoms pack together to make a given substance. This allows us to understand the concept of **density**, which describes how tightly packed the matter in a substance is. The more tightly packed the matter that makes up a substance, the higher its density. In your experiment, then, the syrup had a higher density than the water.

FIGURE 1.2
Democritus

Image in the public domain

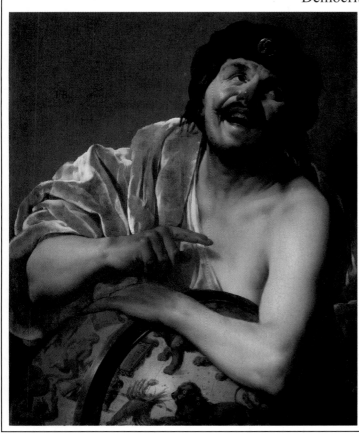

We don't really know what Democritus looked like, but this is how Dutch painter Hendrick ter Brugghen imagined him. He was called the "Laughing Philosopher," but no one is exactly sure why. Some suggest it is because he considered cheerfulness to be an important goal in life. Others suggest it is because he was prone to laugh when he thought someone else was making a stupid mistake.

Although Democritus was right about all things being composed of atoms, he was wrong about most of the details regarding what atoms are really like. He believed, for example, that atoms are indestructible. We now know that is wrong. After all, the atomic bomb and nuclear energy are both based on our ability to split atoms. He also thought that atoms were distinguished based on their shape and size. We now know it is a *lot* more complicated than that.

While Democritus was wrong on many of the details related to atoms, there was one detail he got right. He thought that atoms were in constant motion. For example, if a glass of water is sitting on a table, you might think the water is not in motion. To some extent, you would be right. After all, the water in the glass stays in the glass, and the glass itself stays on the table. At the same time, however, the atoms that make up the water are in *constant* motion. They move around within the confines of the glass, rebounding off the walls of the glass and colliding into each other. You might find it hard to believe that the atoms within a glass of water are in motion when the water itself is not. However, you might find it a little easier to believe after performing the following experiment.

EXPERIMENT 1.2
Atomic Motion

Supplies:

- Two glass canning jars or peanut butter jars (both the same size)
- Food coloring (any color)
- A pan and stove to boil water, and a hotpad to hold the pan
- Eye protection such as goggles or safety glasses

Introduction: By seeing how food coloring gets distributed through two jars of water at different temperatures, you will collect evidence for the fact that atoms are in constant motion.

Procedure:

1. Boil some water. You need to boil enough to fill one of the jars about halfway.
2. Once the water is boiling, take it off the stove (use the hotpad!) and pour it into one of the jars. Pour in enough water so that the jar is about half full.
3. Fill the other jar about halfway with cold water from the tap.
4. Wait until the water in each jar is still.
5. Drop a single drop of food coloring into each jar. Observe what happens over the next several minutes. Record in your laboratory notebook the difference between what happened in each jar.
6. **OPTIONAL**: Let the jar with the cold water sit out for a full day. Record what the jar looks like afterward.
7. Clean up your mess.

What did you see in the experiment? If everything went well, you should have seen the drop of food coloring mix rapidly with the hot water, coloring the entire jar of water relatively quickly. In the jar of cold water, however, the food coloring should not have mixed well at all. Why was there a difference? The answer is found in the motion of atoms. When a substance is hot, its atoms move faster than when it is cold. When you added food coloring to the cold water, then, the atoms in the water collided with the atoms in the food coloring, moving them around. However, since the atoms in the cold water were not moving very quickly, the food coloring did not get moved around much, so it did not mix well with the water. Given enough time, the food coloring will mix well with the water, eventually becoming evenly distributed throughout the jar. When you added the food coloring to the hot water, however, the collisions between the atoms in the food coloring and the atoms in the water were much more violent, because the atoms in the water were moving much more quickly. This moved the atoms in the food coloring around quite a bit, spreading them out evenly throughout the jar of water in a short amount of time.

In the end, then, even though Democritus was wrong about a great many things, he was right about two important ideas. First, all things are, indeed, composed of atoms. Second, those atoms are in constant motion. Now as I said before, Democritus was not well received in his time. Most of his fellow scientists rejected his ideas. In fact, the whole idea of the existence of atoms did not gain much popular support among scientists for almost 2,000 years! This just goes to show you that scientists do not always recognize a good idea when they see one. In fact, the history of science is filled with instances of scientists rejecting good ideas in favor of bad ones. You will see more examples of that as you work through the rest of this course.

ON YOUR OWN

1.2 Based on your results in Experiment 1.1, order the items you used in your experiment (water, vegetable oil, the grape, etc.) in terms of increasing density. In other words, list the item with the lowest density first, followed by items of higher and higher density, and end your list with the item of greatest density.

1.3 Do the atoms in an ice cube move faster or slower than the atoms in a glass of water?

Three Other Notable Greek Scientists

Ancient Greece gave us many more notable scientists. It is impossible to discuss them all in a single chapter, but there are three more that simply must be mentioned. The first is **Aristotle**, often called the father of the life sciences. Aristotle was born shortly before Democritus died. He wrote volumes of works on many things, including philosophy, mathematics, logic, and physics. His greatest work, however, was in the study of living things. He was the first to make a large-scale attempt at the **classification** of animals and plants.

What is classification? It is a lot like filing papers. Remember, science is a two-part process. A scientist must gather facts and then use those facts to draw conclusions about how the natural world works. As you gather more and more facts, they tend to get hard to use unless they can be ordered in some reasonable, systematic way. That's what classification is all about. By the time of Aristotle, Greek scientists had catalogued many plants and animals, but there were so many that keeping track of them was proving to be very difficult. Aristotle came up with a classification scheme that allowed him to group the known plants and animals into an easy-to-reference system. Because Aristotle was financially supported by **Alexander the Great** (you should have read about him in your history books), he was able to obtain plant and animal samples from all over the known world, adding those to his classification scheme.

Although we do not use Aristotle's particular classification scheme today, all fields of science are still committed to the concept of classification. Indeed, scientists who study living things today are still wrestling with producing the ideal classification system for understanding the life sciences. In a future module of this course, you will get a brief introduction to biological classification. You will then see a *lot* more of it when you reach biology in high school.

Although Aristotle was known for a great number of wonderful advances in the sciences, he was also responsible for a great deal of nonsense that hampered science for many, many years. For example, he believed that certain living organisms spontaneously formed from non-living substances. This idea was called **spontaneous generation**.

Spontaneous generation – The idea that living organisms can be spontaneously formed from non-living substances

This idea led scientists to think, for example, that maggots (young flies) spontaneously formed from rotting meat. In other words, if you put rotting meat out, it would simply turn into maggots within a few days.

Of course, we now know that spontaneous generation is impossible. In all our experience, life can only be formed by the reproduction of other living things. People have children, animals produce offspring, and plants make seeds that grow into new plants. These are some of the ways life is formed. Life simply cannot be formed from non-living things. You will learn a lot more of the details regarding the story of spontaneous generation when you take biology. For right now, however, I want to make a point about how science should *not* be done, and spontaneous generation is an excellent example to use in order to make this point.

You see, all great scientists make mistakes. Democritus was thousands of years ahead of his time in proposing the existence of atoms, but he was wrong about most of the details regarding atoms.

Aristotle made great advances in the study of living things, but he believed in spontaneous generation. Aristotle's mistake was much more damaging to the advancement of science than was Democritus's mistakes, however. Why? Because Aristotle was *so well-respected!* You see, Aristotle was considered (rightly so) one of the greatest scientists of his time. Thus, his ideas (even the wrong ones) were revered for *generations!* In fact, the absurd notion of spontaneous generation lasted *well into the 1800s*, more than *2,000 years after* it was proposed by Aristotle.

FIGURE 1.3
Aristotle

Photo © Dhoxax
Agency: www.shutterstock.com

This is a sculpture that was made to honor Aristotle. He was rightly considered one of the greatest scientists in his day, but unfortunately, that hurt science in the long run. The idea of spontaneous generation, for example, lasted for a long, long time because Aristotle championed it. Scientists thought that since Aristotle was such a great scientist, he couldn't possibly be wrong about something so important. Thus, they continued to believe in spontaneous generation despite the evidence against it. In other words, *the reputation of Aristotle*, not scientific evidence, was the reason people believed in the idea. As a result, it took more than 2,000 years for science to show the fallacy of spontaneous generation. This is a great example of how science should *not* be done. Every scientist, no matter how great, will make mistakes. **Thus, no scientist's work should be supported because the *scientist* was great. It should only be supported because the *scientific evidence* supports it!** Sadly, this lesson has not been learned by many of today's scientists! Wrong-headed ideas still survive in science simply because they are championed by respected scientists.

The next Greek scientist worthy of note was **Archimedes** (ark uh me' deez), who lived roughly 100 years after Aristotle. He did great work in mathematics, and he used much of what he discovered in math to advance science. He applied mathematical formulas to explain why certain things happened the way they did. Archimedes was really one of the first scientists to demonstrate how closely mathematics and science are linked.

Archimedes is probably best known for his work with fluids. He was the first to show how you could predict whether or not an object would float in a liquid. His work with liquids led to one of the more entertaining stories in the history of science. The king that Archimedes served, King Hiero, once asked Archimedes to analyze a crown that was made for him. The crown was supposed to be made of gold, but the king was skeptical. Archimedes knew how to determine whether or not the crown was made of gold, but the process required him to know the exact amount of space the crown occupied. This seemed impossible, as the crown was so irregularly shaped that Archimedes could not find a way to measure it accurately.

Well, one day while taking a bath, Archimedes realized that when an item is immersed in water, it displaces the same amount of water as the space that the item occupies in the water. Thus, all

Archimedes had to do was immerse the crown in water and determine how much water it displaced. That would tell him how much space the crown occupied. Archimedes was so excited by this discovery that he ran through the streets screaming "Eureka," which means "I have found it." There was one embarrassing little problem, however. Archimedes was so excited by his discovery that he *forgot to put any clothes on!* In other words, he ran through the streets *completely naked!* While Archimedes himself never wrote of this incident (I would think he was too embarrassed), the story was reported by a Roman writer named Vitruvius about 200 years after it was supposed to have happened.

The last Greek scientist I want to discuss lived about 100 years after Christ's birth. His name was **Ptolemy** (tahl' uh mee), and he studied the heavens. He was one of the first to attempt a complete description of the planets and stars. He assumed that the earth was at the center of the universe, and that the planets and stars orbited about the earth in a series of circles.

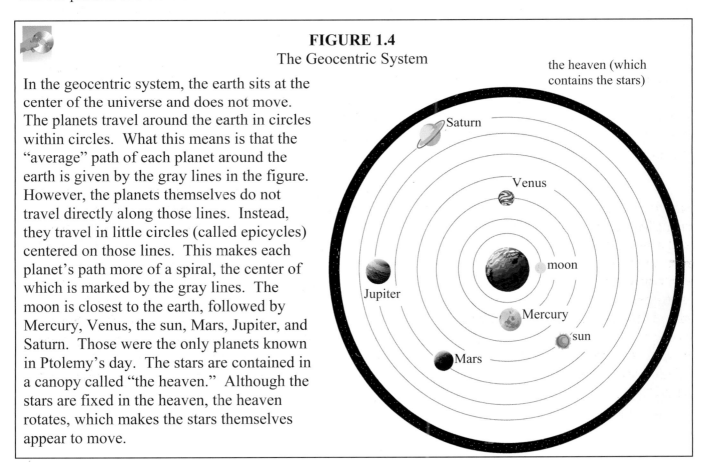

FIGURE 1.4
The Geocentric System

In the geocentric system, the earth sits at the center of the universe and does not move. The planets travel around the earth in circles within circles. What this means is that the "average" path of each planet around the earth is given by the gray lines in the figure. However, the planets themselves do not travel directly along those lines. Instead, they travel in little circles (called epicycles) centered on those lines. This makes each planet's path more of a spiral, the center of which is marked by the gray lines. The moon is closest to the earth, followed by Mercury, Venus, the sun, Mars, Jupiter, and Saturn. Those were the only planets known in Ptolemy's day. The stars are contained in a canopy called "the heaven." Although the stars are fixed in the heaven, the heaven rotates, which makes the stars themselves appear to move.

At the time, Ptolemy could explain a lot of the astronomical data that had been collected using his idea, so it became very popular. Sometimes, his view of the stars and planets is referred to as the **Ptolemaic system**, in an attempt to honor him. Sometimes, it is referred to as the **geocentric system**, to emphasize the fact that Ptolemy thought the earth was at the center of the universe.

The geocentric system was considered the correct explanation for the arrangement of planets and stars in space until about the 1700s. Thus, it was a popular theory for nearly 1,600 years. Once again, however, the reason the geocentric system was so popular had less to do with the scientific evidence and more to do with other considerations. Like Aristotle, Ptolemy was (rightly) considered a great scientist. As data were collected that contradicted the geocentric system, many scientists ignored the data out of reverence for Ptolemy.

There was actually another, probably more important reason the geocentric system became so popular: It fit many scientists' preconceived notions of how things ought to be. In the geocentric system, the earth was at the center of the universe and everything revolved around it. Since most people believed that the earth was the most important part of the universe, the geocentric system "made sense."

Also at this time, many of the scientists were members of the Roman Catholic Church. They were not willing to change their belief system until there was solid proof that the geocentric system was wrong. After all, the church reasoned, since God created man, the earth must be the most important thing in the universe, so it must be at the very center, and everything else must travel around it, just as Ptolemy said.

In the end, it took hundreds of years of scientific data before the church was convinced to give up on the geocentric system. Unfortunately, by that time, the church became viewed as antagonistic towards science, and some people today still hold that view. This is unfortunate because, as you will see in later sections of this module, Christianity is a friend to science. Most of the great scientists in history were Christians, and their Christianity is often credited for their scientific achievements. Nevertheless, many still see Christianity as an enemy of science.

So this little episode from history teaches us several things. You should not hold fast to an idea simply because it fits with your preconceived notions, but it also shows that you should not believe something just because data suggests something different. Science is built on data that is tested time and again, not a person's beliefs. The acceptance or rejection of a scientific proposition, then, should rest solely on the data that has been rigorously tested, nothing more. Today, there is an idea called **evolution**. It is popular among scientists because it fits many scientists' preconceived notions. As you will learn in a later module, there is data for both sides of the argument. Nevertheless, it is still a prevalent idea because many people like the fact that it tries to explain the existence of life without ever referring to God. As a result, they believe the idea without complete proof. Unfortunately, these people have not learned from the history of science. The history of science teaches us over and over again that believing in an idea because of preconceived notions hurts the cause of science; it does not help it!

ON YOUR OWN

1.4 Dr. Steven Hawking is one of the most brilliant scientists of the early twenty-first century. He believes in an idea called "the big bang." This idea tries to describe how the universe was formed. If your friend tells you that you should believe in the big bang because Dr. Hawking is smart and he believes in it, what famous example from the history of science should you tell to your friend?

1.5 What episode from the history of science tells us we need to leave our personal biases behind when we do science?

The Progress of Science Stalls for a While (500 A.D. to 1000 A.D.)

From the time of the first three Greek scientists (Thales, Anaximander, and Anaximenes) until about 400 or 500 A.D., science progressed at a steady rate. Many scientists proposed many ideas trying to explain the natural world. Those ideas were debated and refined. Great houses of learning were established to foster scientific inquiry. Works like those of Aristotle and Ptolemy became the guiding principles behind the progress of science.

After the first few centuries A.D., however, the progress of science stalled dramatically. By that time, the Roman Empire had a great deal of influence throughout the known world, and Rome had a distinct dislike of science. The Roman Empire did not mind inventions, especially those that made work more productive, but it had little use for the practice of explaining the world around us. As a result, real science was actively discouraged in most parts of the world.

Alchemy (al' kuh mee) is one of the best examples of what passed for science during this time period. Alchemists mostly wanted to find a means by which lead (or some other inexpensive substance) could be transformed into gold (or some other precious substance). You see, many people had observed the fact that when you mix certain substances together, they change into other substances. Perform the following experiment to see what I mean.

EXPERIMENT 1.3
A Chemical Reaction

Supplies:

+ A clear plastic 2-liter bottle
+ A balloon (6-inch to 9-inch round balloons work best.)
+ Clear vinegar
+ Baking soda
+ A funnel or butter knife
+ A few leaves of red (sometimes called purple) cabbage
+ A saucepan
+ A stove
+ Measuring cups
+ A few ice cubes
+ Eye protection such as goggles or safety glasses

Introduction: Mixing specific substances together can produce amazing results. This experiment shows you some of what can happen when the right substances are mixed together.

Procedure:

1. Put about 2 cups of water in the saucepan and add several leaves of red cabbage. Put it on a stove burner and heat it so the water boils.
2. While you are waiting for the water to boil, put about 2 tablespoons of baking soda into the balloon. The best way to do this, of course, is to use a funnel. If you do not have a funnel, try picking up the baking soda on the flat end of a butter knife, pushing the knife into the balloon's opening, and then tipping the knife so the baking soda spills into the balloon. It is a tedious process, but you will eventually get all the baking soda you need into the balloon.

3. Once the balloon has about 2 tablespoons of baking soda in it, pour ¾ cup of clear vinegar into the 2-liter bottle.
4. Once the water in the saucepan starts boiling, remove it from the heat. Allow the liquid in the pan to cool by adding some ice. The liquid should have a blue or pink color now.
5. Add ½ cup of the liquid to the 2-liter bottle.
6. Attach the balloon to the opening of the 2-liter bottle by stretching the balloon's opening over the lip of the bottle. In the end, your experiment should look like this:

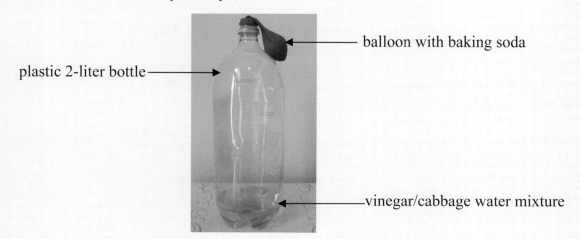

plastic 2-liter bottle

balloon with baking soda

vinegar/cabbage water mixture

7. Once you are ready, lift the balloon so the baking soda falls into the vinegar. Write down what you see in your laboratory notebook.
8. Clean up your mess and put everything away.

What did you see in the experiment? When the baking soda hit the vinegar, the mixture should have bubbled and fizzed, and the balloon should have inflated. At the same time, you should have noticed a color change. The mixture should have turned from a pinkish color to a bluish color. What happened? Well, you witnessed the effect of a **chemical reaction**. In a chemical reaction, one or more substances interact to form one or more new substances.

In your experiment, there were actually two chemical reactions going on. The first occurred when vinegar was mixed with baking soda. Those two substances interacted, forming three new substances: carbon dioxide, sodium acetate, and water. The carbon dioxide, which is a gas, bubbled out of the vinegar and into the balloon, filling up the balloon. The second reaction occurred as the vinegar was being used up in the first reaction. A substance in red cabbage, anthocyanin (an thuh sye' uh nun), interacted with the vinegar to form a pink color. As the vinegar was transformed into new substances by the first reaction, the anthocyanin no longer had vinegar to interact with, so the pink color went away and was replaced by a blue color.

Alchemists saw changes like the ones you saw in your experiment and thought that if they were just able to find the right recipe, they could mix lead with several other substances and make gold. Of course, we now know that this is impossible, because we know that there are severe limitations on how much one substance can change in a chemical reaction. You will learn all about that when you take chemistry. The alchemists didn't know this, however, so they strove to mix substance after substance with lead, hoping one day to find the "magic" mixture that would turn lead into gold.

As alchemists began mixing and recording, many interesting things were observed. These observations were written down, and, every once in a while, one of the mixtures would form some useful substance. The recipe to make this useful substance would then be recorded, and the alchemist would proceed on to the next mixture. Like ancient Egyptian medicine, then, the alchemists (and most "scientists" of this time) really just did things by trial and error. They never tried to use their observations to draw conclusions about how the natural world works. Instead, they were content to just write down their observations and move on to the next experiment, searching for the next useful substance they could make.

Interestingly enough, even though the ideas of Rome held great sway in most of the known world, the Roman Empire itself began to crumble. As that happened, trade and large-scale communication became harder and harder. Since science thrives on the free exchange of ideas from one scientist to another, this put another roadblock in the way of scientific progress. Many historians refer to this period as the **Dark Ages**, because compared to the previous time period in history as well as the next time period in history, little was learned.

So here we find another lesson we can learn from the history of science: **Scientific progress depends not only on scientists, but it also depends on government and culture**. Since the Romans actively discouraged science and concentrated on inventions, the progress of science slowed. Since the crumbling government caused trade and communications to become more difficult, scientific progress slowed even more. For science to proceed, then, the government and the culture must support it.

Although the progress of science slowed during this period, there are a few things worth noting. Most of the knowledge that had accumulated up to this point was carefully preserved by Roman Catholic monks. These monks, and Christians in general, believed that God had revealed Himself to His creation in two ways: through Scripture and through nature. Thus, these monks were committed to preserving *both* means of revelation. They copied and re-copied Scripture so as to preserve it for coming generations. They also did the same with the accumulated scientific knowledge of the time. They created large volumes of scientific observations and speculations, which came to be known as **encyclopedias**. These encyclopedias, with their vast accumulation of data and ideas, were one of the main reasons science was able to flourish in the next period of history.

Another thing worth noting about this period is the fact that although real science stalled dramatically, there were still a lot of people making observations and inventing things. Both Arabs and Chinese during this time period were involved in making careful studies of the heavens. They made observations that were much more detailed and precise than those of the Greek scientists who came before them. Even though there were very few attempts to explain *what those data meant*, at least the data were being collected, and they would be used by later scientists to draw significant conclusions about the world around us.

For example, Chinese records from 1054 A.D. include detailed observations of a phenomenon that Chinese scientists called a "guest star" in the heavens. You see, the scientists were familiar with the stars and knew some formed patterns called **constellations** (kahn' stuh lay' shunz). Well, they recorded in 1054 that a star that had not been seen before suddenly appeared in a certain constellation. Although they did not understand how this "guest star" came to be, they recorded their observations in great detail. Modern scientists have been able to use those observations to determine that the Chinese had seen a **supernova**, which is essentially the explosion of a star. The observations were so detailed that modern scientists were able to look at that same part of the night sky, and when they did, they found a cloud of dust and gas, called a **nebula** (neb' yoo luh). Based on these facts, modern scientists now believe that one way a nebula forms is by the explosion of a star.

FIGURE 1.5
The Crab Nebula

Photo courtesy of NASA

Based on very detailed Chinese records from 1054 A.D., the Crab Nebula is thought to be the remains of a star that exploded.

Once again, then, we come to another lesson in the history of science: **Science progresses by building on the work of previous scientists**. Had the monks of this time period not catalogued and preserved the thoughts and observations of the scientists who had come before them, the scientists who came after them would not have had a foundation upon which to build. Had the Chinese not recorded such detailed observations of the night sky, modern scientists might still not know where the Crab Nebula came from. Thus, in order for science to advance, we must study and preserve the works of the scientists who come before us. As more and more scientific knowledge is accumulated, this becomes a more and more important task.

Another thing worth noting about this time period is that the Christian church (mostly the Roman Catholic Church) was instrumental in continuing the progress of medical treatment. The works of previous scientists were studied in monasteries, because Christians believed it was their duty to aid and comfort the sick. Thus, the medical advances up to this period in history were preserved and practiced throughout the Dark Ages. In addition, although no real understanding of the human body emerged, more trial-and-error medicine such as that practiced by the ancient Egyptians did lead to advances in the treatment of illness.

ON YOUR OWN

1.6 A great many scientists today worry that most students do not appreciate science. As a result, there are those who worry about the future of science. Although it is true that most young people today don't care about science, there are some who do. They will obviously become the scientists of the future. Since there will always be at least a few people who are interested in science, why are today's scientists worried about the future of science?

Science Begins To Pick Up Steam (1000 A.D. to 1500 A.D.)

Towards the end of the Dark Ages, real science slowly began to emerge again, thanks mostly to the Roman Catholic Church. Remember, science slowed considerably at the beginning of the Dark Ages due to the influence of the Roman Empire, which had little regard for real science. One of the reasons it held science in such low esteem was due to the predominant religion of the Roman Empire. The Romans believed in many gods. These gods roamed the universe, alternately torturing or helping humans, depending on their whims. With such a religion, there was no reason to believe the natural world could be explained. After all, the gods' actions were unpredictable. Thus, the Romans reasoned, the natural world itself (which was the creation of the gods) must also be unpredictable. As a result, Romans believed that the natural world simply could not be explained in any consistent way.

By about 1000 A.D., however, Christian scholars began realizing that their beliefs promoted a completely different way of looking at the world around them. They believed in a single God who created the universe according to His laws. Since they believed that God's laws never changed, they realized that the natural laws God set into motion should also never change. As a result, the way that the natural world worked could be explained, as long as scientists could discover the natural laws that God set into motion.

It might seem painfully obvious to you that the natural world must obey certain laws. However, that kind of thinking was relatively revolutionary at the end of the Dark Ages. Now realize that this kind of thinking wasn't really *new*. It was just different from the predominant idea of the day. After all, Greek scientists like Aristotle and Ptolemy also believed that the natural world could be explained by laws that did not change. Nevertheless, that part of their thinking was mostly ignored during the Dark Ages, due to the influence of Roman thought.

A very important figure in this time period was **Robert Grosseteste** (groh' suh test' ee). Grosseteste was a bishop in the Roman Catholic Church in the early 1200s A.D., and he was deeply committed to the idea that the secrets of the natural world could be learned by discovering the laws that God had set in motion. He taught that the purpose of inquiry was not to come up with great inventions, but instead to learn the *reasons* behind the facts. In other words, he wanted to explain *why* things happened the way they did. That's the essence of science.

Grosseteste taught that a scientist should make observations and then come up with a tentative explanation for *why* the observed events happened. The scientist should then make more observations to test his explanation. If the new observations confirmed the explanation, the explanation might be considered reliable. If the new observations contradicted the explanation, the explanation was probably wrong.

As you will learn in the next chapter, that is essentially the method we use in modern science. Thus, Grosseteste is often called the father of the scientific method, because he was the first to thoroughly explain and use it. Grosseteste applied his scientific method to the problem of explaining the rainbow. Although Grosseteste never developed a satisfactory explanation for the rainbow, a Roman Catholic priest who lived roughly 50 years later, **Dietrich Von Freiberg**, built on Grosseteste's work and was able to offer an explanation for why a rainbow appears in the sky. Because of that, Von Freiberg is often called "the priest who solved the mystery of the rainbow." Next year (in physical science), you will learn how a rainbow forms.

Although Grosseteste is considered the father of the scientific method, one of his followers, **Roger Bacon**, is more famous and is sometimes given that title in error. Bacon staunchly advocated the use of Grosseteste's method. He tried over and over again to use science to break the shackles of superstition. For example, conventional wisdom in Bacon's day was that a diamond could be broken only by the application of goat's blood. He proposed experiments that, when performed, showed that goat's blood had no effect whatsoever on diamonds.

Bacon also had a strong belief that science could be used to support the reality of Christianity. A devout Roman Catholic theologian, Bacon believed that the more people learned about science, the more they would learn about God. In addition, Bacon seemed to see the potential of science when few others did. In his writings, he predicted that science would bring about marvels such as flying machines, explosives, submarines, and worldwide travel. People laughed at his ideas back then, but historians today marvel at his insight.

Roughly 70 years after Bacon (in the early 1300s), another important figure, **Thomas Bradwardine** (brad war' deen), emerged on the scene. Bradwardine was a bishop in the Roman Catholic Church, and his work was important on two levels. First and foremost, Bradwardine was a theologian who questioned much of the Roman Catholic Church's teachings. Many church historians consider him the first Reformer, because he emphasized salvation by faith alone, through the grace of God. The more well-known reformers (Luther and Calvin) were heavily influenced by Bradwardine's work.

Not only was Bradwardine an important figure in church history, he was also important in the development of modern science. Bradwardine was one of the first scientists to examine many of Aristotle's ideas critically. He found most of them lacking. He concentrated on understanding motion. He wanted to know why things moved, what kept them moving, and what made them stop. He applied mathematics to his study of motion and actually developed equations in an attempt to describe the details of speed, distance traveled, and so forth. Using mathematics and experiments, he was able to show that most of what Aristotle said about motion was wrong. Although it took nearly 300 more years for science to throw away Aristotle's ideas about motion, it might never have happened without Bradwardine's work.

Another important scientist of this era was **Nicholas of Cusa**. He was also a priest in the Roman Catholic Church in the mid-1400s and became an influential leader in the church toward the end of his life. He was particularly interested in the idea that God was infinite. Because he wanted to learn more about God's infinite nature, he studied the planets and the stars, thinking they were probably the largest (and thus closest to infinite) things that he could study. His studies of the planets were revolutionary because he was one of the first to break from Ptolemy's geocentric view. He (correctly) believed that the earth spins while it travels around the sun. This was in direct disagreement with Ptolemy's ideas, and it laid the groundwork for the scientific revolution that would take place two hundred years later.

Before I end this section, I want to make sure that you have picked up on something. Notice that many of the great scientists of this era were devout Christians. In fact, many were clergy (priests, bishops, etc.) of the Roman Catholic Church. As you read through the rest of this module, you will notice that many of the great scientists from the Dark Ages to modern times were devoted Christians. Once again, that's because the Christian worldview is a perfect fit with science. Science is based on the notion that the world works according to rational laws that do not change. Since Christians believe in a rational Creator whose laws do not change, science and Christianity work very well together.

That last statement surprises some people. Some people actually believe that science and Christianity are at odds with one another. Unfortunately, that myth has developed recently, mostly because the majority of scientists today are not Christian. However, even a quick look at science history tells us that without Christianity, science would never have gotten out of the Dark Ages. The Christian worldview was essential in turning trial-and-error-based observations into true science. The more you learn about the history of science, the more you will see that science would never exist in its present form had it not been for Christianity!

ON YOUR OWN

1.7 Some historians call Grosseteste the first modern scientist. Why does Grosseteste deserve that honor?

The Renaissance: The "Golden Age" of Science (1500 A.D. to 1660 A.D.)

The 16th and 17th centuries (1500 A.D. to 1700 A.D.) were incredibly exciting in the history of science. The excitement took off in 1543, when two very important works were published. The first (and most celebrated today) was published by **Nicolaus Copernicus**. It was a book that laid out his idea about the earth, sun, planets, and stars. Like Nicholas of Cusa, Copernicus believed that Ptolemy's view of the universe was wrong. Rather than placing the earth at the center of everything and believing that the sun and the planets traveled around the earth, Copernicus placed the sun at the center of everything and assumed that the planets (including the earth) traveled around the sun. This view was called the **heliocentric** (he' lee oh sen' trik) **system**, because Helios is the Greek god of the sun. Sometimes, however, it is called the **Copernican system**, in honor of Copernicus.

Copernicus had actually completed his studies and written his book nearly 13 years before it was published. However, Copernicus delayed its publication because the Roman Catholic Church disagreed with the heliocentric system. This fact was a little ironic, as Copernicus himself was part of the church's clergy and had actually done his work at the request of the pope, who was the head of the Roman Catholic Church! Nevertheless, the Roman Catholic Church publicly denounced Copernicus' work and put his book on their list of prohibited reading. As I mentioned in a previous section, the church did this not because of science, but because of preconceived notions. The Roman Catholic

Church believed the idea of the earth being at the center of everything, and they therefore did not want to give up Ptolemy's geocentric view until it was proven beyond a doubt.

FIGURE 1.6
The Heliocentric System

Illustration by Sebastian Kaulitzki
Agency: www.shutterstock.com

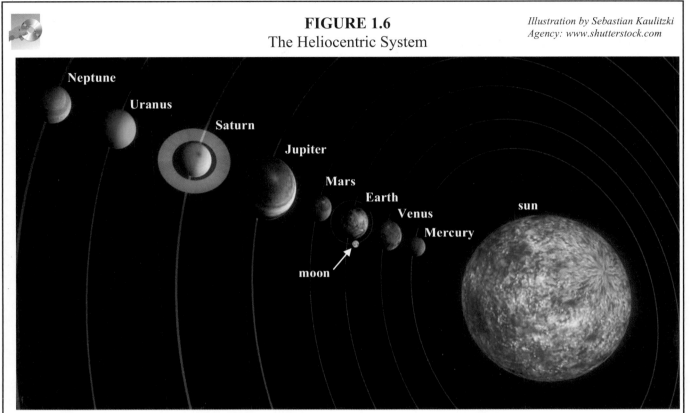

Copernicus championed the heliocentric view, where the planets travel around the stationary sun in circular orbits. Unlike the geocentric view, there are no epicycles. The circles in the drawing show the actual paths of the planets. This is the modern view of how the sun and planets are arranged. Mercury is closest to the sun, followed by Venus, Earth, Mars, Jupiter, Saturn, Uranus, and Neptune. The moon is not a planet, but travels around the Earth while the Earth travels around the sun.

The other important work published in 1543 was written by a doctor named **Andreas Vesalius** (vuh sal' ee us). It was a book that tried to show all the details of the human body. It contained incredibly detailed and amazingly accurate illustrations of the organs, muscles, and skeleton of the human body. This was the first book that illustrated all of the "insides" of the human body, and it revolutionized how medicine was taught.

Although the importance of Vesalius' book was recognized right away, it took longer for people to recognize the importance of Copernicus' work. The main reason was that the Roman Catholic Church banned the book. The church and scientists agreed that although Copernicus had the right idea, he had very little data to back it up. Copernicus promoted his heliocentric system not because he had made a lot of observations that supported this view, but because he knew that there was a lot of evidence *against* Ptolemy's geocentric view. Copernicus also thought that God fashioned the heavens using the heliocentric system because it was the more orderly and pleasing of the two.

Copernicus' heliocentric view became more and more accepted as more and more evidence for it was compiled. One of the most important compilers of such evidence was **Johannes Kepler**. Kepler began making observations of the heavens in the late 1500s. He desperately wanted to be a minister, but he had terrible financial problems that forced him to accept a job as a teacher instead. While he taught, he studied the heavens, hoping his observations would bring glory to God. In a particularly revealing letter, he wrote, "I wanted to become a theologian. For a long time, I was restless. Now, however, behold how through my effort God is being celebrated in astronomy" (*Scientists of Faith*, Dan Graves, Kregel Resources, 1996, p. 49).

Kepler made detailed observations of the planets. His observations were so detailed that he was able to deduce the basic orbits the planets use to travel around the sun. He was even able to describe these orbits mathematically. His mathematical equations became known as "Kepler's Laws," and they became one of the most powerful arguments for the heliocentric system. Kepler's observations of the planets were so detailed and precise that he was able to determine something very interesting about the planets. His data showed that the planets don't really travel around the sun in circles. They actually travel around the sun following an oval pattern, which mathematicians call an **ellipse** (ee' lips). Perform the following "experiment" to learn about how the planets *really* travel around the sun.

"EXPERIMENT" 1.4
Mapping the Paths of the Planets

<u>Supplies:</u>

♦ A pencil
♦ A sheet of paper (8 ½" by 11")
♦ Six thumbtacks or pushpins
♦ A piece of string 8 inches long
♦ A sheet of cardboard larger than or the same size as the sheet of paper

Introduction: Planets travel around the sun in ellipses, not circles. This "experiment" helps you to understand what that means.

<u>Procedure:</u>

1. Lay the sheet of paper on top of the cardboard.
2. Pin it to the cardboard at each corner.
3. Lay one end of the string about 2 inches left of center, halfway down the paper.
4. Pin it to the paper so it is held there.
5. Push the last pin you have through the string about 5 inches away from the pin that is attached to the paper and cardboard.
6. Use this pin to attach the string to the paper about 2 inches to the right of center, straight across from the end of the string that is already pinned down. There will be some excess string dangling off the pin. That's fine.
7. Take the pencil and push the point against the string above the two pins so the string becomes tight.
8. Keeping the string tight at all times, move the pencil from one pin to the other, drawing a curve on the paper. If you keep the string tight, it will guide your pencil. The end result will be a line that begins just above and to the right of the right pin and curves around to and left of the left pin, as shown in the drawing on the right.

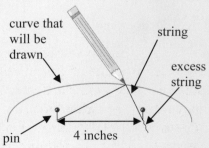

Illustration by Megan Fruchte

9. Repeat the process, this time starting *below* the two pins, keeping the string tight at all times. The result will be a curve that looks like a reflection of the first curve you drew.
10. Now look at what you have drawn. It is an oval, which mathematicians call an ellipse.
11. Pull the right pin off the paper and out of the string.
12. Push that same pin through the very end of the string.
13. Push the pin and string into the paper at the same place the pin was before. This setup should look very similar to the previous one. The pins will be in the same place, but there will be more string in between the pins and no excess string dangling from the right pin.
14. Once again, use the pencil and string to draw two curves: one below the pins and one above them. Keep the string tight at all times, allowing it to guide the pencil in making the curves.
15. Remove the pins and string from the paper and look at the two ellipses you drew.

Both of the drawings you made are ellipses. An ellipse is defined by two points called **foci** (foh' sye – the singular of which is **focus**). In your "experiment," the foci were the two pins. If you were to take any point on the first ellipse you drew and measure the distance from that point to each pin, the sum of those two distances would be 5 inches. That's the property of an ellipse. The sum of the distances from any point on the ellipse to each of the foci is always the same. On the second ellipse you drew, the sum of those distances would be 8 inches, because the string was longer when you drew the second ellipse.

Now don't worry if you do not completely understand ellipses. The main point I want you to understand is the difference between the two ellipses you drew. The second one is more circular than the first, isn't it? That's because the string was longer the second time, but the foci were the same. The ellipses in which the planets travel around the sun are very nearly circular. Thus, they are much more like the second ellipse than the first. Well, if the second ellipse you drew is like the orbit of a planet, where is the sun? The sun is at one of the two foci. In the end then, the planets do not travel around the sun in perfectly circular orbits. They travel in ellipses. Also, the sun is not exactly in the center of the ellipse. Instead, it is at one of the foci.

Other powerful evidence for the heliocentric view came from a scientist named **Galileo** (gal uh lay' oh) **Galilei** (gal uh lay'), who is usually referred to by just his first name. Galileo was a well-known, well-respected scientist for many reasons. He did detailed experiments about motion, confirming the work of Bradwardine and showing the flaws in Aristotle's thinking. Galileo started seriously compiling evidence in favor of the heliocentric system in 1609, when he built his first telescope. While many works claim that Galileo invented the telescope, he did not. He heard about a device that was designed for the military by Hans Lippershey. It was essentially a "tube" with two lenses, and it magnified distant objects. From the description he heard, he was able to determine how this invention worked and quickly built one for himself. So was Hans Lippershey the real inventor of the telescope? We don't really know. However, he is the first name that history associates with the device.

As Galileo worked with telescopes, he made several improvements to the design and also collected volumes of data about the planets and the stars. He was able to show that the planets do not shine on their own. He demonstrated that the planets appear as lights in the night sky simply because they reflect the light of the sun. In addition, he showed that the light coming from Venus went through phases, just like the moon. Facts like these made it clear that the heliocentric view was superior to the geocentric view. Unfortunately, the Roman Catholic Church would not let go of the geocentric view and put Galileo on trial for heresy. In that trial, the church demanded that Galileo publicly recant his belief in the heliocentric system. Because Galileo was a devout Roman Catholic, he obeyed the church and publicly "denounced" the heliocentric view. Nevertheless, he kept collecting data. Well after his death, Galileo's data (along with Kepler's laws) simply proved too powerful for the Roman Catholic Church to ignore, and the heliocentric system was eventually accepted as the correct view of the heavens.

Left Photo © Tomasz Szymanski,
Middle photo © Paul van Eykelen
Agency: www.shutterstock.com

FIGURE 1.7
Scientists Who Corrected Our View of the Heavens

Right photo by Kathleen J. Wile

Copernicus's work argued strongly for the heliocentric system, saying it was the way an orderly God would have created the heavens.

Kepler's observations and the laws he derived from them provided strong evidence for the heliocentric system.

Galileo's telescopic observations could only be explained by using the heliocentric system.

Even though the advances in understanding the heavens take center stage in the history of this time period, many other scientific advances took place as well. **Blaise** (blayz) **Pascal** (pas kal') lived in the mid-1600s. He was a brilliant philosopher, mathematician, and scientist. If you have studied Christian apologetics at all, you might remember him as the author of "Pascal's wager." This argument presents a person's worldview in terms of a bet. He then argues convincingly that Christianity is, by far, the best bet.

In addition to his philosophy, Pascal is also well remembered for his work as a mathematician and scientist. In math, he made several advances in the understanding of both geometry and algebra. In science, he spent an enormous amount of time studying the air and liquids. He demonstrated that the air we breathe exerts pressure on everything, an effect we call **atmospheric pressure** today. In his studies of fluids, he demonstrated a law that we now call "Pascal's Law." The science behind that law allowed us to develop hydraulic lifts, like the lift a mechanic uses to raise a car so he can get underneath it.

ON YOUR OWN

1.8 Galileo faced a very difficult decision in his life. He was convinced by science that the heliocentric system was correct. Nevertheless, his church said that he was wrong and threatened to throw him out if he didn't recant his belief in the heliocentric system. Galileo, in obedience to his church, agreed to publicly recant his belief, even though he knew it was right. Did Galileo make the right choice, or should he have stayed true to his science and been thrown out of the church?

The Era of Newton (1660 A.D. to 1735 A.D.)

Although the Renaissance is often called the "golden age" of science, I personally think that science enjoyed its greatest advancement during the time of **Sir Isaac Newton**. As is the case with many of the great scientists of the past, Newton was a devout (though unorthodox) Christian. He studied science specifically as a means of learning more about God, but he never forgot that the best way to learn about God was by thorough Bible study. He wrote many commentaries on the Bible, concentrating on prophecy. He was particularly drawn to the Book of Daniel. In his later years, he spent a lot more time writing about the Book of Daniel than he did writing about science.

FIGURE 1.8
Sir Isaac Newton

Image in the public domain

To call Sir Isaac Newton brilliant would be an understatement. In his short lifetime, Newton laid down three laws of motion that still guide the science of physics today. He formulated a universal law of gravitation, which is also still used to this day. In his studies of motion, he realized the mathematics of his day was not complete enough to help him understand his data. Thus, he developed an entirely new mathematical field we now call calculus, and it continues to be an essential tool in many fields of science. He also did the famous prism experiment that shows white light is really composed of many different colors of light. In addition, he came up with a completely different design for telescopes, a design that is still used in many of today's telescopes. It is little wonder that many science historians call Sir Isaac Newton the greatest scientist in history.

Newton wrote most of his revolutionary scientific work in a three-volume set we call the *Principia* (prin sip' ee ah). In the first volume, Newton laid down three laws of motion. You will learn about these laws next year when you take physical science. In formulating these laws, Newton made a direct link between mathematics and science. In essence, Newton proposed that a scientific law was useless if it could not be used to develop a mathematical equation that would describe some aspect of nature. The deep link that Newton established between science and math resulted in a major breakthrough. Although many scientists in the past had used mathematics to analyze a scientific problem, Newton was the first to establish an intimate link between the two. This link helped turn scientific research into a detailed, rigorous field of study.

In the second volume of the *Principia*, Newton built on the work of Pascal and added many details to the understanding of the motion of fluids. In the third volume, Newton laid down his universal law of gravitation. The term "universal" has a specific meaning here. You see, scientists in Newton's day thought that the reason an object falls when dropped was due to one physical process, while the reason the planets moved in the sky was due to a completely different process. Newton showed that this was not the case. In volume three of the *Principia*, Newton used detailed experiments and observations to show that gravity was the cause of both effects. The same gravity that attracts objects to the earth (making them fall) also keeps the planets in their orbits around the sun. In addition to his experimental results, Newton had (of course) developed detailed mathematical equations that describe gravity. Those mathematical equations are still considered accurate to this day. The third volume of the *Principia* essentially was the final death blow to the geocentric view of the heavens.

Although Newton took center stage during this time period, there were other great scientists who brought about other significant advances as well. **Robert Boyle**, the founder of modern chemistry, was a contemporary of Newton. He did many experiments with gases, formulating laws that are still used today in chemistry. In fact, when you take chemistry in high school, you will undoubtedly learn about Boyle's Law. Boyle was also a dedicated Christian, who often wrote sermons using nature to give glory to God. His last words to the Royal Society (a group of scientists in England) were "Remember to give glory to the One who authored nature" (*Scientists of Faith*, Dan Graves, Kregel Resources, 1996, p. 63). Unfortunately, those words were eventually forgotten.

Another notable scientist from this period was **Antoni** (an' ton ee) **van Leeuwenhoek** (loo' en hook). Although not educated as a scientist, Leeuwenhoek revolutionized the study of life by building the first **microscope**. His microscope allowed him to see a world that had been invisible up to this point, which enabled him to discover many tiny (microscopic) life forms, including bacteria. The existence of these life forms helped scientists explain many things that had been, up to this point, complete mysteries. Like Boyle, Leeuwenhoek tried to glorify God in all his scientific work. To him, the existence of a microscopic world was just one more testimony to the fact that God made *all* creatures – great and small.

ON YOUR OWN

1.9 Some students think mathematics is too difficult to learn. In order to teach science to such students, there are many science textbooks written today that do not use mathematics at all. What do you think Newton would say about such textbooks?

The "Enlightenment" and the Industrial Revolution (1735 A.D. to 1820 A.D.)

This period in history marks the beginning of a change in the underlying assumptions of science. A philosopher of the time, Immanuel Kant, used the term **Enlightenment** to describe this change. Unfortunately, the change was only partially beneficial to the progress of science, so I always put the term in quotes, because the change that began in this period was only partially enlightened.

What is this change to which I refer? Well, up to this point in history, God was at the center of virtually all science. As you can see from the previous sections, most of the great scientists up to this time in history were devout Christians. Since most of the progress in science was being made by Christians, science had a very Christian flavor to it. You could hardly find a scientific book or paper written that did not mention God reverently. Prayer was at the forefront of most scientific meetings and assemblies. Christianity was the basis of most scientific education. At this point in human history, that began to change.

What caused this change? Ironically, the great advances in science up to this time were indirectly the cause. You see, the advances made in science from the Dark Ages up to this point in history were the result of scientists ignoring the teachings of Ptolemy, Aristotle, and the other scientists whose works had dominated science for so long. As time went on, the scientific community began to learn that scientists should not just accept the teachings of former scientists. Instead, they realized that all scientists make mistakes, and therefore everyone's work must be examined critically. In the end, then, science stopped relying on the authority of past scientists and began relying on experiments and data.

That's the *good* part of the change that occurred during the Enlightenment. Scientists stopped referring to the authority of past scientists and started examining all scientific works critically. As I already pointed out in a previous section, that's the way science *should* be done. Unfortunately, as science began to ignore the authority of past scientists, it also began to ignore the authority of the Bible. That's the *bad* part of the change that occurred during the Enlightenment. Despite the fact that a biblical worldview had brought about the very science they studied, some scientists began to question the truth of the Bible.

Of course, science's departure from a biblical worldview was not abrupt. Many scientists during this time period and beyond were (and are) devout Christians, and God was still mentioned in many scientific works. In addition, many scientists continued to take their direction from the Bible when it came to how they approached science. However, as time went on, fewer and fewer references to God and the Bible could be found in the works of science.

Although this period can be thought of as the beginning of science's departure from a biblical worldview, it is marked in history by the work of a devout Christian, **Carolus** (kair' uh lus) **Linnaeus** (lih nay' us). In 1735, Linnaeus published a book in which he tried to classify all living creatures that had been studied. This work is often used to mark the beginning of the Enlightenment, because it revolutionized the study of living things. The basic classification scheme proposed by Linnaeus is still used today, and we still give living organisms their scientific names according to the rules set down in his book.

Linnaeus was deeply committed to performing science as a means of glorifying God. He called nature God's private garden, and he continually glorified God in his scientific works. Here is a typical quote from his works: "…one is completely stunned by the incredible resourcefulness of the Creator" (*Linnaeus, the Compleat Naturalist*, Wilifrid Blunt, Princeton University Press, 2001, p. 14). In fact, it was Linnaeus' view of God that prompted him to classify living creatures. He believed that God is very organized. Thus, he believed that God's creation should be organized as well. In his mind, the classification scheme he developed was just a means of showing the organization of creation.

As Linnaeus was classifying living organisms, **Antoine-Laurent** (an twon' law rent') **Lavoisier** (luh vwah' see ay) was busy studying chemical reactions. He was the first to analyze chemical reactions in a systematic way, and he was the first to realize that matter cannot be created or destroyed – it can only change forms. This is known as the **Law of Mass Conservation**, and it was Lavoisier's most important contribution to science. Lavoisier was also the first to properly explain **combustion**, which is the process of burning.

Another important scientist in this time period was **John Dalton**. Dalton was a Quaker who attended church at least twice each week. He did many experiments with gases, and proposed many new ideas that helped guide science in the future. Perhaps his most important work was his **atomic theory**. Building on the works of Democritus and others, Dalton proposed a detailed theory about atoms. Although a few of his ideas were wrong, most of them were right, and he is considered the founder of modern atomic theory.

As scientific knowledge grew, many inventors were able to use this knowledge to invent machines that made work faster and more productive. Up to this time period, the production of almost anything was done mostly by hand. Increased scientific knowledge, however, led to the invention of many devices that turned hours of manual labor into just a few minutes of work. This changed forever the way things were made, and so this period in history is also called the **Industrial Revolution**.

The Rest of the Nineteenth Century (1820 A.D. to 1900 A.D.)

During the rest of the nineteenth century, many great advances were made in science. Partially, this is due to the fact that people began to appreciate science more. After all, in the wake of the Industrial Revolution, people realized that the inventions that made their lives better were at least partially the result of scientific knowledge. As a result, there was popular support for science. This popular support translated into better facilities and a better way of life for scientists, which in turn translated into great advances.

This period is probably best known for the work of **Charles R. Darwin**. In 1859, he published a book entitled *On The Origin of Species by Means of Natural Selection or the Preservation of Favoured Races in the Struggle for Life*. Typically abbreviated as *The Origin of Species*, Darwin's book caused a firestorm in the scientific community. In *The Origin of Species*, he proposed a theory that attempted to explain the diversity of life that exists on earth. This theory, now known as the theory of evolution, made no reference to God. Instead, it proposed that the same kinds of processes we see occurring today are, in fact, responsible for all the species on the planet. In effect, Darwin's book proposed to answer the age-old question, "How did we get here?" without ever referring to a supernatural Creator.

You will learn a lot more about Darwin himself and his theory when you take biology. You will also learn some of his theory in a few of the modules of this course. What I want to stress here is the impact of Darwin's work. First and foremost, Darwin's work finished the change that began in the Enlightenment. As Darwin's ideas caught on in the scientific community, those who wanted to ignore the authority of Scripture were empowered. After all, they reasoned, if science can explain how we got here without ever referring to a Creator, why should science continue assuming that the Creator exists? As a result, it became rarer and rarer to find references to God in the scientific literature of this or the next century.

The second impact of Darwin's work was to improve the study of living things dramatically. Now it is important to realize that I (and hundreds of other scientists) think that Darwin's idea of evolution is fundamentally wrong. Nevertheless, even wrong ideas can help advance science! Think about what you have learned up to this point. Most of the ideas proposed throughout the history of science were wrong. Nevertheless, those ideas helped move science ahead, until the correct explanation could be found. Thus, even though Darwin was wrong about much of what he proposed, he still advanced biology enormously.

How did Darwin do that? Well, up until Darwin wrote his book, most scientists thought living creatures stayed the same throughout history. In other words, scientists thought that every type of creature that exists today has existed throughout history. Consider dogs, for example. Scientists of this time period and before thought that Saint Bernards, dachshunds, and chihuahuas always existed. Each of these breeds of dog lived throughout history, essentially unchanged. This idea was called the **immutability of the species**, and Darwin masterfully showed that this just wasn't true. He showed that living organisms can adapt to changes in their surroundings through a process he called **natural selection**. Over time, this can lead to new organisms that are radically different from their ancestors.

FIGURE 1.9
Charles Darwin

Illustration from www.clipart.com

Although a lot of what Darwin proposed has been demonstrated to be incorrect, he did contribute significantly to the advancement of biology by destroying the concept of the immutability of the species. Darwin's work laid the foundations for works that now clearly demonstrate the fact that creatures have the ability to adapt to changes in their surroundings, producing new versions of old creatures. For example, Saint Bernards, dachshunds, and chihuahuas have not always existed. Instead, as the original "dog" spread out to different areas of the world, it encountered different environments. Over the generations, the dogs adapted to these different environments, producing different types of dogs. This was accentuated by breeders choosing which dogs were "desirable" and allowing only those dogs to have puppies. Over the generations, such processes produced the breeds we see today.

Even though this time period is best remembered for Darwin's work, other scientists were producing revolutionary work as well. **Louis Pasteur** was able to finally destroy the idea of spontaneous generation once and for all. He also made great advances in the study of bacteria and other living organisms. He developed a process called **pasteurization**, which he originally used to keep wine from souring. This process is now applied to milk, which is the origin of the term "pasteurized milk." Pasteur is also known for his brilliant work with vaccines. His work laid the foundation for most of today's vaccines, which have saved millions and millions of lives by protecting people from disease.

During this time period, the study of rocks became its own field, known as **geology**. Scientists began to recognize fossils for what they really are: preserved remains of creatures that were once alive. This began to help scientists come up with a better understanding of what kinds of creatures lived in earth's past. **Sir Charles Lyell** was an important figure in this regard. He broke with the scientific view of the time that the earth was a few thousand years old and postulated that the earth took millions of years to form. Once again, although the weight of scientific evidence goes against most of Lyell's ideas, his studies were extremely important to our understanding of modern geology. Another important aspect of Lyell's work is that it exerted a heavy influence on Darwin.

Gregor Mendel also performed his work during this time period. Mendel was an Augustinian monk. He was a devout Christian who devoted much of his life to the study of reproduction. The entire field of modern **genetics**, which studies how traits are passed on from parent to offspring, is based on his work. Although he loved his scientific pursuits, he gave them up in the latter years of his life because of a political struggle between the government and the church. He considered spiritual matters much more important than scientific matters, and he devoted all his energy to fighting what he saw as government encroachment on religious freedom.

During this period in history, science developed a much better understanding of electricity and magnetism. **Michael Faraday**'s experiments and ideas about electricity earned him the title of "the electrical giant." Many of the terms used in the study of electricity today are terms that were first used by Faraday. Faraday's Christian faith was well known in the scientific community. Although humble, he was not ashamed of his Christianity and would argue with any scientist who tried to refute the reality of faith. In fact, his faith led him to lay the foundations of the work of another famous scientist, **James Clerk Maxwell**.

Maxwell is known as the founder of modern physics, which puts him in the same category as Sir Isaac Newton. Maxwell worked with Faraday and was intrigued by Faraday's work and faith. Faraday believed that nature was all interconnected at a fundamental level, because he thought that all nature derived its characteristics from God. Thus, Faraday believed that electricity and magnetism were actually the result of a single process. In other words, he believed that whatever made electricity run through wires also made magnets stick to certain metals. Although Faraday could never offer evidence for this idea, he believed in it fervently.

Maxwell, who was also a devout Christian, shared Faraday's belief. He earned the title of the founder of modern physics because he was able to develop mathematical equations that showed Faraday was right, that electricity and magnetism are both different aspects of the same phenomenon, now called **electromagnetism**. Maxwell is an example of exactly what can be accomplished when you allow your science to be guided by a biblical worldview. Not only did he decide the direction of his research based on his assumptions about how God created the universe, but he was also known to pray while performing his scientific research.

Another very important scientist of this period was **James Joule**. Building on the work of Lavoisier, Joule determined that, like matter, energy cannot be created or destroyed. It can only change forms. This is now known as the **First Law of Thermodynamics**, and it is the guiding principle in the study of energy. He once penned a phrase that should be every scientist's motto: "After the knowledge of, and obedience to, the will of God, the next aim must be to know something of His attributes of wisdom, power, and goodness as evidenced by His handiwork" (*British Scientists of the 19th Century*; J.G. Crowther; K. Paul, Trench, Trubner & Co., Ltd.; 1935; p. 138).

ON YOUR OWN

1.10 As I mentioned in the text, even scientific ideas that are wrong can still lead to advances in science. Besides the scientists mentioned in this section, name another famous scientist that proposed wrong ideas that still advanced science.

Modern Science (1900 A.D. to the Present)

Near the end of the nineteenth century, there were scientists who thought that science had discovered almost all there was to discover about nature. After all, due to the work of Newton and others, scientists could chart the planets in their courses and knew a lot about stars and the rest of space. Those who studied living things had learned volumes about the microscopic world and were in the process of classifying all the organisms known to the human race. With the work of Mendel and others, scientists were finally beginning to understand the complex process of reproduction. Because of the work of Maxwell and others, electricity could be described, and its relationship to magnetism was well understood. The laws of motion as laid down by Newton seemed to explain nearly every aspect of motion that could be studied. As a result, some thought that science had essentially run its course, and there was not much new to be learned.

All this changed in 1900, when **Max Planck** produced a revolutionary idea. In order to explain certain experiments that could not be explained in terms of Newton's laws, Planck proposed an ingenious idea: Much like matter exists in tiny packets called atoms, energy exists in tiny packets, which he called **quanta** (quan' tah). This idea was revolutionary. After all, Newton and the scientists who built on his work believed that you could give *any* amount of energy to an object. If you want to throw a baseball, you can throw it at any speed you desire, as long as you are strong enough. This is not what Planck proposed. He proposed that energy comes in tiny packets. You can give one packet of energy to an object, or you can give two packets of energy to an object. You cannot, however, give an object any amount of energy in between one and two packets.

Now this idea might seem a little weird to you, but it is no weirder than the idea that matter exists in tiny packets called atoms. You can gather one atom of matter or two atoms, but you cannot gather any amount in between. It is essentially the same for energy. Planck produced a lot of evidence for his idea, and after a long while, it became accepted by the scientific community. Eventually, an entirely new way of looking at energy and matter, called **quantum mechanics**, was formed as a result of Planck's idea.

One of the most famous scientists in quantum mechanics was **Albert Einstein**. Einstein used Planck's idea of energy quanta to explain a problem that had perplexed scientists for years. This problem, called the "photoelectric effect" could not be explained by Newton's laws of motion, but could be easily explained by assuming that Planck was right about energy quanta. Despite the fact that Planck produced evidence for his proposition, and despite the fact that Einstein was able to explain a supposedly "unexplainable" problem using the idea of energy quanta, scientists did not want to believe that Planck was right. After all, Newton's laws had been so successful at explaining so much of physics that scientists did not want to believe there was something wrong with them.

As time went on, however, more and more evidence rolled in that showed Planck was right. One of the pivotal cases was made by **Niels Bohr**. Bohr developed a picture of the atom, which we call the **Bohr Model**. This picture of the atom was based on solid mathematics, and it required the assumption that energy comes in small packets. Using the Bohr Model, many of the mysteries of the atom were revealed. In the end, the weight of the evidence overwhelmed the scientific community's devotion to Newton's laws, and quantum mechanics became the new guiding principle in science.

Now it is important to note that quantum mechanics does not really contradict Newton's laws. Newton's laws are still considered valid today. However, we now realize that Newton's laws are simply an *approximation* of quantum mechanics. When the objects you study are large, Newton's laws are valid, because they are equivalent to the laws of quantum mechanics. However, as the size of the object decreases, there are differences between the laws of quantum mechanics and Newton's laws. In those cases, the laws of quantum mechanics are correct. Thus, Newton's laws are useful for large objects (objects we can see), but for tiny objects (like atoms), the laws of quantum mechanics must be used.

FIGURE 1.10

Images in the public domain

Three Important Figures in Quantum Mechanics

Max Planck was the first to propose that energy came in small "packets." This has led science historians to call him the father of quantum mechanics.

Albert Einstein used Planck's idea to develop an explanation for one of the most puzzling effects in physics, known as the photoelectric effect.

Niels Bohr used Planck's idea to develop a mathematical description of the atom. This description allowed scientists to understand experiments they were previously unable to understand.

Although I first mentioned Einstein in terms of the quantum mechanical revolution, he is also an important figure in many other areas of science. For example, Einstein developed a new way of looking at light, matter, and gravity. His **special theory of relativity** explained how matter is really just another form of energy. He used this theory to explain the famous equation $E=mc^2$, which says that matter can be converted to energy and vice versa. Einstein also developed the **general theory of relativity** which is an explanation of *how* gravity works. You will learn more about both of these theories when you take physical science.

Quantum mechanics and relativity have become the guiding principles of science today. The knowledge gained from these ideas has led to numerous advances in medicine, technology, and industry. In many ways, these advances have made life easier for everyone. People live longer today, there are fewer diseases, there is more food per person today than ever before, and increased productivity has led to increased material prosperity. Also, we simply have a clearer picture of *how* creation works. With all these advances, however, do not fall into the trap of thinking we have "figured it all out." Remember, scientists thought that was the case more than 100 years ago. Look what we have learned since then! Science is constantly uncovering new ideas and new ways of looking at things. That's what makes science interesting!

Summing It Up

I hope you have gained something from this overview of science history. If you don't like history, I hope you have at least learned a few lessons from the mistakes scientists have made in the past. If you can learn from those mistakes, you will be a better scientist in the end.

Before you finish with the module, however, I need to make two points. The first is about philosophy. The history of science is rich and detailed. Entire books have been devoted to just portions of the history of science. Thus, there is *no way* I could have covered everything about the history of science in just one module of this course. I am sure there will be some who dispute what I have chosen to cover. Nevertheless, in my opinion, given the constraints of one module, I have presented to you a solid view of how science got to where it is today. I have certainly left a great many things out, so don't think this is the full story. It is, however, a reasonable overview.

The second point I need to make is more practical. You are eventually going to take a test over this. You should be wondering what you need to study. Well, on page 33, you will find a study guide that helps you understand what I consider to be the important material from the module. That ought to help you focus your study for the test. As you work through the study guide, you will see that I do not want you to memorize dates. Rather, I want you to remember the major names and what they were responsible for.

Even though the study guide helps you focus on what to study, there is still *a lot* of information you will need to know for the test. How can you possibly remember it all? Here is a suggestion: Since the study guide covers the material I think is important, make some study aids based on the study guide. For example, I like to make notecards when I have a lot of information to keep straight. On one side of the notecard, I will write a term, a name, or a concept. On the other side, I will write what I need to know about it. For example, the first thing you will see on the study guide is a list of the vocabulary words you need to know. Write the word on one side and the definition on the other. The third question asks, "Who was Imhotep?" Write "Imhotep" on one side of the card and who he was on the other. Once you have done this for the entire study guide, go through your stack of notecards a few times. First, look at one side (the name, for example), and then try to say what is on the other side of the notecard (who he was). Then, *turn the notecards over and go through them the other way*. Thus, when you get to the card about Imhotep, you will look at who he was and then try to say his name. You will be amazed at how well this helps you remember things!

 The multimedia CD has a review of some of the great scientists discussed in this module.

ANSWERS TO THE "ON YOUR OWN" PROBLEMS

1.1 If you look at the definition of science, it contains two parts. Science consists of collecting facts, but it also consists of using those facts to explain the world around us. <u>The Egyptian doctors and the inventors of the ancient world collected lots of facts, but they did not use them to explain the world around them.</u>

1.2 The more tightly packed the matter in a substance, the farther down it fell in the glass. Since density is a measure of how tightly the matter is packed in a substance, the farther the substance fell in the glass, the denser it was. Thus, the least dense item was the cork, and the most dense item was the stone. The vegetable oil was more dense than the cork, but less dense than the water. Continuing that kind of reasoning, then, the order is <u>cork, vegetable oil, ice cube, water, grape, syrup, rock.</u>

1.3 Experiment 1.2 demonstrated that the warmer the substance is, the faster its atoms move. To make ice from water, you must cool the water. Thus, ice is colder than water, which means <u>the atoms in ice move more slowly than those in water.</u>

1.4 Despite the fact that Dr. Hawking is brilliant, he can be wrong, just like many other brilliant scientists. There are many different examples that you could give to your friend that show an example of a brilliant scientist who was wrong. <u>Most importantly, you should tell your friend that we should not make scientific decisions based on *people*. Instead, we should make them based on *data*.</u>

1.5 <u>The story of the geocentric system</u> tells us we must leave personal bias behind when doing science.

1.6 <u>Today's scientists are worried about the future of science because the progress of science depends on cultural support.</u> Science stalled in the Dark Ages due to the Roman culture. If our culture stops supporting science, science will stall again.

1.7 <u>Grosseteste is the first modern scientist because he was the first to work with the scientific method.</u>

1.8 There is no right or wrong answer to this question. You must decide for yourself. Personally, my church means a lot to me. However, I would probably get kicked out rather than give up a belief I truly thought was correct. Since churches are the products of human beings, they are flawed. Only God and Christ are perfect. Thus, a church can be wrong, even about spiritual issues. Of course, I could be wrong, too. If so, I could end up being kicked out of my church for no good reason!

1.9 <u>Newton would not like such textbooks.</u> Newton believed that science had to be linked to math.

1.10 There are several possible answers to these questions. <u>Any one of the first three scientists</u> all advanced science but were wrong. <u>Democritus, Leucippus, Aristotle, Ptolemy, Newton, and many others</u> all advanced the cause of science, but they were all wrong about certain things.

STUDY GUIDE FOR MODULE #1

1. Define the following terms:

a. Science
b. Papyrus
c. Spontaneous generation

2. There were three lessons from the history of science I specifically mentioned in the text. What are they?

3. Who was Imhotep?

4. Although the ancient Egyptians had incredibly advanced medical practices for their time, we do not consider them scientists. Why not?

5. Who were Thales, Anaximander, and Anaximenes?

6. Leucippus and his student, Democritus, are remembered for what idea?

7. Who championed the idea of spontaneous generation and is responsible for it being believed for so long?

8. Who came up with the first classification scheme for living creatures?

9. What is the main difference between the geocentric system and the heliocentric system? Which is correct?

10. What was the main goal of the alchemists?

11. Why don't we consider the alchemists to be scientists?

12. What was the main reason that science progressed near the end of the Dark Ages?

13. Who is considered to be the first modern scientist and why does he deserve that honor?

14. Two great works were published in 1543. Who were the authors and what were the subjects?

15. Although Galileo collected an enormous amount of data in support of the heliocentric system, he was forced to publicly reject it. Why?

16. Galileo built an instrument based on descriptions he had heard of a military device. This allowed him to collect a lot more data about the heavens. What did he build?

17. Who was Sir Isaac Newton? Name at least three of his accomplishments.

18. A major change in scientific approach took place during the Enlightenment. What was good about the change and what was bad about it?

19. What was Lavoisier's greatest contribution to science?

20. What is John Dalton remembered for?

21. What is Charles Darwin remembered for?

22. What does "immutability of species" mean, and who showed that this notion is wrong?

23. What is Gregor Mendel remembered for?

24. James Clerk Maxwell is known as the founder of modern _____.

25. What law did James Joule demonstrate to be true?

26. What is the fundamental assumption behind quantum mechanics? Who first proposed it?

27. What is Niels Bohr remembered for?

28. Einstein was one of the founders of the quantum mechanical revolution. He also is famous for two other ideas. What are they?

"I think this job calls for a quantum mechanic."

Cartoon by Speartoons

MODULE #2: Scientific Inquiry

Introduction

Now that you have a bit of historical context in which to view the human endeavor of science, it is time to figure out exactly what science is all about. You already know the definition of science, and you have already heard terms like "scientific method," so now it's time to learn what science is, and what it is not.

What Science is NOT

The best place to start is to tell you what science is NOT. To learn a bit about what science is not, perform the following experiment.

EXPERIMENT 2.1
How Does Weight Affect the Speed at Which Objects Fall?

Supplies:

♦ A reasonably heavy book
♦ A sheet of cardboard about the same size as the book (The cardboard that comes on the back of a pad of paper works well. You can also cut a piece out of an old cardboard box.)
♦ A sheet of heavy paper (like construction paper or cardstock) about the same size as the book
♦ A sheet of regular paper about the size of the book

Introduction: This experiment will *prove* that heavy objects fall faster than light objects.

Procedure:

1. Hold the book in one hand and the cardboard in another. Hold them both at the same height and parallel to the floor.
2. Drop both at the same time.
3. Note in your laboratory notebook which item hits the ground first.
4. Hold the cardboard in one hand and the heavy paper in another. Hold them just as you held the book and cardboard in step 1.
5. Drop both at the same time.
6. Note in your laboratory notebook which item hits the ground first.
7. Do the same thing once again, this time with the heavy paper and the regular paper.
8. Note in your laboratory notebook which item hits the ground first.
9. Keep the supplies. You will use them again soon.

What did you see in the experiment? If everything went well, you should have noticed that the book hit the ground sooner than the cardboard. The cardboard, however, hit the ground sooner than the heavy sheet of paper, and the heavy piece of paper hit the ground sooner than the regular sheet of paper. What does that tell you? It tells you that heavy things fall faster than light things, right? After all, the book was the heaviest item, the cardboard was the next heaviest item, the heavy paper was next, and the regular paper was the lightest item. Since they all fell the way they did, you can conclude from this experiment that heavy things fall faster than light things, right? Well, not exactly. Perform the following experiment to see what I mean.

EXPERIMENT 2.2
Learning More About Weight and the Speed at Which Objects Fall

Supplies:

♦ All the materials from the previous experiment
♦ A metal paper clip
♦ A small rock (It needs to weigh less than the cardboard, so it should be really small.)

Introduction: In this experiment, you will see that the conclusion I made from the previous experiment is wrong.

Procedure:

1. Hold the book in one hand, as you did in the previous experiment, and the paper clip in the other. Hold them at the same height and drop them simultaneously. Note which hits the ground first.
2. Repeat step 1, this time with the cardboard and the paper clip.
3. Repeat step 1, this time with the heavy paper and the paper clip.
4. Repeat step 1, this time with the regular paper and the paper clip.
5. Repeat steps 1 through 4, substituting the small rock for the paper clip.
6. Wad up the regular paper into a tight, little ball.
7. Repeat step 1, this time using the book and the wadded-up ball of paper.
8. Repeat step 1, this time using the cardboard and the wadded-up ball of paper.
9. Repeat step 1, this time using the heavy paper and the wadded-up ball of paper.

What did you see in this experiment? Well, most likely, the book and the paper clip hit the ground at roughly the same time. In the other trials using the paper clip, the paper clip probably hit the ground first. You should have gotten the same results with the tiny rock. Finally, in steps 7 through 9, the same paper that hit the ground last in every trial of this and the previous experiment probably hit the ground first, with the exception of step 7, when it was dropped with the book. In that step, the wadded-up ball of paper might have hit the ground at the same time or just slightly later than the book.

What do all these results tell us? Well, the first thing they tell us is that our previous conclusion was wrong. After all, the paper clip was certainly lighter than the cardboard and the heavy paper, but it still fell faster than both those objects. The rock was a *lot* lighter than the book, but it hit the ground at the same time as the book. If you chose your rock carefully enough, the rock was lighter than the cardboard, but it still hit the ground sooner than the cardboard. Finally, the same paper that took the longest time to fall in the first experiment suddenly fell faster than the cardboard and the heavy paper when it was wadded up into a ball. Thus, we obviously know that heavy objects do not necessarily fall faster than light objects.

The other thing you might be able to see from this experiment is that the *shape* of an object affects how it falls. After all, when the regular paper was left as a flat sheet, it fell slower than any of the other objects. When it was wadded into a tight ball, however, it fell faster than some of the objects. Also, the small rock and the paper clip had significantly different shapes than all the other objects, and they fell at different speeds. Thus, these experiments seem to indicate that shape has something to do with how quickly an object falls.

Galileo was the first to perform systematic experiments like the ones you have been doing. Based on his work and the work of others, we now know that there is something called **air resistance**. You will learn more about this concept in physical science, but for right now, air resistance refers to the fact that air actually slows objects down as they fall. Several factors affect how strongly air resistance slows an object down, but the object's shape plays a very important role. We now know that if you eliminate air resistance, *all objects fall at the same rate, regardless of weight, shape, or any other characteristic.* This is an important point.

 In the absence of air, ALL objects, regardless of weight or shape, fall at the same rate.

While your two experiments do not demonstrate this fact, many other experiments have.

FIGURE 2.1
Air Resistance

Photo © Thor Jorgen Udvang
Agency: www.shutterstock.com

Despite the fact that this man and his parachute are heavy, he will fall slowly enough to land on the ground safely, because the parachute's fall (and therefore his) is slowed by air resistance. If there were no air, however, he and his parachute would plummet to the ground like a rock.

What can we learn from all this? Well, after the first experiment, we thought we had "proven" that heavy objects fall faster than light objects. We had an experiment with several trials that seemed to demonstrate this fact quite convincingly. Also, the conclusion made sense. After all, if you were to tell most people that heavy objects fall faster than light objects, they would probably agree with you. The statement makes sense and, in general, it is consistent with our everyday experience.

Nevertheless, despite the fact that we had an experiment to back up our conclusion, and despite the fact that the conclusion made sense, it was shown to be wrong. This brings up one thing that science is NOT:

Science is NOT a means by which something can be *proven*.

No matter what you might have thought up to this point, and no matter what you might hear or read, science has never and can never *prove* anything!

Now that last statement might shock you a bit. After all, everyone at one time or another has heard the phrase, "Science has proven...." This is a typical phrase uttered by some people, even some scientists, but nevertheless, it is absolutely wrong. As the two previous experiments (as well as the history of science you read in the previous module) show, scientific conclusions are *continually* being changed based on new information. Ptolemy had an excellent explanation for the arrangement of the planets and stars in the sky. Other scientists had observations and experiments that backed up Ptolemy's view. It turned out, however, that Ptolemy was wrong. Even Copernicus, despite the fact that he proposed a *better* arrangement, was still wrong about a great many things. In fact, even ideas that scientists thought were true just 20 years ago are being changed or discarded due to new data.

In the end, then, all conclusions that scientists draw are *tentative*. All it takes is one experiment to destroy a conclusion based on thousands of years of careful scientific investigation. Consider another example: Suppose a student decided to go to the top of his or her house and start dropping things off the roof. The student starts with small objects like a pen, a shoe, a ball, a pillow, etc. Eventually, the student throws bigger objects like furniture and appliances off the roof. After the student is severely punished by his parents, the student makes this grand proclamation: "My experiments have proven that when an object is dropped from our roof, it will fall."

Is the student correct? Of course not. Despite the fact that the student might have dropped *every object in the house* off the roof, it still does not show that *every* object will fall off the roof when dropped. Suppose you were to drop a helium-filled balloon off the roof. Would it fall? No. It would float high into the air. The helium-filled balloon is what we in science call a **counter example**.

Counter example – An example that contradicts a conclusion

The single counter example provided by the helium-filled balloon shows that the student's conclusion was wrong. It is the same with any scientific conclusion. A single counter example is enough to destroy a conclusion built on thousands of years of scientific work!

So what *can* science do, if it cannot prove anything? Well, when the correct method is followed, science can be used to draw conclusions that are reasonably reliable. Those conclusions will hopefully help us better understand the way creation works, and perhaps we will be able to use those conclusions to build neat things like TVs, VCRs, and air conditioners. However, no matter how reliable we think the conclusions of science are, they are *always* tentative.

To really drive this point home, I want to give you another example from the history of science. In the late 1600s, German scientists Johann Becher and Georg Stahl attempted to explain the observation that some things (like paper and trees) will burn, while other things (like rocks and certain metals) will not. They proposed an idea that all burnable substances contain something called **phlogiston** (fluh jis' tuhn). As a substance burns, it loses phlogiston and, in enough time, the burning will cease because all the phlogiston will be used up. These scientists had detailed experiments to back up their idea, and it became the accepted scientific explanation of combustion for the next 100 years. It took the detailed experiments of Antoine-Laurent Lavoisier (whom you read about in Module #1) to provide counter examples that showed the phlogiston explanation to be wrong. Lavoisier proposed that the process of combustion is actually a chemical reaction in which the chemicals of the substance that is burning react with oxygen in the air, and that there is no such thing as phlogiston. That's what scientists still believe today.

FIGURE 2.2
Combustion

Photo © Stephanie Swartz
Agency: www.shutterstock.com

Contrary to what had been "proven" by Becher and Stahl, these trees are not burning because they contain phlogiston. They are burning because of a chemical reaction with oxygen in the air.

If you are interested in learning more about why science cannot prove anything, you might want to consider reading Karl Popper's book *The Logic of Scientific Discovery*. This book is probably the most important work on the philosophy of science that has been published in the past 100 years, and it is considered one of the major guiding forces in modern science.

ON YOUR OWN

2.1 The First Law of Thermodynamics is a guiding principle of most science today. It basically states that energy cannot be created or destroyed; it can only change forms. In every experiment that has been done properly, the First Law of Thermodynamics has been obeyed. Has science succeeded in proving the First Law of Thermodynamics?

The Scientific Method

As I mentioned in the previous section, although science cannot *prove* anything, as long as you follow the correct method, science can draw conclusions that are reasonably reliable. What is that method? Well, it was first proposed by Grosseteste at the end of the Dark Ages. Today, we call it the **scientific method**. This method provides a framework in which scientists can analyze situations, explain certain phenomena, and answer certain questions. Although you cannot be 100 percent sure that the conclusions you draw from this method are correct, they are more reliable than most other conclusions. Thus, while science doesn't provide a means by which to prove something, it does provide the best means by which you can draw conclusions about the natural world.

The scientific method starts with **observation**. Observation allows the scientist to collect data. Once enough data has been collected, the scientist forms a **hypothesis** (hy pah' thuh sis) that attempts to explain some facet of the data or attempts to answer a question that the scientist asks.

Hypothesis – An educated guess that attempts to explain an observation or answer a question

Once she forms a hypothesis, the scientist (typically with help from other scientists) then collects much more data in an effort to test the hypothesis. If the data are found to be inconsistent with the hypothesis, the hypothesis might be discarded, or it might just be modified until it is consistent with all data that has been collected. If a large amount of data is collected and the hypothesis is consistent with all the data, the hypothesis becomes a theory.

Theory – A hypothesis that has been tested with a significant amount of data

Since a theory has been tested by a large amount of data, it is much more reliable than a hypothesis. As more and more data relevant to the theory get collected, the theory can be tested over and over again. If several generations of collected data are all consistent with the theory, it eventually attains the status of a scientific law.

Scientific law – A theory that has been tested by and is consistent with generations of data

An example of the scientific method in action can be found in the life of Ignaz Semmelweis, a Hungarian doctor who lived in the early-to-mid 1800s. He was put in charge of a ward in Vienna's most famous hospital, the Allegemeines Krankenhaus. He noticed that in his ward, patients were dying at a rate exceeding that of many other wards, even those with sicker patients. Semmelweis observed the situation for quite some time, trying to figure out what was different about his ward as compared to all others in the hospital. He finally determined that the only noticeable difference was that his ward was the first one that the doctors and medical students visited after they performed autopsies on the dead.

Based on his observations, Semmelweis hypothesized that the doctors were carrying something deadly from the corpses upon which the autopsies were being performed to the patients in his ward. Thus, Dr. Semmelweis exercised the first step in the scientific method. He made some observations and then formed a hypothesis to explain those observations.

Semmelweis then developed a way to test his hypothesis. He instituted a rule that all doctors had to wash their hands after they finished their autopsies and before they examined patients in his ward. Believe it or not, up to that point in history, doctors never thought to wash their hands before examining or even operating on a patient! After all, there was no concept of germs at that time. Thus, doctors had no reason to believe that something on their hands could harm a patient. However, based on his hypothesis, Dr. Semmelweis hoped that by washing their hands, doctors would remove whatever was being carried from the corpses to the patients in his ward.

Well, the doctors did not like the new rule, but they grudgingly obeyed it, and the death rate in Dr. Semmelweis's ward *decreased significantly!* To further test his hypothesis, he required that any instruments used on his patients must be washed as well, and the death rate in his ward *decreased to the lowest in the entire hospital*. This, of course, was good evidence that his hypothesis was correct. You would think that the doctors would be overjoyed. They were not. In fact, some got so tired of having to wash their hands before entering Dr. Semmelweis's ward that they actively worked against him. His successor, anxious to win the approval of the doctors, rescinded Semmelweis's policy, and the death rate in the ward shot back up again.

Semmelweis spent the rest of his life doing more and more experiments to confirm his hypothesis that something unseen but nevertheless deadly can be carried from one person to another. Although Semmelweis's work was not appreciated until after his death, his hypothesis was eventually confirmed by enough experiments that it became a scientific theory. Although Semmelweis's hypothesis was ultimately confirmed, he actually died in a mental asylum. It is thought that his despair over the fact that hand-washing could save lives but was not being done drove him crazy.

As time went on, more and more data were gathered in support of Semmelweis's theory. As Antoni van Leeuwenhoek's microscope became a popular tool in medical science, doctors were finally able to see the deadly germs that can be transmitted from person to person. They were able to do experiments that showed germs infecting and harming healthy tissue. In the end, after years of experimentation by Semmelweis and others, Semmelweis's theory became a scientific law. Nowadays, doctors do all that they can to completely sterilize their hands, clothes, and instruments before performing any medical procedure.

Before we leave this story, it might be interesting to note that the Old Testament contains meticulous instructions concerning how a priest is to cleanse himself after touching a dead body. These rituals, some of which are laid out in Numbers 19, are more effective than all but the most modern methods of sterilization. In fact, medical doctor S.I. McMillen says, "In 1960, the Department [of Health in New York State] issued a book describing a method of washing the hands, and the procedures closely approximate the scriptural method given in Numbers 19" (*None of These Diseases*, S. I. McMillen, Fleming H. Revell Co., 1963, p. 18). This, of course, should not surprise you. After all, God knows all about germs. Thus, it only makes sense that He would lay down instructions as to how His people should protect themselves against them. If only doctors had the sense to follow those rules over the past centuries, countless lives would have been saved!

So you see, the scientific method (summarized in Figure 2.3 on the next page) provides a methodical way to examine a situation or answer a question. If a theory survives the scientific method and becomes a law, it can be considered reasonably trustworthy. Even a scientific theory that has not been tested enough to be a law is still pretty reliable, because it is backed up by a lot of scientific data. Nevertheless, you must always remember that the conclusions of science are *tentative*. Just one counter example can destroy a scientific law, and the history of science is filled with such occurrences!

 The multimedia CD has microscopic video and a discussion of germs.

FIGURE 2.3
The Scientific Method

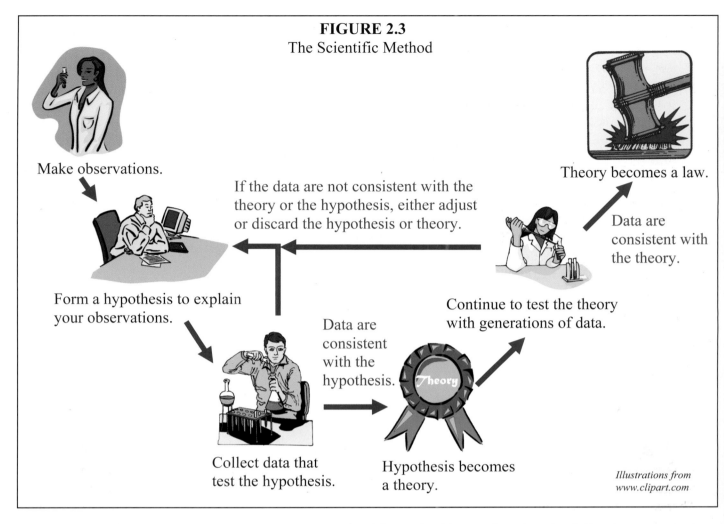

Make observations.

If the data are not consistent with the theory or the hypothesis, either adjust or discard the hypothesis or theory.

Theory becomes a law.

Data are consistent with the theory.

Form a hypothesis to explain your observations.

Continue to test the theory with generations of data.

Data are consistent with the hypothesis.

Collect data that test the hypothesis.

Hypothesis becomes a theory.

Illustrations from www.clipart.com

Now I want you to get some practice using the scientific method by performing the following experiment.

EXPERIMENT 2.3
The Broken Flashlight

Supplies:

♦ A working flashlight
♦ A parent or helper
♦ Eye protection such as goggles or safety glasses

Introduction: In this experiment, you will fix a flashlight that is not working. In the process, you will use the scientific method to determine what caused the flashlight to stop working.

Procedure

1. Tell your parent or helper to look in the solutions and tests guide in order to get their instructions for this experiment. The instructions can be found after the solutions to the test for Module #2. **YOU <u>CANNOT</u> READ THOSE INSTRUCTIONS**. The instructions give your parent/helper an idea of how to make the flashlight stop working. It will be your job to find out what your parent/helper did, so if you read the instructions, you defeat the purpose of the experiment!

2. Once your parent/helper has done something to the flashlight to make it stop working, take it apart. Do this slowly, so you can observe the parts. This will not only help you figure out what's going on, but it will also help you learn how to put the flashlight back together.

3. Once you have taken the flashlight apart and made your observations, write a hypothesis in your laboratory notebook that attempts to explain *why* the flashlight is not working.

4. After you have written your hypothesis down, design an experiment to test your hypothesis. Now please realize that *just fixing the flashlight is not enough*. Science attempts to explain things, not just invent things. If you get the flashlight working, that's nice, but you are doing no more than the ancient Egyptians you learned about in Module #1. They had lots of great inventions and could cure lots of health problems, but they did not understand *why* things happened. In order to do science, you must *explain* the world around you, not just fix things. Thus, you must perform an experiment that specifically tests your hypothesis. Your parent/helper was given some tips, so if you are stuck, get help.

5. Once you have performed your experiment, determine whether or not the experiment confirmed the hypothesis. If so, your hypothesis is now a theory. That's about as far as you can go, because to turn your theory into a law, you would have to test it with several different flashlights, under several different conditions, for several years.

6. If your experiment *did not* confirm your hypothesis, try to come up with another hypothesis and another experiment, and try again.

7. Check with your parent/helper to determine whether or not your hypothesis was correct.

What did you learn from the experiment? Well, hopefully you learned why the flashlight stopped working. That's not the only thing you should have learned, however. You should have learned something about how science is done. You could have just fixed the flashlight and moved on. That would have been fast, easy, and useful. However, that's not what science is all about. When you do science, you must *explain* something, not just fix it. After all, haven't you ever taken apart something that was broken, found nothing wrong with it and then, when you put it back together, it suddenly worked again? That has happened to me more than once. Often, just taking something apart will jostle the components around enough to get them working.

That's why I stressed in the experiment that just getting the flashlight working was not enough. Think about it. You found what you *thought* was wrong with the flashlight in the course of the experiment. You then put the flashlight together and it worked. That *does not* mean you really found the problem. It means that either you found the problem or, in the process of taking the flashlight apart and putting it back together again, you *accidentally fixed the real problem*. Had you not done an experiment to confirm your hypothesis, you would have never known which of those two possibilities actually occurred.

Now the experiment might have seemed a bit tedious. After all, if you find something that looks to be a problem, eliminate it, and then the flashlight works again, most likely you did, indeed, find the source of the problem. Science, however, must be much more careful. Since there were two possible explanations for why the flashlight began to work again, you had to do an experiment that would help you eliminate one of those possibilities. That's how science works. In a scientific experiment, you must be very careful to examine all possible explanations for your observations and then perform experiments to eliminate all but the correct explanation.

ON YOUR OWN

The discovery of Neptune is another excellent example of the scientific method in use. Scientists had noticed that the planet Uranus did not orbit around the sun exactly as Newton's Law of Universal Gravitation predicted. French scientist Urbain Jean Joseph Leverrier assumed this was because a previously undiscovered planet was interfering with Uranus's movement. He made some calculations using Newton's Law of Universal Gravitation and determined where this undiscovered planet had to be in order for Uranus's motion to be consistent with Newton's law. German scientist Johann Gottfried Galle used a telescope to look in the sky at the position Leverrier had predicted, and he saw the planet on the very first night of the search! The planet was named Neptune.

2.2 In this account, what was the observation that led to a hypothesis?

2.3 What was the hypothesis?

2.4 What was the experiment to confirm the hypothesis?

2.5 At the end of the story as written here, was the presence of Neptune in space a scientific law or a theory?

2.6 There is at least one other hypothesis that could have been made based on the observation. Experiments would have eventually shown it to be wrong, however. What is that alternate hypothesis?

Failures of the Scientific Method

Although the scientific method allows us to draw reasonably accurate conclusions about the world around us, those conclusions are not ironclad. In fact, there have been *many* examples of how the scientific method has been used to reach conclusions that are completely wrong. In this section, I want to concentrate on two such examples. Hopefully, these examples will illustrate what I have been trying to stress both in this module and the previous one: **The conclusions of science are *always* tentative**.

In the late 1800s, Italian scientist Giovanni Schiaparelli used a powerful (for its time) telescope to observe the surface of the planet Mars. He noticed several faint lines that seemed to crisscross about the planet. When he published his observations, he said that those lines might be natural or they might be the work of intelligent beings. He was not sure. Upon seeing Schiaparelli's drawings, American scientist Percival Lowell hypothesized that the lines were actually canals that had been dug by the inhabitants of Mars. He assumed that the purpose of the canals was for water distribution. Lowell built an observatory in Arizona to make detailed observations of the planet, which he thought would confirm his hypothesis.

In the early 1900s, Lowell published the results of his observations, providing what he saw as clear and convincing evidence that the lines first observed by Schiaparelli were, indeed, canals built by intelligent beings. He noticed that the lines seemed to change from time to time. He saw this as evidence that the canals were used for water distribution. After all, anyone smart enough to build canals would probably be smart enough to have a system by which they could be opened and closed based on where the water was needed. Thus, the fact that the lines seemed to change from time to time was seen as strong evidence that the lines were actually canals that had been constructed by the inhabitants of Mars.

Also, Lowell noticed that there were blue-green splotches on the planet that would also change from time to time. Sometimes their shape would change; sometimes they would disappear altogether. He assumed that theses splotches were patches of vegetation and that the changing water distribution of the canals (as well as perhaps the changing seasons on Mars) changed where the vegetation flourished and died out.

Lowell's work was received excitedly by many in the scientific community, and other scientists made observations of Mars that seemed to support Lowell's idea that there were canals, vegetation, and intelligent life on Mars. Some even speculated that the inhabitants of Mars must be incredibly advanced to make a planet-wide network of canals that could be opened and closed based on need. Using that assumption, some actually proposed that the two moons orbiting Mars were, in fact, not natural. Instead, these scientists believed that the moons were constructed by the inhabitants of Mars. A few even believed that they were some sort of attack vessels and that the inhabitants of Mars would actually invade earth one day!

FIGURE 2.4
Mars

Photo courtesy of NASA

Mars is named after the Roman god of war, because it often appears as a red dot in the sky. The color reminded the ancients of blood, which reminded them of war. Many scientists have thought that life once existed on Mars. Lowell believed that he saw canals on the planet's surface, and he thought they had been dug by intelligent life. More recently (1996), NASA announced that a meteorite from Mars had been discovered. This meteorite had certain tiny structures that could be seen as evidence of microscopic life, indicating that there was, indeed, life on Mars, at least at one time. Detailed studies of the meteorite, however, indicate that the tiny structures are *not* evidence of microscopic life. Instead, they are structures produced by chemical processes unrelated to life.

At this point in the scientific method, Lowell's original hypothesis could be considered a theory. Based on Schiaparelli's observations, Lowell had formed the hypothesis that canals existed on Mars. He then designed experiments to test his hypothesis (building an observatory and observing

Mars in detail). The results of his experiments confirmed his hypothesis. In addition, other scientists had made observations that seemed to support his hypothesis. Thus, the hypothesis became a theory.

As time went on and more powerful telescopes were built, however, the theory of canals on Mars began to disintegrate. Scientists found that many of the "canals" Lowell and other scientists observed with their telescopes could not be consistently observed by others. Eventually, it was determined that many of the "canals" were really optical illusions caused by the poor optics of the telescopes that Lowell and others had used, along with eye fatigue from long hours of observation through a telescope. The changing blue-green blotches that Lowell and others saw were, in fact, simply collections of dust that were blown about by windstorms that are common on the planet. Many robotic spacecraft have since been sent to Mars, and there are even two robots (Opportunity and Spirit) crawling around its surface, allowing scientists to get very detailed information about what is on that planet. So far, there has not been any evidence collected to indicate that there was once life on Mars.

So you see that following the scientific method does not guarantee that the conclusions drawn are accurate. Lowell and those who believed as he did followed the scientific method to a tee. Nevertheless, they were wrong. Of course, this happened a long time ago. Surely *modern* science doesn't make such mistakes, does it? Yes, it does.

In 1911, Dutch scientist Heike Onnes discovered the phenomenon of **superconductivity**. What is superconductivity? Well, when electricity travels through a wire, the wire resists the flow of electricity. This resistance reduces the energy of the electricity in the wire, and the lost energy is converted to heat, light, or some form of work. In fact, that's how a non-fluorescent light bulb (usually called an "incandescent light bulb") works. The filament in the light bulb resists the flow of electricity, and that resistance generates both heat and light. Onnes discovered that certain substances at *very* low temperatures (about -450 degrees Fahrenheit) did not resist the flow of electricity at all. Thus, electricity could pass through the substance without losing energy. That's superconductivity.

At that time, superconductivity was a complete mystery. Many scientists confirmed Onnes's discovery, but no one knew *how* it could be explained. Everything in science at that time in history indicated that regardless of the substance or temperature, there should *always* be resistance to electricity. As quantum mechanics (see Module #1) became more and more accepted by the scientific community, however, scientists began to see how superconductivity was possible.

In the 1950s, three scientists (Bardeen, Cooper, and Schrieffer) began work on a hypothesis they thought would explain superconductivity. Several experiments confirmed their hypothesis and, by 1960, it was considered a scientific theory. It was actually given the name "BCS theory" in honor of the three scientists who came up with the original hypothesis. BCS theory was put to the test for the next 25 years, and it was confirmed by each and every experiment that was done. BCS theory contained detailed mathematical equations that predicted the results of every experiment done. As a result, BCS theory became the widely accepted explanation of superconductivity. Eventually, physics textbooks started presenting BCS theory as fact, because of the weight of scientific evidence in its favor.

One of the consequences of BCS theory is that there is a certain temperature (roughly -400 degrees Fahrenheit) above which superconductivity is impossible. Regardless of the substance, there could be no superconductivity above a temperature of roughly -400 degrees Fahrenheit. Since BCS theory became accepted as the proper explanation of superconductivity, this consequence was also considered a scientific fact. Thus, scientists as a whole decided that it would be impossible to find superconductivity above that temperature.

Of course, there were a few scientists who were not so convinced about this conclusion. Despite the fact that they were ridiculed by many in the scientific community, these scientists tried to find an example of superconductivity at a temperature higher than that allowed by BCS theory. In 1986, two scientists (J. George Bednorz and Karl Alex Muller) at the IBM research laboratory in Germany found it! Since then, many more examples of superconductivity at higher temperatures than ever thought possible have been found. These superconductors are now called "high-temperature superconductors" and may someday revolutionize the way we use electricity.

So here we have an example of a very modern scientific theory (one considered "fact" by most scientists) that was overthrown by one counter example. As time has gone on, many more counter examples have been discovered. Clearly the original three scientists (Bardeen, Cooper, and Schrieffer) followed the scientific method. Nevertheless, their scientific theory, considered "fact" by many textbooks, was demonstrated to be false!

FIGURE 2.5
A Superconductor and a Magnet

The object floating in the air is a magnet. The dark disk beneath it is a high-temperature superconductor. Because a superconductor excludes magnetic fields, it repels the magnet, causing the magnet to lift into the air. Because this is a "high-temperature" superconductor, it needs to be cooled to "only" -321 degrees Fahrenheit. While this is still very cold, according to BCS theory, no substance should be superconductive at such a "high" temperature.

Now please understand why I brought up these two examples. I certainly do not want to insult the scientists involved. Lowell made many positive contributions to the pursuit of science. For example, he was the first to postulate the existence of a ninth planet. After his death, the ninth planet (now called Pluto) was observed by the very same observatory from which he observed the planet Mars. Although BCS theory turns out to be wrong to some extent, it has still advanced our understanding of superconductivity tremendously. So please don't think I am insulting the scientists in these two stories; they have made *great* contributions to the pursuit of science!

I also do not want to give you the impression that science is a worthless endeavor. Nothing could be further from the truth! Following the scientific method has helped us learn an enormous amount about the world around us. That knowledge has resulted in longer lifespans for people, more productivity for industries, and new inventions like automobiles and airplanes. Clearly, then, science is a *very* worthwhile endeavor.

I brought up these examples to really bring home the point that the conclusions of science are *tentative*. Although Lowell had plenty of evidence for his theory, the evidence was produced with poor telescopes. Thus, the evidence could not be used to support the theory. Although BCS theory had a lot of experiments to back it up, it suffered from a lack of very specific data: the existence of high-temperature superconductors. Thus, no matter how firm a theory or law seems to be, new data might very well destroy it overnight!

ON YOUR OWN

2.7 Lowell's observations of Mars were used to support a theory that has been demonstrated to be false. Are those observations therefore worthless?

2.8 What caused BCS theory to become accepted as the proper scientific explanation for superconductivity?

The Limitations of Science

Now that you have seen some instances in which the scientific method failed to produce reliable conclusions, it seems only natural to discuss the limitations of science. Although science is incredibly interesting and has helped us greatly in our understanding of how creation works, it is not flawless. As I mentioned at the beginning of the module, science cannot *prove* anything. It can provide evidence that a certain idea is true, but it *cannot* prove the idea. It is also not 100 percent reliable. As the history of science clearly shows, scientific theories and laws can be overthrown as the result of new information and ideas.

So science cannot prove anything, and it is not 100 percent reliable. Nevertheless, it is an interesting and useful pursuit. Science has helped us understand an enormous amount about the world around us. It has also led to the development of incredibly useful inventions. Thus, even though it has its limits, science has done a lot to make our lives better. As a result, it is important to understand what science *can* do.

There are those who have a very limited view of science. They say, for example, that science cannot be used to study anything we do not observe happening today. In other words, we can use science to study how cancer forms in the body and how to cure it. After all, we see cancer affecting people every day. We can also design experiments in which we observe whether or not proposed cures actually work. However, these same people say that we cannot use science to examine questions such as the age of the earth, how life originated on earth, or how the earth was formed. After all, they say, no one was around to observe these events. Since the heart of science is observation, there is simply no way that science can be used to study such events.

This is just not true. The only limitations of science are that it cannot prove anything, it is not 100 percent reliable, and it must conform to the scientific method. Can we apply the scientific method to questions such as the ones I discussed above? Of course! We cannot observe the formation of the earth, but we can certainly observe the structure and composition of the earth. We can then form a hypothesis about how the earth came into existence. We can then do more experiments on the earth to learn more about its structure. The data collected from those experiments can be used to test the hypothesis. The hypothesis might have to be refined, but eventually, it might become a theory. More experiments on the structure of the earth can be done, and one day, the theory might even become a law.

In fact, later on in this course we will spend quite some time studying fossils and rocks. You will learn the different ways fossils and rocks form and, by studying the fossils and rocks that are here now, you can learn a lot about what happened in earth's past. Despite the fact that there was not a scientist observing the rocks and fossils forming, you will learn how the scientific method has been applied in an attempt to determine the validity of two competing theories of earth's history.

In the end, then, science is not limited to answering only certain questions. If we apply the scientific method properly, we can use science to attempt to answer virtually *any* question. You must realize, however, that any answer you get from science is tentative. It can always be demonstrated to be wrong, with just one counter example.

So what *can* you do with science? You can study virtually anything and attempt to answer virtually any question. As long as you adhere to the scientific method, you will be using science. You must remember, however, that no matter how well you apply the scientific method, your conclusions could be wrong. The more scientific evidence you have to support your hypothesis or theory, the *less likely* it is that your conclusions are wrong. Nevertheless, science is not 100 percent reliable and cannot prove anything. Thus, your conclusions are always subject to change!

Science and Christianity

Before you finish this module, I want to really emphasize that the scientific method can be applied to *any* subject. Thus, I want to spend some time applying the scientific method to the subject of Christianity. Whether you believe it or not, we can certainly apply the scientific method in studying Christianity. In fact, since the Christian worldview is largely responsible for bringing science out of the Dark Ages, it shouldn't even surprise you that we can use the scientific method to study the Christian faith.

Let's start with an observation. I have met many, many individuals who draw an enormous amount of strength, hope, and encouragement from the Bible. They believe that God speaks to them through Scripture, and they seem quite sincere. Now, of course, there are many other people who draw strength, hope, and encouragement from other sources (the Koran, the Bhagavad-Gita, crystals, humanism, etc.). Thus, just because some people claim God speaks to them through the Bible, that doesn't mean it's true. So we will use the scientific method to help us evaluate their claim.

Based on the observation that many people draw an enormous amount of strength, hope, and encouragement from the Bible, let's form the hypothesis that the Bible is the Word of God. Now we have to collect some data that will either confirm or deny the hypothesis. What kind of data should we collect? Well, let's look at the Bible and see if we can find any evidence that either supports or contradicts our hypothesis.

There is one really obvious place to start. Even a brief reading of the Bible will reveal that it makes a *lot* of predictions about the future. Since parts of the Bible were written a long, long time ago, some of those predictions should have already come true. This is an excellent source of data that relates to our hypothesis. After all, if the Bible is the Word of God, He must have inspired it. Thus, any predictions that it makes about the future *must* be true. However, if the Bible was, in fact, written without inspiration from God, you wouldn't expect it to have a very good track record when it comes to predicting the future. So, let's look at biblical prophecies (specific predictions about the future). Whether or not they have come true will provide us with excellent data that directly relate to our hypothesis.

The prophecies I want to discuss were all written before the events took place. We know this as a result of certain historical facts. First, we know that the entire Old Testament was written by no later than 246 B.C., because the Greek Septuagint, a copy of the entire Old Testament, was initiated in the reign of Ptolemy Philadelphus (285 to 246 B.C.). This is a historical fact. Thus, we know that the Old Testament, in its entirety, existed by about 250 B.C.

The first biblical prophecy comes from the book of Ezekiel, chapter 26, verses 3-21. A subsection of that text says:

> ...therefore, thus says the Lord God, "Behold, I am against you, O Tyre, and I will bring up many nations against you, as the sea brings up its waves. And they will destroy the walls of Tyre and break down her towers; and I will scrape her debris from her and make her a bare rock. She will be a place for the spreading of nets in the midst of the sea, for I have spoken...Also her daughters on the mainland will be slain by the sword...I will bring upon Tyre from the north Nebuchadnezzar king of Babylon...He will slay your daughters on the mainland by the sword; and he will make siege walls against you...Also, they will make a spoil of your riches...and throw your stones and your timbers and your debris into the water...And I will make you a bare rock; you will be a place for the spreading of nets. You will be built no more...

According to the prophecy, things do not look good for Tyre. As mentioned before, we know for certain that this prophecy was written by about 250 B.C. The generally accepted date for the writing of this book, however, is 592-570 B.C. Most historians accept this as a rather strong fact because the book uses a very odd dating system that was used only for a brief time in the early sixth century B.C. Thus, the author was either writing at that time or was a very knowledgeable historian doing everything he could to deceive the reader.

Notice how detailed and precise this prophecy is. Ezekiel calls the city by name. He tells us that many nations will come against her and even singles out the leader of the first nation, Babylon. He is also very specific about Tyre's ultimate fate. He says that Tyre's debris will be thrown into the ocean; it will not be rebuilt; and it will become a place where fishermen can spread their nets to dry.

The other aspect of this prophecy that must be pointed out is the fact that anyone living in Ezekiel's time would consider his predictions to be absurd. Tyre was one of the greatest cities of the ancient world. According to Dr. Wallace Fleming, Tyre was founded more than 2,000 years before this prophecy was written. During that time, it had grown into the most important trading center in that region of the world.

The city was originally built on a large island that lay one-half mile off the coast of Syria. The island had nice ports where trading ships could dock. A smaller island near the original city was eventually linked to the larger island, making the total circumference of the city approximately 2½ miles. The outer wall of the city was up to 150 feet high and was surmounted by battlements. As a result of its prominence as a major trading center, Tyre grew quickly, and an extension of the city had to be built on the mainland. The combination of Tyre's outer walls, its strategic location on an island, and the mainland city as its first line of defense made the city seem invulnerable. In the words of Dr. Fleming, "...Tyre was not only a great city but was considered impregnable." (*The History of Tyre*, Wallace B. Fleming, Columbia University Press: New York, 1915, p. 8)

We see, then, that Ezekiel's prophecy went against the common human wisdom of the day. Had Ezekiel been trying to "make up" a prophecy that would come true, he probably would have tried to predict the fall of a city that seemed a little weaker than the great fortress of Tyre! Instead, Ezekiel pronounced the city's doom, and specifically mentioned many facets of its destruction.

To see just how well this prophecy came true, we only need to consult the history books. According to the ancient historian Herodotus, Nebuchadnezzar, king of Babylon, laid siege to Tyre from 585 to 572 B.C. In the siege, Nebuchadnezzar was able to destroy and take the mainland city, but he was unable to effectively attack the island city. As a result, he simply laid a 13-year siege, stopping all supplies from entering the island city. This pressure forced Tyre to accept Babylonian rule, but the island city remained intact. These historical facts are in perfect agreement with the predictions of Ezekiel.

Since Nebuchadnezzar's siege of Tyre occurred very close to when the prophecy is assumed to have been written, this particular prediction is not all that impressive. It's possible the author wrote this "prophecy" after the fact, thereby ensuring its accuracy. Thus, if this were the only prediction made by Ezekiel, it would not be significant evidence for my hypothesis. The prophecy continues, however, as does the history of Tyre.

The prophecy states that many nations, not just Babylon, will stand against Tyre. It states that Nebuchadnezzar will destroy the mainland city, but it says that "they" will throw Tyre's stones and timbers into the sea. In using the pronoun "they" instead of "he," the prophecy makes the distinction between Nebuchadnezzar and the others that will stand against Tyre. Thus, the pronoun "they" does not refer to Nebuchadnezzar; it refers to the other leaders who will try to destroy Tyre. As history tells us, other leaders did, indeed, march against Tyre.

In 333 B.C., Alexander the Great demanded that Tyre allow him to occupy the island city. The king of Tyre, Azemilcus, was willing to grant Alexander dominion over Tyre, but was unwilling to let him and his army occupy the city. Alexander was thus forced to attack Tyre in order to gain full control over her strategic location. According to the *Encyclopedia Britannica*, Alexander had no fleet with which to attack the island city of Tyre, so he *completely destroyed the mainland city and dumped all its debris into the ocean.* There was so much debris that Alexander was able to construct a wide bridge of debris from the mainland city to the island city, making it possible for his army to march close enough to Tyre to build siege engines (like catapults) and attack the city.

The "bridge" (more properly called a "mole") that Alexander the Great constructed was predicted by Ezekiel almost 250 years before it was built! His prophecy specifically states that Tyre's debris would be thrown into the ocean by someone other than Nebuchadnezzar, and that's exactly what happened! Even the most hardened skeptic would have a hard time arguing that this part of the prophecy was not written down well before the events took place. After all, historians are convinced that the prophecy was written in the sixth century B.C. Even if a skeptic is unwilling to believe the generally accepted date, we know for a fact that the entire Old Testament was copied less than 100 years after Alexander's battle against Tyre. It's very unlikely that a revered document like the Old Testament could be altered so significantly and that the altered version could become generally accepted in less than a century! Clearly, this part of the prophecy *had* to have been recorded before the events took place.

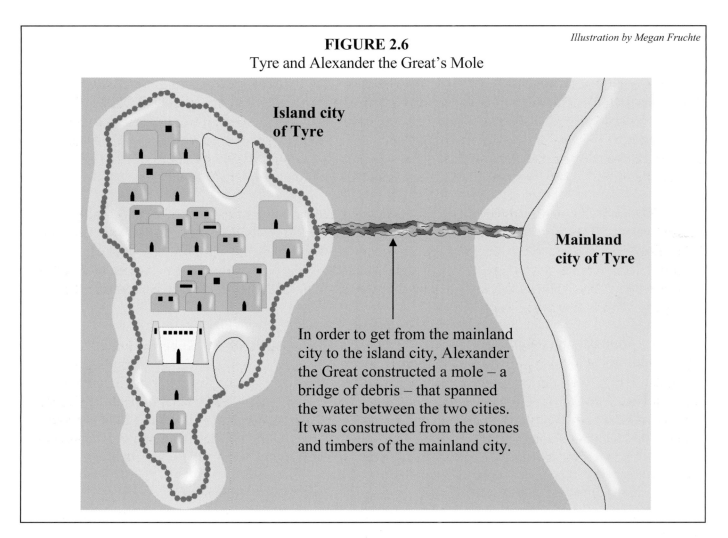

FIGURE 2.6
Tyre and Alexander the Great's Mole

Illustration by Megan Fruchte

Island city of Tyre

Mainland city of Tyre

In order to get from the mainland city to the island city, Alexander the Great constructed a mole – a bridge of debris – that spanned the water between the two cities. It was constructed from the stones and timbers of the mainland city.

Ezekiel also predicted that many nations would march against Tyre, and that's exactly what happened. After Alexander the Great's conquest, the Seleucidae, the Romans, the Moslems, and the crusaders all took turns conquering Tyre. After all this fighting, Tyre lay in ruins. Today, old Tyre is, indeed, scraped down to bare rock. According to historian Nina Jidejian, "The port [of Tyre] has become a haven today for fishing boats *and a place for spreading nets*" (*Tyre Through the Ages*, Nina Jidejian, El-Mashreq Publishers: Beruit, 1969, p. 139, emphasis added).

Think about that for a minute. Ezekiel's prophecy was so precise that it was able to predict the only future use for the city of Tyre – a place for fishermen to spread their nets out so they could dry and be repaired! The prophecy was written down long before Tyre was laid flat by all its conquerors. Only after about 600 A.D. did Tyre become a haven for the spreading of nets. How can all of this be explained? How could Ezekiel have made such an impressive prediction? Was he just really lucky?

If this were the only example of a specific prophecy in the Old Testament that had come true, luck might be a reasonable explanation. There are, however, many such prophecies in the Old Testament. For example, Josh McDowell, in his book *Evidence that Demands a Verdict*, outlines eleven other Old Testament prophecies that predict the future of other major cities in the ancient world. These prophecies were all written down before the events took place, and they all came true in the smallest detail! This is very good evidence in support of our hypothesis. After all, how can anyone except the Creator of time know what will happen in the future? The fact that the Bible is so good at predicting future events long before they take place is evidence that it was inspired by God.

 The most impressive predictions that the Bible makes however, concern the life of Jesus Christ. These predictions, called the "messianic prophecies," provide ample evidence for the divine inspiration of the Bible, as well as the validity of the New Testament itself. The single, unifying theme of the Old Testament is God's promise that He would send a Redeemer to the world. Throughout the Old Testament, there are literally hundreds of predictions made concerning the time the Messiah would come, the type of person the Messiah would be, the place from where He would come, and His activities on earth. Once again, we can be certain that these predictions were written down at least 250 years before Christ ever walked the earth, but they are, nevertheless, detailed prophecies that are incredibly accurate.

The most obvious example of the Old Testament's accurate predictions regarding the coming Messiah relates to His birthplace. In Micah 5:2, we read, "But as for you, Bethlehem Ephrathah...from you One will go forth for Me to be ruler in Israel. His goings forth are from long ago, from the days of eternity." This verse is clearly a prediction that the Messiah will be born in Bethlehem. We know that this verse is talking about the Messiah and not a human ruler, because of the last sentence. No human ruler's "goings forth" are "from the days of eternity."

Interestingly enough, however, there is another Old Testament prophecy, found in Hosea 11:1, which says, "...and out of Egypt I called my Son." Once again, this is clearly a statement regarding the Messiah (no human would be called God's Son in Old Testament times), but this verse predicts that the Messiah would come from Egypt. This seeming contradiction, however, is easily resolved in Jesus Christ. He was, indeed, born in Bethlehem (Matthew 2:1), but He and His parents had to flee into Egypt to avoid Herod's persecution (Matthew 2:14). He ended up staying there until Herod died (Matthew 2:15). At least 250 years before Christ ever walked the earth, his birthplace and flight into Egypt had already been predicted!

The Old Testament's ability to predict events regarding the Messiah doesn't stop there, however. Another excellent example can be taken from Zechariah 11:12-13. In this passage we read:

> I said to them, "If it is good in your sight, give me my wages; but if not, never mind!" So
> they weighed out thirty shekels of silver as my wages. Then the Lord said to me, "Throw it
> to the potter, that magnificent price at which I was valued by them." So I took the thirty
> shekels of silver and threw them to the potter in the house of the Lord.

This passage is a lamentation by the prophet Zechariah. He is furious that the people do not value the Lord more highly. In the end, he quotes God as saying that the people think that He (God) is worth only 30 pieces of silver. Those silver pieces are so worthless in God's sight that they should be thrown to the potter in the house of the Lord.

This passage was a bit hard to understand until its words were finally fulfilled in the life of Jesus Christ, who claimed to be the same as God (John 8:58) and was betrayed by Judas for the "magnificent price" of 30 shekels of silver (Matthew 26:15). Once Judas saw what was happening to Christ as a result of his betrayal, however, he returned to the temple (the house of the Lord) and threw the silver pieces on the temple floor in a fit of remorse and rage (Matthew 27:5). The priests, knowing that the money was tainted, did not want to put it back into the treasury, so they purchased a field for the burial of strangers. The field was named "The Potter's Field" (Matthew 27:7).

In the end, then, we see that this lamentation of Zechariah was actually a prophecy of some rather intricate details related to Christ's betrayal by Judas. It is truly incredible to think that more than 250 years prior to this betrayal, the Old Testament was able to predict how much it would cost, what would eventually happen to the money, and even the name associated with the final purchase!

FIGURE 2.7
Judas's Betrayal of Jesus

Illustration from www.clipart.com

Almost 300 years before the event, Zechariah predicted how much Jesus would be betrayed for, what would happen to the money, and what it would eventually be used to purchase.

If these were the only Old Testament prophecies concerning the coming Messiah, it would be possible to explain them away as wildly improbable coincidences. According to Josh McDowell, however, there are 332 distinct prophecies in the Old Testament that were fulfilled perfectly in the life of Christ! Such a large number of prophecies, all written down at least 250 years prior to the life of Christ, provides strong evidence that the Bible is, indeed, the Word of God!

So, have I just proven that the Bible is the Word of God? *OF COURSE NOT!* Science cannot be used to prove anything! Have I produced an irrefutable argument with which all scientists would agree? *OF COURSE NOT!* There are many, many scientific theories that all have strong evidence to back them up, yet they are not believed by all scientists. You see, just because a hypothesis reaches the level of a theory does not mean that all scientists will accept it! If that were not the case, high-temperature superconductors would never have been found. Indeed, many areas of study have several different theories that all compete to explain the same thing! Each theory has a group of scientists who support it and a group of scientists who do not.

What have I done, then? I have applied the scientific method to show that there is evidence for the hypothesis that the Bible is the Word of God. This means that belief in the Bible is *scientifically reasonable*. It does not prove that the Bible is the Word of God, neither does it demonstrate that all other religions are false. It simply shows that there is *evidence* for such a belief! There is a lot more evidence as well. If you are interested, you can read a book I wrote called *Reasonable Faith: The Scientific Case for Christianity*. It contains a lot more evidence to support the hypothesis. So much evidence, in fact, that the hypothesis can certainly be raised to the level of a scientific theory.

So you see that science can be used to study virtually any subject. After all, there are only three real limitations to science. First, it cannot be used to prove anything. Second, it is not 100 percent reliable. Third, it must conform to the scientific method. As long as you keep these limitations in mind, your study of science will be thought-provoking, stimulating, and rewarding!

ON YOUR OWN

2.9 Some would say that the Bible's ability to predict the future is not all that impressive. After all, psychics predict the future all the time. What is the difference between a psychic's predictions about the future and the Bible's predictions about the future?

2.10 In this section, I used the scientific method to provide evidence for the hypothesis that the Bible is the Word of God. Although the exercise was interesting and could easily bolster someone's faith in the Bible, science should *never* be used as a basis for determining your worldview. Why?

ANSWERS TO THE "ON YOUR OWN" PROBLEMS

2.1 <u>Science has not proven the First Law of Thermodynamics</u>, because science cannot prove anything. A single counter example could demonstrate it to be false, or at least not applicable to all situations.

2.2 <u>The observation was that Uranus did not orbit the sun the way that Newton's Law of Universal Gravitation predicted it should.</u> That needed to be explained.

2.3 <u>The hypothesis was that an undiscovered planet was affecting Uranus's motion.</u>

2.4 <u>The experiment to confirm the hypothesis was the search for the new planet at the position predicted by calculations that assumed its existence.</u>

2.5 <u>At the end of the story, Neptune's existence was a theory.</u> After all, only ONE scientist had seen it. That scientist might have been seeing something else, he might have been looking in the wrong place, or he might have been lying. Also, it might have been sheer coincidence that he found something at the suggested location. Several other scientists had to observe Neptune over a period of time before its existence became a law.

2.6 <u>An alternative hypothesis could have been that Newton's Law of Universal Gravitation was wrong.</u> After all, the observation was that Uranus did not obey Newton's law. Perhaps the problem was not another planet or planets; perhaps the problem was with Newton's law. Of course, that hypothesis would not be confirmed. There are many other possibilities, but this is the one that should come to most students' minds.

2.7 <u>Those observations are far from worthless!</u> They can still be used to gain information regarding the surface of Mars. They just don't support the existence of canals on Mars.

2.8 BCS theory became accepted as the scientific explanation for superconductivity because <u>many scientists did many experiments over the course of several years, all of which confirmed the theory</u>.

2.9 There are two big differences between the predictions of the Bible and the predictions of psychics. First, <u>most psychic predictions are vague, whereas the Bible's predictions are specific</u>. Notice that the prophecies mentioned in the text give names and tell about specific events. Many psychics make vague predictions that can be applied to many events. The biggest difference, however, is that <u>the *vast majority* of a psychic's predictions never come true</u>. A psychic will make hundreds of predictions, most of which never happen. The few that do happen, however, are trumpeted, and the rest are forgotten. All the Bible's prophecies (so far) have come true!

2.10 You should never use science as the basis for your worldview because <u>the conclusions of science are always tentative</u>. Your worldview affects everything in your life (including your science). You should never base something that important on something as tentative as science!

STUDY GUIDE FOR MODULE #2

1. Define the following terms:

a   Counter example
b. Hypothesis
c. Theory
d. Scientific law

2. When someone tells you that "science has proven" something, what should you say?

3. Does a scientific theory have to make sense?

4. A feather and a penny are dropped from the top of a building. Which will hit the ground first?

5. A feather and a penny are dropped down a long tube that has no air in it. Which will hit the bottom of the tube first?

6. What does it take to destroy a scientific law?

Questions 7 through 10 refer to the following story:

In 1682, Edmund Halley studied a bright object that moved in the night sky. After searching other scientists' works, he noted that similar objects that followed a similar path were observed in 1531 and 1607. He decided that those objects were, in fact, the same thing he was studying, and that it passed by the earth roughly every 76 years. He then predicted that the object would be seen again in 1758. On Christmas in 1758, the object was, indeed, seen again. It is now called Halley's Comet, and it comes into view of the earth every 76 years.

7. What was the observation that Halley made to form his hypothesis?

8. What was his hypothesis?

9. What was the experiment that confirmed his hypothesis?

10. Regular appearances of Halley's Comet have been found in history as far back as 2,000 years ago. Is the existence of Halley's Comet a theory or a scientific law?

11. Put the following steps of the scientific method into their proper order:

a. Form a hypothesis
b. Theory is now a law
c. Make observations
d. Hypothesis is now a theory
e. Perform experiments to confirm the hypothesis
f. Perform many experiments over several years

12. If a hypothesis does not agree with the experiment designed to confirm it, what two choices do you have?

13. If a theory does not agree with the experiments designed to test it, what two choices do you have?

14. In the text, I told you about Lowell's belief that there were canals on Mars. Name the observations that led to his hypothesis and the experiments used to confirm it.

15. Why was the discovery of high-temperature superconductors so startling to scientists?

16. What are the three limitations of science?

17. Can science be used to study events that will never, ever happen again?

18. Can science be used to study religious ideas?

19. When I applied the scientific method to Christianity, what were the observations I used to form a hypothesis about the Bible?

20. What was my hypothesis?

21. What were the experiments I designed to confirm the hypothesis?

22. Did I prove my hypothesis?

MODULE #3: How to Analyze and Interpret Experiments

Introduction

Now that you've learned about the scientific method, I want you to spend some time learning the details of how to apply it. The way you apply the scientific method affects the reliability of the conclusions you draw from it. Think for a moment about the failures of the scientific method you read about in the previous module. Why did the scientists come to the wrong conclusions? Well, in the case of Percival Lowell, his experiments were flawed. Indeed, he saw plenty of "canals" on Mars, but they turned out to be the result of bad telescopes and eye fatigue. Had he used better telescopes, and had he allowed more time for his eyes to rest, he might not have been fooled. In the case of BCS theory, there were data missing. High-temperature superconductors were not discovered until *after* the theory had been accepted as the proper scientific explanation of superconductivity. In each case, the investigators followed the scientific method, but because of flawed experiments or missing data, the conclusions they reached were wrong.

To do science well, then, you need to be very careful in designing your experiments and making your observations. You need to try to avoid flaws in your experiments, and you need to think of many different ways to test your hypothesis or theory so as to avoid missing data. The better you are at that, the more reliable your conclusions will be.

Experiments and Variables

In designing an experiment, it is very important that you be able to recognize all the **experimental variables**.

Experimental variable – An aspect of an experiment that changes during the course of the experiment

In order to avoid flaws in an experiment, you must be able to recognize experimental variables and control them. For example, part of the reason Lowell saw "canals" on Mars was the fact that as time went on, his eyes became fatigued. Thus, the strain on his eyes was an experimental variable, because it changed over the course of his observations. Had he recognized this experimental variable, he could have controlled it by taking several breaks in order to rest his eyes. Since he did not recognize and control the variable, his experiments were flawed.

Now don't get the impression that all experimental variables are bad. They are, in fact, very useful. Often, the only way a scientist can learn something in an experiment is by comparing the results of the experiment when different experimental variables change. Thus, experimental variables can be very good. They are bad, however, when they are not recognized or not taken into account. That's when they can lead to flawed experiments.

Experimental variables that are recognized and controlled are often an integral part of an experiment. In fact, the concept behind most experiments is to purposefully change one experimental variable to see how it changes the results of the experiment. Usually, that tells you something about the nature of the variable itself. Perform the following experiment to see what I mean.

EXPERIMENT 3.1
A Floating Egg?

Supplies:

♦   A tall glass
♦   Measuring cups for measuring out 1½ cups of water
♦   An egg (It is best to use one that hasn't been sitting in the refrigerator for a long time.)
♦   A teaspoon
♦   A spoon for stirring
♦   Water
♦   Salt
♦   Eye protection such as goggles or safety glasses

Introduction: Experimental variables can often be used to learn a lot from an experiment. This experiment will show you how.

Procedure:

1. Fill the tall glass with 1½ cups of water. Use the measuring cups to measure out the water.
2. Drop the egg (carefully) into the glass of water. Does it sink or float? Write down the answer in your laboratory notebook.
3. Use the spoon you have for stirring to pull the egg back out of the glass. Try to let it drip in the glass so you don't lose much water. Set the egg aside for the moment.
4. Add one teaspoon of salt to the water and stir with your stirring spoon until the salt is dissolved.
5. Once the salt is dissolved, drop the egg (carefully) into the glass of water. Note the difference (if any) between how the egg behaved before and how it behaved this time.
6. Repeat steps 3 through 5 a total of six times. Each time, note the difference (in your laboratory notebook) between how the egg behaves compared to the previous time. If the egg's behavior does not change even after you have repeated steps 3 through 5 a total of six times, continue to repeat the steps until you see a difference.
7. Clean up your mess. You can rinse off the egg and put it back in the refrigerator as long as it didn't crack during the experiment.

      What did you see in the experiment? If things went well, you saw that the egg sank in water. As you added salt to the water, however, the egg probably didn't sink as quickly as it did before. Eventually, the egg should have actually floated. Before I explain what this means, I want you to analyze the experiment for experimental variables. What changed over the course of the experiment?

      You used the same glass throughout the whole experiment, and you used the same egg. The egg was always pulled out with the same spoon. Thus, none of those things are experimental variables. As I see it, there were two main experimental variables. The first is the most important: the amount of salt in the water. In the first phase of the experiment, there was no salt in the water. Then, one teaspoon at a time, you added salt to the water. After each teaspoon of salt was added, you put the egg back into the water to see what would happen.

      What was the other experimental variable? It was not all that important, but it was, nevertheless, a variable. The amount of water in the glass was somewhat variable. After all, each time you pulled the egg out of the water, you pulled some water out, too. You tried to let the water drip back into the glass, but there was just no way you could have returned *all* the water to the glass. As a result, then, the amount of water in the glass decreased throughout the experiment. Thus, the amount of water was also an experimental variable.

How do these two variables affect what you saw in the experiment? Well, as the amount of salt in the water increased, the egg eventually started to float. Thus, we have learned something: adding salt to water helps eggs to float. What about the second variable? What happened as the result of the amount of water decreasing throughout the course of the experiment? Well, we can use common sense to help us out here. If you added no salt to the water but took a little bit of water out of the glass, would that change whether or not the egg floated in the water? Of course not! In addition, the amount by which the water in the glass changed was rather small, especially compared to the total amount of water in the glass. A few drops that clung to the egg represented just a tiny fraction of the water in the glass. Thus, the second experimental variable probably didn't significantly affect the results of the experiment.

What can we learn about all this, then? Well, do you remember Experiment 1.1? In that experiment, you noticed that objects of lower density floated on objects of higher density. Vegetable oil floated on top of water because vegetable oil is less dense than water. A cork floated on top of the vegetable oil because the cork is less dense than the vegetable oil. Well, in this experiment, an egg sank in pure water but floated once a lot of salt was added to the water. What does that tell us about saltwater? It tells us that **saltwater is denser than pure water**.

A natural example of this fact comes from the Great Salt Lake in the state of Utah. This lake is full of saltwater rather than freshwater, and the added salt makes the water so dense that people can float in it without expending any effort, as shown in the picture below.

FIGURE 3.1
A Young Man Floating in the Great Salt Lake

Photo © Douglas Pulsipher
Agency: World of Stock

In the experiment, then, we had two experimental variables. We thought it through and realized that the second experimental variable (the amount of water in the glass) did not significantly affect the experiment. The first experimental variable, however, did affect the results of the experiment, and we used that experimental variable to conclude something useful from the experiment.

Now it turns out that even though the amount of water didn't affect the results of the experiment *significantly*, it did, in fact, affect the results somewhat. You see, the density of saltwater depends on two things: the amount of salt and the *volume* of the water in which it has been dissolved. The more salt added, the denser the saltwater, and the *lower* the volume of water to which it is added, the denser the saltwater. Since you lost a small amount of water each time you pulled the egg out of the glass, you actually *reduced* the volume of the water, which made the saltwater denser than it otherwise would have been. However, since the amount of water you lost was small compared to the total volume of water, this effect was rather minor. Nevertheless, it is important to make sure you understand *all* the variables in an experiment, because their effect is often not minor!

Before we leave the discussion about this experiment, I want you to spend a little bit of time thinking about the design of the experiment itself. In the experiment, I had you use the same glass each time. If I had made you use a different glass each time, that would have introduced another experimental variable. How would that have affected the results of the experiment? It probably would not have. After all, whether or not the egg sinks in water *should* be independent of the glass in which the water is put. Nevertheless, I had you use the same glass each time just to make sure that the glass was not a variable. Why change something if you don't have to? Even though we *think* the nature of the glass shouldn't matter, we can't be 100 percent sure. Thus, it was safer to just use the same glass each time.

We also could have used a different egg for each trial. Would that have affected the results of the experiment? It probably would have a little. After all, you learned in Module #1 that the density of an object determines whether or not it will float. Well, even though most eggs have similar densities, each egg's density is probably slightly different from the next. After all, eggs come from living creatures. Since no two living creatures are *exactly* the same (even twins have their differences), there is no reason to expect that every egg has *exactly* the same density. I expect the density of eggs doesn't vary a lot, but once again, why take chances? Using the same egg each time eliminated a variable that might have affected the experiment.

In the end, then, when you want to design a good experiment, *you should always reduce the number of experimental variables that are not a necessary part of the experiment*. The amount of salt in the water was a necessary experimental variable. It was used to help us learn something from the experiment. The glass, egg, amount of water, and anything else that could have changed during the experiment were *unnecessary* experimental variables. We would learn *nothing* from them. Thus, we needed to reduce them or get rid of them. We got rid of the glass and egg as experimental variables by using the same one in each trial of the experiment. We reduced the amount of water as an experimental variable by trying to allow all the water to drip off the egg and into the glass before setting the egg down.

Why should you worry so much about experimental variables? Because their effects on an experiment are not always predictable. Even though I explained to you how each of those experimental variables probably would not have affected the final conclusion of the experiment, there is no guarantee that I am right. There may be some subtle effect of which I am not aware or I cannot think. Thus, it was best to get rid of them, because they may have affected the experiment in some unforeseen way.

When designing an experiment, then, you will probably have some kind of experimental variable from which you hope to learn something. You then need to analyze the experiment for all unnecessary variables. When you find them, you either need to eliminate them, or you need to think very hard about how they will affect the experiment. It is best to eliminate them, because no matter how hard you think, you might miss some subtle effect that the unnecessary variable will have.

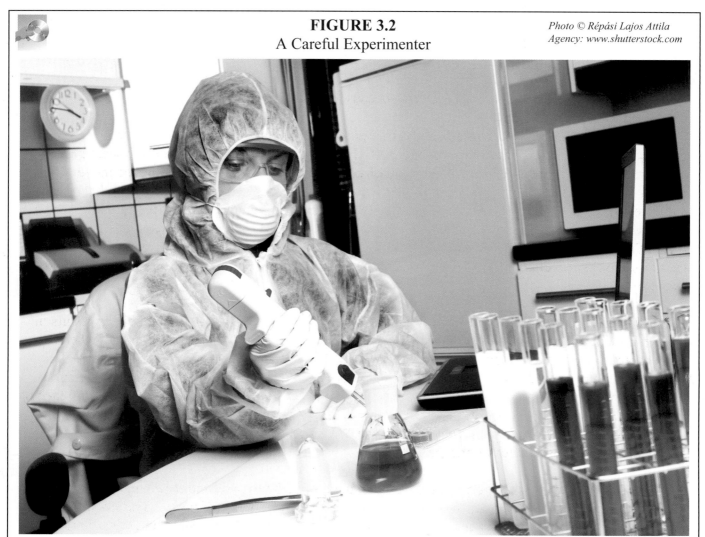

FIGURE 3.2
A Careful Experimenter

Photo © Répási Lajos Attila
Agency: www.shutterstock.com

Aside from the goggles, what this woman scientist is wearing is not for her own protection. Instead, the experiment involves biological substances, and she could accidentally add such substances to the experiment from her skin, hair, or possibly even her breath. Thus, she wears the mask, gloves, and hooded jacket to avoid adding unnecessary experimental variables.

ON YOUR OWN

A student decides to test the effectiveness of different household floor cleaners. He marks off a section of the kitchen floor and scuffs it up with black heel marks. He then divides that section into four equal quarters, and he scrubs each quarter with a different brand of floor cleaner.

3.1 Identify the experimental variables.

3.2 From which experimental variable will the student learn something, and which variables should he try to reduce or eliminate?

3.3 Suggest ways to reduce or eliminate the experimental variables that need to be reduced or eliminated.

Using a Series of Experiments

Now that you know a bit about how to analyze an experiment, you need to understand that most scientists learn very little from a *single* experiment. As a result, scientists generally do a series of experiments to understand whatever they are trying to study. I want you to get some experience seeing how this works.

EXPERIMENT 3.2
Which "Boat" Will Move?

Supplies:

♦ Four sheets of reasonably thick cardboard (A cut-up cardboard box works nicely.)
♦ Scissors that will cut the cardboard
♦ A sheet of facial tissue (Make sure is it not the kind that has been treated with lotion.)
♦ A chunk of soap from a bar of soap
♦ A stick of chewing gum
♦ A bathtub or large sink (A bathtub works best.)
♦ Eye protection such as goggles or safety glasses

Introduction: This experiment will produce an interesting effect that will be explained by further experimentation.

Procedure:

1. Start filling the bathtub with water. Ask your parents if you have "softened" water. If so, ask if the hot water has also been softened. If it has not, fill the tub from the hot tap. If you don't have softened watered or if your hot water is softened, use cold water, so as to save on heating costs. Put a plug in the drain, because you want the water to stand.
2. Stop filling the tub when the water is about 3 inches deep.
3. While you are waiting for the bathtub to fill, use the scissors to cut the cardboard into four equal rectangles. The rectangles should be about 3 inches long and 1 inch wide. If you are using a sink instead of a bathtub, you probably want them to be smaller.
4. Use the scissors to cut a point on one side of each piece of cardboard.
5. Now cut a triangular notch on the side opposite the point, so that each piece of cardboard looks like the drawing on the right.

6. Each one of these pieces of cardboard will be a "boat" in your bathtub. Before you float your boats, however, you need to prepare them with different "motors."
7. Your first motor will be made of chewing gum. Chew the stick of gum until it is soft and pliable.
8. Pull the gum out of your mouth and rip off a small chunk of it.
9. Put the chunk of gum in the notch of one of the boats. Use enough gum so you can cram it into the notch and it stays there.
10. For another boat, you will use facial tissue as your motor. Wet a small amount of facial tissue.
11. Roll the wet piece of tissue into a ball. The ball of wet facial tissue should be about the same size as the chunk of chewing gum you used.
12. Cram the wet facial tissue into the notch of another boat so that it stays there.
13. For the next boat, shave off a chunk of soap about the same size as the chunk of chewing gum you used for the first boat.
14. Cram the piece of soap into the notch so that it stays there.
15. The last boat will have no motor in its notch.
16. By this time, the water in the tub should be rather still. If it is not, wait until it is.
17. Once the water is still, place each boat in the tub in this order: the one with no motor, followed by the one with a chewing-gum motor, followed by the one with the facial-tissue motor, followed by the one with the soap motor. Place them close to one another, pointing in the same direction. Do not put them so close that they touch each other.
18. Observe any differences in the way the boats move. Write your observations in your laboratory notebook.
19. Clean up your mess.

What did you see in the experiment? Well, you should have seen that all the boats except one didn't move much. There are stray winds in every house, and those stray winds probably caused some movement in *all* the boats. However, there should have been one boat that moved a lot more than the others: the boat with the soap motor. Please note that if your water supply is softened, this experiment might not work very well, if at all. That's why I wanted you to use water from the hot tap if your cold water is softened but your hot water is not. If this experiment didn't work as I say it should have, you might try doing it at a house where you can find some water that is not softened.

Before you try to understand why the soap motor caused the boat to move, I want to analyze the experimental variables and their effects on the experiment. We used the same bathtub at the same time for all boats. Each boat was put in a slightly different place in the tub, but that should not have been a big effect. Each boat was put in at a slightly different time, but once again, that should not have been a big effect, either. Each boat was different. I tried to get you to reduce the effect of that variable by making each boat the same size. Nevertheless, the boats were not identical, so that is an experimental variable, too. Likewise, the motors were close to the same size, but not exactly the same size. That's another experimental variable. All these were experimental variables, but they probably had little effect on the results of the experiment.

The big experimental variable, of course, was the "motor" that was used. The first "boat" that you put in the water had no "motor." In experimental terms, we call this the **control** of the experiment.

Control (of an experiment) – The variable or part of the experiment to which all others will be compared

All the other boats can be compared to the control. After all, the point of the experiment was to find a workable motor for a boat. To find out whether or not a given motor was the cause of any motion, we needed something against which to compare the boats. As I mentioned in the experiment, random wind currents could have caused all the boats to move a little. Thus, in order to determine whether or not each of the *motors* caused any motion, we had to see how each boat moved compared to the one with no motor. Since the boat with the soap motor moved a *lot* more than the boat with no motor, we could conclude that the soap motor was doing something to make the boat move. Also, the other boats might have moved, but since they didn't move any more than the control, we can conclude that their motors did not cause any significant motion.

In the experiment, then, the variable you used to learn something was the type of motor. You found out that soap made a workable motor. There is obviously something special about soap, however, because both gum and facial tissue did not make the boats move any more than the control. Now it is time to see if you can figure out *why* soap formed a workable motor.

EXPERIMENT 3.3
What Does Soap Do To Water? – Part 1

Supplies:

♦ A reasonably large bowl
♦ Water
♦ Black pepper
♦ Tweezers
♦ A sheet of facial tissue (The same as the tissue you used in the previous experiment.)
♦ A chunk of soap from a bar of soap (The same as the soap you used in the previous experiment.)
♦ A stick of chewing gum (The same as the gum you used in the previous experiment.)
♦ Eye protection such as goggles or safety glasses

Introduction: This experiment will begin to help you to understand why soap caused the boat in Experiment 3.2 to move.

Procedure:

1. Fill the bowl ¾ full with water.
2. Allow the bowl to sit so the water becomes still.
3. Once the water is still, shake pepper onto the surface of the water. Some of the pepper will sink, but most of it will stay on the surface of the water. Shake the pepper onto the water so the surface of the water is coated fairly evenly with pepper.
4. Touch the surface of the water with the tip of your tweezers. What happens to the pepper? Note that in your laboratory notebook.
5. Put the tweezers down. Allow the water to settle again and, if necessary, add more pepper so that the surface of the water is still coated fairly evenly with pepper.
6. Rip off a small amount of facial tissue, wet it (not with water from the bowl), and roll it into a ball. Use about the same amount of facial tissue as you did in Experiment 3.2.
7. Grab the wet facial tissue with the tweezers and use them to dip the ball of wet facial tissue into the water. Dip the facial tissue so that about half the ball is below the surface of the water and the

other half is above the surface of the water. Note in your laboratory notebook what happens to the pepper.

8. Allow the water to settle again and, if necessary, add more pepper so the surface of the water is still coated fairly evenly with pepper.
9. Chew your stick of gum until it is wet and soft.
10. Pull off a chunk of gum about the size as the wet facial tissue ball you used in step 6.
11. Dip the gum into the water so about half of it is below the surface of the water and the other half is above the surface of the water. Note in your laboratory notebook what happens to the pepper.
12. Allow the water to settle again and, if necessary, add more pepper so the surface of the water is still coated fairly evenly with pepper.
13. Pull off a chip of soap about as big as the wad of gum you just used.
14. Use the tweezers to grab the chip of soap, and wet it with some water (not the water in the bowl).
15. Dip the soap into the water so about half of it is below the surface of the water and the other half is above the surface of the water. Note in your laboratory notebook what happens to the pepper.
16. Clean up your mess.

What did you see in the experiment? If everything went well, the empty tweezers, the wet facial tissue, and the chewing gum did not affect the pepper much. However, the wet soap should have had a dramatic effect. The pepper should have moved away from the soap, as if the soap was pushing it away. This should help you understand why the soap formed a workable motor for the boat. Soap does something that seems to push things on the surface of the water. You can do one more experiment to help you understand what that "something" is.

EXPERIMENT 3.4
What Does Soap Do To Water? – Part 2

Supplies:

♦ Water
♦ Bowl
♦ Metal paper clip (Use a standard-sized paper clip. A big one may not work.)
♦ Toilet paper
♦ Tweezers
♦ A sheet of facial tissue (The same as the tissue you used in the other experiments.)
♦ A chunk of soap from a bar of soap (The same as the soap you used in the other experiments.)
♦ A stick of chewing gum (The same as the gum you used in the other experiments.)
♦ Eye protection such as goggles or safety glasses

Introduction: This experiment will show you what causes soap to affect water the way you observed in Experiment 3.3.

Procedure:

1. Fill the bowl with water.
2. Drop the paper clip into the water. Note what happens.
3. Pull the paper clip out of the water and dry it off.
4. Tear off one square of toilet paper.

5. Cut a rectangle out of that square of toilet paper. It should be about 2 inches longer and 2 inches wider than the paper clip.
6. Set the paper clip on top of the rectangle of toilet paper, in the middle.
7. Carefully lift the rectangle of toilet paper by the corners so the paper clip does not fall off.
8. Gently lay the toilet-paper rectangle on the surface of the water. Watch what happens for a while.
9. Once the toilet paper gets completely soaked, it should fall to the bottom of the bowl. However, the paper clip should continue floating. If that didn't happen for you, try again with a new piece of toilet paper. If you can't get the paper clip to float, you might want to try the experiment with a different metal paper clip or distilled water, which can be found in any major supermarket.
10. Dip the end of the tweezers in the water near the paper clip. If the paper clip moves, follow it with the tweezers. Allow the tweezers to stay in the water for a full minute. Note what happens.
11. Now do the same thing with a wad of chewing gum on the end of the tweezers. The wad should be the same size as what you used in the previous experiment. Note what happens.
12. Repeat step 11 with a wad of wet facial tissue, about the same size as the other tissue wads you have been using.
13. Repeat step 11 with a piece of soap, about the same size as the other soap pieces you have been using.
14. Clean up your mess.

What happened in this experiment? The paper clip sank when you just dropped it into the water. However, when you laid it on the toilet paper, it floated once the toilet paper sank. How is that possible? Well, we can learn something from what happened to the paper clip when you put the soap in the water. The paper clip moved around and eventually sank when the soap was put in the water, but it stayed afloat when you put the facial tissue, gum, and empty tweezers in the water.

What's the explanation for this? Well, first you need to realize that all the things you saw in the experiments occurred on the *surface* of the water. The boats floated on the surface of the water, and the pepper moved on the surface of the water. The paper clip floated on the surface of the water until the soap touched the water. Thus, soap must be doing something to the *surface* of the water. What is it doing?

Well, every liquid has a property called **surface tension**. Surface tension can be thought of as a thin film that stretches across the surface of every liquid. If the film is not disturbed too much, it will tend to hold up things that would otherwise sink in water. Consider the paper clip, for example. It was made of metal, which is clearly a lot denser than water. Thus, you would expect a paper clip to sink when placed in water. That's what you saw when you dropped the paper clip into the water. However, when you used the toilet paper to lay the paper clip on the surface of the water, it floated. That's because of the "film" created by surface tension. The film is thin and fragile, but it is there. When you dropped the paper clip, you broke the film and the paper clip sank. However, when you laid the paper clip on the water gently, you did not break the film, and surface tension was able to hold the paper clip up, causing it to float.

What happened in the experiment when you dipped the soap in the water, however? The paper clip sank. What does that tell you? When the empty tweezers, facial tissue, and gum were dipped in the water, the film of surface tension did not break. Thus, the act of dipping did not cause the paper clip to sink. It was the *soap* that caused the paper clip to sink. What does that tell you about soap's effect on surface tension? *Soap decreases the surface tension of water.*

How does that explain the results of Experiment 3.2? Well, think back to Experiment 3.3. When you dipped the soap into the pepper-covered water, the pepper pulled away from the soap. That's because surface tension had stretched the surface of the water like a thin film. When the soap touched the water, it decreased the surface tension in its general area. However, the surface of the water in the rest of the bowl still had a lot of surface tension. Thus, the film was broken at the center of the bowl but was still stretched hard along the edges. As a result, the film pulled out toward the edges of the bowl, pulling the pepper with it.

In Experiment 3.2, then, the soap in the "boat's motor" was really just reducing the surface tension at the point where the motor was. This caused the "film" on the water to pull back, pulling the boat along with it. Thus, the "boat" moved as if the soap was pushing it.

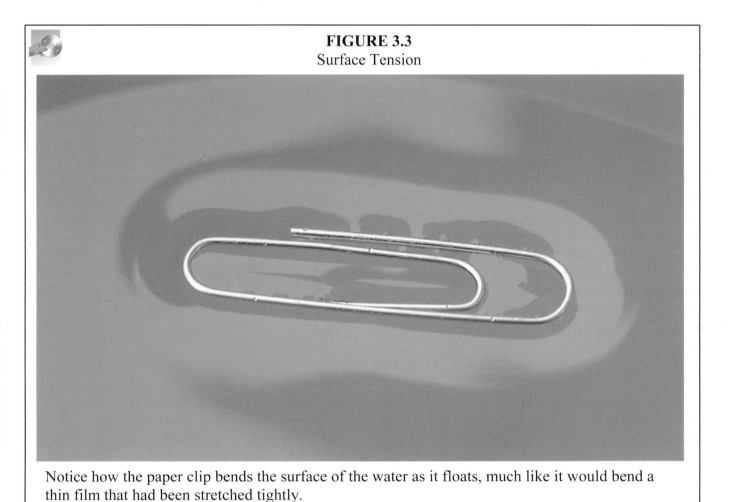

FIGURE 3.3
Surface Tension

Notice how the paper clip bends the surface of the water as it floats, much like it would bend a thin film that had been stretched tightly.

Think about what we did here. We used three different experiments, all with the same important experimental variable. Comparing the results of the experiments helped us explain what soap does to the surface of water. This is typical of how many scientists learn what they want to learn about creation. They look at a single variable's effect in many different experiments, hoping they can draw some general conclusions after several such effects are examined.

ON YOUR OWN

3.4 Suppose you just finished doing a lot of dishes. The dishes were dirty, so you used a lot of soap while doing them. If you put the boat with the soap motor from Experiment 3.2 in the dishwater after you finished the dishes, would the boat move like you saw it move in the experiment?

3.5 Suppose you tried to repeat Experiment 3.4 with vegetable oil instead of water. You try as hard as you can, but you simply cannot get the paper clip to float on the surface of the vegetable oil like you did when you used water. What does this tell you about the strength of the surface tension in vegetable oil as compared to water?

Recognizing Experimental Variables When They Are Not Obvious

Suppose you are sick. You go to the doctor and she tells you that you have a bacterial infection. She gives you some pills she calls antibiotics and tells you to take two of them each day. After the very first day of taking the pills, you start feeling better. After three or four days, you feel completely healthy, but there are still pills left in the container the doctor gave you. The doctor told you to continue to take the pills until they are gone. Nevertheless, you feel fine, so you stop taking the pills. In a week, you get sick again with the same thing.

When you go to the doctor again, she examines you and immediately tells you that you did not take *all* the pills she gave you. She gives you some more pills and tells you to continue to take them until they are gone, no matter how you feel. This time, you follow her instructions to the letter, and you get better. Not only do you get better, but you do not come down with the same thing again.

How did the doctor know a pill would help you get better? How did she know how many pills to give you? How did she know you had to continue to take *all* the pills, regardless of how you felt? The doctor knows all these things because of the results of many *experiments* that had already been done on other people.

You see, when medical scientists come up with a new drug they think will treat a particular illness, there are many, many experiments they must do before the drug can be given to the general public. Typically, the experiments start with animals. Animals with an illness similar to the one the drug is supposed to treat are given the drug to see whether or not it is effective in the animals. If the drug has no severe side effects and is effective at treating the illness, a new series of experiments will be done with other animals. Eventually, if the animal-based experiments are successful, experiments will be performed on people.

Now first you need to know that the people in these experiments are volunteers. Sometimes they are paid money to be in the experiment. Sometimes they are willing to volunteer because they have the illness and no effective treatment currently exists. In any event, long before doctors can prescribe the drug to you and me, several experiments are performed on volunteers.

I want to discuss the typical method used in these drug studies, because it illustrates an important point about doing experiments. Suppose, for example, I came up with a new drug that was supposed to relieve severe headaches. Suppose further that the drug was tested in several experiments with animals and the drug seemed both safe and effective. At this point, it is ready for human testing. How would I test it on people?

First, I would get a group of volunteers, all of whom had trouble with severe headaches. These would be my test subjects, but what would I do next? I could give out a bunch of pills to everyone and tell them to take a pill whenever they feel a severe headache coming along. In addition, I could have them record whether or not they felt better after taking the pill, and if so, how long it took before they started feeling better. After a few weeks, I could gather up the records of each person and then decide whether or not the drug really worked, right?

Well, I *could* do it that way, but there are a few experimental variables I would be missing. First, remember that I am working with a bunch of different people in this study. Each person has his own definition of a headache. Also, each person has his own idea of what it means to "feel better." For some people, they feel better as soon as the pain is no longer distracting. Others don't feel better until all the pain is gone. Also, every person has a different level of pain that makes them uncomfortable. Some people can experience a lot of pain and barely notice it, while others can experience just a little pain and be miserable. This is called a person's **pain threshold**.

Thus, there are a *lot* of experimental variables here. How do I deal with them? Well, the first thing to do is to set up a control group. Remember, when you are trying to learn about whether an aspect of an experiment has any effect on the results, you can compare your results to a control. In Experiment 3.2, for example, the control was the boat with no motor. In Experiments 3.3 and 3.4, the control was the empty set of tweezers. When you compared the results of the experiment to what happened with the control, you were able to determine when something interesting happened.

In the case of my drug study, then, I need to establish a control. To do that, I need to withhold the drug from a group of the volunteers. I can then compare the reports of the control group to the reports of the volunteers who took the drug. If the reports of the volunteers who took the drug differ dramatically from the reports of the control group, the drug had an effect, right?

Well, once again, I am *still* missing an important experimental variable. There is still a big difference between the control group and the volunteers who actually took the drug. The people in the control group *know* that they are not taking anything that will make them better. The volunteers who are taking the drug *know* that they are taking something that *I think* will make them better. As a result, the control group does not *expect* anything great to happen to them, while the volunteers who take the drug might expect something great to happen to them. It turns out that this is an important experimental variable. Studies have shown that some people can get relief from an illness by simply *thinking* they are being cured. Thus, I must control or eliminate this experimental variable as well.

How do I do that? I can give my control group *fake pills* to take. In most drug studies, the fake pills, called **placebos** (pluh see' bohz) are usually just made out of sugar. They are made to look identical to the drug being tested, so the volunteers do not know whether or not they are taking the drug or the placebo. As a result, they *all* think they are being given a drug that will help them. Thus, that experimental variable is eliminated. These kinds of studies are called **blind experiments**.

Blind experiments – Experiments in which the participants do not know whether or not they are a part of the control group

This term comes from the fact that the participants are "blind" to whether or not they are getting the actual treatment being tested.

So is that the best way to design a study? Not quite. You see, as long as I know who is a part of the control group and who is not, it might affect the way I examine the reports. If I know a person is a part of the control group, I don't *expect* anything great to happen to him. Thus, I will probably not look at his report very carefully. I might also try to explain away instances where the placebo seemed to help his headache. On the other hand, if I know a person is part of the group taking the real drug, I will probably look very closely at his or her report. I might also note the smallest of relief in headache pain as something much more important than what it really is.

How do I take care of this variable? That's easy. I become "blind" myself. I have someone else keep track of who is in the control group and who is taking the real drug. When I look at each report, then, I have no idea whether to expect great things or not-so-great things. Thus, I will analyze each report in the same way. After I have finished my analysis, the person who knows which volunteers are in the control group can then see if my analysis of the reports differs between those in the control group and those not in the control group. These kinds of studies are called **double-blind experiments** because neither the participants nor the people analyzing the results know who is in the control group and who is not.

Double-blind experiments – Experiments in which neither the participants nor the people analyzing the results know who is in the control group

FIGURE 3.4
Blind Studies

Photo © Leah-Anne Thompson
Agency www.shutterstock.com

If the subject (left) doesn't know whether or not the scientist analyzing the data (right) is giving her the actual pills that are being tested, the experiment is a blind experiment. If the scientist also doesn't know, it is a double-blind experiment. If the scientist knows but the subject does not, it is often called a **single-blind experiment** to emphasize that only the subject is blind to whether or not she is being given the actual pills.

Notice, then, that there are at least two experimental variables that are not very obvious. Both of these variables can have dramatic effects on the results of the experiment, so both have to be controlled or eliminated. Think for a moment about *why* these variables exist in the experiment. They exist because the data are **subjective**. In other words, the data being collected depend to some extent on the opinions of people. Whether or not a headache is more or less intense is a matter of opinion from person to person. The analysis of such data is subjective as well. This leads to experimental variables that must be controlled.

Other experiments do not have such variables. Suppose, for example, I am testing the effectiveness of different types of fertilizers. I grow the same type of plant in several different pots that are all the same size and contain the same kind of soil. I expose the plants to all the same conditions. I water the plants each day with the same amount of water. To one plant, I add no fertilizer. I give each of the other plants a different brand of fertilizer, but I use the same amount of fertilizer in each case. I then measure the height of each plant each day.

I have a control in this experiment. It is the plant with no fertilizer. Do I need the study to be blind or double-blind? Of course not! The height of each plant is a measurable number. It is not subjective; instead, it is **objective**. With objective data, there is no way opinion can affect the experimental results, so there is no need to go to the trouble of having a double-blind experiment. When designing an experiment, then, you must think carefully about whether or not the data taken are subjective. If the data are subjective only on the part of the subjects, you might be able to do it as a single-blind study. If the data are subjective not only to the subjects but also to those analyzing the data, it should be a double-blind experiment. If the subjects can't be influenced by opinion (if the subjects are plants, for example) and the data are objective, there may be no reason to do any kind of blind study.

Now notice I said that there "may be" no reason to do blind studies when the data are objective and the subjects aren't influenced by opinion. Also, I said an experiment in which the data are subjective only to the subjects "might be" done as a single-blind study. Why "may be" and "might be"? Well, sometimes, even when the data are objective, the people analyzing the data will still be made blind to what or who is in the control. They do this to avoid the *appearance* of subjectivity. For example, if I am the maker of a new pill, I want the results of the experiments to demonstrate that the pill I made was effective. If I am not very honest, then, I might "tweak" the results in favor of my pill. However, if I don't know who is actually getting the pill, then I cannot even be accused of interfering with the results. As a result, some scientists choose to remain blind during the course of an experiment in order to either avoid the temptation for dishonesty or avoid any accusations of dishonesty.

ON YOUR OWN

3.6 Many studies have been done on homeschooled students. In one popular type of experiment, the homeschooled students take the same standardized tests that publicly schooled students take. The scores of the homeschooled students are then compared to those of publicly schooled students. You can think of the publicly schooled students as the control group in such a study. Should such a study be done as a single-blind study, a double-blind study, or neither?

3.7 Another way homeschooled students are studied relates to their social skills. In one experiment, psychologists examined several students at play. Some of the students were homeschooled and some were publicly schooled. The psychologists examined the students at play and determined who was socially well-adjusted and who was not. You can think of the publicly schooled students as the control group in such a study. Should such a study be done as a single-blind study, a double-blind study, or neither?

Interpreting the Results of Experiments

At this point, you have a good idea of how to design an experiment. You know how to use and recognize experimental variables. You also know how to control or eliminate the experimental variables that might affect the results of your experiment in a bad way. Now it is time to look at a couple experiments and get some practice interpreting their results. I want to start with an experiment that deals with ocean water.

Before you can understand the experiment, however, you need to learn a few things. In Experiment 3.1, you mixed salt with water. You mixed the salt so thoroughly with the water that it actually seemed to "disappear." It did not disappear, of course. Had you tasted the water, it would have tasted salty. Thus, the salt was still there; it was mixed so thoroughly with the water, however, that you could not see it. As you probably know, we say that the salt **dissolved** in the water, and instead of salt and water, you had a **solution** called saltwater.

Well, it turns out that *lots* of things can dissolve in water, including gases. When you drink soda pop, for example, the "fizz" comes from carbon dioxide that is dissolved in the soda pop. Carbon dioxide is a gas, but it can dissolve in water and other liquids. When it is dissolved in water, the result is a solution that has a specific taste. Many people like the taste, which is why soda pop is made with dissolved carbon dioxide.

In the same way, oxygen gas can dissolve in water. In fact, that's where fish and other underwater creatures get their oxygen. Fish, for example, have **gills** that remove the dissolved oxygen from water and allow the fish to use the oxygen to support their life functions. So please understand that fish do not "breathe water." They breathe oxygen that has been dissolved in water.

Whether or not water can support fish depends, in part, on how much dissolved oxygen is in the water. If there is not enough dissolved oxygen in the water, the fish will suffocate, just like you and I would suffocate if there wasn't enough oxygen in the air. If you have seen a fish tank with lots of fish in it, you probably saw something in the tank that was bubbling. The bubbling was caused by a device that pumps air into the water. Most of the air bubbles out of the water, but some of the oxygen in the air dissolves in the water, keeping the amount of dissolved oxygen in the water high enough to support the fish in the tank.

"But wait a minute," you might be saying to yourself. "I have seen fish live long, healthy lives in a fishbowl that has no air bubbling through it. How did the fish in the fishbowl breathe?" Well, remember that there is air above the surface of the water in any fishbowl or fish tank. There is oxygen in that air, and *some* of the oxygen in the air dissolves into the water of the fishbowl. However, only so much oxygen can dissolve into the water that way. If only a couple fish live in a fishbowl, the amount of oxygen dissolving into the water from the air above the fishbowl will probably be enough to support them. However, if several fish live in a bowl or tank, they will use up the dissolved oxygen faster than more can dissolve in from the air above. That's when you need to pump air into the tank.

Thus, the amount of dissolved oxygen is important for any water being used to support fish and other underwater life. This includes the ocean. To see how "healthy" the water in the Bering Sea is for fish, a scientist studied the amount of dissolved oxygen at different depths. After making his measurements, he graphed his results as follows:

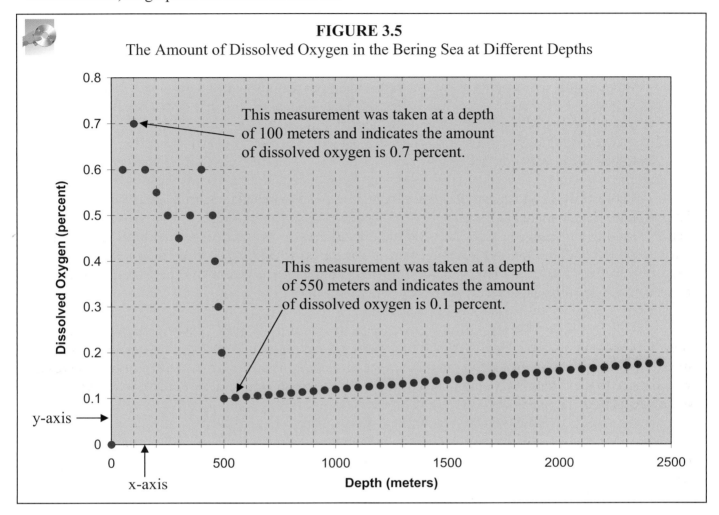

FIGURE 3.5
The Amount of Dissolved Oxygen in the Bering Sea at Different Depths

It is important for you to become familiar with reading graphs like this, because a lot of experimental data is communicated in this way. What does this particular graph show us? Well, the horizontal scale on the graph (usually called the **x-axis**) tells us the depth at which the measurement was taken. Notice that the depth is in meters. If you are not familiar with meters, don't worry. A meter is about the same distance as a yard. The important thing to see is that as you move to the right along the x-axis, the numbers get bigger. Thus, the farther to the right on the graph, the deeper the measurement was made. The vertical scale on the graph (usually called the **y-axis**) tells us how much oxygen was in the ocean water. Notice that this measurement was done in percent. The numbers get bigger the higher they are on the y-axis, so the higher on the graph, the more oxygen there is in the water.

Now let's look at the graph. Each dot on the graph represents a measurement. The first dot is on the bottom left-hand corner of the graph. Looking at the x-axis, it is right on the 0. This means it was taken at zero meters in depth, or right on the surface. Looking at the y-axis, it is on the zero as well. This means there was zero percent dissolved oxygen there. Now look at the next dot. It is not very far to the right of zero, but it is pretty high on the graph. The dot after that one (the one to which an arrow is pointing) is just a little higher up on the graph. Let's figure out what that dot means.

If you look at the x-axis, you will see a little vertical bar with "500" below it, which means that position on the x-axis represents a depth of 500 meters. Now the point we are looking at isn't nearly that far to the right, is it? It is somewhere between the "0" on the x-axis and the "500" on the x-axis. Thus, this measurement was made at a depth somewhere between 0 and 500 meters. If you notice, it takes five vertical bars to go from the 0 to the 500. What does that tell you? It tells you each line is worth 100. Since the dot is right on the first line, you know that it was taken at a depth of 100 meters. Now look at the y-axis. You can see it is on the line marked by a 0.7 on the y-axis. So, this particular point tells you that at a depth of 100 meters, the amount of oxygen is 0.7 percent.

Do you see how to read the graph? The horizontal position of each dot represents the depth at which the measurement was taken. The vertical position of each dot represents the amount of dissolved oxygen at that point. In the case of the dot I just discussed, it was easy, because the dot was on lines for both the x-axis and y-axis. However, look at the other dot being pointed out. It is in between the line representing a depth of 500 meters and the one indicating a depth of 600 meters. So, what is the depth? Well, the dot is about halfway between 500 and 600, so that must mean it was measured at 550 meters. At that depth, the amount of oxygen is 0.1 percent. Thus, when dots are between two markings on either axis, you must "guestimate" the values by noting which lines the dot is between as well as how far between them it is.

Now that you know how to read the graph, what does it tell us? Well, once you actually get below the surface (at depths greater than 0), the amount of dissolved oxygen is pretty large. After all, the dots just to the right of 0 are high on the graph. Since a high vertical position indicates a lot of dissolved oxygen, depths between 0 and 400 meters seem to have a lot of dissolved oxygen. The dot at 100 meters is the highest one on the graph. This means there is more dissolved oxygen at that depth than any other measured depth. Once the measurements go below a depth of 400 meters, the amount of dissolved oxygen really starts to decrease. The dot at 500 meters has the lowest amount of dissolved oxygen. Thus, we can say that of all the measurements taken, the amount of oxygen is lowest at 500 meters.

What happens for depths larger than 500 meters? Well, as the dots get farther and farther to the right of 500 meters, they start to get higher and higher. The effect is not large, but it is definitely there. This tells us that at depths greater than 500 meters, the amount of dissolved oxygen increases slowly with increasing depth.

Okay. That was a lot of information, so let's review. The higher the dot is on the graph, the more dissolved oxygen is in the water. The farther to the right the dot is on the graph, the deeper the measurement was taken. The data indicate that at depths less than 400 meters, the amount of dissolved oxygen in the water is relatively high. It is highest at 100 meters. At depths between 400 and 500 meters, the amount of dissolved oxygen decreases very quickly as the depth increases. Then, after 500 meters, the amount of dissolved oxygen increases slowly with increasing depth.

So what does this data tell us? Well, remember the trend of the data. The majority of the oxygen is at the shallower depths. What does that tell us about *where* the oxygen is coming from? It is, most likely, coming from at or near the surface of the water. Let's think for a moment about what's at or near the surface of the water. Air is right there at the surface of the water. What's air got in it? It has oxygen. Thus, this experiment gives us evidence that most of the oxygen in the Bering Sea comes from the air. Oxygen in the air gets dissolved in the water as it hits the surface of the water, and then it gets mixed into the water at somewhat lower depths. Since the amount of oxygen drops off quickly from 400 to 500 meters, we can say that the mixing of oxygen to depths below 400 meters is rather inefficient.

Given this data, where is the water healthiest for fish in the Bering Sea? Based on oxygen alone, the healthiest depth is 100 meters. Of course, there are many other factors that affect fish health, but we can say fairly certainly that most of the fish are going to spend the majority of their time at depths shallower than 500 meters, because that's where they will find a lot of oxygen to breathe.

Now that you have seen how to interpret a graph of experimental data, try to interpret the next one on your own.

ON YOUR OWN

A student decides to find the ideal amount of fertilizer to add to plants. He grows ten individual plants (all of the same type), each one treated with a different amount of the same fertilizer. After a few weeks, he measures the height of each plant and produces the following graph:

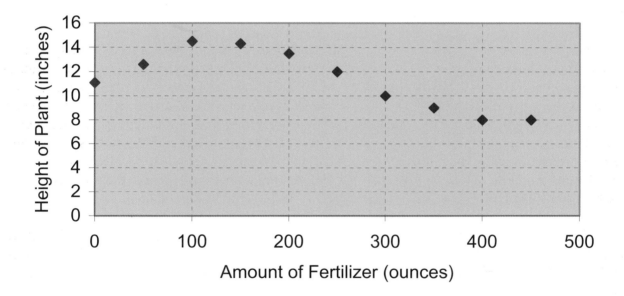

3.8 What is the ideal amount of fertilizer to use, if you want tall plants?

3.9 A student hypothesizes that no matter what amount of fertilizer you use, it's better than using no fertilizer at all. Does this experiment support the hypothesis?

3.10 Suppose a farmer uses an automated fertilizing system that cannot put a precise amount of fertilizer on the plants. Instead, the farmer must indicate a range of 100 ounces. For example, the farmer can specify ranges like 25 to 125 ounces or 500 to 600 ounces. What range should the farmer specify?

ANSWERS TO THE "ON YOUR OWN" PROBLEMS

3.1 There are at least three experimental variables here. First, <u>the brand of floor cleaner used</u> is a variable, because he uses a different brand on each quarter. Second, <u>the amount of black heel marks in each quarter</u> will be different. There is just no way he can scuff up the floor equally on all quarters. Third, <u>the amount and effectiveness of the scrubbing</u> will vary. Most likely, he will get tired as time goes on. Thus, he will scrub less vigorously in the last quarter than on the first quarter. There may be more, but those are the ones most obvious to me. Do not worry if you didn't get them all – just use this as a learning experience.

3.2 <u>The student will learn something from the brand of floor cleaner used</u>. That's the whole purpose of the experiment. The cleanest quarter will indicate the best floor cleaner. <u>He should reduce or eliminate the variable amount of black heel marks on each quarter and the variable amount and effectiveness of the scrubbing.</u>

3.3 <u>He can reduce the variable amount of black heel marks by examining each quarter closely and trying to even out the amount of black heel marks so they are the same on each quarter. He can reduce the variable amount and effectiveness of the scrubbing by taking breaks to ensure he is not tired. He could also count the number of strokes and make sure he scrubs with the same number of strokes on each quarter.</u>

3.4 <u>The boat will probably not move very much</u>. Remember, the boat moved because of a decrease in surface tension caused by the soap. If a lot of soap is already in the water, the surface tension is already decreased substantially. Thus, the effect of the soap on the boat will most likely be insignificant.

3.5 <u>Vegetable oil has a lower surface tension than water</u>. If the paper clip could float on water because of its surface tension, a liquid on which it cannot float must have a lower surface tension.

3.6 <u>The study should be done as a single-blind study, but there is no need for a double-blind study</u>. I would make it blind to reduce the competition factor. If the publicly schooled students knew they were being treated as a control for a comparison to homeschooled students, they might try harder than they normally would in order to "beat" the homeschoolers. The homeschooled students might also have similar competitive instincts if they knew they were being compared to publicly schooled students. Since the data are not subjective, however, there is no reason to make the person analyzing the data blind. Remember, the researcher needs to be blind only if the data are subjective. In the case of this experiment, a test score is an objective measurement that leaves no room for interpretation. Thus, there is no way the researcher's preconceived notions can affect the results. Now, of course, if the researcher wants to avoid all appearance of subjectivity, he could make it a double-blind study just to be on the safe side, but from a scientific point of view, there is no reason to do so. In case you are wondering, homeschooled students usually score significantly higher than publicly schooled students in these kinds of studies.

3.7 <u>The study should be double-blind</u>. First, if students knew who was homeschooled and who wasn't, that would affect how they behave toward one another. So the students have to be blind as to whether they are a part of the control or the studied group. In the same way, the psychologists analyzing the students' behavior must be blind as well. Otherwise, their preconceived ideas on homeschooling versus public schooling might affect how they analyze each student. In case you were wondering, such studies report that there are only small differences between homeschooled students and publicly schooled students. The observable differences are typically that homeschooled students don't break the rules as often as publicly schooled students. Also, some of these studies have shown that homeschooled students tend to play with others regardless of race, gender, or age. Publicly schooled students, on the other hand, tend to exclude those who are not of the same race, gender, and age.

3.8 The plants grow tallest with <u>100 ounces</u> of fertilizer, because the dot at 100 ounces of fertilizer is highest on the graph. Thus, that amount produces the tallest plants.

3.9 <u>This study does not support the hypothesis.</u> With no fertilizer, the plants grow taller than with 300 to 450 ounces of fertilizer. You can see this because the dot for 0 fertilizer is higher than the dots for 300, 350, 400, and 450 ounces.

3.10. <u>The range should be 100 to 200 ounces.</u> Since there must be a range, you need to establish the range over which the plants grow tallest for that range. Since 100 ounces is the ideal amount, you might have thought 50 to 150 ounces would be a good range, because that would have 100 as the average amount of fertilizer. Look at the data, however. Plants grown with 50 ounces are smaller than plants grown with 150 and 200 ounces of fertilizer. Thus, the best 100-ounce range is between 100 and 200 ounces.

Jerry never understood the proper way to do a blind experiment.

Cartoon by Speartoons

STUDY GUIDE FOR MODULE #3

1. Define the following terms:

a. Experimental variable
b. Control (of an experiment)
c. Blind experiments
d. Double-blind experiments

2. When is an experimental variable good and when should it be reduced or eliminated?

Questions 3 through 7 refer to the following story:

A consumer laboratory decides to test the effectiveness of different laundry detergents. Five white shirts are stained with grass stains and put into five different washers. In one washer, no laundry detergent is used. In the other four washers, four different types of laundry detergent are used, one type in each washer. Water from the same source is used to fill each washer. The washers are then turned on for the same amount of time and same kind of cycle, and once they are finished, the shirts are examined by eye to see which is the cleanest.

3. What is the control for this experiment?

4. What is the experimental variable that will be used to learn something from the experiment?

5. What are the experimental variables that need to be reduced or eliminated?

6. What could be done to reduce or eliminate the unwanted experimental variables?

7. Are the data collected objective or subjective?

8. Why can a carefully placed needle float on water, even though a needle is denser than water?

9. What does soap do to the surface tension of water?

10. A student tries to float a needle on water. He succeeds, but only after several attempts. He then tries to float the same needle on another liquid. Although the needle sinks when dropped in the liquid, it is much easier to lay the needle on the surface of this liquid and make it float than it was to get the needle to float on water. Compare the surface tension of this liquid to the surface tension of water.

11. A new, fat-free potato chip comes out on the market. A few months later, there are reports that some people get severe stomach cramps a few hours after eating the chips. You must do an experiment to see if the chips cause severe stomach cramps. A group of people volunteer for the study. Describe how you would design the experiment. Also, indicate whether the experiment should be single-blind, double-blind, or neither.

12. A study is done to see if a certain herb can increase a student's concentration skills. A group of students volunteer for the experiment, which consists of giving the students a pill made of either sugar or the herb. The students then take a series of math tests. The test scores of the students who take the

herb will be compared to those who took the sugar pills. If there is a difference between the average test scores of the groups, it could very well be the result of the herb. Should this be a single-blind experiment, a double-blind experiment, or neither?

13. A farmer has four different cornfields. The government pays him to experiment with three different kinds of herbicides (weed killers). He sprays nothing on one field, and he sprays each of the other fields with a different brand of herbicide. He then records the number of tons of corn he produces from each field, and reports back to the government about which herbicide produced the best crop. Should this be a single-blind experiment, a double-blind experiment, or neither?

14. A researcher is trying to determine if there are any differences between how homeschooled students play and how publicly schooled students play. She plans to get a group of publicly schooled students and a group of homeschooled students together and observe how the children play with one another. She will record her observations and then try to see if the ways in which the homeschooled children play with each other are different from the ways in which publicly schooled children play with each other. Should this be a single-blind experiment, a double-blind experiment, or neither?

15. A scientist comes up with a revolutionary drug that he thinks will allow people to lose weight without dieting. They simply need to take the pill and their excess weight will slowly disappear. He decides to test the pill by getting two groups of volunteers together. The first group will take a fake pill, and the second group will take his new drug. Each volunteer will be weighed once a week for 12 weeks. Should this be a single-blind experiment, a double-blind experiment, or neither? What results will indicate that the new drug is effective?

(The study guide continues on the next page.)

Questions 16 through 19 refer to the following story:

A student is playing with a spring and notices that the more weight he hangs on it, the more it stretches. He therefore decides to do an experiment. He suspends the spring from the ceiling and puts a hanger on the bottom of the spring. He then starts putting more and more weight on the hanger. He measures the length of the spring each time he adds weight, and he comes up with the following graph:

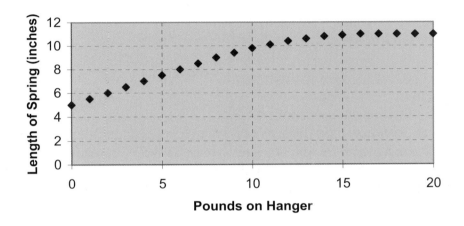

16. How long is the spring when it is not stretched out at all?

17. How many pounds are necessary to stretch the spring to 8 inches?

18. At about what weight does the spring no longer stretch in response to more weight being put on it?

19. The student does this experiment on several more springs. Although the actual numbers vary from spring to spring, the graph always has the same basic shape. What does this tell you about the ability of a spring to stretch when pulled?

MODULE #4: Science, Applied Science, and Technology

Introduction

By working through the previous three modules, you have probably gotten a good idea about what science is and how to do it. That's good, because in the next module and the three that follow it, I will introduce you to the fascinating fields of geology and paleontology. These are two of the most controversial fields in science, so you need to have a firm grounding in the nature of science in order to know how to deal with the controversies you will encounter. In *this* module, however, I want to spend some time on a distinction that is rarely made but is *very* important.

The Distinction Between Science, Applied Science, and Technology

The distinction between science, applied science, and technology is rather simple. Despite this fact, it is rarely made in textbooks today. As a result, many students grow up thinking that these three pursuits are the same. In fact, they are not. The distinction between them is the *motivation* behind each one. Science is motivated by curiosity to understand. A scientist does experiments designed to explain some facet of creation. The scientist does not care one whit about whether or not the knowledge gained is *useful*. The scientist just wants the knowledge to satisfy her own curiosity.

Applied science is quite different. In applied science, experiments are aimed at trying to find something useful. For example, an applied scientist will look at a job and say, "There must be an easier way to do that job." He will then start doing experiments aimed at the goal of building a process or machine that will make the job easier.

Do you see the difference? In science, we are just trying to answer questions. We want to know *why* something in creation happens as it does. Thus, we make observations, form hypotheses, do experiments, and eventually come up with theories and laws that explain *why*. In applied science, we have a completely different goal. In applied science, we want to use science *to make something better*.

What about technology? It is related to, but different from, both science and applied science. Technology is a new process or machine that makes life better or makes a job easier. Now although that sounds a lot like applied science, it is not. Technology is often the *result* of applied science, but it is also often the result of science. In addition, it can be the result of accident.

Now if all this is a bit confusing, let me clear it up with a few examples. I will start out with a simple one. You already learned that the ancient Egyptians had the best medical practices of anyone in the known world back in ancient times. One of their medical practices was to put moldy bread on an open wound. This is an example of technology that was the result of accident. The ancient Egyptian doctors tried several different treatments for open wounds. Many of those treatments made the patient sicker, so the doctors stopped using them. Eventually, someone tried putting moldy bread on an open wound. The wound healed quickly and cleanly, and eventually, the practice became a standard medical procedure.

The practice of putting moldy bread on open wounds is an example of technology. The process itself makes life better because it allows people's wounds to heal more efficiently. This should illustrate an important point. When most people think of "technology," they think of machines like computers, televisions, and automobiles. Although those are all examples of technology, they are not the only kinds of examples. Any invention or process that makes life better or a job easier is technology. Medical treatments, nutritional programs, and the like are all considered technology. The ancient Egyptians, then, had a lot of technology, but it was mostly the result of accident.

Technology can also be the result of applied science. Consider the computer, for example. The origin of computers can actually be traced back more than 1,000 years. However, one of the more important forerunners of the computer was produced by **Blaise Pascal** in 1642. As you learned in Module #1, Pascal was a great scientist, mathematician, and philosopher. Although he practiced science, he also practiced applied science. One of the things he wanted to do was to make the job of adding and subtracting numbers easier. After years of experiments trying to come up with a "machine" that could add and subtract, he eventually invented the **adding machine**.

As time went on, many advances were made to the adding machine, all in an attempt to make the job of keeping track of numbers easier. Eventually, adding machines were made that could multiply and divide as well. As time went on, people figured out how to make these machines work on more and more complex problems. All this was done with machines composed of gears, rods, and shafts.

Computers eventually took a giant step forward in 1947 when American scientists John Eckert and John Mauchly invented **ENIAC**, the first electronic computer. ENIAC stood for "Electronic Numerical Integrator and Computer." It used electronic devices known as **vacuum tubes** (almost 18,000 of them!) to produce several hundred multiplication steps every second. Although this computer was fast compared to all the adding machines that had come before it, it was huge (as shown below) and incredibly expensive.

FIGURE 4.1
A Portion of ENIAC

U.S. Army photo from
http://ftp.arl.army.mil/~mike/comphist/

Applied scientists began to work on ways to reduce both the size and expense of building an electronic computer. Since vacuum tubes were both large and costly to build, they decided to attack the problem at that point. Some applied scientists worked on making vacuum tubes smaller and cheaper, while others worked on finding a replacement. In 1947, three applied scientists from Bell Telephone Laboratories (Walter Brattain, John Bardeen, and William Shockley) developed the **transistor**. It could perform the function of a vacuum tube at a much cheaper price, and it was also tiny in comparison. That discovery made it possible to build small, inexpensive computers, and it ushered in the computer age that we are in today.

Now look at how the computer was invented. It started out as a device that Pascal made specifically to help people who had to keep track of a lot of numbers. Pascal did not invent the adding machine by trial and error. He used the scientific method – forming hypotheses on how to make such a device, performing experiments, etc. Thus, Pascal was doing science. However, his goal was not to learn about some aspect of creation. Instead, it was to make life easier for certain people. Thus, Pascal was doing applied science.

In each stage of the computer's history, you can see that nearly every advance was the result of applied science. Scientists working on new computers were interested in making the adding machine faster, more efficient, and able to do more things, all with the expressed purpose of making it easier to keep track of numbers. Thus, the computer is a result of (mostly) applied science.

Although you would think that most technology we have today is the result of applied science, that's not necessarily true. Consider, for example, the use of X-rays in modern medicine. When a doctor thinks you might have broken a bone, he has an X-ray done of that bone. The X-ray allows the doctor to look at the bone without cutting you open, which makes the diagnosis much faster and safer.

X-rays were discovered in 1895 by German scientist **Wilhelm Conrad Roentgen**. Roentgen was not trying to come up with a new medical procedure. Instead, he was studying electricity and trying to understand *what* it was. He was passing electricity through a tube that was partially filled with gas. He noticed that even though the tube was encased in black cardboard, whenever the electricity passed through the tube, a nearby screen would glow. He hypothesized that the tube was emitting some sort of rays whenever the electricity passed through it. Since he had no idea what those rays were, he called them "**X-rays**." He performed further tests and demonstrated that X-rays could form images on photographic film, just like visible light could.

Medical scientists quickly understood the value of these X-rays. After all, they could form images on photographic film even when the source was enclosed in a black box. Soon, doctors were using X-rays to form images of the insides of people's bodies. They were used to find bullets inside shooting victims and, as the technology developed further, they were eventually used to diagnose problems with bones and internal organs.

The technology of X-rays, then, is really the result of science. A scientist who was just trying to figure out the nature of electricity ended up discovering a process that advanced medical diagnosis and treatment immensely. Not all technology, then, is the result of applied science. Some of it is the result of accident, and some is the result of science.

FIGURE 4.2

X-Ray Image of a Person's Hands

Photo © JolaM
Agency: www.shutterstock.com

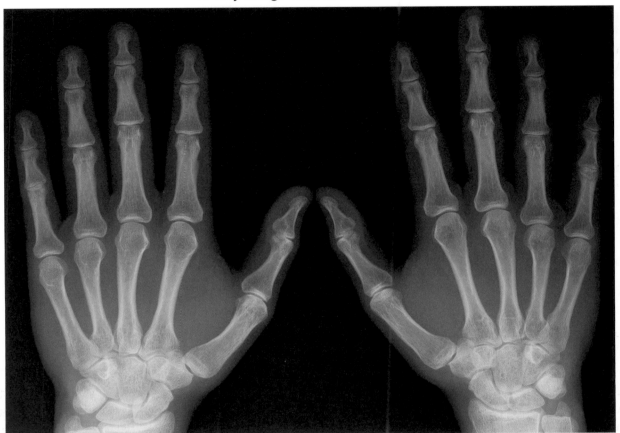

Since X-rays don't pass through bone as easily as skin, you can use them to take a "photograph" of a person's bones.

Sometimes, science and applied science interact to produce technology. The history of the computer gives us an example of that. As you just learned, computer technology made a great leap forward when mechanical adding machines were replaced by electronic computers. The principal component of an electronic computer at that time was the vacuum tube – a glass tube from which most of the air had been removed. The tube contained electrical wires and plates and, when electricity was passed through it in a certain way, the vacuum tube could be used to run a computer. Vacuum tubes were first developed by scientists to study electricity. Later, applied scientists realized that these same tubes could be used to run computers. Thus, without scientists studying electricity, there would have been no vacuum tubes to make electronic computers! Science and applied science, then, often work together to make technology.

ON YOUR OWN

4.1 Identify each of the experiments described below as a science experiment or applied science experiment.

a. An experiment designed to figure out why rainbows form in the sky
b. An experiment designed to determine how to make a field produce more crops
c. An experiment designed to make a television have a sharper picture
d. An experiment designed to determine the factors that influence the speed of wind

4.2 Which of the following would be considered technology?

a. An explanation of how clouds form
b. A microwave oven
c. A recipe to make cement
d. A description of the lifecycle of a grasshopper

Simple Machines

Since the rest of this course is going to concentrate on science, I thought I would spend the rest of this module discussing technology and applied science. The best way to discuss both of these subjects is to introduce the concept of **simple machines**.

Simple machine – A device that either multiplies or redirects a force

To understand this definition, you obviously have to know what force is.

Force – A push or pull exerted on an object in an effort to change that object's velocity

So what does all this mean? Let's start with force.

A force is used to change the velocity of an object. For example, if a car is stalled and you need to get it to a service station, you push on it to get it moving. When you do that, you are exerting a force in an attempt to change the car's velocity. The car's initial velocity is zero, but if you push hard enough, you will change that and give the car a velocity so it can move. Thus, the push changes the car's velocity from zero to some value that is not zero. Suppose you get the car rolling and you reach a hill. The service station is, thankfully, at the bottom of the hill. You allow the car to roll down the hill, but now it is going much too fast for you to pull into the station. What do you do at that point? You hit the brakes. The brakes push against the wheels to stop the car. Once again, the brakes apply a push to alter the velocity of the car. This time, the velocity changes from a large number to zero.

Now that you know what force is, you know what a simple machine is. A simple machine magnifies a force or changes its direction. Generally, this is done to make a task easier to complete. There are six basic kinds of simple machines: **the lever, the wheel and axle, the pulley, the inclined plane, the wedge,** and **the screw**. Most non-electronic machines are really just combinations of these six simple machines.

The Lever

The lever is a simple machine that magnifies either force or motion. It consists of a rigid bar that rotates around a fixed point called the **fulcrum**. The best way to understand the lever is to do an experiment that uses one.

EXPERIMENT 4.1
The Lever

Supplies:

♦ A wooden pencil
♦ A wooden ruler

♦ At least five quarters, preferably more
♦ Eye protection such as goggles or safety glasses

Introduction: A lever allows you to use a small force to lift a heavy load. This experiment will demonstrate that fact.

Procedure:

1. Lay the pencil down on a flat tabletop or desktop.
2. Lay the ruler across the pencil so that the pencil is at the center of the ruler, as shown below:

Illustration by Julia Marie Ciferno   ruler

pencil

3. Don't worry if your ruler doesn't stay horizontal. It will probably tilt so one side hits the tabletop. That's fine.
4. Place two quarters on the end that is resting on the tabletop.
5. Place a single quarter on the other end.
6. Now think about the setup. The end of the ruler that is resting on the tabletop has two quarters on it. The weight of those two quarters is pressing down on that end of the ruler. The other side has a single quarter on it. The weight of that single quarter is pressing down on that side of the ruler.
7. Keeping the ruler still, begin moving the pencil over toward the side with two quarters on it. Move it a little bit at a time, and stop in between each move to see what happens. Eventually, you should see the ruler tilt so the side with the single quarter falls and hits the tabletop, and the side with two quarters is raised up in the air.
8. What did you just accomplish? You just used a lever to make the weight of one quarter lift up the weight of two quarters. The ruler is the rigid bar, and the pencil is the fulcrum. By moving the fulcrum towards the larger weight, you could actually make the small weight lift the larger weight.
9. Add another quarter to the stack of two quarters. The ruler should once again tilt so the side with three quarters is touching the table, and the side with one quarter is in the air.
10. Begin moving the pencil toward the stack of quarters again, like you did in step 7. Continue to do this until the ruler tilts so the side with the single quarter rests on the table, and the side with the three quarters is in the air. You have now used a lever to make the weight of one quarter lift the weight of three quarters.
11. Continue the experiment, adding more quarters to the stack. Each time, move the pencil toward the stack, and you should see that the weight of a single quarter can lift many, many other quarters. When I did this experiment, I was able to get the weight of a single quarter to lift *20 quarters*!
12. Clean up your mess.

In the experiment, you made a lever. The ruler was the rigid bar, and the pencil was the fulcrum. The single quarter represented what we call the **effort**, which is the force being applied to the lever. The stack of quarters is called the **resistance**, which identifies the weight that's being lifted. Thus, the basic parts of a lever are the bar, the fulcrum, the effort, and the resistance. Using a lever like the one you made in the experiment, you can move objects that it would otherwise be impossible to lift. In the experiment, for example, you used an effort equal to the weight of one quarter to lift a resistance of several quarters. The lever, then, magnified the effort so a large resistance could be lifted.

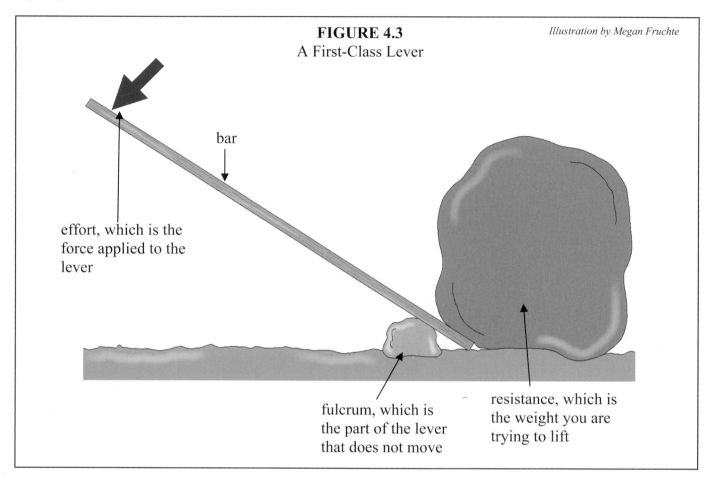

FIGURE 4.3
A First-Class Lever

Illustration by Megan Fruchte

bar

effort, which is the force applied to the lever

fulcrum, which is the part of the lever that does not move

resistance, which is the weight you are trying to lift

As you saw in your experiment, a lever gives the person using it an advantage. A lever like the one you used in your experiment, for example, allows a person to lift heavy objects with a relatively small force. Thus, the person receives a **mechanical advantage** by using a lever.

Mechanical advantage – The amount by which force or motion is magnified in a simple machine

In your experiment, when you used the weight of a single quarter to lift three other quarters, the lever was providing a mechanical advantage of 3. The effort was magnified three times so one quarter could lift three quarters.

What determines the mechanical advantage of a lever? Mechanical advantage is determined by the distance between the effort and fulcrum as compared to the distance between the resistance and the fulcrum. Remember what happened in the experiment. In order to get the one quarter's weight to lift a stack of quarters, you had to move the pencil (the fulcrum) toward the stack of quarters (the resistance). The closer the fulcrum was to the resistance, and the farther it was from the effort, the more weight the effort could lift.

If the fulcrum is put precisely in between the effort and the resistance, there is no mechanical advantage. If you wanted to lift 100 pounds with the lever, you would have to supply 100 pounds of force. However, if you move the fulcrum closer to the resistance, the amount of force you would have to use goes down. How much does it go down? Well, you can calculate the mechanical advantage of a lever using a rather simple mathematical formula:

For a Lever
Mechanical advantage = (distance from fulcrum to effort) ÷ (distance from fulcrum to resistance)

Suppose, for example, you made a lever in which the fulcrum was 6 inches from the resistance and 60 inches from the effort. In that case the mechanical advantage would be calculated by replacing "distance from fulcrum to effort" with "60" and "distance from fulcrum to resistance" with "6":

Mechanical advantage = (distance from fulcrum to effort) ÷ (distance from fulcrum to resistance)

Mechanical advantage = 60 ÷ 6 = 10

This means you could lift a resistance *10 times as heavy as the effort*. Thus, you could lift a 100-pound rock using only 10 pounds of force!

I will come back to the concept of mechanical advantage when I do a couple examples at the end of this section. Before I do those examples, however, I want to tell you a few more things about levers. Notice that I called the lever in Figure 4.3 a **first-class lever**. What did I mean by that? Did I mean that it was just a really great lever? No! It turns out that there are three different kinds of levers, and the one illustrated in Figure 4.3 is an example of the first kind. There are also **second-class levers** and **third-class levers**. What separates these three classes? The position of the fulcrum relative to the resistance and effort.

In a first-class lever, the fulcrum is positioned between the effort and resistance. In a second-class lever, the fulcrum is at one end of the bar and the resistance is between the fulcrum and the effort. In a third-class lever, the fulcrum is at one end of the bar and the effort is between the fulcrum and the resistance.

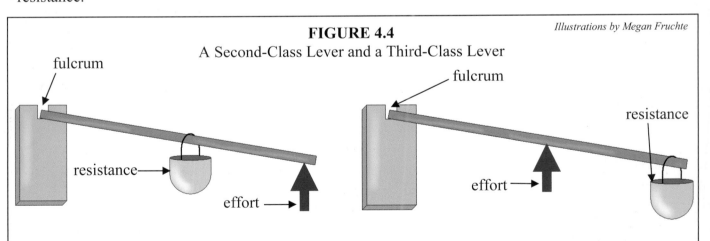

FIGURE 4.4
A Second-Class Lever and a Third-Class Lever

Illustrations by Megan Fruchte

A Second-Class Lever
In this lever, the fulcrum is at one end of the bar and the resistance is between the fulcrum and the effort.

A Third-Class Lever
In this lever, the fulcrum is at one end of the bar and the effort is between the fulcrum and the resistance.

Both a second-class lever and a third-class lever provide mechanical advantage, and that mechanical advantage can be calculated using the same mathematical equation I showed you earlier. However, the nature of the mechanical advantage is *different* between these levers. A second-class lever, like a first-class lever, magnifies force. If the mechanical advantage is 10, you can lift a resistance of 100 pounds with only a 10-pound effort. In a third-class lever, force is not magnified. In fact, the effort is usually larger than the resistance in a third-class lever. What's the mechanical advantage, then? Well, even though it takes more force to lift the resistance, the resistance moves a lot *faster* than the effort. Thus, a third-class lever magnifies speed, not force.

I want you to notice one other thing about these three classes of levers. What happens to the *direction* of the force being applied to the lever? In the first-class lever pictured in Figure 4.3, the effort pushes *down* and the resistance moves *up*. Thus, a first-class lever not only magnifies the effort, but it also changes the direction of the effort. Now look at the second-class lever pictured in Figure 4.4. Notice that the effort pushes *up*, and the resistance moves *up* as well. A second-class lever, then, magnifies force, but does not change the direction of the force. In the third-class lever pictured in Figure 4.4, the effort pushes *up* and the resistance moves *up* as well. Thus, a third-class lever magnifies speed and does not change the direction of the force.

Believe it or not, there are many, many common examples of all three classes of levers. Figure 4.5 illustrates a few of them:

FIGURE 4.5

A Common Example of Each Class of Lever

Illustrations from
www.clipart.com

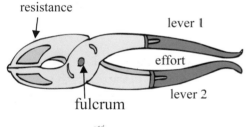

Pliers are an example of two **first-class levers**. The fulcrum is between the effort and resistance. You can grasp an object with a much firmer grasp when using pliers, because the force of your grasp is magnified.

A wheelbarrow is an example of a **second-class lever**. The fulcrum is at one end, and the effort (where you lift) is at the other. The resistance is between the effort and the fulcrum. You can lift more weight in a wheelbarrow than you can with your arms, because the lever magnifies the force with which you lift.

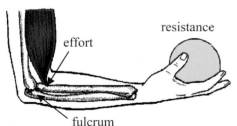

Your forearm is an example of a **third-class lever**. The fulcrum is at one end (your elbow), and the effort (provided by the muscle) is between the resistance and the fulcrum. You exert more force with your muscle than the weight you lift, but the speed at which the weight moves is much faster than the speed at which your muscle moves.

In the past few pages, I have thrown a lot of information at you, so I want to step back and review before I continue. First, a lever consists of four parts: a bar, a fulcrum (the part that does not move), an effort (the force being applied), and a resistance (the load you want to move). In a first-class lever, the fulcrum is between the effort and the resistance. Because of this arrangement, the direction of the effort is reversed. If you press down, the resistance will move up. Also, a first-class lever magnifies the effort, providing a mechanical advantage that can be calculated. A second-class lever has the fulcrum at one end of the bar, and the resistance is between the fulcrum and the effort. This arrangement does not change the direction of the effort. If you lift up, the resistance moves up. It does, however, magnify the effort, providing a mechanical advantage that can be calculated. Finally, third-class levers also have the fulcrum at one end of the bar, but the effort is between the fulcrum and the resistance. This arrangement does not change the direction of the effort. It also does not magnify the effort. Instead, it magnifies the speed at which the effort moves, providing a mechanical advantage that can be calculated. Although the effort moves slowly, the resistance will move quickly.

Before I leave this discussion of levers, I want to revisit the equation for mechanical advantage. It is important for you to learn that the more science you do, the more you will see that math is an integral part of science. The mechanical advantage equation is your first introduction to this fact, so I want to highlight it. Study the following example to make sure you understand how to use the mechanical advantage equation.

EXAMPLE 4.1

A person constructs a first-class lever to move a 200-pound rock. The fulcrum is placed 5 inches from the rock, and the person applies force 100 inches from the fulcrum. What is the mechanical advantage of this lever?

To calculate mechanical advantage, you use the equation I gave you earlier. Since the distance between the effort (the applied force) and the fulcrum is 100 inches, we replace "distance from fulcrum to effort" with 100. Since the resistance (the load the person is trying to move) is 5 inches from the fulcrum, we replace "distance from fulcrum to resistance" with 5.

Mechanical advantage = (distance from fulcrum to effort) ÷ (distance from fulcrum to resistance)

Mechanical advantage = 100 ÷ 5 = 20

The mechanical advantage, then, is <u>20</u>.

Now remember what we calculated here. This is far from a meaningless number! It tells us that whatever force the person applies, the force used to move the rock will be *20 times greater*. This means that to move the 200-pound rock, the person need only push with 10 pounds!

ON YOUR OWN

4.3 Tweezers are an example of a lever. To which class of levers do tweezers belong?

4.4 A person constructs a second-class lever in which the fulcrum is 1 foot from the resistance, while the effort is 3 feet from the fulcrum. What is the mechanical advantage of this lever?

4.5 If a lever has a mechanical advantage of 10, what does that mean?

The Wheel and Axle

The next simple machine I want to discuss is the wheel and axle. In a wheel and axle, a large circular wheel is attached to a smaller cylinder, which is like a solid tube. When the wheel turns, so does the axle. When the axle turns, so does the wheel. If both parts do not turn together, it is not the simple machine we are discussing. The function of the *simple machine* known as a wheel and axle depends on the fact that both the wheel and the axle turn together.

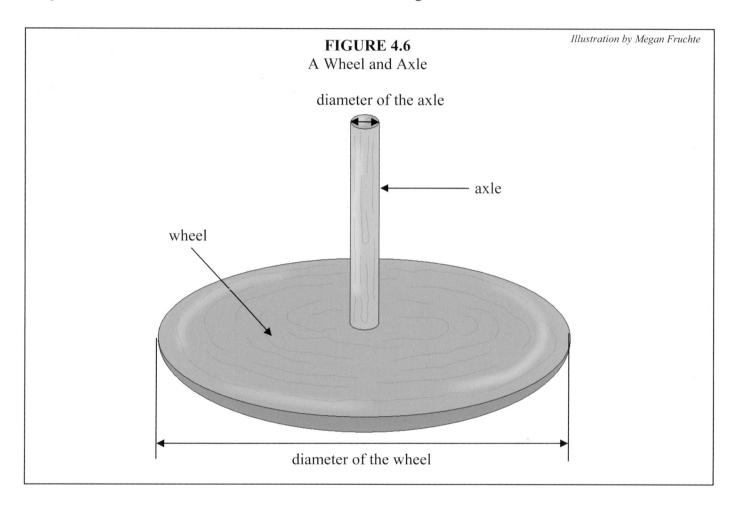

FIGURE 4.6

A Wheel and Axle

Illustration by Megan Fruchte

diameter of the axle

axle

wheel

diameter of the wheel

A wheel and axle has two applications, both of which can be found in an automobile. In the first application, the engine turns an axle, and the axle causes the wheels to turn. The turning of the wheels causes the car to move. In this application, then, the force is applied to the axle and used to turn the wheel. The second application can be found in the steering wheel. The driver turns the steering wheel, which causes the axle below the steering wheel to turn. In this case, then, the effort is applied to the wheel, making the axle turn.

A wheel and axle also offers a mechanical advantage. Like the mechanical advantage of a lever, it is relatively easy to calculate. First, you need to know the **diameter** of the wheel and the diameter of the axle. Now you might not be familiar with the term "diameter," so I want to define it.

Diameter – The length of a straight line that travels from one side of a circle to another and passes through the center of the circle

The diameter, then, is a measure of the size of a circle. From Figure 4.6, you can easily see that the diameter of the wheel is much bigger than that of the axle.

Once you know the diameter of the wheel and the diameter of the axle, the mechanical advantage can be calculated, once again by a relatively simple equation:

For a Wheel and Axle
Mechanical advantage = (diameter of the wheel) ÷ (diameter of the axle)

Notice that *this* equation for mechanical advantage is similar to, but different from, the equation for the mechanical advantage of a lever. This is an important point. A wheel and axle is completely different from a lever. They both offer a mechanical advantage, but because they are different, the equations for mechanical advantage are different. This is common in science. Often you can calculate the same thing for different situations, but the equations will be slightly different. You have to get used to that. Thus, if you are asked to calculate the mechanical advantage of a wheel and axle, you have to use a different equation from the one you would use to calculate the mechanical advantage of a lever.

Before I show you an example of calculating the mechanical advantage for a wheel and axle, I need to tell you what the mechanical advantage does in a wheel and axle. That depends on which way you use the wheel and axle. Suppose you turn the wheel in order to make the axle turn. In that case, the mechanical advantage magnifies the force you are applying. If the mechanical advantage is 10, and you turn the wheel, the axle turns with a force ten times as large.

Have you ever seen the inside of a big, 18-wheel truck? If you have, you probably noticed that the truck's steering wheel is *significantly* bigger than a typical car's steering wheel. This is because a truck requires more force to turn than does a car. Since the mechanical advantage of a wheel and axle increases as the diameter of the wheel gets bigger, a truck's steering wheel magnifies the force with which the driver turns much more than does the steering wheel of a car.

If you use the other application of a wheel and axle (turning the axle in order to make the wheel turn), the force with which you turn is not magnified. In fact, you will need to apply a greater force. However, the mechanical advantage will cause the edge of the wheel to turn with much greater speed. In an automobile, the engine turns the axle with a certain speed. The mechanical advantage of the wheel and axle, however, magnifies that speed, so that the car can travel faster than it would if the wheels were the same size as the axle.

Have you ever compared the size of a dragster's tires to those of a normal car? A dragster's wheels are *much* larger than a normal car's wheels. Once again, the mechanical advantage of a wheel and axle increases when the size of the wheel increases. To get more speed, then, a dragster has bigger wheels. This increases the mechanical advantage, increasing the speed of the car for drag races.

EXAMPLE 4.2

A wheel has a diameter of 24 inches, while its axle has a diameter of 2 inches. What is the mechanical advantage of this wheel and axle?

Since this is a wheel and axle, we must use the mechanical advantage equation for a wheel and axle, not a lever:

Mechanical advantage = (diameter of the wheel) ÷ (diameter of the axle)

The diameter of the wheel and that of the axle are both given, so we can put them in the equation:

Mechanical advantage = 24 ÷ 2 = 12

The mechanical advantage, then, is <u>12</u>.

What does this mechanical advantage mean? Well, it depends on the application you use. If you are turning the wheel, the force with which you turn will be magnified by 12. Thus, the axle will turn with 12 times the force applied to the wheel. If you are turning the axle, the speed will be magnified by 12. Thus, the wheel will turn with a speed 12 times faster than that of the axle.

ON YOUR OWN

4.6 When is a wheel and axle similar to a first-class or second-class lever? When is it similar to a third-class lever?

The Pulley

A **pulley** consists of a grooved wheel that rotates freely on a frame. A pulley is operated by laying a rope in the pulley's groove. When one end of the rope is pulled down, the wheel rotates and the other end of the rope is lifted up.

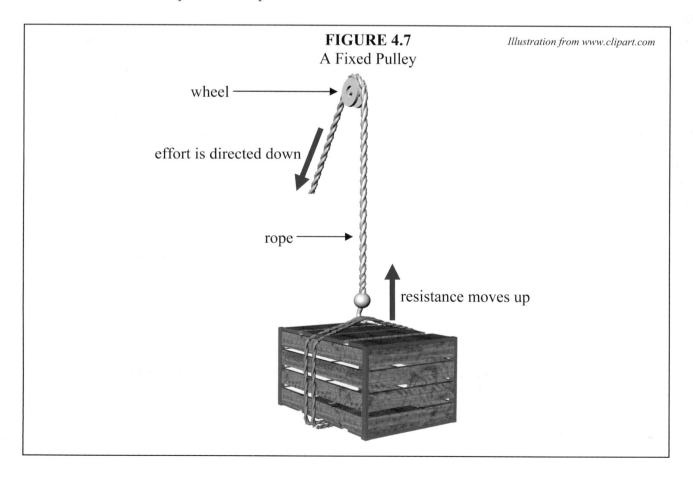

FIGURE 4.7
A Fixed Pulley

Illustration from www.clipart.com

wheel

effort is directed down

rope

resistance moves up

Notice that I labeled Figure 4.7 a "fixed pulley." That doesn't mean the pulley was broken at one time. It means the wheel can only rotate. It is fixed to an anchor and thus cannot move up, down, left, or right. As you will see in a moment, we can arrange things so that pulleys move, and that changes things a bit. A single, fixed pulley offers no mechanical advantage. However, it does change the direction of the force. This, in itself, is useful, because most people can pull down with more force than they can lift up. Thus, if you want to lift a heavy object, you can attach a rope to it, thread the rope through a pulley, and pull down on the rope. The pulley will change the direction, lifting the heavy object.

Although a single, fixed pulley offers no mechanical advantage, a series of pulleys can. Perform the following experiment to see what I mean.

EXPERIMENT 4.2
A Simulation of Using Multiple Pulleys

Illustrations from www.clipart.com

Supplies:

♦ Two brooms or a broom and a mop (You basically need two implements with long handles. The experiment works best when the handles are very smooth.)
♦ Several feet of rope (Nylon rope works best because it is slick.)
♦ Two reasonably strong people to help you

Introduction: In this experiment, you will use broom handles to simulate pulleys, and you will see how multiple pulleys can provide mechanical advantage.

Procedure:

1. Have your helpers stand about 3 feet apart, facing one another.
2. Tie one end of the rope to one of the brooms. It works best if you can tie the rope to the place where the bristles attach to the broom handle. There is usually a bulge there, and if you tie the rope just below the bulge, it will stay secure.
3. Have one helper hold the broom handle with both hands so the broom is parallel to the floor. Have the other helper hold the other broom in the same way.
4. Loop the rope around the handle of the broom to which it is not tied. Make sure that the rope is between the hands of the helper holding that broom. In the end, your experiment should look something like this:

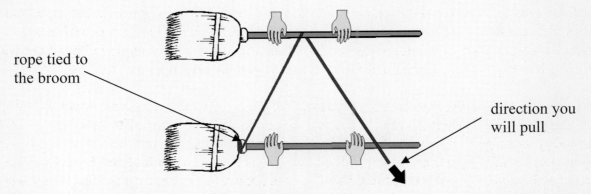

rope tied to the broom

direction you will pull

5. While you pull back on the rope as shown by the arrow in the drawing above, have your helpers pull back on each broom with all their might.

6. While they are pulling, try to pull your helpers together by pulling hard on the rope. Unless you are stronger than they are, you probably will not be able to pull them together. Even if you can pull them together, get an idea of how hard it was to do so.

7. Now you need to change your experiment a bit. This time, loop the rope first around the handle of the broom to which it is not tied, then loop it around the handle of the broom to which it is tied, and then loop it again around the handle of the broom to which it is not tied. Make sure that the rope is in between the hands of your helpers when it loops around the broom handles. Now your experiment should look something like this:

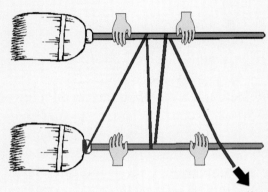

direction you will pull

8. Once again, tell your helpers to resist with all their might, and try to pull them together with the rope. Notice any difference?

9. You can continue the experiment by looping the rope around the broom handles a few more times. You should notice a pattern to the number of times the rope is looped around the broom handles and how difficult it is to pull your helpers together.

10. Put everything away.

What did you learn in the experiment? When the rope was looped around the broom handle once, it was difficult to pull your helpers together. However, when you looped the rope around the broom handles three times, it suddenly got a *lot* easier. If you continued the experiment, you should have found that the more you looped the rope around the broom handles, the *easier* it was to pull your helpers together.

Although you were not using pulleys in the experiment, you were simulating the use of pulleys. As long as the broom handles were reasonably smooth, the ropes moved around the broom handles much as they would have moved through the wheel of a pulley. Thus, even though the ropes were not on pulleys, they behaved much like they were. Therefore, you can think of the first trial in the experiment as a simulation of using a single pulley. Because it was only a single pulley, there was no mechanical advantage. Thus, it was hard for you to pull your helpers together.

When you looped the rope around the broom handles a total of three times, however, things changed, didn't they? Suddenly, it got much easier to pull your helpers together, didn't it? Why was it easier to pull your helpers together? Well, when you looped the rope around the broom handles three times, you were simulating the use of multiple pulleys. When you use multiple pulleys, you gain a mechanical advantage. You should have noticed the mechanical advantage by the fact that it was easier to pull your helpers together. If you didn't notice a big difference, the rope probably did not move on the broom handles very easily. In that case, your experiment didn't simulate pulleys very well, so you didn't get a mechanical advantage.

You can, therefore, gain a mechanical advantage with pulleys by using more than one. Thus, the force with which you pull will be magnified. When multiple pulleys are used, we often call the resulting system a **block and tackle**. A block and tackle consists of one or more fixed pulleys and one or more moveable pulleys. The more pulleys you have in a block and tackle system, the more mechanical advantage you get. In fact, in a block and tackle system, the mechanical advantage is simply given by the number of pulleys you use.

For Pulleys in a Block and Tackle
Mechanical advantage = number of pulleys used

Now I want to point out something very important. In all three of the simple machines I have shown you so far, a mechanical advantage can be attained. In first-class levers, second-class levers, a wheel and axle (if used properly), and multiple pulleys, that mechanical advantage can be used to multiply force. The person using the simple machine, then, gets "something good" by using the machine. The person gets his or her force magnified. Is there anything "bad" they have to take in return? Is there anything negative that accompanies the positive effect of the force being magnified? Yes, there is. I want to illustrate this using a block and tackle system.

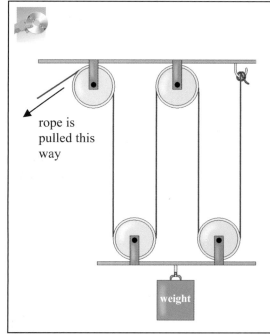

FIGURE 4.8
A Block and Tackle

Illustration by Megan Fruchte

rope is pulled this way

weight

This is one way to build a block and tackle. Notice that there are two fixed pulleys fastened to the top bar, which represents the ceiling or some other unmoving frame to which the system is attached. The two pulleys near the weight are moveable. When the left end of the rope is pulled down, the moveable pulleys and the weight will be pulled up. Since there are a total of four pulleys in the system, the mechanical advantage is 4. As a result, when you pull on the rope, the force with which you pull is magnified by 4, making it much easier to lift the weight. Thus, if this system is used to lift a 400-pound weight, only 100 pounds of force will need to be exerted in order to lift the weight. If more pulleys were added, it would require even less force.

Since you don't have to use a lot of force to lift the weight using the block and tackle in the figure, you are (in some way) saving yourself some work. However, you actually "pay" for that savings in another way. Suppose you want to lift the weight in the figure 1 foot in the air. How much rope will you have to pull? Well, each of the four strands of rope coming up from the moveable pulleys will have to rise 1 foot. So the rope on the left must shorten by 1 foot, the rope next to it on the right must shorten by 1 foot, etc. Each rope must shorten by 1 foot. How much rope will you need to pull, then? You will need to pull *4 feet of rope*. So in order to "save" yourself work by magnifying the force by 4, you "pay" for it by having to pull four times as much rope!

As your parents have probably already told you, you almost never get something for nothing. That saying is very true when it comes to understanding creation. The natural world will never "give" you something without "taking" something in return. Thus, when you use two pulleys in a block and tackle, the force with which you pull the rope is magnified by a factor of 2. There is a drawback, however. When you do that, you end up pulling twice as much rope in order to move your load. Thus, if you want to lift the load 5 feet, you must pull 10 feet of rope. The mechanical advantage offered by several pulleys, then, makes it easier to lift a load. However, you "pay" for that by having to pull a lot more rope.

This is true of any mechanical advantage offered by any simple machine. If you use a simple machine to magnify force, you "pay" for that by having to use that force over a longer distance. When you use a first-class lever in which the fulcrum is closer to the resistance than the effort, you have to push the lever farther than the load will raise up. If the mechanical advantage is three, for example, the force you exert is magnified by 3, but you will have to push the lever three times as far as the load will be lifted.

On the other hand, suppose you are using a third-class lever or you are using a wheel and axle to magnify speed. When that happens, you "pay" for the magnified speed by using a lot more force. If the mechanical advantage of a third-class lever, for example, is 3, the load will move three times faster than the speed at which the effort moves, but the effort will be three times larger than it would be if you just lifted the load without the lever. No matter what, then, you always "pay" for a mechanical advantage. If you use a simple machine to magnify force, you will have to apply that force over a much longer distance. If you use a simple machine to magnify speed, you will have to apply a much larger force.

ON YOUR OWN

4.7 A person tries to lift a load with a single pulley. He has just enough rope to get the job done. However, no matter how hard he pulls, he cannot lift the load. A smart student who just finished reading this section tells him to set up a four-pulley system. That will make it much easier for him to lift the load. The smart student also tells him to go out and get more rope. How many times more rope will the person need?

The Inclined Plane

The inclined plane is perhaps the simplest of the simple machines. It makes lifting a load easier, because you can slide the load up the inclined plane rather than lifting it straight up.

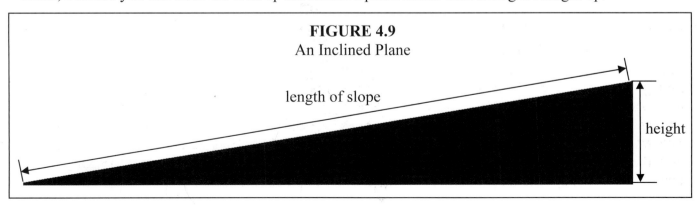

FIGURE 4.9
An Inclined Plane

length of slope

height

Although you may have never used a lever or a pulley, you have *certainly* used an inclined plane. Any time you chose to walk up a ramp, roll something up a ramp, or push something up a ramp, you used an inclined plane. The mechanical advantage of an inclined plane can be easily calculated, as long as you know the dimensions of the inclined plane:

> **For an Inclined Plane**
> Mechanical advantage = (length of the slope) ÷ (height)

Like all simple machines, you "pay" for the mechanical advantage of an inclined plane. The way you pay for it is by having to push the load farther. If your goal is to raise the load up to a certain height, you can either lift it up directly, or you can push it up an inclined plane. If you lift it directly, you will move it a distance equal to the height. If you push it up an inclined plane, you will move it the length of the slope, which is always longer than the height. Thus, you push the load farther, but you need not push it as hard.

ON YOUR OWN

4.8 What is the mechanical advantage of an inclined plane whose slope is 8 feet long and whose height is 2 feet? If the slope were 10 times as long, the mechanical advantage would be huge. What would be the drawback, however?

The Wedge

The **wedge** is often confused with the inclined plane, because both simple machines look the same. They are used differently, however, so they are considered to be different machines. Figure 4.10 illustrates how these two machines are used.

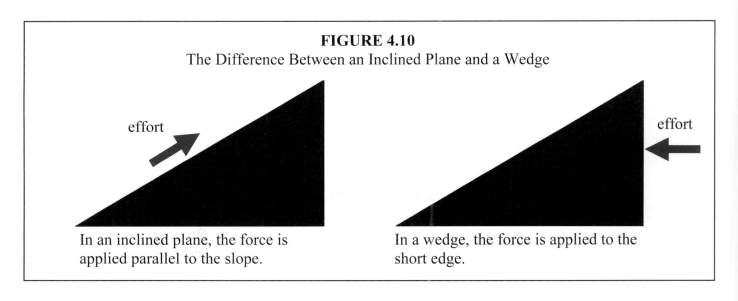

FIGURE 4.10
The Difference Between an Inclined Plane and a Wedge

effort

effort

In an inclined plane, the force is applied parallel to the slope.

In a wedge, the force is applied to the short edge.

Since these machines are used differently, it makes sense that they serve different purposes. An inclined plane is meant to ease the force required to lift a load. A wedge, on the other hand, is generally used to separate things.

When you strike the vertical edge of a wedge, the pointed end of the wedge applies a force to whatever it is in contact with. Have you ever watched someone split wood? If you have logs with a large diameter, you need to split those logs into smaller pieces in order to fit them into a normal fireplace. As a result, many people with fireplaces must split wood. If the wood is old enough, it is possible to split a log by simply striking it with an axe. However, most logs are not that easy to split. In order to split wood, then, most people use wedges. The pointed end of the wedge is placed in contact with the log, and a hammer is used to hit the vertical edge of the wedge. The pointed end travels into the wood, pulling the wood apart at the point of contact. With enough strikes of the hammer, the wedge will split the log. A modified version of the wedge is the **double wedge**, which is shown below:

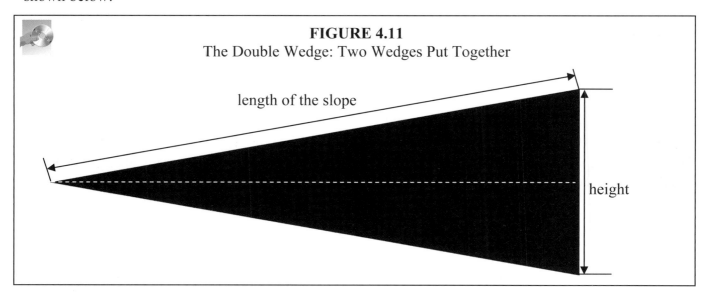

FIGURE 4.11
The Double Wedge: Two Wedges Put Together

length of the slope

height

Regardless of whether it is a double wedge or a single wedge, the mechanical advantage of a wedge can be calculated with the same equation that relates to the inclined plane.

For a Wedge (and an Inclined Plane)
Mechanical advantage = (length of the slope) ÷ (height)

Like that of all other simple machines, the wedge's mechanical advantage must be "paid" for. You must push the wedge in farther than the things you are separating will move apart. Thus, if you are splitting wood, you will need to drive the wedge into the wood farther than the two halves of the wood will be moved apart.

ON YOUR OWN

4.9 Suppose you have two single wedges with identical slopes and heights. Do you gain more mechanical advantage by using just one of those wedges, or by using both wedges as a double wedge?

The Screw

The last simple machine I want to discuss is the screw, which is actually an inclined plane wrapped around the axle of a wheel and axle.

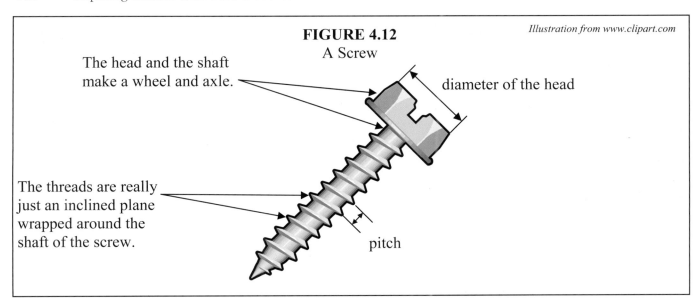

FIGURE 4.12
A Screw

Illustration from www.clipart.com

The head and the shaft make a wheel and axle.

diameter of the head

The threads are really just an inclined plane wrapped around the shaft of the screw.

pitch

As is illustrated in the figure, the inclined planes on a screw are usually called threads. The vertical distance between the threads is called the **pitch** of the screw. A full turn of a screw will result in the screw traveling into an object by a distance equal to its pitch.

What is the mechanical advantage of a screw? Well, that's an interesting question. A screw itself has some mechanical advantage. You can calculate the mechanical advantage of a screw with the following equation:

For a Screw
Mechanical advantage = (circumference) ÷ (pitch)

This equation, of course, means nothing unless you know what **circumference** is.

Circumference – The distance around a circle, equal to 3.1416 times the circle's diameter

To get the circumference of a circle, then, you find its diameter and multiply by 3.1416. You might recognize that number. It is actually an approximation of a number we call **pi**. You will learn a lot more about pi when you study geometry, so I don't want to go into that now.

What does all this mean? Well, suppose a screw has a pitch of 0.1 inches. The same screw might have a head with a diameter of 0.2 inches. To calculate the mechanical advantage, then, we must first determine the circumference of the head:

Circumference = 3.1416 x (diameter)

Circumference = 3.1416 x 0.2 = 0.62832

Now that we have the circumference, we can calculate the mechanical advantage:

Mechanical advantage = (circumference) ÷ (pitch)

Mechanical advantage = 0.62832 ÷ 0.1 = 6.2832

What does this mean? It means that if you grasp the screw by the head and turn it with your fingers, you can get the screw into the wood with 6.2832 times less force than what it would take to hammer the screw into the wood.

Now that sounds like a big mechanical advantage, but if you have ever worked with screws, you know that it is *awfully* hard to get a screw into wood using your fingers! Instead, you typically use a screwdriver. Somehow, that's a *lot* easier. Why is it easier? Well, a screwdriver has a circumference that is much larger than the head of the screw. Since you are using the screwdriver, then, the circumference you use in the mechanical advantage equation is the circumference of the *screwdriver*, not the screw!

Suppose a screwdriver has a diameter of 1 inch. If you use that screwdriver to turn the same screw I discussed earlier, the mechanical advantage is totally different:

Circumference = 3.1416 x (diameter)

Circumference = 3.1416 x 1 = 3.1416

Mechanical advantage = (circumference) ÷ (pitch)

Mechanical advantage = 3.1416 ÷ 0.1 = 31.416

Instead of 6.2832, then, the mechanical advantage of the screw is 31.416 when you use a 1-inch diameter screwdriver!

Have you ever had trouble getting a screw into wood? What did you do? Well, if you were smart, you went to the toolbox and got a screwdriver with a larger diameter. The "fatter" the screwdriver, the more mechanical advantage you get from the screw. Thus, a larger-diameter screwdriver makes it easier to screw a screw into wood. Notice that the *length* of the screwdriver does not enter into the mechanical advantage. Only the *diameter* of the screwdriver matters when it comes to determining how easy it is to screw in a screw.

EXAMPLE 4.3

A screw has a pitch of 0.05 inches. Its head has a diameter of 0.30 inches. What is the mechanical advantage of the screw if you grasp it on the head and screw it in?

To get the mechanical advantage of a screw, we must have the circumference. To get that, we multiply the diameter by 3.1416:

Circumference = 3.1416 x (diameter)

Circumference = 3.1416 x (0.30) = 0.94248

Now that we have the circumference, we can get the mechanical advantage:

$$\text{Mechanical advantage} = (\text{circumference}) \div (\text{pitch})$$

$$\text{Mechanical advantage} = 0.94248 \div 0.05 = \underline{18.8496}$$

What is the mechanical advantage of the same screw if you turn it with a screwdriver that has a diameter of 1.5 inches?

When you use a screwdriver, the mechanical advantage is calculated using the circumference of the *screwdriver*, not the *screw*. Thus, we need to determine the circumference of the screwdriver:

$$\text{Circumference} = 3.1416 \times (\text{diameter})$$

$$\text{Circumference} = 3.1416 \times (1.5) = 4.7124$$

Now we can calculate the mechanical advantage:

$$\text{Mechanical advantage} = (\text{circumference}) \div (\text{pitch})$$

$$\text{Mechanical advantage} = 4.7124 \div 0.05 = \underline{94.248}$$

So once again the mechanical advantage is much greater with a screwdriver!

Before I leave this section, I want to make a quick point. A screwdriver in itself is a simple machine. What kind of simple machine is a screwdriver? Well, when you turn the round handle, it turns the round shaft that turns the screw. What is that? It's a wheel and axle! Thus, the combination of a screw and screwdriver is really just a combination of two simple machines: a screw and a wheel and axle. Of course, since a screw is really just a combination of another wheel and axle with an inclined plane, you can say that when you use a screwdriver to imbed a screw into wood, you are using three simple machines: two wheel and axles and an inclined plane.

ON YOUR OWN

4.10 A screw has a pitch of 0.02 inches. The head has a diameter of 0.20 inches and the screwdriver with which the screw is being turned has a diameter of 1 inch. What is the mechanical advantage of the screw when it is turned with the screwdriver?

ANSWERS TO THE "ON YOUR OWN" PROBLEMS

4.1 Experiments (a) and (d) are science experiments, while (b) and (c) are applied science experiments. The goals of experiments (a) and (d) are simply knowledge. Now, that knowledge might be useful, but its use is not the goal. The knowledge is the goal. Thus, these are science experiments. In experiments (b) and (c), making something useful is the goal. That makes it applied science.

4.2 Options (b) and (c) are both examples of technology. Options (a) and (d) are knowledge. Option (b) is a machine, which is obviously technology. Option (c) is not a machine, but it directly makes life easier by allowing you to make sturdy structures. Thus a recipe for cement is technology, just like a microwave oven is.

4.3 Tweezers are an example of a third-class lever. The fulcrum is the part that does not move. Thus, it is the top end of the tweezers. The resistance is grasped with the other end of the tweezers. You pinch them in the middle, so the effort is in between the fulcrum and resistance. That's the definition of a third-class lever.

Photo from www.clipart,.com

4.4 To solve this, we use the mechanical advantage equation:

Mechanical advantage = (distance from fulcrum to effort) ÷ (distance from fulcrum to resistance)

Mechanical advantage = 3 ÷ 1 = 3

4.5 It means different things depending on the type of lever. For first-class and second-class levers, it means that the effort will be magnified by 10. For third-class levers, it means the resistance will move at ten times the speed of the effort.

4.6 A wheel and axle is similar to a first-class or second-class lever when the wheel is turned by the effort. In that case, the effort is magnified, just as it is in first-class and second-class levers. A wheel and axle is similar to a third-class lever when the axle is turned by the effort. At that point, speed is magnified, not effort. That's what happens in a third-class lever.

4.7 The person will need 4 times the amount of rope. Since he changed to a four-pulley block and tackle, he now has a mechanical advantage of 4. He pays for that, however, by needing four times as much rope.

4.8 We can calculate the mechanical advantage using the equation for an inclined plane:

Mechanical advantage = (length of slope) ÷ (height)

Mechanical advantage = 8 ÷ 2 = 4

An inclined plane with a slope 10 times as long would give a lot more mechanical advantage, but you would have to push the load ten times farther. At some point, the extra pushing just isn't worth the effort you save due to the mechanical advantage.

4.9 Remember, the mechanical advantage is determined by taking the length of the slope and dividing by the height. In this case, the double wedge would have twice as large a height as the single wedge (see Figure 4.11). If you divide by a large number, the result is a small number. Thus, the larger the height on a wedge, the lower the mechanical advantage. <u>The single wedge, therefore, would give the most mechanical advantage</u>. Why would you use a double wedge, then? Well, remember that you "pay" for the mechanical advantage. A single wedge would require less force, but you would have to push it a long way to get the needed separation. A double wedge would require more force, but it would not have to be pushed in as far to get the desired separation.

4.10 First, notice that the screw is not being turned by grasping its head. Thus, the diameter of the head is *irrelevant* in this problem. You have to be on your guard for that. Sometimes I will throw in useless numbers just to see how closely you are paying attention! This is one such case.   Since the screwdriver is being used, we need to know *its* circumference:

$$\text{Circumference} = 3.1416 \text{ x (diameter)}$$

$$\text{Circumference} = 3.1416 \text{ x } 1 = 3.1416$$

Now we can use the mechanical advantage equation for a screw:

$$\text{Mechanical advantage} = \text{(circumference)} \div \text{(pitch)}$$

$$\text{Mechanical advantage} = 3.1416 \div 0.02 = \underline{157.08}$$

STUDY GUIDE FOR MODULE #4

1. Define the following terms:

a. Simple machine
b. Force
c. Mechanical advantage
d. Diameter
e. Circumference

2. How is applied science different from science?

3. What gives rise to technology?

4. Identify each of the following as a science experiment or an applied science experiment:

a. An experiment to determine how to make electronic circuits smaller
b. An experiment to understand what factors affect how electricity runs in an electronic circuit
c. An experiment to figure out how to reduce electronic noise in an electronic circuit
d. An experiment to figure out the speed of electrons as they flow through an electronic circuit

5. Which of the following would be considered technology?

a. A classification scheme for all animals
b. A vaccination that will keep all animals from contracting the flu
c. A new diet for dogs that will lead to longer life
d. An understanding of what causes urinary-tract infections in cats

6. List the six types of simple machines.

7. Which two simple machines look identical?

8. What is the mechanical advantage of a first-class lever in which the fulcrum is 10 inches from the resistance and 40 inches from the effort?

9. What does the mechanical advantage in problem #8 mean?

10. A shovel is an example of a lever. To what class does a shovel belong?

11. A child's see-saw is a lever. To what class does it belong?

12. What is the mechanical advantage of a wheel and axle when the wheel has a diameter of 15 inches and the axle has a diameter of 3 inches?

13. If a person turned the wheel of the wheel and axle in problem #12, what would the mechanical advantage do?

14. If a person turned the axle in the wheel and axle in problem #12, what would the mechanical advantage do?

15. A block and tackle is composed of six pulleys that all work together. What is the mechanical advantage of the block and tackle system?

16. Using the block and tackle system in problem #15, how many feet of rope would have to be pulled if a person wanted to lift a load 1 foot?

17. What is the mechanical advantage of an inclined plane with a slope of 6 feet and a height of 2 feet?

18. What is the mechanical advantage of a wedge with the same dimensions as the inclined plane in problem #17?

19. A screw with a pitch of 0.1 inches is turned with a screwdriver whose diameter is 2 inches. What is the mechanical advantage?

20. If you are having a hard time turning a screw, should you get a longer screwdriver or a fatter one?

MODULE #5: The History of Life – Archaeology, Geology, and Paleontology

Introduction

In the previous quarter of this course, I spent time discussing what science is and what it is not. I discussed the scientific method, how to perform and analyze experiments, and the difference between science, applied science, and technology. For the rest of the course, I want to concentrate on just one area of science: **life science**.

Life science – A term that encompasses all scientific pursuits related to living organisms

You can tell by the definition that life science is a *big* area of science. This means you've got a *lot* to learn!

When I started discussing science at the beginning of this course, where did I start? I started with the history of science. After all, in order to understand something, you need to see how history has shaped its development. The same is true for a study of life science. In order to really understand what life is, we must first look at the history of life.

How Do We Learn About the History of Life?

When I discussed the history of science, it was easy to understand where I got my information. All the things I covered had been recorded by historians. How do we learn about the history of life? Well, the first way is to go back to the historians. After all, there are historical records that are several thousands of years old. Many of these records tell us about people, nations, animals, and plants that lived a long time ago. This gives us some information about the history of life. That's not the end of the story, however.

In order to really learn about the history of life, we have to go beyond historical records. After all, historical records get more and more scarce the further you go back in history. Thus, we need something to help supplement the historical record. The first tool we can use to accomplish this task is **archaeology** (ar kee awl' uh jee).

Archaeology – The study of past human life as revealed by preserved relics

Scientists in the field of archaeology try to learn more about the people who lived in the past by studying what those people left behind.

If you think about it, even when you combine archaeology and historical records, you still don't get a good view of the history of life. After all, history usually centers on what happened to *people* in the past. Archaeology concentrates on studying human relics and **artifacts**.

Artifacts – Objects made by people, such as tools, weapons, containers, etc.

Thus, history and archaeology are excellent tools for learning about the history of *human* life, but how do we learn about the history of all the animals and plants that have lived on earth in the past? To accomplish this task, we must focus on two fields of science: **geology** (gee awl' uh jee) and **paleontology** (pay' lee uhn tall' uh jee).

<u>Geology</u> – The study of earth's history as revealed in the rocks that make up the earth

<u>Paleontology</u> – The study of life's history as revealed in the preserved remains of once-living organisms

These two fields of science are incredibly interesting and can reveal much about what went on during earth's past. However, as you will come to find out, they are also two of the most ill-used and misinterpreted fields of science. Thus, we must take great pains to make sure we understand exactly what these fascinating fields of science tell us.

<u>Archaeology and History</u>

I will spend the majority of this quarter discussing geology and paleontology, since those fields cover the history of all living creatures. For now, however, I want to spend some time on archaeology. From a scientist's point of view, archaeology is a bit limited because it concentrates on artifacts left by people. Nevertheless, it is still a valuable resource for learning about the history of life.

Archaeology can give us some clues about civilizations for which we have few or no historical records, but archaeology's main strength lies in uncovering and clarifying the history of civilizations for which we *do* have historical records. Consider, for example, some of the world history you already know. You probably know that there was an empire called the "Roman Empire." You probably know the names of some of the emperors. You have probably spent some time reviewing the history of great countries like Egypt and China. How do we know that the historical facts you have read are actually true?

Think about it. I could write a history of ancient Greece tomorrow and try to get it published. It could be full of all sorts of lies and errors. How would anyone know that my history of ancient Greece is wrong? Well, you might say that it would contradict the history of ancient Greece we already know. But how do we know *that* history is right? After all, our knowledge of history comes from books. How do we know that the authors of *those* books weren't writing lies and errors?

Photo © Kharidehal Abhirama Ashwin
Agency: www.shutterstock.com

FIGURE 5.1
Hieroglyphics

This is an example of ancient Egyptian writing known as **hieroglyphics** (hi' ruh glif' iks). In essence, it is writing that uses symbols and pictures to represent concepts and sounds. This series of symbols, then, relates a story. Some of what we know about ancient Egypt comes from translating hieroglyphics. But how do we know the accounts in these hieroglyphics are true? Couldn't the people who left them have been lying or making several errors as they wrote?

In historical science, any document (a clay tablet, a scroll, a book, etc.) that claims to be a work of history is put through three tests. They are called the **internal test**, the **external test**, and the **bibliographic** (bib lee uh graf' ik) **test**. If the work passes those three tests, it is considered a legitimate work of history. If it fails even one of those tests, it is not considered an authentic historical work. It might have other values, but as a historical document, it is not reliable.

Each of the three tests I mentioned above are very important, and they each test a different facet of a supposedly historical work. The first test is straightforward and easy to describe. The **internal test** simply tests to see whether or not the document in question is internally consistent. In other words, the internal test says that a valid work of history cannot contradict itself. This, of course, makes an enormous amount of sense. After all, if a historical document makes a statement at one point and then completely contradicts that statement later on, it probably isn't a very reliable document!

Now you might think it is easy to determine whether or not a document passes the internal test. After all, you just have to read the document and look for any contradictory statements, right? Well, not exactly. You must remember that many documents that deal with ancient history are written in ancient languages. For example, if an archaeologist finds a scroll that claims to be a history of ancient Greece, it is probably written in Greek. Now, of course, Greek is a language spoken today, but most likely the *version* of Greek used in the scroll is quite different from the version of Greek spoken today. Languages change over time, and what people call Greek today is *significantly different* from the Greek spoken and written even a few hundred years ago.

I really want to drive this point home, because it is *very* important. Languages change over time, sometimes quite dramatically. Consider, for example, the following phrase:

> Whan that April with his showres soote
> The droughte of March hath perced to the roote
> And bathed every vein in swich licour
> Of which vertu engendred is the flowr

In what language is that passage written? Believe it or not, it is written in *English!* This passage is from the General Prologue of Geoffrey Chaucer's *The Canterbury Tales*. This collection of stories was written in *English* approximately 600 years ago! Does this give you an idea of how languages change over time? A mere 600 years ago, a passage from a work of English is barely recognizable as English. In fact, if you were to hear this passage read with the correct pronunciation (you can find it on the multimedia companion CD that comes with this course), you would realize that it *sounds* even less like English than it looks!

The point to this discussion is quite simple: Languages change over time. The more time that has elapsed since a document was written, the harder it will be to *understand* the language. This, of course, makes it difficult to *spot* inconsistencies within a document. What seems like a contradiction might not be a contradiction once the original language and its usage are taken into account. Thus, when applying the internal test to a document, historical scientists use **Aristotle's dictum**.

Aristotle's dictum – The benefit of the doubt is to be given to the document itself, not assigned by the critic to himself.

Aristotle's dictum states that when you apply the internal test to a document, you must give the document some leeway. If two passages seem to contradict each other, they are not to be counted as a contradiction if a legitimate explanation can be offered to explain away the contradiction. In the next section, you will get a concrete example of how to apply Aristotle's dictum, so if you don't completely understand it right now, don't worry.

The second test that is applied to supposedly historical documents is the **external test**. This test asks another simple question: Does the document contradict other known historical facts? There are two ways that historical scientists apply the external test. First, they compare the document of interest to other documents that have already passed the three tests. Since those documents are considered reliable, anything that contradicts them is probably unreliable. Unfortunately, the older the document, the fewer the documents to which it can be compared. Luckily, however, the external test has another component. The external test also compares the statements in the document to known *archaeological* facts. For example, if a supposedly historical document references a city, archaeology might be able to confirm or deny the existence of that city. The older the document, the more important this component of the external test becomes.

FIGURE 5.2
Archaeology and the External Test

Photo by Kathleen J. Wile

Archaeology confirms that this place in Athens, Greece, is the famous Areopagus (also called Mars Hill), where trials were held and people came to argue and debate. Its existence can be used to provide evidence for or against a historical document. For example, the Bible tells us that Paul went there to debate Christianity with the Athenians (Acts 17:16-34). The fact that it puts Paul at the proper place for debate in Athens provides external evidence for the truth of the account.

The final test, the **bibliographic test**, is probably the most important of the three. To be a reliable document, the work must contain either direct eyewitness accounts or a second-hand report *based on* eyewitness accounts. The problem with such accounts, however, is that they were recorded shortly after the events took place. Given that fact, how do we know they have not been altered over time? You see, we have *virtually no original documents from any truly ancient work of history*. This is a very important point. Nearly every document we have concerning the history of ancient Egypt, the Roman Empire, etc. are all *copies* of some original document that has been lost.

Well, if we are working with copies of the original work, how do we know that the words on the copy are truly the words from the original? This is probably the *biggest* problem with historical works. After all, back in ancient times the only way to copy was by hand. This was a time-consuming, error-riddled process. It was also usually quite expensive. In order to make a copy of a document, someone who could read and write (skills not always easy to find in ancient times) would have to carefully read a few words and then write them legibly. This would sometimes take hours for a single page! The cost of both the supplies and the person's wages could quickly become astronomical.

FIGURE 5.3
An Ancient "Copier"

Image from www.photos.com

Because copying was done by hand in ancient times, it took an enormous amount of time. It also took a lot of manpower. Often, to ensure accuracy, one man would copy the document while another looked on. This helped reduce mistakes. Nevertheless, making copies in ancient times was far from perfect. Often scribes would miss errors in the copy process. Also, anyone who had the resources and the power to command that a copy of a document be made would also be able to command the copier to change things he didn't like. Suppose, for example, a king ordered his scribes to make a copy of a history of his realm. In that history, suppose that the original author made some negative statements regarding one of the king's ancestors. The king might order those statements stricken from the work or, worse yet, revised to remove their negative meaning.

Mistakes associated with copying and the deliberate changes made at the request of the person paying for the copy corrupt an otherwise reliable document. Thus, a document might have been reliable when it was first written, but if it was altered during the copy process, what we have today might not be a reliable document. As a result, we need to be able to evaluate the version of the document we have today to see if it is faithful to the original.

How can we tell whether or not a historical document has been altered as a part of being copied over the years? Well, that's where the bibliographic test comes in. The bibliographic test asks two questions. First, it asks how many years passed between when the original work was written and the time of the first copy we have. The shorter the time span, the more reliable the document is. After all, if only a short time elapsed between the writing of the original and the making of the copy, there would have been little chance for alterations to occur. Alternatively, the longer the time span between original and copy, the more chance there was for alteration. Second, the bibliographic test asks how many *different* copies made by *different* people exist for the document of interest. If many copies made by many different people exist, and if they are all basically the same, it is very unlikely that the original was modified. After all, the same modifications would have to have been made by all copiers, and given the difficulty of communication in ancient times, that is rather unlikely.

So the bibliographic test measures the time between copy and original as well as the number of copies made by different people. The shorter the timespan and the larger the number of copies made by different people, the more reliable the document is. As a point of terminology, copies of a work made by different people are often called **supporting documents**, because they can be used to support the validity of the document of interest. Thus, many historians would say it this way: the bibliographic test requires a short timespan between original and copy as well as many supporting documents for the copy of interest. If you are a bit confused about the bibliographic test at this point, don't worry too much. I will discuss it later with some concrete examples, and that will help.

In the next three sections, I want to talk about each of the three tests individually. The best way to do that is to actually apply them to a specific historical document. That will give you the best understanding of the tests and how they are used. To what document will I apply these tests? I want to use the Bible as my example. After all, the Bible is certainly a work of history. I believe it is much more than that, but it does contain many historical accounts from the ancient past. Thus, it is a good document to use as an example. There are other reasons I want to use the Bible, however. First, I think you might be surprised at how well the Bible actually passes these tests, indicating that *science* tells us you *can* believe the accounts in the Bible. Second, I want to reinforce a statement I made in a previous module. We can apply science to *any* question, as long as we use the right methodology. Thus, we can use historical science to evaluate the Bible, despite the fact that it is a work of religion.

ON YOUR OWN

5.1 An archaeologist discovers a document that claims to be a history of the Sumerian people. It mentions a battle that was fought at a great fortress in a certain region of the Sumerian Empire. Archaeologists look in that area and find the remains of a tiny village, but no indications of a fortress or a great battle. Which test does this document fail?

5.2 A document being evaluated as a history states that a certain city was built in 117 A.D. Later in the document, it references a battle that was fought for control of the city, and it indicates the battle occurred in 105 A.D. Which test does the document fail?

The Internal Test

In order to show you how historians evaluate historical documents using the internal test, I want to apply the internal test to the Bible. Have you ever heard someone say that the Bible contradicts itself? If you haven't, you will! It is a common misconception. For example, William Henry Burr, in his book *Self-Contradictions of the Bible*, claims that the Bible contradicts itself at least 144 times. Clearly, if that is the case, the Bible should not be considered a trustworthy source of history.

Is William Burr right? Is the Bible riddled with contradictions? Not at all. However, William Burr's examples of supposed biblical contradictions make excellent illustrations of how difficult it is to apply the internal test to an ancient document. Without the proper analysis, many historical documents seem to contradict themselves. However, once the linguistic and historical details of the document are investigated, these apparent contradictions mostly disappear.

For example, one "contradiction" he lists concerns the genealogies of Christ. In the New Testament, there are two genealogies of Christ. One is presented in the Book of Matthew, chapter 1, and the second is recorded in the Book of Luke, chapter 3. At first glance, they seem to be completely contradictory. They don't even agree on Jesus' grandfather. Matthew 1:16 says, "Jacob was the father of Joseph, the husband of Mary" whereas Luke 3:23 says Jesus was the "the son of Joseph, the son of Eli." One account, then, says that Jesus' grandfather was Jacob, whereas the other says he was Eli. While these two genealogies seem contradictory, they are actually complementary. That's because the genealogy presented in Matthew is *Joseph's* family line, whereas the passage in Luke traces *Mary's* family line.

If you understand the culture within which the text was written, this becomes clear. Since women were not considered very historically important to the ancient Jews, their names did not appear in genealogies. Thus, when a historian needed to trace the family line of a woman, he would often use the name of the woman's husband instead of her own name. We know from history that Luke was a very educated person, and such an educated person would know that whether or not a person is Jewish is based solely on the mother. If your mother is a Jew, you are a Jew. If your mother is not a Jew, you are not a Jew. Of course, Luke was also educated enough to know that women should not be mentioned in genealogies, so that's why he uses Joseph's name. We see, then, that after examining the cultural context of the passage, this apparent "contradiction" fades away. This is true of many of the supposed contradictions that occur in the Bible.

Other supposed "contradictions" occur because of the difficulty in translation. An example of that can be found in the Book of Acts.

FIGURE 5.4
The Conversion of Paul

Image in the public domain

The conversion of Paul (depicted here in the famous Caravaggio panting) is reported three times in the Book of Acts. All three accounts say that while traveling to Damascus, Paul had a vision of Christ. Two of the accounts also add that the vision temporarily blinded him. Those two accounts, however, supposedly contradict each other concerning the men who were with him on the journey. In Acts 9:7, the Bible says, "And the men which journeyed with him stood speechless, hearing a voice, but seeing no man" (KJV). According to this account, then, the men with Paul heard the voice coming from the vision. However, Acts 22:9 says, "And they that were with me saw indeed the light, and were afraid; but they heard not the voice of Him that spake to me" (KJV). In this account, it seems that the men with Paul *did not* hear the voice coming from the vision. This seems like a clear contradiction. Did the men hear the voice from the vision, or didn't they?

Although the account of Paul's conversion in Acts 9 seems to contradict the account in Acts 22, the passages are, in fact, complementary, not contradictory. All you have to do is understand the original language in which the New Testament was written: Greek. In each passage, the Greek word "akouo" is translated as the verb "to hear." In Greek, however, when verbs are constructed in different cases, their meanings differ.

In Acts 9:7, "akouo" is constructed in the genitive case, whereas in Acts 22:9, the accusative case is used. When this word is used genitively, it implies only that sounds were heard; however, when constructed in the accusative case, the word implies that speech was both heard *and* understood. In English, we use the same construction for both cases. For example, when a person says, "I hear you, man," he may mean that your voice is reaching his ears, or he may mean that he understands what you are saying. So, once again, a detailed look at these passages yields no contradiction at all. In fact, by looking at both passages we learn something. We learn that Paul's attendants did, indeed, hear *sounds* coming from Paul's vision, but they could not distinguish any *understandable speech* from those sounds. In fact, most modern translations make this clear. The New American Standard Bible (NASB), for example, translates Acts 22:9 as, "And those who were with me saw the light, to be sure, but did not understand the voice of the One who was speaking to me."

The vast majority of apparent contradictions in the Bible can be cleared away by examining linguistic, cultural, and literary context. There are some apparent contradictions that don't have such simple answers, however. An example of this comes from the Book of Genesis. In the first two chapters of this book, the Creation of the world is discussed. Chapter 1 gives an overview of the creation, while chapter 2 goes back and discusses Creation with Adam and Eve as its focus. These two passages seem to differ on the order in which things were created. In Genesis 1:25-27 the Bible says:

> God made the beasts of the earth after their kind, and the cattle after their kind, and everything that creeps on the ground after its kind; and God saw that it was good. Then God said, "Let Us make man in Our image, according to Our likeness; and let them rule over the fish of the sea and over the birds of the sky and over the cattle and over all the earth, and over every creeping thing that creeps on the earth. God created man in His own image, in the image of God He created him; male and female He created them.

Thus, according to this passage, the animals of the earth were created first, and then man was created. In Genesis 2:18, 19, however, we read:

> Then the Lord God said, "It is not good for the man to be alone; I will make him a helper suitable for him. Out of the ground the Lord God formed every beast of the field and every bird of the sky, and brought them to the man to see what he would call them; and whatever the man called a living creature, that was its name.

In this passage, it seems that the animals were created after man, not before him as was stated in the previous passage.

Is this a contradiction? No. Remember, the Old Testament was written in ancient Hebrew. Hebrew is an especially difficult language to translate, because many of the words have several meanings, and context is supposed to guide the reader as to how to interpret what is written. It has been suggested by Hebrew scholars that a proper translation of the Hebrew verb (yatsar) used in Genesis 2:19 is "had formed" rather than simply "formed." If this is the case, the contradiction disappears. After all, if you replace "formed" with "had formed" in Genesis 2:19, the passage does not imply that man was created before the animals. It simply mentions that God had already made the animals out of the ground, and at this point in the account, He brought them to Adam. However, the situation is not as clear-cut as was the translation situation in Acts that I discussed previously. Although this explanation is accepted by some scholars, it is rejected by others. So, unlike the previous example, there is no conclusive evidence that this is not a contradiction. On the other hand, there is also no conclusive evidence that it *is* a contradiction.

Do controversial passages such as these keep the Bible from passing the internal test? If they did, almost no ancient work of history would pass. It turns out that most ancient works have a few difficult passages that are hard to reconcile with each other. Consider, for example, the works of the historian Josephus. His works are considered accurate sources of history, yet his books seem to contradict each other when it comes to his descriptions of the temple at Jerusalem. Some historians argue that the descriptions differ because he is describing the temple at two different times. Between those times, there had been some major renovations, so one would expect the descriptions to be different. While there is no conclusive evidence that this explanation is true, it is a reasonable way to explain around the apparent contradiction. Since situations like this one do not cause the works of Josephus to fail the internal test, they should not make other documents fail the internal test.

In the end, then, if an apparent contradiction doesn't have conclusive evidence indicating it is, in fact, a contradiction, historians label it a "difficulty." As I mentioned previously, when applying the internal test to ancient documents, historians must follow Aristotle's dictum. This means the reader can't assume he knows what happened back then and automatically label a difficulty as a contradiction. Instead, the document must be given the benefit of the doubt. If a contradiction cannot be conclusively demonstrated, the document does not fail the internal test. Since we cannot show conclusive evidence for a contradiction between Genesis 1 and 2, this difficulty does not cause the Bible to fail the internal test.

Contrary to what some might claim, if you examine the Bible in its entirety, you find no passages that clearly contradict one another. Thus, the Bible passes the internal test. In fact, the Bible has fewer "difficulties" from an internal test point of view than some of the other historical documents of its time. As a result, it passes the internal test as well as the histories of the Roman Empire, etc., that make up most of what we know concerning life at and before the time of Christ.

I hope this brief discussion has given you some idea of how difficult it is to apply the internal test to ancient documents. What seem to be clear contradictions in the *translation* of an ancient document simply vanish when the document is examined in light of the language and culture of the time. Even apparent contradictions that do not have ironclad explanations are not enough to keep a document from passing the internal test. The contradiction itself must be indisputable. It is important to remember this when working with *any* historical document, including the Bible.

ON YOUR OWN

5.3 Another famous "contradiction" in the Bible comes from Matthew 27:5 and Acts 1:18. They seem to give different accounts of how Judas died. Do a little research to find out why this is not a contradiction. You might want to ask a pastor, priest, or someone else who knows the Bible well; you might want to go to the library and get a book on supposed biblical contradictions (there are many); or you might want to get on the Internet and find out.

The External Test

Once a document passes the internal test, the next test applied is the external test. This test determines whether or not the document contradicts any "external" sources of historical facts. If other histories of the time exist, the document in question must be consistent with them. In fact, the document in question should, to some extent, overlap with other accepted historical works so as to lend even more credibility to the document. The more overlap that occurs, the better the document passes the external test. In addition to other accepted historical texts, the document in question must also be consistent with any archaeological discoveries for that time period. Once again, the more archaeological facts that support the document, the better the document passes the external test.

Applying the external test to the Bible is a daunting task because it is a work that covers a long time period. Many parts of the Old Testament report on events that occurred so long ago that they have no external historical works with which they can be compared. In addition, the focus of the Bible is rather narrow; thus, many historians do not comment on anything related to the Bible's accounts. Finally, a scientist must exert hefty skepticism when examining works that are contemporary with the New Testament, because many of the authors of that time period were sympathetic to the Christian church. The works of such authors cannot be considered truly objective when they speak of matters reported in the New Testament. In addition, many historical documents written over the New Testament time period were written by Jewish leaders who were vehemently anti-Christian. These accounts must also be taken with a grain of salt.

Reasons such as these lead most historians to consider archaeological discoveries as the primary data used in applying the external test to the Bible. In this section, most of the discussion related to the external test will consist of archaeological data; nevertheless, I will spend some time comparing the works of external authors to the New Testament. First and foremost, I will reject all works by authors who are sympathetic to the Christian cause. Although many of these authors (Tertullian, Iraeneus, Polycarp, etc.) do provide us with accurate portraits of the events of the time, their objectivity is in question. A good scientist must always try to reduce the bias in any data with which he or she works. Thus, we must reject obviously pro-Christian authors from our external test. After disregarding these possibly biased authors, who is left?

Cornelius Tacitus, a Roman, wrote several works that are considered quite accurate histories of the first century A.D. In his major work, *Annals*, he mentions the existence of Christ and his death by Pontius Pilate, in perfect agreement with the accounts written in the Bible. He also mentions certain cities and rulers that are also discussed in the Bible. In each case, Tacitus's reports are consistent with those of the New Testament.

Another well-respected, non-Christian historian of the day was Flavius Josephus, who I mentioned previously. Josephus was a Jew who wrote a history of the Jewish people in an attempt to create better feelings between the Romans and the Jews. In his major work, *Antiquities of the Jews*, he not only mentions Christ's death at the order of Pontius Pilate, but he also mentions Christ's resurrection! Here is the quote from the 18th chapter of *Antiquities* (3:63–65):

> Now there was about this time Jesus, a wise man, if it be lawful to call him a man, for he
> was a doer of wonderful works – a teacher of such men as receive the truth with pleasure.
> He drew over to him both many of the Jews, and many of the Gentiles. He was the Christ;
> and when Pilate, at the suggestion of the principal men among us, had condemned him to

the cross, those that loved him at the first did not forsake him, for he appeared to them alive again the third day, as the divine prophets had foretold these and ten thousand other wonderful things concerning him; and the tribe of Christians, so named from him, are not extinct at this day (*The Works of Josephus*, William Whiston, Hendrickson, 1998, p. 480).

Josephus also mentions rulers and cities discussed in the Bible, and his reports are consistent with those of the Bible. In addition, Josephus mentions the life and execution of John the Baptist and the existence of Christ's brother James, in agreement with the New Testament.

FIGURE 5.5

Image from www.photos.com

Flavius Josephus

This is a fanciful representation of Flavius Josephus that appears in a William Whiston translation of his work. The fact that many of the accounts in the Bible (including that of Christ's resurrection) are confirmed in the works of Josephus is important, because Josephus *was not* a Christian. He was a Jew who wrote in an attempt to make Rome more sympathetic toward the Jews. Thus, he was not trying to make Christianity "look good" in his work. Instead, he was reporting what he considered historical facts that happened during his time. While some have suggested that the account of Christ's resurrection in his *Antiquities of the Jews* was added during the copying process, there is no serious evidence to back up the claim. The bibliographic test should produce evidence for such an alteration, but it does not.

Two other non-Christian historians who lend support to the New Testament are Thallus and Phlegon. Both of these historians mention a darkness that covered the land on the day that Christ died, in perfect agreement with the account given in Matthew 27:45.

When compared to archaeological discoveries, the Bible truly stands out as an accurate source of history. Whether one is studying data related to the New Testament or the Old Testament, archaeology provides incredibly convincing evidence for the historical validity of the Bible. For example, William F. Albright, one of the greatest archaeologists of the twentieth century, says, "There can be no doubt that archaeology has confirmed the substantial historicity of the Old Testament..." (*Archaeology and the Religion of Israel*, William F. Albright, Johns Hopkins, 1953, p. 176). In addition, F. F. Bruce, author and historian, says, "...it may be legitimate to say that archaeology has confirmed the New Testament record" (*Archaeological Confirmation of the New Testament: Revelation and the Bible,* Carl Henry, Ed., Baker Book House, 1969, p. 331). Perhaps the best summation of how archaeology has confirmed the Bible was made by Nelson Glueck, a Jewish archaeologist. He says, "…it may be stated categorically that no archaeological discovery has ever controverted a biblical reference. Scores of archaeological findings have been made which confirm in clear outline or exact detail statements in the Bible" (*Rivers in the Desert*, Nelson Glueck, Jewish Publications Society of America, 1969, p. 31).

It would be an impossible task to even briefly sketch all the archaeological discoveries that have confirmed specific passages in the Bible. As one scholar states, "The digestion of the data uncovered is overwhelming even for professional archaeologists, not to mention scholars of related subjects" (*Archaeology of the Land of the Bible*, Amihai Mazar, Doubleday, 1992, p. xv). Since the volume of such data is overwhelming, I want to concentrate on a few specific examples. These examples are ironic, because they represent cases in which archaeologists originally thought the Bible was in error. More data, however, revealed that the archaeologists were in error, not the Bible. It is important to note that the following examples are not isolated incidents. As another historian notes, "There are a number of striking cases where specific passages have been doubted...and have [later] been directly confirmed" (*The Stones and the Scriptures*, Edwin Yamauchi, J. B. Lippencott, 1972, p. 20).

A particularly startling example of such a reversal comes from the Old Testament book of Genesis, chapter 14. This chapter details a series of battles fought between two ancient alliances. During one of the battles, Abram's nephew, Lot, was captured. Abram led a group of men against the alliance that captured Lot, defeated the alliance, and rescued his nephew. In the early part of this century, most archaeologists believed that this account was a total fabrication. Indeed, in 1918, William F. Albright wrote an article in the *Journal of Biblical Literature* in which he stated that all of Genesis 14 was either borrowed from a legend or made up entirely.

Since 1918, however, a great number of archaeological discoveries have put the historicity of this tale beyond doubt. Discovery of the Mari Tablets in 1933 provided evidence that the kings mentioned in the account did, in fact, exist and that such long-distance battles were, indeed, fought at that time. In addition, Albright himself discovered significant archaeological evidence that the cities mentioned in the account were at war during that time. In the end, the evidence forced Albright to reverse his earlier belief. In a commentary that he wrote in 1948, Albright stated that archaeology (some of it his own) has confirmed the reliability of Genesis 14.

FIGURE 5.6
One of the Mari Tablets

Image in the public domain

The Mari Tablets are stone tablets discovered by French archaeologists in 1933. There are 23,000 in all, and they contain quite a bit of information about the kingdom of Mari, an ancient kingdom on the west bank of the Euphrates River. It existed before and during the lives of Abraham, Isaac, and Jacob, so the tablets deal with much of the same history as the Old Testament. They describe the customs of the Mari kingdom, as well as giving names of people who lived during that time. These tablets mention King Arioch from Genesis 14, indicating that he was a real person. In addition, they mention Nahor, a city discussed in Genesis 24:10.

The most important aspect of this particular example is that the same archaeologist who originally doubted the historical accuracy of Genesis 14 ended up being forced to change his mind in light of the evidence. Clearly, Albright did not give Genesis 14 the benefit of the doubt while studying the relevant archaeological discoveries. He believed it was a fabrication. In the end, however, the data forced him to admit that he was in error. Remember, this is the same archaeologist I originally quoted as saying that archaeology has confirmed the historicity of the Old Testament. This example provides a lot of credence for such a conclusion. Here is an archaeologist who did not want to believe that the Old Testament was an accurate historical work. However, after a lifetime of archaeological study, he was forced to concede the point. Clearly, he would not make such a statement if the data were not convincing.

It is important to note that the Old Testament has been shown by archaeology to be accurate not only in the "big" issues of kings, battles, cities, and dates, but also in "little" issues as well. Archaeologists are constantly being amazed at the Old Testament's accurate attention to detail. For example, in the Old Testament account of Joseph and his coat of many colors (Genesis, chapters 37 through 47) it is stated that Joseph's brothers sold him into slavery for the price of twenty shekels (Genesis 37:28). Many archaeologists have doubted this price, because, based on early archaeological evidence, slaves sold at slightly later times than Joseph's were significantly more expensive. Once again, however, more archaeological data vindicated the Old Testament. In 1966, the data were so convincing that author K. A. Kitchen wrote,

> ...the price of twenty shekels of silver...is the correct average price for a slave in about the eighteenth century B.C.: Earlier than this, slaves were cheaper (average, ten to fifteen shekels), and later they became steadily dearer. This is one more little detail true to its period in cultural history (*The Ancient Orient and the Old Testament*, K. A. Kitchen, Leicester, 1966, pp. 52, 53).

This, then, is yet another example of a biblical passage that was doubted by archaeologists and historians but was later confirmed by the data.

Finally, the New Testament is also just as archaeologically sound as the Old Testament. Consider the case of The Pavement, where the passage in John 19:13 says Christ was tried before Pilate. Prior to about 1950, there was no archaeological confirmation of such a place; thus, many archaeologists believed that it never really existed. In 1960, however, William F. Albright demonstrated that The Pavement was the court of the tower of Antonia, the headquarters of the Roman military. The reason it had not been discovered before was that it had been buried during one of the times Jerusalem had been rebuilt, and it was not uncovered until the 1950s.

Based on the weight of the somewhat fragmentary historical evidence and the huge amount of archaeological evidence, then, we can say without question that the Bible passes the external test. In fact, more archaeological attention has been paid to the Bible than any other source of ancient history. We can therefore say that the Bible passes the external test better than any other source of ancient history!

ON YOUR OWN

5.4 In "On Your Own" question 5.1, I mentioned a document that seemed to fail the external test. Suppose that the passage in question is one of *only a few* that are not consistent with archaeology. Based on what you have read here, should you conclude that the document fails the external test? Why or why not?

The Bibliographic Test

The last test we need to apply to a document of history is the bibliographic test. Remember, a good work of history is composed of either eyewitness accounts or the accounts of those who heard from eyewitnesses. Well, if the document is old, it must have been copied several times in order to survive to the present day. The bibliographic test tries to determine whether or not the copies we have today are really true to the original.

Now remember, in order for a document to pass the bibliographic test, there must be a relatively short amount of time between copy and original, and there must be several copies made by different people. Before I examine how the Bible fares in the bibliographic test, I want you to get an idea of how other documents of ancient history fare.

The histories written by Cornelius Tacitus are considered accurate accounts of the events that took place in the Roman Empire during the first century A.D. His works give us a substantial amount of the facts we know concerning the Roman Empire. Currently, there are 20 copies of his major work (*Annals*) and only one copy of a collection of his minor works. The earliest copy of his major work was made almost 1,000 years after the original was written, and the single copy of his minor works was made roughly 900 years after the originals were penned. By comparison, consider the work of Pliny the Younger, who was also a historian of the first century A.D. His *History* is currently supported by seven different copies, the earliest of which was made 750 years after the original.

For works of ancient history, the numbers quoted above are pretty commonplace. Some works are supported by more copies, some by fewer. The works of Sophocles (sah' fuh kleez), for example, have 193 different copies with which they can be compared. This is one of the larger numbers you will see in conjunction with ancient works of history. Unfortunately, the earliest of these copies was written nearly 1,400 years after the original. Alternatively, the 750 years that elapsed between the original works of Pliny the Younger and the earliest existing copies represents one of the smaller time spans related to ancient works of history.

Compare these numbers to those of the New Testament, which is supported by *over 24,000 different copies*, the earliest of which was written a mere *25 years after the original*! The differences between the 24,000 copies are trivial, indicating that the New Testament we have today is completely faithful to the original text. Let these numbers sink in for a moment. The New Testament passes the bibliographic test *better than any other historical work of its time.*

What about the Old Testament? Does it pass the bibliographic test as well as the New Testament? Not quite, but then again, you wouldn't expect it to. After all, the works in the Old Testament are significantly more ancient. Nevertheless, the Old Testament still passes the bibliographic test better than any other historical document of its time. The best way to illustrate this is with the example of the Dead Sea scrolls.

Prior to 1947, the earliest existing copy of parts of the Hebrew Old Testament came from the *Cairo Codex*, which was written in about 895 A.D. Since the last events of the Old Testament were supposed to have occurred approximately 450 B.C., this represents a significant time lag between the original writings and the first available copies. In 1947, however, the Dead Sea Scrolls were discovered. These scrolls contain copies of parts of several hundred ancient books. One of the scrolls contained a complete copy of the Old Testament book of Isaiah. The scroll was dated by archaeologists as having been written in 125

B.C. This version of Isaiah proved to be word-for-word identical with the standard Hebrew Bible in more than 95 percent of the text. The 5 percent of variation consisted mostly of obvious slips of the pen and variations in spelling. In over 1,000 years, then, the Book of Isaiah (and presumably the rest of the Old Testament) was copied faithfully. This adds great evidence to the already convincing data that support the bibliographic reliability of the Old Testament.

FIGURE 5.7

Dead Sea Scrolls

Photo © Brand X Pictures

This is a picture of one of the Dead Sea Scrolls on display in The Shrine of the Book, a wing of the Israel Museum. The circular case in the center is the display case holding the scroll, a closer view of which is given in the bottom portion of the picture. The initial discovery of the Dead Sea Scrolls was an accident. Bedouin shepherds were exploring caves on the northwest side of the Dead Sea, and they came across several sealed jars. When the jars were opened, well-preserved documents were found inside. Since that discovery, eleven other document-containing caves have been found. Most of the documents are made of animal skins, but some are papyrus, and there is at least one document written on a copper plate. It is thought that the scrolls were preserved and hidden in the caves so they would not be destroyed in the first Jewish-Roman war that started in 66 A.D. The entire collection of scrolls contains both biblical and non-biblical writings. While most of them are written in ancient Hebrew, some of them are written in Aramaic.

In the end, then, the Bible passes the bibliographic test better than any other work of ancient history. As William Green puts it, "...it may be safely said that no other work of antiquity has been so accurately transmitted" (*General Introduction to the Old Testament*, William Green, John Murray [Pub.], 1898, p. 181). Thus, we can be sure that the Bible we read today is faithful to the original eyewitness accounts. Combine that with the fact that the Bible passes the internal test just as well as any ancient document of history and that it passes the external test *better* than any document of its time, and you come to the *scientific* conclusion that the stories and accounts in the Bible are more trustworthy than any of the other accounts we have about the Roman Empire and other facets of ancient life!

ON YOUR OWN

5.5 Suppose archaeologists found a new historical document (a copy of a much older document) in a ruin. A few years later, several copies of that same document were discovered in a nearby location, and it is determined that the same king who commissioned the first copy also commissioned the other copies. Would those copies help the document in passing the bibliographic test? Why or why not?

Archaeology in the Absence of Historical Documents

Although archaeology is of immense value in determining the validity of historical documents, it can also stand alone as a means of learning about people and civilizations not recorded in historical documents. After all, almost every civilization leaves behind artifacts. We can learn a lot about ancient people from those artifacts, as long as we are careful to understand that in just examining artifacts, we do not have a complete picture. Thus, all conclusions we draw must be very tentative.

When an archaeologist discovers an ancient artifact, one of the first things he or she asks is, "How old is this thing?" Unfortunately, it is often difficult to provide an exact answer to this question. After all, how in the world would you know how old something is if you just dig it up from the ground? Well, sometimes, the artifact itself can give you the answer. Ancient coins, for example, might have the year they were made printed on them. Also, an artifact might be referenced in a work of history. For example, suppose a work of history mentions the date at which an Egyptian king died. If an archaeologist can find that king's tomb, the tomb and the artifacts buried in it can be dated by the reference in the historical document.

Sarcophagus photo from www.photos.com

FIGURE 5.8
Artifacts With Known Dates

Column photo by Kathleen J. Wile

This sarcophagus (a fancy name for a coffin) held the body of King Tutankhamen. Since his death is referenced in works of history, we know how old the sarcophagus is.

This column from the ancient city of Ephesus has a date written on it, so we know how old it is.

When the age of the artifact can be determined one of these two ways, archaeologists say the artifact has a **known age**.

Known age – The age of an artifact as determined by a date printed on it or a reference to the artifact in a work of history

Unfortunately, few artifacts have known ages. Thus, archaeologists must employ other means by which to determine how old an artifact is. One of the more reliable methods is called **dendrochronology** (den' droh kron awl' uh jee).

Dendrochronology – The process of counting tree rings to determine the age of a tree

During the life of a tree, its trunk expands. If you cut down a tree and look at the inside of the trunk, you will see that it is made up of a series of rings, which are commonly called "tree rings." A tree typically grows one ring each year. Thus, if you cut a tree down and count the tree rings, you can determine how old the tree is. If there are 123 rings, the tree is, most likely, 123 years old.

FIGURE 5.9
Tree Rings

Photo © Mikhail Olykainen
Agency: www.shutterstock.com

one
ring

This tree grew a ring each year. A complete ring consists of a light band of wood ending in a dark band of wood. Note the variation in width.

Counting tree rings is a good method for determining the age of a tree, but how does that help determine the age of artifacts in archaeology? Well, the first thing you have to realize is that the *appearance* of a tree ring depends on several environmental factors for the year in which the ring was formed. The length of the growing season, the amount of rain, the average temperature, and several other factors all play a role in determining how wide the ring being grown that year will be, as well as the darkness of its dark band. As you look at a tree's rings, then, you will see patterns of varying thickness. You will also see variation in the darkness of the dark bands that mark the end of a tree ring. Those patterns are a result of the weather patterns that occurred in the tree's environment over its lifetime.

Okay, fine, but how does that help an archaeologist? Well, since the weather in a given region affects the appearance of tree rings, archaeologists studying a certain region can cut down an old tree that is still alive. They can then look for distinct patterns of tree rings that correspond to several years of a given weather pattern for that region. Counting from the outside of the tree to the start of this special pattern will then tell archaeologists *how many years ago that weather pattern occurred.* Archaeologists find several such patterns and catalog them as **master tree ring patterns** for that region of the world.

So, when an archaeologist discovers a log that was once used to build a home or something like that, she can look at the rings in the log to find one of those master tree ring patterns. If the archaeologist finds one, then she knows how many years ago the ring patterned formed, because that has already been determined. Since the archaeologist knows when that ring pattern was formed, she can then count the remaining rings on the tree that was discovered and determine when the tree was cut down. That will tell the archaeologist how long ago the people who cut down the tree were alive, and that will determine the age of the artifacts left by those people.

Perhaps an example will help you understand exactly how this is done. Suppose an archaeologist finds a log that was used in the construction of a building. She examines the tree rings and finds a pattern in the rings that corresponds to a master tree ring pattern. Dendrochronologists have already determined that this particular master tree ring pattern corresponds to the weather in the area during the years 200 to 300 A.D. This tells the archaeologist that the tree she is examining formed those rings from 200 to 300 A.D. She then finds that from the end of that pattern to the edge of the log, there are 200 more rings. This tells the archaeologist that the tree stopped forming rings 200 years *after* the end of the master tree ring pattern. Thus, the tree stopped forming rings at 500 A.D. Why did the tree stop forming rings? Because it was cut down. Thus, the tree was cut down in 500 A.D. That's when construction of the building must have been taking place.

Archaeologists have cataloged master tree rings patterns that have allowed them to date certain artifacts to as far back as 6600 B.C. Now before I go any further, I have to point out something very important. You must pay close attention here:

The only ages that are certain in archaeology are the KNOWN ages.

I cannot stress this point enough. Although dendrochronology is considered one of the best dating tools that exists, it is still fraught with difficulties. These difficulties lead to uncertainties in the ages calculated using this method. Thus, unless the date is written on the artifact, or unless a reference to the artifact can be found in a reliable historical document, the age determined by archaeologists is uncertain.

One of the big problems with dendrochronology is that trees *sometimes* grow more than one ring a year. This, of course, will lead an archaeologist to believe that a tree is older than it really is. The farther an archaeologist goes back in history, the worse this problem becomes. Thus, the dates determined by dendrochronology are usually considered *upper limits*. In other words, when dendrochronology determines that an artifact is 2,000 years old, it means that the artifact is *at most* 2,000 years old. It could be younger. This, then, is an important point:

Ages determined by dendrochronology are upper limits for the age of an artifact.

Typically, the older the artifact, the more error there will be in the process of tree-ring counting.

Even though dendrochronology allows archaeologists to get a pretty good idea of how old an artifact is, it is still a pretty limited dating method. After all, in order to use dendrochronology, an archaeologist must discover a log that has identifiable tree rings. That's not enough, however. There also has to be a master tree ring pattern in the log so the archaeologist knows the age of some portion of the log. Thus, an archaeologist cannot use dendrochronology to date just anything! As a result, archaeologists try to use other dating methods to determine an artifact's age.

One very popular method archaeologists use is called **carbon-14 dating**. This dating method is actually a part of a much broader group of dating methods called **radiometric dating**.

Radiometric dating – Using a radioactive process to determine the age of an item

You will learn a lot more about radiometric dating when you take physical science next year, including the fact that radiometric dating is usually unreliable. There is one exception to this general rule, however. The radiometric dating technique called carbon-14 dating is about as reliable as dendrochronology as long as the item being dated is less than 3,000 years old. You will learn the details of why this is the case next year.

When an archaeologist uses dendrochronology or radiometric dating to determine the age of an object, the archaeologist says that the object has an **absolute age**.

Absolute age – The calculated age of an artifact from a specific dating method that is used to
            determine when the artifact was made

Now it is important for you to understand what "absolute" means in the term "absolute age." It *does not mean* "correct" or "sure." The term "absolute age" simply means that an actual date has been assigned to the artifact. Thus, if an archaeologist uses dendrochronology to determine that an artifact was made in 40 B.C., the archaeologist will say that the artifact has an absolute age. However, any good archaeologist will be quick to point out that the age is really just an upper limit to the *true* age of the artifact, due to the problems with dendrochronology. As a result, "absolute" does not imply "true." It simply means that a dating method has been used to assign a date to the artifact. This is an important distinction to remember!

ON YOUR OWN

5.6 An archaeologist is trying to determine the age of an ancient village that has just been discovered, and he would like to use dendrochronology. What *two* things must he have in order to determine the age of the village in this way?

5.7 If an artifact has no date written on it, is there any way you can determine its age with certainty?

Before I leave this section, I want to make a very important point. If you go to a museum or read certain history books, you will find that some archaeologists believe that they have found artifacts that are hundreds of thousands (or even millions) of years old. You need to be very skeptical about such ages. Remember, the most reliable absolute dating method is dendrochronology, and it can only provide ages of 8,000 years or so. Even though such ages are pretty reliable, they still only provide an upper limit on the true age of an artifact.

About the only absolute dating methods that produce ages like hundreds of thousands or millions of years are radiometric dating methods. As you will learn in physical science next year, these dating methods are incredibly unreliable. Thus, the dates obtained by using them must be viewed with healthy skepticism. The problem is, many scientists love to use radiometric dating because they want to believe that the earth is billions of years old and that man has been living on earth for hundreds of thousands or even millions of years. It turns out that radiometric dating can provide such ancient ages, and thus many scientists like to use radiometric dating.

In my opinion, and in the opinion of many other scientists, radiometric dates are not at all reliable, with the notable exception discussed above. Thus, anytime you hear that some artifact has an absolute age of tens of thousands, hundreds of thousands, or millions of years old, you have to realize that the dating method used to calculate such an ancient age is viewed as unreliable by many in the scientific community.

Relative Dating and the Principle of Superposition

If an archaeologist is not able to find the known age or an absolute age for an artifact, he can still get some idea of how old the artifact is. Archaeologists often determine the **relative age** of an object. When trying to determine an object's relative age, an archaeologist is not trying to get a firm number for how old the object is. Instead, the archaeologist is trying to determine whether the object is older or younger than some other object of interest.

If you don't know the age of an object, how can you tell whether it is older or younger than something else? You can use the **Principle of Superposition**.

The Principle of Superposition – When artifacts are found in rock or earth that is layered, the deeper layers hold the older artifacts.

The Principle of Superposition is used heavily in archaeology and geology, so I want to make sure you understand it.

When an archaeologist or geologist digs into the earth, he or she will usually find that the soil and/or the rock tend to have distinct layers, which are called **strata**. Archaeologists assume that when these layers were formed, they were formed one at a time. As you will see later on in this course, that's not a good assumption in many cases. Nevertheless, it is an assumption used quite heavily in archaeology and geology.

If the layers in a formation of soil or rock were, indeed, formed one at a time, we can draw a rather obvious conclusion. We can say that the deeper layers are older than the shallow layers. After all, if the layers formed one at a time, the bottom layer must have formed first, the layer on top of it must have formed next, the layer on top of that one must have formed next, and so on. Thus, the bottom layer in any formation is the oldest one; the layer on top of it is the next oldest layer, and so on. The layer at the very top of the formation is the youngest layer. To see how this works, examine Figure 5.10.

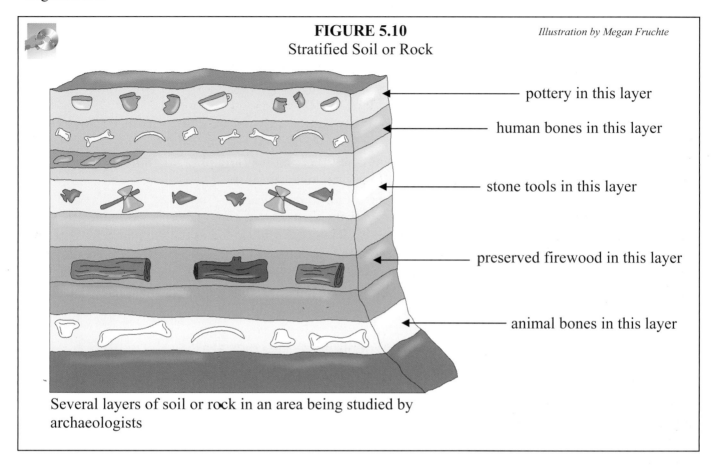

FIGURE 5.10

Illustration by Megan Fruchte

Stratified Soil or Rock

pottery in this layer

human bones in this layer

stone tools in this layer

preserved firewood in this layer

animal bones in this layer

Several layers of soil or rock in an area being studied by archaeologists

If the Principle of Superposition is true, any artifacts found in the bottom layer will be the oldest artifacts in this area, and any artifacts found in the top layer will be the youngest. Thus, even though an archaeologist might not be able to determine an absolute date for any of the artifacts in the figure, he or she could say that the firewood is older than the stone tools. In addition, he could say that the stone tools are older than the pottery. The archaeologist might even be able to determine more than that. Suppose, for example, the archaeologist can use dendrochronology to determine an absolute age for the firewood. Suppose, based on dendrochronology, the firewood is determined to be 1,000 years old. The archaeologist could then say that although there is no way to give an absolute date for the animal bones, they are older than 1,000 years, because they are found in a layer below the layer in which the firewood was found.

The Principle of Superposition, then, can at least give the archaeologist an idea of how old an artifact is *relative to another artifact*. This can be useful, but once again, it must be viewed with a bit of skepticism. As you will learn later on in this course, layers of rock and soil are not always laid down one by one. Sometimes, they are laid down simultaneously as the result of certain catastrophes. Thus, the underlying assumption for the Principle of Superposition is not true in all cases. Unfortunately, it is hard to tell when the Principle of Superposition is true and when it is false, so this can lead to a lot of confusion when discussing the relative ages of artifacts.

ON YOUR OWN

5.8 Based on the Principle of Superposition, list the artifacts pointed out in Figure 5.10 in terms of *increasing* age. In other words, list the youngest artifact first and the oldest one last.

5.9 What is the underlying assumption of the Principle of Superposition?

<u>What Do We Know About Human History?</u>

I have spent a lot of time discussing archaeology and history and how they interact. However, I have not spent a lot of time discussing what archaeology and history actually tell us about human life in the past. I have done this on purpose. I think it is more important for you to learn the *science* of history and archaeology than it is to learn about their conclusions. After all, unless you know *how* history and archaeology are done, you will not know *how to interpret* the things that historians and archaeologists tell you.

Now that you know a bit about how history and archaeology are done, however, I do want to spend a few moments on what history and archaeology tell us about the past. The first thing they tell us is that the history of human life as given by the Bible is an accurate account of what has happened in the past. Thus, one of the best things you can do to learn about human history is to read the Bible.

Now remember, the Bible passes the tests of historical science better than any of the histories that cover the same time periods covered by the Bible. Thus, science tells us we can believe the accounts given in the Bible better than the accounts given in other historical documents for the relevant time periods. This means that the overall history of human life on earth is best provided by the Bible. As a result, we have solid scientific reasons to believe in the events of the past as related by the Bible.

Now wait a minute, you might think. Doesn't the Bible give accounts of events that are rather hard to believe? What about the Flood during Noah's time, for example? The Bible tells us that the entire world was destroyed by a worldwide flood caused by God. The only people who survived the flood were members of a family led by a man named Noah, who had built an ark by the Lord's command. Isn't that just a little hard to swallow?

Well, perhaps it might be hard to swallow for some, but there are ample reasons to believe it is true. First, if you choose not to believe the most historically valid document of that time period, it is awfully hard to understand how you can believe *any* history we currently know. After all, the same historical tests used to evaluate all other works of history tell us that the Bible is, by far, the most reliable. If you start deciding to reject parts of biblical history, you have really departed from the science of history and are more or less making up the rules as you go.

Also, there is ample external evidence (evidence from sources other than the Bible) to believe that a worldwide flood did, indeed, happen in the past. As you will learn a little later on in this course, there is quite a lot of geological evidence for a worldwide flood. In addition, history gives us even more evidence that a worldwide flood happened sometime in earth's past.

There are many stories of a worldwide flood from many different cultures. For example, Babylonian tablets that date back to 2000 B.C. (absolute age) contain a story called the "Gilgamesh

Epic." This story tells about a king who seeks out a wise man. The wise man and his family are described in the story as the sole survivors of a great flood. In Greek mythology, the king of Phthia, Deucalion, and his family are said to be the sole survivors of a flood that the god Zeus sent to destroy humanity because of man's wicked ways. The natives of Polynesia, the aborigines (ab uh rij' uh neez) of Central America, the aborigines of South America, the natives of South Asia, the Chinese, and the Japanese all have similar stories.

FIGURE 5.11

Photo from www.photos.com

The Gilgamesh Tablet

This is part of the tablet upon which the Gilgamesh Epic was written. In this tale, King Gilgamesh was one-third man and two-thirds god. He was very powerful, but he was a tyrant. As a result, the sky god makes Enkidu, a wild man, to defeat him. However, a woman causes Enkidu to lose some of his powers. Enkidu and Gilgamesh fight, and Gilgamesh wins. Afterward, they become fast friends. They adventure together, doing great things. Enkidu dies, however, and Gilgamesh sets out to find the secret of immortality from the one wise man who survived the great flood. The man tells him the story of the flood and of a plant that restores youth, but Gilgamesh fails the test needed to use it. He goes back home still a mortal, but much wiser. He lives the rest of his life as a great, benevolent king.

It is virtually impossible that all these cultures learned the tale of a worldwide flood from each other! The Chinese and Japanese had no contact with the Greeks or the Jews until well after the flood stories had been recorded. The aborigines of Central and South America are separated from all the other cultures I mentioned by an ocean! How is it that all these cultures would have such similar legends if they weren't all derived from an actual event?

Thus, the history of human life as given by the Bible is probably the best place to start if you want to find out what happened to people in the past. There is, of course, more to history than what's mentioned in the Bible, but the Bible is the best historical framework in which to view all the other history we know.

ON YOUR OWN

5.10 Since there are many different stories about a worldwide flood that come from many different cultures, why should we believe the Bible's account? Why not believe the story of the worldwide flood as given in Greek mythology or one of the aboriginal legends?

ANSWERS TO THE "ON YOUR OWN" QUESTIONS

5.1 The document seems to be contradicted by archaeological research. Thus, it fails the external test.

5.2 The document seems to contradict itself. How could a battle be fought over a city that had not yet been built? The document fails the internal test.

5.3 These passages are not contradictory. Instead, they are complementary. One states that Judas hanged himself, and the other states he fell headlong into a field. In the Jerusalem area, there are many cliffs with trees that grow so their branches hang over the edge of the cliff. These were often used for suicide, because a person could tie the rope to the branch, tie the other end to his neck, and just jump. Oftentimes, however, the tree branch would break under the person's weight, causing the person to fall to the bottom of the cliff. This is probably what happened in Judas's case. Remember, in Acts 1:18 Judas ended up with his "intestines gushed out." Thus, he must have fallen from a height. So the two passages together tell us more than each individual passage. One eyewitness saw the body afterward, and decided that Judas fell. The other might have watched the event or interviewed someone who did. He would conclude that Judas hung himself. Both would be right.

5.4 The document might not really fail the external test, because later archaeological research might confirm the existence of the fortress. After all, the archaeologists might not be looking in exactly the right place, or the village that the archaeologists found could have been built on top of the ruins of the fortress, which lie below, still undiscovered. Once again, the conclusions of science are *tentative*.

5.5 These copies would not help the document in passing the bibliographic test. The copies of a document have to be made by a different source in order to be used in the bibliographic test. Remember, one thing the bibliographic test guards against is the process by which text is added or removed from a document at the direction of the person ordering the copies.

5.6 In order to use dendrochronology, the archaeologist must find a preserved log with identifiable rings in the remains of the ancient village. He also must find a master tree ring pattern in the preserved log. The log gives the archaeologist something with which to use dendrochronology, and the master tree ring pattern allows him to figure out how old the log is.

5.7 There is another way to get a known age for an artifact. If the artifact is mentioned in a document of history and a date is given there, the artifact will have a known age.

5.8 The Principle of Superposition states that the artifacts found in the lower layers will be older than those found in the upper layers. Thus, in order of increasing age, you have pottery, human bones, stone tools, preserved firewood, and animal bones.

5.9 The Principle of Superposition assumes that each layer of soil or rock is formed one at a time. We know this is not always true.

5.10 We should believe the biblical account because the Bible is more historically reliable than any of the other documents, as demonstrated by the internal, external, and bibliographic tests.

STUDY GUIDE FOR MODULE #5

1.   Define the following terms:

a.   Life science
b.   Archaeology
c.   Artifact
d.   Geology
e.   Paleontology
f.   Aristotle's dictum
g.   Known age
h.   Dendrochronology
i.   Radiometric dating
j.   Absolute age
k.   The Principle of Superposition

2.   If you wanted to learn about the history of life other than human life, would you use archaeology or paleontology?

3.   Name the three tests used to evaluate documents that claim to be historical.

4.   Give a brief description of each of the tests listed in #3.

5.   In what test is Aristotle's dictum used? Why must we use it?

6.   There are two reasons to believe that the copy of an ancient document might not be the same as the original. One is that the person making the copy might have made some unintentional mistakes. What is the other reason?

7.   What two things help a document pass the bibliographic test?

8.   Does the Bible contain any contradictions that make it fail the internal test?

9.   Does the Bible have any difficult passages that might seem like contradictions?

10. Why are the two accounts given in Acts 9:7 and Acts 22:9 not contradictory? Feel free to use your Bible to look up those verses.

11. Why are the two genealogies of Christ given in Luke 3 and Matthew 1 not contradictory? Once again, you can use your Bible.

12. Why can we say that the Bible passes the external test better than any other document of its time?

13. Suppose a document passes the internal and bibliographic tests but some of the conclusions of archaeologists go against what the document says. If the document has some other external support (other historical documents or some archaeological evidence), why should you not automatically say that it fails the external test?

14. Why can we say that the New Testament passes the bibliographic test better than any other document of its time?

15. Does the Old Testament pass the bibliographic test?

16. The age of an ancient settlement is determined by using dendrochronology on some firewood that had been chopped down but never used by the inhabitants. Does the settlement have a known age or an absolute age?

17. A coffin of a great king is discovered. The date of the king's death is recorded in a document of history. Does the coffin have a known age or an absolute age?

18. If an archaeologist gives an absolute age for an artifact, does that mean we know for certain how old the artifact is?

19. Why does an archaeologist use master tree ring patterns?

20. What is the underlying assumption of the Principle of Superposition?

21. Suppose an archaeologist uses dendrochronology to determine that a city was built in 2500 B.C. Several years later, another archaeologist is digging deeper under the site of the city and, in a lower layer of soil, he finds the remains of another city. Unfortunately, there is nothing he can use for any dating technique. He can still conclude something about the age of the city. Assuming the Principle of Superposition is true in this situation, what can he conclude?

22. Besides being discussed in the most accurate historical document of its time, what other historical evidence exists to indicate that a worldwide flood actually did occur?

MODULE #6: Foundations of Geology

Introduction

In the previous module, I spent considerable time on the science of archaeology and how it relates to history. Hopefully, you now have a better appreciation for where the "historical facts" you have read about in your history courses actually come from. I now want to move into another branch of science that often deals with history: the science of geology. Although geology has many uses other than history, no one can truly understand the history of life or the history of this planet without understanding geology. In this module, then, I want to give you a brief introduction to this fascinating science. Once you have a grasp on the basic concepts in geology, you will then be able to understand paleontology, which I will discuss in the next module.

When we start using geology as a tool for understanding what happened in earth's past, we immediately encounter a problem. We can make observations of the rocks, minerals, etc., that make up the earth, but we do not know for sure *how* they were formed or how they came to have the characteristics we observe. No one was around to observe the rocks forming, so we do not have any direct observations that allow us to determine how the rocks came to be. Nevertheless, if we want to use geology to learn about earth's history, we *must* know how the rocks we are observing today were formed.

Are we stuck, then? Of course not! As I have stressed several times in this course, science does not depend solely on direct observation. Science depends only on the scientific method. Thus, we can still use science to help us understand earth's history. We simply must start with a hypothesis, test the hypothesis with experiments, etc., etc. As long as we perform our geological investigations that way, we will be able to learn a lot about earth's past.

FIGURE 6.1
Rock Formation at the "Garden of the Gods" in Colorado Springs, Colorado

Although no one observed how these beautiful rocks formed, we can use the scientific method to help us find an explanation.

So we need to start by forming some hypotheses. This is where we run into a bit of trouble. You see, there are (at least) two different viewpoints when it comes to forming hypotheses about earth's past: **catastrophism** (kuh tas' troh fiz uhm) and **uniformitarianism** (yoo' nuh form' uh tair' ee uhn iz uhm).

Catastrophism – The view that most of earth's geological features are the result of large-scale catastrophes such as floods, volcanic eruptions, etc.

Uniformitarianism – The view that most of earth's geological features are the result of slow, gradual processes that have been at work for millions or even billions of years

You can think of each of these as a starting hypothesis. Most scientists take one view or the other and then start their scientific inquiries from there. This leads to two very different views of earth's past.

Well, you might be thinking, what's the problem? One of these hypotheses is right and the other is wrong. Let's use the scientific method to find out which can be confirmed by the data. *That's* the problem. Some geological data support one hypothesis, while other geological data support the other. Thus, there are scientific arguments that favor each of the hypotheses! Which do you choose? Well, that depends *a lot* on which data you consider to be the most important. In my scientific opinion, the most important data support catastrophism, and the data in support of uniformitarianism are rather limited and can mostly be "explained away." However, other scientists see the data in support of uniformitarianism as much more important and "explain away" the data in support of catastrophism. In the end, then, we are left with two views of geology that are quite at odds with one another.

In general, more scientists believe in uniformitarianism than catastrophism. If you remember my discussion of the history of science, however, that should not count for much in your mind. The history of science is *full* of cases in which the majority of scientists were dead wrong. We do not do science by majority vote; we do it by the data. The catastrophism view has been around for a lot longer. Once again, however, that shouldn't count for much, either. After all, the history of science is full of wrong ideas that stayed around for a long, long time. Thus, the only way to determine which point of view is better is to review the data for yourself and make up your own mind.

In order to help you do this, I want to tell you about the main geological *features* of the earth. It will take me almost two modules to complete that task. After that, however, I will dedicate more than a full module to explaining these features from both the uniformitarian view and the catastrophist view. Now remember, I think that catastrophism is the better hypothesis. Thus, even though I will try to be even-handed, my discussion will be slanted in that direction.

ON YOUR OWN

6.1 Many people believe that the earth is billions of years old. Others believe that the earth is "young," which usually means less than 10,000 years old. Is it possible to believe in a "young" earth using the uniformitarianism approach to geology? Is it possible to believe in a "young" earth using the catastrophism approach to geology? Is it possible to believe in an earth that is billions of years old under the uniformitarianism hypothesis? Is it possible to believe in an earth that is billions of years old under the catastrophism hypothesis?

<u>Soil, Rocks, and Minerals</u>

If you go outside and start digging, you will first encounter a lot of dirt, which we call **soil**. Soil is actually composed of several different things. First, the topmost layer of soil (called **topsoil**) is rich in **humus** (hyoo' mus).

<u>Humus</u> – The decayed remains of once-living creatures

Although it sounds kind of gross, humus is a very important part of the soil. It contains nutrients that plants use to stay healthy. Soil that has a lot of humus is ideal for planting gardens, trees, etc. As you dig deeper in the soil, you will find its other components: **gravel, sand, silt,** and **clay**. Not all soil has each of these components, but most does. It turns out that the relative amounts of gravel, sand, silt, and clay in soil will determine how well the soil holds water. This will also affect how well plants grow in the soil. You will learn more about that in a couple of years when you take biology.

As you dig deeper and deeper in the soil, you will eventually find rock. I don't mean a large rock buried in the soil. I mean a solid layer of rock. That's because all the earth's soil is actually sitting on top of earth's **crust**, which is made of solid rock. Although one rock might look like any other rock to you, there are basically three different kinds of rocks that make up the earth's crust: **sedimentary** (sed uh men' tuh ree) **rock, igneous** (ig' nee us) **rock**, and **metamorphic** (met uh mor' fik) **rock**.

Sedimentary rock is formed, as you might expect, from **sediments** (sand, silt, minerals, and other components of soil) that are laid down by water or some other agent. As these sediments begin to pile up, they can be cemented together due to chemical reactions, as well as heat and pressure. This hardens the sediments into a solid substance, which is called sedimentary rock. Although sedimentary rock actually makes up only about 8 percent of earth's crust, it covers most of the earth's surface. It is usually the topmost layer of earth's crust, so it is the most common kind of rock people encounter. The rock formation in Figure 6.1, for example, is made of sedimentary rock.

Igneous rock forms from molten rock, which is usually called **magma**. When a volcano erupts, the lava that it spews forth is magma. When that molten rock cools, it solidifies, forming igneous rock. Although the only time we see magma is when a volcano erupts, magma often flows underground as well. You will learn more about that next year in physical science. Since magma often flows underground and never reaches the surface, many igneous rocks are formed underneath the surface of the earth. You usually find igneous rock at the surface of the earth only as a result of volcanic activity. There is, however, a lot of igneous rock under the surface of the earth due to underground magma. Please note that the only difference between magma and lava is location – lava is on the earth's surface, while magma is below the earth's surface.

Metamorphic rock is rock that has undergone change, usually due to heat and/or pressure. Both igneous rock and sedimentary rock can form metamorphic rock. Because of the chemical changes that form metamorphic rock, it is typically very hard. Limestone, for example, is a sedimentary rock. Marble, however, is metamorphic limestone and is much harder than limestone.

Now it is important to realize that just as matter has basic building blocks we call atoms, rocks also have basic building blocks. They are called **minerals**.

<u>Minerals</u> – Inorganic crystalline substances found naturally in the earth

What in the world does that definition mean? Well, first you need to know that the term "inorganic" simply means that the substance in question did not come from a living being. Thus, it can't be the remains of some dead organism or the product of a living one. The term "crystalline" is a term from chemistry that refers to a specific kind of structure. The best way for you to understand this term is by experiment.

EXPERIMENT 6.1
"Growing" Crystals

Supplies:

- Alum (a white powder you can find in the spice section of any large supermarket)
- A small glass (like a juice glass)
- A spoon for stirring
- Some thin, rough string (Thread will work, but the rougher the string, the better the results.)
- Two weights (washers, nuts, fishing sinkers, etc.)
- A large plate
- A few rocks from outside (Small pebbles actually work best.)
- A sheet of dark paper (blue, black, etc.)
- A magnifying glass
- A stove
- A pot to heat water
- Gloves to protect your hands from the heat
- Sugar (optional)
- Food coloring (optional)
- Eye protection such as goggles or safety glasses

Introduction: In this experiment, you will turn powdered alum back into its natural crystalline form. You will also see how different the physical structure of a mineral is compared to that of a rock.

Procedure:

1. Add about 2 cups of water to the pot and heat until it is boiling.
2. While you are waiting for the water to boil, cut a piece of string so it is 2½ times as long as your juice glass is tall.
3. Attach a weight to each end of the string.
4. Once the water is boiling, take it off the stove and wait for the boiling to stop.
5. As soon as the boiling stops, add alum to the hot water with the spoon. It should dissolve readily.
6. Continue to add alum until you cannot get any more to dissolve. You will know you have reached that point when the water gets cloudy and will not clear up regardless of how much you stir.
7. Let the pot stand for a few moments, and the undissolved alum will settle to the bottom of the pot, making the solution above it reasonably clear.
8. Once the solution in the pot is pretty clear, carefully pour some of the liquid into the empty glass. Do this slowly and carefully, trying not to disturb the alum that has settled to the bottom of the glass. Pour until you have filled the glass ½ full. Try to avoid pouring any of the alum that has settled to the bottom of the pot into the glass. This process is called **decanting**, and it is used quite a bit in chemistry.
9. Now you should have a reasonably clear solution of alum in the glass. Put on the gloves to protect your hands from the heat, and put the glass on the plate.

10. Drop one end of the string in the glass. The weight will keep that end in the glass.
11. Put the other end on the plate. Your setup should look like this:

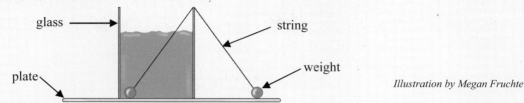

Illustration by Megan Fruchte

12. Draw this setup in your laboratory notebook.
13. Let the setup sit for several hours. The best thing to do is stop science for today and look at it when you start science tomorrow. It will not hurt to let it sit for several days.
14. After the setup has been left alone for several hours, carefully pull the string out of the solution. Draw a picture of what the string looks like.
15. What you see clinging to the string are **crystals** of alum. This is an example of what a mineral often looks like in its natural form.
16. Lay the dark paper out on a table and shake the string so some crystals fall onto the paper.
17. Use your magnifying glass to examine the crystals.
18. Put a few rocks next to the crystals and, with your magnifying glass, compare the rocks to the crystals. You should see a difference. Write that difference down in your lab notebook.
19. **OPTIONAL**: You can use this same kind of experiment to make rock candy. If you clean out the glass and pot thoroughly and use new string, you can repeat this experiment using sugar instead of alum. The crystals that grow on the string will be sugar crystals, which you can eat. If you want the sugar crystals to have color, add some food coloring to the solution before you put in the string. Note that the sugar crystals are NOT minerals. Sugar is an organic substance, so it does not fit the definition of a mineral. Also, note that it will take a LOT of sugar, as sugar dissolves very well in hot water.

What did you see in the experiment? Well, you should have seen what scientists mean by the term "crystalline." A crystalline substance usually has a sharp, geometric shape. When you compared the alum crystals to the rocks, you should have noticed a strong difference. The crystals have sharp edges and smooth sides that formed an obvious geometric pattern. The rock might have had a few edges here and there, but no distinct geometric pattern.

So how does this help us with the difference between rocks and minerals? Well, a mineral is the same throughout. In other words, the chemical makeup of a mineral does not change no matter where you look at it. The alum you started the experiment with was a mineral, because all the powder in the jar was the chemical known as alum. There weren't any other chemicals in the powder. When you made alum crystals, each crystal was composed only of alum. There was nothing else in the crystals. The difference between the powder you started with and the crystals you ended up with was simply the appearance. You started with powdered alum and ended up with crystals of alum, but it was alum the whole time. Typically, when you find a mineral in the earth, you find it as a crystal. The powdered alum you started with was simply crystals of alum that had been smashed into a powder.

When you looked at the rocks, you didn't see a geometric pattern, because a rock contains more than one mineral. In other words, if you were able to chemically analyze the rocks you looked at in the experiment, you would have found that each rock had at least two (probably more) separate chemicals in it. Because of the mix of chemicals in a rock, it will not form a distinct geometric pattern like you see in a crystal.

In the end, then, we can say that minerals are pure substances. No matter where you look in a mineral, you will always see the same chemical. A rock, however, is usually a combination of two or more minerals. Thus, a rock is generally composed of two or more chemicals. From a *practical* standpoint, however, you can usually distinguish between a rock and a mineral simply by looking at it. Minerals often form nice crystalline shapes, while rocks do not.

Left: Photo © Mirka Moksha
Agency: Shutterstock.com

FIGURE 6.2
Minerals and Rocks

Right: Photo © Olga Sweet
Agency: Shutterstock.com

These beautiful crystals are made of amethyst. No matter where you take a sample, the only chemical you will find in the crystals is the mineral amethyst.

These are granite rocks. They are made of three different minerals – feldspar, quartz, and mica. As a result, they don't have the sharp, crystalline shape of a pure mineral.

ON YOUR OWN

6.2 You are looking at a shiny, beautiful object that has a nice, distinct geometric pattern. When chemically analyzed, it is found to be composed of three separate chemicals. Is it a rock or a mineral?

6.3 You are looking at two different samples of rock. The first is harder than the second. Suppose you are told that one rock is sedimentary and the other is the metamorphic version of that sedimentary rock. Which is which?

Strata in Sedimentary Rock

Now that you are familiar with the different types of rocks and minerals that make up the earth's crust, it is time to get an idea of how those rocks are arranged on the earth. The best way to do this is to study an example. One dramatic example would be the **Grand Canyon**. This 277-mile long canyon can be found in Arizona. It ranges in width from 4 miles to 18 miles, and at one point, it is more than a mile deep. While most people visit the Grand Canyon to observe its beauty and grandeur, it can also serve as an excellent tool for the study of geology. The walls of the canyon are composed mostly of sedimentary rock, so just looking at the canyon gives you a good idea of some of the basic characteristics of this rock type. Consider Figure 6.3, which gives you one view of the Grand Canyon.

FIGURE 6.3
A Portion of the Grand Canyon

Photo © Bryan Brazil
Agency: Shutterstock.com

Isn't God's creation marvelous? Aside from the incredible beauty, what characteristic is immediately obvious in the picture? If you look at the walls of the canyon, you will see that the rocks form obvious *layers*. These layers are called **strata**, and they are the most distinguishing aspect of sedimentary rock. The figure below shows yet another striking example of the strata that form in sedimentary rock.

FIGURE 6.4
Strata in Sedimentary Rock

Photo © Nelson Sirlin
Agency: Shutterstock.com

While looking at the strata in sedimentary rock, the first thing you might ask yourself is how those layers actually formed. Well, once again, we don't know for sure, because there was no one there to observe their formation. Nevertheless, the following experiment will demonstrate one way that such strata might have formed. This is another experiment that must sit overnight. Thus, it is best to perform the experiment as the last science you will do today.

EXPERIMENT 6.2
Separation of Sedimentation

Supplies:

♦   A large glass jar with a lid
♦   Some dirt from outside (Dig straight down into the ground so you get dirt from many depths.)
♦   Some sand
♦   Some gravel composed of various sizes of rocks
♦   Water
♦   Eye protection such as goggles or safety glasses

Introduction: In this experiment you will see how water can separate sediments into layers.

Procedure:

1. Fill the jar about one-fifth of the way with dirt.
2. Add an equal amount of sand.
3. Add an equal amount of gravel.
4. Put the lid on the jar and then invert the jar to mix the contents. Invert the jar several times so the sand, gravel, and dirt are all mixed up.
5. Draw a picture of the jar and its contents.
6. Add water to the jar so the water level is about an inch from the top of the jar.
7. Put the lid on and invert the jar to once again mix up the contents.
8. Invert the jar several times so all the gravel, dirt, and sand get shaken up in the water.
9. Let the jar sit for about an hour.
10. After about an hour, invert the jar again several times to once again mix everything up.
11. Repeat step 10 at least twice more before you go to bed. Be sure to let the jar sit for at least an hour between each repetition.
12. Draw a picture of the jar and its contents after it has set undisturbed overnight.
13. Dump the contents of the jar outside wherever your parents tell you it should be dumped, and clean up your mess.

What did the contents of the jar look like after it sat overnight? Well, it should have looked a lot different from the way it looked before you added the water. Most likely, the gravel is now at the bottom, and the soil and sand have settled out in layers. The lighter substances are probably on top, and the heavier substances are probably on the bottom.

So we see that water has the ability to separate sediments into layers. When you mixed up the contents of the jar, you simulated a body of water in motion. You simulated currents in rivers, tides in the ocean, etc. As water moves, it can separate sediments. When the sediments settle out of the water, they can settle out in layers. Although there are other processes that deposit sediments onto the ground, water processes are, by far, the most common. Thus, when water deposits sediments on the ground, the sediments can be separated out into layers. Once water has deposited sediments onto the ground, the sediments can then form sedimentary rock as the sediments are cemented together due to chemical reactions. Now, of course, there are other explanations for how sedimentary rocks form layers, and you will learn about them in the next module. The experiment was designed to give you just one possible explanation.

It is important to note that the strata formed by sedimentary rock vary greatly in thickness and appearance. For example, compare the strata shown in Figure 6.5 to those shown in the previous two figures.

FIGURE 6.5
More Strata in Sedimentary Rocks

Photo © Steve Estvanik
Agency: Shutterstock.com

Notice that the layers in this rock formation come in various thicknesses. As you can see, some are really quite thin. When a single layer of rock is less than 1 centimeter (0.39 inches) thick, it is called a **lamination**. Several of these layers together are called **laminae** (lam' uh nee). Thus, we would say that this rock formation contains many laminae.

ON YOUR OWN

6.4 The Grand Canyon is in the northwestern part of a state that has many of the characteristics of a desert. There is little rain in Arizona and few lakes. Does it really make sense to think that the sedimentary rock in the Grand Canyon was laid down by water?

Weathering of Rocks

Once you have been awed by the beauty of the Grand Canyon, and once you have learned about sedimentary rocks and their strata, another thought should come to your mind. How did all of that rock in the Grand Canyon get exposed? After all, you typically find rock *underneath* the soil. Thus, you have to dig in order to get to the rock. Why, then, is the sedimentary rock in the Grand Canyon exposed so you can see it without doing any digging?

The answer to that question is "erosion," but to understand erosion, we must begin with *weathering*. Remember, sedimentary rock forms when sediments are laid down, and then, by chemical reactions, those sediments are cemented together to form rock. Well, if sediments can form rocks, doesn't it make sense that rocks can be turned back into sediments? We call that process **weathering**.

Weathering – The process by which rocks are broken down to form sediments

There are two types of weathering: **physical weathering** and **chemical weathering**. I want to give you examples of each, and the best way to do that is by experiment.

EXPERIMENT 6.3
Physical Weathering: The Power of Plants

Supplies:

♦ Plaster of Paris
♦ A medium or large margarine tub
♦ A few lima beans
♦ Water
♦ Paper towels
♦ Eye protection such as goggles or safety glasses

Introduction: This experiment will demonstrate that plants have the power to break down rocks.

Procedure:

1. Mix up the plaster of Paris as the instructions indicate so you get a nice, creamy mixture.
2. Pour the plaster into the margarine tub until it is about half full.
3. Right away, place a few lima beans into the plaster. They should sink into it a little.
4. Allow the plaster to dry. This will take a while. You can start the next experiment while you wait for the plaster to dry.
5. Once the plaster has dried, fold a paper towel so it will fit in the tub, covering the beans and plaster.
6. Wet the paper towel and place it in the tub so the beans are all covered.
7. Place the tub near a window and periodically check to make sure the paper towel stays wet. If it gets dry, wet it again.
8. Every day, pull the paper towel up and check on the beans.
9. What happens to the plaster when the beans sprout?
10. When you are done, you can put the entire experimental setup in the trash.

EXPERIMENT 6.4
Chemical Weathering

Supplies:

- ♦ Vinegar
- ♦ A large glass
- ♦ A limestone rock (Most gravel is limestone. You can also go to a home improvement store's garden section and ask for limestone. The rock needs to be small enough to fit in the glass.)
- ♦ Some steel wool (You can get this at any hardware store.)
- ♦ A small bowl
- ♦ Eye protection such as goggles or safety glasses

Introduction: Rocks can be broken down by chemical weathering. This experiment will give you two examples of how that happens.

Procedure:

1. Put the rock in the large glass.
2. Fill the glass ¾ full with vinegar.
3. Watch the rock for a few minutes. You should eventually see tiny bubbles forming around the rock and rising in the vinegar. These bubbles are the result of a chemical reaction that occurs between the vinegar and the limestone.
4. Let the glass sit overnight.
5. Place the steel wool in the bowl.
6. Pour vinegar over the steel wool. Pour in enough vinegar so about half of the steel wool is soaking in it.
7. Let the bowl and steel wool sit.
8. A few times throughout the evening, turn the steel wool so the other half soaks in the vinegar.
9. In the morning, examine the glass with the rock in it. Swirl the vinegar around a bit. You should see sediments in the vinegar. Those sediments have come from the rock.
10. Now examine the steel wool. What do you see floating in the vinegar?
11. Clean up everything.

Although Experiment 6.3 will take a while to finish, you will eventually see that as the beans sprout, the plaster will crack and break into pieces. This is an example of physical weathering. The plaster is an example of sedimentary rock. As plants grow on and near sedimentary rock, the roots of those plants will sink into the sedimentary rock, trying to get water and nutrients for the plant. The roots are strong enough to break the rock apart, turning sedimentary rock back into sediments.

There are other types of physical weathering as well. When wind picks up sand and other gritty materials and slams them into rocks, the rocks will wear away. That's another example of physical weathering. Changing temperatures also cause physical weathering. When rocks heat up, they expand. When they cool, they contract. Constant changes in temperature cause the rocks to expand and contract over and over again. This stresses rocks, causing them to crack and break. These processes and many others tend to break rocks down into sediments.

Experiment 6.4 provides you with two examples of chemical weathering. In the first example, you saw how vinegar can break down limestone into sediments. This is the result of a chemical reaction between the vinegar and the limestone. As you will learn in biology and chemistry, vinegar is a weak acid. Lime reacts with vinegar to make carbon dioxide (a gas) and other chemicals. In your experiment, you saw the carbon dioxide in the form of bubbles that were coming out of the rock. As this chemical reaction occurred, the rock started getting broken down. The sediment you saw in your experiment was the result of that breakdown.

Another example of chemical weathering was demonstrated by the steel wool. Steel wool is made mostly of iron, which tends to rust. The vinegar in the experiment increased the speed at which the iron in the steel wool rusted, and in the end, some of the steel wool turned into an orange powder, which is commonly called "rust." There are many rocks in the earth's crust that have iron in them. As that iron rusts, it crumbles into a powder. Much of the red color you see in Figures 6.3 and 6.4 comes from this process. Well, as the iron in the rock crumbles, that makes the portions of the rock surrounding the iron crumble as well. Once again, the result is that rock breaks down into sediment.

"Now wait a minute," you might be thinking. "There isn't a lot of vinegar in the desert! How can Experiment 6.4 be an example of the kind of weathering that takes place in the Grand Canyon?" Well, remember what I told you vinegar is. It is a weak acid. It turns out that the rain falling from the sky is also weakly acidic. You will learn more about that when you take chemistry. Thus, rain also promotes rusting. Now vinegar is a stronger acid than rainwater, so it promotes rusting faster than rain water does. Nevertheless, over time, rainwater can produce the same effects as what you saw in your experiment.

Can you see the difference between chemical and physical weathering? In physical weathering, the rocks get broken down, but the little pieces of rock that result still have the same basic composition as the rock had originally. After all, in Experiment 6.3, the plants broke the plaster into small bits. Thus, before the weathering you had plaster. After the weathering you also had plaster; the plaster was just in smaller pieces. If you could cement those pieces back together, you would have a big sample of plaster again. In chemical weathering, the *composition* of the rock changes. In Experiment 6.4, the lime in limestone was turned into carbon dioxide bubbles and other chemicals. The sediment left over in the vinegar no longer had lime in it. Thus, any rock formed by these sediments would not be limestone any more. The same can be said about what happened to the steel wool. The steel wool turned into rust and was no longer steel.

One way to think about the difference between physical weathering and chemical weathering is to think about the sediments that remain after the weathering. If the sediments that remain are the same as the original rock but just smaller pieces, you know the rock underwent physical weathering. If the sediments that remain have a different composition from the original rock, you know the rock underwent chemical weathering.

Using that kind of reasoning, you can tell that the plaster in Experiment 6.3 underwent physical weathering because the only difference between the plaster before the weathering and after the weathering was the size of the plaster pieces. Before the weathering, you had one piece of plaster. After the weathering, you had many, many small chunks of plaster. Nevertheless, in the end you still had plaster. Thus, the makeup of what you had did not change. In Experiment 6.4, however, the results were different. The rock was limestone before the weathering, but the lime in the limestone turned into gas (as evidenced by the bubbles) and other chemicals as a result of the weathering. Since the resulting sediments no longer had lime in them, they were *different in composition* from the original limestone. As a result, you know the limestone underwent chemical weathering.

Generally, the process of weathering takes time. Thus, it is hard to see it happening on a day-by-day basis. Nevertheless, you can see the accumulated effects of weathering if you look in the right places. Consider the gravestones pictured below.

FIGURE 6.6
Weathered Gravestones

Photo © Jim Mills
Agency: Shutterstock.com

You can see from the picture that there is writing on the gravestones, but it is very hard to read. Why? Over time, the rock weathered, which discolored it and broke it down. As the rock broke down, the engraving became shallow, and combined with the discoloration, it became hard to read.

ON YOUR OWN

6.5 A rock contains a large amount of the mineral called forsterite. Over time, the forsterite reacts with carbon dioxide and water to make magnesium bicarbonate and silicic acid. This breaks down the rock. Did the rock experience chemical or physical weathering?

6.6 A rock breaks into little pieces after a larger rock falls on it. Did the rock undergo physical weathering or chemical weathering?

Erosion

Weathering is often the first step in a process called **erosion**, which is responsible for shaping geological structures and landscapes into what we see today.

Erosion – The process by which rock and soil are broken down and transported away

As was the case with weathering, erosion is best demonstrated by experiment.

EXPERIMENT 6.5
Erosion

Supplies:

- A shoebox
- A gardener's spade (or something else you can use to dig)
- Scissors
- A spot in the yard in which you can dig
- A water hose and water
- A large rock
- Eye protection such as goggles or safety glasses

Introduction: This experiment demonstrates erosion and two of the major factors that affect it.

Procedure:

1. On one of the short sides of the shoebox, cut out a triangle that is wide at the top of the box and narrows down to a point halfway down the side. Your shoebox should look like this:

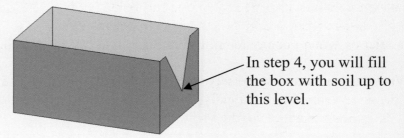

In step 4, you will fill the box with soil up to this level.

2. Ask your parents where you can dig in the yard. You will end up replacing what you dig up, but it won't look the same as it did before.
3. Use the spade to peel off a layer of sod from the ground. What you want is the grass, roots, and soil that make up the top portion of the yard. You can get what you need by shoving the spade into the ground just under the grass roots and pulling up the soil, roots, and grass in one clump. You want to gather enough to cover the bottom of the box. You need not try to get all of it in one clump of sod. Get several clumps that, when laid down in the box, will cover the bottom. Don't actually put the sod in the box yet. Just peel it off and set it aside.
4. The soil underneath the grass should now be exposed. Fill the box with that soil so you have an even layer of soil in the box all the way up to the point of the triangle that you cut out earlier.
5. Use the rock to prop up the end of the box that does not have the triangle cut out of it. This will make the box and its contents slope toward the triangle.
6. Turn on the hose so it emits a constant, slow stream of water.
7. Hold the hose a few inches above the box near the propped-up end, so the water strikes the soil and runs down the slope toward the triangle.
8. Hold the hose there for a few moments and observe what happens. Notice how the water forms gullies in the dirt.
9. Increase the speed of the water coming out of the hose and see how that affects the gullies being formed in the dirt.
10. After a while, turn off the hose and tilt the shoebox so the excess water runs out of the box.
11. Use the spade to even out the soil so there are no gullies and the surface is reasonably flat.

12. Place the sod you collected in step 3 on top of the soil. Arrange it so the sod covers all of the soil, leaving no bare soil exposed.
13. Pat the sod down with the spade or your hand so it sits securely on the soil.
14. Repeat steps 6-10 again, and note the difference the sod makes.
15. Return the soil to the hole you dug and then pat the sod on top to cover the soil. That way, the part of the yard that you dug up won't look so bad.
16. Clean yourself and everything else up.

What you saw in the first part of the experiment is an example of erosion. As water ran over the soil, it carried some of the soil away, forming gullies in the landscape. Although it might be a bit hard to imagine, water can do the same thing to rock. As it runs across rock, it can pick up bits of the rock and carry them away, especially if the rock is weathered. As time goes on, this can form a gully in the rock. That's (most likely) how the Grand Canyon was formed. Running water eroded the rock, digging a gully in the ground, exposing rocks on both sides of the gully. The exposed rocks then weathered, producing the beauty you see now.

Notice that in the experiment, the speed of the water strongly affected the speed at which the gullies were dug out. Slow-moving water dug the gullies slowly, while fast-moving water dug the gullies much more quickly. This is also true for rocks. Slow-moving water cuts through rock very slowly, while fast-moving water can cut through rocks more quickly. That point will become important later on when I compare uniformitarianism to catastrophism.

What did you notice in the second part of the experiment? The addition of grass on top of the soil kept the water from digging a gully, right? That's because the roots of plants tend to hold soil together, and erosion cannot take the soil away.

Although running water is the most common agent of erosion, there are others. Rain can be an agent of erosion. As raindrops strike soil and rock, they hit hard. The hit of a raindrop can weather a tiny part of a rock, and then the flow of rainwater will carry away the sediment made from that physical weathering. Wind can also weather and erode a rock. The physical force of windborne particles can weather a rock, and the motion of the wind can pick up the sediment formed and whisk it away.

Since erosion by water is the most common form of erosion, it is worth concentrating on for a moment. One thing you might ask yourself is: What happens to the sediments that are eroded by water? Well, that depends on what kind of water did the eroding in the first place. Suppose, for example, a river is rushing over rocks. The river picks up bits of the rock and carries them away. Where do they go? Well, a river has to end somewhere. Many rivers dump their water into a large lake or ocean. That's typically where the sediments carried by a river end up.

Consider, for example, the Nile River, which is considered by most scientists to be the longest river in the world. It measures over 4,100 miles in length from its beginning at Lake Victoria in Central Africa to its end at the Mediterranean Sea, where it dumps its water. The river carries an enormous amount of water, especially in the summer, when heavy rains in that region of the world cause the river to flood its banks every year. At the point where the Nile reaches the Mediterranean Sea, it deposits a lot of its sediments in a fan-shaped area called the river's **delta**. Figure 6.7 gives you an aerial view of this huge structure. The rest of the sediments end up in the Mediterranean Sea.

FIGURE 6.7
Satellite Photo of the Nile River's Delta at the Mediterranean Sea

*Photo courtesy of
the NSSDC / NASA*

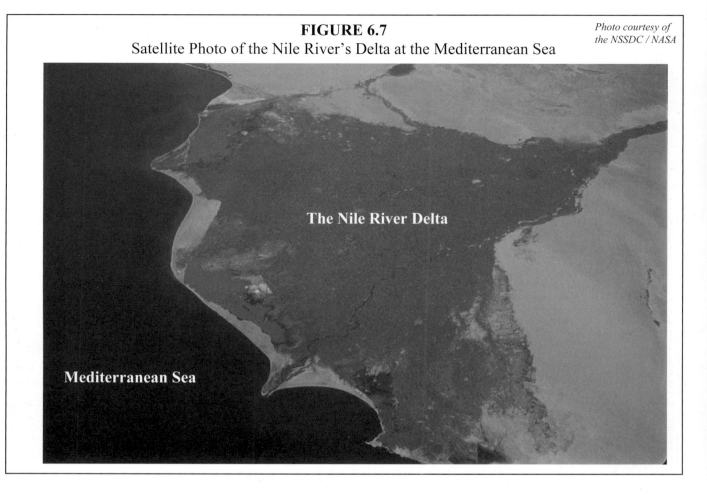

The Nile River Delta

Mediterranean Sea

Many of the sediments carried along by rivers, then, end up getting deposited at the river's delta. Some make it past the delta and flow into the sea into which the river empties.

What about sediments in other bodies of water? When rain erodes sediments into lakes and the ocean, the sediments can settle to the bottom of the lake or ocean. They can also be deposited at the shoreline. In the case of oceans, the tide might bring some sediments in and deposit them on the shore, or it might erode the shore and take sediments out to sea. Where sediments end up actually depends on many factors such as the size of the sediments and the energy associated with the process bringing them to the lake or ocean.

Erosion, then, is creation's way of "recycling" sediments. Rivers, rains, winds, etc., erode rocks. The sediments get deposited in river deltas, at the bottoms of lakes or oceans, on the shore of the oceans, etc. Those sediments, if laid down properly under the right conditions, might eventually form sedimentary rock, which might once again erode, starting the process all over again.

Although I have concentrated on the kind of erosion that occurs at the surface of the earth, there is also a great deal of erosion that occurs underground. As you will learn in physical science, a large fraction of earth's freshwater supply actually flows underground. This **groundwater** can also erode rock. We can see the effects of this erosion by looking at a **cavern**. Caverns often form giant mazes under the earth that stretch for miles in all directions. In the Kentucky area of the United States, for example, there is a system of interconnected caverns called Mammoth Cave. The total length of the tunnels in this system exceeds 365 miles!

Caverns are often damp places. Many contain streams or lakes, and most have groundwater seeping into them. This water drips down to the floor of the cave. Often, as the drip forms on the ceiling, a small amount of sediment (usually calcium carbonate) is deposited on the ceiling. When the drop hits the floor, a bit of sediment might be deposited as well. Eventually, those deposits build up, sometimes forming beautiful structures that hang from the ceiling or rise from the floor in the cave.

FIGURE 6.8
Stalactites and Stalagmites in a Cave

Photo by Kathleen J. Wile

stalactites

stalagmites

When the deposits start on the ceiling and form an icicle-like structure hanging down, the structure is called a **stalactite** (stuh lak' tyt). When the deposits form a structure that rises from the ground, the structure is called a **stalagmite** (stuh lag' myt). If you examine stalactites or stalagmites up close, you will usually see they are wet. After all, the dripping water that formed them is, mostly likely, still dripping. As a result, most stalactites and stalagmites continue to grow. In fact, sometimes a stalagmite forms underneath a stalactite, and eventually, they grow until they meet each other. The resulting structure is called a **column** or a **pillar**.

Caves are not the only place that stalactites, stalagmites, and columns form. Many statues made out of stone (the Lincoln Memorial, for example) have basements underneath them. As years of rain have eroded those statues or monuments and soaked into their basements, stalactites and stalagmites have formed there. Those stalactites and stalagmites show how powerful a force erosion can be, as well as how quickly stalactites can form.

ON YOUR OWN

6.7 Although erosion can form beautiful views like the Grand Canyon, it can also be a problem. Suppose, for example, a house is built near the edge of a steep hill. Heavy rains can erode the soil and rock on the hillside, taking away the support of the house and potentially causing the house to fall down the side of the hill. What could the owner of the house do to help reduce the amount of hillside erosion?

6.8 An experienced cave diver goes to the bottom of a lake in a large cave. When she reaches the bottom of the lake, she finds it is covered in stalagmites. She concludes that this must have been an empty cavern at one time and that the lake must have formed a while after the cave formed. Why?

<u>Bringing It All Together: The Basic Structure of the Grand Canyon</u>

Now that you have learned the basics of sedimentary rock, weathering, and erosion, it is time to look at the Grand Canyon in a bit more detail. Examine Figure 6.9.

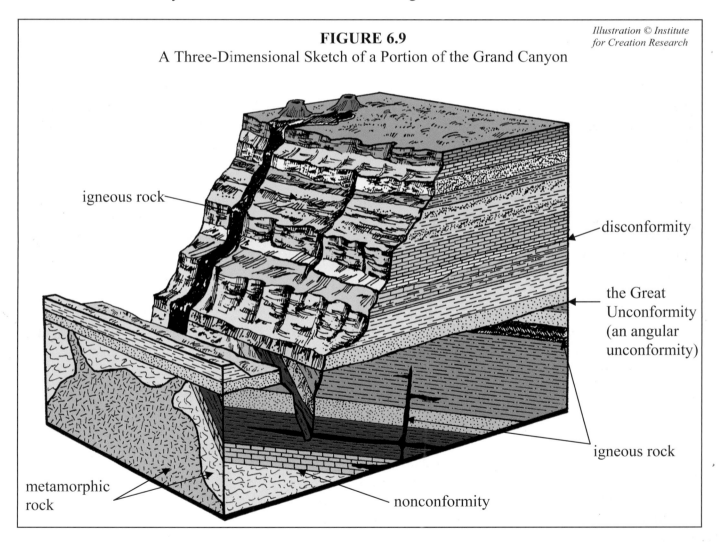

FIGURE 6.9
A Three-Dimensional Sketch of a Portion of the Grand Canyon

Illustration © Institute for Creation Research

igneous rock

disconformity

the Great Unconformity (an angular unconformity)

igneous rock

metamorphic rock

nonconformity

The first thing you should notice from the figure is that most of the rocks are stratified. The igneous and metamorphic rocks are indicated in the figure, and the strata are composed of sedimentary rock. Thus, the majority of rock in the Grand Canyon is sedimentary, and the sedimentary rock is formed in layers. The upper layers are horizontal, but the lower layers are tilted relative to the upper layers. Notice the boundary between those two sets of layers. It is an example of a very important kind of boundary, called an **unconformity**.

<u>Unconformity</u> – A surface of erosion that separates one layer of rock from another

It is important to understand that an unconformity is not just a separation between rock strata. It is a separation in which the top of the layer *below* the unconformity was eroded *before* the layer above the unconformity formed. This isn't the case with many geological strata. Often, one layer of rock sits smoothly on top of another layer, without any evidence of erosion in between. Thus, an unconformity is a special kind of separation between strata – it is a separation marked by all the indications of erosion.

Not surprisingly, we see different kinds of unconformities in the geological record. For example, the unconformity I am talking about now is labeled the **Great Unconformity**. It is given that name because it is probably the most striking unconformity in the Grand Canyon. It is striking, of course, because the rock strata below are tilted relative to the rock strata above. This kind of unconformity is called an **angular unconformity**, because the strata of rocks below it lie at an angle relative to the strata of rocks above it.

What formed the Great Unconformity in the Grand Canyon? Well, uniformitarians and catastrophists argue over the details, but they both agree that the rocks below the angular conformity were tilted by some major event like an earthquake, and then the rocks above the angular unconformity were laid down. I will discuss this more when I compare and contrast uniformitarianism and catastrophism.

Now please understand that the term "unconformity" is a general term that simply refers to the surface of erosion between two layers of rock. An angular unconformity is a *specific kind* of unconformity. Not surprisingly, there are other specific kinds of unconformities in the geological record. When sedimentary rock rests on top of igneous or metamorphic rock, the unconformity that lies between them is called a **nonconformity**. I have labeled one of the Grand Canyon's nonconformities at the bottom of Figure 6.9.

Another specific kind of unconformity is called a **disconformity**. In a disconformity, the strata are parallel. Notice the disconformity I have labeled in the figure. The strata above and below are both horizontal, so they are not tilted relative to each other. As a result, it is not an angular unconformity. In the same way, both layers are sedimentary, so it is not a nonconformity. If a geologist examines the layer below the disconformity, she will see the obvious signs of erosion, so it is definitely an unconformity. Thus, this particular kind of unconformity is called a disconformity.

Now don't get confused here. Not all boundaries between rock strata are unconformities. When you performed Experiment 6.2, for example, you were able to see strata form out of the various sediments in the jar. Although there were clear differences between each layer, there were no unconformities between the layers. An unconformity is marked by a surface that has been eroded. Since the layers were deposited right on top of each other, and since there was no rushing water or blowing wind to erode the surface of one layer before the other was laid down, there were no unconformities in your experiment. Thus, an unconformity is more than just a separation between layers of rock. It is a separation that has been eroded. So not all the parallel lines in Figure 6.9 represent unconformities. There are many identifiable boundaries between rock strata in the Grand Canyon, but a lot of them give no evidence of erosion, so they are not unconformities.

In the end, then, we call a boundary between strata an unconformity only if there is clear evidence of erosion between the layer below and the layer above. Once we have identified such a boundary, we call it an unconformity. To further identify which *type* of unconformity it is, we look at the rock layers above and below the boundary. If the layers are tilted relative to one another, we call it an angular unconformity. If the rock below is igneous or metamorphic and the rock above is sedimentary, we call it a nonconformity. If both layers are sedimentary and parallel, we call it a disconformity.

There is actually one more type of unconformity, but it is strange. Sometimes there is a layer of rock that geologists *believe* contains an unconformity, but it cannot be physically identified. There is no evidence of erosion, but because of certain assumptions some geologists make, they assume there *must be* an unconformity there. Such unidentifiable unconformities are called **paraconformities**. You will learn more about paraconformities in Module #8. For now, just think of them as unconformities that some geologists assume must exist, but without physical evidence to mark the unconformity.

The next thing I want you to notice in the figure is the igneous rock pointed out in the center of the figure near the bottom. These "veins" of igneous rock shoot right through several layers of sedimentary rock. This is called an **intrusion**, and it forms when magma from underneath the sedimentary rock gets injected in the cracks and fissures of the sedimentary rock. In technical terms, the "veins" of igneous rock that run in the same direction of the strata are called **sills**. The "veins" running perpendicular to that direction are usually called **dikes**.

Now I want you to see where another major igneous rock formation is. It is on the surface of the Grand Canyon and, as you might have guessed, it is the result of volcanic activity. As I told you earlier, much of the igneous rock you actually see is like this rock. It is the result of volcanic activity. Do you remember, however, that I also told you some igneous rock forms as the result of magma flowing underneath the ground? Now you know I was talking about intrusions.

Notice, then, that the rocks in the Grand Canyon tend to fall into four basic groups. First, there are the igneous and metamorphic rocks that form the base of the canyon. Then, there is the group of sedimentary (and one layer of igneous) rock that form strata that lie below the Great Unconformity. The third group of rocks contains the sedimentary rocks that form horizontal strata above the Great Unconformity. Finally, there are the igneous rocks formed at the surface due to volcanic activity. The explanation of how these four groups came to be is a matter of lively debate between uniformitarians and catastrophists. When I compare and contrast those views in the next module, you will see what I mean.

The Grand Canyon is a spectacular sight in the United States, and few other sights can match its beauty and grandeur. The reason I highlighted it here is that it is a good example of some of the geological features of our planet. It contains all three basic rock types (igneous, metamorphic, and sedimentary), it has many strata, and it has unconformities, one of which is rather striking. Thus, it contains many of the geological features you will find on earth. In addition, some of the rocks contain fossils. Since fossils are very important in the study of life on this planet, any discussion of geology as it relates to the history of life on earth must include a discussion of fossils.

In the next module, then, I will discuss fossils. I will tell you how fossils form and dispel some myths you might have heard about them. In addition, I will discuss the specific kinds of fossils that have been found in the Grand Canyon. Then, in the next module, I will sum it all up with a comparison between the uniformitarian view of life's history and the catastrophist view. Hopefully, this will give you an idea of how fascinating the study of the earth's history is!

ON YOUR OWN

6.9 In the picture below, an unconformity between two layers of sedimentary rock is pointed out. What type of unconformity is it?

unconformity

Photo © kavram
Agency: Shutterstock.com

6.10 You learned about the principle of superposition in the previous module. Assuming it is true, which group of rocks in the Grand Canyon is older: the sedimentary rocks that form horizontal strata or the rocks below the angular unconformity?

ANSWERS TO THE "ON YOUR OWN" PROBLEMS

6.1 It is impossible to believe in a young earth using the uniformitarian approach to geology. The definition itself states that millions of years are assumed. It is possible to believe in a young earth with the catastrophism view. Catastrophes can mold the geological features of the earth very quickly. It is possible to believe in a billions-of-years-old earth with the uniformitarian approach. In fact, uniformitarians *must* believe in a very, very old earth. It is possible to believe in a billions-of-years-old earth with the catastrophism approach. Although catastrophes cause big changes quickly, there could have been several that occurred millions or billions of years apart from one another.

6.2 Although the fact that it's shiny and has a distinct geometric pattern indicates it might be a mineral, it is composed of multiple chemicals. A mineral is composed of the same chemical throughout. Thus, this must be a rock. Perhaps someone cut and shined the rock to make it look like a mineral.

6.3 Metamorphic rock tends to be harder than the rock from which it formed. Thus, the first is probably metamorphic and the second is probably sedimentary.

6.4 Yes, it makes sense to think that the sedimentary rock in the Grand Canyon was laid down by water. There is not a lot of water in Arizona *now*, but at some time or times in the past, there could have been water there. You have already learned that there is a lot of evidence for the fact that a worldwide flood occurred. There certainly would have been water in Arizona then!

6.5 This is an example of chemical weathering. Even though you have no idea what these chemicals are, you see that the names changed. Forsterite changed to magnesium bicarbonate and silicic acid. Thus, after the weathering, the rock no longer contained forsterite, so it underwent chemical weathering.

6.6 This is an example of physical weathering. The only difference between before and after the weathering is the size of the rock. The pieces are just little versions of the original rock, so no change in composition occurred.

6.7 The homeowner could plant a lot of plants on the hillside. As your experiment showed, plants tend to reduce the effects of erosion.

6.8 Remember that stalagmites form as the result of groundwater that seeps in the ceiling of a cave and drips down to the floor, depositing its sediment on the floor. If the lake had always been a part of the cave, no stalagmites would have formed, because water would have dripped onto the surface of the lake and the sediments would have been spread throughout the lake.

6.9 This is a disconformity. The strata are parallel to one another.

6.10 The rocks below the angular unconformity are older, according to the Principle of Superposition, because they are below the other rocks.

STUDY GUIDE FOR MODULE #6

1. Define the following terms:

a. Catastrophism
b. Uniformitarianism
c. Humus
d. Minerals
e. Weathering
f. Erosion
g. Unconformity

2. Which hypothesis (uniformitarianism or catastrophism) requires that the earth be billions of years old?

3. What are the three basic types of rocks?

4. How is each type of rock mentioned in #3 formed?

5. What agent is responsible for laying down most of the sedimentary rock we see today?

6. A rock in the desert is constantly bombarded by bits of sand that are carried on the wind. Sometimes the sand hits the rock so hard that tiny chips of the rock are broken off. As time goes on, the constant beating of the sand on the rock wears the rock down, and it gets much smaller. Has the rock experienced physical or chemical weathering?

7. When limestone is exposed to weakly acidic water, it breaks down, forming a gas in the process. Is this chemical or physical weathering?

8. A geologist is comparing the erosion that occurs as a result of two different rivers. The first river flows quickly while the second flows slowly. Which river do you expect to cause the most erosion?

9. Two hillsides in the same community experience a very heavy rain. The first hillside is covered with grass and flowers, while the second is mostly bare. Which hillside will experience the most erosion?

10. What causes a river to form a delta?

11. What kind of water is responsible for eroding underground caverns?

12. What is the difference between a stalactite and a stalagmite?

13. What causes stalactites and stalagmites to form?

Questions 14 through 19 refer to the side-on view of the Grand Canyon below:

Illustration by Julia Marie Ciferno

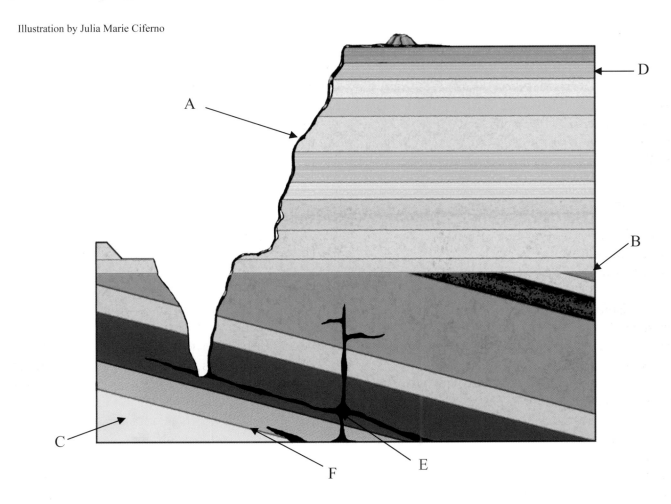

14. Which letter identifies metamorphic rock?

15. Which two letters identify igneous rock?

16. Which letter identifies sedimentary rock?

17. Which letter identifies an angular unconformity?

18. Which letter identifies an intrusion?

19. Which letter identifies a nonconformity?

20. If an unconformity exists between two parallel strata of sedimentary rock, what kind of unconformity is it?

MODULE #7: The Fossil Record

Introduction

Now that you know some of the basic types and formations of the rocks in the earth's crust, it is time to look inside those rocks and see what they contain. As you have already learned, rocks contain minerals. Minerals are interesting to study, and some (like diamonds and rubies) are considered precious. From a scientific point of view, however, some rocks contain even more precious items: fossils. Although I have already mentioned fossils and you probably have a good idea of what a fossil is, I want to give you a formal definition.

<u>Fossil</u> – The preserved remains of a once-living organism

A fossil, then, gives us information about what happened in the past, as it is a preserved record of something that was once alive. If the fossil is old enough, it can give us information about a time in earth's past before there was a lot of recorded history.

Before we move on, go back and look at the definition. There is a very important word there – *preserved*. What usually happens when an organism dies? Typically, it *decomposes*. If you have a garden, you might have even seen this process in action. Gardeners will often gather leaves in the fall and spread them over the area in which they want to plant a garden next spring. Over the course of the winter, many of the leaves will decompose, forming the nutritious humus that adds to the topsoil. This humus makes the soil more fertile, which can result in a rich, lush garden.

Remember, leaves are part of a living plant. When they fall off the plant, they die and eventually decompose to form nutritious topsoil. Although you have probably not witnessed it firsthand, the same thing happens to animals when they die. Their skin, hair or feathers, organs, and even their bones eventually decompose and form rich humus that will be later used by plants as a source of nutrition. When you take biology, you will find out that there are all sorts of living organisms (called "decomposers") that have been created by God for the specific purpose of aiding this decomposition process.

If you think about it, then, the formation of a fossil is an exception to the general rule of nature. In general, dead organisms are not preserved. Instead, they decompose. When you find the preserved remains of an organism, then, you know there must be something special about the way in which it was formed. The special conditions that lead to fossil formation are quite rare; thus, only a tiny fraction of once-living organisms gets fossilized. The vast majority simply decompose. In the next few sections, I want to discuss the various special conditions that can lead to the formation of a fossil.

The Making of Fossils Part 1: Casts and Molds

The most common means by which a dead organism can be preserved is by the formation of a **mold** and the making of a **cast**. In this process, the organism itself is not actually preserved. Instead, rocks are formed in the image of the plant or animal. The best way to understand this process is to actually do it yourself.

EXPERIMENT 7.1
Making a Fossil Cast

<u>Supplies:</u>

♦ Modeling clay (Play-Doh® will work)
♦ Plaster of Paris
♦ A paper plate
♦ A shell or something else with a distinctive shape or design
♦ Vaseline® or another petroleum jelly
♦ Eye protection such as goggles or safety glasses

Introduction: Many fossils form by a natural process that involves a mold being made and then filled with a substance that hardens into rock. In this experiment, you will use clay as the substance from which the mold is made and plaster as the rock.

<u>Procedure:</u>

1. Cover the outside of the shell (the part you will fossilize) with Vaseline.
2. Roll the clay out on the paper plate so it covers an area larger than the shell.
3. Choose the most interesting part of the shell and firmly press it into the clay, so an imprint forms in the clay.
4. Pull the shell away, and you should see a nice impression of the shell in the clay. At this point, you have made a **mold** of the shell.
5. Mix the plaster according to the directions on the package and pour the plaster into the impression. Fill the impression so full that the plaster spills a little over the clay and onto the paper plate.
6. Allow the plaster to harden.
7. Once the plaster has hardened, pull it off the paper plate and remove the clay from it. What do you see? This is called a **cast** of the shell.
8. Optional: You can use this method to make a fossil of almost anything. Try making a fossil of your hand, your foot, or anything else you would like to preserve!
9. Clean up your mess.

       Believe it or not, the process you performed in the experiment happens throughout creation. Consider, for example, a seashell that gets buried in sediment. As the sediment hardens and turns to rock, the rock surrounding the shell hardens around the shell. This results in a shell encased in sedimentary rock. As time goes on, water that seeps through the sedimentary rock will weather both the rock and the shell. If the shell is affected by weathering a lot more than the rock, it is possible that the shell will disintegrate before the rock. Alternatively, the shell can decompose inside the rock. If either of these things happens, you have a mold where the shell originally was. This mold, much like the mold you made, will have the general shape and design of the shell.

       Sometimes, paleontologists will split open a rock and find an empty mold like that. Other times, the rock will weather away to reveal a portion of the mold. This can tell the paleontologist about the shell that was once there. Although it is possible to find such molds, it is relatively rare. It is much more common for something to fill the mold. For example, other sediments can seep into the sedimentary rock that contains the mold, and those sediments might fill the space left by the mold. As time goes on, those sediments will harden, forming a cast of the original shell. In your experiment, the plaster acted in this way. It filled the mold like sediments filling a space in a rock, and when the plaster hardened, a likeness of the shell was made.

FIGURE 7.1
Molds and Casts

Photos © Stephen Krausse (left), Russell Shively (right)
Agency: Shutterstock.com

The picture on the left shows a mold. Notice how the organism left an impression, but it is not filled in. The picture on the right shows a cast. Notice how the fossil is quite different from the rock in which it was found. That's because the material that flowed into the mold was quite different from the rock that made it. The fossil is of a trilobite, which you will learn about at the end of this module.

In your experiment, then, you first formed a mold by pressing the shell into clay. If you had allowed the clay to harden, you would have had a preserved mold, much like what you see on the left side of Figure 7.1. That would be considered a fossil of the shell. Usually, a mold formed like the one that you made does not last very long. If an animal leaves footprints in mud, for example, you could consider those molds of the animal's feet. However, as soon as the next rain comes, those footprints will, most likely, be washed away. Molds formed on the surface of mud or clay, then, rarely are fossilized, because they are likely to erode more quickly than the mud or clay in which they were formed can harden.

This, of course, is not always the case. There are fossil footprints preserved in the geological record. Thus, molds formed on the surface of mud, clay, and sediment *can* become fossilized, but such an occurrence is extremely rare. Molds are much more commonly formed when the plant or animal is completely buried in the sediment. That way, the sediment can harden right around the plant or animal, and the resulting mold cannot be eroded as easily.

Once you made your mold, you then filled it with plaster, making a cast, like the fossil on the right side of Figure 7.1. This can happen naturally, as sediments find their way into a mold and then harden. Magma intrusions can also naturally fill a mold, making an igneous cast of the fossil. Although many casts form naturally, sometimes it is useful to make artificial casts. Crime scene investigators, for example, will make plaster casts of footprints made in the mud near the scene of the crime. Since the footprints in the mud will wash away quickly, making a cast preserves them for use in the crime investigation. Also, paleontologists will often make casts of fossil molds they find so the fossils can be studied without handling the molds directly.

Although I talked about casts and molds being formed to fossilize seashells, virtually any remains of a plant or animal can be fossilized in this way. Bones, for example, will often be preserved in casts. Preserved footprints have been found in both cast and mold form. Typically, hard substances are more likely to form molds and casts because a hard substance can withstand the pressure of the sediments that surround it without being crushed.

ON YOUR OWN

7.1 Is it possible for a mold to form without a cast? Is it possible for a cast to form without a mold?

The Making of Fossils Part 2: Petrifaction

Another way the remains of once-living organisms can be preserved is through the process of **petrifaction** (peh truh fak' shun), which is also called "petrification."

Petrifaction – The conversion of organic material into rock

In the definition of mineral, you learned that the term "inorganic" means "not from a living creature." Well, the term "organic" means "from a living creature." Thus, petrifaction is the process by which the remains of a once-living organism are turned into rock.

Petrifaction is the result of a creature's remains being exposed to water that contains minerals. You see, living tissue like bone and wood contains pores – spaces in which water can flow. As mineral-rich water swirls around an organism's remains, some of that water fills the pores. Over time, however, the water will evaporate. What happens when the water evaporates? Perform the following experiment to find out.

EXPERIMENT 7.2
Minerals in Water and Evaporation

Supplies

- A cup of water
- A small glass
- Table salt
- A measuring spoon that measures one-eighth of a teaspoon
- A clean glass baking pan (A large rectangular one works best)

Introduction: When mineral-rich water evaporates, something important happens to the minerals. You will find out what that is in this experiment.

Procedure:

1. Put 1 cup of warm water into the glass.
2. Add one-eighth teaspoon of salt and stir so it all dissolves and the resulting solution is clear.
3. Look at the glass baking pan and make sure it is clean. Hold it up to the light at several different angles to make sure. If you see any smudges or residue on the pan, clean it so the glass is clear.
4. Pour a *small amount* of the water into the glass baking pan and tilt the pan around so the water spreads out. The more you can spread the water out, the better.
5. Wait ten minutes. By then, all the water should have evaporated. If not, wait a bit longer.
6. Observe the pan and note whether or not it is still clean.
7. Clean up your mess.

What did you see in the experiment? Once the water evaporated, the pan was no longer clean, was it? It had white streaks on the bottom, didn't it? What were those streaks? They were made of salt. Like any mineral dissolved in water, salt cannot evaporate with the water, so it is left behind when the water evaporates. The same thing happens in petrifaction. As mineral-rich water evaporates from the remains of an organism, the minerals are left behind, deposited in the dead organism. As time goes on, the organic materials begin to decompose, and the deposited minerals are all that is left behind. If this process is allowed to complete, the remains can be entirely replaced, and the result is a stony substance that is a replica of the creature being preserved.

Petrifaction works best on the hard remains of a creature, like bone and wood, because hard remains do not decompose quickly. This allows time for minerals to be deposited as the remains slowly decompose. The figure below, for example, shows you a piece of petrified wood. Although you can still see the familiar ring pattern that indicates you are looking at part of a tree trunk, the fossil is no longer wood, but hard stone.

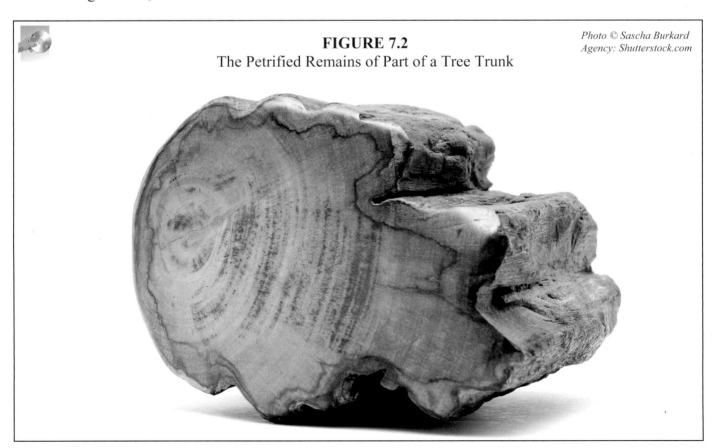

FIGURE 7.2
The Petrified Remains of Part of a Tree Trunk

Photo © Sascha Burkard
Agency: Shutterstock.com

A very famous example of this kind of petrifaction can be found in the state of Arizona. At a United States National Park called the Petrified Forest, you can find one of the largest concentrations of petrified wood in the world. As you walk through the park, you will find huge pieces of wood just lying on the ground. While they often look like chunks of wood recently cut from a tree, when you actually touch them, they feel like solid stone. That's because they have been petrified.

In certain cases, petrifaction can happen very quickly, faster than the time it takes for the creature being fossilized to decompose. Under these conditions, the minerals can combine with the organic materials in the creature's remains rather than replace them. As a result, the organic materials can be made resistant to decomposition and are therefore preserved. This is especially valuable to paleontologists, because few fossils actually have any of their organic materials preserved. Thus, petrified remains of this kind are considered quite precious!

It is instructive to compare fossils formed by casts to those formed by petrifaction. In each case, you get a hard, stony likeness of the creature's remains. However, it is important to note the differences between the two. When a mold is formed, the shape of the creature's remains is preserved, as are any obvious bumps or grooves on the surface. When the sediments or magma fill the mold to form a cast, the result is something that has the same shape as the creature's remains as well as the same surface characteristics. The inside of the cast, however, is just solid rock. On the other hand, when petrifaction occurs, the original parts of the remains are either replaced bit by bit or are preserved. As a result, you get an actual replica of the creature's remains, including details not just on the surface of the remains. This, of course, provides more information to the paleontologist, but it is also a much rarer form of fossilization.

ON YOUR OWN

7.2 The Petrified Forest tells us that although Arizona is a dry, desert-like place today, it must have had a plentiful supply of water at some time in the past. Why?

<u>The Making of Fossils Part 3: Carbonized Remains</u>

So far, I have discussed two means of fossilization. These processes, as I have already stated, tend to preserve the hard remains of plants and animals such as wood, bones, or shells. Now I want to discuss an entirely different fossilization process. When an organism is buried in sediment, the pressure can cause liquids and gases in the organism's remains to be forced right out into the surrounding sediments. Since water makes up a large part of any organism (the human body is about 60 percent water, for example), this means the majority of the organism's remains are lost. Chemical reactions take place, leaving a thin, filmy residue composed mostly of carbon. This process, called **carbonization**, often forms a detailed "drawing" of the creature in stone.

Plant fossils are probably the most common carbonized fossils, because the structure of plant tissue is particularly suited to carbonization. This is fortunate for paleontologists, since many plants (like grasses) do not have any hard tissues. Even the plants that have hard tissue (like the wood in a tree), still have soft parts (like leaves) that are incredibly important when it comes to identifying and understanding them. Thus, the carbonization process preserves organisms that are often not preserved by molds, casts, or petrifaction. Even though animal tissue is not ideally suited to carbonization, some carbonized fossils of soft-bodied animals (like jellyfish) are found. Even some fish have been preserved by carbonization.

Plant fossil photo by Shizhao and published under the Creative Commons Attribution ShareAlike 2.5 License: http://creativecommons.org/licenses/by-sa/2.5/

FIGURE 7.3
Carbonized Remains

Fish fossil photo © Anthro Agency: Shutterstock.com

Carbonized Plant Fossil

Carbonized Fish Fossil

I want you to get a better idea of how the carbonization process works by performing the following experiment. While it is not a perfect model of carbonization, it gives you a good idea of how such remains are formed.

EXPERIMENT 7.3
A Model of the Carbonization Process

Supplies:

♦ At least two (preferably more) leaves (They should not be dried out. You can pick them off the tree or get recently fallen ones that are not yet dried out.)
♦ Two sheets of blank, white paper per leaf
♦ Many thick books (You can use fewer books if you have some heavy weights you can put on the books.)

Introduction: The process of carbonization requires chemicals from the organism being fossilized to be transferred to the rock in which it has been trapped. This experiment gives you a model for how that happens.

Procedure:

1. Place a leaf between two sheets of paper.

2. Put the leaf and sheets of paper on a hard, flat surface, and stack several books on them so they are subject to a lot of pressure.
3. Repeat steps 1 and 2 for each leaf, but each time, vary the weight of books stacked on the leaf. You want at least one leaf with only a bit of weight on it, and one with a *lot* of weight on it. Preferably, you have many leaves, and you should have a different amount of weight on each.
4. Let the leaves sit for at least a week. Two weeks would be better.
5. After the waiting period is over, peel the sheets of paper away from each leaf. Note what each sheet of paper looks like. Also, note how the sheets of paper differ with different amounts of weight.
6. You can throw the leaves away, but keep the papers and put them in your lab notebook. If you want, you can cut out the parts that have leaf prints on them and keep just those parts.
7. Clean up your mess.

When the waiting period is over, you should find that each sheet of paper has a leaf print on it. Why? Well, there are chemicals in the leaf, and the pressure of the books caused some of those chemicals to be transferred to the paper. Since the pressure is important, you will see that different weights caused different amounts of detail in the leaf print. This is similar to the process of carbonization. Even though carbonization requires heat as well as pressure, the basic process is the same.

If you think about it, carbonization gives us different information about the organism from petrifaction or the formation of molds and casts. Not only is the detail in a carbonized fossil often quite exquisite, the fossil does actually contain some of the chemicals that were initially in the organism. While those chemicals might have been transformed by reactions, they nevertheless contain some information about the organic parts of the organism, which are typically lost in the petrifaction and mold/cast formation processes.

ON YOUR OWN

7.3 Form a hypothesis about how the amount of weight in Experiment 7.3 will affect the leaf imprint on the paper you find. Write it down now, and see how well the results of the experiment support your hypothesis.

The Making of Fossils Part 4: Avoiding Decomposition

Although all the fossilization processes I have discussed so far will preserve *parts of* or the *major features of* a dead organism, none of them produce ideal specimens for a paleontologist to study. Molds, casts, and petrifaction typically preserve only the "hard" parts of a plant or animal such as wood, shells, and bones. Carbonized remains can provide stunning detail as to what a plant or animal looked like, but at best, only a small fraction of the organic remains of the organism is left behind, and they might be quite different from their original chemical composition, due to reactions that have occurred over the years. Also, carbonized remains are flat, so you do not get information regarding the "thickness" of the organism. In the end, then, all these fossils give the paleontologist information, but the information is scant at best. A living creature is full of soft tissue, organs, skin, hair, etc., that are rarely fossilized by any of these means. Without being able to analyze these parts of an organism, our knowledge of that organism will always be incomplete.

Even though *most* fossils do not contain complete information about the fossilized creature, there are a few strikingly spectacular specimens that come close. For example, in 1977 in a remote area of Siberia, the preserved remains of a baby mammoth were found. We have never found a living example of a mammoth; however, we know that mammoths must have existed because their fossils have been found.

The fossil found in Siberia in 1977 was remarkable in that skin, hair, and many soft body parts that normally are not preserved were well preserved. Why? Well, the mammoth was found inside a tomb of frozen mud. The ice that surrounded the mammoth's remains protected it from the organisms that aid in decomposition, and the frigid temperature slowed down many of the chemical reactions that cause organic matter to decompose. In the end, then, the mammoth's remains were preserved because it was frozen, much like we preserve food by putting it in the freezer. Since then, frozen mammoths have been found that are even more remarkably preserved. Because of these fossils, scientists know a lot more about mammoths than they know about many other extinct animals.

Ice tombs like the one that enclosed the baby mammoth provide excellent preservation, but they are not the only way to get beautifully preserved fossils. Consider, for example, the fossil in the figure below.

FIGURE 7.4
A Honeypot Ant in Amber

Photo by Joachim Scheven
Courtesy of LEBENDIGE VORWELT *museum*

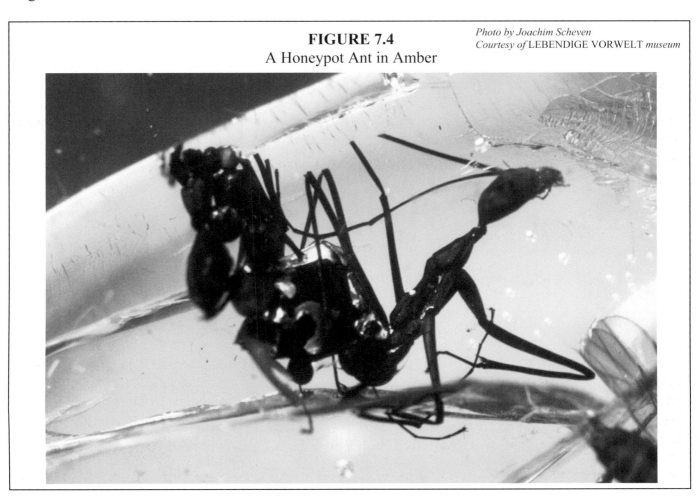

This remarkable specimen is encased in **amber**, which is a kind of **resin**.

<u>Resin</u> – A thick, slowly flowing liquid produced by plants that can harden into a solid

Many plants produce resin as a protective measure. It can seal in moisture if water is scarce, and it can be used as a protection against very cold weather. Since it is often sticky, it can also be used to trap insects that are trying to eat the plant. It is possible that the ant in Figure 7.4 is a fossil for that very reason. It might have been trying to eat the plant but got caught in the sticky liquid as it was crawling on the plant. As the plant produced more resin, the ant was eventually covered, and when the resin hardened, the ant was "sealed in."

The sealed amber tomb has preserved the ant very well. You must realize, however, that although the ant appears to be intact, it is definitely not. Amber preserves the creatures entombed in it because once it hardens, amber does not allow any of the creatures that aid in decomposition to get to the creature. Nevertheless, the chemicals that make up this ant have been decomposing on their own since the ant first died. Thus, many of the ant's internal structures are already completely decomposed. Nevertheless, because no creatures can aid the decomposition, it is very slow, and many parts of the ant do remain.

Paleontologists have actually succeeded in extracting DNA from some insects fossilized in amber. As you will learn in biology class, DNA is a huge molecule that exists in every living creature. The molecule contains all the information that a living creature needs to grow, develop, and live. Needless to say, then, the DNA extracted from insects fossilized in amber can tell us a lot about what those insects were like in the past. Interestingly enough, the DNA extracted from such fossils indicates that overall, DNA does not change very much. For example, if you compare the DNA extracted from an insect fossilized in amber to a living insect of the same species, you will see very little difference between the DNA from the fossil and the DNA from the living insect.

ON YOUR OWN

7.4 Some paleontologists actually classify insects fossilized in amber as fossil molds. Why is an insect in amber like a fossil mold?

Three General Features of the Fossil Record

Now that you have learned a bit about the fossilization process, it is time for you to learn some of the things we can observe about the fossils that have been discovered. Usually, the sum total of all discovered fossils is referred to as the **fossil record**. After all, fossils are the remains of once-living organisms. Thus, fossils are really a record of life in earth's past.

What can we observe about the fossil record? Well, one of the first things that becomes apparent when studying the fossil record is that most fossils are found in sedimentary rock. This should make sense to you. After all, igneous rock is formed from magma and lava. Most creatures unlucky enough to be trapped in lava would probably be burnt to a crisp rather than fossilized. This is not always true, however. Fossil trees have been found in igneous rock, as have some fossil bones. In general, however, finding fossils in igneous rock is extremely rare. In the same way, finding fossils in metamorphic rock is extremely rare. Thus, most fossils are found in sedimentary rock.

Now remember that most sedimentary rock is laid down by water. Based on this fact and the fact that most fossils are found in sedimentary rock, we can easily come to the conclusion that most fossils have also been laid down by water. This is an important point. Without the action of water, most fossils would not be formed. Indeed, one of the fossilization processes (petrifaction) needs sediment-laden water in order to work! Thus, water is a very important part of the fossilization process.

The next aspect of the fossil record is usually not mentioned by paleontologists, because it is considered a rather boring fact. Nevertheless, it is a very important feature of the fossil record. *The vast majority of all fossils on this planet are the fossils of hard-shelled organisms, like clams!* I suspect you might have already read a great deal about fossils before taking this course. By the time I was your age, for example, I had read every book about dinosaurs I could find. I had also read a lot about fossils in general. I had never, ever read about this important aspect of the fossil record, however!

Most people think about fossil dinosaurs, insects trapped in amber, and woolly mammoths when they hear about the fossil record. However, fossils like this make up a tiny, tiny minority of what's actually in the fossil record. In fact, if you really break down the fossil record, here's what you find: The vast majority of all fossils we recover are of hard-shelled creatures, like clams. They can be found in every region of the earth. Of the small fraction that remains, the vast majority are bony marine animals, like fish. Of the tiny fraction that remains after bony marine animals, the vast majority are insects. Only the very, very tiny fraction that remains is made up of reptiles, birds, plants, and mammals. Think about that for a moment. If you read most textbooks on fossils, you will think that there are countless fossils of dinosaurs and the like. There aren't. In fact, fossils of anything other than clam-like creatures are rare, and fossils of reptiles or mammals are *exceedingly* rare.

Now if you think about it, this should make sense. After all, the harder something is, the more likely it is to fossilize. Since clams and the like have hard shells, they are more likely to fossilize. Also, remember that water is incredibly important in the fossilization process. Thus, hard-shelled creatures that live in water *should* be the most likely kind of fossil you find. Using the same kind of reasoning, fish should be the next most likely fossils to find, since fish have hard bones and live in water. Thus, it is not *surprising* that the vast majority of fossils are hard-shelled creatures and fish. However, if you read most discussions of fossils, this important fact is left out!

The next thing that is easy to notice about the fossil record is that it contains the remains of some organisms still living today. For example, consider the fossilized honeypot ant shown in Figure 7.4. The same species of ant can be found alive today in Australia. This is true of many, many fossils. Interestingly enough, when paleontologists compare such a fossil to its living counterpart, they find that the fossil and the living counterpart are incredibly similar. Based on the fossil evidence, then, we can conclude that organisms that have survived throughout earth's history experience little change. Now please understand that there is a *major* difference between "little change" and "no change at all." The fossil record (indeed, even the history of recorded science) tells us that organisms do change a bit over time. Finches, for example, tend to develop shorter, stouter beaks over several generations if those generations are all exposed to dry conditions. Nevertheless, the main features that make those birds finches (instead of eagles, for example) do not change.

Although many of the fossils that paleontologists find have living counterparts today, some do not. For example, consider the mammoth I discussed earlier. Although it is easy to find elephants alive today, we cannot find a living version of a mammoth. What are the differences between mammoths and elephants? Examine Figure 7.5.

FIGURE 7.5
Mammoth Compared to an Elephant

Drawing of What We Think a Mammoth Looked Like   African Elephant

Although there are many similarities between mammoths and elephants, there are important differences as well. Both have hair, but a mammoth was covered in thick, shaggy hair, whereas elephants are covered mostly in bare skin with small patches of hair. The back of a mammoth was shaped rather differently from that of an elephant, and a mammoth's tusks were bigger and more curved than those of elephants.

There are no mammoths living today. Nevertheless, we know that mammoths lived at one time, because we have their fossilized remains. Thus, we say that the mammoth is now **extinct**.

Extinct – A term applied to a species that was once living but now is not

So one of the general features of the fossil record is that it contains fossils of species represented by organisms currently living on earth, but it also contains fossils of animals *scientists think* are extinct today. Please note, however, that scientists are not always right when they think an animal is extinct. As you will learn in the next module, some species were thought to be extinct, but then living individuals were discovered. For example, in 2006, living examples of ants called *Gracilidris* (grass' uh lih dris) were discovered in South America. This was a huge surprise, because until then, we had only found fossils of them. Thus, they were thought to be extinct, but we now know they are not.

Before I go any further, I want to answer a question that you *should* be asking yourself. In Figure 7.5, I present a drawing of a mammoth. You should be wondering how in the world we know what a mammoth looks like, since no mammoths are alive today. Well, the answer is simple, but I need to make sure you really understand it. We know a lot about what mammoths used to look like because we have fossils of mammoths. Remember, however, that most of the time, fossils are terribly incomplete. In addition, only the hard parts of an organism are fossilized. If soft parts are fossilized, it is usually in the form of a carbonized fossil, which gives only some information about the organism. As a result, most fossils are not detailed enough for us to draw a reliable picture of what the organism actually looked like.

In the case of mammoths, however, we have a few incredibly well-preserved fossils that do have remains of hair, skin, and other soft parts. For example, the frozen baby mammoth discussed in the previous section gave paleontologists examples of mammoth hair, skin, etc. Thus, the *only* reason we have a good idea of what mammoths looked like is that we have a few incredibly well preserved fossils. This is *very rare* in the fossil record. We do not have such fossils for most of the extinct animals we have found in the fossil record. Thus, we really do not know a lot about them. So when you see drawings of dinosaurs and the like, you need to view them very skeptically. Most of the fossils upon which those drawings are based contain nothing but a few bones and some teeth. Most of the details in these drawings, therefore, are the result of imagination, not data!

Before I discuss the final feature of the fossil record, I want to take a moment to discuss extinction. Scientists estimate that since 1600, 484 species of animals and 654 species of plants have become extinct. We can therefore *see* extinction occurring throughout history. Some of those extinctions were the result of human activity. Some were the result of the natural ebb and flow of creation. Thus, we see that extinction occurred in earth's past by examining the fossil record. We also can see that it occurred by examining historical records.

The reason I bring this up, however, is that extinction is a favorite topic of misinformation for many people who call themselves "environmentalists." If you read the literature of such people, you will see claims that 10,000 to 60,000 species of plants and animals go extinct *every year*. Most of the time, these people blame this calamity on human activity. Such statements are outright lies, however. The people who call themselves "environmentalists" tend to get away with such lies, because their facts are rarely checked.

If you read the literature of the scientists who are actually doing research on extinctions throughout history, you will find that in the last 400 years, just over 1,100 species of plants and animals have become extinct, and many of those extinctions don't have any apparent connection to human activity. Of course, the extinction of *some* species can be blamed on people. The Passenger Pigeon, for example, was hunted to extinction by people in North America. In addition, the activities of people indirectly caused some animals to become extinct. The Australian bird known as the Robust White-eye, for example, went extinct because Europeans inadvertently brought rats to Australia on their boats. The rats preyed on the bird and its eggs, driving it to extinction. What we can say for sure about extinction, however, is that for the past 400 years, only a little more than 1,100 species have gone extinct, and only a portion of those extinctions are a result of the activities of people.

ON YOUR OWN

7.5 Suppose you are studying the fossils of animals that are thought to be extinct. You have three fossils: one of a species of wasp about 2 inches long, one of a sea-dwelling fish about 20 feet long, and one of a land-dwelling mammal about 3 feet long. If you had to speculate, which of the three would you think is the most likely to actually be extinct?

A Fourth General Feature of the Fossil Record

The final general feature of the fossil record I would like to point out is that the fossils found in different strata of rock tend to be quite different. Remember, the majority of fossils in the fossil record are found in sedimentary rock. As you learned in the previous module, sedimentary rock tends to form layers that geologists call strata. Well, if you find fossils in a sedimentary rock formation, you will usually find significant differences between the fossils in each layer.

For example, in the previous module, you saw a diagram of various rock strata in the Grand Canyon. If a paleontologist were to examine the fossils found in each stratum (the singular of "strata"), he would find some similarities, but he would also find significant differences. First of all, nearly every layer of rock would contain fossilized clam-like animals. Remember, after all, that the vast majority of the fossils on this planet are of hard-shelled creatures like clams. Thus, they are in several of the strata of the Grand Canyon. Once you get rid of all those fossils, however, you notice some striking differences. Examine the figure below to see what I mean.

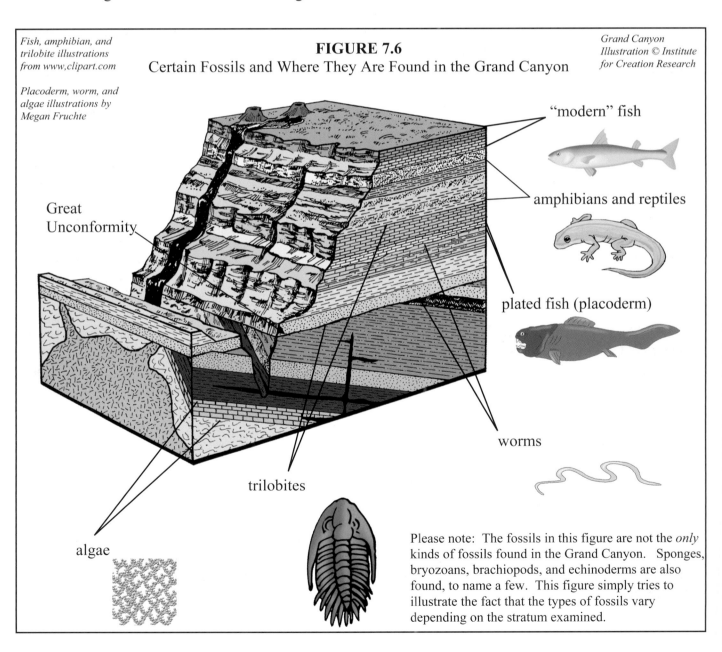

Fish, amphibian, and trilobite illustrations from www.clipart.com

Placoderm, worm, and algae illustrations by Megan Fruchte

FIGURE 7.6
Certain Fossils and Where They Are Found in the Grand Canyon

Grand Canyon Illustration © Institute for Creation Research

"modern" fish

amphibians and reptiles

plated fish (placoderm)

Great Unconformity

worms

trilobites

algae

Please note: The fossils in this figure are not the *only* kinds of fossils found in the Grand Canyon. Sponges, bryozoans, brachiopods, and echinoderms are also found, to name a few. This figure simply tries to illustrate the fact that the types of fossils vary depending on the stratum examined.

The most striking thing about the fossils in the Grand Canyon is that there are very few in the strata below the Great Unconformity (pointed out in the figure). There aren't even any hard-shelled creatures in those strata! In fact, there are no animal fossils at all. A careful paleontologist will find a few fossils of microscopic creatures such as algae and bacteria (you will learn a lot about those organisms in biology class). Above the Great Unconformity, the strata have significantly more fossils in them.

There are fossils of **trilobites** (try' luh byts) in many of the layers above the Great Unconformity. Trilobites lived in water. Most lived on the ocean bottom, where they plowed through the mud looking for food. They were protected by a hard outer covering known as an "exoskeleton," much like a lobster. Trilobites are assumed to be extinct, as no living one has ever been discovered. The most common form of trilobite fossil is a cast fossil. In some of the layers above the Great Unconformity, actual fossils of trilobites have not been found. In those layers, however, fossils of their tracks have been found, indicating the presence of trilobites.

In the three layers just above the Great Unconformity, there are fossils of worm burrows, indicating the presence of worms. In only one layer of the Grand Canyon (pointed out in the figure), you will find fossils of **placoderms** (plak' uh durms). Placoderms are strange-looking fish that are also assumed to be extinct. They had bony plates covering their heads rather than the scales you see covering the heads of fish today. There have been no fossils of placoderms found in any other layer of the Grand Canyon. Fish that look like the ones we see today (labeled "modern" fish in the figure) are found only in the topmost layers of the Grand Canyon.

Interestingly enough, there are no fossils of mammals or birds in the Grand Canyon. However, there are fossils of **amphibians** (most likely salamanders) and **reptiles** in the three layers pointed out in the figure. If you are not familiar with the term "amphibian," it refers to creatures that live both in and out of water. Frogs, salamanders, and toads are all examples of amphibians. The reason I have to say that the fossils are "most likely salamanders" is that they are not bones, carbonized fossils, or molds/casts of the amphibians. Instead, they are fossils of amphibian tracks. The tracks seem to be the kinds of tracks that a salamander makes; thus, most paleontologists consider them to be fossils of salamanders. There are also tracks that most likely came from small reptiles, like lizards.

The point to this rather long discussion is very important. You can find fossils of trilobites in the Grand Canyon, but you cannot find them just anywhere in the Grand Canyon. You must look in the layers above the Great Unconformity. You can also find fossils of worms, but you must look in the three strata directly above the Great Unconformity. If you are looking for fish that look like the fish that live today, you can find fossils *only* in the topmost layers. It turns out that in virtually every geological formation that contains strata and fossils, the fossils found in one layer can be significantly different from the fossils found in another layer.

Why are there different types of fossils in different strata? Well, the answer to that is full of controversy. As I stated in the previous module, much of what you conclude from the sciences of geology and paleontology depends on whether you start with the hypothesis of uniformitarianism or the hypothesis of catastrophism. Uniformitarians have one explanation for why the fossils found within different strata are so different. Catastrophists have another explanation. Hopefully, looking at the two explanations will help you on your way to determining which you think is the better hypothesis.

Before I move on to a discussion of the uniformitarian and catastrophist explanations for the major features of the fossil record, I want to sum them up for you so you can remember them easily.

GENERAL FEATURES OF THE FOSSIL RECORD

1. **Fossils are usually found in sedimentary rock. Since most sedimentary rock is laid down by water, it follows that most fossils were laid down by water.**
2. **The vast majority of the fossil record is made up of hard-shelled creatures like clams. Most of the remaining fossils are of either water-dwelling creatures or insects. Only a tiny, tiny fraction of the fossils we find are of plants, reptiles, birds, and mammals.**
3. **Many of the fossils we find are of organisms that are still alive today. Many of the fossils we find are of organisms that are now extinct.**
4. **The fossils found in one layer of stratified rock can be considerably different from the fossils found in another layer of stratified rock.**

As you read about both explanations of the fossil record, it is important to keep these features in mind.

ON YOUR OWN

7.6 A geologist shows you a rock and says it was taken from a layer of the Grand Canyon that contained fossils. You can ask the geologist one question about the fossils found in the layer from which the rock was taken, and then you must tell the geologist whether the rock was found above or below the Great Unconformity. What question should you ask the geologist, and how will that help you determine from where the rock was taken?

Geology and Paleontology from the Uniformitarian Perspective

Any explanation of the fossil record begins with the explanation of the geological record that you learned about in the previous module. After all, since fossils are found in rocks, the formation of rocks will obviously affect the formation of fossils! Whether we are discussing uniformitarianism or catastrophism, then, we must explain both the geological record and the fossil record together.

The uniformitarian starts with a very important assumption when trying to explain the geological and fossil records. The assumption is best summed up with the phrase:

The present is the key to the past.

This statement means that in order to understand what happened in the past, we merely have to study what is happening today. The uniformitarian believes that nothing "really special" happened in earth's past. Instead, the same processes we see happening today were going on throughout earth's past. Since that is the case, it stands to reason that the same processes we see happening today are responsible for forming the rocks and fossils we study in geology and paleontology. What we must do, then, is see how sedimentary rock is forming today, and that will tell us how sedimentary rock formed in the past. In the same way, we need to see how fossils are forming today, and that will tell us how they formed in earth's past.

So how is sedimentary rock formed today? One way it forms is by catastrophes. While uniformitarians acknowledge that catastrophes are responsible for *some* geological formations we see today, they do not think that *most* of the geological formations we see today were formed by catastrophes. After all, not many catastrophes that form geological structures occur today, and when they do, they are isolated to certain regions of the planet. Since the uniformitarian geologist wants to understand the entire earth's geological formations based on what is happening today, catastrophes just won't do. Thus, other processes must be examined.

It is hard to point to an example of sedimentary *rock* forming today by means other than catastrophes, but it is very easy to point to examples of sediments *being deposited* today. For example, geologists have studied the deltas of rivers and have shown that each year, the depth of the sediment in the delta has increased. After all, rivers are constantly depositing sediment in their deltas. As time goes on, then, the sediments will get thicker and thicker. The same basic observation can be made in today's oceans. Geologists have analyzed mud being deposited on the bottom of the oceans. As time has gone on, the thickness of the mud has increased. The speed at which geologists have observed this mud accumulating varies enormously on the conditions under which it is deposited, but the average rate is rather slow. In addition, we can even see that the sediments are often deposited in layers, just like the strata we see in sedimentary rock.

Not only do we see sediments being deposited by rivers and settling out of oceans, we also see water evaporating, leaving behind accumulations of sediments. One excellent example of this is the Dead Sea, which lies on the border between Israel and Jordan. Because of the weather in that region of the world, the water from the Dead Sea evaporates very quickly (at a rate of about 120 inches per year). In fact, the Dead Sea is shrinking because water is evaporating from it faster than water is being added to it by rain and rivers. The water in the Dead Sea is full of sediments (mostly salt sediments), and as the water evaporates, those sediments accumulate. As a result, there are large accumulations of salt sediments that form a "ring" around the Dead Sea, as you can see from Figure 7.7.

FIGURE 7.7
The "Salt Ring" Around the Dead Sea

Photo © Marta Mirecka
Agency: Shutterstock.com

Observations such as these and countless others have led uniformitarian geologists to think that the sediments making up the sedimentary rock we see today were, in fact, laid down by the same kinds of processes. For example, uniformitarian geologists think that the strata in the Grand Canyon were (with the possible exception of one layer) all laid down with the aid of water. In most cases, uniformitarians believe that these rocks are the result of sediments being slowly deposited by large bodies of water that advanced and retreated across North America.

In the uniformitarian framework, Arizona was once (at least partially) covered by a body of water, like an ocean. As time went on, sediments accumulated at the bottom or near the shore of that ocean. After a long time of sediment accumulation, the ocean retreated due to several factors, and the layer of sediment remained. That layer of sediment hardened into sedimentary rock and was subject to weathering and erosion. That's how one layer of sedimentary rock formed. Eventually, the ocean advanced again and once again (at least partially) covered Arizona, and the layer of sedimentary rock formed before became the bottom of the ocean. Once again, sediments began to be deposited on the ocean floor or near the ocean shore; thus, sediments were deposited on top of that original layer of sedimentary rock. Eventually, the ocean retreated again, and the whole process was repeated over and over again.

A given layer of sedimentary rock in the Grand Canyon, according to uniformitarians, represents a time when that part of Arizona was covered by a body of water. The sediment that accumulated during that time period later solidified (most likely when the body of water retreated), and the result was a new layer of sedimentary rock. Thus, as you look at the many layers of sedimentary rock in the Grand Canyon, what you are really observing is the slow accumulation of sediment at the bottom of a body of water, a retreat of that body of water, a time period where there was no body of water, and then the formation of another body of water to start the process again. Since these bodies of water changed, disappeared, and reformed because of differing conditions, the sediments they deposited on Arizona were different in composition. This explains why there are so many different kinds of rocks in the strata of the Grand Canyon.

The thing you have to remember about this view of geology is that it depends on enormous amounts of time. The sedimentation rates we observe today indicate that sediments are deposited very slowly. Although rates vary significantly, the sedimentation that has been observed today indicates it would probably take more than a thousand years to form a 1-foot-thick layer of sediment. Thus, the sediments deposited over Arizona, from the uniformitarian point of view, must have taken thousands or millions of years to be deposited. Also, uniformitarians generally assume that the time it took to deposit the sediments is actually smaller than the time between deposits. In other words, it might have taken a few million years for a layer of sediment to be deposited while the a body of water covered Arizona, but once that body of water was gone, the sediments were probably exposed for as much as 100 million years before another body of water covered Arizona again.

In this framework, it is easy to see how the Great Unconformity was formed as well. After all, since uniformitarians believe that a great amount of time passes between the formation of each layer of sedimentary rock, there are many things that can happen after one layer of rock is formed and before another is laid down. Suppose, for example, that after several layers of rock had been formed, an earthquake occurred, shifting the land in the Arizona area. All the rocks that had been laid down in nice, horizontal layers by the slow deposition of sediments would have been tilted one way or the other by the earthquake. As time went on, erosion probably smoothed out any edges exposed as the result of the tilting. Then, when the ocean advanced across Arizona again and began depositing sediment, the sediment would be deposited horizontally, even though the strata below the ocean had been tilted.

Is it reasonable to think that Arizona was once covered by a body of water? Of course it is.
We see the ocean level rise and fall today based on different weather factors on the earth. It is
possible, therefore, that the ocean level was much higher in the past, possibly high enough to cover all
or part of Arizona. In addition, climate conditions in a given region can change dramatically. Thus,
even though Arizona is much like a desert now, it might not always have been that way. It could very
well have been covered by the ocean or some other body of water at one time.

Once the rocks in the Grand Canyon had formed, something had to happen in order to cut that
incredible canyon out of those rocks. Uniformitarians believe that the river we now see running
through the bottom of the canyon (the Colorado River) could have done just that, given enough time.
Remember, Experiment 6.5 showed you that running water can cut gorges in sediment. In the
uniformitarian view, the Colorado River began slowly eroding the rocks of the Grand Canyon about 6
million years ago. This began cutting a gorge into the rocks. The erosion of the river was then
enhanced as earthquake-like motions caused the rocks in that area to rise. These two processes plus 6
million years ended up forming the gorgeous canyon we see today.

Now, given this view of how the strata in the Grand Canyon were formed, it becomes very
obvious why you only find certain fossils in certain layers of rock. Since uniformitarians believe that
each layer of rock was laid down one at a time, the Principle of Superposition applies to these rock
layers. In other words, the lower the rock layer, the longer ago those sediments were deposited. The
fact that paleontologists can only find algae and other such organisms below the Great Unconformity is
an indication that only those kinds of organisms lived in the oceans of Arizona back during that time in
earth's ancient history. The fact that you can find trilobites in many layers of the Grand Canyon above
the Great Unconformity is simply due to the fact that trilobites lived in the waters of Arizona during
the time those strata were deposited. However, since trilobite fossils cannot be found below the Great
Unconformity, there must not have been any trilobites living during the period when those sediments
were deposited.

In the end, then, each layer of rock in a geological formation is, according to uniformitarians, a
record from a certain period in earth's history. Usually, that period is 10 to a few hundred million
years. If you find fossils in a layer, you know those creatures lived during that time period in earth's
past. If you consistently do not find fossils of a creature in a layer, it might mean that the creature did
not live during that time period.

ON YOUR OWN

7.7 Use the uniformitarian view to arrange the organisms in Figure 7.6 according to how long ago
they lived. Start with the organism that lived during the earliest times in Arizona's past and end with
the creature that lived in the most recent part of Arizona's past.

Geology and Paleontology From the Catastrophist Perspective

The catastrophist starts with a completely different point of view from the uniformitarian.
While the uniformitarian believes that essentially the same processes we observe today are responsible
for forming most of the geological features of the earth, catastrophists believe that a good fraction of
the geology we see today is the result of processes that occurred once in earth's past and will not be

repeated. This is, obviously, a huge difference in viewpoint. This huge difference in viewpoint usually results in a huge difference in what is concluded from the geological and fossil records.

Many catastrophists refer to the Bible's account of the creation of the world as well as its account of the worldwide flood to explain a good fraction of the geological record. While there is still a lot of vigorous debate among catastrophists (as there is among uniformitarians) as to the precise interpretation of the geological record, many catastrophists think the layers of rock below the Great Unconformity were formed when God first created the earth. The igneous and metamorphic rocks that lie below the Great Unconformity are assumed to have been formed as a part of the initial creation of the earth (the first day of creation as recorded in the Bible). Most of the sedimentary rock strata below the Great Unconformity are also assumed to have been formed during Creation week, but not before the third day, which is when the Bible says the oceans and dry land were formed. As that happened, there would have obviously been a lot of erosion and deposition as well as earthquake-like movements. This would have formed sediment layers very quickly.

From many catastrophists' point of view, there probably wasn't a lot of geologically important activity between the end of Creation week and the worldwide flood. There were, most likely, a few volcanic eruptions and small floods that covered only certain regions of the earth. Those catastrophes (called "local" catastrophes) might well have produced some of the strata that lie below the Great Unconformity. Nevertheless, compared to the geological violence of Creation week and the worldwide flood, these catastrophes were small and would have therefore contributed only a little to the geological features below the Great Unconformity.

The layers of rock above the Great Unconformity are assumed by catastrophists to have been formed during and after the worldwide flood. Before the Flood, or perhaps as a part of its early stages, the layers of rock that had already been formed could have been tilted as the result of earthquakes. The surface could then have been eroded by the enormous amounts of wind, rain, and rushing water that began to form the Flood. The majority of the strata above the Great Unconformity could have then been deposited by the floodwaters themselves.

Now catastrophists do not believe the worldwide flood caused a nice, calm ocean to cover the earth. Think about it for a moment. According to the Bible, God opened the "fountains of the great deep" and the "floodgates of the sky" (Genesis 7:11) in order to create the Flood. This tells us that underground water shot up out of the ground (and the bottom of the ocean) to begin covering the earth, and a fierce rain fell for forty days and forty nights (Genesis 7:12). Since the Bible says that even the tallest mountain of the earth was covered (Genesis 7:19), there was obviously a *lot* of water released from underground and from the floodgates of the sky. This would have resulted in a *violent* surge of water. According to catastrophists, then, the Flood covered the whole earth, but not in a gentle sea! The earth was covered in surging, rushing water that probably was composed of violently shifting currents.

These violently shifting currents would, according to catastrophists, cause huge changes in the depth, speed, and direction of the floodwaters as they moved. When the waters were deep and advancing, that's when one kind of sediment was deposited, forming one type of rock layer. As the waters settled down a bit and became more gentle, another kind of sediment would form, forming another type of rock layer. When the Flood waters were shallow and retreating, another kind of rock layer could be formed. In the end, then, the different rock layers you see above the Great Unconformity were laid down during different stages of the Flood, as the floodwaters changed depth, direction, and speed.

After the floodwaters retreated from the land and the rocks of the Grand Canyon were formed, catastrophists believe that another catastrophe actually cut the canyon out, exposing the rocks and forming the amazing view we see today. Thus, catastrophists and uniformitarians believe that the Grand Canyon was cut through the rocks after they formed. The difference is that catastrophists believe the canyon was cut very quickly as a result of a catastrophe like a local flood, while uniformitarians rely on slow erosion caused by the Colorado River. Catastrophists also believe that some of the very top layers of rock (such as the igneous rock formed as a result of volcanic activity) were formed after the Flood, as a result of smaller catastrophes.

Is it reasonable to believe in this kind of framework for the formation of geological structures? Of course it is. You have already seen how the scientific method shows the Bible to be an excellent source of history. Thus, it is reasonable to believe in the Creation week as reported by such an excellent source of history. You have also already seen that there is evidence from outside the Bible that a global flood did, in fact, occur. Using these historical events to explain geology, therefore, is reasonable, as long as it is consistent with the data.

Does it make sense that so many different types of sediment could have been deposited by a worldwide flood in so many layers at such thicknesses as what we see in the Grand Canyon? Of course. After all, we know that most sedimentary rock is laid down by water. We also know that the speed at which water flows affects the erosion it causes. The violent, rushing waters of the Flood could have easily eroded enormous amounts of sediment that were later deposited during different stages of the Flood. Variations in depth, direction, and speed of the floodwaters could easily be responsible for the different kinds of sediment that composed the Grand Canyon. In addition, we have actually seen catastrophes form large sections of sedimentary rock, complete with strata. You will learn more about such geological formations in the next module.

Using the catastrophism viewpoint I just discussed as a reference, then, you can also see why different fossils appear in different layers. There are few fossils below the Great Unconformity because those rocks were formed during Creation week and afterwards. Thus, there was little to fossilize. The strata above the Great Unconformity contain many more fossils because there were plenty of creatures that could be fossilized by the time of the Flood. In fact, since the Flood killed all air-breathing animals but those on the ark, there would be an ample supply of dead things to fossilize! Also, since the Flood waters rose in different places at different times, they caught different creatures at different stages in the Flood. In addition, since the sediment was laid down based on the depth, direction, and speed of the floodwaters, the creatures being fossilized in any given layer would have, most likely, been caught in the floodwaters in a given region.

In the catastrophist point of view I discussed, then, the different layers of rock do, to some extent, represent different times in earth's history. The deepest rocks are the result of Creation week as well as some local catastrophes that occurred between Creation week and the Flood. They therefore represent the earliest parts of earth's history. Most of the remaining rocks are the result of the worldwide flood and thus represent that portion of earth's history. Some of the topmost rocks are the result of recent local catastrophes and thus represent the very recent part of earth's past.

However, according to catastrophists, the fact that different fossils can be found in different layers is not because each layer of rock represents a different part of earth's history. Instead, catastrophists believe that the rocks of Creation week will have few fossils in them because of the very nature of Creation week. The rocks formed during the Flood, however, will be teeming with fossils.

In this framework, the different fossils in different strata are simply an indication that the Flood trapped and fossilized different creatures at different stages of the Flood, depending on the depth, direction, and speed of the floodwaters.

Before I end this section, I want to make it clear that the "catastrophist view" I presented here is not the only view held by catastrophists. For example, while many catastrophists think the evidence indicates that the rocks below the Great Unconformity were formed during Creation week, not all catastrophists concur. Some think, for example, that while the Great Unconformity marks the point at which the rising ocean reached Arizona, some (if not many) of the rock layers below the Great Unconformity were formed by the geological activity and rains that began the Flood. As a result, they think that at least some of those rocks were formed well after Creation week. It is not surprising that there are differences among catastrophists when it comes to such details, as people weigh and interpret evidence in different ways. Uniformitarians are also often divided when it comes to how this rock layer formed or how that geological structure was produced, so it is not surprising that catastrophists are as well.

ON YOUR OWN

7.8 Suppose a paleontologist were to find fossils of trilobites in a layer of Grand Canyon rock below the Great Unconformity. Using the catastrophist framework, was the rock most likely formed during Creation week or during a local catastrophe between Creation week and the Flood?

Uniformitarianism or Catastrophism: Which View Is Correct?

You have just been given a very sketchy introduction to both the uniformitarian and catastrophist view of geology. They are very different, so either one or both of them is wrong. Assuming one is correct, which one is it? Well, no one knows for sure. Remember, the nature of science is that it cannot prove anything. Thus, we cannot say for sure that one is right and one is wrong. Even though we cannot say *for sure* which is right and which is wrong, we can examine the data and see which viewpoint is consistent with the data and which is not. That's what I want to do in the next module. I want to look at each view and see how it stands up to the relevant data.

Before I leave this module, however, I want to make one very important point about catastrophism and uniformitarianism. You might think that the hypothesis of catastrophism is not as testable as the hypothesis of uniformitarianism. After all, uniformitarians believe that we can explain most of the geological and fossil records in terms of processes we see today. Thus, we can test some of the ideas of the uniformitarian view by observing how sedimentation and fossilization occur today. Catastrophism, on the other hand, refers to events that took place once in history and will not be repeated. Thus, we cannot test the catastrophist view because we have nothing to observe today.

This idea is a common misconception. First of all, although we will never be able to observe the worldwide flood, we can observe smaller catastrophes that occur around the world. If we see how those catastrophes have affected the geological record, we can predict what a much greater catastrophe might have done. Indeed, some great advances in catastrophic geology have occurred as the result of detailed studies of Mount Saint Helens' eruption in 1980 and hurricanes such as Donna in 1960. You will learn more about that in the next module.

Well, you might say, although we can have *some idea* of what a global flood would do to the geological record, we still must include some speculation. A local flood might allow you to observe changes in the local geology, but you still must speculate on how those changes would be amplified by a global flood. We will never know that for sure, so there is an enormous amount of speculation involved. In uniformitarianism, there is no speculation needed. After all, we *see* those events occurring right now. Thus, uniformitarianism uses a much more direct approach.

Once again, that is a common misconception. Although it is true that uniformitarians can directly view the processes they think formed all the geology we see today, they also have to speculate. You see, using all the history at our disposal, we can only see how those processes have worked for, at most, a few thousand years. Uniformitarians, however, require hundreds of millions of years in order for the processes we see today to form the geological and fossil records. Thus, uniformitarians must also speculate. They must speculate on how these processes are affected by the time span of hundreds of millions of years.

In the end, then, both uniformitarians and catastrophists must speculate. They must speculate on different things, but they both do it. Neither framework is any more "scientific" than the other. Each relies on many assumptions and even more speculation. This is one of the reasons we cannot yet say which one is correct. Since they both involve a large degree of speculation, it is difficult to come up with hard data that clearly rule out one or both of the views.

ON YOUR OWN

7.9 As you can see from the previous section, catastrophism (at least the kind that I discuss in this course) relies heavily on the Bible. Some would say, therefore, that catastrophism requires quite a bit of faith, since a catastrophist must believe in the events described in the Bible. It is important to point out that uniformitarians must exercise a bit of faith as well. List an article of faith in which a uniformitarian must believe. Indicate (based on your own bias) which view (catastrophism or uniformitarianism) requires the most faith.

7.10 Consider the explanations given by uniformitarians and catastrophists regarding why the fossils found in different strata are so different. Which one appeals more to you? Why?

ANSWERS TO THE "ON YOUR OWN" PROBLEMS

7.1 <u>A mold can form without a cast, but a cast cannot form without a mold</u>. Remember, the mold is made first, when the creature's remains disintegrate and the surrounding rocks retain the original shape. After the mold is formed, a cast can be formed when new sediment fills the mold. Thus, a mold can form, and if no sediment fills the mold, a cast will never form. A cast must have a mold, however, so no cast will form unless a mold forms first.

7.2 <u>Petrifaction will not occur without a good supply of mineral-laden water</u>. Since wood was petrified in Arizona, there must have been a lot of water in Arizona at one time.

7.3 <u>There is no real answer to this question, since it depends on the results of your experiment</u>. In general, however, a minimum amount of weight is needed to make a print. After that, the more weight you add, the more detail you find in the print. Eventually, however, too much weight crushes the leaf too much, reducing the detail once again.

7.4 <u>An insect in amber is like a mold because the amber surrounds the insect and then the insect begins to decay</u>. As a result, there is an insect-shaped hole in the amber, with some organic material still inside. The insect-shaped hole can be thought of as a mold.

7.5 As I mentioned, you can never be sure an animal is extinct. However, the easier an animal is to find, the less likely it could escape the notice of scientists. Thus, easy-to-find animals (like mammoths) thought to be extinct are more likely to actually be extinct than hard-to-find mammals. A 2-inch wasp would be hard to find. Since there is so much ocean in the world, and so little of it has been explored, you could also imagine a fish (even a large one) escaping notice for a long time. However, a 3-foot mammal would be rather easy to spot, especially since there is so little land on the world compared to ocean. Thus, <u>of the three mentioned, the mammal is probably the most likely to actually be extinct</u>.

7.6 Remember, the strata below the Great Unconformity do not contain animal fossils. They contain only the remains of algae and bacteria. <u>You need to ask the geologist whether or not animal fossils were found in that layer of rock. If the answer is yes, you know it comes from above the Great Unconformity. If the answer is no, you know it comes from below the Great Unconformity</u>.

7.7 In the uniformitarian view, the Principle of Superposition applies. In other words, the deeper the layer, the older it is. Thus, the fossils found at the bottom are the oldest, and the fossils found at the top are the youngest. This means that the order of fossils from oldest to youngest is: <u>algae, trilobites and worms, plated fish, amphibians and reptiles, and modern fish</u>. You really can't make the distinction between trilobites and worms, because they are both found in the layer right above the Great Unconformity and neither is found any lower. Thus, you have to say that they lived at the same time.

7.8 The reason catastrophists believe that there are few fossils below the Great Unconformity is because most of the layers were formed during Creation week, when there were few things to fossilize. However, if a local catastrophe were to have occurred between Creation and the Flood, then there would have been the chance that creatures such as trilobites would be fossilized. Thus, <u>the layer of rock was probably formed in a local catastrophe that happened between Creation week and the Flood</u>.

7.9 There are at least two articles of faith I can think of. You need only list one. <u>One thing that a uniformitarian must have faith in is that the Bible's account of the worldwide flood is NOT literally true</u>. After all, if there was a worldwide flood as reported by the Bible, it would have radically altered the geology of the earth in a single, non-repeatable event. That cannot fit into the uniformitarian view. I consider this a hard article of faith to believe. Since the Bible has been shown to be very historically accurate, it is hard to believe that the Flood either never happened or was some local event that was mischaracterized as a global one. Others have a different view, however. <u>Another article of faith for uniformitarians is that the earth is old enough to allow for the hundreds of millions of years they need for their view</u>. In my opinion, the most compelling scientific evidence indicates the earth is only thousands of years old. Thus, I find it very hard to believe in the millions of years required by the uniformitarians. Others, however, have a different view. Thus, I think the uniformitarian view requires the most faith, but others may differ with me on that point.

7.10 There is no right or wrong answer here. I want you to think about it deeply enough to write an answer, though. That will help you prepare for the next module.

"I'm not sure, but I think it's a fossil cast."

Cartoon by Speartoons

STUDY GUIDE FOR MODULE #7

1. Define the following terms:

a. Fossil
b. Petrifaction
c. Resin
d. Extinct

2. When a plant or animal dies, what is the most likely thing that will happen to its remains?

3. Which forms first: a fossil mold or a fossil cast?

4. Describe the process of a cast forming, indicating when the mold has formed and when the cast has formed.

5. What is required in order for petrifaction to occur?

6. Why does petrifaction usually produce fossils with more information than fossil casts?

7. Can you learn much about the thickness of an organism from carbonized remains?

8. What type of organism is most likely to leave carbonized remains?

9. What is so nice about fossils that have been encased in amber or ice?

10. What are the four general features of the fossil record?

11. What kinds of creatures make up the vast majority of the fossil record?

12. Approximately how many species of plants and animals have gone extinct in the last 400 years: a hundred, a thousand, ten thousand, or a hundred thousand?

13. What is a trilobite? Are trilobites extinct?

14. What is a placoderm? Are placoderms extinct?

15. What is the uniformitarian explanation for how most sedimentary rocks formed?

16. What is the catastrophist explanation for how most sedimentary rocks formed?

17. What is the uniformitarian explanation for why different fossils are found in different strata?

18. What is the catastrophist explanation for why different fossils are found in different strata?

19. What major speculation must uniformitarians make when studying geology?

20. What major speculation must catastrophists make when studying geology?

MODULE #8: Uniformitarianism and Catastrophism

Introduction

Now that you have learned the basics of uniformitarianism and catastrophism, I want to spend some time contrasting these two views of earth's history. The contrast will be very interesting, because you will see how these two hypotheses lead to dramatically different views of what happened in earth's past. Hopefully, I will be as even-handed as possible, but please remember that *all* scientists are biased. It is impossible to be otherwise. Thus, I am biased as well. In my scientific opinion, the data leans heavily in favor of catastrophism. So I am sure my discussion will as well! Please remember that as you read.

Uniformitarianism and the Geological Record

Remember what uniformitarians believe about the strata we see in the geological record? They believe that each one represents a certain period of time in earth's past. The deeper layers represent time periods farther back in earth's past, whereas the layers near the top represent more recent periods in earth's past. From a uniformitarian point of view, then, it would be very useful to know *which* layers represent *which* time period.

How do uniformitarians do this? Well, the first thing you have to realize is that uniformitarians do not believe that sedimentary rock formed in *all* regions of the earth during *all* time periods. After all, in order for sedimentary rock to be formed, sediments must be deposited. In order for sediments to be deposited, there must be some agent to do the depositing. Typically, that agent is water, but it also could be wind. Thus, for sedimentary rock to form in a certain region, there must be water or the right kind of wind around to deposit sediments to begin with. Well, those conditions are not going to exist in *all* regions of the world during *all* time periods.

Thus, when uniformitarians look at the rock layers in a given part of the world, they do not expect to find a layer of rock for each time period in earth's past. Instead, they expect to find some layers in some regions of the world and other layers in other regions of the world. How do they determine which layers belong to which time period? They use **index fossils**.

Index fossils – Fossils that are assumed to represent a certain period in earth's past

Remember, there are many fossils of organisms that are now extinct. Since uniformitarians believe that each layer of rock represents a given time period, the fossils in any given layer are of organisms that lived during the time period during which the layer was deposited. Well, if you find a certain kind of fossil in one layer of rock that does not appear in higher or lower layers of rock, *that* fossil can be related to *that* layer of rock and therefore *that* time in earth's past. As a result, if a uniformitarian is looking at rock strata from different parts of the world, he can assume that any rock layer containing that particular kind of fossil was laid down at the same time as any other layer of rock containing that particular kind of fossil.

In the end, then, uniformitarian geologists have certain index fossils they think indicate certain times in earth's past. If a paleontologist finds an index fossil in a certain layer of rock, that tells the geologists *what time period* the layer of rock represents. Now this is a difficult concept, so if you are having trouble understanding it, don't worry. I want you to perform a simple "experiment" to help you see what I mean.

"EXPERIMENT" 8.1
A Simulation of Using Index Fossils to Order Rock Layers

Supplies:

- 18 index cards (The size is irrelevant, as is the presence or absence of lines.)
- A parent or someone else to write on the cards and hold the key

Introduction: Uniformitarians use index fossils in order to determine when a particular layer of rock was laid down. This activity will help you understand how they do that.

Procedure:

1. Your parent/teacher needs to set up this experiment. She needs to draw a symbol on each index card. Six symbols should be used: a star, a circle, a square, a triangle, a straight line, and an "X." Each card should have only one symbol on it. Thus, your parent/teacher needs to draw a star on three index cards, a circle on three other index cards, etc. In the end, she will have three index cards with a star on each, three index cards with a circle on each, three index cards with a square on each, and so on.

2. Now your parent/teacher needs to put these cards in three piles. She should do this while you are somewhere else, so you do not see the way your parent makes the piles. Each pile needs to have one card with each symbol on it. Thus, each pile will have a card with a star, a card with a circle, a card with a square, and so on. The *order* in which these symbols appear in each pile must be the same. For example, your parent/teacher can put the card with the star on the bottom of the pile, the card with the circle next, the card with the square next, the card with the triangle next, the card with the line next, and the card with the "X" on top. If the first pile has those cards in that order, then *each of the other piles must have those cards in the same order*.

3. Once that is done, your parent/teacher needs to write down the order in which the symbols appear in the piles and hide that list from you.

4. Now your parent/teacher needs to remove two cards from each pile. She should remove the card with the star and the card with the "X" from one pile, the card with the square and the card with the line from the next pile, and the card with the circle and the card with the triangle from the last pile. Your parent/teacher *should not* change the order of the cards that remain; she should just remove two cards from each pile. In the end, there should be three piles, each of which has four cards.

5. Now it's your turn. You need to look at the three piles of cards and use them to determine the order in which your parent originally laid down all six cards. Remember, each pile is missing two cards, so you are missing two symbols in each pile. Nevertheless, the cards that remain are still in the same order in which they were laid down. There are just two cards missing from each pile. Using all three piles, however, you should be able to reconstruct the order in which the six original cards were laid down.

6. Write down your reconstruction and check with your parent to see if you are correct.

Did you get the reconstruction right? It really doesn't matter. What's important is that you thought through the process. This gives you an idea of how uniformitarians interpret the fossil record. When they look at the strata in any region of the earth, they see several layers and assume each layer represents a certain period of time in earth's history. They know, however, that at any given place, there is not necessarily a layer from *each* period of earth's history. Thus, much like each pile in your experiment was missing a couple of cards, a given location's rock record can be missing some layers of rock. However, just like you were able to reconstruct the order in which the cards were laid down by your parent, uniformitarian geologists think they can reconstruct the order in which the rocks were laid down by comparing different geological formations from different regions of the earth.

How do they do that? Well, they do it the same way you reconstructed the order of the cards in your experiment. Remember, each card had a symbol on it. According to uniformitarian geologists, each layer of rock contains index fossils that indicate what time in earth's past the rock was formed. Thus, just like you used the symbols on the cards to determine the order in which the cards were originally laid down, uniformitarian geologists use the index fossils in each layer to determine the order in which the rock layers were laid down.

Because this is such an important point, and because you still might be a bit confused, I want to explain this again with a figure.

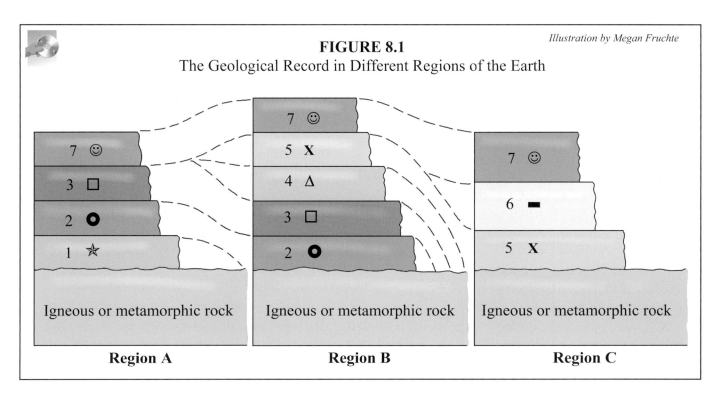

FIGURE 8.1
The Geological Record in Different Regions of the Earth

Illustration by Megan Fruchte

In this figure, regions "A," "B," and "C" represent different regions on the earth. In each region, a geologist finds sedimentary rock strata sitting on top of igneous or metamorphic rock. The sedimentary rock layers all have fossils in them. The index fossils they contain are represented by the symbols in each layer. Thus, the star in the bottom layer of region "A" represents the type of index fossils found in that layer. If two layers have the same symbols, that means they have the same index fossils, which means the uniformitarian believes they were laid down during the same time period in earth's past.

Suppose you were a uniformitarian geologist. How would you interpret the geological records in these three regions of the earth? Well, first you would look for layers that had the same index fossils. The layer that is second to the bottom in region "A" and the layer at the bottom of region "B," for example, both have circles in them. This means they contain the same index fossils. Thus, a uniformitarian geologist would assume that these two layers represent the *same time period* in earth's past. Why are there no layers with circles in region "C"? Well, the uniformitarian would assume that during this time period in earth's past, the conditions were not right for the formation of sedimentary rock in region "C." Either that, or sedimentary rocks were laid down in region "C" during that time frame, but they eroded away before more rocks could be laid on top of them. As a result, there are no layers of rock representing that time period in region "C."

Since the two layers in regions "A" and "B" have the same index fossils (represented by circles in the figure), they are assumed to represent the same time period in earth's past. Thus, they should be labeled the same. I labeled them with a "2." Why? Well, in region "A," there is a layer *below* the layer with the circle. What does the Principle of Superposition tell us? It tells us that the older rocks are lower than the younger rocks. Thus, the layer *under* the layer with circles must be *older* than the layers with the circles. I therefore labeled *that* layer as "1" and the layers with the circles as "2." According to a uniformitarian, then, the layer labeled "1" is the oldest layer of rock, while the layer labeled "2" is a bit younger. Why is there no layer "1" in regions "B" and "C"? Once again, the uniformitarian would say that either the conditions weren't right for sedimentary rock to be laid down in regions "B" and "C" during that time period, or the rock eroded away after it was laid down.

Using this same kind of reasoning, the uniformitarian geologist can determine the order in which each layer in regions "A" through "C" was laid down. Think about how you determined the order in which the cards were laid down in your experiment. You matched the symbols on the cards to determine which cards were equivalent. In the same way, a uniformitarian matches rock layers based on the index fossils found in each layer. After matching the symbols, you used the fact that the cards were laid down one at a time. Thus, if one card was *under* another card, you knew that it was laid down *before* the other card. In the same way, a uniformitarian geologist assumes that the Principle of Superposition works for sedimentary rock layers. Thus, the geologist assumes that if one layer is *under* another, it is the *older* layer.

In the end, then, the uniformitarian geologist can use the same reasoning you used in your experiment to determine the order in which all the layers in Figure 8.1 were laid down. By matching the index fossils from layer to layer, the geologist assumes that he or she can identify which layer in each region of the earth represents the same time period as a layer in another region of the earth. In the figure, for example, the top layer of each region has the same index fossils (represented by smiley faces). Thus, they all represent the same time period in earth's past. Also, the geologist uses the Principle of Superposition to determine which layer was laid down first, which was laid down second, etc. Once again, think about the top layer in the figure. Since it is on the top in each region of the earth, it must represent the most recent time period in earth's past.

Using this kind of reasoning, the uniformitarian can order each layer in terms of when it was laid down in earth's past. That's what the numbers in the figure represent. The layers with the low numbers were laid down first, followed by the layers with the larger numbers. Thus, in this figure, the lower the number of the layer, the *older* the layer. If a certain number does not appear in a region, it means that either the conditions were not right for forming sedimentary rock in that region of the earth at that time, or the rock that was laid down in that region eroded away. The dashed lines, then, connect the layers in one region of the earth with the corresponding layers in another region, if those layers exist.

If the uniformitarian assumptions are correct, you can use this kind of reasoning to order all the sedimentary rock layers of the earth in terms of when they were laid down. When you do that, you notice a pattern. It seems that the kind of creatures that lived at different times in earth's past were quite different. The figure below illustrates what I mean.

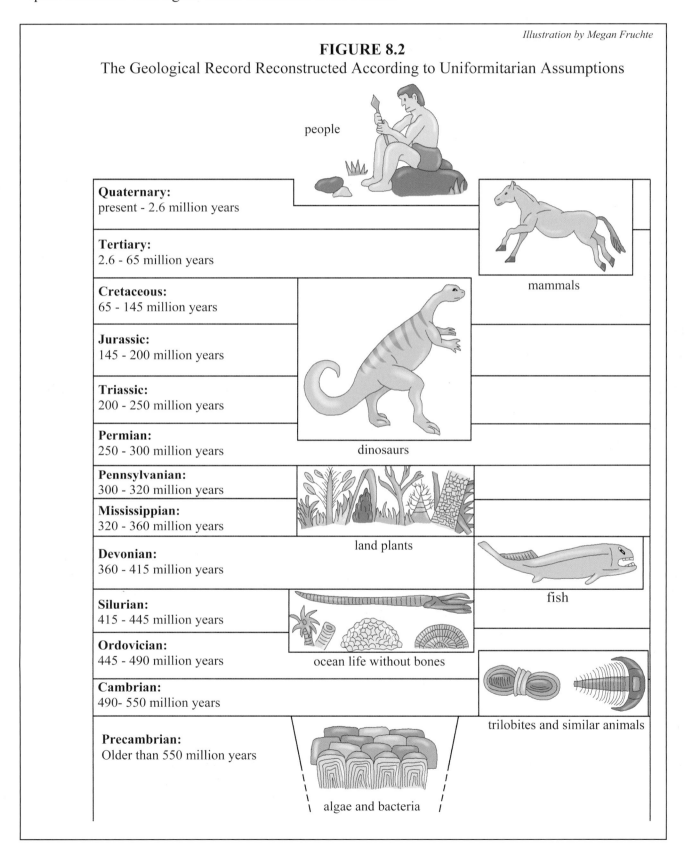

Illustration by Megan Fruchte

FIGURE 8.2
The Geological Record Reconstructed According to Uniformitarian Assumptions

people

Quaternary:
present - 2.6 million years

Tertiary:
2.6 - 65 million years

mammals

Cretaceous:
65 - 145 million years

Jurassic:
145 - 200 million years

Triassic:
200 - 250 million years

Permian:
250 - 300 million years

dinosaurs

Pennsylvanian:
300 - 320 million years

Mississippian:
320 - 360 million years

land plants

Devonian:
360 - 415 million years

fish

Silurian:
415 - 445 million years

Ordovician:
445 - 490 million years

ocean life without bones

Cambrian:
490- 550 million years

trilobites and similar animals

Precambrian:
Older than 550 million years

algae and bacteria

A drawing like the one shown in Figure 8.2 is typically referred to as a **geological column**.

Geological column – A theoretical picture in which layers of rock from around the world are
meshed together into a single, unbroken record of earth's past

Although this is rarely pointed out in most geology textbooks (even the ones written at the college
level), it is *very* important that you understand that the geological column is an abstract concept. You
cannot go anywhere on earth and find all the layers of the geological column complete with their index
fossils. This is a theoretical picture. It assumes that each layer of rock represents a period in earth's
past, and it further assumes that the index fossils found in a given layer of rock are, in fact, accurate
indicators of *which* time period the rock was formed. If either of these assumptions is wrong, the
geological column is probably not accurate.

In the figure, each rectangle represents a layer of rock, and each layer has layers *within* it, so a
more detailed geological column would have many more rectangles. According to uniformitarian
assumptions, each layer represents a time period in earth's past. The time period covered by a
collection of layers is usually referred to as an **era**, and each is given a name, as listed in the figure.
While geological columns can be more or less detailed, the one given in the figure includes what most
uniformitarian geologists consider the "major" eras of the geological column.

Notice that each layer in the figure also has a range of years associated with it. These years
represent how long ago uniformitarian geologists assume these layers were laid down. The
Precambrian layer of rock, for example, is assumed to have been laid down more than 550 million
years ago, while the Cambrian layer right above it was laid down during a time period that started 550
million years ago and ended 490 million years ago. How do uniformitarian geologists get these ages?
Well, that's a complicated process to explain. In addition to uniformitarian assumptions, it relies
heavily on radiometric dating, which you will learn more about in physical science. For right now,
you just need to know that the dates are determined by a process more complicated than the process
used to determine the order of the layers, and it relies heavily on radiometric dating, a process whose
reliability is controversial.

Now notice in the figure what kinds of plant and animal fossils are found in the different layers
of rock. In Precambrian rock, for example, fossils of only algae, bacteria, and other "simple" forms of
life exist. In Cambrian rock and the lower layers of Ordovician rock, however, fossil trilobites are
found. In the upper parts of Ordovician rock and in Silurian rock, ocean-dwelling creatures with no
backbones (a creature without a backbone is called an "invertebrate") are found. As you get into rocks
that are younger (according to the geological column), you eventually find fossils of fish. Younger
rocks reveal fossils of plants, then dinosaurs, and then mammals. Finally, the youngest rocks
(Quaternary rocks) contain fossils of human beings. It is important to note that although trilobites are
shown only in Cambrian and Ordovician layers in the figure, they are actually found in rock layers all
the way up to the Permian era. However, in Cambrian and lower Ordovician layers, they are the most
common fossil you find (aside from hard-shelled organisms such as clams, of course).

There is one other important thing to note about Figure 8.2: we know it is wrong to some
extent. The geological column has been represented this way for many, many years, and so it has
become an icon in geology. However, over the years, fossil evidence has made it clear that the lower
layers of the geological column are not an accurate representation of earth's history. That's because
over time, paleontologists have found fossils in Cambrian rock that, according to the geological

column, should not exist in rock older than Ordovician or Silurian rock. In other words, the science of geology has changed over time, but the geological column as presented in most textbooks has not. We now know that life forms uniformitarian geologists once thought did not exist until 415 to 445 million years ago actually existed more than 500 million years ago, according to uniformitarian time scales. As a result, a more accurate geological column would have trilobites and similar animals, as well as ocean life without bones, all together in Cambrian, Ordovician, and Silurian rock. Unfortunately, most textbooks do not present such an accurate picture.

ON YOUR OWN

8.1 What are the two major assumptions that uniformitarian geologists use in constructing the geological column?

8.2 If either assumption listed in 8.1 is wrong, what can you conclude about the geological column?

8.3 In the previous module, you learned that the layers below the Great Unconformity in the Grand Canyon contain few fossils. The fossils found there are typically of algae and bacteria. What time period would a uniformitarian say those layers represent?

Uniformitarianism and Evolution

Now if you look once again at Figure 8.2, notice that according to the geological column, there seems to be a "progression" in the organisms that lived during earth's past. In the oldest rocks (Precambrian), we see only "simple" life forms such as algae and bacteria. In the younger rocks layers (like the Cambrian rocks, for example) there are more complicated life forms such as trilobites. In even younger rocks (Ordovician), there are more complicated ocean-dwelling creatures. Even younger rocks (Devonian) show fish, which are some of the most complicated ocean-dwelling animals. Eventually, fossils of plants, dinosaurs, and even mammals begin to appear as the rocks get younger and younger. Finally, in the youngest rock layers, we see fossils of human beings.

According to uniformitarians, this provides excellent evidence for the **Theory of Evolution**.

The Theory of Evolution – A theory stating that all life on this earth has one (or a few) common
ancestor(s) that existed a long time ago

Now what does this definition mean? Well, the Theory of Evolution states that long, long ago, there was only one (or a few) simple life form(s) on this planet. As that life form began to reproduce, certain differences appeared between the parent and some of the offspring. In human beings, for example, we know that two brown-haired parents can have a baby with blond hair. Thus, even though a child will have many things in common with his or her parents, there will also be differences between the parents and the child.

The Theory of Evolution states that as millions of years passed and the offspring of this simple life form continued to reproduce, and their offspring reproduced, and so on, these small differences between parent and offspring began to "pile up." As this went on, there were eventually so many differences that the offspring being produced looked nothing like the original life form that began this process. In this way, a "simple" life form gave rise to a more complicated life form. This happened over and over again as time went on, producing more and more complex organisms over earth's history.

For example, consider the case of a fish. Suppose a fish was born that had slightly longer fins than its parents and its siblings. This might make the fish able to swim faster than all its siblings. Thus, this fish could get food faster than its siblings. It also would be better able to swim away from other fish that were trying to eat it. As a result, this long fin would give the fish an advantage. That advantage would ensure the fish lived to reproduce. When the fish did reproduce, most likely, a few of its offspring would have long fins as well.

Now suppose that one of those offspring reproduced and one of *its* offspring had a bit more control over the end of its fin compared to all the other fish. Suppose it could open and close the end of the fin, almost like it was a hand. This would be an advantage for the fish, because it could dig in the sand at the bottom of the ocean for food.   When that fish reproduced and its offspring reproduced and so on and so on, the fin might continually change so as to start looking more and more like a leg or arm rather than a fin. Eventually, then, after millions and millions of years of reproduction with plenty of differences cropping up between parent and offspring, a fish with legs and arms might be produced. If, as time went on, this fish and its offspring kept reproducing, a fish with legs and arms and the ability to breathe air might eventually be born. At that point, the creature would no longer be a fish. Instead, the creature would be some other life form, perhaps a salamander or some other amphibian. The figure below shows how a uniformitarian might think this happened. Please note that all the drawings are based on fossils that have been found in the fossil record.

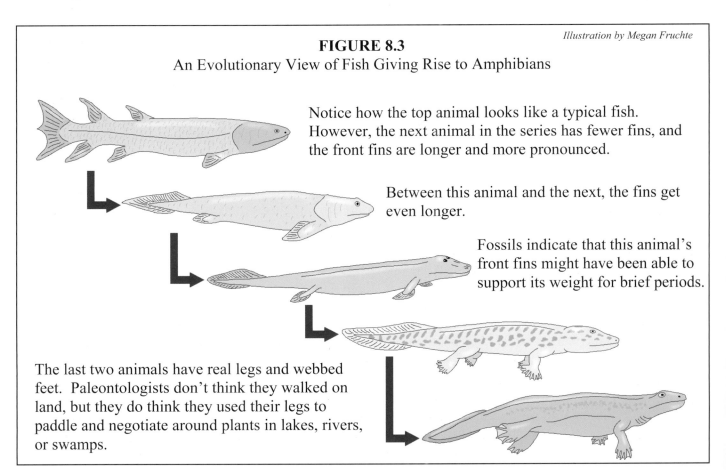

Illustration by Megan Fruchte

FIGURE 8.3
An Evolutionary View of Fish Giving Rise to Amphibians

Notice how the top animal looks like a typical fish. However, the next animal in the series has fewer fins, and the front fins are longer and more pronounced.

Between this animal and the next, the fins get even longer.

Fossils indicate that this animal's front fins might have been able to support its weight for brief periods.

The last two animals have real legs and webbed feet. Paleontologists don't think they walked on land, but they do think they used their legs to paddle and negotiate around plants in lakes, rivers, or swamps.

In the end, then, the Theory of Evolution states that starting with a single (or a few) life form(s) and progressing through hundreds of millions or perhaps billions of years of reproduction, the differences that occur between parent and offspring can "pile up" so as to make completely new life forms. If you look at the geological column in Figure 8.2, that's what the fossil record seems to indicate. After all, the oldest rocks contain only simple life forms, while the younger rocks contain more and more complicated life forms.

According to an evolutionist, then, the simple life forms you see in Precambrian rock began reproducing. As the differences between parents and children continued to pile up, the life forms began to change. Those changes piled up to such a degree that eventually, trilobites were formed. As a result, an evolutionist would say that over millions of years, bacteria and algae **evolved** into trilobites.

Continuing this line of reasoning, the creatures that lived in Cambrian times eventually evolved into the ocean-dwelling creatures with no bones that we see in the Ordovician and Silurian rocks. Those creatures eventually evolved into the fish we see in Devonian rock. The plants that lived in Devonian times eventually evolved into the land plants of the Mississippian and Pennsylvanian eras. Eventually, the fish in the oceans evolved into amphibians (like salamanders and frogs) and then into the dinosaurs and other reptiles you see in the Permian, Jurassic, Triassic, and Cretaceous eras. The creatures in those eras eventually evolved into the mammals of the Tertiary period, which eventually evolved into people. All the life forms we see today, then, are really just the descendants of a single (or a few) simple life form(s) that existed hundreds of millions or billions of years ago.

The geological column, then, seems to be a record of how this evolution occurred. You start with very simple life forms in the oldest rocks and you simply follow the fossils through to see how those life forms evolved into what we see today. Of course, you have to remember that the geological column itself is simply a theoretical construct. It doesn't actually exist anywhere. In fact, there is no place on earth you can go to see fossils in the order of ocean life without bones, fish, amphibians, reptiles, and mammals. Thus, the whole idea that life appeared on earth in that order is based on the geological column, which in turn is based on certain assumptions and a particular way of looking at the geological record. If the assumptions upon which it is based are not true, the Theory of Evolution is probably not true, either.

There is one other thing I must stress. I told you this in the last module but I need to remind you of it now. Remember, the fossil record looks very little like what is drawn in Figure 8.2. In fact, what you are looking at in Figure 8.2 constitutes a tiny, tiny fraction of the fossil record. The vast majority of the fossil record is composed of hard-shelled creatures like clams. Thus, what you are looking at here is a tiny, tiny subset of what has been preserved for us in the form of fossils.

In summary, then, following uniformitarian assumptions provide you with two major conclusions: First, uniformitarians believe they can construct a theoretical geological column that provides them with a chronological record of life on this earth. Even though such a record doesn't exist in any one place, given a few assumptions, earth's geological history can be "meshed" together to construct the chronological record. Second, uniformitarians believe that according to this record, life started out simple and gradually got more and more complex. Using the geological column as evidence, evolutionists believe that the great number of plants and animals we see today were formed from a single (or a few) simple life form(s) that existed hundreds of millions, if not billions, of years ago. That process is called evolution. You will learn *a lot* more about evolution in biology class.

ON YOUR OWN

8.4   Many students who first hear about the Theory of Evolution ask, "If evolution happened in the past, why don't we see one kind of life form evolving into another kind of life form today?" How would an evolutionist answer this question?

8.5   Since the geological column is only a theoretical construction, the Theory of Evolution would be better served by more direct evidence. If the Theory of Evolution is true, what kind of direct evidence for it would you expect to find in the fossil record?

Catastrophism and the Geological Record

Now that you have seen the way a uniformitarian interprets the geological record, it is time to see how a catastrophist interprets the same record. Now remember, the catastrophist believes that most of the geological record we see today was formed as the result of one or more catastrophes. The worldwide flood as described in the Bible (and confirmed by writings from many other cultures) is the biggest of these catastrophes and thus is responsible for a good fraction of the geological record. In addition to that catastrophe, however, other local catastrophes such as hurricanes or volcanic eruptions have produced some of the geological structures we see today.

The first thing you might ask a catastrophist is whether or not there is any evidence that geological structures can form in this way. Uniformitarians, after all, have some evidence for their view. We see sediments accumulating today that fit right in with the uniformitarian view. In addition, the nature of this sediment accumulation indicates that over time, the sediments could, indeed, form the kinds of rock we see in the geological record today. Thus, uniformitarians have some present evidence for their ideas about the past. Do catastrophists have any such evidence? Yes, they do, and the evidence is rather dramatic.

On May 18, 1980, an earthquake started in the southwestern part of the state of Washington. That earthquake caused a landslide that ripped the top off of one of the most beautiful mountains in the region: **Mount Saint Helens**. Geologists knew that Mount Saint Helens was a volcano, but it had been inactive since 1857. However, in early 1980, a column of magma began pushing up the inside of the mountain, causing the northern face of the mountain to bulge outward. When the top of the mountain was ripped away in the earthquake, that released the magma, and the volcano erupted. The eruption lasted from May 18 to October 18. It killed 57 people, severely damaged life in an area of about 70 square miles, and covered an even larger area with ash and debris. The total energy released in the explosion is estimated to be equivalent to the explosion of *430 million tons of TNT*, which is about the same as the energy released in the explosion of *33,000 atomic bombs*. During the main part of the eruption, the volcano was releasing energy at the rate of *one atomic bomb per second*. This energy release leveled entire forests and caused massive mudflows.

What were the geological results of this amazing sequence of events? Well, geologists have been studying the data for more than a generation, and they still don't completely understand it. However, there are a few rather amazing things we have learned. First and foremost, Mount Saint Helens has taught us that stratified sediments can be laid down in a matter of hours: not days, not years, not millions of years, not billions of years. Consider, for example, the photo shown in Figure 8.4.

FIGURE 8.4

Stratified Sediments That Formed in Less Than Five Hours (The geologist in the photo provides scale)

During the eruption, there were periods when huge volumes of steam were released. This ground-hugging steam, mixed with volcanic ash, formed a "river" of mud that moved across the ground at speeds greater than 100 miles per hour. As sediments were deposited by this "river," they formed layers, which you can clearly see in the photograph. If you look closely at the formation, you can see that the strata are of varying thickness. Some strata are reasonably thick, and others are very thin, as shown below.

FIGURE 8.5

A Close-Up of the Formation in Figure 8.4

Much like the photos shown in the previous module, then, these sediments were deposited in layers. Regular strata of different thickness, as well as laminae, are present.

So we see that the same kind of stratified formations uniformitarians assume take millions of years to form can, in the case of a catastrophe, form in a matter of hours. Stratified sediments are not the only kinds of geological formations that were formed rapidly as a result of the Mount Saint Helens eruption. Remember how uniformitarians assume the Grand Canyon was formed? Once the rocks of the Grand Canyon were formed, uniformitarians believe that the Colorado River began eroding those rocks. They estimate that this took approximately six million years.

While it is certainly conceivable that a river could slowly erode a canyon like the Grand Canyon over a period of millions of years, Experiment 6.5 demonstrated that the speed at which erosion takes place depends on the speed at which the eroding agent travels. In that experiment, you saw that a slowly flowing stream eroded a landscape slowly, while a quickly flowing stream eroded the landscape very quickly. In the eruption of Mount Saint Helens, there were many, many agents of erosion (water, steam, mud, etc.) that traveled very quickly over the landscape. If you look at the results of these eroding agents, you will be amazed.

In the figure below, there are two canyons. The canyon on the right is known as "Engineers' Canyon." The canyon on the left was formed in less than a day as a result of a mudflow that took place during the Mount Saint Helens eruption.

Photo by Dr. Steven A. Austin

FIGURE 8.6
A Canyon Formed in a Day

© Institute for Creation Research

Canyon Formed in a Day

Engineers' Canyon

Interestingly enough, the canyon that formed in a day has much in common with the Grand Canyon. The general shape of the canyon is the same, and the size of the canyon is roughly one-fortieth that of the Grand Canyon. This has led some geologists to call this rapidly formed canyon the "Little Grand Canyon."

We see, then, that canyons can be formed rapidly as the result of catastrophic events. In fact, Mount Saint Helens has taught us something else about canyon formation. It has taught us that appearances can be *very* deceiving. You see, the reason uniformitarians believe the Colorado River eroded the Grand Canyon is that the Colorado River is at the *bottom* of the Grand Canyon. Thus, it seems only logical to conclude that the river formed the canyon. Although this seems like a logical assumption, we now know that it is not necessarily a *correct* assumption. Consider, for example, the photo in Figure 8.7.

Photo by Dr. Steven A. Austin   **FIGURE 8.7**   © *Institute for Creation Research*
Another View of Catastrophic Erosion

A person to provide scale for the photo

140-foot-high cliff face. It is important to note that the *rock* was not formed in the eruption. It was already there. The erosion that exposed the cliff face was caused by a mudflow that was caused by the eruption.

The important thing to know about this river is that it formed *after* the canyon was formed.

If a uniformitarian geologist were to study this canyon without the benefit of knowing what happened, he or she would most likely assume that the river pointed out in the figure eroded the canyon over a period of millions of years. After all, that's what makes sense. The river is at the bottom of the canyon, and the rock on both walls of the canyon is exposed. Thus, the river carved the canyon through a slow process of erosion, right? Not in this case. You see, people *observed* this canyon form as a result of the Mount Saint Helens eruption, and it was formed *first* as a result of the eruption's mudflows. *Later on,* the river was formed in the canyon. In this case, then, the river did not form the canyon. *Instead, the canyon formed the river*!

What does all this tell us? Does it tell us that the uniformitarian assumptions about the formation of stratified rock and canyons are wrong? Of course not! It just tells us that they *could be* wrong, and they are certainly not the *only possible explanation*. This is a very important point and cannot be overemphasized. Uniformitarian geologists are fond of explaining *exactly* what happened in earth's past to form this layer of rock or that canyon. If you go to the Grand Canyon and take a tour, for example, the tour guide will tell you without a doubt that the Colorado River carved the Grand Canyon out through the slow process of erosion over a period of 6 million years. However, the only canyons whose formation we have *actually observed* did not form that way. Why, then, are uniformitarian geologists so confident that the Grand Canyon formed that way? They are confident only because they fervently believe in the uniformitarian hypothesis. Direct observation, however, tells us that the catastrophism hypothesis can also explain such formations.

Now think about all that you've learned for just a moment. When I mentioned that the total energy released as a result of the Mount Saint Helens eruption was roughly equivalent to the explosion of 33,000 atomic bombs, you probably decided that the Mount Saint Helens eruption was an enormous catastrophe. Well, in terms of loss of life and damage to the surrounding area, that is probably true. On a *geological scale*, however, the Mount Saint Helens eruption was rather ordinary. Several much more severe catastrophes have happened during the course of recorded history. Thus, the geological features that formed as a result of the Mount Saint Helens eruption are, most likely, *rather limited* compared to the geological features that would be formed by a *serious* catastrophe!

So, let's take the word of the most historically accurate document of ancient history and assume that there was a worldwide flood. In addition, let's make the logical conclusion that every major culture has a worldwide flood story because there was, indeed, a worldwide flood. Think of the enormous geological implications of such a catastrophe. Compared to a worldwide flood, the Mount Saint Helens catastrophe would be hardly noticeable! If the Mount Saint Helens catastrophe can build layers of stratified sediment that are several feet high, it stands to reason that a worldwide flood could form layers of stratified sediment that are hundreds or thousands of feet high. If the Mount Saint Helens catastrophe can carve out canyons that are one-fortieth the scale of the Grand Canyon, a large, post-Flood catastrophe could certainly carve out the Grand Canyon itself.

ON YOUR OWN

8.6 Does the data from the Mount Saint Helens eruption prove that the Grand Canyon was formed quickly as a result of a catastrophe?

8.7 The Mount Saint Helens catastrophe was a volcanic eruption, not a flood. Nevertheless, catastrophists assume that many of the structures formed by the volcanic eruption could also be formed by a flood. Why is this a reasonable assumption?

Catastrophism and the Fossil Record

Now remember what you learned in the previous module. Many catastrophists believe the rocks you see in the geological record belong to four distinct groups. First, there are the rocks associated with God's creation of the world. Many of the igneous and metamorphic rocks are the "foundations" of the earth that God initially formed. The sedimentary rocks that sit directly on top of those rocks are, in general, the result of the creative acts involving water. Most of those happened between days three and six of the Creation event as described in the Bible. Second, a few of those rocks might have resulted from certain local catastrophes (like volcanic eruptions) that occurred after Creation week but before the worldwide flood. Third, the majority of sedimentary rock we see today is a direct result of the Flood itself. Fourth, there are some sedimentary and igneous rock formations that are the result of local catastrophes that have occurred since the Flood. Mount Saint Helens is an example of such a catastrophe.

In this view, then, the fossils found in these rocks can be split into three basic groups. The fossils in the pre-Flood rocks are the remains of the creatures that lived before the Flood. The fossils in the rocks that were laid down by the Flood are the remains of the creatures that lived roughly at the time of the Flood. Fossils in the post-Flood rocks are the remains of creatures that lived after the Flood. In some ways, then, the catastrophist believes that the geological record does provide you with a glimpse into different periods of earth's past. However, unlike the uniformitarian view, those periods represent three broad eras rather than several distinct periods of time.

Now remember, catastrophists think that most of the sedimentary rocks (and therefore most of the fossil-bearing rocks) we see today were laid down during the Flood itself. Thus, when the catastrophist looks at the fossil record, he or she assumes that most of the fossils are the result of the kinds of processes that happen during a flood. As I mentioned in the previous module, catastrophists explain the fact that different fossils appear in different layers of the geological record not because each layer represents a separate period in earth's history, but because each layer was formed during a different stage of the Flood. The creatures caught in these layers would be different, depending on the details of the Flood and the region of the earth. Using this assumption, there are certain aspects of the fossil record that become quite easy to understand.

First of all, there is the existence of the fossils themselves. It is important to note that paleontologists have uncovered huge numbers of fossils in the geological record. Sometimes, those fossils are concentrated in enormous deposits often called **fossil graveyards**. In a series of rocks in Africa called the Karoo Beds, for example, the fossils are so plentiful that one paleontologist estimated there are more than 800 billion fossils of creatures that had backbones (which biologists call "vertebrates"). Many of these creatures were fish.

Now think about that for a moment in terms of the fossilization processes you learned about in the previous module. In order for something to be fossilized, it must be buried in sediment, amber, mineral-rich water, or ice very quickly. In the case of the Karoo Beds, the creatures had to be covered in sediment in order to be preserved, because they are found in sedimentary rock. In the catastrophism viewpoint, this is not at all surprising. After all, the Flood probably forced these creatures to move in an effort to escape the nasty conditions caused by the rapidly moving floodwaters. This probably concentrated them into a small region. Eventually, the huge amounts of moving sediment and mud caused by the raging floodwaters overtook the creatures, burying them quickly. As the floodwaters continued to deposit more and more sediment on the creatures, the creatures were fossilized.

In terms of what we know about fossilization, this makes an enormous amount of sense. We know for a fact that fossil deposits like the ones seen in the Karoo Beds are simply not formed today. In the Gulf of Mexico, for example, there is a phenomenon called a **red tide**. You will learn more about red tides in biology class. For right now, you just need to know that red tides kill massive numbers of fish when they occur. In the Gulf of Mexico, it is not unusual for a single red tide to kill a million fish. What happens to those fish once they die? Do they fossilize? NO! They simply decay away. Thus, there must have been something *special* that fossilized billions of fish in the Karoo Beds. In the catastrophist view, that something special was a worldwide flood. The Flood would tend to concentrate creatures, and then the huge amounts of sediments carried by the Flood could bury and preserve them rapidly.

Fossil graveyards are common in the fossil record. It would be hard for me to mention even a fraction of the fossil graveyards uncovered by paleontologists. However, I must mention another one because it provides still more evidence that many fossils were formed by a worldwide flood. Consider, for example, the fossil graveyard found in the Cumberland Bone Cave in Maryland. In this cave, there are thousands of fossils that range through dozens of different types of creatures. In this *one cave*, paleontologists have found fossils of wolverines and grizzly bears, both of which are found in very cold climates. In addition, they have found fossils of peccaries (a form of pig) and antelopes, which are found in warm, wet climates. They have found fossils of groundhogs, rabbits, and coyotes, which are found in temperate, dry prairies. Finally, they have found fossils of water-loving creatures such as beavers and muskrats.

Now think about that for a moment. In this single cave, paleontologists have found fossils of land creatures from very cold climates, land creatures from warm and wet climates, land creatures from temperate and dry climates, and water creatures. These fossils are not found in different strata. They are found all mixed up together in the Cumberland Bone Cave. Other caves *in the very same part of Maryland* exhibit no fossils at all! How can we explain all this? In the catastrophism view, it is quite simple. Remember, a flood was supposed to have covered the entire world. Thus, the flood would have killed creatures from *all* climates. The waters could have easily mixed these fossils together and, as a result of currents from the floodwaters advancing and retreating, those mixed-up fossils would end up being deposited in just one area. While the explanation for these fossil graveyards is simple in the catastrophism framework, it is hard to explain them in terms of uniformitarianism.

The massive fossil deposits in fossil graveyards, then, are evidence for the catastrophist view of the geological record. In addition, the mere existence of the number of fossils we see today is best understood in the catastrophist framework. As you learned in the previous module, fossilization is the exception, not the rule. Under normal conditions, a dead plant or animal will decay. In order to be preserved, the animal must be buried rapidly. The catastrophist view provides the easiest way to understand how this could happen to the extent we see in the fossil record.

In addition, sometimes the fossils themselves indicate they were preserved very rapidly. In fact, there are museums that carry carbonized remains of a large fish in the process of eating a small fish. If you go to the Creation Museum run by Answers in Genesis, for example, you can see an example of such a fossil. Think about how such a fossil could be formed. A fish doesn't die in the middle of a meal and then lie around for millions of years while both it and its meal are encased in sediment. Instead, the best way to understand such a fossil is to realize that the fish were *buried in an instant*, without warning. Most likely, the large fish was eating when the Flood's waters brought in a huge amount of sediment, burying the fish in mid-swallow. This killed both the fish and its potential meal. Since they were buried by sediment, the process of forming a carbonized fossil then began. Figure 8.8 shows you a photo of one such fossil.

FIGURE 8.8
A Fish Fossilized in the Middle of a Meal

Photo © Ken Lucas / Visuals Unlimited

Fossils like this one seem to capture a moment in time, and they speak of rapid, catastrophic death.

Now, of course, the real issue is not how quickly an organism is killed. The real issue is how quickly an organism's remains can be preserved. Remember, in order for a dead organism to become a fossil, the normal process of decay must be slowed so the process of preservation can occur before the remains decay away. This can happen in several ways. As I already discussed, an animal can be encased in amber or in frozen mud. These kinds of "tombs" slow down the decay process, allowing preservation to occur. In addition, even rapid burial in sediment will help to slow down the decay process by making it harder for decomposing organisms and chemicals to get to the creature's remains.

However, slowing down the decay process isn't the only issue involved in making a fossil. The preservation process must still be quick enough, or even a slow decay process will eliminate any record of the dead organism. So, one big question is: How long does it take a fossil to actually form? Since we tend to use fossils to learn about the periods of time before recorded history, most people assume fossils take a long time to form. However, we know that this is not always the case. Consider, for example, the photos shown in Figure 8.9.

FIGURE 8.9
Fossils of Items That Are Not Prehistoric

This waterwheel was built roughly 70 years ago. Today, it is almost completely petrified due to the mineral-rich water that has been flowing over it.

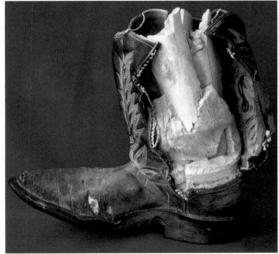

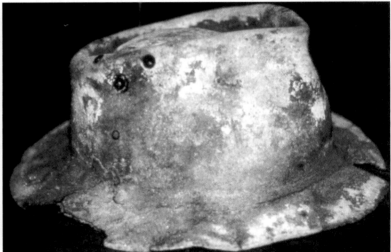

This boot is clearly not prehistoric, but it contains hardened sediments encasing bones that are at least partially fossilized.

This hat is also not prehistoric, but it is as hard as a rock because it has been petrified.

    The unusual fossils in the photos demonstrate that fossilization can occur quickly, given the right conditions. Clearly, none of these fossils are very old. Leather boots, waterwheels, and hats haven't been around for millions of years. Nevertheless, these recently made things have been at least partially fossilized, all because they were exposed to the proper conditions. Catastrophists think that this is the *normal* mode of fossilization. Without the proper conditions, fossils will not form at all. If the proper conditions exist, catastrophists think fossils form rapidly.

ON YOUR OWN

8.8 Why are fossil graveyards like the Cumberland Bone Cave a problem for uniformitarians?

Uniformitarianism or Catastrophism: Which Is Better?

Now that I have given you the basics of both uniformitarianism and catastrophism, I want to examine them in the light of certain data I consider important. Now remember, as I have warned you several times, I think that catastrophism is a superior view with which to analyze the data. Thus, my examination of these two viewpoints will be biased towards catastrophism. That is unavoidable. If you pick up a uniformitarian's book on geology, catastrophism might not even be mentioned. If it is mentioned, it will probably be shown in a poor light. In the end, every book is biased because every author is biased. If you truly want to be educated in the subjects of geology and paleontology, you should probably read authors from both viewpoints and try to come to your own conclusions.

So given the fact that I am biased, how do these two theories stack up in light of the data? To begin with, catastrophism seems to do a much better job at explaining the number of fossils found in the fossil record, including fossil graveyards. As I have said before, most dead organisms decay. They do not fossilize. Thus, fossilization is a rare event. Usually, something special must occur in order for a dead organism to fossilize. Catastrophes such as volcanic eruptions and floods, especially the worldwide flood, would provide lots of these special events. This explains well the huge number of fossils that exist. Uniformitarianism has a much harder time explaining such things. Fossil graveyards like the Cumberland Bone Cave compound this problem. How did so many fossils from so many climates come to rest in a cave, especially when the other caves in the surrounding area have no fossils at all? Catastrophism offers a ready explanation – uniformitarianism does not.

There are also certain fossils for which catastrophism offers a better explanation than does uniformitarianism. For example, in March 2005, the journal *Science* published a report from Dr. Mary Schweitzer and her colleagues. In this report, the scientists showed strong evidence that they had found soft, unfossilized tissue in the fossilized thigh bone of a *Tyrannosaurus rex*, which is a type of dinosaur. This is a stunning find, since uniformitarians believe that the bone is over 65 *million* years old. Now remember, most tissue decays rapidly, and a fossil forms only when a preservation process such as petrifaction can work faster than the decay process.

Now most of the *Tyrannosaurus rex* bone was petrified. In fact, the soft tissue was found by accident, because the appearance of the fossil led scientists to believe it was completely petrified. However, paleontologists were forced to break open the thigh bone in order to move the fossil, and that's when the discovery was made. The discovery clearly shows that the *Tyrannosaurus rex* thigh bone was not *completely* petrified. Now it is hard to believe that after 65 million years the petrifaction process had not been completed, but it is even harder to understand how soft tissue could have survived for such a long time without decaying away. Nevertheless, uniformitarians are working on trying to understand how this could have happened. Of course, in my opinion, the very fact that you can find soft tissue in such a fossil tells you that the fossil is not millions of years old, because soft tissue simply cannot be preserved for that long, even under the best of conditions. At best, you could imagine soft tissue to be preserved for thousands of years. Thus, it is more reasonable to assume that the *Tyrannosaurus rex* bone is thousands, not millions, of years old.

Of course, this is a point at which you could put both uniformitarianism and catastrophism to the test. If the *Tyrannosaurus rex* bone really is millions of years old, the fact that preserved soft tissue can be found in it is nearly miraculous. Thus, you would not expect to find soft tissue in many other bones found in the same strata. However, if such bones are only thousands of years old, you would expect to find more examples. Now please realize that even over thousands of years, the vast majority of tissue will decay away. Nevertheless, the chance of soft tissue remaining after only a few thousand years is much higher than after a few million years. Thus, paleontologists should start looking into lots of dinosaur bones they think are millions of years old. If they find soft tissue in several other bones, it is hard to imagine how the bones could all be millions of years old.

So why don't you find paleontologists going into the collections and breaking open a bunch of dinosaur fossils? Well, remember that dinosaur fossils are *incredibly rare*. Take away the fossils of clams and other hard-shelled creatures, and there aren't many fossils left. Take away insect and fish fossils, and you have even fewer left. Thus, dinosaur bones are *amazingly valuable*. In reality, they are more valuable than most other things people hold dear. Imagine that your mother has a vase from China that is 2,000 years old. Do you think she would want you to break it open to see if you can find something hidden in the ceramic? Of course not! Well, dinosaur bones are even more precious than a 2,000-year-old Chinese vase. Thus, it is very hard for paleontologists to bring themselves to just break them open. Nevertheless, if we are ever to find out whether or not soft-tissue preservation is incredibly rare or somewhat common, it will probably have to be done.

Moving away from individual fossils, let's take a look at the uniformitarians' geological column. Remember, this is a construct, based on uniformitarian assumptions. The construct is assembled using index fossils. According to uniformitarians, there are certain fossils that are representative of specific times in earth's history. For example, trilobites are used as index fossils. Trilobites are assumed to have existed from Cambrian times (550 million years ago) through Permian times (250 million years ago). Thus, when a paleontologist finds a trilobite in a layer of rock, he or she assumes that the rock represents an age from Cambrian to Permian times. If the number of trilobites is particularly large, then it is usually considered Cambrian rock.

Now think about that for a moment. In order for this to really be true, trilobites must be extinct now. After all, if they represent the eras mentioned above, they *could not have lived before or after those eras*. The problem is that we *don't really know* whether or not trilobites are extinct. We assume they are because we have not *found* any living examples. That doesn't mean they don't exist, however. It only means that we have not found them! There is a *lot* of ocean bottom to explore, and we have not come close to covering most of it yet. Thus, they *could* still exist, hidden away where scientists have not looked yet.

But how likely is that? I mean, could scientists have just missed trilobites after all this time? Well, consider the Wollemi pine. Until 1994, this tree was known only by its fossils, which are only found in Jurassic rock. This led uniformitarians to believe that it died out 145 million years ago. In fact, finding a Wollemi pine fossil was considered evidence that you were looking at Jurassic rock. However, in 1994, living Wollemi pines were found in Australia's Blue Mountains. Now these trees are not small. Some specimens are nearly 100 feet high. Nevertheless, they escaped science's notice until very recently. If these huge trees (living on land) could escape notice, why couldn't tiny trilobites that live at the bottom of the ocean do so as well?

Two questions come to mind when faced with the discovery of these trees. First, if Wollemi pine fossils are used to identify Jurassic rock, how accurate can such an identification be? Second, *why can't paleontologists find fossil Wollemi pines in other strata?* After all, 150 million years is a long time. Shouldn't one or two Wollemi pine fossils be found in strata from more "recent" times, since they have been living all along? In my opinion, this brings the whole idea of the geological column into doubt. If those strata *really do* represent different eras in earth's past, then you *should* find some fossil Wollemi pines in rocks that are more recent than Jurassic rock. Nevertheless, paleontologists cannot. Why? Uniformitarians do not have a satisfactory answer to that question.

Now if this was the only example of such a situation, you might be able to explain it away. However, it is not. A more well-known example is the **coelacanth** (see' luh kanth). This was a kind of fish whose fossils are very prevalent in the geological column from Devonian (415 million years ago) times to Cretaceous times (65 million years ago). No fossils of coelacanths can be found in rock "younger" than Cretaceous rock or "older" than Devonian rock. Therefore, uniformitarian geologists concluded that there have been no living coelacanths on earth for the last 65 million years. However, in the winter of 1939, *The London Illustrated News* reported on the discovery of a living coelacanth. We now know they are relatively common in a region off the coast of South Africa and in another region between Africa and Madagascar. Once again, you have to ask why the geological column seems to indicate that no coelacanths have existed for 65 million years when, in fact, living coelacanths exist today! Is it really possible that coelacanths avoided being fossilized for 65 million years when they were fossilized with such regularity prior to that? There are several examples of both plants and animals that were assumed to be extinct but have now been found alive today. This remains a difficult problem if you choose to believe the uniformitarian viewpoint.

Not only are these kinds of fossils difficult to understand in terms of uniformitarian assumptions, there is another disturbing use of index fossils that is often necessary in order to interpret the geological record in terms of uniformitarian assumptions. In Module #6, I introduced the term "unconformity." As you should recall, an unconformity is a surface of erosion that separates one layer of rock from another. I mentioned that there were four types. The first three were easy to understand, but then I mentioned the last type of unconformity: a **paraconformity**.

Paraconformities are rather common in geology. In the Grand Canyon, for example, there are layers of rock that contain Cambrian index fossils in the lower parts of the layer and Mississippian index fossils in the upper parts of the same layer. According to uniformitarian assumptions, Cambrian times were supposed to have ended 490 million years ago, and Mississippian times were not supposed to have begun until 360 million years ago. Thus, these time periods should be separated by a clear unconformity. After all, in other parts of the Grand Canyon, there is a clear unconformity between Devonian and Cambrian rock. Thus, the uniformitarian MUST assume that there was a break in the deposition of sediments between Cambrian times and Mississippian times. Nevertheless, in parts of the Grand Canyon, you find Cambrian index fossils and Mississippian index fossils with no unconformity in between.

The way the uniformitarian gets around this problem is to suggest that there is a paraconformity in the rock. A paraconformity is an unconformity that has been "disguised" so that it does not look like an unconformity at all. Thus, even though the layer in question has no evidence of erosion, the uniformitarian geologist assumes there *must* be an unconformity at that point because there must have been millions of years between the deposition of the index fossils. As a result, the uniformitarian geologist simply assumes that an unconformity exists there, and it is called a paraconformity. Paraconformities are, perhaps, one of the biggest problems for uniformitarians. One reason they are such a problem is that there are so many of them. The other reason is that there is simply no evidence for them. Regardless of the lack of evidence, however, uniformitarians must believe in them, or the whole geological column is useless.

Please note that index fossils and paraconformities are of no worry to the catastrophist. The catastrophist thinks that the different fossils found in different strata represent different conditions and stages of the worldwide flood. Thus, it is not surprising to find fossils of Wollemi pines and coelacanths in some geological strata but not others. After all, whether or not a creature gets fossilized depends on where it is and what the conditions of the Flood were in that region. If a catastrophist finds coelacanths in deep strata but not shallow ones, that just means that coelacanths were fossilized early in the Flood and not later in the Flood. Nevertheless, there is no reason to assume that they do not exist any more. In the same way, there is no reason for a catastrophist to assume the presence of an unconformity that does not seem to exist. If "Cambrian" index fossils and "Mississippian" index fossils are found in the same layer, it tells the catastrophist that in that region of the world, those creatures lived near one another during the time of the Flood and were caught by sediment deposits at roughly the same stage of the Flood.

The whole concept of unconformities does bring me to a problem with the catastrophist viewpoint, however. This problem is (understandably) considered serious by uniformitarians. Catastrophists have yet to offer a description of how unconformities can exist between certain layers of rock formed in the Flood. Remember, not all layers of rock are separated by unconformities, but some are. These unconformities seem to indicate that erosion took place after the lower layer was deposited and before the upper layer was deposited. There was not a lot of time during the Flood for erosion to take place. Thus, the way in which unconformities formed can be a problem in the catastrophist viewpoint.

There are, of course, other difficulties with catastrophism. For example, there are many limestone formations in Europe and North America that have what geologists call "*in situ* growth structures." These structures have the appearance of being formed slowly over time by creatures that were living in the sediments as the sediments were being deposited. If we assume that these sediments were laid down by the Flood, it is hard to understand how the fossil structures could have formed. The problem is even more significant due to the fact that these fossils are found in what seem to be their *natural* growth positions. Thus, it really *does* look like they were formed during a "business as usual" period in earth's past. The worldwide flood would certainly not be "business as usual," so this presents catastrophists with a problem.

Speaking of limestone brings me to another problem with catastrophism. Limestone is a broad term that includes different kinds of geological structures. One particular form of limestone is **chalk**. It is made up mostly of the remains of animals that make hard shells. In fact, while you might think of clams when you think of animals with hard shells, there are countless microscopic creatures that live in water and produce hard shells to protect themselves. When those creatures die, their remains settle to the bottom of the water where they live, and they form chalk deposits.

An example of a chalk deposit can be seen in the White Cliffs of Dover, which are on the coast of England. These cliffs, which reach heights of 350 feet, are composed of chalk. The problem for catastrophists is that these chalk cliffs seem to have all the characteristics of chalk deposits that are currently forming *very slowly* by the death and subsequent sinking of microscopic creatures. It is very hard to see how all the microscopic organisms needed to produce chalk structures like the White Cliffs of Dover could have been killed by the Flood, selectively transported to individual locations such as

Dover, and then deposited in such a way as to make it look like they slowly settled out of the ocean. Thus, chalk structures like the White Cliffs of Dover are a problem for the catastrophist view.

FIGURE 8.10
The White Cliffs of Dover

Photo © Sally Wallis
Agency: Shutterstock

While some catastrophists have made attempts to tackle the problem of how these kinds of chalk deposits could have been formed during the Flood, the details are still very difficult to understand in the framework of catastrophism.

So, *both* uniformitarianism and catastrophism have difficulties. Regardless of which view you take, you will run into puzzling problems. Which, then, is the better framework in which to view geology? Well, that depends on how many problems you see with each view and how important those problems are to you. In my opinion, for example, the problems with catastrophism are small compared to the problems associated with uniformitarianism. Thus, I think that the more scientifically accurate viewpoint is the catastrophist viewpoint. Nevertheless, knowledgeable scientists can view the same data and come to the opposite conclusion. Thus, this is a decision that you must make on your own, depending on how you view the data.

ON YOUR OWN

8.9 If the whole idea of index fossils is ignored, what evidence exists for paraconformities?

Evolution: Can It Provide Evidence for Uniformitarianism?

One of the most important aspects of the uniformitarian viewpoint is the concept of evolution. If you believe that the geological column is real, it is easy to believe that life on this planet started out as a "simple" life form and slowly evolved into all the creatures we see today. After all, that's what the geological column indicates happened. Of course, if you think that the construct of the geological column is not correct because of problems like the ones I pointed out in the previous section, you have no real reason to believe in the process of evolution.

Evolution, then, becomes something we can use to support or deny the reality of the geological column. If there is independent evidence for evolution, that would be evidence in favor of the reality of the geological column. After all, if we can independently show evidence for evolution, it would support the idea that the geological column is giving us an accurate view of earth's history. So what about that? Is there independent evidence for the process of evolution or not? Well, the short answer to this question is "**no**." You will learn more about evolution when you take biology. For right now, however, let's look at what should be the main line of data that relates to evolution.

Now remember what evolution says. It says that life started out simple, and through hundreds of millions (or perhaps billions) of years, the simple life forms became more complex. This happened as differences between parent and offspring began "piling up" in generation after generation. In this way, fish evolved into frogs, frogs evolved into reptiles, reptiles evolved into birds and mammals, and mammals evolved into humans. If this really happened, then at some time in earth's past, a creature had to exist that was part fish, part frog. This kind of creature is called an **intermediate link**, because it represents a "link" between one type of creature and another. If evolution really happened, then, there should be evidence of such creatures in the fossil record. The fact is, however, paleontologists can find only a few examples of such creatures, and those are highly questionable.

The scientist who first proposed a strong argument for evolution (Charles Darwin) noticed this lack of intermediate links in the fossil record. To him, it was the most difficult problem he had with his own hypothesis. In fact, in his book, he stated:

> Geological research, though it has added numerous species to existing and extinct genera, and has made the intervals between some few groups less wide than they otherwise would have been, yet has done scarcely anything in breaking the distinction between species, by connecting them together by numerous, fine, intermediate varieties; and this not having been affected, is probably the gravest and most obvious of all the many objections which can be raised against my views (*The Origin of Species*, 6th ed, 1962, Collier Books, New York, p. 462).

Notice what he says here. Evolution says that one species eventually led to another. Thus, there should be "fine, intermediate varieties" of fossils in between species. The fact that none (or few) could be found was a problem he called "grave."

Although Darwin could not find good examples of intermediate links in the fossil record, he had a hope. He wrote his book in the mid-1800s. As a result, he figured geology was still in its infant stage as a science and that geologists just hadn't found the intermediate link fossils yet. He was convinced that as time went on, geologists would find these intermediate links. Thus, he said that the intermediate links were currently just "missing" from the fossil record, but they would be found in time. Critics of evolution quickly coined the phrase "missing link" to emphasize that the fossil record was devoid of any direct evidence for evolution.

Well, what of these missing links? Has geology uncovered them? The answer to that is an unequivocal **NO**. Consider, for example, this evolutionist's summary of the fossil record:

> …according to Darwin...the fossil record should be rife with examples of transitional forms leading from the less to more evolved...Instead of filling the gaps in the fossil record with so-called missing links, most paleontologists found themselves facing a situation in which there were only gaps in the fossil record, with no evidence of transformational intermediates between documented fossil species (Jeffrey H. Schwartz, *Sudden Origins*, 1999, John Wiley & Sons, New York, p. 89).

So Dr. Schwartz says (and most experts on the fossil record agree) that the missing links are still missing! Darwin saw this fact as strong evidence against evolution, and Dr. Schwartz says that the situation is no better now. The fossil record, then, is strong evidence against evolution.

At this point, you might be thinking, "Wait a minute, haven't I seen museum exhibits, television programs, and books with detailed, evolutionary sequences? Where have they come from if the fossil record is so devoid of evolutionary intermediate links?" Well, they come either from misinterpretations of the fossil records or from the imaginations of those who really want to believe in evolution. In biology, you will learn about some of these misinterpretations. In this module, I want to concentrate on the imagination part. Perhaps the most famous fossil presented as evidence for evolution is *Archaeopteryx* (ark ee op' ter iks), which evolutionists want to believe is an intermediate link between reptiles and birds.

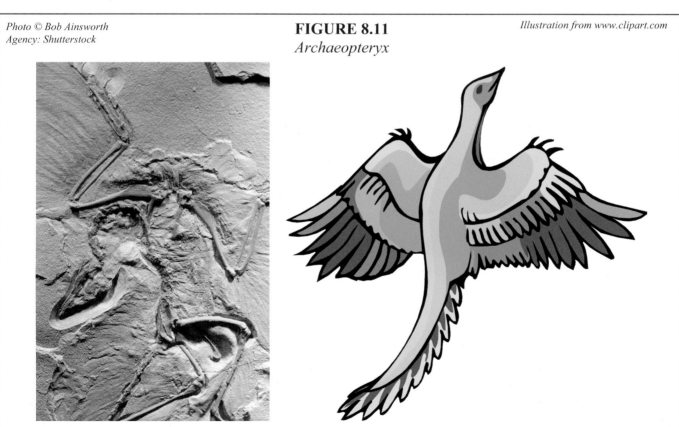

Photo © Bob Ainsworth
Agency: Shutterstock

FIGURE 8.11
Archaeopteryx

Illustration from www.clipart.com

The photo on the left is of an *Archaeopteryx* fossil. The drawing on the right is an artist's impression of what *Archaeopteryx* might have looked like.

Those who believe in evolution think that *Archaeopteryx* is an intermediate link between reptiles and birds. They think this because *Archaeopteryx* has some unique features you don't see in living birds today. The fossil impression clearly shows teeth in the mouth. No living bird has teeth, but reptiles have teeth. In addition, there are claws on the wings. No living adult bird has claws on its wings. Reptiles, however, have claws for their front feet. The tail is also longer and has more bones than that of the living birds we see today. Reptiles usually have long, bony tails. Thus, since this fossil is clearly a bird (the impression shows feathers), but it has some characteristics we normally associate with reptiles, many think that this fossil qualifies as an intermediate link between reptiles and birds.

The problem is that intermediate-link status is mostly in the imagination of those who want to believe in evolution. Look at the sketch of what *Archaeopteryx* might have looked like. If you saw something like that today, what would you call it? You would call it *a bird*. Indeed, detailed studies indicate that *Archaeopteryx* was an excellent flyer, as you would expect of a fully developed bird. Thus *Archaeopteryx* seems to be just a bird with certain special features that no living bird today has.

Along with *Archaeopteryx*, there are a few other supposed intermediate links that paleontologists can find. In each case, however, the fossil looks so much like one of the two creatures it is trying to link, that it is hard to believe it is evidence for evolution. For example, paleontologists believe that a creature called *Australopithecus* (aw stray' loh pih' thih kus) is an intermediate link between apes and humans. Since apes are similar to humans in many ways, evolutionists believe that apes evolved into humans. The problem is that *Australopithecus* is almost entirely ape. If you saw one, you would consider it to be an ape. Nevertheless, because of a few minor differences between the apes we see today and the fossils of *Australopithecus*, it is assumed to be an intermediate link. However, since it looks like an ape, it probably is nothing more than an ape with a few special characteristics.

In the end, then, there are almost no intermediate links in the fossil record, and the few that paleontologists believe are intermediate links are highly questionable. If evolution really occurred, however, there should be *many* intermediate links. The fact that only a few questionable ones can be found is strong evidence against evolution.

Another excellent example of this is given by Figure 8.3. Evolutionists want you to believe that the sequence of animals shown in that figure represent strong evidence for the evolution of fish into amphibian. However, if you study the figure closely, you will see that the supposed intermediates between fish and amphibian are so close to either fish or amphibian that they cannot really be considered intermediate links.

Look, for example, at the first three drawings in the figure. They are all of fishes with fins, right? The fins vary in number and shape, but that is true of fishes alive today. There is a huge variety in terms of both the number of fins on fishes alive today as well as the shapes of those fins. Thus, these are just three different kinds of fishes. Then look at the fourth animal pictured. It looks a lot like a salamander, but notice it no longer has fins at all! It has legs that end in claws. According to evolution, those legs and claws had to develop over generations. Where are the intermediate stages? Nowhere. Basically, we go from three different kinds of fishes with fins to an animal that has functional legs and claws. How did the fins develop into legs? Did the claws develop before the legs? Did they develop with the legs? There is no way to know, because there are no real intermediate links between the fins and the legs.

In then end, then, direct fossil evidence for evolution in the form of intermediate links is lacking. When you get to the point where you take biology, you will find that the balance of the biological evidence goes against the idea of evolution producing what we see today from one (or a few) simple life forms(s). Thus, evolution simply cannot explain the living world of today.

Now please understand that while positive evidence for evolution would also be evidence for the uniformitarian view of geology, evidence against evolution is not necessarily evidence against the uniformitarian view. After all, the uniformitarian view of geology is about how rocks form and what the fossils in the rocks tell us about life in earth's past. Essentially, the uniformitarian view of geology says that rocks form mostly as the result of slow, gradual processes, and the fossils in those rocks indicate that the earliest organisms were rather "simple," and that as time went on, they became more and more complex. While evolution asserts the same thing, it is not the only way to explain the uniformitarian view of life and earth's history.

In fact, there are *creationists* who are also uniformitarians. They believe in the uniformitarian view of geology, but they also agree that the Theory of Evolution is not a valid explanation of life's history on earth. One such group is referred to as **progressive creationists**. Probably the most popular author in this camp is Dr. Hugh Ross. In his view, God created simple creatures, allowed them to live, reproduce, etc., and then, after a long while, He created slightly more complex creatures. Once again, He then paused and allowed them to "do their thing" for a long while, and then He created even more complex creatures. After enough time, of course, this would produce all the basic kinds of organisms we see today.

Notice that progressive creationism is consistent with the uniformitarian view. The uniformitarian view simply says that "simple" organisms lived on earth first, and as millions and millions of years passed, more and more complex creatures appeared. Well, according to progressive creationists, that's what happened, because God created, waited a long time (millions of years even), and created more, waited another long time, created more, etc.

Please note that while progressive creationism is consistent with uniformitarianism, it is not consistent with catastrophism. Thus, even people who consider themselves creationists can disagree on the details of the geological record – some creationists are uniformitarians, while others are catastrophists. This is why it is important for you to investigate both sides of this issue. All this disagreement among many different scientists indicates that the issue is far from settled!

ON YOUR OWN

8.10 If a scientist believes that God created each type of creature individually, would he or she expect to find intermediate links in the fossil record? How does that expectation compare to the data we have?

ANSWERS TO THE "ON YOUR OWN" PROBLEMS

8.1 <u>First, they assume that the Principle of Superposition works for sedimentary rock. Second, they assume that the index fossils found in a layer of rock will indicate which time period the layer represents.</u>

8.2 If either of those assumptions is wrong, <u>the geological column is probably not accurate.</u>

8.3 Uniformitarians would say that those are <u>Precambrian rocks.</u> Looking at Figure 8.2, you can see that only simple fossils like algae are found in Precambrian rocks.

8.4 The evolutionist would say that you do not see evolution happening today because <u>evolution occurs too slowly to see it happening.</u> Remember, evolution takes place over hundreds of millions of years. True science has only been around for a few thousand years. That's such a small time compared to the millions of years required for evolution that you would not be able to see evolution happening.

8.5 <u>You would expect to see fossils of creatures that look like a cross between creatures we see today.</u> For example, if fish evolved into frogs, then there should be fossils that are part fish and part frog. While you might think Figure 8.3 provides such evidence, it does not. I will explain that in the final section of this module.

8.6 <u>No, it does not prove anything.</u> Remember, science does not prove anything. The data from Mount Saint Helens provides evidence for a catastrophic formation of canyons like the Grand Canyon. This evidence is not conclusive, but to many scientists it is very convincing.

8.7 While the volcanic eruption of Mount Saint Helens triggered the catastrophe, <u>the geological structures discussed in this book were formed by a "river" of mud flowing at high speeds.</u> A flood would also produce "rivers" of sediment-laden waters flowing at high speeds.

8.8 <u>Fossil graveyards are a problem for uniformitarians because they assume that creatures are fossilized one at a time by accident.</u> To make a fossil graveyard, then, that accident would have to happen over and over again in a certain region. Also, when fossil graveyards contain creatures from many climates, it is hard to understand how this could have happened in one place.

8.9 <u>There is no evidence for paraconformities other than index fossils.</u> Remember, a paraconformity is an imaginary line drawn in rock to separate index fossils that are supposed to identify "old" rock from index fossils that are supposed to identify "younger" rock. If index fossils don't exist, there is no reason to drawn that imaginary line.

8.10 <u>If God created each creature, a paleontologist would expect no intermediate links.</u> This is what we see in the fossil record, so the direct evidence from the fossil record supports creationism. Note that this evidence is consistent with catastrophism, but it is also consistent with certain kinds of creationist uniformitarians, such as the progressive creationists.

STUDY GUIDE FOR MODULE #8

1. Define the following terms:

a. Index fossils
b. Geological column
c. The Theory of Evolution

2. How are index fossils used by uniformitarian geologists?

3. Explain, in your own words, how the geological column is constructed.

4. Is it possible to go somewhere in the world and see all major layers of the geological column and its fossils in one geological formation?

Using Figure 8.2 as a guide, answer questions 5 through 7

5. According to the uniformitarian view, which creatures lived on earth first: trilobites or fish?

6. If a paleontologist finds only fossil algae in a layer of rock, roughly how old does the paleontologist think the rocks are?

7. A geological formation with only two layers of rock is studied. One has fossils of mammals only, and the other has fossils of fish only. According to uniformitarian assumptions, which layer should be on the bottom and which should be on the top?

8. Why is the geological column considered evidence for evolution?

9. Why is the geological column not really evidence for evolution?

10. What do the data from Mount Saint Helens tell us about the time it takes to form stratified rocks?

11. If you see a canyon with a river flowing at the bottom of it, should you assume that the river eroded the canyon?

12. On a geological scale, was the Mount Saint Helens eruption a major catastrophe? What does that tell you about the kinds of geological formations that could be formed in a major catastrophe?

13. What did the Mount Saint Helens eruption have that a major flood would also have?

14. What is so important about the Cumberland Bone Cave when it comes to the question of uniformitarianism versus catastrophism?

15. Do fossils require millions of years to form?

16. What is a paraconformity?

17. List at least four problems with uniformitarianism as discussed in the text.

18. What are the three problems with catastrophism that were discussed?

19. Why does the fossil record offer no evidence for evolution?

20. Why does the fossil record offer evidence for the idea that God created each plant and animal individually?

While he never made his position clear in class, most students who visited his office thought Professor Johnson was a catastrophist.

Cartoon by Speartoons

MODULE #9: What Is Life?

Introduction

Now that you've gotten a good view of the history of life, I want to examine the whole concept of life in a little more detail. After all, if we are going to study life science, we need to know what life is! Now to some extent, you already have an idea of what life is. If I were to ask you whether or not a rock is alive, you would easily answer, "No!" On the other hand, if I were to ask you whether or not a blade of grass is alive, you would quickly answer, "Yes!" Most likely, you can distinguish between life and non-life by just giving examples of what is alive and what is not.

Even though this is the case, scientists must be a little more detailed in describing what it means to be alive; thus, they have developed several criteria for life. If something meets all these criteria, we can say scientifically that it is alive. If it fails to meet even one of the criteria, it is not alive. These criteria are:

1. **All life forms contain deoxyribonucleic (dee ahk' see rye boh noo klay' ik) acid, which is called DNA.**

2. **All life forms have a method by which they extract energy from the surroundings and convert it into energy that sustains them.**

3. **All life forms can sense changes in their surroundings and respond to those changes.**

4. **All life forms reproduce.**

When put together, these criteria describe what it means to be alive, at least as far as science is concerned. Anything that meets these criteria is called a **living organism**. Now if you're not sure exactly what each of these criteria means, don't worry. I will discuss each of them in detail.

DNA and Life

Our first criterion states that all life contains **DNA**. Now you've probably heard about DNA before (I mentioned it briefly in Module #7). Most likely, however, it is still a big mystery to you at this point. Why is DNA so special when it comes to life? Well, DNA provides the *information* necessary to take a bunch of lifeless chemicals and turn them into a living system. You see, if we were to analyze an organism and determine every chemical that made up the organism, and if we were then to go into a laboratory and make all those chemicals and throw them into a big pot, we would not have made something that is alive. We would not have even made something that resembles the organism we studied. Why?

In order to make life, we must take the chemicals that make it up, and we must *organize* them in a way that will promote the other life functions mentioned in our list of criteria for life. In other words, just the chemicals themselves cannot extract and convert energy (criterion #2), sense and respond to change (criterion #3), and reproduce (criterion #4). In order to perform those functions, the chemicals must be organized so they work together in just the right way. Think about it this way: Suppose you go to a store and buy a model airplane kit. When you get it home, you unpack the box and pile all the parts on the table. At that point, do you have a model airplane? No, of course not. In order to make the model airplane, you have to assemble the pieces in just the right way, according to the instructions. When you get done, all the parts are in just the right place and work together with the other parts. This produces a model airplane.

In the same way, DNA is the set of instructions that takes the chemicals that make up life and arranges them in just the right way so as to produce a living system. Without this instruction set, the chemicals that make up a living organism would be nothing more than a pile of goo. However, directed by the information in DNA, these chemicals can work together in just the right way so as to make a living organism. Now of course, the exact way in which DNA does this is a little complicated. When you take biology, you will learn a great deal about how DNA does its job. In this course, I want you to concentrate on what DNA looks like instead of the details of how it does its job. If you really learn about the structure of DNA now, it will be easier for you to understand how DNA works when you take biology.

FIGURE 9.1
A Model Airplane Kit

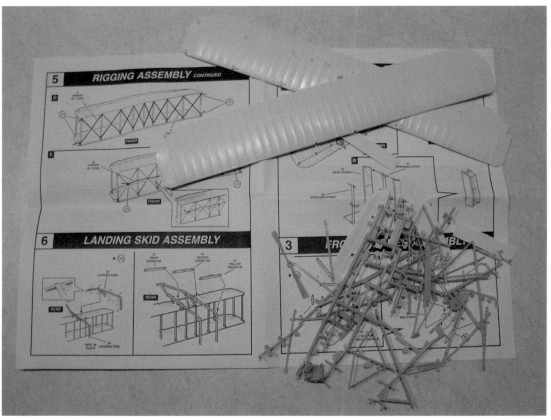

The pieces that make up this kit do not make a model airplane. In order for the model airplane to be made, the pieces must be assembled according to the instructions. In the same way, the chemicals that make up a living organism require the instructions in DNA in order to form a living organism.

Okay, then, what does DNA look like? Well, first of all, you need to know that DNA is a **molecule**. In physical science next year, you will learn a lot more about atoms and molecules. For right now, just remember that atoms are the basic building blocks of matter.

Atom – The smallest chemical unit of matter

Everything you see (this book, the chair upon which you sit, your body) is made up of little units of matter called atoms. Currently, scientists know of 116 different kinds of atoms in creation. This number increases as time goes on because, every once in a while, scientists produce a new kind of atom. In a few years, then, the number of basic kinds of atoms in creation will probably be a little larger. That's why I say there are "about" 116 different kinds of atoms in creation.

If this were the end of the story, the universe would be pretty boring. After all, if everything you see is made up of atoms, and if there are only about 116 different kinds of atoms in creation, then there are only about 116 different substances in creation, right? Of course not! Although God used atoms as the basic building blocks of creation, He designed those atoms to link together to form larger building blocks called **molecules**.

Molecule – Two or more atoms linked together to make a substance with unique properties

These larger building blocks make up most of the substances with which you are familiar. Table salt, water, sugar, etc., are all made up of molecules, which are, in turn, made up of atoms.

DNA is a molecule. This means that it is made from several atoms that link together. Well, it turns out that DNA is actually a *really big* molecule. Most molecules in creation are made up of somewhere between 2 and 100 atoms linked together. DNA, however, is made of *millions* of atoms linked together! Now if you think about that, it should make sense. After all, DNA contains all the information necessary to make life. Thus, DNA must contain a *lot* of information. It has been estimated that if one could translate into English all the information in a single human DNA molecule, it would fill up *1,000 books, each of which would be 500 pages long*! That amount of information requires a large molecule!

Now let me point out that although DNA is large *compared to other molecules*, it is remarkably small when you consider all the information it stores. A DNA molecule, in fact, represents *the most efficient means of storing data in all of creation*. Many people today marvel at how much information can be stored in a tiny laptop computer. However, the best computer disk made today cannot even *come close* to storing information as efficiently as does DNA. In fact, computer scientists have been trying for years to make computers that store information the way DNA does, and they *can't do it*.

Now think about that for a moment. Human science can't produce anything that stores information as efficiently as DNA does. Suppose one of your friends showed you the hard disk from a computer. Suppose further that you used the computer to look at the information on the disk and found that the disk contained detailed drawings and instructions for assembling a bicycle. If your friend told you that the disk and all its contents were formed as the result of lightning striking a pile of garbage that contained plastic and metal, would you believe him? Of course not. Why?

Well, first, the disk itself is a complicated piece of technology that can be used to store a lot of useful information. Things like that do not result from accidents. They are made as a result of careful design and manufacturing. Also, the instructions for assembling the bicycle (which are stored on the disk) could not form by accident, either. There is just too much information there. The instructions were clearly *created* by someone who knows how to make bicycles. Thus, it would be obvious to you that neither the disk nor the information on that disk could be the result of some accidental event like lightning striking a pile of plastic and scrap metal. Nevertheless, if you are a scientist and do not believe in God, you are *forced* to believe that a data-storage device *significantly more advanced* than humankind's best computer disk, and information *significantly more extensive* than the instructions for assembling a bicycle, both came about as the result of an accident! Scientists who believe in God need not believe such silly things! Just as computer disks and bicycle-assembly instructions are designed and made by intelligent engineers, DNA and the information necessary for life are designed and made by the most intelligent engineer of all: God!

ON YOUR OWN

9.1 In general, which is smaller: an atom or a molecule?

9.2 Think about a cookbook. A cookbook is, in some ways, like DNA. How?

The Structure of DNA

In the previous section, you learned that DNA stores an enormous amount of information. How does it store information? The answer to that question lies in the structure of DNA. The figure below represents a simplified view of a portion of a DNA molecule.

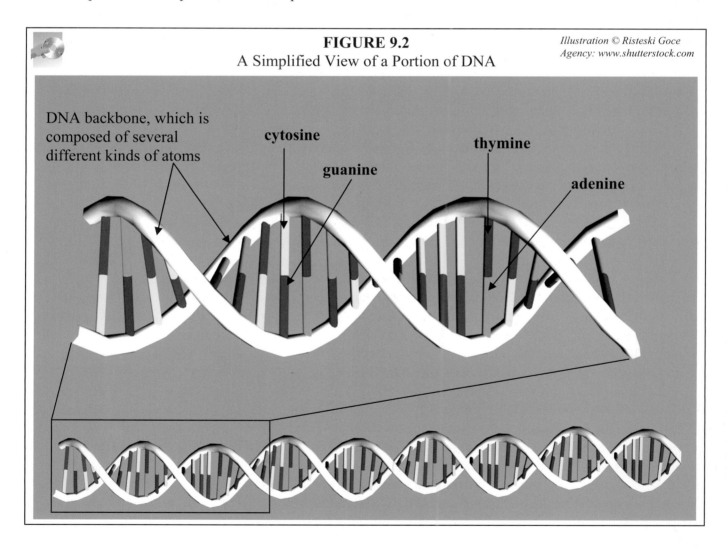

FIGURE 9.2
A Simplified View of a Portion of DNA

Illustration © Risteski Goce
Agency: www.shutterstock.com

DNA backbone, which is composed of several different kinds of atoms

cytosine

guanine

thymine

adenine

A DNA molecule is shaped like a **double helix**. If you don't know what that means, don't worry. You will be making a model of DNA in a little while, and you will see what it means then. The double helix is formed by two long strands of atoms linked together in just the right way. These strands make up the **backbone** of the DNA. Each strand has little units attached to it. These units are called **nucleotide** (noo' klee oh tide) **bases**. There are four different nucleotide bases in a DNA molecule. Their names are **adenine** (ad' uh neen), **thymine** (thy' meen), **guanine** (gwah' neen), and **cytosine** (sy' tuh zeen).

In the figure, the DNA backbone is represented by the silver ribbons. Adenine is represented by the green bars, thymine is represented by the red bars, cytosine is represented by the yellow bars, and guanine is represented by the blue bars. Notice that the nucleotide bases link together. This is what holds the double helix together. Notice also that there are no cases of blue bars linking with red bars or green bars. In each case, green bars link with red bars and blue bars link with yellow bars. This represents the fact that the four nucleotide bases of DNA cannot link together in just any way. Only adenine and thymine can link together, and only cytosine and guanine can link together. You will learn more about this in a moment.

Now how in the world does this molecule store information? Well, have you ever heard of something called **Morse code**? In 1836, Samuel F.B. Morse invented the telegraph, in which electrical signals were sent over a wire whenever a button on the telegraph was pressed. The electrical signal generated an indentation on a moving piece of paper at the other end of the wire. This, of course, could be used to send messages from one place to another very quickly. However, in order to allow such a device to send meaningful messages, a code had to be established. When the indentation was short, it was called a "dot," and when the indentation was long, it was called a "dash." Morse code allowed all 26 letters in the alphabet as well as the numerals 0 through 9 to be represented by a series of dots and dashes. For example, the letter "S" was represented by 3 dots, and the letter "O" was represented by 3 dashes. If you were in trouble and had a telegraph, you could send three dots followed by 3 dashes followed by three dots. The person receiving your transmission would translate that as "SOS," which is the internationally-recognized abbreviation for "I need help."

Although Morse code was often used to send short messages like "SOS," it was also used to send very detailed messages as well. After all, using just dots and dashes, you could spell out *any* word in the English language. Thus, if you wanted to, you could send this entire book (just the words, not the pictures) to someone via Morse code. It would be *very* tedious, but it *could* be done. Well, just as all the information in this book could be represented by a series of dots and dashes in Morse code, all the information necessary for life is stored in a coded series of the four nucleotide bases (adenine, thymine, cytosine, and guanine) in DNA.

However, just as someone must *translate* from Morse code back to English so you can understand a message sent in Morse code, the series of nucleotide bases in DNA must also be translated into something that a living organism can understand. It turns out that there is a host of chemical processes that occur in order do just that. The details of these processes are far beyond the scope of this course, but when you take biology, you will learn about some of them. For right now, I want you to realize that DNA stores information as series of the four nucleotide bases adenine, thymine, cytosine, and guanine. With the proper chemical translation equipment, this information can be translated into something useful to a living organism. To make sure you have a good picture of DNA's structure in mind, I want you to build a model of DNA that is similar to the illustration shown in Figure 9.2.

EXPERIMENT 9.1
All photos by Kathleen J. Wile
Building a Model of DNA

<u>Supplies:</u>

♦ Long pipe cleaners (the longer the better)
♦ Four different colors of beads (They need to have holes in them large enough for the pipe cleaners to fit through. You can get beads like that at any craft store.)
♦ Scissors strong enough to cut the pipe cleaners
♦ Eye protection such as goggles or safety glasses

Introduction: Although a drawing of DNA is nice, a model is even better. In this experiment, you will build a model of DNA to help you understand its structure.

<u>Procedure:</u>

1. Sort the beads out by color. Assign a color to represent each nucleotide base. In the pictures you see on the next page, for example, red represents thymine, and green represents adenine. Blue represents guanine, and yellow represents cytosine.
2. Make several small loops in one of the pipe cleaners. The best way to do this is to wrap the pipe cleaner once around a pencil. Shape the pipe cleaner so it is straight and so all of the loops are on just one side. Your pipe cleaner should look something like this:

3. Do the same thing with another pipe cleaner, and then lay them side by side so the loops face each other, as show in the drawing below:

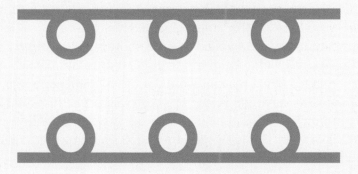

3. Cut a pipe cleaner into small segments. You need to make one segment for each pair of loops that face each other. Each segment should be long enough so that two beads can be threaded into the pipe cleaner and there will still be excess pipe cleaner sticking out each end. There should be enough excess pipe cleaner for each side to be wrapped into a loop. That way, you can use these pipe-cleaner segments with their beads to connect the two pipe cleaners you made in steps 2 and 3.
4. Put two beads (each a different color) on each pipe-cleaner segment. On a given segment, you should put either one bead that represents adenine and one bead that represents thymine or one bead that represents guanine and one bead that represents cytosine.
5. Once the beads are threaded into a pipe-cleaner segment, use the excess pipe cleaner on each side of the segment to attach the segment to the loops. The segment will therefore join the first pipe

cleaner with loops to the second pipe cleaner with loops. In effect, then, you will make a "ladder" that looks something like this:

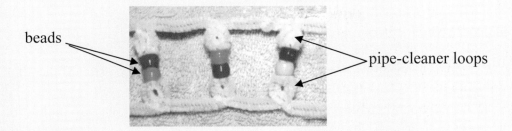

beads   pipe-cleaner loops

Remember, in this case, red represents thymine and green represents adenine. Thus, on a given segment there can be a red bead and a green bead, but not a red bead and yellow bead. The two beads can be in any order, but only red and green (representing thymine and adenine) or blue and yellow (representing guanine and cytosine) can be together.

6. You have now built the basic structure of DNA. The pipe cleaners with loops in them represent the backbone of the DNA, and the beads represent the nucleotide bases. There are only two things left to do. First, you need to make your model longer. Do this by making another "ladder" like the one you just made. Then, twist the pipe cleaners on the end of the first "ladder" with the pipe cleaners on the end of the second "ladder" so that you now have a single "ladder" that is twice as long:

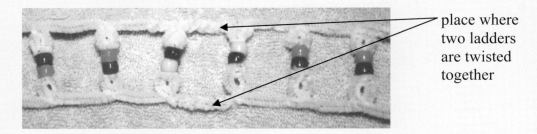

place where two ladders are twisted together

7. Repeat step 6 several times so your "ladder" grows longer and longer.
8. The final step is to twist the "ladder" into a double helix like DNA. Do this by holding each end and twisting them in opposite directions. In the end, your DNA model should look something like this:

9. Your DNA model will not stay twisted unless you hold it in its twisted form for quite some time. You can do this by twisting the DNA model so it looks right and then anchoring the ends to a table or other surface with tape. That will hold the model in its shape. After a few hours, you can release the tape and the model should stay twisted.

Look at your DNA model. I have said before, the pipe cleaners with the loops in them represent the backbone of the DNA. The twists in the model show you what a "double helix" structure looks like. The beads represent the nucleotide bases. If you followed the directions properly, only the nucleotide bases representing adenine and thymine or the nucleotide bases representing guanine and cytosine touch each other. This represents the fact that in DNA, adenine only links to thymine and cytosine only links to guanine. In living organisms, the sequence of nucleotide bases in the DNA (represented by the sequence of colored beads in your model) is a code that can be translated into the information necessary for life. When you take biology, you will learn the basics of how this is done.

I need to make one more point about your model. In real DNA, each side of the "ladder" is really its own molecule. The reason the two sides of the "ladder" stay together is because adenine "likes" to link up to thymine, and guanine "likes" to link up to cytosine. Thus, two sides are connected by the nucleotide bases that link up. In your model, then, the place where the beads touch each other is really a link that holds one side of the ladder to the other side. If you were to cut the pipe cleaner in between the two beads, your model would begin to unravel into two halves. In real DNA, this happens as a part of the process that decodes the sequence of nucleotide bases into information. You will learn more about this process when you take high school biology.

What I want you to understand right now is that in order to figure out the sequence of nucleotide bases in DNA, you only need to know about the sequence of nucleotide bases on one half of the DNA. Suppose, for example, some mean person cut your DNA model right in between each bead. As I told you before, this would cause your model to unravel into two halves. Suppose further that this mean person took one half of your DNA model and left the other half. When you see the half he left sitting on the table, you see the following:

Using just what you see there, you can figure out what the sequence of nucleotide bases on the other half of the DNA model was.

Remember, thymine (represented by red) links only to adenine (represented by green). Thus, since the first bead on the half you have is red, you know the first bead on the half that was stolen must have been green, because thymine (red) links only to adenine (green). Similarly, since yellow represents cytosine and blue represents guanine, the second bead on the side of the DNA that was stolen must have been blue, because cytosine (yellow) links only to guanine (blue). Using this kind of reasoning, you could completely reconstruct the other half of the DNA, even though it was stolen:

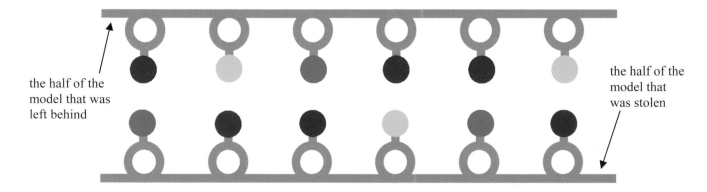

the half of the model that was left behind

the half of the model that was stolen

The point of this discussion, then, is that since we know thymine links only to adenine, and cytosine links only to guanine, if you know the sequence of nucleotide bases on one half of a portion of DNA, you can determine the sequence of nucleotide bases on the other half of DNA.

ON YOUR OWN

9.3 A scientist analyzes one half of a portion of DNA. She determines the following sequence:

adenine, thymine, cytosine, adenine, guanine, cytosine, thymine

What is the sequence of nucleotide bases on the other half of this portion of DNA?

9.4 Suppose that any nucleotide base could link up with any other nucleotide base. If this were the case, would there be any way of reconstructing the nucleotide base sequence from one half of a portion of DNA, like you did in the previous problem?

Energy and Life

I spent so much time talking to you about DNA that you probably forgot what I was originally discussing. In the first section of this module, I gave you four criteria for life. DNA was involved in the first criterion. Now I want to proceed to the second:

2. All life forms have a method by which they extract energy from the surroundings and convert it into energy that sustains them.

What does this mean? Well, it basically says that all living organisms have to "eat" in some way. You see, everything around you (plants, paper, rocks, wood, everything) has energy in it. When you eat food, you are actually taking energy from the food and transferring it to your body. Thus, you are taking in energy from the surroundings (food) and converting it to energy that sustains you.

Why didn't I just word this criterion for life as "all living organisms must eat to survive"? Well, that's because the word "eat" is too restrictive. You see, some living organisms (plants, for example) actually produce their own food, so they do not need to eat in the strict sense of the word. Perform the following experiment to see what I mean.

EXPERIMENT 9.2
Finding Food in Plants
Supplies:

- Eye protection such as goggles or safety glasses
- One slice of potato (uncooked)
- A pale green leaf (The paler the green, the better this experiment will work.)
- Rubbing alcohol (available at any drugstore)
- Iodine (available at any drugstore)
- A jar with a lid
- Two shallow dishes
- Tweezers

Introduction: This experiment allows you to detect stored food in plants.

Procedure:

1. Place the leaf in the jar and fill the jar with about 1 cup of rubbing alcohol.
2. Put the lid on the jar and let it sit overnight.
3. The next day, open the jar and dump out the alcohol. Keep the leaf.
4. In one shallow dish, place a potato slice. Pour just a little iodine on the white part of the potato slice. Note what happens.
5. Place the leaf in the second shallow dish. Pour enough iodine into the dish so that the leaf is covered.
6. Wait for a few moments and then grab the potato slice with the tweezers. Wash the potato with water. Try to avoid getting iodine on your hands, because it will stain them. Notice the color change that has occurred on the white part of the potato. Be sure and wash out the sink you are using with LOTS of water. Any iodine left in the sink will rust flatware and other metal objects placed in the sink, so you need to get rid of ALL iodine.
7. Wait about two hours and then pull the leaf out of the iodine with the tweezers. Once again, wash the leaf with water and look at it. Do you see a color change?
8. Clean everything up. Be sure and clean the sink with plenty of water!

In the experiment, you took a potato and added iodine to it. The result was that the white part of the potato turned blue. In fact, it might have turned such a dark blue it was nearly black. Why? Well, the potato contains **starch**. That's why we eat it. Starch is a chemical we use as a food source. The starch contains energy, and our bodies break the starch down and convert the energy contained in it into energy our bodies use to keep us alive. Iodine is often used to test for the presence of starch, because when iodine is mixed with starch, the mixture turns a deep blue color. That's the blue color you saw on the potato.

Well, when you put the leaf in the alcohol, the alcohol broke down the protective coating (called the "cuticle") that coats the leaf. It also partially pulled out a chemical (chlorophyll) that gives the leaf its green color. This left a pale leaf with no protective coating. When you added iodine to the leaf, you should have seen part or all of it turn blue. That's because starch is also in the leaf. Leaves actually produce food in the form of a chemical called **glucose** (gloo' kohs). If the plant needs energy, it takes the energy from the glucose and converts it into energy it uses to survive. If the plant has plenty of energy, it converts any unused glucose into starch (or one of a few other chemicals), which can be broken back down into glucose when the plant needs energy.

Plants (potato plants, house plants, trees, or any other kind of plant), therefore, produce their own food. Thus, they don't "eat" in the same way you and I eat. Nevertheless, they do convert energy from their surroundings into energy that sustains them. Therefore, they do meet the second criterion for life. How do plants produce their own food? Well, they take water from the ground and a gas called carbon dioxide from the air. Aided by the energy of sunlight, they chemically combine carbon dioxide and water to make glucose, the chemical I mentioned above. This process is called **photosynthesis** (foh' toh sin' thuh sis).

Photosynthesis – The process by which green plants and some other organisms use the energy of
         sunlight and simple chemicals to produce their own food

You will learn a lot more about this process in biology. One of the byproducts of photosynthesis is oxygen. Thus, plants help renew our oxygen supply so we can continue to breathe.

Since plants make their own food, they do not need to get food from their surroundings. This can be demonstrated with a long-term experiment.

EXPERIMENT 9.3
A Simple "Self-Sustaining" System

Supplies:

♦ A large jar with a lid
♦ A small potted plant that can fit inside the jar with room to spare
♦ Water
♦ An area of the house that gets sunlight almost every day
♦ A piece of masking tape or a marker

Introduction: Since plants produce their own food, they need not get it from an outside source. Under the right conditions, then, plants are self-sustaining.

Procedure:

1. Water the plant so the soil in the pot is moist.
2. Put the potted plant into the jar and close the lid so the plant is enclosed in the jar.
3. Use a marker or a piece of masking tape to mark the height of the plant on one side of the jar.
4. Place the jar next to a window or in some other area that is well-lit. It can even be left outside as long as the outside temperature stays pleasant.
5. Check on the plant every few days. Note whether or not it grows. Let it sit for at least 30 days. You can even let it sit for longer if the continued experiment is interesting to you. In fact, you can use this kind of experiment for a science-fair project.

In the experiment, you will see that the plant will stay alive and even grow, despite the fact that it is enclosed in the jar. If a mouse, insect, or any other animal were unlucky enough to be enclosed in the jar, it would quickly die due to lack of food and water. Nevertheless, the plant will live and grow. Why? Well, you provided it with some water, and there was some carbon dioxide in the air that was in the jar. Since you placed the plant in sunlight, the plant will use the energy of sunlight, the water in the soil, and the carbon dioxide in the air surrounding it to make glucose and oxygen.

When the plant needs energy, it will convert the glucose into energy. It takes oxygen to do that, but oxygen will be produced when the glucose is made, so there will be plenty of oxygen available. When the glucose is converted to energy, water and carbon dioxide will also be produced. You probably will see some of that water as droplets that form on the inside of the jar. That water and carbon dioxide will later be used to produce more glucose. Do you see what will happen, then? The plant will use carbon dioxide and water to make glucose, but those two chemicals will be made when the glucose is used. In the same way, it will use up oxygen to convert the glucose to energy, but that oxygen will be made again when the glucose is made. Thus, the plant will be almost self-sustaining.

The plant will not be *completely* self-sustaining, however. It will need the energy from the sunlight. Thus, the plant takes energy from its surroundings (in the form of light) and converts it into glucose, which it can use to make energy to sustain itself.   As long as disease doesn't enter into the picture, the plant should continue to live its complete life without any input other than light. The light doesn't even have to come from the sun. If it is bright enough, light from a lamp will sustain the plant.

You probably should be asking yourself a question at this point. What about fertilizer? You know that farmers and gardeners often use some form of fertilizer in order to help their plants grow. Why won't your plant need fertilizer? Well, contrary to popular belief, fertilizer does not *feed* a plant. A plant uses only water, carbon dioxide, and light to make its food (glucose). Any excess food is stored as starch or one of a few other chemicals, like sucrose (table sugar). Thus, fertilizer is not something a plant eats. Fertilizer has several chemicals in it that help some of the plant's other functions (fighting disease, repairing injuries, etc.). Thus, fertilizer is kind of like a "vitamin pill" for plants. Just like you and I don't *need* vitamin pills to stay alive, a plant does not *need* fertilizer to stay alive. However, just as vitamin pills can help make us healthier, fertilizer can make a plant healthier.

Whether a living organism makes its own food or eats its food, it then converts the food into energy. The process by which food is broken down and converted to energy is called **metabolism** (muh tab' uh liz um).

Metabolism – The sum total of all processes in an organism that convert energy and matter from
              outside sources and use that energy and matter to sustain the organism's life functions

The process of metabolism is incredibly interesting. You will learn a lot more about it when you take biology.

As you continue to check on your experiment, you will probably notice water droplets on the inside of the jar from time to time. As I mentioned before, that is because water and carbon dioxide are produced when the plant converts glucose into energy. In fact, water and carbon dioxide are produced by the metabolism of nearly every living organism. You can see that human metabolism produces water. Just hold a glass surface near your mouth and exhale onto the glass. You will see the glass cloud up. That's because you exhale water as a product of your metabolism. The water then forms tiny droplets on the glass, clouding it. I also noted that in converting its food to energy, the plant needed oxygen. That is true for the vast majority of living organisms (not all, but most) on the earth. Most of them need oxygen in order to convert their food into energy, which is why most living things need oxygen to survive. So even though plants make oxygen by photosynthesis, they also *use* oxygen when they burn their food. They make more food than they burn, however, so overall, plants make more oxygen than they use. This is why plants are considered a source of oxygen.

  The multimedia CD has a video about eating and metabolism.

ON YOUR OWN

9.5 Some fertilizers are advertised as "high-quality plant food." What is wrong with such an advertisement?

9.6 Several science-oriented stores will sell you an "aquatic biosphere," which is a closed glass container that holds water, underwater plants, underwater snails, and perhaps some shrimp. The biosphere is completely closed off, but the occupants will live for quite a long time, as long as you provide the biosphere with one thing. What one thing must you provide?

Sensing and Responding to Change

Moving down the list of our criteria for life, we come to the third one:

3. All life forms can sense changes in their surroundings and respond to those changes.

It is important to realize that in order to meet this criterion, an organism's ability to sense changes is just as important as its ability to respond. After all, even a rock can respond to changes in its environment. If a boulder, for example, is perched on the very edge of a cliff, a slight change in the wind patterns around the boulder might be enough for it to fall off the cliff. In this case, the boulder is responding to the changes in its surroundings. The reason a boulder doesn't meet this criterion for life is that the boulder cannot *sense* the change and then respond.

Living organisms are equipped with some method of receiving information about their surroundings. Typically, they accomplish this feat with **receptors**.

Receptors – Special structures that allow living organisms to sense the conditions of their internal or
external environment

Your skin, for example, is full of receptors. They give you a sense of touch, allow you to feel pain, etc. Have you ever heard of leprosy? This terrible disease causes people's skin receptors to cease functioning properly. This causes them to lose the sense of touch, pain, etc. that comes from their skin. Now you might think it is good to lose the ability to sense pain, but consider the figure below.

FIGURE 9.3
The Feet of a Person With Leprosy

Photo © Karen Low Phillips
Agency: www.istockphoto.com

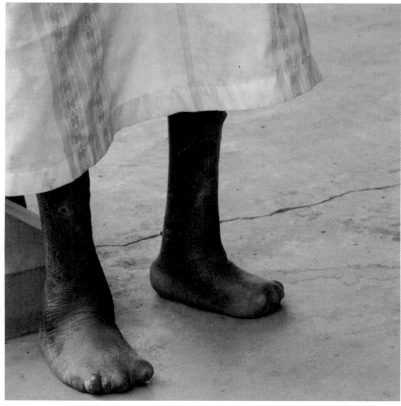

The feet you see belong to a person with leprosy. The leprosy did not eat away at his toes, however. This man has no toes because the leprosy prevented him from feeling pain. Most likely, the man's toes were cut, but because he could not feel the pain, he did not know they were being cut. It is possible that his toes were simply cut off because he did not know to pull away from whatever was cutting them. It is also possible that his toes were not cut off, but the wound became infected, and because there was no pain from the infection, they were never cleaned. Eventually, they had to be surgically removed. This might have happened all at once, or he might have lost a few toes at a time.

So you see that the inability to feel pain is *not* a good thing. Pain tells us that something is wrong, which causes us to react. We can pull away from a painful sensation to avoid more damage. We can also investigate the area that hurts to care for it properly. If your arm gets cut, for example, you know it, and you can clean and bandage the wound before it gets worse. Since people with leprosy cannot *feel* the pain, they can be cut and not even know it. People with leprosy must examine themselves several times each day to detect injuries that you or I would immediately know exist!

Now before I move on, I need to make sure you understand that the term "leprosy" as we use it today is not the same as the term used in the Bible (see 2 Kings 5, for example). In biblical times, the disease "leprosy" referred to a variety of skin disorders that were probably caused by an infectious agent. Since leprosy can cause all sorts of skin problems due to the lack of pain sensation, there are some *similarities* between what the Bible calls "leprosy" and what we call "leprosy" today. Nevertheless, they are two completely different ailments. This is common when dealing with ancient literature. The meanings of words change over time, which is why it is important to study history and language in order to have a complete understanding of the Bible (or any other ancient work).

Of course, not only people, but *all* living organisms must sense and respond to change. Thus, all living organisms have receptors. Perform the following experiment to see that even earthworms can sense and respond to change.

EXPERIMENT 9.4
Sensing and Responding to Change

Supplies:

- A few earthworms (Get them at a live bait shop if you can't find them outside.)
- A container that will hold the earthworms and soil
- Soil
- Some water
- A bright light

Introduction: All living organisms sense and respond to changes in their environment. This experiment shows how earthworms respond to light and water.

Procedure:

1. If you bought your earthworms, they probably already came in a container with soil. If not, get a container and fill it at least halfway with soil.
2. Put the earthworms on top of the soil and leave the lid off the container.
3. Put the container under the light.
4. Let the whole system sit for 30 minutes or more and see what happens to the earthworms.
5. Turn off the light and make the room reasonably dim.
6. Pour water on the soil so as to make it really wet.
7. Once again, wait for 30 minutes or so and see what happens to the earthworms.
8. Clean everything up. Let the earthworms go, or use them as an excuse to go fishing!

What did you see in the experiment? If all went well, you should have seen that in the first phase of the experiment, the worms dug themselves into the soil. Why did they do that? Well, worms do not have eyes like you and me, but they can sense light, because they have light-sensitive receptors on their skin. When they sense light, they crawl away from it. Why? Earthworms actually breathe through their skin. In order for that to work, their skin must stay moist. When earthworms sense light, they think it is the sun. Since the sun tends to dry out things that are moist, the earthworms know that they must avoid long-term exposure to the sun, or their skin will dry, suffocating them. Thus, when earthworms *sense* light, they *respond* by moving away from it.

In the second part of the experiment, the earthworms should have crawled out of the soil to the top of the soil. Once again, this is because they sensed a change in the environment and responded to it. In this case, the change was that the soil got very wet. In response, the earthworms came up to the surface. There are at least two reasons for this. First, if the soil gets too wet, the earthworms can have trouble breathing through their skin. Also, when the soil is wet, there is less danger of the earthworm's skin drying out. Thus, being on the surface is safer for the earthworm when the soil is wet. Earthworms often come up out of ground at night (once again, because there is less chance of their skin drying out then), and that is why some people call earthworms "nightcrawlers."

A living organism's ability to sense and respond to changes in its surrounding environment is a critical part of survival. If earthworms could not sense and respond to light, they would die. If we did not experience pain, the consequences could be terrible. You see, God's creation is always changing. Weather changes, seasons change, landscapes change, and the community of organisms in a given region changes. As a result, living organisms must be able to sense these changes and respond to them, or they will not be able to survive.

ON YOUR OWN

9.7 Although it might be hard to believe, plants sense and respond to change in their surroundings. After all, they are living organisms. Name at least one example that shows how plants sense and respond to change.

Reproduction and Life

We now come to the final criterion that determines whether or not something is alive:

4. All life forms reproduce.

We instinctively know this, of course. After all, dogs have puppies, cats have kittens, and people have children. There is, of course, a very simple reason *why* living organisms must reproduce. If they do not, they will eventually die out completely. Thus, reproduction is a means by which living organisms ensure that their kind will continue. Of course, sometimes this is not enough. As we learned from geology and paleontology, some organisms become extinct. This can be for a variety of reasons, but in the end, it comes down to one thing: the organisms died off faster than they could reproduce. As a result, eventually, there were just no more of those organisms left. Reproduction, then, is God's way of making sure that life continues.

In order to get a little bit of experience observing the process of reproduction, perform the following experiment:

EXPERIMENT 9.5
Fruit Fly Reproduction

Supplies:

♦ Large jar (It must be large enough to fit a banana inside.)
♦ Nylon stocking large enough to stretch over the mouth of the jar
♦ Rubber band large enough to fit around the mouth of the jar
♦ A banana

Introduction: In this experiment, you will see the process of reproduction in fruit flies. **Please note:** If you are on a "normal" homeschooling schedule, you might have to delay this experiment, as it will not work well in the winter unless you live in a part of the world that is warm in winter.

Procedure:

1. Peel the banana.
2. Open the jar and stick the banana in the jar.
3. Leave the jar open and look at it daily. Eventually, you should see some small flies hovering around the banana. As you might expect, they are **fruit flies**. If you don't see any fruit flies, try leaving the uncovered jar outside for a day or so. Try to put it on a table or other raised platform away from roofs and trees to reduce the chance of crawling insects making their way inside.
4. Once you get some flies, trap them in the jar by stretching the nylon stocking over the mouth of the jar and holding it in place with the rubber band. The stocking must cover the entire mouth of the jar. It has tiny holes that will allow air into the jar so the flies can breathe, but the holes are too small for the flies to squeeze through. Thus, they will stay in the jar and continue to live. In case you are wondering, this is not cruel. The flies have a huge food source and are not bothered by anything trying to eat them. They are as content as flies can be.
5. Observe the jar daily over the next two weeks. Note what you see. Make drawings of what the flies look like initially, and then make drawings when the situation changes.
6. You need to observe things for at least two weeks. After that, you can release the flies outside or continue to observe, whichever you prefer. This is another experiment that can be used as a science fair project.

What will you see in the experiment? Well, if things go well, you will see that after a few days, little white crawling things will appear on the banana. Those are **maggots**. When flies reproduce, they make maggots. Thus, the maggots are "baby" flies. As the maggots mature, they become the flies you originally saw in the jar. Over the period of two weeks, you should have seen maggots form and mature into adult flies. The process of maggots turning into flies is called **metamorphosis** (met uh mor' fuh sis). When you take biology, you will learn more about this fascinating process.

Since reproduction is something common to all living organisms, and since there are so many different kinds of living organisms in creation, you can imagine that reproduction takes many different forms. For example, while many organisms need a partner for reproduction, many do not. A bacterium, for example, simply makes copies of itself. Some flatworms actually tear themselves in half, and then each half regenerates so that there are two flatworms where there once was only one. These organisms, then, don't need help from another organism for reproduction to occur. Even among organisms that need a partner for reproduction, there are differences. Consider, for example, the difference between reproduction in dogs and reproduction in people. Dogs and people both need mates in order to reproduce, but the reproduction strategy is still quite different.

FIGURE 9.4
Reproduction in Dogs and People

Photo © rgbspace (left) David Jenks (right)
Agency: www.shutterstock.com

When dogs reproduce, *several* puppies are born to a single mother dog each time. There are so many puppies that they are called a **litter**. These Siberian husky puppies were all born to the same mother over a period of a few hours. Also, they are born with their eyes closed. They will not be able to open their eyes and see for two to three weeks.

When people reproduce, usually one baby is born at a time. Every once in a while there will be two (we call the babies **twins**), and even more rarely more than two will be born. One baby at a time, however, is the norm. While not independent from his or her parents, the baby is more developed than a puppy. The baby's eyes are functional at birth, for example.

Why do dogs produce so many puppies at one time when people usually produce only one baby at a time? Well, the answer is simple. God has designed each living organism's reproduction strategy to meet that organism's survival needs. In the wild, dogs die frequently, because they live reasonably dangerous lives. As a result, if dogs had few puppies, more dogs would die each year than the number of puppies born that year. As a result, every year there would be fewer and fewer dogs until there were no more dogs at all. Thus, since a dog's life is dangerous, dogs must have several puppies in order to keep the population of dogs steady. Human beings, however, live significantly less dangerous lives. As a result, the population of people will stay steady even when most people have only two or three babies their entire lives.

The number of offspring that a living organism has, therefore, depends on how many offspring are necessary to keep the population level up. Rabbits, for example, have a *lot* of offspring. The typical rabbit can begin producing offspring about six months after birth. They produce three to eight rabbits in each litter. A mother rabbit can have as many as *six litters each year*! Since the average rabbit lives about 10 years, you can see how many baby rabbits can be produced! Why do rabbits need to reproduce so much? They lead incredibly dangerous lives. There are *many* other animals that hunt and eat rabbits. As a result, *a lot* of rabbits die each year. Thus, they must produce lots of new rabbits to keep the rabbit population steady.

Have you heard anything about earth's "population problem"? There are some people out there who think that there are just too many people on earth. They consider this a real problem, arguing that eventually, earth will not be able to support the number people it holds. As a result, they say, there will be widespread famine and disease because there will be simply too many people living on the planet.

Is this a real problem? Not at all! Anyone who does any research into this supposed problem will find out that there is no need to worry about the human population growing too quickly for the earth to support it. To understand why, you need to learn a few details about the issue. First and foremost, the earth's population is growing. There is a simple reason for that. More babies are born each year than the number of people who die each year. It turns out that the average mother must have 2.2 babies in order to keep the population of humans steady.

Why does the average mother have to have 2.2 babies in order to keep the human population steady? Well, it takes two people (a mother and a father) to have a baby. Thus, each couple needs to have two babies, one to "replace" the mother and the other to "replace" the father. However, there are *some* children that die due to disease or accident. These children will not "replace" the adults they are supposed to replace, because they did not live long enough to have their own children. If there aren't a few "extra" babies born each year, the parents of those children will not get "replaced" when they die, and the human population will slowly decrease. Thus, the average mother must have just a little more than two babies in order to "replace" the mother, the father, and those children who die early.

It turns out that in *many* countries like the United States, the United Kingdom, Canada, and Italy, mothers are having *fewer* than 2.2 children in their lifetime. As a result, mothers in these countries are not having enough babies in order to keep the human population steady. In addition, the *number* of countries in which mothers are having fewer than 2.2 babies is actually *increasing*! Thus, there are many countries in which the mothers are not having enough babies to replace the people who are dying, and the number of countries in that situation is growing!

Despite these facts, the human population is still growing because of countries like India, in which mothers are having significantly more than 2.2 babies in their lifetime. However, the average number of babies being born to mothers in countries such as India is also *decreasing*. Thus, even though the human population is still increasing, it is not increasing all that quickly. In addition, the speed at which the human population is growing *decreases every year*. As a result, it is only a matter of time before the human population stops growing. In fact, while predictions such as these are often unreliable, the United Nations predicts that the world's population will stabilize by the year 2300.

"Wait a minute," you might think. Even if the speed at which the population is growing is slowing down, the population will still increase for a while. Are we in danger of the population becoming too large *before* it stops growing? The answer to that question is a very firm "No." How can I say that? Well, probably the biggest indicator of whether or not there are too many people on earth is the amount of food per person. After all, if there really are too many people for earth to support, the first thing that you would see is starvation. There would simply not be enough food for every person on the planet.

Is the amount of food per person decreasing? Absolutely not! In fact, the opposite is true. Every year since it has been studied, the amount of food per person on the earth actually *has increased*. Over the past 250 years, for example, the population of the earth has increased by a factor of 6. This means there are six times as many people living today than there were in the mid-1700s. Now that sounds like a lot, but consider this: *The amount of food produced over that same time period has risen by a factor of 1,700!* Thus, there is more food per person on earth now than there *has ever been in history*.

If this is the case, why are there people who are starving today? That is the result of evil, not food shortage. People starve because they are in countries whose leaders hoard the wealth and food. In countries where the leaders do not hoard the food and wealth, people starve because they refuse to work, or because they do not take advantage of the charitable organizations that will feed them. If all of the food on earth were divided equally among the people of the earth, we could all eat to our hearts content and still have extra.

There are other indicators you can look at to determine whether or not there are too many people on earth. The price of raw materials used in manufacturing is also a great indicator. After all, if there were too many people on earth, people would have to fight over the materials we use for building things. If that were the case, the price of these materials would go up and up. In fact, the price of *almost all* raw materials (in inflation-adjusted dollars) has *decreased every generation* since these things have been measured.

In the end, then, the human population on earth is *not* a problem. The rate at which it is growing decreases every year. We therefore know that the population of people will eventually level off and then, most likely, decrease slowly. Meanwhile, the amount of food per person on earth is increasing, and the cost of raw materials is decreasing. Thus, there are no population problems to worry about. God has designed the earth as our home, and He would not skimp on the design. His gift to us will provide for our needs as long as He sees fit.

Of course, there are more differences in reproduction among the creatures of the world than just the number of offspring they have. Some animals hatch from eggs, for example, while others are born live. Even once they are born or hatched, there are differences among animal offspring. Some animals, for example, are born ready to take care of themselves. Sea turtles, for example, hatch from eggs and need no care from their parents. They immediately make a mad dash for the sea and begin a dangerous but normal life. Scientists call them **precocial** (prih koh' shul).

Precocial – A term used to describe offspring that are born able to hear, see, move about, regulate body
            temperature, and eliminate waste without a parent's help

Horses have precocial offspring, as do many types of reptiles, fish, and ground-nesting birds.

Other animals have offspring that require a lot of parental care in order to survive. Scientists call these animals **altricial** (al trih' shul).

Altricial – A term used to describe offspring that are born without at least one of the following
            abilities: hear, see, move about, regulate body temperature, or eliminate waste

Dogs, for example, have altricial offspring. Puppies can do many things that precocial offspring can do, but they cannot see. Puppies, then, are more "helpless" than newly hatched sea turtles and therefore require more parental attention. Interestingly enough, very similar animals can have remarkably different offspring. Hares, for example, look a lot like rabbits. Even though they look similar, hares have precocial young, while rabbits are born without hair and with their eyes closed. Thus, rabbit offspring are altricial, because they cannot see or regulate their body temperature (which is what hair allows a mammal to do).

ON YOUR OWN

9.8 The bombardier (bom buh deer') beetle is a very interesting insect you will learn about in biology class. It is an ugly beetle with a powerful chemical weapon that wards off any creature wanting to eat it. As a result, bombardier beetles live a very safe life. Would you expect bombardier beetles to produce a lot of offspring or only a few?

The Cell: Life's Smallest Unit

Now that you know the basic criteria that determine whether or not something is alive, it is important for you to see *how* living organisms meet these criteria. For example, all living organisms have DNA. Where is the DNA? All living organisms convert energy from their surroundings into energy that sustains them. Where and how does that happen? All living organisms sense and respond to change in their surroundings. How? All living organisms reproduce. What are the details?

Well, the answers to many of those questions are too detailed for this course. You will learn some of the answers when you take biology. However, I can *begin* to answer some of those questions by introducing you to life's most basic unit: the **cell**.

Cell – The smallest unit of life in creation

What is a cell? Let's start with a figure.

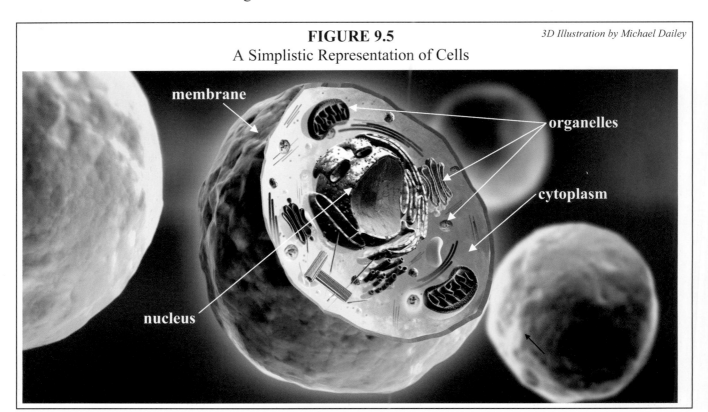

FIGURE 9.5
3D Illustration by Michael Dailey
A Simplistic Representation of Cells

membrane

organelles

cytoplasm

nucleus

The spheres in the figure represent cells. First, notice that the cells in the drawing are surrounded by an outer covering called a **membrane**. The central cell has been cut away so you can see inside the membrane. A jellylike substance called **cytoplasm** (sye' tuh plaz' uhm) fills the cell, and **organelles** (or guh nelz') are suspended in the cytoplasm. These organelles have individual tasks they must accomplish to keep the cell alive.

Believe it or not, your entire body is made up of cells. In fact, just as everything you see is made up of atoms, all life is made up of cells. There are roughly one hundred trillion cells that make up your body! These cells work together to make you the person that you are. You see, every cell in your body has particular tasks it must accomplish. You have cells in your eye that detect light, and based on what they detect, they send electrical signals to your brain. This allows you to see. You have cells in your skin that protect your body from foreign substances. You have cells in your blood that transport oxygen to all the cells in your body. This allows your body's cells to burn your food for energy. All the different cells in your body work with each other to accomplish the things that keep you alive.

Interestingly enough, the cells in you are very similar to the cells we find in cats, dogs, and other animals. Even the cells in an elephant are very similar to the cells you have in your body. Of course, it takes many more cells to make an elephant than to make you, and it takes fewer cells to make a dog or a cat. Also, the tasks these cells perform and the ways in which they work together are different. That's a large part of why a dog is different from a cat, and an elephant is different from you. Nevertheless, the cells themselves are very similar.

You will study cells in *great detail* when you take biology, but I do want you to know a few things about them right now. First of all, they are very small. That is obviously the case, since there are about a hundred trillion of them in your body! The cells in your body range in size, but the average cell is about *1 to 3 ten thousandths of an inch* across. That's pretty small! The largest cell in the body is a few hundredths of an inch across. Thus, you cannot see most cells with your naked eye. You must use a microscope.

The second thing you need to know about cells is that it does not necessarily take a lot of them to make a living organism. Although people, cats, insects, and many, many other organisms are composed of trillions of cells, there are *billions and billions* of living organisms that are composed of *only one* cell. Indeed, there is an entire microscopic world of which you are mostly unaware. You will learn a bit about that world in the next module. The organisms that make up this microscopic world are often made up of just one cell! A single cell *can* perform all the functions of life. Thus, a *single cell* is considered alive.

The third thing I want to point out is that cells themselves can reproduce. They must be able to, or they would not be considered alive. What you might not have considered, however, is that there are cells in your body that are reproducing *right now* as you read this text. After all, in order to grow, you need more cells. Where do those cells come from? They come from the reproduction of other cells. Also, you have cells in your body that die all the time. For example, millions of red blood cells in your body die *every second*. Those cells must be replaced. Thus, your cells are constantly reproducing in order to replace cells that have died and in order to make new cells so you can grow.

The fourth thing I want you to know is the identity of one of the organelles in the cell. It is called the **nucleus** (noo' klee us), and it is pointed out in Figure 9.5. The nucleus is probably the most important organelle in the cell. It is where you will find most of the organism's DNA. You can find DNA in another organelle, called the mitochondrion (my tuh kahn' dree uhn), but that is very specific DNA with very specific functions. The main DNA of a cell is found in its nucleus.

The last thing you need to know about cells is that there are three basic kinds in creation. The ones sketched in Figure 9.5 are **animal cells**. They are the cells you find in animals. Plants have a slightly different kind of cell, and it is called, as you might imagine, a **plant cell**. Finally, there is a third kind of cell that is typically found in the tiniest single-celled organisms. These organisms are called **bacteria**, and a cell from such an organism does not have a nucleus. There is still DNA in the cell; it is just not housed in the nucleus, because there is no nucleus. This is one reason that the nucleus is considered an important organelle in the cell. The presence or absence of a nucleus in a cell can help identify what kind of cell it is. You will learn more about cells without a nucleus in the next module.

In order for something to be living, it must meet all the criteria listed at the beginning of this module. If that is the case, then it will *definitely* be composed of cells. Thus, you could add a fifth criterion for life: All life forms are composed of at least one cell. This, however, is usually not done, since anything that meets the other criteria *must* be composed of cells. Since the cell is the smallest unit that can satisfy all four criteria for life, the cell is considered the most basic unit of life itself.

Now even though the cell is the most basic unit of life, it is ***not*** simple. Please do not confuse "basic" with "simple." Life is exceedingly complex, and even the most basic unit of life is amazingly complicated. It is so complicated that, in fact, human science still cannot understand the details of even the most basic kind of cell. Over the years, we have made huge progress in our understanding of how cells work, but we are still far from understanding all the details. The fact that the greatest minds of science cannot yet completely understand how a cell works gives you some idea of how complicated cells are!

ON YOUR OWN

9.9 A mule is the offspring of a female horse and a male donkey. Most mules are sterile, which means they cannot produce offspring. Does this mean they are unable to meet the fourth criterion for life and are therefore not considered alive? Why or why not?

9.10 Suppose a scientist is looking at cells from the following organisms under a microscope:

a bacterium (the singular form of bacteria)
b. onion
c. mouse
d grass
e. horse

Which cells would look very similar to each other under the microscope?

ANSWERS TO THE "ON YOUR OWN" PROBLEMS

9.1 Remember, atoms link together to make molecules. Therefore, molecules must be bigger than atoms, because there are two or more atoms in a molecule. Thus, <u>atoms are smaller</u>.

9.2 A cookbook has many recipes in it. These recipes have information that tells you how to take many individual things that you would probably not eat and put them together in such a way as to make them something you would eat. <u>Like a cookbook, DNA has information that takes many individual chemicals that are not alive and puts them together in such a way as to make life.</u>

9.3 Remember, DNA is held together by nucleotide bases on one half of the molecule linking up with nucleotide bases on the other half. Only adenine and thymine can link together, and only cytosine and guanine will link together. Thus, the other side must be:

<u>thymine, adenine, guanine, thymine, cytosine, guanine, adenine</u>

9.4 <u>There would be no way to do it</u>. The way we determined the first nucleotide base on the other half of the DNA molecule in the previous problem was by recognizing that only thymine can link to adenine. If any nucleotide base could link to adenine, there would be no way to know which nucleotide base would be there.

9.5 <u>Fertilizers are **not** plant food</u>. Plants make their own food. Fertilizers are plant "vitamins."

9.6 <u>You must provide light</u>. The plant will make food for itself, and the other creatures will eat either the plant or microscopic organisms you cannot see. Those microscopic organisms most likely will eat the plant. The plant will also make enough oxygen for all the organisms, but it needs light to make its own food and produce oxygen.

9.7 There are many ways that plants sense and respond to change. Here are a few:

<u>Plants can sense where the greatest amount of light is, and they grow toward that light.</u>

<u>Plants can sense when they touch a structure, and if the structure is right, they will wind themselves around the structure for support.</u>

<u>Plants can sense which way is up, and they will always grow that way.</u>

<u>Plants can sense when it is night and respond. For example, many plants close their flowers at night and open them in the morning.</u>

There are other examples, but these are the most common. You will experiment with some of these later on in the course.

9.8 Since the bombardier beetle leads a pretty safe life, there will not be a lot that die before having babies. Thus, they do not need a lot of extra "replacements." Therefore, you would think that <u>bombardier beetles have few offspring.</u>

9.9 Although the mule itself cannot produce offspring, each of its cells can reproduce. Otherwise, it would not grow or be able to heal if it is hurt. Thus, <u>the mule still meets the fourth criterion of life, but it does so because of its cells' ability to reproduce.</u>

9.10 <u>Cells (b) and (d) would look very similar, because they would be plant cells. Similarly, cells (c) and (e) would look very similar, because they are animal cells.</u> The bacterium cell would not look like any of the others, as it lacks a nucleus.

"Why are you reading that? You're already an expert on cells."

Cartoon by Speartoons

STUDY GUIDE FOR MODULE #9

1. Define the following terms:

a. Atom
b. Molecule
c. Photosynthesis
d. Metabolism
e. Receptors
f. Precocial
g. Altricial
h. Cell

2. What are the four criteria for life?

3. What does DNA provide to a living organism?

4. Compared to other molecules, is DNA big or small?

5. Does DNA store its information more efficiently or less efficiently than a computer?

6. DNA is made up of two basic parts: the backbone and the nucleotide bases.

a.   Which part stores the information?
b.   Which part forms the double-helix structure?

7. Which nucleotide base will link to adenine? Which will link to cytosine?

8. One half of a portion of DNA has the following sequence:

cytosine, guanine, adenine, guanine, thymine, thymine

What is the sequence of nucleotide bases on the other half of this portion?

9. One half of a portion of DNA has the following sequence:

thymine, guanine, cytosine, adenine, thymine, guanine

What is the sequence of nucleotide bases on the other half of this portion?

10. What is the name of the chemical that plants make for food?

11. What is the name of the chemical that plants often store their food as?

12. For most organisms, metabolism requires food and something else. What is that something else?

13. Metabolism produces energy and usually two other things. What are they?

14. An organism's receptors no longer work. Which of the four criteria of life will the organism not be able to perform?

15. Consider the difference between a shark and an anchovy. Both are fish. The first is a fierce hunter that rarely is eaten by any other animal. The second is a major source of food for many other fish in the sea. Which would you expect to have more offspring: two shark parents or two anchovy parents?

16. Every once in a while, a female cat will be born sterile. This means that the cat cannot have kittens. Does this mean that the cat is not alive, since it cannot reproduce?

17. Is the population of people on this earth becoming a problem?

18. Indicate what the arrows are pointing at in the cell drawn below:

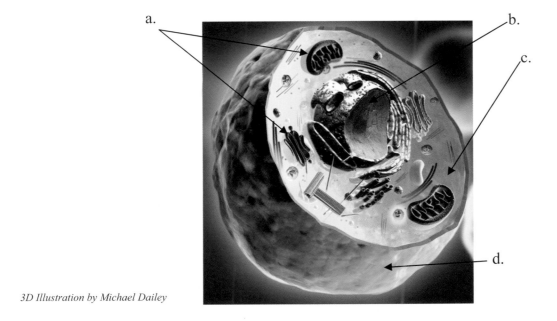

3D Illustration by Michael Dailey

19. In which organelle is most of the DNA stored?

20. How many basic kinds of cells are there? Name them.

21. If a scientist uses a microscope to examine a cell from a mouse, a cell from a leaf, and a cell from a cat, how many different basic kinds of cells will she see?

MODULE #10: Classifying Life

Initial Experiment Setup

In the third section of this module (kingdom Monera), you will be studying bacteria. Although it is impossible to see bacteria without the aid of a nice microscope, I want you to perform an experiment that will help you learn a bit about bacteria. This experiment must sit for two days, however, so I want you to start it now, which will ensure it is ready when you reach that section of the module.

EXPERIMENT 10.1 - Part 1
Factors That Affect Bacterial Growth

Supplies:

♦ One chicken bouillon cube
♦ Table salt
♦ White vinegar
♦ Four small glasses
♦ One large glass
♦ One measuring cup
♦ One teaspoon
♦ Masking tape
♦ Marker or pen
♦ Eye protection such as goggles or safety glasses

Introduction: This experiment allows you to see how bacteria grow despite the fact that you cannot see them without the aid of a microscope.

Procedure:

1. Dissolve the bouillon cube in $1\frac{1}{3}$ cups of hot water from the faucet. Do this in the large glass. The entire cube may not dissolve. That's fine.
2. Equally divide the solution between the four small glasses.
3. Add a teaspoon of salt to one of the glasses and stir until the salt is dissolved. Label this glass with masking tape that has the word "salt" on it.
4. Add a teaspoon of vinegar to the second glass and stir. Label this glass with masking tape that has the word "vinegar" on it.
5. Label the third glass with masking tape that has the word "control" on it.
6. Label the fourth glass with masking tape that has the word "cold" on it.
7. Put the fourth glass in the refrigerator.
8. Do not cover any of the glasses.
9. Allow the glasses to sit for a few days. While the glasses are sitting, continue with the module.

Introduction

In the previous module, you learned in detail the different criteria for life. If something satisfies those four criteria, it is alive. If it fails to meet even one of the criteria, it is not alive. Thus, based on those four criteria, we can *distinguish* between life and non-life. In other words, we have·

formed a **classification system**. In this classification system, we identify all things around us as either alive or not alive. A rock is not alive, but a houseplant is alive. Thus, there are two categories in this classification system.

If you think about it, you use classification systems all the time. You classify other students as publicly schooled, privately schooled, or homeschooled. You also classify them as people you like, people you can tolerate, or people you don't really like. In both of these classification systems, other students belong to one of three categories. In the end, then, you are already familiar with the use of classification systems.

Why do you use classification systems? Well, a classification system takes an enormous amount of data and orders it in an easy-to-access, meaningful way. Consider, for example, the idea of classifying students based on how they are educated. Although there are many differences from one homeschooled student to the next, homeschooled students share much in common. In the same way, all publicly schooled students share common experiences, despite the fact that every individual student is unique. Finally, privately schooled students also have many things in common, despite their individual characteristics. By placing students into one of those three categories, you are "ordering" them in an easy-to-access system of reference.

So what? What does that do for you? Well, suppose you wanted to study different kinds of educational methods. If you gave a bunch of students a few standardized tests, you could take all the publicly schooled students' test scores and average them. You could then figure out a separate average test score all the privately schooled students. Finally, you could compute the average test score of all the homeschooled students. If you then compared those three averages, you might learn something about the effectiveness of each type of educational process. In fact, many such studies have been done. In general, homeschooled students have the highest average test scores, privately-schooled students have lower average test scores, and publicly schooled students have the lowest average test scores.

See what this classification system has allowed us to learn? By grouping students together in a few distinct classifications, we have been able to learn something about the effectiveness of the various types of schooling. Without the classification system, having a bunch of students take standardized tests doesn't tell you anything except the amount of knowledge that each individual has. By putting the students in categories and comparing the test scores between those categories, however, you have learned something more.

Classification, then, is a way of grouping things in terms of similarities that they share. This takes a large amount of data and organizes it in a way that helps us learn something about those things we are classifying. Well, since the goal of science is to learn, it makes sense that scientists want to classify things, too. In fact, you have already learned some classification systems in this course. In an earlier module, you learned that there are three kinds of rock: sedimentary, igneous, and metamorphic. That's a classification system for rocks, and it contains three distinct categories.

In this module, you will learn a five-category classification system for living organisms. This is one of the more popular classification systems used throughout the life sciences, but it is not the only one. Several different classification systems exist, and they each have their strengths and weaknesses. However, they all have this in common: They attempt to take the enormous amount of information that pertains to life and order it in some meaningful, easy-to-use way.

The Five-Kingdom System

The study of life is often referred to as the science of **biology**. In biology, the **five-kingdom system** is a convenient way to classify living organisms. In this system, the main categories are called "kingdoms." As you might expect, there are five of them. The names of these kingdoms are **Monera** (muh nihr' uh), **Protista** (pruh tist' uh), **Fungi** (fun' jye), **Plantae,** and **Animalia.** We capitalize the names of the kingdoms because they are considered proper names.

Now first of all, you should not be afraid of these names. I expect they are mostly new to you, but that's okay. You will be studying these five kingdoms throughout this entire module, so you have plenty of time to learn the names. Right now, you should focus on the things you recognize about them already. For example, look at the last two. Those are just Latin names for "plants" and "animals." Thus, you already know two of these five kingdoms. They are the kingdoms that contain plants and animals. You might even be familiar with the third kingdom as well. Have you every heard a mushroom referred to as a fungus? Well, "fungi" is just the plural form of "fungus." Thus, kingdom Fungi contains mushrooms. It contains other organisms, too, like molds that grow on bread and fruit.

What about those other two kingdoms? Well, remember from the previous module that there is a tiny, microscopic world of which you are mostly unaware. Those two kingdoms (Monera and Protista) contain most of the organisms in that microscopic world. The five-kingdom system, then, isn't so bad. The first two kingdoms are Monera and Protista, which contain mostly microscopic organisms. The third kingdom is Fungi, and it contains organisms like mushrooms. The fourth kingdom (Plantae) contains plants, and the fifth kingdom (Animalia) contains animals.

Top middle photo by Kathleen J. Wile
Both bottom photos by Dawn M. Strunc

FIGURE 10.1
The Five-Kingdom System

Photos © Ed Phillips (top right), © Sebastian Kaulitzki (top left) Agency: www.shutterstock.com

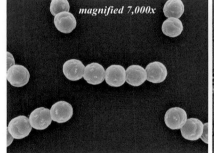

Kingdom Monera contains bacteria, like these streptococci.

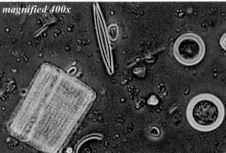

Kingdom Protista contains microscopic organisms like these diatoms.

Kingdom Fungi contains fungi, like the mold growing on this strawberry.

Kingdom Plantae contains the plants, such as this calla lily.

Kingdom Animalia contains the animals, like this rhinocerous.

Now, how do we know what organisms go into which kingdom? Well, we group organisms together based on similar characteristics. Since we are trying to put *all* living organisms in creation into one of five categories, these similarities have to be pretty basic. For example, the first and most basic distinction we make between organisms is the number and type of cells the organism has.

Remember from the previous module that there are three kinds of cells: plant cells, animal cells, and cells without a nucleus. Let's spend some more time on the differences between those cells. Cells that have a nucleus are called **eukaryotic** (yoo kehr ee aht' ik) cells. Cells without a nucleus are called **prokaryotic** (pro kehr ee aht' ik) cells. Now remember, the nucleus is an organelle. If a cell has no nucleus, we say it has no other distinct, membrane-bound organelles. Thus, we can define these two types of cells as follows:

Prokaryotic cell – A cell that has no distinct, membrane-bounded organelles

Eukaryotic cell – A cell with distinct, membrane-bounded organelles

Study the following figure to see the difference between prokaryotic and eukaryotic cells.

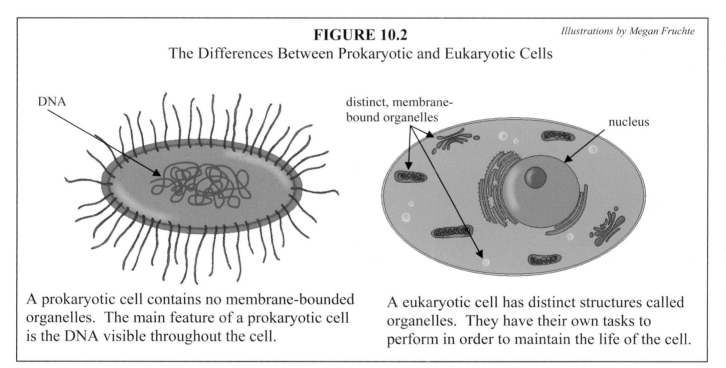

FIGURE 10.2

Illustrations by Megan Fruchte

The Differences Between Prokaryotic and Eukaryotic Cells

A prokaryotic cell contains no membrane-bounded organelles. The main feature of a prokaryotic cell is the DNA visible throughout the cell.

A eukaryotic cell has distinct structures called organelles. They have their own tasks to perform in order to maintain the life of the cell.

Now that you know the distinction between these two basic cell types, I can discuss how to split organisms up into the five different kingdoms. Kingdom Monera contains all organisms composed of prokaryotic cells. Bacteria are the most well-known members of kingdom Monera. They are made of a single, prokaryotic cell. I will discuss bacteria in more detail in the next section of this module.

The next kingdom is called Protista. It contains those organisms composed of only one eukaryotic cell. It also contains organisms referred to as **algae** (al' jee). Algae are composed of eukaryotic cells and look like water plants, but they are not really plants. Plants have specialized components like roots, leaves, stems, etc. Algae do not. Seaweed is an example of algae. Realize, then, that although many of the organisms in this kingdom are microscopic, others are not. The single-celled organisms contained in this kingdom are microscopic. Even some of the algae contained in this kingdom are microscopic. However, there are certain forms of algae (like seaweed) that are composed of many cells and are not microscopic.

Moving out of the microscopic world (for the most part) and into the macroscopic world (the world we can see with the naked eye), we come to kingdom Fungi. This kingdom contains mostly the organisms that feed on dead organisms. Please understand what I mean when I say that an organism "feeds on dead organisms." Lions, for example, kill their food before they eat it, but they do not feed on dead organisms. They kill live organisms and eat them. An organism that feeds on dead organisms finds something that is *already* dead (and usually has been dead for a while) and then feeds on it. As I have noted before, mushrooms are placed in kingdom Fungi. They typically feed on decaying plant material. Most fungi are visible to the naked eye and therefore are composed of trillions of cells. However, there are examples of single-celled organisms we place in kingdom Fungi. Yeast is the most common example of a single-celled member of kingdom Fungi. Whether they are made of one cell or many, all fungi have eukaryotic cells.

The next kingdom, Plantae, is composed of organisms that are made of many eukaryotic cells and produce their own food. Trees, grass, bushes, etc., are all members of kingdom Plantae. The last kingdom, Animalia, also contains organisms made of many eukaryotic cells. Members of kingdom Animalia are separated from kingdom Plantae by the fact that they eat other (usually living) organisms (fungi, plants, or other animals) rather than making their own food. Of course, members of kingdom Animalia are called "animals." Grasshoppers, birds, cats, fish, and snakes are all members of kingdom Animalia.

ON YOUR OWN

10.1 An organism is made up of one prokaryotic cell. To what kingdom does it belong?

10.2 An organism is made up of many eukaryotic cells. It makes its own food and has specialized structures like roots, stems, and leaves. To what kingdom does it belong?

10.3 An organism is made of many eukaryotic cells. It eats only dead organisms. To what kingdom does it belong?

Kingdom Monera

With kingdom Monera, we begin to discuss the incredible microscopic world that exists all around us. This world was unknown to human beings until the 1670s, when Antoni van Leeuwenhoek crafted a crude magnifying lens system that was strong enough to see it. This "miniature creation" is home to an incredibly large number of microorganisms. Amazingly enough, the combined weight of all microscopic organisms far exceeds the combined weight of all other living organisms on earth! Bringing this fact a little closer to home, the number of organisms in kingdom Monera that live in your intestines and on your skin is larger than the number of cells in your entire body! Thus, even though microorganisms are small, they are an important part of life on earth.

Organisms in kingdom Monera are interesting on many different levels. First of all, these organisms are not well understood by biologists. There are several facets of their structure and function that are still a complete mystery to science. This is interesting, since scientists consider them the "simplest" form of life. It tells you something about the nature of life when even the simplest creature is far too complicated for us to understand!

Second, some members of kingdom Monera can survive in habitats that are deadly to other organisms. For example, they live on dust particles floating 6 kilometers (almost 4 miles) above the surface of the earth. They thrive and multiply in temperatures too extreme for any other organism. In fact, microbiologists have found certain organisms from kingdom Monera living in a *nuclear reactor*. They survived even *while the reactor was running full blast*! Finally, members of kingdom Monera represent the smallest organisms in creation. The average member of this kingdom is less than *one ten-thousandth of an inch* across! Clearly, then, these interesting organisms are worth studying.

Without a very nice microscope, you will never be able to see bacteria. To give you an idea of what bacteria look like and how small they are, look at the following photograph, taken with a very specialized microscope called an "electron microscope." The organism pictured is a bacterium (that's the singular form of bacteria) which is called *Pseudomonas* (sue' duh mohn' us). The picture made by the electron microscope is 36,000 times the actual size of the bacterium shown!

FIGURE 10.3
The Bacterium *Pseudomonas* Magnified 36,000 Times

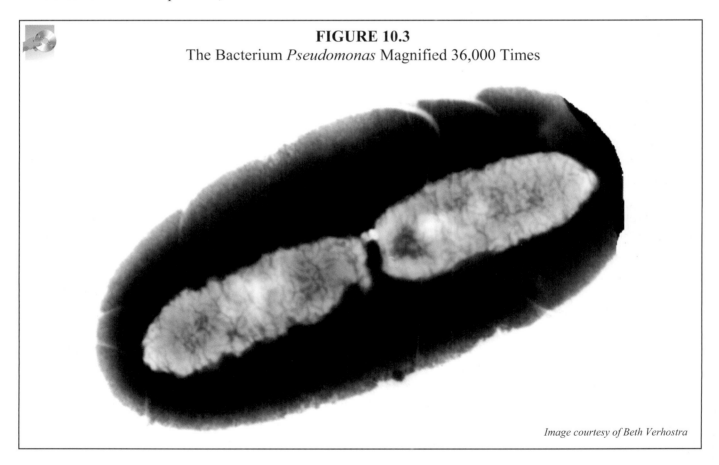

Image courtesy of Beth Verhostra

Even though it is impossible to see bacteria without the aid of a nice microscope, the experiment you started at the beginning of this module should allow you to see them indirectly. The instructions that follow tell you how to finish that experiment.

EXPERIMENT 10.1 - Part 2

<u>Supplies</u>:

♦ The four glasses and eye protection from the beginning of the experiment
♦ White paper (no lines if possible)
♦ A brightly colored marker or crayon

Introduction: This is a continuation of the first experiment. You will now be able to see bacteria in an indirect way.

<u>Procedure</u>:

1. Use the marker or crayon to write "HELLO" at the bottom of the white paper. The letters should be large, but they should not be taller than the level of liquid in the glasses.
2. Put the paper behind the glass labeled "control" so the word "HELLO" is behind the liquid in the glass.
3. Try to look through the liquid and see if you can read the word from the other side of the glass. Note whether you can clearly see it, can mostly see it, can barely see it, or cannot see it at all.
4. Repeat steps (2) and (3) with the other glasses. Each time, note how easy it is to see the word "HELLO" through the liquid in the glass.
5. Dump the liquids down the drain, thoroughly rinsing the sink with HOT water.
6. Wash your hands *thoroughly* with soap and warm water.

What did you see? If things went well, you probably were not able or were just barely able to see the word through the liquid in the "control" glass. However, you were probably able to see the word somewhat through the liquid that had salt in it as well as the liquid that had been in the refrigerator. In addition, you should have been able to see the word very clearly through the liquid that had the vinegar in it.

How does all of this relate to bacteria? During the two days the liquid sat out, bacteria were able to enter the liquid. Most likely, they were deposited in the liquid by dust particles that settled on the surface. In addition, there were probably some in the glass before you added the liquid. The chicken bouillon acted as a food source for those bacteria, allowing them to grow and reproduce. As the two days went by, more and more bacteria began populating the liquid. Their presence caused the liquid to become cloudy. Thus, the cloudier the liquid, the more bacteria there were in the liquid.

Since the control was the cloudiest, we can conclude that bacteria grow and reproduce very well in water with bouillon at room temperature. Since the liquid with salt was not as cloudy, we can conclude that salt tends to hurt the growth and reproduction of bacteria. In the same way, since the refrigerated liquid was less cloudy than the control, we can conclude that very low temperatures tend to hurt the growth and reproduction of bacteria. Finally, since the liquid with vinegar was pretty clear, we can conclude that vinegar really hurts the growth and reproduction of bacteria.

I want to get back to that point in a minute. First, however, I want to explain why I told you to rinse the sink out thoroughly with HOT water and to wash your hands thoroughly with soap and warm water. You see, it was very important that you get rid of all the bacteria that grew in your experiment, because many bacteria are **pathogenic**.

<u>Pathogen</u> – An organism that causes disease

Pathogenic bacteria, then, are bacteria that cause disease. In fact, many of the ailments that plague humanity, plants, and animals are caused by pathogenic bacteria.

The bacterium *Clostridium* (claw strid' ee um) *botulinum* (bot' yool in uhm), is one of the principal causes of food poisoning, for example. If food has not been properly cooked to rid it of bacteria, this is one of the most likely contaminants. Eating food infected with these bacteria can cause botulism. Mild cases of botulism involve severe nausea, diarrhea, and high fever. However, severe cases of botulism can cause you to stop breathing entirely, which will lead (of course) to death.

Bacteria known as *Salmonella* (sa muh nell' uh) are common contaminants of eggs and poultry. Since these bacteria are present in nearly every bird, about the only way to make sure you get rid of them is by cooking the meat or eggs thoroughly. The heat will kill most of the bacteria. If you eat poultry that hasn't been cooked well enough, you can be infected by these bacteria. Once again, while mild cases of *Salmonella* poisoning cause just nausea and diarrhea, severe cases can cause death.

This list could go on and on and on. Since many bacteria are pathogenic, it is important to try to limit our exposure to them. That's why I told you to rinse the sink thoroughly, so all the bacteria would go down the drain. If any bacteria were left in the sink and you used a dish that had been in the sink and not washed well, you could be exposing yourself to the bacteria you grew in the experiment. It was also important to wash your hands so any bacteria that got on your hands during the second part of the experiment (or during cleanup) also went down the drain.

Since it is important for us to limit the amount of exposure we have to bacteria, it is instructive to look at the results of the experiment again. The experiment demonstrated that bacteria grow and reproduce reasonably well in liquid that has a food source at room temperature. You can reduce the growth and reproduction somewhat by adding salt or refrigerating the liquid. You can reduce the growth and reproduction more by adding vinegar.

Now think about those results in terms of what we do with our food. When you buy meat, eggs, milk, and things like that at the store, what do you immediately do when you get home? You put the food in the refrigerator. Why? Well, most people would say that it keeps the food from spoiling, at least for a while. That's true, but why? The answer is that a *lot* of what we call "food spoilage" is caused by bacteria. Milk curdles, for example, because of bacteria. Meat gets rancid because of bacteria. Thus, putting food in the refrigerator reduces the growth and reproduction of bacteria, which keeps the food from spoiling for a while.

Do you know how people stored meat before we had refrigeration? Typically, they *salted* it. As your experiment demonstrated, salt reduces bacterial growth and reproduction just about as well as refrigeration. As a result, salt was a precious substance before refrigeration was widely available. Of course, the problem with using salt is that it changes the taste of the food you are trying to store. For meat, salt usually adds flavor, so that's not a problem unless the amount of salt required to stave off bacterial growth overwhelms the flavor of the meat. Of course, you would definitely *not* want to salt milk! Thus, although salt does help increase the time that some foods could be stored, it is not as widely applicable as refrigeration.

What about using vinegar? After all, your experiment demonstrated that the addition of vinegar reduced bacteria growth and reproduction even more than salt or refrigeration. Well, some people still use vinegar to preserve food for long periods of time. We call it "pickling." When you pickle food, the process involves adding vinegar, which nearly stops bacteria growth and reproduction. Pickling, then, is an excellent way to store food. Like salting, however, is it not reasonable for many foods, because it affects the taste significantly.

There are other ways to reduce the growth and reproduction of bacteria. For example, bacteria *must* have moisture to survive. Thus, **dehydrated food** (food in which almost all the water has been removed) can be stored for a long, long time without fear of significant contamination by bacteria. In addition, you can severely reduce the amount of bacterial growth and reproduction by killing most of the bacteria in the food initially and then sealing it away from the outside. Remember, the liquids in your experiment were exposed to the air, and bacteria were introduced into them from the dust particles floating in the air. If you had sealed the liquids, they would have not had as many bacteria in them. In addition, had you boiled the liquid to kill most of the bacteria and *then* sealed it, the bacterial growth and reproduction would be almost non existent. That's the idea behind canned foods. Canned foods are cooked or treated in some other way to kill the bacteria already in the food. Then, when they are put it the can, they are sealed away from the air. Thus, no bacteria can get in, and therefore canned foods can be stored for a long time.

Before I finish this section, I want to make sure you understand that *not all bacteria are pathogenic*. I have spent so much time talking about pathogenic bacteria and how to limit your exposure to them that you might get the idea that all bacteria are bad for you. That's just not true.

There are bacteria that live inside you that help you immensely. For example, one of the byproducts of bacteria that live in your intestines is vitamin K, a substance your body needs. Intestine-dwelling bacteria also secrete chemicals that help your body digest the food you eat. In addition, some bacteria in your gut actually keep pathogenic bacteria from growing and reproducing there. These bacteria, then, actually keep you healthy!

Bacteria also help us make cheese. When starter bacteria are added to milk, they feed on the milk and produce a chemical called lactic acid. This begins to separate the milk solids (called "curds") from the liquids in the milk (called "whey"). The whey is then drained off, and the curds are used to make the cheese. Depending on the starter bacteria used, the time and temperature over which they act, and how you process the curds, you get different kinds of cheese.

Bacteria not only help us make food, but they also help make the earth hospitable to life. Cyanobacteria, for example, use photosynthesis to make their own food, and that gives us oxygen to breathe. Other bacteria decompose dead organisms, which recycles chemicals so that other living organisms can use them.

ON YOUR OWN

10.4 A biologist looks at three milk samples under a microscope. The milk samples were all taken from the same bottle of milk, but they were put in three different glasses. The first glass was covered and placed in the refrigerator for 15 hours. The second was left sitting on a counter uncovered for 15 hours. The third was left sitting out on the same counter for 15 hours, but it was covered during that time period. In which sample would the biologist find the most bacteria? In which sample would the biologist find the least bacteria?

Kingdom Protista

The next kingdom I want to discuss has some things in common with kingdom Monera. For example, like kingdom Monera, most of the organisms in kingdom Protista can be seen only with the aid of a microscope. There are two major differences, however. First, members of kingdom Protista are made of eukaryotic cells, while the members of kingdom Monera are composed of prokaryotic cells. Second, the members of kingdom Protista are much bigger. Typically, single-celled organisms in kingdom Protista are about 10 to 100 times larger than the members of kingdom Monera.

This kingdom is usually split into two groups: protozoa and algae. Protozoa are mostly single-celled and tend to behave like little animals. They can move around, and most of them eat other organisms. Some produce their own food, but they can at least move around. Algae, on the other hand, are more like plants. They do not have a plant's specialized structures like roots, stems, and leaves. However, they do make their own food, just like plants. They also aren't able to move around on their own. They can move with the currents in a stream, for example, but they can't move of their own accord.

As I mentioned in the previous module, plants (and algae) make their own food through the process of photosynthesis. One of the substances used up in the process of photosynthesis is carbon dioxide, and one of the byproducts is oxygen. In other words, the process of photosynthesis uses up carbon dioxide and produces oxygen. It turns out this is very useful for animals, because when animals breathe, they use up oxygen and produce carbon dioxide. Thus, the process of photosynthesis gets rid of the excess carbon dioxide produced by animals and puts more oxygen back into the air so the animals can breathe it again.

A lot of students already know that. They know that photosynthesis is absolutely essential to keep the earth's supply of oxygen plentiful. What most students *do not know*, however, is that *algae are the most important source of photosynthesis on earth*, and they produce significantly more of the earth's oxygen supply than plants produce. Thus, in terms of earth's oxygen supply, the members of kingdom Protista are extremely important!

Like bacteria, members of kingdom Protista need moisture to live. Wherever there is water, there will probably be protozoa, algae, or both. They live in freshwater ponds, streams, and lakes as well as saltwater oceans and lakes. They even live in soil and inside the bodies of animals and people. While many members of this kingdom are essential for life, some are pathogenic to people, animals, and plants.

For example, one protozoan, *Entamoeba* (ent' uh mee' buh) *histolytica* (his' toh lih' tih kuh), causes dysentery. This illness produces severe diarrhea, intestinal cramping, fever, and often vomiting. How do you get this terrible protozoan? It is often spread through contaminated water. Countries that do not carefully sterilize their water supply often have lots of this protozoan in their water supply. This is where the phrase "Don't drink the water" comes from. If you drink water contaminated with this pathogenic protozoan, you can contract dysentery. In some cases, the infection can spread to your liver and brain, causing death!

In order to give you some idea of the members in this kingdom, I want to show you a couple figures. Let's start with the protozoans of kingdom Protista.

FIGURE 10.4
Some Protozoa From Kingdom Protista

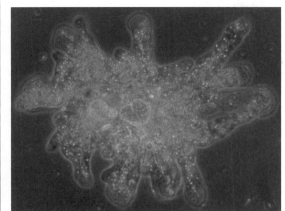

Amoeba (uh mee' buh) – magnified 400x

These organisms do not have any defined shape. Instead, they exist as a "blob" that is constantly changing its shape. The "arms" you see in the photo are called pseudopods (soo' duh pods). In order to move, amoebas stretch a pseudopod out and force cytoplasm into the pseudopod. By repeating this process several times, amoebas can slowly move from one place to another.

Photo © A. Rakosy/Custom Medical Stock Photo

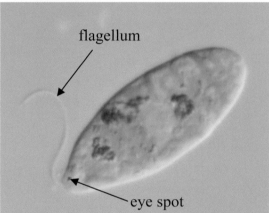

Euglena (yoo glee' nuh) – magnified 1,000x

These organisms are typically smaller than an amoeba. They have a "tail" called a flagellum (fluh jel' uhm) that they use to move through the fluid in which they live (usually water). Although they do eat other organisms, they also can produce food by photosynthesis. The red dot you see near the base of the flagellum is an "eye spot." It is not an eye, but it can sense light, which the euglena needs for photosynthesis.

Photo © JL Carson/Custom Medical Stock Photo

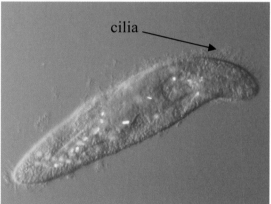

Paramecium (pehr uh mee' see um) – magnified 250x

These organisms are some of the largest protozoa. They move by beating the "hairs," called cilia (sil' ee uh), back and forth like little oars in the water. This requires a lot of energy, so paramecia and protozoa like them consume more food than most other protozoa. Paramecia and organisms like them are often called "ciliates," after their cilia.

Photo © JL Carson/Custom Medical Stock Photo

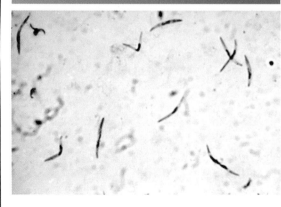

Plasmodium (plas moh' dee um) – magnified 400x

These organisms cause the disease known as malaria. They are usually transmitted through mosquito bites. In fact, the microscopic image you see here are plasmodium spores that are found in the saliva of a mosquito. When the mosquito bites a person, these spores enter the person's bloodstream and go to the liver. In the liver, they mature and reproduce.

Photo © NMSB/Custom Medical Stock Photo

Of course, the protozoa represent only part of kingdom Protista. The rest of the kingdom is made up of different forms of algae.

FIGURE 10.5
Some Algae From Kingdom Protista

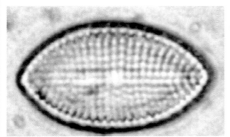

Diatom – magnified 400x

This organism is just one of many different kinds of diatoms. Diatoms are responsible for more photosynthesis than any other group of algae.

Photo by Kathleen J. Wile

Kelp – no magnification

Although this looks like a water plant, it is not. It has no specialized structures like roots, stems, or leaves. It is one of the many forms of what is commonly called "seaweed." Unlike the microscopic members of kingdom Protista, kelp can grow to be very large, in excess of 100 feet high!

Photo © Peter Ajtai, Agency: www.shutterstock.com

Red algae – no magnification

This is another form of seaweed. It is interesting because of its red color. Most organisms that perform photosynthesis are green. Red algae are exceptions to that general rule.

Photo © Mike Guiry, NUI, Galway

ON YOUR OWN

10.5 A scientist shows you an organism that was pulled from a lake. It is large and green and cannot move on its own. It makes its own food by photosynthesis. How can you tell whether this organism is a plant (and therefore belongs to kingdom Plantae) or a form of algae (and therefore belongs to kingdom Protista)?

Kingdom Fungi

Have you ever gone mushroom hunting? I mean, other than in a store. Where did you search for the mushrooms? Most likely, you looked for them in decaying mats of leaves, piles of dead tree limbs, or other places where the remains of dead plants and animals are found. Why? Well, mushrooms are a part of kingdom Fungi, and most of the organisms in this kingdom feed on dead organisms. By feeding on dead organisms, they decompose dead matter. As a result, these organisms are called **decomposers**.

<u>Decomposers</u> – Organisms that break down the dead remains of other organisms

Guess what results from decomposers breaking down the dead remains of organisms? Nutrients for plants and other organisms! Fertilizer, for example, can be made simply by taking dead matter from other organisms and adding some decomposers. In a few months, you will have rich fertilizer that will act as a source of vitamins for plants.

The role of the decomposers in creation is very important. In a single autumn, the average elm tree will drop as much as *400 pounds* of leaves on the ground. If it were not for the members of kingdom Fungi, those leaves would continue to pile up, until the tree choked on its own dead leaves in just a few seasons! Because of the decomposers, however, the leaves are broken down into fertilizer that can then be reused by the tree.

The very presence of decomposers in creation is another example of the Creator's ingenuity. Think about it for a moment. The planet He gave us has its own recycling system built right into it! Think about the design and planning that had to go into such a system. Suppose a team of brilliant scientists spent their careers trying to devise a system in which many different organisms could survive for a long period of time. Do you think they could come up with a plan this elegant and this well-designed? Of course not!

Indeed, a team of scientists tried to design and build a self-contained system for supporting life. It was called "Biosphere 2" and was supposed to be a microcosm of life on earth. It contained a variety of animals and plants and was designed to be completely self-supporting. The scientists thought they had it all worked out. They spent seven years and $200 million designing and building this air-tight, enclosed facility that spans 3.15 acres in Arizona. Despite the best that technology and science had to offer, however, Biosphere 2 could not support life for even two years! After about 16 months, oxygen levels could not be maintained. They had to start pumping oxygen in from the outside. Many of the animal species that had been put in Biosphere 2 became extinct, at least within the confines of the biosphere. In the end, Biosphere 2 was a failure.

Why was Biosphere 2 a failure? Well, there were many reasons, but one of them was that the designers had not anticipated the number and variety of decomposers they needed. As a result, the dead matter in Biosphere 2 was not decomposed quickly enough. This meant there were not enough nutrients available to be used by the plants and members of kingdom Protista that were supposed to supply oxygen through photosynthesis. Without those nutrients, these organisms could not live in a healthy manner, so they in turn could not produce oxygen efficiently.

If a team of brilliant scientists could not come up with a workable system for sustaining life (even after spending seven years and $200 million), how in the world could this perfectly balanced system we call earth have come about by chance? Nevertheless, any scientist who does not believe in God is forced to believe that very thing! In all of our experience, well-designed systems *do not* occur by chance. They only result from careful design and construction. This planet is the most well-designed system that anyone has ever studied. Thus, it is only logical to assume that it is the result of careful design and construction as well!

Since decomposers are an important part of creation, you should learn a little bit about them. Let's start with the decomposer you know best: the mushroom. A mushroom, since it is a part of kingdom Fungi, is more appropriately called a "**fungus**." The figure below is a sketch of the individual parts of the fungus that you and I call a mushroom.

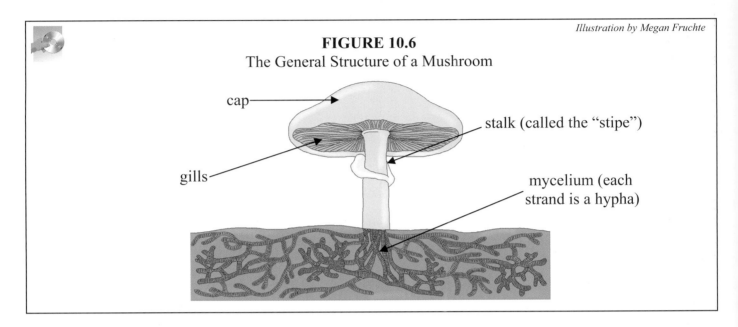

Illustration by Megan Fruchte

FIGURE 10.6
The General Structure of a Mushroom

cap

stalk (called the "stipe")

gills

mycelium (each strand is a hypha)

You should notice from the sketch that the part you call the mushroom is really only a portion of the fungus. Underneath the ground (or underneath the surface of the dead material), there is a vast network of interwoven filaments, each of which is called a hypha (hi' fuh). This network is called the **mycelium** (my sell' ee uhm), and believe it or not, the mycelium is *the actual fungus*.

The part you call the mushroom (the stalk, gills, and cap) is the only part of the fungus that is visible above the surface. Thus, it is the only part you see. However, that part is really just a means by which the fungus reproduces. Thus, the stalk, gills, and cap are only present for a short amount of time: the time during which the fungus reproduces. The fungus is always around, however. It just lives beneath the surface where you can't see it unless you really look for it. Next time you see a mushroom, carefully dig around it, looking just beneath the surface. It might help if you have a magnifying glass. Look for thin filaments that weave in and out of each other. *That's* the real fungus!

Now don't be fooled by this drawing. The mycelium is *not* a root system for the mushroom. Although it might look a lot like roots in the drawing, there are *many* differences between a root system and the mycelium of a mushroom. A root system, for example, has one purpose: to pull nutrients and water from the soil so they can be transported to the rest of the plant. The mycelium of the mushroom, on the other hand, is the *main part* of the fungus. The stalk, cap, and gills of a mushroom exist only at a certain stage of the mushroom's life. The mycelium, however, exists throughout the entire life of the mushroom. Thus, whereas the root system is really just an extension of the tree; a mushroom's stalk, cap, and gills are really just extensions of the main body – the mycelium. One more point: the gills on a mushroom are NOTHING like the gills on a fish. The gills on a fish help the fish breathe. The gills on a mushroom are necessary for reproduction, not breathing, so don't get them confused. You will learn more about *both* kinds of gills when you take biology.

Although mushrooms are probably the most familiar members of kingdom Fungi, there are other types of organisms in this kingdom. Figure 10.7 gives you three examples.

Shelf fungi photo from the
MasterClips Collection

FIGURE 10.7

Mold and yeast photos
by Kathleen J. Wile

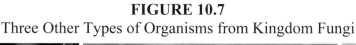
Three Other Types of Organisms from Kingdom Fungi

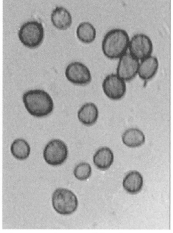

Shelf Fungi	Mold	Yeast (magnified 400x)
These fungi are typically found growing out of dead (or dying) trees. The mycelium is underneath the tree bark.	There are many different kinds of molds. They grow on rotting fruit, stale bread, and many other decaying food items. This mold is growing on a tomato.	The yeast used in baking bread is actually a single-celled fungus.

You have probably seen **shelf fungi** growing on dead or dying trees when you have taken walks in the woods. Much like mushrooms, the "shelves" you see are only extensions of the *real* fungus, which grows beneath the bark of the tree. Just as you've seen shelf fungi before, I am sure you have seen **mold** before. Mold is a general term used for many different fungi that grow on fruit, bread, and other foods.

You might be surprised to see yeast pictured in Figure 10.7. Yes, yeast are fungi. They are one of the examples of fungi that are composed of a single cell. Just so you understand that yeast are, indeed, fungi, and also so you can see what decomposers do, perform the following experiment.

EXPERIMENT 10.2
Yeast Is a Decomposer

Supplies:

♦ Baker's active yeast (available at any supermarket)
♦ Banana
♦ Water
♦ Two zippered plastic bags (like Ziploc® sandwich bags)
♦ A butter knife
♦ A teaspoon
♦ A marker or some masking tape
♦ Eye protection such as goggles or safety glasses

Introduction: This experiment will demonstrate the function of decomposers using yeast, one of the members of kingdom Fungi.

Procedure:

1. Peel the banana and cut two slices from it with the butter knife. The slices should be roughly the same thickness and size.
2. Wet each slice with water. Don't use a lot. Just make sure each slice is wet.
3. Use the teaspoon to scoop out some yeast. Sprinkle the yeast on one of the two slices. Do not put any yeast on the other slice.
4. Place each slice of banana in a different zippered plastic bag. Label the one containing the banana slice that has yeast on it. You can label it with the marker or some tape. Just be sure it is labeled in a way that you know means, "This bag contains the banana slice upon which I sprinkled yeast."
5. Seal the bags with the zippers.
6. Place them on a counter or a shelf.
7. Check the bags daily for about a week. Note the differences you see in the two bags.
8. After a week (you can observe them for longer if you like), throw the bags away.

    Although it will take up to a week for you to see results, you should notice a big difference between the contents of the two bags. Wait until then to answer the second "On Your Own" question (question 10.7) below.

ON YOUR OWN

10.6 A student wants to study a mushroom to learn more about the organism. He finds a mushroom growing in his backyard and pulls it out of the ground, getting the entire stalk, cap and gills. What is the student missing? What must he do to get what he is missing?

10.7 After a few days of checking the bags in Experiment 10.2, what difference did you see between them? How can you explain the difference?

Kingdom Plantae

    Now I want to move on to a kingdom with which you are more familiar. Kingdom Plantae contains the plants of creation. In the beginning of this module, I said that kingdom Plantae contains the organisms that make their own food. You learned, however, that kingdom Protista also contains a few organisms that make their own food (algae). Do you remember what distinguishes algae from plants? To help you remember, perform the following experiment.

EXPERIMENT 10.3
Vegetative Reproduction

Supplies:

♦ A houseplant (Ivy works best, but most houseplants will work. If you have a few varieties of houseplants and ivy is not among them, you might try a few instead of just one.)
♦ A glass
♦ Scissors

♦ Some water
♦ Eye protection such as goggles or safety glasses

Introduction: In this experiment, you will be reminded of what distinguishes plants from algae. You will also see one way in which many plants reproduce.

<u>Procedure</u>:

1. Fill the glass ¾ full of water.
2. Use the scissors to cut a stem from the plant. The stem should have at least a couple of leaves on it, and it should be reasonably long.
3. Place the stem in the glass so a large part of the stem is in the water but the leaves are hanging on or above the top of the glass.
4. Set the glass somewhere that is comfortably warm and well lit. The best place would be somewhere near where the rest of the plant is kept.
5. Check the glass daily, keeping it ¾ of the way full of water. Note any new developments.

What will you see in the experiment? Eventually, you should see roots forming in the water. If you see that happening, you can actually plant the stem in some soil. As long as the newly-formed roots are underneath the soil and you take care to keep the soil moist, the stem should eventually grow into another full-fledged plant. This process is called **vegetative reproduction**.

<u>Vegetative reproduction</u> – The process by which one part of a plant can form new roots and develop
into a complete plant

Vegetative reproduction is not the only way plants reproduce, of course. Plants typically reproduce by forming seeds. However, vegetative reproduction is another form of reproduction that plants have at their disposal. Gardeners often use this to grow several plants from one. They usually refer to it as "growing a new plant from a cutting of an old plant." You will learn a lot more about how plants reproduce when you take biology.

Although Experiment 10.3 demonstrates the process of vegetative reproduction rather well, it is not the real point of the experiment. The real point is to visually show you the difference between algae and plants. As I mentioned in a previous section of this module, plants have very specific parts. The **roots** absorb water and nutrients from the soil, while the **stems** help transport the nutrients and water to the **leaves**. The leaves are the main place where photosynthesis takes place in most plants. Thus, there are three specific kinds of structures in plants (roots, stems, and leaves), and they each perform their own tasks. Algae are not like that. Although one portion of an alga (singular of "algae") might look different than another portion, there are not specific structures that have different roles related to the functions of life.

 The multimedia CD has a video of plants growing to show the development of stems and leaves.

I want to make one other point about the members of this kingdom before moving on. As I mentioned in Module #9, plants have cells that are different from animal cells. Plant cells have a nucleus and organelles, just like animal cells, but there are some important differences. As a result, a scientist can generally distinguish between a plant cell and an animal cell by looking at them under a microscope. To give you an idea of the differences between the two, a simplified sketch of a plant cell is shown in Figure 10.8.

FIGURE 10.8

3D Illustration by Michael Dailey

A Simplified Sketch of a Plant Cell

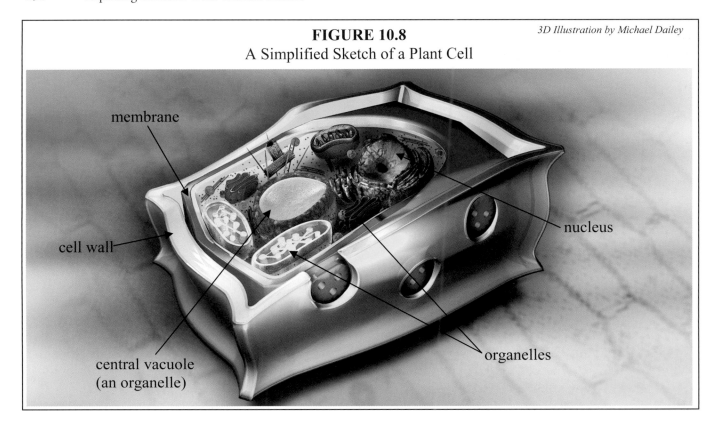

membrane

cell wall

central vacuole
(an organelle)

nucleus

organelles

Notice some of the differences between an animal cell (such as the one in Figure 9.5) and the plant cell drawn above. First, most plant cells are a bit squarer than animal cells. This isn't always true, but it is true for the majority of plant cells. Second, while a plant cell has a membrane around it (like an animal cell), it also has a **cell wall** surrounding the outside of the membrane. Animal cells do not have cell walls. The cell wall is a rigid structure that has holes in it. The holes allow nutrients and other chemicals to pass through so they can travel to and from the membrane.

A third difference between plant and animal cells can be found near the center of the cell. There, you will find an organelle called the **central vacuole** (vac' yoo uhl). The central vacuole can be thought of as a kind of water balloon. It fills with water, increasing in size. This pushes the organelles and cytoplasm in the cell against the cell wall. The cell wall is strong, however, so it pushes back against the force created by the expanding central vacuole. When a plant cell is functioning normally, the pressure caused by the central vacuole pushes against the cell wall, and the cell wall pushes back against the pressure. This results in a rigid cell. What happens when the cells are rigid? Perform the following experiment to find out.

EXPERIMENT 10.4
Turgor Pressure

<u>Supplies</u>:

♦ A stalk of wilted celery with the leaves still on it
♦ A glass
♦ Some water
♦ A reasonably sharp knife
♦ Some food coloring (preferably blue)
♦ Eye protection such as goggles or safety glasses

Introduction: The pressure inside a plant cell due to the increasing size of the central vacuole is called **turgor pressure**. This experiment will show you what turgor pressure does for a plant.

Procedure:

1. Fill the glass ¾ of the way with water.
2. Add a few drops of food coloring to the water and stir so the water is blue.
3. Cut a small slice off the bottom of the wilted celery stalk. The bottom is the end opposite the leaves.
4. Put the stalk of celery into the water so the bottom of the celery rests at the bottom of the glass.
5. Allow the celery to stand in the water overnight. This should end your science work for today.
6. Check the celery the next morning. What differences do you notice?
7. Clean everything up.

What happened overnight? Well, you should have noticed two differences between the celery yesterday and the celery today. First, you should have noticed that the leaves and some of the top of the celery stalk turned blue. Second, you should have noticed that the celery is no longer wilted. Why? Well, when you cut a small slice off the bottom of the celery, you made a "fresh cut," allowing the celery to absorb some water. That water traveled all the way to the top of the celery, being absorbed by cells wherever it was needed. The blue color shows that the water from the cup was, indeed, transported to the very top of the celery.

Why is the celery no longer wilted? Well, as the cells that needed water absorbed it, their central vacuoles began to expand. This increased the turgor pressure in the cells, causing the cells to go rigid. That rigidity allowed the celery to stand straight up. Thus, the turgor pressure in a plant's cells helps the plant to stand upright. Without turgor pressure, plants look wilted and don't stand up straight.

FIGURE 10.9
A Wilted Plant

Photo © Scott Rothstein
Agency: www.shutterstock.com

This flower is wilted because it was unable to absorb enough water to keep its turgor pressure up. As a result, its cells could not stay rigid enough to help the stem support the flower at the top.

A wilted plant is not necessarily a dead plant – it is just a plant that lacks water. Now, of course, if a plant has too little water for too long, it will die. However, a wilted plant can become quite healthy again if it is given more water and is able to absorb that water to recreate the turgor pressure it needs.

It is important to note that the appearance of wilting can be caused by things other than a loss of water. When plants are infected by certain pathogenic organisms, they look like they are wilting.

ON YOUR OWN

10.8 I told you that *most* of a plant's photosynthesis takes place in its leaves. Does the rest of the photosynthesis take place in its stems or its roots?

10.9 What would happen to a plant cell if it did not have a cell wall?

Kingdom Animalia

If an organism is not a single-celled prokaryotic cell, not a single-celled eukaryotic cell, not a form of algae, not a fungus, and not a plant, it is an animal and belongs in kingdom Animalia. This tells us that *most* of the organisms with which we are familiar are animals. Earthworms, for example, are animals. Insects are animals. Fish are animals. Cats and dogs are animals. Birds are animals. In fact, from a biological point of view, even humans are a part of kingdom Animalia.

Now don't get all upset here. I am not saying that humans are animals. Clearly, humans are not animals. Humans are made in the very image of God. Animals are not. Thus, there is a huge difference between people and animals. However, from a *biological point of view*, people belong in the same kingdom as animals. We are made up of the same basic kinds of cells that the animals are made of, and we do not have any characteristics that place us in the other kingdoms. Thus, we *are* members of kingdom Animalia. We are, however, very special members.

As you can see, then, there is a lot of diversity in this kingdom. Everything from earthworms to butterflies to turtles to blackbirds to cats to humans belongs in it. In fact, you might not realize it, but there are actually *microscopic animals* as well. Figure 10.10 shows you one such animal, called a **cyclops**.

FIGURE 10.10
A Cyclops, Magnified 100x

Photo courtesy of the United States Environmental Protection Agency (EPA)

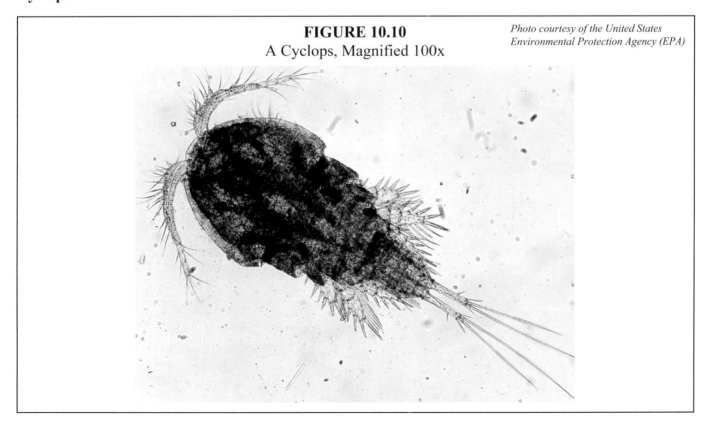

This interesting animal is part of a large group of small, water-dwelling animals called "copepods" (coh' pee pods). They are called "cyclops" because they have only one eye. The eye can't see images, but it is able to detect light. These tiny animals are not good swimmers. Instead, they tend to float in the water, going wherever the currents take them. Some hunt even smaller organisms to eat, others filter the water they are in looking for food, and some are even parasitic.

It is important to realize, then, that the members of kingdom Animalia can be quite different from what you normally think of when you think about animals. Now, instead of trying to give you an overview of the animal kingdom, in the next module I am going to begin a discussion of the incredible human body. Not only will you learn the basics of how you are built, but you will also learn some of the amazing processes that go on to keep you alive. As I discuss how people perform all the functions of life, I will also show you how other organisms accomplish those same essential tasks. In that process, you will learn a lot more about kingdom Animalia, along with organisms in other kingdoms as well.

 The multimedia CD has a video about kingdom Animalia.

ON YOUR OWN

10.10 Suppose you were able to look at a single cell under a microscope. The cell might be just one cell from an organism that has many cells, or it might be the only cell in the organism. There are two kingdoms to which you could automatically assign the organism based *only* on the cell you see. What two kingdoms are they?

ANSWERS TO THE "ON YOUR OWN" PROBLEMS

10.1 All organisms made of prokaryotic cells belong to <u>kingdom Monera</u>.

10.2 It most likely belongs to <u>kingdom Plantae</u>. It could belong to kingdom Protista. As you will learn later, there are some organisms (algae) in kingdom Protista that are made up of many eukaryotic cells and that make their own food. However, these organisms do not have specialized structures like roots, stems, and leaves.

10.3 If the organism eats only dead organisms, it is most likely a member of kingdom <u>Fungi</u>. It is not a part of kingdom Monera, as it is made of eukaryotic cells. It is not in Protista, as it is made of more than one cell. It is not in Plantae because it does not make its own food. It could be in Animalia, but most organisms that feed only on dead organisms are in kingdom Fungi.

10.4 <u>The biologist will see the most bacteria in the sample from the glass that was left sitting uncovered on the counter. The biologist will see the least bacteria in the sample from the glass that was placed in the refrigerator.</u> As you learned from Experiment 10.1, refrigeration slows the growth and reproduction of bacteria. What about the glass that sat covered on the counter? Well, that will have a lot of bacteria in it, but not as much as the uncovered one. Remember, I told you that bacteria were introduced into the liquids in your experiment through dust particles in the air. By covering the glass, you reduce the number of bacteria introduced in that way.

10.5 <u>You can tell the difference by looking for specialized structures like roots, stems, and leaves.</u> If it has such structures, it is a member of kingdom Plantae, not kingdom Protista.

10.6 <u>The student is missing the mycelium</u>, which is the most important part of the fungus. <u>The student must dig into the ground and get the filaments that make up the mycelium.</u>

10.7 <u>The banana slice with the yeast on it should be mushy and squished, while the other banana slice should just look brown, but should have retained its original shape. This is because the yeast decomposed the banana, turning it into mushy goo.</u> Since the banana without yeast did not have a decomposer on it, it did not decompose very rapidly. The bag with the yeast in it will probably be partially inflated, too, since gas is a product of decomposition.

10.8 <u>The rest of the photosynthesis takes place in the stems.</u> It could not take place in the roots, because the roots are underground, and there is no light underground.

10.9 <u>Without a cell wall, a plant cell would explode.</u> There would be nothing to fight against the pressure caused by the central vacuole.

10.10 <u>Members of kingdoms Monera and Plantae can be classified based only on their cells.</u> After all, if the cell is prokaryotic (lacking organelles), the organism comes from kingdom Monera. If it is a plant cell (having a central vacuole and a cell wall), the organism comes from kingdom Plantae. Members of the other kingdoms are made of cells that look like animal cells. Thus, identifying a cell as an animal cell only narrows the classification down to three kingdoms.

STUDY GUIDE FOR MODULE #10

1. Define the following terms:

a. Prokaryotic cell
b. Eukaryotic cell
c. Pathogen
d. Decomposers
e. Vegetative reproduction

2. Name the five kingdoms we used in our classification system.

3. An organism is made up of several eukaryotic cells and eats only dead organisms. To which kingdom does it belong?

4. An organism is made up of several eukaryotic cells and makes its own food. It has specialized structures that perform individual tasks. To which kingdom does it belong?

5. An organism is made up of one prokaryotic cell and eats only dead organisms. To which kingdom does it belong?

6. An organism is made up of several eukaryotic cells and makes its own food. It has no specialized structures. To which kingdom does it belong?

7. An organism is made up of one eukaryotic cell and eats other, living organisms. To which kingdom does it belong?

8. An organism is made up of several eukaryotic cells and eats only living plants. To which kingdom does it belong?

9. Why can dehydrated food be stored for a long time without worry of it being contaminated by bacteria?

10. Why did people salt meat before refrigeration was available?

11. When you store food for a long time, why does covering it reduce the amount of bacterial contamination?

12. A member of kingdom Protista can move on its own. Is it part of the protozoa or the algae?

13. Are there any pathogenic organisms in kingdom Protista?

14. Why are decomposers essential to creation?

15. Are all members of kingdom Fungi made of many cells? If not, give an example of a single-celled member of kingdom Fungi.

16. Icebergs are dangerous to ships because the visible part of an iceberg is actually very small. Most of an iceberg is underwater where it cannot be seen. How is a mushroom like an iceberg?

17. What is the main part of a mushroom: the cap, the stalk, the gills, or the mycelium?

18. A cell has a cell wall and a central vacuole. Is it a prokaryotic cell, a plant cell, or an animal cell?

19. What is turgor pressure and what does it do for a plant?

20. To which kingdom do people belong?

MODULE #11: The Human Body: Fearfully and Wonderfully Made

Introduction

Now that you know a little bit about the amazing diversity of life in creation, I want to try to explain how incredibly well God has designed it all. The best way to do this is to show you God's ultimate feat of design: the human body. As I discuss some of the most basic aspects of the human body, you will get a deep appreciation for how carefully and thoughtfully God put everything together. As Scripture says, we are indeed "fearfully and wonderfully made" (Psalm 139:14).

In order to give you a slightly broader view of creation, from time to time I will compare the structures of the human body to the structures of other organisms. Hopefully, this will allow you to learn about other organisms in creation. I also hope that it will teach you one of the most important facts of biology: **There is no such thing as a simple life form**. As human beings, we tend to think of organisms like insects and microorganisms as "simple" creatures. Although you can argue that such life forms are, indeed, less complex than human beings, it is very apparent that they are not at all *simple*. Even the most basic organism in creation is exceedingly more complex and well designed than the most impressive piece of technology ever produced by people! The more you study life, the clearer it becomes that not even the tiniest organism in creation could possibly be the result of chance.

The Superstructure of the Human Body

Where do I start? The human body is so amazing and so complex that it is incredibly difficult to decide where my discussion should begin. Nevertheless, I have to start somewhere, so I will begin with what holds your body up and keeps it together: the **superstructure**.

The body's superstructure is composed of three basic units: **the skeleton, the muscles,** and **the skin**. There are 206 separate bones in an adult's skeleton. Children actually have more bones than adults, because while children mature, some of the separate bones in the body fuse together to become one. These bones work together to support the body. They also work with the muscles to allow you to move. In addition, some bones are specifically designed to protect vital organs. Finally, a substance inside your bones, the red **bone marrow,** actually produces the cells in your blood.

In order to help you move, your body has about 640 different **skeletal muscles.** In addition to those muscles, there are also **smooth muscles,** which control the movements necessary for your body's internal organs and blood vessels to function. Finally, there is special muscle called **cardiac** (kar' dee ack) **muscle.** This muscle is found only in the heart, and it controls how the blood is pumped throughout your body.

The last element of your body's superstructure is your skin. It has two functions. First, it protects your body by preventing certain substances from getting inside. Second, it helps sense the outside world and then sends messages about those sensations to the brain. This can also be thought of as a means of protecting the body. For example, if you put your hand in hot water, nerves in your skin tell your brain that the water is hot, and the brain then instructs your skeletal muscles to pull your hand out. This protects your body from the heat of the water.

Although you may think that you are pretty familiar with your skin, you probably are not aware that your hair, fingernails, and toenails are all really a part of your skin. You see, skin cells harden in a process called **keratinization** (kuh' rat uh nuh zay' shun). This process is what forms your hair, nails, and the outer layer of your skin.

Consider how these three elements of your superstructure (skeleton, muscles, and skin) work together. Go find a ball. Pick it up in your hand, and then throw it (preferably outside!). Now think about what had to go on in order to allow you to perform this relatively simple act. Your skin sent information to your brain telling it about the size, shape, and texture of the ball. Your brain then sent instructions to your skeletal muscles to move so you could grasp the ball. Your muscles then moved the bones in your hand according to those instructions, allowing you to grasp the ball.

All those processes were necessary just for you to grasp the ball! In order to throw it, your brain sent lots of different instructions to the muscles of your arm and hand. The muscles moved according to those instructions, causing your bones to move. As your bones moved, the skin kept sending information to your brain, and at some point, your brain decided it was time to let go of the ball. Thus, while still sending instructions to the muscles in your arm, the brain also sent instructions to the muscles that control your hand to move in a certain way. When the muscles followed those instructions, the bones in your hand moved so as to release the ball, and the ball then flew through the air, hopefully where you intended it to go.

Now think about all that for a moment. The actions I just described are all very precise. They require incredible coordination between your brain, muscles, skeleton, and skin. As you think about that, remember that your body is performing *millions of other processes at the same time.* After all, while you were throwing the ball, you continued to breathe, your blood continued to flow, and you continued to see, smell, and hear. All these things continued on as normal while your body performed this well-coordinated set of actions!

Do you think that we could build a robot that could accomplish all this? Absolutely not! We could build a robot that has an arm capable of grasping and throwing a ball. However, in order to perform all of the coordinated actions it takes to throw a ball, it would require a large amount of computing power. There is no way to give the robot enough computing power and functionality to do all that *and* simultaneously perform many other tasks that also require a large amount of coordination.

In other words, despite the amazing technology that can be designed and created by us today, we cannot make a machine that can do even a fraction of what you can do with your own body! Nevertheless, if you do not believe in God, you have to assume that this incredible "machine" we call the human body – a machine that far surpasses anything our best applied scientists can build – had to have been the result of *random chance.* After all, without God, you have to believe that the human body is the product of evolution, and evolution occurs by random chance. If our greatest applied scientists cannot build anything that comes anywhere close to performing the functions of the human body, how likely is it that the human body evolved by chance? In my opinion, the answer is, "There is no likelihood whatsoever."

ON YOUR OWN

11.1 One treatment for certain types of cancer is a bone marrow transplant. In this procedure, a portion of the patient's bone marrow is replaced with different bone marrow. Besides the bone marrow itself, what else would change in the patient's body as a result of this procedure?

<u>Bones</u>

Now that you know a bit about your body's superstructure as a whole, I want to discuss the individual parts in a bit more detail. Let's start with the skeleton. As you know, your skeleton is made up of **bones**. However, you are probably not aware of how incredible your bones really are. First of all, bones are as strong as steel but at the same time as light as aluminum. To this day, applied scientists cannot come up with any material that is both as strong and light as bone. Antoni Tomsia is a scientist who works for Lawrence Berkeley National Laboratory in California. His team is trying to produce "artificial" bone tissue, but cannot produce anything close to what your body naturally makes. He says, "[We] want a strong, light, and porous material, which is almost a contradiction in terms, but nature does it…Bone is made from [chemicals] which are…extremely weak. But nature mixes them together at room temperature and without toxic chemicals to create something that is very tough — this fascinates us" (www.lbl.gov/Science-Articles/Archive/MSD-artificial-bone.html – retrieved 09/22/07).

EXPERIMENT 11.1
Minerals in Bone

<u>Supplies</u>:

♦ An uncooked chicken bone (preferably a wishbone or wing)
♦ A jar with a lid
♦ Vinegar (preferably white)

Introduction: Bones are both strong and light. They are also somewhat flexible. In this experiment, you will learn what makes them strong and how flexible they would be without it.

<u>Procedure</u>:

1. Clean the bone of all meat and tendons. Make it as bare as possible.
2. Allow the bone to dry overnight.
3. The next day, test the bone by trying to gently bend it. Do not use so much force that you break it! Notice that the bone bends a bit, but it is still mostly rigid.
4. Fill the jar with enough vinegar so that the bone will be fully immersed.
5. Drop the bone in the jar and close the lid.
6. Every day, pull the bone out of the vinegar and test it as you did in step 3.
7. Note the difference you observe.
8. Put the bone back into the vinegar and close the jar again.
9. Continue this process for seven days or more.
10. Once the seven days are over, pour the vinegar mixture down the drain, throw the bone away, and clean up your mess.

What will you see over the course of seven days? Well, at first, the ends of the bone will get soft. As time goes on, the entire bone will get rubbery so that it can be bent and flexed very easily. It is a nice effect, so you should definitely keep the experiment going until the bone reaches that state. Why will the bone get rubbery? To answer this, I need to tell you what bones are made of. Bones consist of cells surrounded by a substance called the **bone matrix.** This matrix is composed principally of two things: **collagen** (kahl' uh jin) and **minerals.** Collagen is a flexible, thread-like substance that belongs to a class of chemicals known as **proteins.** The minerals in bones are rigid, hard chemicals that contain calcium. I'm sure you've heard that milk builds strong bones. That's because milk contains calcium, and the minerals in your bones are made with calcium. Thus, drinking milk helps supply your body with the calcium it needs to make the minerals in your bones.

Collagen and minerals work together to make your bones both strong and flexible. The collagen gives bones their flexibility, while the minerals give bones their hardness. In your experiment, the vinegar dissolved the minerals in the chicken bone. As time went on, then, there were fewer and fewer minerals in the chicken bone, so the bone got more and more flexible. Eventually, the vinegar dissolved many of the minerals in the bone, and you were left with a bone made mostly of collagen. Without the minerals, your bones would be as rubbery as that chicken bone, but without the collagen, your bones would be rigid and brittle. As a result, if your bones had no collagen, they would break instead of bend when you fell. Because of the unique blend of collagen and minerals in bones, however, your skeleton is both flexible and strong.

Figure 11.1 illustrates the makeup of a typical bone in the human body. Now don't get worried. I am not going to require you to memorize this drawing. I just want you to see the general structure of a typical bone.

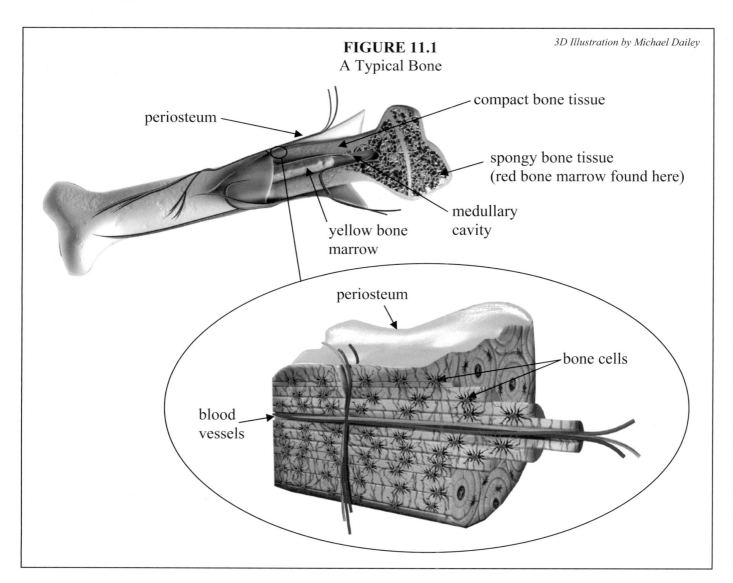

FIGURE 11.1
A Typical Bone

3D Illustration by Michael Dailey

periosteum

compact bone tissue

spongy bone tissue
(red bone marrow found here)

medullary cavity

yellow bone marrow

periosteum

bone cells

blood vessels

Along the length of a long bone's center runs the **medullary** (med' you lar ree) **cavity**. This cavity contains bone marrow and blood vessels. Red bone marrow produces the cells in your blood. Yellow bone marrow, on the other hand, is composed of fats that are being stored by your body. In bones such as the one drawn in Figure 11.1, the bone marrow is generally red in younger people and yellow in adults.

The medullary cavity can be surrounded by two types of bone: **spongy bone** and **compact bone.** Both of these kinds of bone are made of the same substances. The main difference between compact bone tissue and spongy bone tissue is how the minerals and collagen are packed together. In compact bone tissue, they are packed together tightly, forming a hard, tough structure that can withstand strong shocks. In spongy bone tissue, on the other hand, there are open spaces in the network of solid bone. This gives the tissue a spongy look. Although the bone looks spongy, it is quite hard, providing support without adding much weight. It also contains red bone marrow, which produces red blood cells. You will learn about these cells in a later module.

The compact bone tissue is made up of tiny "rods" that are packed together. A more detailed view of these rods is shown in the lower portion of the figure. Notice that there are blood vessels running through the center of each rod as well as out to the edges of the rods. These are necessary because there are living **bone cells** that need oxygen and nutrients. The bone cells are in those spidery-looking spaces in the figure. Thus, even though you might not think of them that way, your bones are actually alive. In fact, bone cells continue to make more spongy and compact bone tissue, allowing your bones to grow along with your body. Also, there are special bone cells that break down worn bone tissue so that strong, new bone can replace it. Thus, your bones change throughout your life, growing and changing shape based on the needs of your body.

The compact and spongy bone tissue are both surrounded by a sheath of tissue called the **periosteum** (pehr' ee ah' stee uhm). This layer contains blood vessels that supply nutrients to the bones. Remember, there are cells in the bones, and they need food and oxygen. They also need to get rid of wastes. The periosteum also contains nerves that can send pain signals to your brain if the bone is damaged.

Because bone is composed of living tissue, it continually changes to meet your body's needs. In fact, your bones *increase or decrease their mass as needed*! For example, bones that bear weight must be firm. Thus, if you walk around, exercise, and exert yourself, your bones will be stressed and will respond by increasing their mass to become more firm. On the other hand, if you are bedridden or very inactive, that stimulation isn't there. As a result, bone tissue will be taken away. In addition, if you gain a lot of weight, your bones will have more weight to bear and will therefore increase their mass to be able to do their job. If, on the other hand, you lose a lot of weight, your bones need not bear as much weight, and they will lose some of their mass.

Not only do your bones change to meet your body's needs, they also grow as you grow. In fact, some bones actually fuse together as you mature. As a result, babies are born with up to 350 bones, but mature adults have only 206 bones. These bones come in all shapes and sizes. The smallest bone in an adult's body is found in the middle ear and is only one tenth of an inch long. The largest bone is the femur, and it represents nearly 25 percent of a person's height. The skull, which you might think is only one bone, is actually composed of 29 separate bones. Figure 11.2 gives you an overview of the bones in an adult's body.

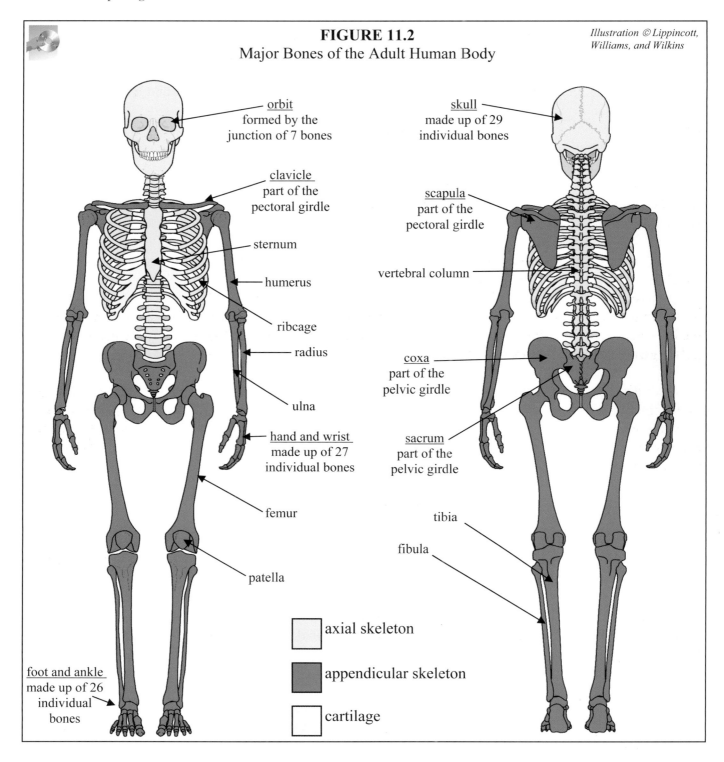

FIGURE 11.2
Major Bones of the Adult Human Body

*Illustration © Lippincott,
Williams, and Wilkins*

orbit
formed by the
junction of 7 bones

skull
made up of 29
individual bones

clavicle
part of the
pectoral girdle

scapula
part of the
pectoral girdle

sternum

vertebral column

humerus

ribcage

radius

coxa
part of the
pelvic girdle

ulna

hand and wrist
made up of 27
individual bones

sacrum
part of the
pelvic girdle

femur

tibia

fibula

patella

axial skeleton

appendicular skeleton

cartilage

foot and ankle
made up of 26
individual
bones

The sum total of all bones in the body is called the **endoskeleton.** You have probably heard it called just the "skeleton," but in the next section of this module, you will see why it needs to be called the endoskeleton. From a biologist's point of view, the most important part of the endoskeleton is the **vertebral column**, which is often called the backbone. The presence or absence of a vertebral column in a creature is one means of classification in biology. All creatures that have a vertebral column are called **vertebrates** (ver' tuh brayts). Humans, therefore, are vertebrates since they have backbones. Cats, dogs, elephants, fish, and most of the other animals with which you are familiar are vertebrates.

Like the endoskeleton of most vertebrates, the human endoskeleton can be split into two major sections: the **axial skeleton** and the **appendicular** (ah pen dihk' you luhr) **skeleton.**

Axial skeleton – The portion of the skeleton that supports and protects the head, neck, and trunk

Appendicular skeleton – The portion of the skeleton that attaches to the axial skeleton and has the limbs attached to it

As you can see from the figure, the vertebral column, ribs, and skull make up the axial skeleton. On the other hand, the limbs (arms and legs) as well as the bones to which they attach make up the appendicular skeleton.

A person's upper limbs are connected to the axial skeleton by means of the **pectoral girdle**, which is made up of the clavicles and scapulae (plural of scapula). What you call "the arm" is split into two regions – the **arm** (made up of the humerus) and the **forearm** (made up of the radius and ulna). In the same way, what you call "the leg" is composed of the **thigh** (made up of the femur) and the **leg** (made up of the tibia and fibula). These limbs connect to the axial skeleton by means of the **pelvic girdle**, which is composed of three bones – two coxae (plural of coxa) and the sacrum.

Although I have spent most of my time talking about bone, that is not the only substance found in the human endoskeleton. There is also quite a bit of **cartilage** (car' tih lej). This substance is not as firm as bone. Instead, it is more flexible. You can see from the figure that cartilage attaches the ribs to the sternum, holds the vertebral column together, and attaches the two coxae to one another. As you will learn shortly, it also caps the parts of bones that form joints.

ON YOUR OWN

11.2 When people get older, their bones break more easily. For example, if you trip and fall, it will most likely hurt, but your bones will almost certainly not break. However, a very old person can easily break a bone simply by tripping and falling. What substance is lacking in an older person's bones?

11.3 Suppose you are holding two bones in your hand. They are roughly the same size and shape; however, the first bone is significantly heavier than the second. Which bone has more compact bone tissue?

Skeletons in Other Organisms

Now that you know a little bit about the human endoskeleton, you should learn about the other kinds of support structures that God has used in His creation. As I mentioned in the previous section, all creatures we call vertebrates have a backbone. In fact, the endoskeleton of most vertebrates is similar to that of humans. Most vertebrates have both an axial and an appendicular skeleton, for example. Most vertebrates have ribs, a skull, and limbs as well. Thus, animals such as cats, dogs, fish, and the like all have endoskeletons similar in many ways to the human endoskeleton.

Even though most vertebrates have similar skeletons, don't get the idea that they are all the same. For example, many vertebrates don't have bones in their endoskeleton! Instead, vertebrates like sharks have an endoskeleton made almost entirely of cartilage. Such endoskeletons are not as firm as those of other vertebrates, but they are very flexible.

Of course, not all animals are vertebrates. Organisms from kingdom Animalia with no backbone are called **invertebrates** (in ver' tuh brayts). Believe it or not, there are more invertebrates in kingdom Animalia than there are vertebrates! Figure 11.3 shows some examples of invertebrates.

FIGURE 11.3
Examples of Invertebrates

Photos from www.clipart.com

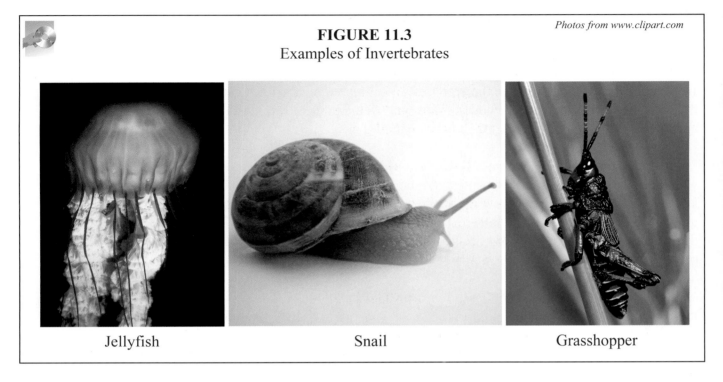

Jellyfish   Snail   Grasshopper

An invertebrate does not have an endoskeleton for one of many reasons. In the case of a jellyfish, for example, there is no need for one. A jellyfish floats in the water. The water helps support the creature, so jellyfish and invertebrates like them do not need a support structure of their own. Snails, clams, and other shelled animals find protection and support in their shells. Finally, insects (grasshoppers, for example) have an external support structure call an **exoskeleton.**

Exoskeleton – A body covering, typically made of chitin, that provides support and protection

Actually, grasshoppers represent just one of the many kinds of animals with exoskeletons, which biologists call **arthropods** (ar' thrah podz). There are more arthropods in creation than *all other animals combined!* Crayfish, lobsters, spiders, scorpions, and insects are all examples of arthropods.

As the definition above states, an exoskeleton is generally made of **chitin** (kye' tin). This chemical has the useful property of being both tough and flexible (much like the chemical mixture that makes up bone). In addition to chitin, there is usually a mineral substance in the exoskeleton of an arthropod that makes it hard (much like the calcium minerals in bone). The hard, tough exoskeleton can be thought of as a suit of armor that an arthropod wears. It is flexible enough to move with the creature, but is tough enough to provide a good measure of protection and support. Some biologists say that the best way to get an idea of what an arthropod's exoskeleton is like is to examine your own fingernails. The structural qualities of an arthropod's exoskeleton are much like those of your fingernails.

Now invertebrates are not the only organisms in creation without a backbone. Invertebrates are *the members of kingdom Animalia* that do not have a backbone. The organisms in the other four kingdoms do not have backbones, either. Why not? Well, think about it. The members of kingdoms Monera and Protista are mostly composed of one cell. The cell membrane gives them the support they need. The members of kingdom Protista that are composed of many cells (algae) all float in the water. Like the jellyfish, then, the water supports algae. As you learned in Experiment 10.4, the members of kingdom Plantae have turgor pressure in their cells that helps support them.

What about the members of kingdom Fungi? Well, like arthropods, they are covered with chitin. Biologists do not consider this an exoskeleton because, unlike endoskeletons and exoskeletons, the chitin covering of fungi cannot move around. Nevertheless, it does support the fungi. Without its chitin covering, for example, the mushroom part of a fungus could never stand up. It would simply flop over from its own weight, much like a wilted plant.

ON YOUR OWN

11.4 Classify each of the following as a vertebrate, invertebrate, or neither:

   a. worm   b. alligator   c. grass   d. yeast   e. starfish   f. bass (a fish)   g. clam

Skeletal Muscles

Now that we have discussed a bit about the human endoskeleton, I want to move on to the next component of the superstructure – the muscles. As I mentioned briefly in a previous section of this module, there are three main types of muscles in your body: skeletal muscles, smooth muscles, and the cardiac muscle. In this section, I want to concentrate on the skeletal muscles. As their name implies, these muscles mostly exist to move the endoskeleton. This, of course, allows your body to move.

What you may not realize, however, is that your skeletal muscles do perform some other tasks. For example, they help you maintain posture. Think about standing up straight and perfectly still. Once you are standing and in position, do you think it takes muscle activity to stay standing still? You bet it does! Even though you are standing still, your skeletal muscles constantly make fine adjustments to keep you in that position. Without muscle activity, you would collapse like a rag doll! Muscles also help keep us warm. On a cold day, you stay warmer if you do a little exercise instead of just standing around. When you are really cold, your body moves its muscles to make you shiver. That's your body's way of generating heat through its muscular system.

One important feature of skeletal muscles is that they are **voluntary muscles**. This means you can control them by thinking about it. For example, if you want to move your arm to touch something, you think about the motion, and your muscles perform it. Please note, however, that you do not *have* to think about controlling certain skeletal muscles. Do you think about breathing? Of course not. However, as you will learn later, the muscles that control breathing are skeletal muscles and are therefore voluntary. You don't have to consciously think about breathing, however, because some automatic processes in your brain take care of that for you. But then why do I say that the muscles involved in breathing are voluntary? Well, if you think about it, you can stop them, at least for a while. After all, if you think about it, you can hold your breath. That involves stopping the movement of the voluntary muscles involved in breathing. So while voluntary muscles *can* be controlled by conscious thought, they *don't have to be* controlled that way.

Figure 11.4 gives you an overview of the skeletal muscles in the human body. Now don't get all worried here. I am not going to make you memorize these muscles. I just want to give you an idea of how complex it all is.

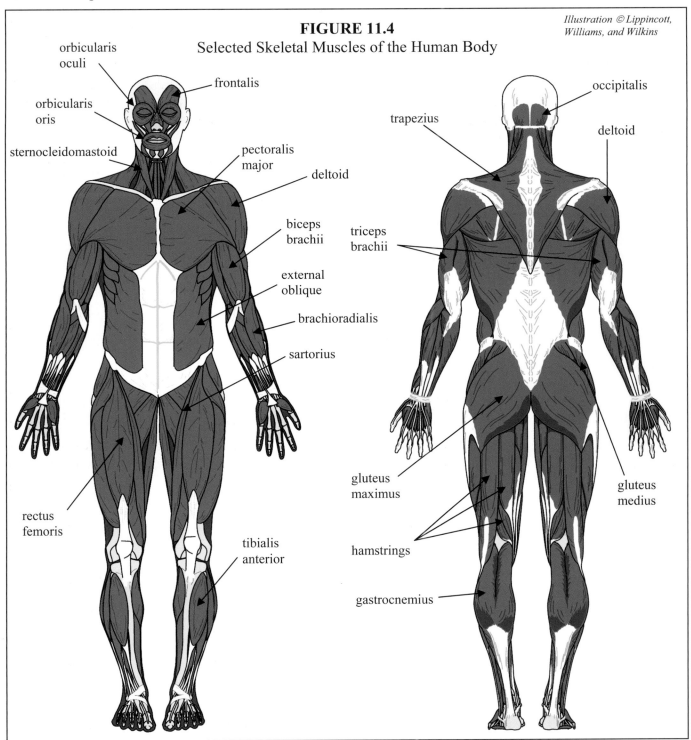

FIGURE 11.4
Selected Skeletal Muscles of the Human Body

Illustration © Lippincott, Williams, and Wilkins

orbicularis oculi

frontalis

orbicularis oris

sternocleidomastoid

pectoralis major

deltoid

biceps brachii

external oblique

brachioradialis

sartorius

rectus femoris

tibialis anterior

occipitalis

deltoid

trapezius

triceps brachii

gluteus maximus

hamstrings

gluteus medius

gastrocnemius

The first thing to realize about skeletal muscles is that they do not attach directly to the skeleton. Instead, the muscles typically taper as they get near the skeleton, and they end in a **tendon**, which attaches to the skeleton. Notice, for example, the arm muscle labeled "brachioradialis" (bray' kee oh ray' dee ay' lis) in Figure 11.4. Do you see how it tapers down to a white strip that goes toward the thumb? That white strip is the tendon connecting that end of the muscle to the skeleton.

The second thing to realize about skeletal muscles is that they would do little good if it were not for the **joints** in the skeleton. Muscles allow us to move because the skeleton is jointed. Think about it: Suppose your arm was supported by one long bone that went from your shoulder to your hand. If that were the case, you could not bend your arm without breaking the bone! Thus, your upper limb is *jointed* about halfway between your shoulder and hand. This joint, called the "elbow joint," separates the arm bone (the humerus) from the two forearm bones (radius and ulna). Because that joint is there, you can bend your arm at the elbow. There are four major kinds of joints in the human body, and they are illustrated in Figure 11.5.

Illustrations © Lippincott, Williams, and Wilkins

FIGURE 11.5
Major Types of Joints in the Human Body

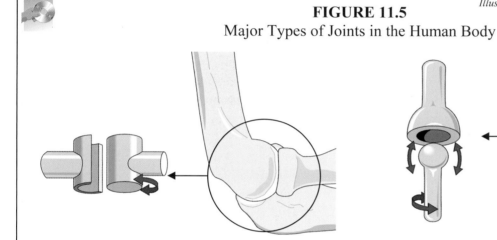

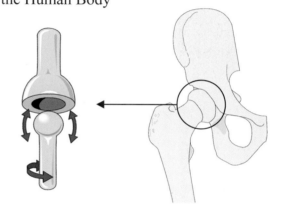

Hinge Joint
Elbows and knees are hinge joints. They offer a limited range of motion but are very stable.

Ball-and-Socket Joint
Hips and shoulders have ball-and-socket joints. They offer a wide range of motion but are less stable than hinge joints.

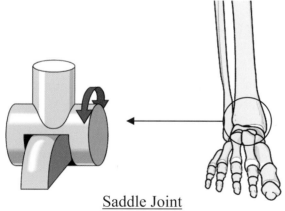

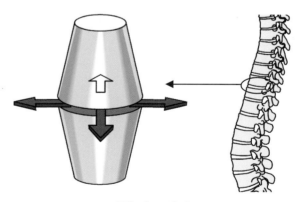

Saddle Joint
The ankle has a saddle joint. The range of motion is less than a ball-and-socket but more than a hinge.

Washer Joint
Washer joints appear only in the backbone. They allow you to bend and twist your back.

As mentioned in the figure, **hinge joints** can be found at the elbow and the knee. They act like the hinges on a door, allowing up and down (or left and right) motion, but that is all. For a joint, that is fairly limited motion. However, because the motion is limited, the stability of the joint is enhanced. This is especially important for the knee, because it holds an enormous amount of weight.

Ball-and-socket joints have a ball-shaped head that fits into a bowl-shaped socket. This design allows for a wide range of motion. The ball can roll around in the socket, providing left and right motion *along with* up and down motion. The hip joints and shoulder joints are good examples of ball-and-socket joints. Although ball-and-socket joints all have the same basic design, there are differences between one ball-and-socket joint and another. For example, the socket part of the shoulder joint is rather shallow. That allows for a large range of motion. However, the ball can be pushed or knocked out of the socket, causing a dislocated shoulder. In the hip joint, the socket is deeper. This results in slightly less freedom of motion for the hip, but the ball is more secure in the socket, so there is less chance of dislocating the hip joint as compared to the shoulder joint.

To understand the difference in the amount of motion provided by ball-and-socket joints as compared to hinge joints, try moving your forearm without moving *anything* else. Keep your wrist, hand, and shoulder rigid and still, and just move your forearm at your elbow. Notice the rather limited range of motion you have. Now, keep your entire forearm, wrist, and hand still, and move your entire arm at the shoulder. Notice how much more you can do by moving your arm at the shoulder. You can move your arm in circles, up and down, even back and forth. That's the difference in motion between a hinge joint (elbow) and a ball-and-socket joint (shoulder).

The **saddle joint** is more or less in between a hinge joint and a ball-and-socket joint. Saddle joints are composed of two saddle-shaped bones that fit together. The saddles can slide along each other, allowing left to right motion as well as up-and-down motion, but the bones are not as free to move as they are in a ball-and-socket joint. Your ankle joint is a good example of a saddle joint. Notice that your ankle joint does allow more motion than your elbow, but not nearly as much as your shoulder.

The last major kind of joint is the **washer joint**, and it exists only in your backbone. Your backbone is made up of individual bones called **vertebrae** (ver' tuh bray). Each vertebra (singular of "vertebrae") is connected to the other with a washer joint made of a cartilage disk. Each joint allows a small range of motion. Together, however, all the washer joints in your backbone allow you to bend and arch your back.

Now, joints by themselves are not as useful as you might think. They allow the skeleton to bend at certain places, but they cannot *cause* the motion. Also, remember that bone is hard. If joints were made of bone and nothing else, there would be a *big* problem. The bones in the joint would rub against each other. This would cause LOTS of pain and severe bone damage. To get around this problem, the bones in a joint do not actually touch. Instead, the bones in a joint are covered with **articular** (ar tik' yuh lur) **cartilage**. This cartilage is tough, but it is also flexible. Similar in feel to hard plastic, it is firm but smooth and resilient. As a result, the cartilage-covered bones of a joint can rub up against each other without damage. In addition, the resilient nature of the cartilage allows it to act as a shock absorber so that jarring movements (such as jumping) do not destroy the joints.

Now that's amazing enough, but I am not done yet! If two bones are jointed together, the cartilage will allow them to rub against each other without damage, but the joint would not necessarily stay together, would it? Consider a ball-and-socket joint, for example. What keeps the ball in the socket? Well, the two bones that are jointed together are held together by strips of tissue called

ligaments (lig' uh mints). Ligaments are much like strips of stiff elastic that go from one bone to the other. This holds the bones in the joint, but because of the slightly elastic nature of ligaments, the bones can be pulled apart from one another for brief times due to large stress, and then they will "snap" right back into place, provided that the stress does not last too long or is not too severe.

Okay, that's all there is to a joint, right? WRONG! Although cartilage and ligaments allow joints to move and keep the bones together, our bodies are designed to be incredibly efficient as well. If a joint had just cartilage in between the two bones, the joint would be able to move, but not without a lot of effort. Thus, in order to make the motion in joints smooth as well as not too difficult, the joints are also *lubricated*! Most joints are surrounded by a "bag" called the **articular capsule**. This bag is made of two layers – the **fibrous capsule** and the **synovial** (sih no' vee uhl) **membrane**. The cells in the synovial membrane produce a fluid, called **synovial fluid**. The synovial fluid in the articular capsule is slippery, like raw egg white. That slippery quality allows the fluid to lubricate the joints so that their motion is smooth and easy. This kind of joint, called a **synovial joint**, is shown below.

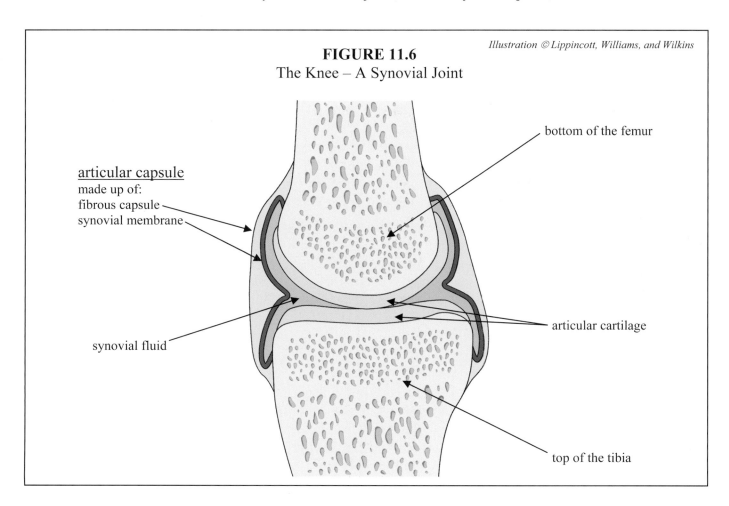

FIGURE 11.6
The Knee – A Synovial Joint

Illustration © Lippincott, Williams, and Wilkins

articular capsule
made up of:
fibrous capsule
synovial membrane

synovial fluid

bottom of the femur

articular cartilage

top of the tibia

Now that you know about joints and how they work, I can finally describe to you how skeletal muscles move the bones around those joints. They accomplish this by relaxing or contracting in concert with other muscles. This is a very complicated process which is best illustrated by example. I want to use Figure 11.7 (on the next page) to show you how certain muscles in your neck work so you can tilt your head from side to side.

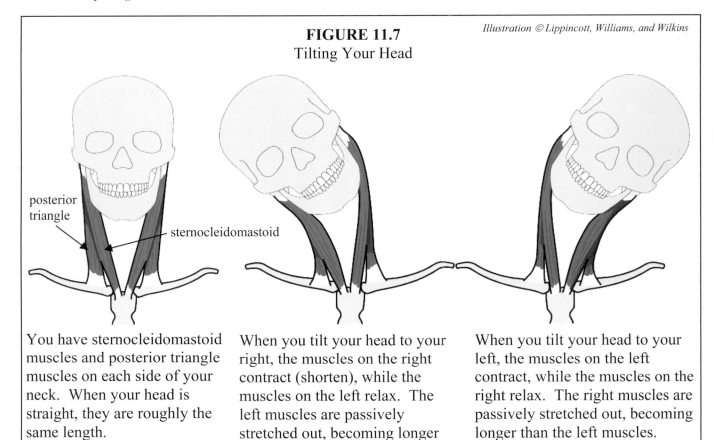

FIGURE 11.7
Tilting Your Head

Illustration © Lippincott, Williams, and Wilkins

posterior triangle

sternocleidomastoid

You have sternocleidomastoid muscles and posterior triangle muscles on each side of your neck. When your head is straight, they are roughly the same length.

When you tilt your head to your right, the muscles on the right contract (shorten), while the muscles on the left relax. The left muscles are passively stretched out, becoming longer than the right muscles.

When you tilt your head to your left, the muscles on the left contract, while the muscles on the right relax. The right muscles are passively stretched out, becoming longer than the left muscles.

The main players when it comes to tilting your head are the **sternocleidomastoid** (ster' noh klee' doh mas' toyd) muscles and the **posterior triangle** muscles. You have one of each on your left and one of each on your right. When you want to tilt your head, the muscles on one side contract, while the muscles on the other side relax. The contracted muscles shorten, pulling on your head as well as the relaxed muscles. Since the relaxed muscles offer no resistance, they just stretch out. If you tilt your head to the right, then, the muscles on the right contract, while the muscles on the left relax. This causes the muscles on the right to shorten, which passively stretches the muscles on the left and tilts the head to the right.

This is typical of how skeletal muscles work. They work in groups that are opposite of one another. When one group contracts, the opposite group relaxes, and motion in one direction is caused. Motion in the other direction is caused when the groups switch jobs, and the first relaxes while the second contracts. To give you another example, suppose you want to flex your forearm to show someone your muscle. The bigger the bump that forms on your arm, the more impressed an observer should be. Well, that bump is essentially your biceps brachii (bray' kee eye), which contracts to move your forearm at the elbow. Its partner is the triceps brachii, which relaxes and is passively stretched out while the biceps brachii contracts. When you straighten your arm out again, the biceps relaxes, and the triceps contracts. Now even though the examples I have given involve only a few muscles, most muscles work in large groups of ten, twenty, or even thirty or more, depending on the joints involved.

I want you to sit back and think about all this for a moment. The human skeleton is full of joints. There are four major designs for these joints, depending on the motion that the joint needs to perform. In addition, there are variations within those designs (shallow or deep sockets in the ball-and-socket joint, for example) in order to meet the individual requirements for the joints. The bones within the joints are cushioned with cartilage to reduce wear and pain. The bones are held together with ligaments that secure the bones in the joints but allow for some flexibility when the joint is stressed. The joint is then encased in a bag that makes its own fluid that lubricates the joint. Finally, the joint is moved by muscles that work *in concert* with other muscles. Sometimes the muscles work in pairs, but many movements we make require the concerted motion of more than *thirty* individual muscles.

Has applied science ever come up with anything so marvelous? Of course not! Think about an automobile, for example. An automobile has several moving parts that rub up against each other, much like the bones in a joint rub up against each other. Those parts are not cushioned like bones are, however. In addition, automobiles use oil, like joints use synovial fluid, to lubricate the moving parts. However, automobiles don't make their own oil! Instead, you have to buy it and put it in the engine. Joints make their own! Even a marvel of technology like an automobile is *primitive* compared to the human muscular and skeletal systems.

Have you ever seen a robotic arm? Several industries use robotic arms to perform repetitive tasks over and over again. Have you ever watched how jerky their movements are? That's because the hydraulics that control their motion are not nearly as smooth or efficient as muscles. Also, the energy required to move a robotic arm is *significantly greater* than the energy required to move your arm.

In the end, then, the human muscular and skeletal systems produce motion much more efficiently, much more elegantly, and at a much lower energy cost than the best machines that applied science can produce. Despite this fact, there are scientists who believe that the human body is the result of evolution, which requires *random chance*! Think about that for a moment. Suppose I showed you a car and told you that it was formed as the result of a tornado that ran through a junkyard. Suppose I told you that all the metal in the junkyard was thrown together in just the right way by chance, and a car was produced. Would you believe it? Of course not! The car is just too well designed to be the product of random chance. How, then, can anyone who has really studied the human body (which is much more elegantly designed than any car) ever believe it is the result of evolution?

ON YOUR OWN

11.5 Athletes and other people who stress their joints can damage the cartilage and ligaments of the joints. If the cartilage of a joint is damaged, what bad thing can happen to the bones of the joint? If the ligaments are damaged, what bad thing can happen?

11.6 Suppose a man's triceps brachii muscle stops working properly. The triceps can never contract. It can only remain relaxed. Will the man be able to flex his forearm at the elbow? Will the man be able to straighten his arm?

Smooth Muscle and the Cardiac Muscle

Smooth muscles are quite different in both structure and function from skeletal muscles. As their name implies, smooth muscles appear smoother than skeletal muscles. Under a microscope, skeletal muscles are long and have an orderly, striped appearance. Smooth muscle cells, on the other hand, are smaller and look smooth and unstriped. Smooth muscles are not connected to the bone, but form layers that are arranged so they can help make your organs work.

Consider, for example, what happens when you eat. Food you eat goes down into your stomach. You will learn the details of this in an upcoming module, so I don't want to dwell on how that happens right now. I just want to talk about what happens when the food lands in your stomach. In order to do its job, the stomach must churn the food around, mixing it with the liquid in the stomach. How is that accomplished? It is accomplished through the action of three layers of smooth muscles that line the stomach wall. They contract and relax, mixing the food with the liquids in the stomach to spur on the digestion process.

Unlike your skeletal muscles, your smooth muscles are controlled without any conscious thought. Thus, the movements they cause are called **involuntary movements**, because you do not do them by choice. They happen as a normal part of life with no thought on your part. Since smooth muscles cause involuntary movement, they are often called **involuntary muscles**. Because the stomach is controlled by smooth muscles, you never have to think about "working" your stomach. It happens involuntarily. That's how all your internal organs work. If you always had to think about contracting and relaxing the muscles that control your organs, you would die right away. That doesn't happen, though, because your brain does it all for you without you having to think about it at all!

The cardiac muscle is another muscle that works involuntarily. Under a microscope, a cardiac muscle cell is striped like a skeletal muscle cell, though the stripes are smaller. However, since it is controlled involuntarily, it is like a cross between a skeletal muscle cell and a smooth muscle cell. The heart muscle is controlled by both the brain and a small patch of cells, called the **sinoatrial** (sine' oh aye' tree uhl) **node**, that resides within the heart. The sinoatrial node sets the pace at which the cardiac muscle contracts and relaxes. It does this by generating an electrical signal that turns on and off about 100 times each minute. When the electrical signal turns on, the cardiac muscle contracts. When it turns off, the cardiac muscle relaxes. That's how your heart beats. Because the sinoatrial node sets the "pace" at which your heart beats, it is often called the **pacemaker**.

"Wait a minute," you should be thinking. My heart doesn't usually beat 100 times a minute! That's right. Remember, I said that the brain also has some control over the cardiac muscle. Based on the information that your brain is getting from the receptors all over your body, the brain can slow down or speed up the rate at which the sinoatrial node produces electrical signals. Under normal circumstances, your brain usually slows your heartbeat to between 60 and 80 beats per minute. When you exercise heavily, or when you are nervous, your brain can speed the rate up so that your heart beats faster.

You probably know of someone who has an artificial pacemaker. Worldwide, more than 200,000 artificial pacemakers are surgically implanted into people each year. Thus, odds are that you know of or at least have heard of someone who has one. These people have a condition that causes their sinoatrial node to malfunction. As a result, the implanted pacemaker generates the electrical signals that cause the cardiac muscle to contract and relax. A pacemaker, then, is an artificial sinoatrial node. Like most of the marvels of technology, however, it pales in comparison to the biological wonder that it imitates. For example, it is *huge* compared to the sinoatrial node. Also, while a pacemaker can vary the rate at which it produces signals, its range is limited. It cannot react to meet the body's needs like the sinoatrial node can. Thus, those who have pacemakers must watch their activity level, because their heart cannot adjust to the demands of the body the way it would if the sinoatrial node were working properly.

ON YOUR OWN

11.7 There are muscles in your blood vessels that expand and contract in order to regulate the way that blood flows throughout your body. Are these smooth or skeletal muscles? What about the muscles that cause your fingers to open and close? Are they smooth or skeletal muscles?

Muscles and Movement in Other Organisms

Most animals have muscles that allow them to move. Although some details differ between the muscles of a frog and the muscles of a human, the basic structure and function of muscles are reasonably consistent throughout most of kingdom Animalia. One thing that I would like to point out, however, is that the *placement* of the muscles can be quite different in some animals as compared to others. Consider the arthropods, for example. Remember, these animals have exoskeletons. Thus, while our muscles (and all vertebrate muscles) lie *on top of* the skeleton, the muscles of arthropods are attached *underneath* the skeleton. In other words, while our muscles pull on the skeleton from on top of the bone, arthropod muscles pull on their skeleton from underneath the chitin.

What about the other kingdoms? Well, the members of kingdom Monera can, indeed, move from one place to another. They do not utilize muscles, however. Most members of kingdom Monera have little tails called **flagella** (fluh jel' uh). They spin these tails like little outboard motors, allowing them to move through the water (or other liquid) they inhabit. Some members of kingdom Protista (the algae) do not really move much on their own. Others (the protozoa) rely on specific structures that allow them to move. Some have flagella, while others have tiny hairs called **cilia** (sil' ee uh). These hairs beat back and forth, acting like little oars that row the organism through the water.

The members of kingdom Fungi do not move around a lot. They certainly have no muscles. The members of kingdom Plantae do not have muscles, but they manage to move in a few ways. Perform the following experiment to see what I mean.

EXPERIMENT 11.2
Phototropism and Gravitropism in Plants

Supplies:

♦ Two houseplants. Make sure that your parents won't mind one of them looking really funny once the experiment is over.
♦ A few books
♦ A sunny window

Introduction: In this experiment, you will see two specific situations that cause plants to move.

Procedure:

1. Set one of the plants in front of the window, a few feet away from it. Allow it to sit for three days.
2. Make a pile of books on the floor.

3. Tilt the second plant so that its pot lies against the books. Steady it so that the plant stays tilted, leaning against the books.
4. After three days, turn the first plant (the one that is not tilted) 180 degrees, so that the side of the plant that did not face the window now faces the window.
5. Note what you see in both plants after a few days.

For the first plant, you will see that it slowly moves so that most of its leaves face the window. The tendency of plants to grow so that they face the light is called **phototropism** (foh' toh trohp' iz uhm). Although most houseplants take a few days in order to move so that they face the light, some plants can do so much more quickly. While they are budding, sunflowers actually turn throughout the day so they follow the sun as it travels across the sky!

What will happen to the second plant is an illustration of **gravitropism** (grav' uh trohp' iz uhm), which is the tendency for a plant to sense which way is "up" and to grow that way. Both gravitropism and phototropism are caused by special chemicals, called growth hormones, that accelerate plant growth. These hormones are affected by gravity and light. As a result, different parts of plants grow at different rates depending on the position of the plant. This has the net effect of "moving" the plant so that it faces the light and always grows upward.

If you think about it, of course, such movements are very helpful to plants. Since plants make their food using the energy of sunlight, the more they face the light, the more food they can make. Phototropism, then, allows the plant to take as much advantage of the sun's light as possible. This can be especially important in forests, where taller plants (like trees) can block the sun from smaller plants (like bushes or young trees). Phototropism allows a plant to "grow around" the shade so as to find the sunlight.

How do plants benefit from gravitropism? Think about it: You don't have to worry about planting a seed "right side up." No matter which way the seed falls, the plant grows up out of the soil. That's because of gravitropism. Plants have other means of movement as well. You will learn more about them when you take biology.

Skin

Now that we have covered the skeleton and muscles, the only other portion of the body's superstructure we need to cover is the **skin**. This, of course, is the thin layer that covers your entire body. You might think of skin as just a "wrapper" that holds your body together, but it is so much more than that! Your skin is your body's primary line of defense. It protects your inner tissues from drying out. It also provides you with a sense of touch, grows hair and nails, and even keeps pathogenic microorganisms out of your body. In response to sunlight, your skin also starts the process of making vitamin D, which helps the digestive system absorb the calcium it needs from your diet. This, of course, helps your skeletal system. Interestingly enough, the skin's job is so tough that it must be constantly renewed. As a result, your body is always replacing its skin. In fact, the skin cells you will have about 30 days from now will be completely new compared to the skin cells you have today.

In order to do its job, the skin is composed of many different parts. To help you understand just what a marvel your skin is, Figure 11.8 shows you a cutaway representation of a block of human skin. It is truly amazing to think that something as thin as our skin has this much detail!

FIGURE 11.8
A Simple Diagram of Human Skin

Illustration by Megan Fruchte

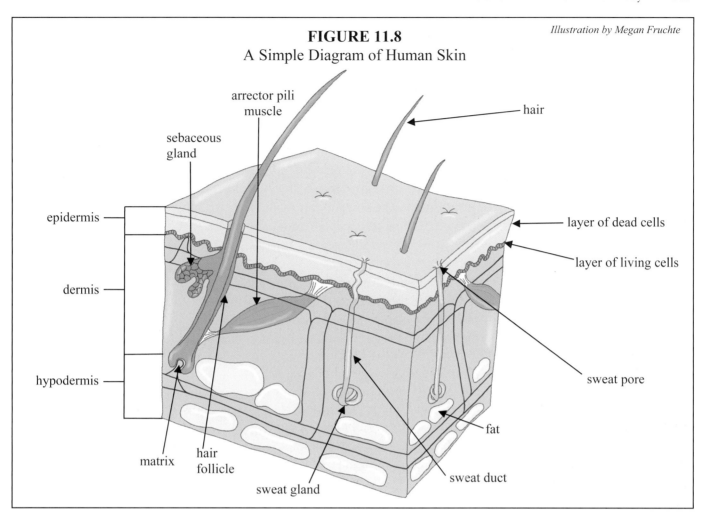

Your skin is composed of two basic layers. The outer layer is called the **epidermis** (ep uh dur' mis), and the inner layer is called the **dermis**. Below the dermis lies the **hypodermis** (hi poh dur' mis). Composed mostly of fat, it is not technically considered part of the skin. It binds the skin to the underlying tissues.

Notice that the epidermis is composed of two layers – a layer of living cells with a layer of dead cells above. The living cells of the epidermis are continually reproducing. After a new living cell is formed, it is slowly pushed toward the top of the epidermis and, as it moves upward, its cytoplasm is transformed. Now remember, the cytoplasm of a cell (as described in Module #9) is a jelly-like substance that makes up most of the cell. The cell's organelles are located in the cytoplasm, and the cell's membrane holds the cytoplasm in place. Well, as a living skin cell moves upward in the epidermis, the cytoplasm is transformed because the cell makes a waterproofing protein called **keratin** (kair' uh tin). This process, called keratinization, actually kills the cell, but makes the dead cell quite sturdy and hard to destroy. This is how your body continually renews your skin.

The dead cells in the epidermis are what really do most of the skin's protective work. Because these cells are firm and sturdy, it is difficult for pathogenic organisms (mostly bacteria and fungi) to penetrate the epidermis. In addition, the waterproof keratin prevents your skin from easily drying out. Because the topmost skin cells are dead, however, they are constantly falling from the skin's surface. Thus, the layer of living epidermal cells must continually reproduce so that new cells can be keratinized and sent to replace the cells that fall off. A good fraction of the dust you find in your home is composed of the dead epidermal cells that have fallen from your family's (and your pets') skin.

Your skin also has **hair**. Almost all of your skin produces hair. Even though you might not be able to see it without the aid of a magnifying glass, there is hair on almost every part of your body, except for certain areas such as the palms of your hands and soles of your feet. Like the outer layer of the epidermis, hair is made from keratinized cells, but the keratin is harder in these cells than in the skin's cells. Thus, hair is dead as well. The cells that are keratinized to make hair do not come from the lower layer of the epidermis. Instead, they come from a structure known as a **hair follicle** (fall' uh kul), which is like a tiny "pit" of epidermis. The lowest part of the hair follicle, called the **matrix**, is composed of cells that rapidly reproduce. The cells produced by the matrix become keratinized and form a cylindrical hair, which pushes upward within the hair follicle.

Hair grows at different rates based on the activity of your hair follicles. The hair follicles on your head, for example, are very active for months at a time. As a result, the hair on your head can grow very long. The hair follicles on your arms and legs, however, are active for only short periods of time and have long periods of "rest." Thus, they produce hair that is much shorter than the hair on your head.

Why does your skin grow hair? Well, hair has two main functions: insulation and sensation. First of all, your hair helps keep you warm. Hair helps trap warm air next to your skin. Have you ever gotten "goose pimples"? Typically, they are caused by cold air or by nervousness. Goose pimples are formed by hair. You see, each hair follicle is connected to a small smooth muscle in the dermis called the **arrector** (uh rek' tor) **pili** muscle. When you get cold (or when you are very nervous), this muscle automatically contracts, pulling the hair straight up. This increases the amount of warm air trapped next to the body. It also pulls on the epidermis beside the hair follicle, causing a little bump to form. That bump is what we call a goose pimple.

Hair's second purpose is sensation. The hair is surrounded by nerves in the dermis. When your hair is moved, those nerves send signals to your brain, telling it that the hair is being moved. Your brain then tells you that something is touching your skin. Since hairs move so easily, this is a very sensitive system. Even a gentle breeze will move your hair, sending signals to your brain so that you know a gentle breeze is blowing. The skin has other receptors (which I will discuss in a later module) that provide your sense of touch. However, your hair is a very sensitive receptor when it comes to something touching you.

Sebaceous (suh bay' shus) **glands** are connected to the hair follicle in the dermis. These glands produce oil that coats the hairs and also gets ejected onto the skin at the openings where the hairs emerge. This oil softens the hair and the skin. If you have ever experienced dry, chapped skin, you know how painful it can be. This oil keeps dry skin from becoming an everyday occurrence. The oil also helps protect the body from harmful organisms, as it makes it harder for certain bacteria to attach themselves to the skin. These glands are absolutely necessary for healthy skin, but they are also a nuisance for young people. During most students' teen years, the sebaceous glands are extremely active, producing a *lot* of oil. Bacteria feed on the contents of the oil, disrupting the normal operation of the hair follicle. Too many cells are produced there, and they clump together, which causes the hair follicle to get plugged up. Oil then forms underneath the plug, forming a bump with a white top (usually called a "whitehead"). When the building pressure bursts the whitehead, the bacteria further irritate the tissue, causing a red bump, the tell-tale sign of acne.

The other structures illustrated in Figure 11.8 govern the process of sweating. Sweat is produced in your sweat glands, travels up through the dermis in the sweat duct, and then pours out onto your skin through your sweat pores. Sweating serves at least two purposes. When we sweat, we cool ourselves down. You will learn more about *how* sweating cools you down next year when you take physical science. For right now, just realize that sweating cools your skin. Secondly, sweat helps feed bacteria and fungi that *live on your skin!* Now wait a minute. Doesn't the skin do everything it can in order to keep bacteria and fungi out of your body? Well, not exactly. The skin does everything it can to keep *pathogenic* bacteria and fungi out of your body. However, not *all* bacteria and fungi are pathogenic. In fact, many are beneficial to us.

You see, there are certain bacteria and fungi that produce acid (primarily a substance called lactic acid) as a byproduct of the processes keeping them alive. This lactic acid is an incredibly effective defense against many types of pathogenic bacteria and fungi. Thus, your body encourages these acid-producing bacteria and fungi to live on your skin. These beneficial bacteria and fungi then cover your skin in acid, protecting it from harmful bacteria and fungi.

If you don't know much about chemistry, you might wonder how in the world having acid covering your skin could possibly be good for you. Well, when you take chemistry in a few years, you will learn that only a few acids are dangerous. Many are quite gentle. In fact, if you drink fruit juice, soda pop, or milk, you are drinking acid. Thus, acids are not necessarily dangerous chemicals. Many are quite good for your body, including the lactic acid produced by the bacteria and fungi that live on your skin.

Now I want you to think about this for a moment. Your skin's primary function is to protect your body from harm. One of the most obvious threats the body faces is infection by pathogenic bacteria and fungi. Although your skin alone provides a lot of defense against such infections, it is just not enough. Thus, your skin actually produces *food* for bacteria and fungi that can *help* it do its job! Isn't that amazing? Without your skin producing food, the bacteria and fungi that live on it would die. Without those bacteria and fungi, your body would be much more susceptible to infection. In other words, this is a case in which *several organisms help each other* so as to benefit all the organisms concerned. The bacteria and fungi on your skin benefit from the food your skin provides, and you benefit by staying healthier.

Although this process is rather surprising, it is very common throughout creation. In fact, it is so common that biologists have a term for it. The term is **symbiosis** (sim by oh' sis).

Symbiosis – A close relationship between two or more species where at least one benefits

As you will learn in biology, there are actually three different kinds of symbiosis in creation, but for now, this is the only one with which you need to be concerned. To make it clear exactly how common symbiosis is in creation, consider the words of Dr. George D. Stanley, Jr.: "Symbiosis is the most relevant and enduring biological theme in the history of our planet." [*Science* **312**:857, 2006]. This "enduring biological theme" is an incredible testament to God's forethought in designing His creation. You see, survival is all about solving problems. The better an organism can solve the problems related to staying alive, the longer and more productive that organism's life will be. Thus, in order to help these organisms solve problems, God has made it so that many organisms can work together. Just as a volleyball team is much more effective than a single player, the "teams" formed via symbiosis make all the organisms involved more effective at living.

Can you imagine how such "teams" could form by chance? After all, teams are formed when a leader (coach, team captain, etc.) begins choosing players and assigning them to play certain positions. The team leader has some idea of the capabilities of each player, and he assigns each player to a position that the player has the ability to play. The same thing must be true of symbiosis. Organisms don't just randomly go around looking for other organisms to help! Think about it: There are a host of bacteria and fungi that your skin fights. How would your body know to make a special type of food that only attracts *certain types* of bacteria and fungi? Well, the "team captain" (God), designed your body to attract the correct players (the beneficial bacteria and fungi) and then "assigned" those players to the position of making an acid that is good for your skin and fights off pathogens.

The idea that such a team could be put together by random chance is absurd. Nevertheless, if you do not believe in God, you are forced to believe that the process of symbiosis has happened over and over again in nature as the result of random chance! Those who do not believe in God truly have amazing faith! They have enormous faith in the ability of random chance to produce the awesome design we see in creation.

 The multimedia CD has a video about symbiosis.

Now that I have shown you the basics of your skin, I want to address one subject that you are probably wondering about: skin color. Why is it that people have such a wide range of skin color? Skin has cells deep in the epidermis that make a chemical called **melanin** (mel' uh nin). This chemical is called a **pigment**, because it tends to give color to whatever it is in. This particular pigment tends to darken skin. If someone has a lot of melanin, he has dark skin. If someone has only a little melanin, he has light skin. There is a certain condition call **albinism** (al' buhn iz uhm), in which a person has no melanin at all. These people have skin that is extremely light.

What affects how much melanin a person has in his or her skin? There are many factors, and the following experiment demonstrates one of them.

EXPERIMENT 11.3
Skin Color

Supply:

♦ A plastic bandage, such as a Band-Aid®

Introduction: In this experiment, you will see how light affects the production of melanin.

Procedure:

1. Put the bandage around one of your fingers so that it covers your skin.
2. Leave the bandage on for two days. Try to get out in the sun as much as you are able, because that will enhance the effect.
3. At the end of two days, pull the bandage off and compare the skin that was under the bandage to the rest of your finger.
4. After you are done with the experiment, answer "On Your Own" question 11.10.

Hair gets its color essentially the same way skin does. Dark hair has a lot of melanin in it, while light hair has very little. Red hair contains a mixture of melanin and red pigment. If a person produces a lot of red pigment and only a little melanin, his hair is "strawberry blonde." The more melanin produced, the deeper the red color becomes. Without any melanin (in the case of albinism, for example), hair is white. In an older person, the cells can stop making melanin for the hairs. As a result, the hairs are white, and we say that the person has "gray hair."

ON YOUR OWN

11.8 Suppose a medical researcher comes up with a way of shutting down the activity of the sebaceous gland. Although teenagers everywhere rejoice, the Food and Drug Administration (FDA) decides to *not* allow the process to be performed in the United States. Why would teenagers everywhere rejoice at such a discovery? Assuming that the procedure itself is safe, why wouldn't the FDA allow it to be performed in the United States?

11.9 When a person gets burned enough that she must be hospitalized, the doctors and nurses know that certain problems are likely to occur because of the severe damage to her skin. Can you list at least two of these problems?

11.10 Based on the results of Experiment 11.3, does sunlight tend to increase or decrease the amount of melanin in your skin?

Skin in Other Organisms

Most organisms in creation have some kind of outer covering that protects them. Thus, almost all organisms have some kind of "skin." However, the "skin" of many organisms is not nearly as complex as human skin. Most members of kingdoms Monera and Protista, for example, have just a membrane surrounding their single cell. Some bacteria (kingdom Monera) have a sheath of sticky goo (called a "capsule") that covers their membrane. This capsule protects them to a greater degree than does the membrane by itself.

Most plants (kingdom Plantae) have an epidermis. Unlike human skin, however, the epidermis of plants is often just one layer of cells. Even though that's pretty simplistic when compared to human skin, it does offer a lot of protection for the plant. In kingdom Fungi, the organisms are typically covered with chitin. This covering is strong. It serves to hold parts of the fungus up (as I mentioned previously), but it also offers excellent protection for the fungus.

Most of the organisms in kingdom Animalia also have a skin of some sort. The makeup of the skin is often used to help classify organisms in this kingdom. For example, if an organism's skin produces hair, it is considered a **mammal**. Mammals are a group of organisms that all have similar characteristics, one of which is skin that makes hair. In addition, most mammals give birth to live young (as opposed to laying eggs), nourish their young with milk that they produce, and possess a heart with four chambers. As you can tell from the description, humans are mammals, as are cats, dogs, elephants, rabbits, etc. You will learn more about mammals when you take biology.

If an organism's skin produces feathers, it is a **bird**, not a mammal. On the other hand, if the organism's skin produces scales, the organism is probably either a **fish** or a **reptile**, depending on other characteristics the organism has. If the organism's skin is an exoskeleton, the organism is an **arthropod**. Some organisms, like **amphibians** (frogs, toads, and salamanders), even *breathe* with their skin. Obviously, then, the structure and function of an organism's skin varies quite a bit in creation!

Summary

Before you finish with this module, I want you to take a moment and think about what you have learned. The human body is truly amazing in its design! Think of all the structures I have taught you about in this module, and then consider this: I have *barely even scratched the surface* of the human superstructure. I have deliberately left out many of the more difficult aspects of the human skeletal system, the human muscular system, and human skin, simply because you do not have the chemistry to understand them! Now I want you to think about one other fact: The human body is so amazingly complex that there are still many aspects that are a *complete mystery* to science! Despite our best efforts, we have yet to understand many of the processes that make the human body work! This should give you profound respect for the God who actually designed and created it, and it should also convince you that there is simply no way such an elegantly designed system could ever be formed by random chance!

Based on the words of a popular phrase,
Henry looks for beauty somewhere between
the dermis and the hypodermis.

ANSWERS TO THE "ON YOUR OWN" PROBLEMS

11.1 <u>The patient's blood would change as well</u>. Since bone marrow produces blood cells, a bone marrow transplant will actually change the patient's blood. That is, in fact, the reason bone marrow transplants are done.

11.2 As a person gets older, the relative amount of <u>collagen</u> in his bones decreases. Remember, the minerals in bone make them hard but brittle. The collagen makes them flexible. Bones with the right amount of each are hard but do not break easily. With too few minerals, the bones are too soft (like the chicken bone in your experiment). With too little collagen, the bones are hard and brittle.

11.3 Compact bone tissue is much heavier than spongy bone tissue. Thus, the <u>first bone</u> has more compact bone tissue because it is heavier.

11.4 You don't have to know a lot about these creatures to determine whether or not they are vertebrates. You just have to remember a couple of things. First, if the organism is in *any* kingdom other than Animalia, it is neither a vertebrate nor an invertebrate. If it is an animal, then it is a vertebrate if it has a backbone. For your purposes, you can assume that if it has an endoskeleton at all, it has a backbone and is therefore a vertebrate.

a. A worm is an animal, but it is too squishy to have an endoskeleton. Thus, it is an <u>invertebrate.</u>

b. An alligator is an animal, and it has an endoskeleton. Thus, it is a <u>vertebrate.</u>

c. Grass is a plant. Thus, it is <u>neither</u> an invertebrate nor a vertebrate.

d. Yeast is a fungus. Thus, it is <u>neither</u> an invertebrate nor a vertebrate.

e. This is a hard one. A starfish is covered with a hard, outer covering. If you look inside, there are no bones. Thus, it is an <u>invertebrate</u>. Don't worry if you got that one wrong!

f. Fish have endoskeletons. Thus, a bass is a <u>vertebrate.</u>

g. A clam has a nice, hard outer shell, but it has no endoskeleton. It is an <u>invertebrate</u>.

11.5   Cartilage cushions the ends of the bones so that they don't scrape together in the joints. <u>Damage to the articular cartilage will cause great pain and bone damage as the bones of the joint scrape together</u>. Ligaments hold the bones in the joints. Thus, <u>damaged ligaments will make it easy to dislocate the joint</u>. Interestingly enough, however, the pain and swelling from the damaged ligament actually helps prevent further dislocation.

11.6   The triceps contracts to extend the forearm, making the arm straight. It relaxes so that the biceps can flex the forearm. Thus, <u>the person will be able to flex the forearm at the elbow but not extend it</u>.

11.7   <u>The muscles that regulate blood flow are smooth.</u> You know that because you don't have to think about regulating your blood flow. Your body does it automatically. Thus, they are involuntary muscles and are therefore smooth. <u>The muscles that open and close your fingers are skeletal muscles</u>.

You know this because you have to think to move your fingers. Thus, the muscles are voluntary. Also, the fingers are part of the skeleton. To move the skeleton, you have to use skeletal muscles.

11.8   <u>Teenagers everywhere would rejoice because without the oil from the sebaceous gland, there would be no acne</u>. Remember, acne starts with a plugged-up sebaceous gland. <u>The FDA would not approve the procedure because you need that oil for healthy skin</u>. It keeps the skin from painfully cracking, and it also makes it harder for harmful bacteria to attach to your skin.

11.9   Since the skin provides waterproofing, <u>the person might have a problem with water loss, which can cause dehydration</u>. Since the skin provides sensation, <u>the person might have trouble with sensations</u> like touch, temperature awareness, etc. Since the skin provides protection from pathogenic microorganisms, <u>the person might have trouble with infections</u>. Since the sweat glands in the skin help control body temperature, <u>the person might have trouble controlling her own body temperature</u>.

11.10   In your experiment, the skin covered with the bandage should have been lighter than the rest of your skin. Since the rest of your skin was exposed to light, that means light makes skin darker. That's why you can suntan. Since increasing the amount of melanin in skin makes it dark, <u>light must increase the amount of melanin in your skin</u>.

STUDY GUIDE FOR MODULE #11

1. Define the following terms:

a. Axial skeleton
b. Appendicular skeleton
c. Exoskeleton
d. Symbiosis

2. What three things make up the human superstructure?

3. What are the two main differences between smooth muscles and skeletal muscles?

4. Where is cardiac muscle found? Is it an involuntary muscle or a voluntary one?

5. What is produced in the red bone marrow?

6. What is keratinization? What is it used for?

7. What two principal substances make up bone? What qualities do they each provide to the bone?

8. What is the difference between compact bone tissue and spongy bone tissue?

9. Are bones alive?

10. What is the difference between an invertebrate and a vertebrate? Is it possible for an organism to be neither?

11. Are your arms part of the appendicular skeleton or the axial skeleton? What about your neck?

12. What is the difference between an endoskeleton and an exoskeleton? What do we call organisms with exoskeletons?

13. Order the following joints in terms of increasing range of motion, then order them in terms of increasing stability: ball-and-socket, hinge, saddle

14. What purpose do ligaments serve in the joints? What about cartilage?

15. How do skeletal muscles attach to the skeleton?

16. Describe how the sternocleidomastoid and posterior triangle muscles on each side of the neck work together in order to tilt the head.

17. Are the muscles in your stomach smooth muscles or skeletal muscles?

18. When it is budding, a sunflower will actually turn throughout the day so that it follows the sun across the sky. What is the term we use to describe this?

19. What are the two main functions of hair?

20. What are the two main functions of sweat?

21. Why do your skin cells constantly fall off your body?

22. What do the sebaceous glands produce, and what are the substance's two main purposes?

23. For the following animals, classify each as mammal, bird, reptile, or amphibian:

    a.   An animal with hair
    b.   An animal that breathes through its skin
    c.   An animal with scales
    d.   An animal with feathers

MODULE #12: Energy and Life

Introduction

Now that you know a little bit about the skeleton, muscles, and skin, I want to discuss something they all use: **energy**. The muscles use energy to contract and relax, the bones use energy to grow and make blood cells, and the skin uses energy to produce hair, skin cells, and nails. In fact, energy is used in all parts of our bodies. Indeed, energy is such an important component of life that it is central to our second criterion for life:

All life forms have a method by which they extract energy from their surroundings and convert it into energy that sustains them.

In this module and the next, I want to give you an introduction to how that happens in your body as well as how it happens in many other organisms.

Life's Energy Cycle

Before I start discussing the ways in which your body satisfies the second criterion for life, I want to spend some time on a few fundamental concepts. First, I want ask you a very simple question: Where does all this energy come from? After all, the second criterion for life says that living organisms take energy from their surroundings and convert it into energy that sustains them. Well, if living organisms *take* energy from the surroundings, it must already be there waiting to be taken. Where does it come from?

Almost all the energy used by living organisms comes from one place: **the sun**. There are some bacteria that get their energy from certain chemical reactions involving sulfur or methane, but most organisms in creation get their energy from the sun. Now that might sound a little strange to you. After all, you know that you get your energy from the food you eat and the liquids you drink. If you were to stop eating and drinking and simply lie out in the sun all day, you would die. You wouldn't be able to satisfy your energy needs that way! How, then, can I say that the energy in your body (and the bodies of most organisms) originated in the sun?

Well, think about it. When light from the sun hits the earth, plants (and other organisms like algae) convert that energy into food for themselves. We call such organisms **producers**, because they produce food for themselves.

Producers – Organisms that produce their own food

It is easy to see how the energy a producer uses comes from the sun. Through the process of photosynthesis, producers use energy from the sun, carbon dioxide, and water to make a sugar called glucose. That glucose is then used by the plant as food. The plant, then, converts the energy of the sun into glucose, and it uses the glucose as food for energy.

That's not the end of the story, however. God has designed producers to make a lot more food than they need. They store this excess food, usually in some chemical form other than glucose. Plants, for example, usually store their excess food as starch or fat (as in seeds). When animals eat those plants, they are using that starch or fat to produce their energy. Thus, even though these animals cannot get energy *directly* from the sun, they get it indirectly, by eating the food that the producers made. We call such creatures **consumers**, because they consume other organisms to get their food.

<u>Consumers</u> – Organisms that eat living producers and/or other consumers for food

Human beings are consumers. We eat plants, and we eat meat, which comes from animals. Those animals ate either plants or creatures that had eaten plants. In the end, then, the energy of life comes from the sun, because the producers produce the food from the sun's energy, and the consumers eat the producers, or they eat other consumers that have eaten the producers.

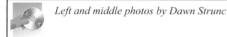

FIGURE 12.1
Producers and Consumers

The plants in this lush South African landscape are producers. They make their own food from sunlight.

This giraffe is a consumer, because it eats plants, which are producers.

This person is a consumer, because she eats plants and animals.

There is actually a third group of organisms I have not mentioned yet – the **decomposers** you learned about in Module #10. Although you *could* classify such organisms as consumers (after all, they do not produce their own food), they are classified separately because they play a distinct role in creation. Decomposers "recycle" dead organisms. You see, as a decomposer eats a dead organism, the organism is broken down into chemicals that act as fertilizer for producers. Now remember, fertilizer is *not* plant food. However, fertilizer does act like "vitamins" that make plants healthier. As a result, producers use the products of the decomposers. This makes the decomposers different from the consumers.

Now I need to make a very important point. Not all organisms that eat dead things are decomposers. Vultures, for example, eat dead animals. However, the process of a vulture eating a dead animal does not produce fertilizer for plants. Thus, a vulture is not a decomposer. As you will recall from Experiment 10.2, yeast is a decomposer. That's because when yeast eats dead organisms, the organisms are broken down into substances used by producers.

Throughout this discussion so far, I have classified organisms by whether they are producers, consumers, or decomposers. However, we can get a bit more detailed than that. If an organism is a consumer, it can be further classified. Remember, giraffes are consumers because they eat producers. Lions are also consumers, but they do not eat producers. They are consumers because they eat *other* consumers. Also, people are consumers, because we eat *both* producers and consumers.

If a consumer eats only producers, it is called a **herbivore** (ur' bih vor).

<u>Herbivore</u> – A consumer that eats producers exclusively

If a consumer eats only other consumers, it is called a **carnivore** (kar' nih vor).

<u>Carnivore</u> – A consumer that eats only other consumers

Finally, if a consumer eats both producers and other consumers, it is an **omnivore** (ahm' nih vor).

<u>Omnivore</u> – A consumer that eats both producers and other consumers

From these definitions, then, you can see that giraffes are herbivores, lions are carnivores, and humans are omnivores.

 The multimedia CD has a video about herbivores, carnivores, and omnivores.

ON YOUR OWN

12.1 Classify each of the following as a consumer, producer, or decomposer:

a. grass   b. horse   c. tree   d. yeast   e. sparrow   f. shark

12.2 A creature's diet includes leaves, fruit, and certain bugs. Is this creature a carnivore, herbivore, or omnivore? If one of the three items from that list were removed, the creature would be classified differently. What one thing would have to be removed, and what would its new classification be?

Now before I leave this section, I want to bring up something I mentioned in passing before. While *the vast majority* of energy used by living things comes from the sun, some of it does come as a result of specific chemical reactions that do not need the energy of sunlight. One place you can find such chemical reactions in creation is at the bottom of the very deep parts of the oceans. In the deep oceans, sunlight cannot penetrate to the ocean floor. Nevertheless, you can find producers there. These producers live near fissures in the ocean's bottom, called **hydrothermal vents**.

As you will learn in physical science, the interior of the earth is very hot. Hydrothermal vents expose this hot interior. When a hydrothermal vent is at the bottom of the ocean, it spews forth superheated water that is rich in various chemicals, some of which can be used by bacteria to make their own food. Even though these bacteria do not use sunlight, we would still call them producers, because they produce their own food.

Well, what do you think the presence of producers at the bottom of the ocean causes? You guessed it! It causes the presence of consumers that are looking for a meal. Thus, hydrothermal vents at the bottom of the ocean support a rich community of producers and consumers, all of which take advantage of the energy stored in the chemicals that are spewed into the ocean. Because it is a relevant and enduring theme in the study of life, you also find examples of symbiosis in these communities, as shown in the figure below.

FIGURE 12.2
A Hydrothermal Vent and an Example of the Community of Organisms It Can Support

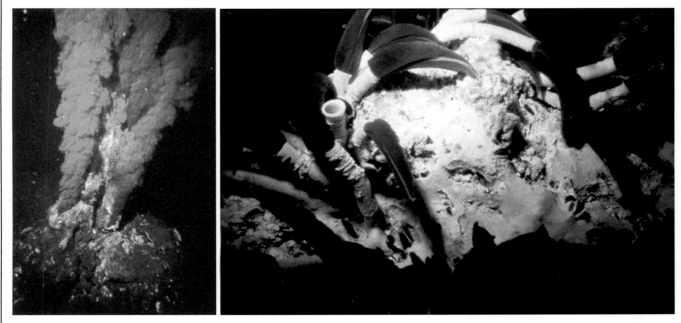

The hydrothermal vent on the left is called a "black smoker." You can see the hot, chemical-laden water rushing from it. The creatures on the right are tubeworms. The worms' red "plumes" house bacteria that produce energy from the chemicals at the hydrothermal vent. In exchange for this "housing," they give some of that energy to the tubeworms.   *Photos courtesy of the NOAA*

How Do Organisms Get Energy From Food?

So now you now know that producers make their own food (usually from the sun's energy), and consumers eat that food by eating producers or eating animals that have eaten producers. Also, you know that decomposers eat dead organisms and "recycle" those dead organisms back into creation. However, I still haven't told you *how* organisms actually get energy from food. Well, that's not an easy question to answer. In fact, I will spend the rest of this module *and the next* just giving you an introduction to how this is done. The process is quite fascinating and well worth the time it will take to discuss!

In short, organisms get energy from food by *burning* their food. Now don't get the wrong idea here. There aren't little fires going on in your body. Nevertheless, the chemical process by which organisms get energy from food is a **combustion** reaction. Combustion reactions are what occur when wood, paper, and other flammable materials are burned. Thus, much like we can get energy to heat our home by burning wood in a fireplace or natural gas in a furnace, organisms get the energy they need for life by burning their food.

Of course, the burning process that goes on in organisms is quite different from the burning process that goes on in a fireplace or a furnace. Nevertheless, there are a few similarities. I want you to perform the following experiment to see some of those similarities.

EXPERIMENT 12.1
What Combustion Needs

Supplies:

♦ A small candle (It needs to be in some kind of heavy holder, but the holder should not be tall. A small tealight candle in a glass holder, like the one in the figure under step 5, is ideal.)
♦ A glass that will cover the candle
♦ A deep bowl (The bowl should be deep enough so that when the candle is placed at the bottom of the bowl, the sides of the bowl are above the flame of the candle.)
♦ One cup of vinegar
♦ One tablespoon of baking soda
♦ Matches
♦ Eye protection such as goggles or safety glasses

Introduction: In this experiment, you will see that oxygen is essential for combustion. Please note that you are going to be working with open flames in this experiment. **BE CAREFUL!!**

Procedure:

1. Put the candle on a table or countertop and light it.
2. Put the glass upside down over the candle so it covers the candle completely.
3. Watch the candle for about a minute or so. Note what happens.
4. Add the vinegar to the bowl.
5. Place the candle in the bowl. The candle holder needs to be heavy enough so the candle rests on the bottom of the bowl. It should not float in the vinegar. Now light the candle. In the end, your setup should look like this:

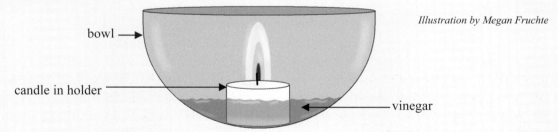

Illustration by Megan Fruchte

bowl →

candle in holder ——

— vinegar

Notice how the vinegar surrounds the candle but the candle is taller than the height of the vinegar. Also notice that the sides of the bowl are taller than the candle and its flame.

6. SLOWLY sprinkle the tablespoon of baking soda into the vinegar. Make sure the baking soda lands in the vinegar, not in the candle. You will see bubbles in the vinegar. Add the baking soda slowly so that the bubbles do not rise high enough to spill over into the candle. Distribute the baking soda all the way around the candle so that the bubbles surround it.
7. Watch the candle. What happens?
8. Wait until the bubbling stops, and then use a match to try to relight the candle. Don't move the candle. Try to relight it right where it is. What happens?
9. Clean everything up.

What did you see in the experiment? If everything went well in steps 1-3, you should have watched the flame on the candle slowly dim until it went out altogether. Why did that happen? The flame of a candle comes from the combustion of the wax that makes up the candle. Combustion requires oxygen. When you put the glass over the candle, the oxygen in the air surrounding the candle could not be replenished. Thus, when all the oxygen was used up, combustion could no longer occur, and the flame went out.

The second part of the experiment demonstrates the same fact, but in a much more interesting way. You see, when baking soda and vinegar mix, a chemical reaction occurs. This chemical reaction produces carbon dioxide gas. That's what the bubbling was all about. The bubbles you saw were the result of carbon dioxide gas forming in the chemical reaction between baking soda and vinegar.

Well, as the baking soda and vinegar produced carbon dioxide gas, the gas began to fill up the surrounding area. In other words, the carbon dioxide gas began filling up the bowl. To make room for itself, the carbon dioxide pushed away the air that was in the bowl. Eventually, then, there was no more air surrounding the candle – only carbon dioxide. As you will learn in physical science, air is a mixture of gases. One of the gases in that mixture is oxygen. Since the air was pushed out of the way by the carbon dioxide, the oxygen was pushed away along with it. Once most of the oxygen was pushed away from the candle, the flame went out, because combustion requires oxygen.

Now, what happened when you tried to relight the candle? Well, you struck a match, and it began to burn. However, as you moved the match towards the candle, it suddenly extinguished. Why did that happen? Remember that the carbon dioxide produced by the chemical reaction was still there, surrounding the candle. It stays there until the breezes that blow in your home eventually mix air back into the bowl. Now, as long as the match was exposed to the oxygen in air, it burned. As you lowered the match into the bowl, however, the match eventually was surrounded by only carbon dioxide. At that point, there was no longer any oxygen near the match, so combustion could not occur. Once again, at that point, the flame went out.

Hopefully, then, the experiment demonstrated to you that combustion requires oxygen. This is an important point.

Combustion requires oxygen.

Now let me ask you a question: Why do you need to breathe? Nearly everyone can answer that question. You need to breathe in order to get oxygen. Okay, let me ask you another question: Why do you need oxygen? The answer to that question should be a little more obvious now. Your cells need oxygen in order to burn your food for energy. Without oxygen, combustion cannot occur. Combustion is what your body uses to convert the food you eat into energy your body can use. In order for that conversion to occur, you must have oxygen. Without oxygen, you die. After all, you can be completely full of food, but if you have no oxygen with which to burn your food, you can never get energy from it. Without energy, all the systems that keep you alive simply stop.

As a side note, many fire extinguishers use carbon dioxide to put out fires. Such extinguishers are best used on fires that involve flammable liquids (such as gasoline) or electrical equipment. They work by simply pushing the air away from the fuel of the fire, surrounding it with carbon dioxide instead. This removes the oxygen necessary for combustion, which puts out the fire. If you have ever seen such a fire extinguisher work, it sprays what looks like a white mist at the fire. However, that's not really what happens. Carbon dioxide is a colorless gas, but as it leaves the fire extinguisher, it gets very cold. You will learn *why* this happens when you take physical science. Water vapor in the air condenses around this cold gas, forming droplets of liquid water (and ice) that make it look like a white mist is shooting out of the fire extinguisher.

Okay, so you now know that combustion requires two things. First, it requires something to burn. In the case of a candle, the wax is what burns. In your cells, food is what burns. The second thing that combustion needs is oxygen. We know that combustion produces energy. After all, the flame of a candle gives off both heat and light. Those are both forms of energy. In your cells, combustion produces the energy you need to live. Does combustion produce anything else besides energy? Yes, it does. Perform the following experiment to find out the other products of combustion.

EXPERIMENT 12.2
The Products of Combustion

Supplies:

♦ A mirror (A hand-held mirror is best, but any mirror will do.)
♦ A paper towel
♦ Red (sometimes called purple) cabbage (You only need a few leaves.)
♦ Distilled water (You can get it at any large supermarket. You need about ½ gallon.)
♦ Two drinking straws
♦ A saucepan
♦ A stove
♦ Three small glasses (like juice glasses)
♦ A ¼-cup measuring cup and a 1-cup measuring cup
♦ A 2-liter plastic bottle (the kind soda comes in)
♦ A balloon (6-inch or 8-inch round balloons work best.)
♦ A small spoon (like a ¼ measuring teaspoon)
♦ Vinegar
♦ Baking soda
♦ Eye protection such as goggles or safety glasses

Introduction: Combustion usually produces energy and two substances. This experiment will help you learn what those substances are.

Procedure:

1. Rinse the saucepan out twice with distilled water.
2. Place a few leaves of red cabbage in the pan.
3. Rinse out the measuring cups twice with distilled water.
4. Use the 1-cup measuring cup to add 2 cups of distilled water to the saucepan.
5. Put the saucepan on the stove and heat it until the water boils.
6. While you are waiting for the water to boil, perform the first experiment, which is described below.

The first experiment:

7. Use the paper towel to clean and dry the mirror.
8. Hold the mirror close to but not touching your mouth.
9. Breathe on the mirror three or four times.
10. Examine the mirror. Note what happened.

The second experiment:

11. Once the water begins to boil, turn off the stove and remove the pan from the heat. Allow the pan and water to cool.
12. Look at the color of the liquid in the pan. It should be purplish or bluish. If it is red or pink, you need to do steps 1-6 over. Be sure to rinse out the pan thoroughly with distilled water, because a red or pink liquid at this stage of the experiment indicates you have a contaminant in the pan.
13. While the pan and water are cooling, fill the 2-liter bottle about one-eighth full of vinegar.
14. Get a balloon ready.
15. Use the small spoon to add baking soda to the vinegar in the bottle. Add two or three spoons worth.
16. As soon as you've added the baking soda, quickly cover the opening of the bottle with the mouth of the balloon. Make the seal between the balloon and bottle as airtight as possible, so that the balloon begins to fill up with the carbon dioxide being produced. You do not need to fill the balloon very full at all. As long as the balloon is at least partially inflated, you have all the carbon dioxide you need.
17. Let the balloon and bottle sit for three minutes. As long as the seal between the balloon and bottle is airtight, you will not lose the carbon dioxide inside the balloon.
18. Rinse the three small glasses out twice with distilled water.
19. Use the ¼-cup measuring cup to scoop out ¼ cup of the solution in the saucepan. Try to avoid getting cabbage leaves in the cup, but it will not hurt the experiment if you do. **BE CAREFUL. THE SOLUTION WILL BE HOT!!!**
20. Pour that solution into one of the small glasses.
21. Repeat steps 19 and 20 twice more so that all three glasses have ¼ cup of cabbage water in them.
22. Remove the balloon from the 2-liter bottle. Pinch the neck of the balloon so you do not lose much carbon dioxide.
23. Place one end of the straw in the cabbage water solution in one of the three glasses. Next, use the balloon to blow carbon dioxide through the other end of the straw and into the cabbage water. Do this slowly, so that the solution does not splatter you! Don't worry about getting *all* the carbon dioxide into the straw. You will lose *a lot* in the process. The main thing is to make sure that at least *some* of the carbon dioxide goes through the straw and into the cabbage water. You will know this is happening because you will see bubbles coming out the end of the straw.
24. After you are done, note the color as compared to the cabbage water in either one of the remaining glasses.
25. Get another straw and place one end in the cabbage water that is in one of the two remaining glasses.
26. Blow through the other end with your mouth so that your breath goes down the straw and bubbles up through the cabbage water. Do this several times.
27. Compare the color of the cabbage water to the color you saw in step 23 as well as the color of the cabbage water in the remaining glass.
28. Clean everything up.

What did you see in the experiments? Well, let's start with the first one. When you breathed on the mirror, it fogged up, didn't it? What made that fog? Water vapor made it. When you breathe out, one of the things you are exhaling is water vapor. Where did that water vapor come from? Most of it came from the combustion reactions that are burning up your food. That's one of the products of combustion: water vapor. When you go outside on a cold day, you can "see your breath." In a way, that's true. On a cold day, the water vapor you exhale immediately becomes liquid water as soon as it leaves the warm confines of your mouth. The "fog" you see coming out of your mouth is composed of little droplets of exhaled water. There are other gases you are exhaling, but you cannot see them. However, you do see one gas that is being exhaled: water. Most of that water comes from the combustion reactions that burn your food.

You now know two of the things produced by combustion: energy and water. There is one more thing, and it is illustrated by the second experiment. What happened in that experiment? Well, you should have seen that the cabbage water in all glasses initially had a blue/purple color. When you used the balloon to bubble carbon dioxide through the cabbage water in the first glass, it turned a pink/red color. The same thing should have happened when you blew your own breath through the cabbage water in the second glass. The cabbage water should have turned pink/red. Especially when you compared the color of the cabbage water in the first two glasses to the cabbage water in the third glass, the color change should have been rather striking.

What does this mean? Red cabbage contains a chemical that changes color based on other chemicals to which it is exposed. You will learn more about this in chemistry, but the chemical in red cabbage is called an "indicator," because it indicates the presence of other chemicals known as acids and bases. Well, when carbon dioxide is bubbled through water, a chemical reaction occurs that makes an acid (carbonic acid). In the presence of acid, the chemical in red cabbage turns pink/red. So, when you bubbled carbon dioxide through the cabbage water, the carbon dioxide reacted with the water to make an acid. That acid caused the chemical from the red cabbage to turn pink/red.

Well, what happened when you blew your own breath through the cabbage water? It turned the same pink/red color. What does that tell you? It tells you that your breath also contains carbon dioxide. Where does the carbon dioxide come from? You guessed it: It comes from the combustion reactions that burn your food! So now you know the three products of most combustion reactions:

Combustion produces energy, carbon dioxide, and water.

To sum all this up, you burn your food in order to give your body energy. You inhale oxygen because combustion requires oxygen. Without that oxygen, you could not burn your food and therefore could not get the energy you need to live. You exhale carbon dioxide and water because carbon dioxide and water are both produced by combustion.

ON YOUR OWN

12.3 Some science books tell you that the sun "burns" its fuel, producing the light that comes to earth. Based on the fact that astronauts must wear space suits that provide oxygen when they are in space, what can you say about such a statement?

12.4 Many experienced growers emphatically believe that plants grow better when their caretakers talk to them. Assuming that plants can't really hear us when we talk, what have you learned in this section that might explain such a phenomenon?

12.5 Describe an experiment that would provide evidence for the explanation you provided in question 12.4.

What Actually Gets Burned for Energy?

Now that you know a few details about the combustion process itself, I want to discuss *exactly* what your body burns for energy. After all, we eat *a lot* of things for food (meat, vegetables, fruits, breads, dairy products, sweets, etc.). Does your body just take it all in and burn it? No! In fact, your body is rather picky about what it burns. There are only three things your body can burn effectively: **carbohydrates** (kar boh hi' drayts), **fats**, and **proteins**. Your body even has a preference. It would rather burn carbohydrates. If it can't burn carbohydrates, it will resort to burning fats. If it can't get either of those, it will burn proteins.

Collectively, carbohydrates, fats, and proteins are called the **macronutrients** (mak' roh new' tree uhnts), because we must eat a lot of them every day. I want to discuss each of the macronutrients individually, and since the body prefers to burn carbohydrates, I want to discuss them first. There are many different forms of carbohydrates. Simple carbohydrates are called **monosaccharides** (mon' oh sak' uh rydz). Sometimes, they are also called **simple sugars**. Glucose, the chemical that plants produce for food, is an example of a monosaccharide. The monosaccharide called "fructose" (frewk' tohs) is the sugar that gives fruits their sweet taste. There are other carbohydrates, however. Two monosaccharides can link together to become a **disaccharide**. Perhaps the best know disaccharide is table sugar, which is formed when glucose links up with fructose. The scientific name for table sugar is **sucrose** (soo' krohs). Finally, if many monosaccharides link together, they form a **polysaccharide**. The polysaccharide with which you are most familiar is starch, which is the main component of a potato. It is made from many glucose molecules linked together. Figure 12.3 illustrates the different kinds of carbohydrates.

FIGURE 12.3
Carbohydrates

Illustrations by Megan Fruchte

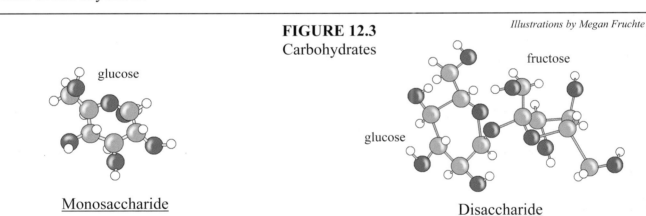

Monosaccharide

These are the simplest carbohydrates. Glucose is pictured as an example.

Disaccharide

When two monosaccharides link up, they form a disaccharide. The one pictured here is sucrose.

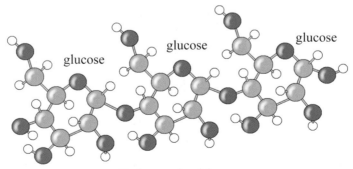

Polysaccharide

When several monosaccharides link up, they form a polysaccharide, such as starch. There is not enough room to picture a real starch molecule, as it has many glucose molecules linked together.

As I mentioned before, your body tends to burn carbohydrates first. In fact, the cells in your brain will *only* burn carbohydrates for energy. They cannot burn fats or proteins. As a result, when your body starts to run low on carbohydrates, it will burn fat and proteins in other parts of the body and save the carbohydrates for use by the brain. Interestingly enough, however, when it comes to carbohydrates, the cells in your body can only burn monosaccharides. Thus, in order for the body to use disaccharides and polysaccharides, it must first break them down into monosaccharides.

The next macronutrient I want to discuss is fat. There are many, many different types of fats in the food we eat, but they can all be put into one of two classifications: **saturated fats** or **unsaturated fats**. Generally speaking, saturated fats are solid at room temperature, while unsaturated fats tend to be liquid at room temperature. Fried foods are cooked in hot fat. If the fat is solid at room temperature (such as butter or lard), it is most likely made of saturated fats. If it is liquid at room temperature (such as vegetable oil), it is most likely made of unsaturated fats.

Although many weight-conscious Americans think of fat as a bad thing, it is absolutely essential for a healthy body. As you learned in the previous module, your skin has a fat layer that is used to insulate the body. Without that insulation, you could not keep your body at the proper internal temperature. Many organs have a layer of fat for cushion and insulation. Also, much of the fat in your body serves as a great storehouse of energy in case you are unable to eat for an extended amount of time. Finally, there are certain vitamins (A, D, E, and K) that can *only* be stored in the body's fat reserves. Thus, fat is a necessary part of life.

Your body can actually produce most of the fats it needs from excess carbohydrates and proteins. In other words, if you eat more carbohydrates than your body needs, it can convert those carbohydrates into fat as a way of storing them for future use. There are also two types of fat your body needs but cannot produce itself. They are called **essential fats** and are typically found in vegetable oils. A good diet must contain plenty of those fats.

Of course, even though fat is a necessary part of life, too much fat can be bad for you. A host of health problems (diabetes, heart disease, even some forms of cancer) can be traced back to too much fat in the body. Thus, like most things in life, you need to be moderate in your fat intake. Except for certain people with specific conditions, everyone needs to eat fat. In fact, many "low fat" foods neglect the essential fats you must eat, and some nutritionists call essential fats the most neglected nutrient in the United States. Eating too much fat (or eating so many carbohydrates that your body makes too much fat), however, can be bad for you as well.

Proteins are the third macronutrient. Your body burns these molecules only if you have too many of them, because they are essential to many other chemical processes that occur in your body. Like polysaccharides, proteins are formed when smaller chemicals, called **amino** (uh me' no) **acids**, link together in long chains. Nearly every chemical reaction that occurs in the body is affected by proteins. Even the reactions that burn food for energy are controlled by proteins. Thus, next to DNA, proteins are probably the most important chemicals for life.

In fact, the information stored in DNA is used to tell the cells in your body how to make proteins. How does it do that? You will learn the details when you take biology. For right now, however, just realize that each cell in your body contains amino acids. The cell reads the information contained in DNA and, based on that information, starts linking its stored amino acids together in long chains to make proteins.

To make the proteins necessary for life, then, the cells in your body use their DNA and their accumulated amino acids. The DNA is in the nucleus of the cell, but where do the amino acids come from? Well, your cells can actually manufacture 11 of the 20 amino acids they need. However, there are nine amino acids, called **essential amino acids**, which your cells cannot manufacture. In order to get these amino acids, you must eat proteins that contain them. The best sources of these essential amino acids are meat, milk, fish, or eggs. That's because animal proteins contain all of the essential amino acids.

Have you ever talked to a true vegetarian (someone who not only refrains from eating meat, but does not eat *any* animal products)? Such individuals often refer to themselves as "vegans." They will tell you they must eat a wide variety of plant products so as to get enough protein in their diet. Actually, that's not quite true. All living organisms contain proteins, because proteins govern virtually all the chemical reactions of life! Thus, there are plenty of proteins in plants. The problem is that plant proteins rarely contain all nine essential amino acids that our bodies cannot produce. Thus, true vegetarians must eat a wide variety of plant products in order to get *the right kind of proteins* in their diet. They can eat all the protein they want, but unless the proteins they eat contain the nine essential amino acids, it does little good. In order to get all nine essential amino acids, true vegetarians must eat a wide range of plants and seeds.

The main reason you need to eat protein, then, is not as a source of energy. Instead, the proteins you eat are a source of the amino acids your body cannot produce itself. Without a steady supply of amino acids, your body would not be able to manufacture the proteins it needs to manufacture, and the consequences can be terrible. Children who do not get the nine essential amino acids, for example, typically suffer severe brain damage, resulting in mental retardation.

When you eat proteins, then, your body does not keep them intact. It breaks the proteins down into their individual amino acids. Those amino acids are then sent to the cells throughout your body so that your cells can use them to manufacture the proteins the cells need. Under normal circumstances, that's how your body uses the amino acids in the proteins you eat. If you eat too many proteins, your body ends up having more amino acids than it needs. If that happens, the excess amino acids are converted into carbohydrates and fats. If your body suddenly runs low on both carbohydrates and fats, however, it can burn the amino acids directly for energy.

Athletes can very often have situations in which they burn amino acids for energy. Typically, an athlete stresses his or her body by demanding a large amount of energy in a short time period. Under those circumstances, the athlete's muscles may need energy faster than the body can supply monosaccharides and fats to those muscles. As a result, the muscles will begin to burn the amino acids that are there in the muscle cells. Because of this, athletes often eat high-protein diets, because they burn more proteins than the average person. However, it is never a good idea to eat too much of anything, including protein. If your body doesn't need the amino acids, and if it doesn't burn them for energy, proteins are converted to fat, and once again, being overweight has been connected to several health problems. Thus, the idea that you can "bulk up" by eating a lot of proteins isn't really true. You might "bulk up," but unless you need those proteins, the bulk will be fat, not muscle.

In the end, then, the food we eat provides us with three macronutrients, which in turn provide energy for our daily lives. These macronutrients are used in different ways, depending on the situation. Figure 12.4 illustrates this.

FIGURE 12.4
Food and the Macronutrients

Food illustration from www.clipart.com
Molecule illustrations by Megan Fruchte
Energy starburst by Speartoons

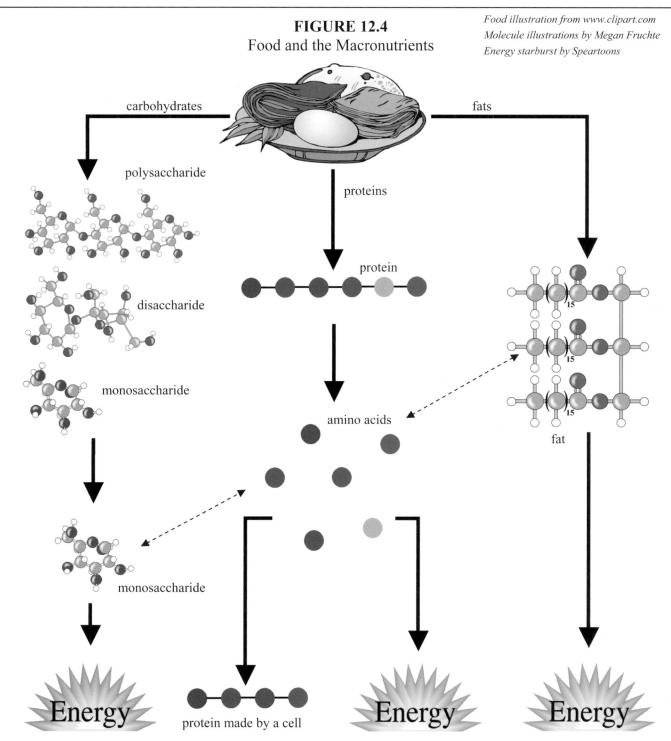

The carbohydrates in your food get broken down into monosaccharides and then burned for energy. Excess carbohydrates can be converted to fats in order to store the energy for later use. They can also be used to make amino acids if the cells need them.

The proteins in your food get broken down into amino acids. If your body has too many amino acids, they will be converted into fat or carbohydrates. Otherwise, they will be used by the cells to make the specific proteins the cells need to make. Under conditions of low carbohydrates and fats, they can be burned for energy.

The fats in your food can be used for insulation, cushioning, vitamin storage, or energy storage. Some fats are essential for other body functions as well. They can be burned for energy or used to make carbohydrates or amino acids. Fats are usually burned when your body runs low on carbohydrates.

Before I finish with this section, I want to make two points. First, please realize that food contains other things your body needs besides just macronutrients. In fact, food contains a huge number of chemicals (like vitamins and minerals) that we call **micronutrients**. These micronutrients are important for healthy living as well. However, micronutrients are not used for energy, and energy is what I am stressing in this module. Thus, I am ignoring the micronutrients, even though they are important. In case you are wondering, we call carbohydrates, fats, and proteins "macronutrients" because you need a lot of them every day. The prefix "macro" means "large," so "macronutrients" refers to the substances we need in large quantities. The micronutrients are important, but we need them in much smaller quantities. That's why we call them micronutrients.

Second, I want to remind you of something I told you before. The chemical process by which we convert the macronutrients into energy is combustion, but it is unlike any combustion you have ever seen. Thus, do not think there are little fires going on in your body! True, we do burn the macronutrients for food, but the burning process is carefully controlled and regulated by a whole host of chemical machinery. Although the end result is identical to combustion, the process is completely different from anything you have ever seen. I will discuss that process to some degree at the end of this module. You will learn even more about it when you take biology. For now, just realize that it is a very interesting form of combustion and is unlike any burning process with which you are familiar!

ON YOUR OWN

12.6 A man puts himself on a no-fat diet. As a result, his macronutrient intake is almost all carbohydrates and protein. An analysis of his body's fat content was done before he started the diet and several weeks afterward. To his shock, the level of fat in his system actually *increased* after being on the diet. Where did the excess fat come from?

12.7 A woman goes on a high-protein diet. As a result, she begins eating a lot more protein than she used to eat. If her cells were short of amino acids before she went on the diet, what will happen to the extra protein she is now eating?

Energy Use in the Body

The macronutrients in food provide us with the energy we need to survive, but for what purposes do our bodies use this energy? Well, remember that in the previous module, I told you about involuntary muscles. They control the workings of our organs. Even though we don't need to think about their actions, they are continually contracting and relaxing in order to keep our bodies working. Thus, our bodies need energy to keep the involuntary muscles going. Of course, your skeletal muscles also require a lot of energy. Whenever you move any part of your body, specific sets of skeletal muscles contract or relax. When muscles contract, they use energy. Whether you are moving your legs to walk or moving your eyes to look at something new, your skeletal muscles are using energy to make that motion occur.

There is another thing we never think about but nevertheless requires an enormous amount of energy. Perform the following experiment to see what it is.

EXPERIMENT 12.3
Body Temperature

Supply:

♦ An oral thermometer (The kind you use to take a person's temperature. Do not use one of those strips you put on your forehead. Use the kind of thermometer you stick in your mouth.)

Introduction: You know that your body stays warm. In this experiment, you will see that your internal body temperature does not change significantly, regardless of the conditions.

Procedure:

1. Take your temperature while you are sitting down. Follow the normal instructions for your thermometer. It usually involves keeping the thermometer under your tongue for a few minutes.
2. Once you have taken your temperature, put the thermometer back in your mouth, and go somewhere cold. It could be outside; it could be right next to an air conditioner; you could even open the refrigerator door and stand as close as you can to the refrigerator. **Now be reasonable about this.** The idea is to get uncomfortably cool, but NOT dangerously cold! If the temperature outside is sub-zero, don't go outside. Instead, go to a room in your house that is uncomfortably cold. If you have a garage attached to your house, for example, it will probably be cool if it is really cold outside. Like I said, be *uncomfortably* cold, *not dangerously* cold!
3. Allow the thermometer to stay in your mouth for another three minutes while you are uncomfortably cold.
4. Go to a warm place and look at the temperature reading again. Compare it to your previous temperature reading.
5. Put the thermometer down and put on a sweater. Then, do 5 minutes of vigorous exercise. You could do jumping jacks, run in place, or something like that. The point is to get uncomfortably warm as a result of the exercise.
6. Take your temperature right after you are finished with the exercise. **Be careful!** You are probably not used to taking your temperature when you are out of breath.
7. Compare your temperature now to the other two measurements.
8. Wash the thermometer and put it away.

What did you see in the experiment? Well, as long as you took your temperature correctly each time, you should have seen very little difference between the three temperature measurements. The measurement you made in step 3 might be a bit lower than the first one you made, and the measurement in step 5 might be a bit higher than the first one you made. In general, however, even though you felt uncomfortably cold in step 3, your *internal temperature* did not change much. Once again, even though you felt uncomfortably warm in step 5, your *internal temperature* did not change much.

Why is that? Well, human beings are **endothermic** (en' doh thur' mik). This means we use energy for the purpose of keeping our internal temperature relatively constant. In other words, we are "warm-blooded." Not all organisms are like that. In fact, the *vast majority* of organisms are **ectothermic** (ek' toh thur' mik), which means they do not have a means by which they can control their internal temperature. In other words, they are "cold-blooded." If it is cold outside, ectothermic creatures get cold on the inside. If it is warm outside, ectothermic creatures are warm on the inside.

Now don't get me wrong. The internal temperature of an ectothermic creature is not necessarily *the same* as the outside temperature. However, the outside temperature strongly affects the internal temperature of an ectothermic creature, but it does not strongly affect the internal temperature of an endothermic creature.

Ectothermic organisms require less food than endothermic organisms, because it takes *a lot* of energy to maintain a constant internal temperature. Since ectothermic organisms do not maintain a constant internal temperature, they expend less energy in order to stay alive and thus require less food. Endothermic creatures, however, generally are faster at responding to the outside world than are ectothermic creatures. That's because high temperatures increase the rate at which most chemical reactions occur. Thus, a higher internal temperature means faster chemical reactions inside the body. Since an organism is ultimately controlled by chemical reactions, the faster the reactions go, the faster the organism can react.

A good way to see the effect of outside temperature on the movement of ectothermic creatures is to go to a zoo and watch how the reptiles move on a cool day. Typically, they move very slowly if at all. On cool days, most reptiles try to find a sunny rock upon which to lie, because a sunny rock is the warmest place to be. On warm days, however, the reptiles move around a lot more. That's because reptiles are ectothermic. On warm days, their internal temperature is higher, so the chemical reactions in their bodies run faster. This allows them to move more quickly.

You think of your body's energy use when you exercise or do other strenuous activities. However, that's just one way your body uses energy. It also uses energy to control all the involuntary muscles that keep your organs and internal processes functioning properly. In addition, it uses energy to keep your internal temperature at a constant 98 to 99 degrees Fahrenheit. Also, your cells constantly use energy to perform hundreds of tasks, such as making proteins from amino acids as I discussed earlier. Thus, even when you are sitting quietly, your body is still using energy. In the next section, I will explain how we measure the energy your body uses.

ON YOUR OWN

12.8 You are comparing two animals – one that is ectothermic and one that is endothermic. The first eats three times its own weight in food each day, while the other eats less than its own weight in food every day. Most likely, which one is the endothermic animal?

Calories and Food

I am sure you've heard about calories. If you have ever tried to lose weight, or if you have ever talked to someone who is trying to lose weight, you have probably heard about "counting calories." In this section, I want to tell you what a calorie is and what it measures. A **calorie** is actually a unit used to measure energy. You will learn a lot about that unit when you take chemistry, so I don't want to go into the definition of calorie and all that right now. I just want you to realize that a calorie represents a certain amount of energy.

Well, since food provides you with macronutrients, and since macronutrients provide you with energy, one way to measure the macronutrient content in food is to measure the number of calories of energy the food gives you. The more energy in the macronutrients that the food contains, the more calories it provides. Now it turns out that there is a bit of confusion over the definition of a calorie. Chemists have a very specific definition, but nutritionists have another. The result of this confusion is that a food calorie is actually worth 1,000 chemistry calories. Thus, please realize that in this discussion, I will always talk in terms of food calories. When you take chemistry later, you will see the difference in the definitions and the confusion it causes.

Since the calorie is a unit of energy, it can be used to measure both the amount and the type of macronutrients in food, as well as the amount of energy your body needs in order to live. I want to talk about both those concepts in this section. First, let's talk about the energy your body uses. The total rate at which your body uses energy is called your **metabolic** (met uh bah' lik) **rate**. Your metabolic rate has two factors. The first is the rate at which your body burns energy just to perform the minimum functions that will keep you alive. This is called your **basal** (bay' sul) **metabolic rate**, which is often abbreviated as **BMR**.

Basal metabolic rate – The minimum amount of energy required by the body in a day

Now please realize that the BMR is not a measure of the total energy used by the body in a day. Notice the definition. The BMR is a measure of the *minimum* energy required by the body every day. In other words, suppose you did *nothing* all day but sit quietly in a room. Your body would still need a lot of energy to maintain your body temperature, keep your cells working, keep you breathing, etc., etc. Your BMR is the amount of energy necessary to perform those minimum functions in a day. It varies based on many things including your height, weight, general athleticism, age, genetics, and gender. Two very similar people can have significantly different BMRs.

The second factor in determining your metabolic rate is the amount of activity you engage in every day. For example, suppose you sleep in on Saturday. Once you get up, you sit quietly and read for a while, and then you spend the rest of the day in quiet conversation with your family. On a day like that, you don't burn up much more energy than what is determined by your BMR. Suppose on Sunday, however, you get up early and go to church. After church, you get together with your friends and play some games, roughhouse a little, and generally cause a ruckus. All that activity requires a lot of energy above and beyond what is demanded by your BMR. On Sunday, then, you would use a lot more energy than you did on Saturday. Thus, your *total* metabolic rate (the sum of your BMR and the energy needed to sustain your activity level) would be much higher on Sunday than on Saturday, even though your BMR would be the same for both days.

Scientists have done a lot of work studying human metabolic rates. Although metabolic rates vary from person to person, there are some general trends that tend to be fairly accurate on average. Table 12.1 lists the average energy requirements for people of different ages and genders. Now please understand that this table lists the *total* energy needed each day, which includes both your BMR and the energy needed to sustain your activities.

TABLE 12.1
Average Daily Energy Needs Based on Gender and Age

Gender	7-10 yrs	11-14 yrs	15-18 yrs	19-24 yrs	25-50 yrs	51 yrs +
Male	2,000 Cal	2,500 Cal	3,000 Cal	2,900 Cal	2,900 Cal	2,300 Cal
Female	2,000 Cal	2,100 Cal	2,200 Cal	2,200 Cal	2,200 Cal	1,900 Cal

Notice that, in general, girls and women need less energy than boys and men. That's because, in general, a woman's BMR is lower than a man's BMR. Also notice that as children grow, they need more energy. Once they reach maturity (after age 18), however, their energy needs level off and even decrease with age.

Now remember, calories can be used to measure your macronutrient intake as well. For a healthy life, the number of calories worth of macronutrients you eat every day should roughly equal the number of calories you use every day. Thus, the average 13-year-old male should eat roughly 2,500 calories worth of macronutrients, because that's what Table 12.1 says the average 13-year-old male uses each day. If you eat significantly fewer calories than you use, you will lose weight. If you eat significantly more calories than you use, you will gain weight.

As you might imagine, however, a healthy life requires more than just eating the proper number of calories every day. Because the three macronutrients are used differently in the body, you need a certain distribution of macronutrients in your food. Many nutritionists in the United States think that about 70 percent of the calories you eat each day should come from carbohydrates. Roughly 20 percent should come from fat, and the balance should come from protein. According to these nutritionists, this mixture of macronutrients is ideal for the human body. However, there is no real consensus among nutritionists. That's because there are still too many things we do not understand about the human body! Now please remember that I am not addressing the micronutrients at all. There are many micronutrients you need in order to stay healthy as well. Thus, all the information I am giving you in this module relates only to the macronutrients.

ON YOUR OWN

12.9 Consider two roommates in college who are both essentially the same height, weight, and age. They eat essentially the same amount of the same cafeteria food each day. They also participate in essentially the same activities each day. However, one roommate loses weight during his first college year, while the other gains weight. How is that possible?

Metabolic Rates Throughout Creation

The metabolic rates of organisms vary greatly throughout creation. In general, ectothermic organisms have lower metabolic rates than endothermic organisms, because ectothermic organisms need not expend energy in order to keep their internal temperature constant. As I mentioned previously, however, that lower metabolic rate comes at a cost. Ectothermic creatures are, in general, slower to react to the outside world than are endothermic creatures. They are also limited in where they can live, since the outside temperature affects their internal systems significantly.

However, metabolic rates vary dramatically even among similar creatures. For example, consider the organisms in kingdom Protista. In Module #10, I told you about different protozoa in this kingdom. All protozoa are composed of a single cell, and the majority of them have means by which they can move from place to place. Thus, you would think they are all rather similar. Nevertheless, their energy needs vary dramatically from organism to organism. For example, the paramecium pictured in Figure 10.4 has significantly higher energy needs than does the euglena pictured right above it.

Perhaps the best example of how metabolic rates vary among similar creatures is to consider the metabolic rates of different mammals. Remember, I already told you that mammals are animals that share similar characteristics. They all have skin that produces hair, they are all endothermic, they give birth to live young, and they nurse their young with milk they produce. Thus, mammals are similar in many ways. Nevertheless, their energy needs vary considerably.

Now before I tell you how mammal metabolic rates differ from one another, I have to introduce a concept called **normalization**. When we normalize two things, we do something to make them more comparable. For example, consider an elephant and a mouse. Which do you think eats more? The elephant, of course. Why? Because the elephant is so much *bigger* than the mouse. However, if I truly want to compare an elephant to a mouse when it comes to how much food they eat, it makes more sense to divide the amount that each animal eats by its own weight. That way, I am comparing the animals' food intake on a *per-pound* basis. When you do it that way, it turns out that the mouse eats considerably more than the elephant. Depending on the situation, elephants eat 300 to 500 pounds of food each day, but that is only about 3 to 5 percent of an elephant's body weight. A mouse eats only about one-tenth to one-fifth of an ounce of food each day, but that is 10 to 15 percent of its body weight. Thus, ounce for ounce, a mouse eats more than an elephant. If you normalize all mammals' metabolic rates by their weight (so you get their metabolic rate *per pound*), you see an interesting trend.

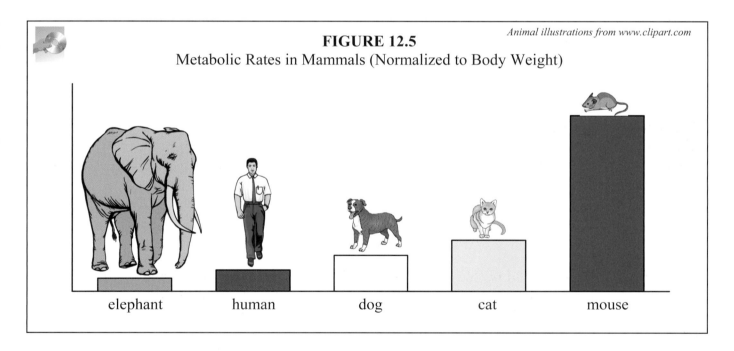

FIGURE 12.5

Metabolic Rates in Mammals (Normalized to Body Weight)

Animal illustrations from www.clipart.com

elephant   human   dog   cat   mouse

Do you see a trend in the figure? The smaller the mammal, the larger the normalized metabolic rate. That's a general trend among mammals throughout creation. Why? Well, it turns out that small creatures have a larger percentage of their total body exposed to the outside air. Thus, a mouse has a larger portion of its body in contact with the air than does an elephant. As a result, a mouse loses more heat than an elephant. Since they are both mammals, however, they both must keep their internal temperature constant. Because the mouse loses more heat than the elephant, it must expend more energy to keep its internal body temperature constant. As a result, the normalized metabolic rate of a mouse is much higher than that of an elephant.

How Combustion Works in Living Organisms

Throughout this module, I have been telling you that you burn your food for energy. I have also been telling you that the combustion occurring in your body is significantly different from the combustion that occurs in a candle, fireplace, or furnace. In this last section of the module, I want to give you a simplistic view of how combustion occurs in most living organisms.

First, you have to realize that your food is burned in your cells. Remember, the cell is the basic unit of life. Thus, all your energy needs originate in your cells. Your muscle cells need energy in order to contract your muscles, your living skin cells need energy to reproduce and react to outside stimuli, etc. Thus, the combustion that takes place in a living organism takes place inside the organism's cell or cells.

In order to simplify things somewhat, I am going to concentrate only on how monosaccharides are burned for energy. Amino acids and fats can be burned for energy, but those processes are even more complicated. As you will see in a moment, the combustion of monosaccharides is hard enough to understand, so I don't want to get any more complex than that. I will also choose the specific monosaccharide called glucose, which happens to be the favorite food of most cells in your body.

The combustion of a monosaccharide takes place in three basic steps that are carefully controlled so as to not occur too quickly. This is already significantly different from the combustion of wax in a candle or wood in a fireplace. Those kinds of combustion happen very quickly, producing lots of energy in a short amount of time. If the combustion of monosaccharides were to happen that quickly, the cell would instantly burn up! Thus, in order to make the release of energy gentle, cells break up the combustion process into three carefully controlled steps.

The first step is called **glycolysis** (gly kol' uh sis). In this step, the monosaccharide glucose is broken into two parts. This results in a small release of energy and a little bit of hydrogen. The two parts of the glucose and the hydrogen are then sent to a particular organelle in the cell called the **mitochondrion** (my' toh kon' dree uhn).

In the mitochondrion, the process continues with the second step, called the **Krebs cycle**. In this step, the two pieces of glucose react with oxygen to produce carbon dioxide and hydrogen. That results in a small release of energy as well. This is also where the carbon dioxide you exhale comes from. Once that carbon dioxide is produced, it leaves the cell, is picked up by your blood, and is sent to your lungs, where you breathe it out. (As a side note, there is a process that occurs at the end of glycolysis to prepare the two pieces of glucose for the Krebs cycle. More detailed biology books consider this a separate step, so you will often hear that there are four steps to the process of combustion in living organisms. I don't want to get that detailed, but don't worry, you'll learn all about it when you take biology!)

The hydrogen from glycolysis as well as the hydrogen released in the Krebs cycle go through the third step, called the **electron transport system**. In the electron transport system, oxygen combines with all that hydrogen to make water. This results in a large release of energy. Since the majority of energy release occurs in this step, and since this step takes place in the mitochondrion of the cell, the mitochondrion is often referred to as the "powerhouse" of the cell.

Now don't worry if some of this is a little confusing. It is difficult stuff. However, it is important enough to look at again, so I want you to study the following figure.

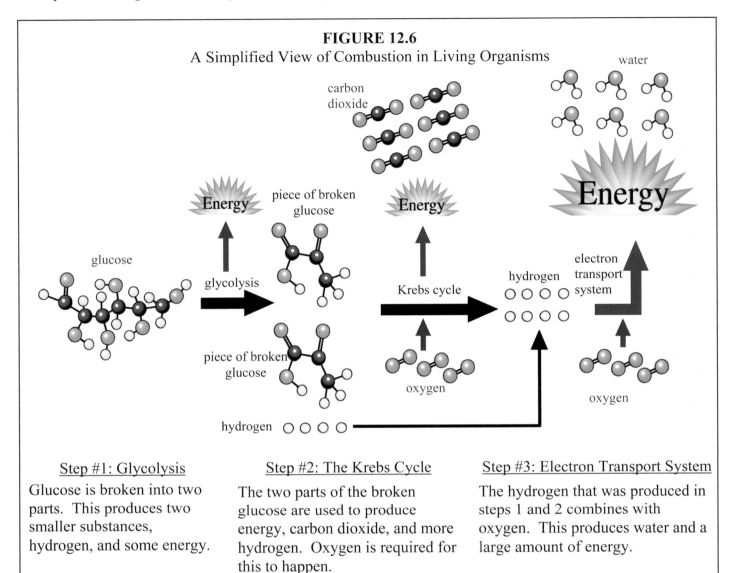

FIGURE 12.6
A Simplified View of Combustion in Living Organisms

Step #1: Glycolysis

Glucose is broken into two parts. This produces two smaller substances, hydrogen, and some energy.

Step #2: The Krebs Cycle

The two parts of the broken glucose are used to produce energy, carbon dioxide, and more hydrogen. Oxygen is required for this to happen.

Step #3: Electron Transport System

The hydrogen that was produced in steps 1 and 2 combines with oxygen. This produces water and a large amount of energy.

Although this figure is complicated, try to break it down. The blue words and arrows represent things that are *added* to the process. Thus, a glucose molecule and oxygen molecules are the only things added to the process. The red arrows represent things that are made. Thus, carbon dioxide, water, and energy are made. Overall, then, this process takes glucose and oxygen and converts it into water and carbon dioxide. As the steps occur, energy is released. Now let's walk through the steps while you look at the figure.

In the first step, a glucose molecule is broken into two parts. This results in two pieces of a glucose molecule, some hydrogen, and some energy. The hydrogen produced in this step makes its way to step 3. The two pieces of the broken glucose molecule proceed to step 2. In step 2, the two broken pieces of the glucose are further broken down into carbon dioxide, more hydrogen, and some energy. This process requires oxygen. Finally, in step 3, oxygen combines with the hydrogen made in both previous steps. This produces water and significantly more energy than the other two steps combined.

So, although the overall process Figure 12.6 describes is combustion, the complex nature of the process makes it a very *gentle* combustion. In other words, this is a way of burning monosaccharides without releasing so much energy that the cell is destroyed in the process. It allows the organism to produce energy the same way a fire produces energy, but in a much more controlled and gentle way. Now don't worry if this is all a little above your head. I wanted to expose you to it for two reasons. First, when you take biology, you will need to learn this process in more depth. If you are exposed to it now, it will be *easier* to learn the next time. Second, I wanted to give you an idea of how *complicated* this all is.

Think about it for a moment. The process by which living organisms get energy from food is amazingly complicated. Even the "simple" organisms in kingdom Protista burn food this way! Make no mistake about it: I have not even scratched the surface of this incredible process. The details of each step of the process are amazingly hard to understand. They are so hard to understand, in fact, that many scientists *never* learn the process in detail. There are so many chemical processes governing each step that it takes a detailed knowledge of chemistry and biology to truly understand it.

Are you beginning to see why I told you that there is *no such thing* as a simple life form? One of the most basic processes occurring in all living organisms is exceedingly complex. It has to be. Otherwise, living organisms could not get the energy they need in a way that keeps them from burning up! Nevertheless, if you deny the existence of a divine Creator, you are *forced* to believe that this exceedingly complex system, a system that very few scientists truly understand, has all come about *by chance*! How can anyone possibly believe such a thing? The design inherent in this system alone cries out in witness of a Supreme Designer!

Like I said before, don't be concerned if this is all a little over your head. The main things I want you to pull from this section are as follows:

1. **The process of combustion in living organisms is amazingly complex. It has to be in order to provide energy in a gentle but efficient fashion.**

2. **The combustion process occurs within the cell and is done in three steps to allow for a gentle release of energy.**

3. **Two of the three steps in the combustion process occur in an organelle called the mitochondrion.**

4. **Since the majority of the combustion process takes place within the mitochondrion, biologists refer to the mitochondrion as the powerhouse of the cell.**

Even though these are the only things you have to understand about how organisms get energy, the more you understand this discussion, the easier it will be for you when you revisit this topic with much more detail in biology.

ON YOUR OWN

12.10 If there were no oxygen available to an organism, could it produce any energy? **HINT**: Consider each step in Figure 12.6 individually.

ANSWERS TO THE "ON YOUR OWN" PROBLEMS

12.1 a. Grass is a <u>producer</u>, because it is a plant and therefore makes its own food.

b. A horse is a <u>consumer</u>, because it eats other organisms (grass, for example).

c. A tree is a plant and is therefore a <u>producer</u>.

d. Yeast is part of kingdom Fungi, so it is a <u>decomposer</u>.

e. A sparrow eats other organisms, so it is a <u>consumer</u>.

f. A shark eats other organisms, so it is a <u>consumer</u>.

12.2 The creature is an <u>omnivore</u>. However, <u>if you removed bugs from the list, the creature would be an herbivore</u>.

12.3 <u>The statement is wrong</u>. The sun does not burn anything, because there is no oxygen in space, where the sun is. The sun uses thermonuclear fusion, a process you will learn about in physical science, to produce the light that reaches earth.

12.4 We know that plants use carbon dioxide, water, and energy from the sun to make their own food (glucose). Well, when we talk to plants, our exhaled breath tends to hit the plants. <u>The carbon dioxide from our exhaled breath increases the amount of food that the plant can make, and that makes the plant more healthy</u>.

12.5 There is an easy way to test the hypothesis in question 12.4. <u>Make three groups of plants. The first you take care of without talking to them at all. Take care of the other two groups in exactly the same way, with these two exceptions: To the second, play a tape of someone talking, but do not actually talk to them. To the third, do not talk to them, but breathe on them for the same amount of time you play the tape to the second group</u>. If the hypothesis is right, the first and second group will look nearly the same, but the third group will be healthier.

12.6 Remember, excess carbohydrates and proteins can be converted to fat. <u>The fat came from excess carbohydrates and/or proteins</u>.

12.7 <u>The extra proteins she is now eating will be broken down into their amino acids, and the amino acids will be sent to the cells so they can make their own proteins</u>.

12.8 <u>Most likely, the first animal is endothermic</u>. Endothermic animals need a lot more energy in order to keep their internal temperature fairly constant.

12.9 <u>The roommates have different BMRs</u>. Although they basically do the same activities, that just tells you the energy they need *above their BMRs* is the same. The total energy they use also includes their BMRs, however. If those are different, the number of calories they burn each day will be quite different.

12.10 <u>Yes, the organism could still produce *some* energy</u>. Look at Figure 12.6. Oxygen is not needed until step 2 (the Krebs cycle). Thus, step 1 does not need oxygen. Since there is *some* energy produced in step 1, the organism could produce that energy, even if oxygen isn't present. For most organisms, however, the energy produced in step 1 is not enough. Thus, the organism would still most likely die.

STUDY GUIDE FOR MODULE #12

1. Define the following terms:

a. Producers
b. Consumers
c. Herbivore
d. Carnivore
e. Omnivore
f. Basal metabolic rate

2. From where does the energy in most living organisms ultimately originate?

3. Label each of the following as a consumer, producer, or decomposer:

a. mushroom   b. evergreen bush   c. worm   d. algae

4. What is the name of the chemical process that converts food into energy?

5. What does combustion require?

6. What does combustion produce?

7. What are the three macronutrients?

8. What is the main thing that macronutrients provide?

9. Do we need to eat more macronutrients or micronutrients?

10. Which is larger: a monosaccharide, a disaccharide, or a polysaccharide?

11. Is glucose a monosaccharide, a disaccharide, or a polysaccharide?

12. What are the two basic kinds of fat? How can you distinguish them?

13. What are proteins made of?

14. In what order does the body prefer to burn the macronutrients?

15. When proteins are eaten, they are broken down into their amino acids. If your cells are short on amino acids, what happens to the amino acids that come from the proteins you eat? What happens if your cells have plenty of amino acids?

16. Why is it important to eat either animal protein or a wide variety of plant protein?

17. Which type of animal has a higher BMR: an endothermic animal or an ectothermic animal?

18. Which type of animal cannot be active on a very cold day: an endothermic animal or an ectothermic animal?

19. What do calories measure?

20. Consider two men. While they sleep, they burn about the same number of calories. However, the first man needs significantly more calories than the second in order to keep his weight constant. Which man is less active during the day?

21. Jean and Wanda are essentially the same height, weight, and age. If Jean needs to eat more calories than Wanda in order to keep her weight constant, can you immediately conclude that Jean is more active than Wanda?

22. When normalized by weight, which has a higher BMR: a horse or a mouse?

23. Where does the combustion of food take place?

24. Why is the mitochondrion called the "powerhouse" of the cell?

25. How many basic steps are involved in the combustion of food? Why do cells do it in such a complex way?

MODULE #13: The Human Digestive System

Introduction

In the previous module, I spent a lot of time discussing the energy we get from food. I discussed the process of combustion, the three macronutrients, and how combustion occurs in living organisms. However, I really didn't tell you *how* the food you eat gets broken down into the three macronutrients you end up burning for energy. That's what I want to cover in this module. Along the way, you will also learn a little bit about the micronutrients. In the previous module, I glossed over them. In this module, I want you to learn a little more about them.

The Process of Digestion

When you eat your food, your body must break it down in order to get the nutrients contained within. That process is called **digestion**.

Digestion – The process by which an organism breaks down its food into small units that can be absorbed by the body

The process of digestion starts with **ingestion**. When you eat food (or drink liquid), you are ingesting it. The process of digestion starts at that point. To get an idea of what the process of digestion entails, perform the following experiment.

EXPERIMENT 13.1
Seeing a Part of the Digestive Process

Supplies:

- A saltine cracker
- A tablespoon
- Iodine (This is available at most drugstores. You used it in Experiment 9.2.)
- Two small glasses
- Eye protection such as goggles or safety glasses

Introduction: The process of digestion involves two different kinds of action. In this experiment, you will see both of them.

Procedure:

1. Break the saltine cracker in half. Crumble half of the cracker and allow the crumbs to fall into one of the two glasses.
2. Add two tablespoons of water to the cracker crumbs and swirl the glass to mix the cracker crumbs with the water.
3. Chew the other half of the cracker really well. **DO NOT SWALLOW**, but spend a lot more time chewing the cracker than you normally would before swallowing.
4. Spit the stuff in your mouth out into the other glass. Okay, it's gross, but science is gross sometimes. Deal with it!
5. Add two tablespoons of water to the chewed-up mess and swirl the glass.
6. Note any differences you see in the two glasses.

7. Add equal amounts of iodine to both glasses. It doesn't need to be a lot – just a drop or two.
8. Swirl each glass.
9. Note any difference you see in the two glasses.
10. Clean everything up.

What did you see in the experiment? Well, the first thing you should have noticed was that the cracker you chewed was reduced to much smaller pieces than the cracker you crumbled. In fact, that's the first part of digestion: breaking up food into small pieces. We call that **physical digestion**, because it doesn't change the chemical nature of the food. It simply breaks it into tiny pieces.

The second thing you should have noticed is how differently the two "cracker solutions" acted in response to iodine. The unchewed half of the cracker should have produced a dark blue color. Depending on how well you chewed the other half of the cracker, it should have produced a much lighter blue. If you chewed the cracker really well, you might have seen no blue color at all in that glass.

What do the results of this experiment show us? When iodine mixes with starch, it produces a deep blue color. The deep blue color you saw when you put the iodine in the glass with the unchewed cracker told you that saltine crackers have starch in them. Remember what starch is. It is a polysaccharide. When you added the iodine to the water that contained the chewed cracker, the much lighter blue or absence of blue told you there was less starch in the chewed cracker.

Where did the starch go? Well, the **saliva** (some people call it "spit") your mouth produces contains chemicals that break down starch. Remember, our bodies must break polysaccharides (like starch) down into monosaccharides before they can be used. The saliva in your mouth starts this process by breaking down starch into disaccharides. This is the second component of digestion: **chemical digestion**. It is not enough to just break down the food into tiny pieces. Your body must also change the chemical nature of the food in order for it to be absorbed into your blood.

Digestion, then, has two different components. Some parts of the process of digestion are aimed simply at breaking down the food you eat into smaller pieces. Other parts of the digestive process are designed to take those pieces of food and chemically alter them so your body can absorb them. The unusable parts of the food then get removed from your body.

ON YOUR OWN

13.1 In which part of the digestive process are your teeth a major participant: physical digestion or chemical digestion?

The Human Digestive System

As you might imagine, the human digestive system is large and complex.   I want to discuss many of the parts of the digestive system in greater detail, but to start, I want to give you a general overview. I will start with a figure. Please note that some structures in the figure, including the **nasal cavity**, **larynx** (layr' inks), and **trachea** (tray' key uh), are in the figure but are not a part of the digestive system. They are labeled in blue and are there just for reference.

FIGURE 13.1
An Overview of the Human Digestive System

Illustration © Lippincott, Williams, and Wilkins

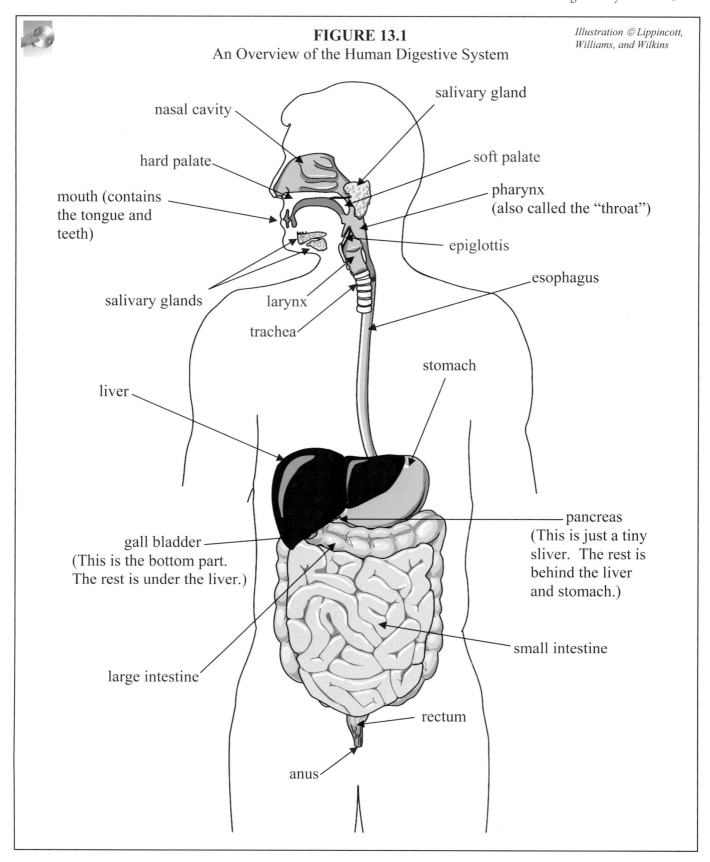

Now that you've seen the figure, here's an overview of how it all works. First, food enters your body through your **mouth**. It is cut, crushed, and ground into little pieces by your **teeth**. It is also moistened by saliva, which is produced in your **salivary glands**. Your **tongue** moves food around your mouth. It also provides most of the taste sensation you get when you eat. The food is then passed from your mouth to your **pharynx** (fare' inks), where it is then passed into your **esophagus** (ee sof' uh gus). Notice in the figure that the pharynx has a "fork" in it. One path of the fork leads to the esophagus, and the other path leads to the larynx. When I talk about the details of the mouth, pharynx, and esophagus in the next section, I will talk about the incredible process that occurs to make sure food goes down the fork that leads to the esophagus, while air goes down the path that leads to the larynx.

Once in the esophagus, the food goes to your **stomach**, where it is churned and mixed with juices that are made by the stomach lining. Your stomach temporarily stores the food that has been thoroughly mixed with juices and then gradually releases it into your **small intestine** (in test' in). There, the food is broken down chemically, and most of the micronutrients and macronutrients are absorbed by the bloodstream through the lining of your small intestine. The nutrient-filled blood then passes through your **liver**, which picks up many of those nutrients. That's not the only thing your liver does, however. It is one of the largest organs in your body. It also cleans the blood of toxins and wastes, and it produces a substance called **bile**, which is necessary for the digestion of fats. In addition, it makes certain proteins your body needs from the amino acids absorbed in digestion, and it stores many of the micronutrients and macronutrients it picks up from the blood.

The bile from your liver is concentrated (to make it stronger) and stored in your **gall bladder**. Your gall bladder then injects this concentrated bile into your small intestine, where it aids in the digestion of fats coming from the stomach. Your **pancreas** (pan' kree us) produces other digestive juices, which are also injected into the small intestine to aid in the digestion process.

Once the food is digested in your small intestine, what was not absorbed is sent to your **large intestine**. By the time food reaches this point, most of the micronutrients and macronutrients have been removed. Most of the food that makes it into your large intestine, then, is waste and must ultimately be ejected from your body. Water is absorbed from the waste, turning the waste into **feces** (fee' sees), which are then sent to your **rectum** and expelled from your body through your **anus**.

Please note that there are parts of the digestive system that never actually come in contact with the food being digested. For example, while the gallbladder is a part of the digestive system, food never passes through it. The sum of the parts of the digestive system through which food actually passes is often called the **alimentary canal** or the **digestive tract**. However, that doesn't represent the *entire* digestive system, as there are some digestive organs through which food never travels.

That's the basic outline of what happens in order for your body to digest the food you eat. How long does all this take? Well, it depends on the individual as well as the kind and amount of food that is ingested. However, on average, it takes less than 1 minute for food to get chewed in the mouth and transferred to the esophagus. It is in the esophagus for only a couple of seconds and ends up in the stomach. Typically, a meal remains in the stomach for 2 to 4 hours before being sent to the small intestine. The small intestine usually takes 1 to 4 hours to digest the food, and then the food gets sent to the large intestine. The amount of time the waste products stay in the large intestine varies *greatly* depending on the person involved and the type of food that was eaten. The shortest time the waste products spend in the large intestine is about 10 hours, but some waste products take *several days* to make it through the large intestine. In the end, then, the food you eat can spend as little as 13 hours in your body or as long as several days. Remember, however, that most of the micronutrients and macronutrients have been absorbed by the time the food leaves the small intestine. Thus, your body gets most of the nutrients from the food you eat within 3 to 8 hours.

ON YOUR OWN

13.2 Using Figure 13.1 as a guide, name the organs that are a part of the digestive system but not a part of the alimentary canal.

13.3 Blood vessels run through all the organs of the body, supplying nutrients and oxygen to the organs' cells as well as picking up the cells' waste products. One organ of the digestive tract, however, has many blood vessels that *pick up nutrients* in order to distribute them throughout the body. Which organ has a lot of these blood vessels?

The Mouth, Pharynx, and Esophagus

Now that you have seen the digestive system as a whole, I want to break it down into several parts so you can learn more details about how it works. I want to start with a more detailed view of the mouth, pharynx, and esophagus.

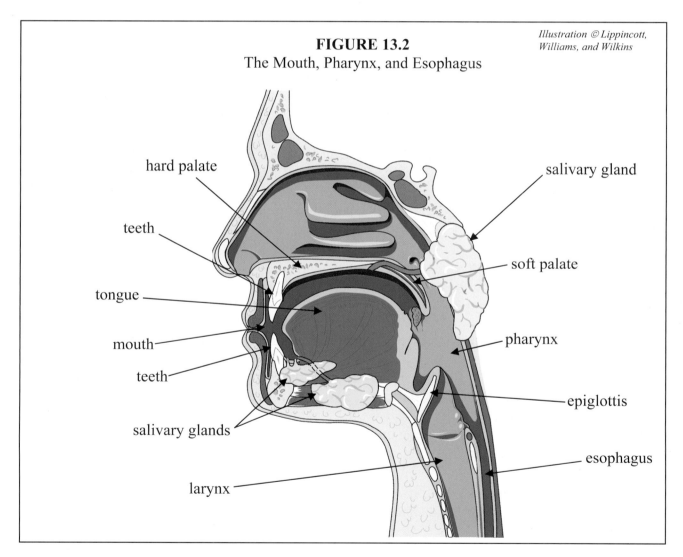

FIGURE 13.2
The Mouth, Pharynx, and Esophagus

Illustration © Lippincott, Williams, and Wilkins

hard palate

teeth

tongue

mouth

teeth

salivary glands

larynx

salivary gland

soft palate

pharynx

epiglottis

esophagus

As you learned in Experiment 13.1, the digestion of food starts in the mouth. The teeth cut, grind, and crush the food into small bits for physical digestion. It is important to know your mouth has specific kinds of teeth, each designed for a different purpose. Figure 13.3 illustrates this fact.

FIGURE 13.3

3-D illustration © Tara Urbach
Agency: Shutterstock

The Basic Kinds of Teeth in an Adult's Mouth

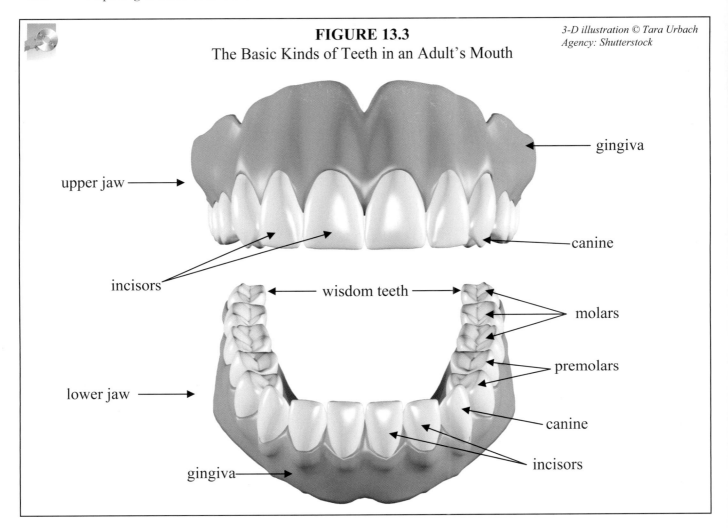

Your teeth are made of hard, bonelike material and are surrounded by soft, shock-absorbent **gingiva** (jin' juh vuh), which most people call "gums." The **incisor** (in size' or) teeth are sharp and used to cut food. The **canine** (kay' nine) teeth are used to tear food, while the **premolars** and **molars** are used to crush and grind food. The third molars (the ones in the very back) on each side of upper and lower jaw are called **wisdom teeth**, because they generally appear much later than your other teeth, usually between the ages of 16 and 24. For some people, they grow in wrongly and must be extracted so they don't negatively affect the other teeth.

Once the food is cut, torn, and ground into small bits, those bits are mixed with saliva that comes from the salivary glands. Saliva contains a digestive juice that begins to chemically digest the food. As you learned in the experiment, one thing saliva helps to do is break down starch. It also lubricates the mouth, making chewing and swallowing easier, and it aids in physical digestion by moistening the food.

How do your salivary glands put saliva into your mouth? Well, as shown in Figure 13.2, there are ducts that run from the salivary glands into your mouth cavity, both underneath and above your tongue. The saliva that has been produced in the salivary glands travels through those ducts and into your mouth. It is important to realize that the salivary glands do not put saliva into your mouth all the time. Instead, they do it mostly when you are eating. How do the salivary glands "know" you are eating? Well, the senses of taste and smell (you will learn about these senses later in the course) and the feeling of hunger send signals to the salivary glands, telling them to "turn on." That causes the salivary glands to release saliva into your mouth. You can actually see how this works the next time you are really hungry. Before you start eating, smell your food by inhaling deeply through your nose. What happens? Your mouth begins to fill with saliva, even though you haven't put food in it!

A Russian physiologist (a scientist who studies how the systems of the body work) by the name of Ivan Pavlov demonstrated that a body can be **conditioned** to produce saliva using senses other than taste and smell. In 1889, he did experiments in which he rang a bell every time he fed a dog. Eventually, the dog's salivary glands would produce saliva whenever the bell was rung, regardless of whether or not there was food for the dog to eat. Pavlov called this a **conditioned response**, because the dog had become conditioned to expect food whenever the bell was rung. As a result, its body responded by salivating. If you ever hear the term "Pavlovian response," it refers to a response that is brought on by conditioning.

Once the teeth have cut, crushed, and ground the food, and once the food has been mixed with saliva, your tongue moves the food around so it forms a soft lump called a **bolus** (bowl' us). The tongue then rises to move the bolus to the back of the mouth, and the **soft palate** rises, sealing off the nasal cavity. The bolus then moves out of the mouth and into the pharynx.

Have you ever been drinking something (like milk) and started laughing? Did the liquid you were drinking squirt out of your nose? If so, that's because your laughing caused the soft palate to move, breaking its seal on the nasal cavity. As a result, the milk traveled into your nasal cavity and out your nose.

Once the bolus gets to your pharynx, the muscles there contract, squeezing the food so it moves into your esophagus. Now although that *sounds* pretty simple, it is actually a rather complex procedure involving the coordination of several muscles at once. You see, the pharynx is a passageway for two things: air and food. When you inhale, air passes through the pharynx to the larynx and then into the lungs. However, when you eat, the bolus moves through the pharynx and then into the esophagus. How does your body know that air goes down one "pipe" and food goes down the other?

Well, the act of swallowing causes the muscles at the base of the larynx to contract, causing the larynx to rise up. If you put your hand on your larynx as you swallow, you can feel it rise. This motion causes a small flap of cartilage called the **epiglottis** (ep uh glah' tis – see Figure 13.2) to cover the larynx. When the food passes into the pharynx, then, there is only one opening: the esophagus. Thus, the bolus goes into the esophagus, because the larynx is covered by the epiglottis. When you inhale, the muscles at the base of the larynx relax. This causes the epiglottis to uncover the larynx, and air can pass down through the larynx, into the trachea, and on into the lungs.

Although this is an incredibly well-coordinated system, every once in a while something goes wrong, and the trachea can be uncovered when food gets into the pharynx. When this happens, part or all of the bolus can fall into the larynx instead of the esophagus. To prevent problems caused by such failures, God designed a backup mechanism for this system. The linings of the larynx and trachea are *very* sensitive. If anything other than air passes down the larynx, a signal is sent to the brain and muscles cause you to cough. This pushes any food in the larynx back into the pharynx. If you have ever eaten and then started coughing uncontrollably, someone probably asked you if your food "went down the wrong pipe." In fact, that's most likely what happened! Food probably got into your larynx, and your body's cough mechanism kicked in, making you expel the food.

Once the bolus is in the esophagus, the muscles of the esophagus contract above the bolus and relax below it. As you might expect, this is a well-coordinated system in which several groups of muscles contract and relax in perfect time relative to one another, making a "wave" of muscle activity that pushes the bolus down the esophagus and into the stomach. Since all of this muscle activity goes on without conscious thought, the muscles involved are smooth muscles.

ON YOUR OWN

13.4 Although many animals have teeth, they don't necessarily have all the teeth that humans have. For example, there are certain animals that do not have canine teeth. Would you expect carnivores, herbivores, or omnivores to lack canine teeth?

13.5 Why do you cough when you inhale smoke?

The Stomach and the Small Intestine

Once the bolus of food gets to the end of the esophagus, it is deposited in the stomach. The rest of the digestive process takes place either there or in the intestines. Figure 13.4 gives you a cutaway view of the stomach and the first part of the small intestine.

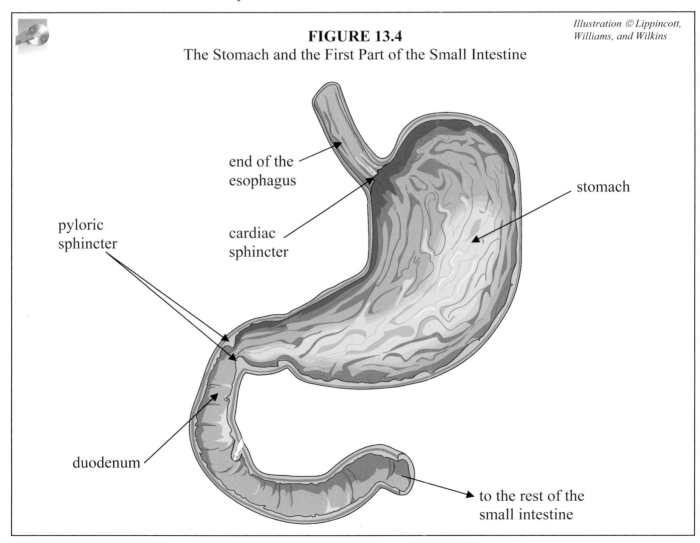

Illustration © Lippincott, Williams, and Wilkins

FIGURE 13.4
The Stomach and the First Part of the Small Intestine

end of the esophagus

stomach

pyloric sphincter

cardiac sphincter

duodenum

to the rest of the small intestine

As the bolus travels down the esophagus, the **cardiac sphincter** (sfink' ter) opens to allow it to land in the stomach. The sphincter then quickly closes to prevent backup of the bolus. Notice in the figure that the inside wall of the stomach has folds in it. They are called **rugae** (roo' gee), and they exist to allow the stomach to expand. As you fill the stomach with food, it stretches, smoothing out the rugae. When the stomach empties, it gets smaller because the tissue folds back into rugae.

In the stomach, the bolus is mixed with a liquid called **gastric juice**. Gastric juice is actually a mixture of many different chemicals, the most important of which is **hydrochloric** (hi' droh klor' ick) **acid**. This chemical is a powerful acid whose main function is to activate digestive chemicals that are in the gastric juice. It also kills pathogenic microscopic organisms (like bacteria) that might have been eaten along with the food. In addition, hydrochloric acid helps dissolve the food so that it is easier to digest. The hydrochloric acid found in the stomach is often called "stomach acid."

If you have ever eaten too much food, you might have felt your stomach acid in the form of **heartburn**. Heartburn is a burning sensation you feel in the middle or upper part of your chest. It is called heartburn because you feel a burning sensation in the general vicinity of your heart. Although it is called heartburn, it has nothing to do with the heart. Instead, it is the result of excess stomach acid leaking up and out of the stomach into the esophagus, irritating the lining of the esophagus. When you feel heartburn, you are told to take an antacid. Why? Perform the following experiment to find out.

EXPERIMENT 13.2
Stomach Acid and Antacids

Supplies:

♦ Tums® antacid tablets (Try to get white ones, or at least a tub of Tums that has some white ones in it.)
♦ Toilet bowl cleaner (It should contain hydrochloric acid, also called hydrogen chloride, as an ingredient. The best kind to get is colorless. If you cannot get colorless, get a clear kind that has a light tint of color to it. DO NOT get the kind that clings to the bowl.)
♦ Red (sometimes called purple) cabbage
♦ A small glass (like a juice glass)
♦ A teaspoon
♦ A spoon for stirring
♦ A saucepan
♦ A measuring cup
♦ Distilled water (You can get it at any large supermarket. You need about ½ gallon.)
♦ A stove for boiling water
♦ Eye protection such as goggles or safety glasses

Introduction: In this experiment, you will get a good idea of the properties of stomach acid as well as the function of antacids.

Procedure:

1. You need to make the same indicator solution you made in Experiment 12.2. Start by rinsing the saucepan, measuring cup, stirring spoon, and small glass with distilled water.
2. Place several leaves of red cabbage in the saucepan and add 2 cups of distilled water.
3. Heat the saucepan until the water boils and allow it to boil for a few minutes.

4. Turn off the heat and allow the pan and its contents to cool for a while.
5. Add one teaspoon of toilet bowl cleaner to the small glass. **BE CAREFUL WHILE HANDLING THE TOILET BOWL CLEANER.** If you get it on your hands, immediately rinse them with LOTS of water. Toilet bowl cleaner will burn your skin.
6. Once the saucepan and its contents have cooled somewhat, fill the measuring cup with the cabbage water. **BE CAREFUL - IT COULD STILL BE VERY HOT.** If you get a few cabbage leaves in the measuring cup, use the stirring spoon to remove them.
7. Pour the cup of cabbage water into the small glass. Use the spoon to stir the contents so the teaspoon of toilet bowl cleaner mixes with the cabbage water. The color of the contents should be pink or red. If not, the color of your toilet bowl cleaner is too strong and you need to try a different kind of toilet bowl cleaner.
8. Add an antacid tablet to the small glass. Try to use a white one.
9. Note what happens when the tablet hits the cabbage water/toilet bowl cleaner mixture.
10. After you have watched the tablet for a few moments, start stirring it. You want the tablet to completely disappear. This will take a little while. You can speed the process up by using the spoon to cut up and crush the tablet.
11. Note the color change that begins to occur.
12. Once the tablet is gone, note the color. If you do not see purple or blue, add another tablet and continue to stir. Your goal is to get the solution to be purple or blue.
13. Once you get to the purple or blue color, add another teaspoon of toilet bowl cleaner. What happens?
14. Clean everything up.

What did you see in the experiment? Well, if everything went well, the antacid tablet or tablets should have turned the toilet bowl cleaner/cabbage water solution from red/pink to blue/purple. The addition of more toilet bowl cleaner should have turned the color back to red/pink. Why did this happen?

If you remember from Experiment 12.2, red cabbage contains a chemical we call an "indicator," because it indicates the presence of two other types of chemicals: **acids** and **bases**. You will learn a lot more about acids and bases when you take chemistry. For right now, you can think of these two chemicals as opposites of one another. Acids have certain chemical properties that cause them to react in certain ways, and bases have different chemical properties that cause them to react in pretty much opposite ways. The key point to know right now is that acids and bases tend to cancel one another out. If you take an acid and add just the right amount of base to it, the base will cancel out the chemical properties of the acid, and the acid will cancel out the chemical properties of the base. This is called **neutralization**, because acids neutralize the properties of bases, and bases neutralize the properties of acids.

In your experiment, you started with toilet bowl cleaner. The active ingredient of toilet bowl cleaner is usually an acid. In many toilet bowl cleaners, that acid is hydrochloric acid, which is the same acid your stomach produces. In the experiment, then, the toilet bowl cleaner represented stomach acid. When the chemical in red cabbage is exposed to acids, it turns a red/pink color. When it is exposed to bases, it turns a blue/purple color.

In the experiment, then, you added the cabbage water to the toilet bowl cleaner. Since the toilet bowl cleaner had acid in it, the cabbage water turned red/pink in response to the acid. When you added the Tums tablet, however, things should have gotten interesting. The tablet should have started bubbling and fizzing, getting smaller and smaller. This is because the Tums tablet (or any traditional antacid tablet) contains a base. In the case of Tums, the base is calcium carbonate, the same chemical that makes up a stick of chalk. Another common base in antacid tablets is magnesium hydroxide. In your experiment, the base in the tablet chemically reacted with the acid in the toilet bowl cleaner. This chemical reaction allowed the base to start neutralizing the acid.

As the neutralization took place, you should have noticed the color of the solution begin to change. It got less red and more blue. Eventually, it turned either blue or purple. This indicated that the base had neutralized all the acid. That's what antacid tablets do in your stomach. They add a base to your stomach, neutralizing some of the acid in your stomach. This gets rid of extra acid, which hopefully removes the cause of heartburn. In your stomach, there is a *lot* more acid than in the experiment, however, so even several antacid tablets will not neutralize *all* the acid in your stomach. However, they will neutralize some of it, so that not as much acid can leak out into the esophagus.

In your experiment, you did one more thing. After you saw the color change to blue/purple, you then added more toilet bowl cleaner. This should have turned the solution red again. Why? Well, think about it. The reason the solution turned blue was because all the acid had been neutralized by the base. When you added more toilet bowl cleaner, however, you added more acid. That extra acid neutralized all the base in the solution and left it with extra acid. Thus, the solution had acid in it again, and the chemical from the cabbage water turned red/pink again. This will happen over and over again if you keep adding base and then acid.

Okay, then, let's go back to what happens to the bolus of food once it gets into your stomach. In addition to the hydrochloric acid we discussed, the stomach produces a few chemicals that begin chemically digesting the bolus of food. Smooth muscles in the stomach relax and contract, churning the bolus with the gastric juice until it is turned into a liquid mush called **chyme** (kyme).

Chyme passes from the stomach to the small intestine in spurts that are controlled by a ring of muscles called the **pyloric** (pie lor' ik) **sphincter**. In the small intestine, the chyme is mixed with several more digestive chemicals that come from the **gall bladder** and **pancreas**. One other interesting thing takes place at this point. The chemicals that continue the digestion process in the small intestine cannot work properly in the presence of acid. The chyme, however, is full of hydrochloric acid from the stomach. So as the food passes through the small intestine, it is mixed with bases that come from the pancreas, gall bladder, and small intestine. These bases quickly neutralize the stomach acid, allowing the digestive chemicals in the small intestine to do their job.

Most of the rest of the digestion takes place in the first part of the small intestine, which is called the **duodenum** (do uh dee' num). After that, the digested food continues through the small intestine and, along the way, the blood absorbs the nutrients from the food so they can be transported to different places in the body. This absorption process is slow and time-consuming. That's why the small intestine is so long. If you stretched an adult's small intestine into a straight tube, it would be nearly 20 feet long! Since it is long, it takes the digested food quite a while to pass through it. That way, there is plenty of time for the absorption of nutrients.

In fact, the small intestine is a great testimony to the design ingenuity of our Creator. As I mentioned, the absorption of digested food is a slow process. Thus, the digested food must spend a long time in the small intestine to get absorbed. However, that time would have to be *significantly* greater if it weren't for the clever design of the small intestine. Unlike many organs, the inside wall of the small intestine is not smooth. Instead, it is covered with millions of projections called **intestinal villi** (vil' eye), illustrated in the figure below:

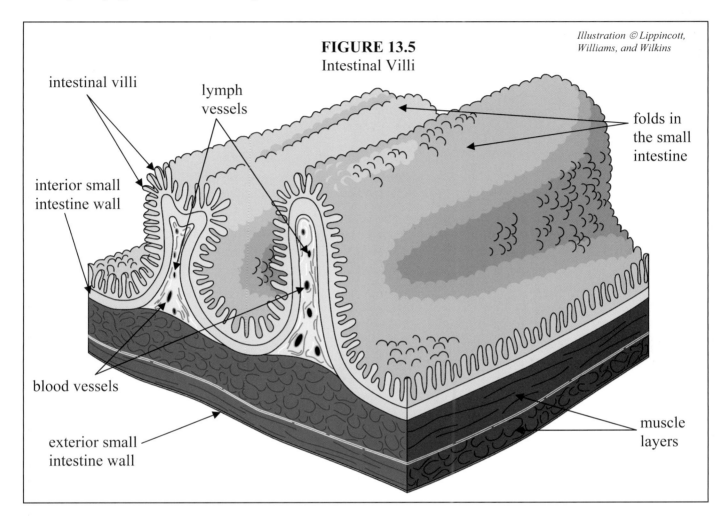

FIGURE 13.5
Intestinal Villi

Illustration © Lippincott, Williams, and Wilkins

intestinal villi

lymph vessels

folds in the small intestine

interior small intestine wall

blood vessels

exterior small intestine wall

muscle layers

These villi increase the amount of intestinal wall that comes in contact with the food, speeding up the absorption process. If the inside wall of the small intestine were smooth rather than covered with villi, the small intestine would need to be *2¼ miles long* in order to allow enough time for the absorption of food!

Altogether, the intestinal villi make the wall of the small intestine look like it is covered with velvet. Each one looks like a tiny finger that waves around the interior of the small intestine. This mixes the chyme and allows the villi to come into contact with it. Each one of these villi is covered with a single layer of cells that specialize in absorbing nutrients. As nutrients are absorbed by these cells, they are passed to the blood vessels, which then send the nutrients throughout the body.

The small intestine, because of its amazing design, can absorb almost all the useful nutrients from the chyme by the time it has traveled the entire length of the small intestine. Thus, when the chyme passes from the small intestine into the large intestine, it is mostly composed of indigestible material that the body considers waste. The large intestine's job, then, is to treat this waste so it can be expelled from the body.

The large intestine is actually composed of three parts: the **cecum** (see' cum), the **colon** (kohl' un), and the **rectum**. The colon, which is the largest part of the large intestine, encircles the small intestine. As a result, food traveling through it first goes up toward the liver (in the **ascending colon**), across the body from right to left (in the **transverse colon**), and then down toward the rectum (in the **descending colon**). It is called the "large" intestine because its diameter is larger than the diameter of the small intestine. It is actually about ¼ the length of the small intestine, or roughly 5 feet long. A cutaway view of the end of the small intestine, along with the entire large intestine, is shown below.

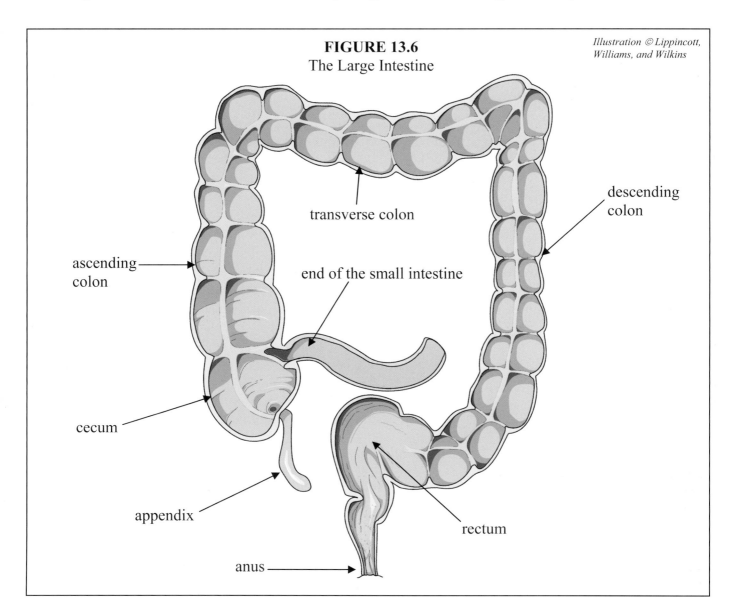

FIGURE 13.6
The Large Intestine

Illustration © Lippincott, Williams, and Wilkins

transverse colon

descending colon

ascending colon

end of the small intestine

cecum

appendix

rectum

anus

The cecum is at the beginning of the large intestine. Chyme enters the cecum from the small intestine, and smooth muscles in the cecum push chyme into the colon. The main function of the colon is to absorb water that is in the chyme. This consolidates the waste in the large intestine and provides water for your body. Other things happen in the colon, however.

For example, there are many bacteria that live in your large intestine. These bacteria feed on the chyme as it travels through the large intestine. Since they digest some of the chyme for their own life processes, the chyme is further reduced, consolidating the waste even further. Not only that, but some of the byproducts of the bacteria feeding on the chyme are useful to your body. One particular vitamin, vitamin K, is produced by bacteria that live in both the large intestine and the small intestine. You will learn a little more about vitamin K in the final section of this module. Other chemicals that are a part of the B-vitamin family are also the byproducts of bacteria feeding off the chyme in the large intestine.

These chemicals (vitamin K and certain B vitamins) are absorbed in the large intestine and distributed throughout the body. Without the bacteria living in your large intestine, your body would not have enough of these chemicals, and your health would suffer. The bacteria living in your large intestine are yet another example of the Creator's forethought in His design. Just like the bacteria on your skin, the bacteria in your intestines help keep you healthy. In exchange, your body provides food for them. As you learned in Module #11, this is called "symbiosis." The total number of bacteria in your intestines is *over 100 trillion (100,000,000,000,000)!* Together, they weigh about 3 pounds!

Although your body *benefits* from having bacteria in your large intestine, those same bacteria would be pathogenic in other parts of your body. In healthy individuals, then, the bacteria are confined to your intestine. However, if the walls of your intestine are torn, those bacteria that were being helpful can invade other parts of your body and cause serious damage!

The last part of the large intestine is the rectum. Any waste products that make it to this point are called **feces** (fee' sees) and must be expelled from the body. The feces are pushed into the rectum via the contraction and relaxation of smooth muscles in the colon. Once the feces have entered the rectum, they pass out of the body through the anus. About one-third of a person's feces are composed of bacteria that were originally in the large intestine. Most (not all) of the bacteria are dead by the time they leave the body.

Although I have not gone over every part of the digestive system yet, the parts I have covered (mouth, pharynx, esophagus, stomach, small intestine, and large intestine) are collectively called the digestive tract or alimentary canal. Any internal structure through which food actually passes is part of the digestive tract. Although other organs are a part of the digestive system, they are not a part of the digestive tract, because food does not pass through them.

ON YOUR OWN

13.6 Where in the digestive tract does most of the absorption of nutrients occur?

13.7 Although there are bacteria in the large intestine, there are essentially none in your stomach. Why?

No, It's Not Useless!

Notice there is a structure in Figure 13.6 that I have not discussed – the **appendix**. This little, worm-shaped tube branches off the large intestine at the cecum. Only apes and humans have an appendix, so it is obviously a very specialized organ. For reasons we do not understand, the appendix can become infected and filled with pus. This results in pain and cramps near the right hip bone. This pain is usually accompanied by fever, nausea, and vomiting. If the appendix is not removed at that point, it will eventually burst, and the infection can spread throughout the stomach area. If untreated, this can actually lead to death. As a result, infected appendices are usually removed with a surgical procedure called an "appendectomy" (ap un dek' tuh me).

For most of the history of the study of human anatomy, many scientists believed that the appendix actually served no purpose whatsoever in the human body. In fact, there are some uninformed scientists who still believe that to this day! They call the appendix a **vestigial** (ves tih' gee uhl) **organ**, which means it is a useless remnant of the process of evolution. In other words, these scientists think that at one time, the appendix did serve some useful purpose. According to these scientists, apes probably needed their appendix at one time. However, as they changed through the process of evolution, some other organ (or process) took over the appendix's job. However, the appendix continued to form in apes, but there was no longer anything for it to do. Since these same scientists think that humans evolved from apes, they think that humans inherited the ape's useless appendix.

In the late 1800s, evolutionists listed 180 organs in the human body that were supposedly vestigial. This list included such things as the thyroid gland, the thymus gland, the pineal gland, and the tonsils. All 180 organs were thought to be vestigial because science had supposedly demonstrated that they served no useful purpose. We now know that all those organs (including the appendix) are useful, important, and sometimes *vital* organs. You see, the human body is so complex and well designed that there are still aspects of it which are a *complete mystery* to modern science. As a result, it is not surprising that scientists have had a tough time discovering what the appendix's job is. Nevertheless, science recently figured it out, at least partially.

So what does the appendix do? Well, at least one function of the appendix is to "reboot" the intestines after a bad illness. What do I mean by "rebooting the intestines"? Well, do you remember the bacteria that live in your intestines? You receive many benefits from them, but in some illnesses (like cholera), they can be virtually wiped out. However, the slim appendix with its "dead end" provides a safe harbor for some of the bacteria, allowing them to ride out the illness. Once the illness has passed, the bacteria leave the appendix and repopulate the intestines so the person will once again receive their benefits. Of course, this is just *one* function the appendix serves. There are probably other functions yet to be identified.

As a brief aside, I must point out that evolution *predicts* the presence of vestigial organs in people and animals. This can be seen by the fact that over the years, evolutionists have *assumed* many organs, including the appendix, to be vestigial. Creationists, however, have always stated that the appendix is not useless. As a result, they predicted that a function would eventually be found for it. As is the case with many other issues in science, the creationist prediction has been demonstrated to be the accurate one, while the evolutionist prediction has been demonstrated to be false. It is truly unfortunate that a hypothesis like evolution, which has so many failures when compared to the data, is still a popular view among scientists.

The Liver, Pancreas, and Gall Bladder

Although not a part of the digestive *tract*, the liver, pancreas, and gall bladder are nevertheless important to the human digestive system. They are illustrated in Figure 13.7. On the left-hand side of the figure, you see them along with the stomach, liver, and transverse colon. However, in that arrangement, the gall bladder and pancreas are almost completely hidden. Thus, the right side of the figure shows you the view with the stomach, liver, and transverse colon removed.

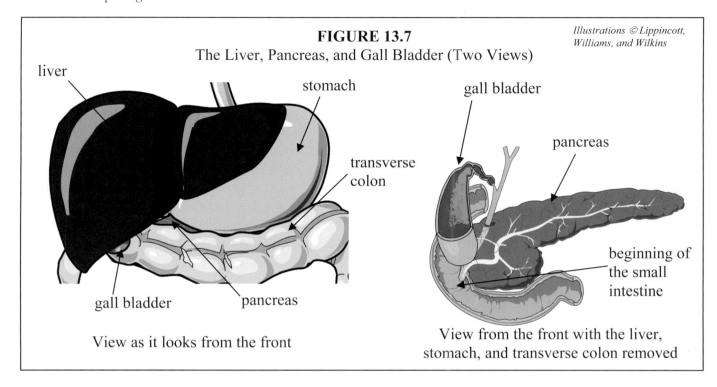

FIGURE 13.7

The Liver, Pancreas, and Gall Bladder (Two Views)

Illustrations © Lippincott, Williams, and Wilkins

View as it looks from the front

View from the front with the liver, stomach, and transverse colon removed

The liver is, by far, the most complicated organ in the digestive system. It has an enormous number of jobs, yet it is able to perform them all with incredible efficiency. Its most direct role in terms of digestion comes from the fact that it makes bile. Bile is a mixture of chemicals that prepares fats for digestion. The bile made by the liver is sent to the gall bladder. The gall bladder's job is twofold. First, its walls remove about 90 percent of the water from the bile. Chemists say this makes the bile "concentrated," which increases its strength. Then, when chyme enters the small intestine, the gall bladder contracts, shooting bile into the chyme. The bile then prepares the fats in the chyme so that other chemicals can digest them.

The liver performs many more functions than just making bile! For example, the blood vessels that pick up nutrients from the small intestine carry their blood directly to the liver. If the body is not in need of a large amount of energy, the liver takes the monosaccharides coming from the intestines and converts them into glucose, which is then converted into the polysaccharide known as **glycogen** (gly' kuh juhn). The liver then stores the glycogen until the body needs energy. When energy is needed, the liver breaks down the glycogen and sends it to where it is needed. The liver can also store fats. When energy is needed and no glycogen is readily available, the liver can chemically transform parts of the fat into glucose. In addition, if the liver receives amino acids, it can use them to make proteins. It can also convert the amino acids to glucose if glycogen is not readily available.

Not only does the liver store and transform macronutrients, but it can also produce other chemicals the body needs. The principal components of cell membranes, for example, are produced in the liver. Thus, the liver is much like a chemical plant combined with a chemical warehouse. It takes raw materials coming from the small intestine and then, based on conditions in the blood, it "decides" what to do with those chemicals. It might store them for future use, or it might use them to make something the body needs right away.

The liver is also a detoxification center. There are certain chemicals you get from your food that can be dangerous. In addition, there are chemicals you inhale from the air (pollutants, for example) that are poisonous. Either way, there are toxic chemicals that make their way into your bloodstream. The liver takes those chemicals and can recycle them for use in making bile, or it can transform them into less harmful substances so they can be excreted in the urine. For example, when amino acids are used for energy, a chemical similar to ammonia is formed. This chemical is toxic to the body, so the liver transforms it into urea, which your body can easily get rid of in your urine.

If that's not enough, there is at least one more task the liver performs. It helps to warm the blood. Remember, humans are endothermic. That means our internal temperature is held relatively constant. One of the reasons our body temperature stays constant is the function of the liver. Blood that passes through the liver is warmed so that its temperature stays the same. How does the liver warm the blood? Well, many of the chemical processes performed by the liver produce heat as a byproduct. That heat is what warms the blood as it passes through the liver.

All this should give you a good idea of why the liver is so large. It has many, many functions that are absolutely essential to the body. A typical liver is 9 inches wide, 7 inches tall, and 5 inches thick. A healthy adult liver weighs about 3 pounds. An enormous amount of blood (about 1½ quarts *each minute*) passes through the liver.

The pancreas is the only organ in the digestive system that I have not yet covered. A typical adult pancreas is roughly 5 inches long. It is widest on the right, near the beginning of the small intestine, and tapers down significantly along its length. The pancreas has two main functions. It makes several digestive juices that are squirted into the small intestine as chyme passes through the pyloric sphincter. In addition, it produces a base known as sodium bicarbonate. You know this chemical better as "baking soda." Perform the following experiment to see what sodium bicarbonate does in your body.

EXPERIMENT 13.3
The Effect of Sodium Bicarbonate on Stomach Acid

Supplies:

♦ Baking soda
♦ Toilet bowl cleaner (the kind you used in the previous experiment)
♦ Red (sometimes called purple) cabbage
♦ A small glass (like a juice glass)
♦ A teaspoon
♦ A separate spoon for stirring
♦ A saucepan
♦ A measuring cup
♦ Distilled water (You can get it at any large supermarket. You need about ½ a gallon.)
♦ A stove for boiling water
♦ Eye protection such as goggles or safety glasses

Introduction: This experiment will show you what happens when the sodium bicarbonate from your pancreas is mixed with the stomach acid in the chyme that comes from your stomach.

Procedure:

1. You need to make the same indicator solution you made in Experiment 13.2. Start by rinsing the saucepan, measuring cup, stirring spoon, and small glass with distilled water.
2. Place several leaves of red cabbage into the saucepan and add 2 cups of distilled water.
3. Heat the saucepan until the water boils and then allow it to boil for a few minutes.
4. Turn off the heat and allow the pan and its contents to cool for a while.
5. Add one teaspoon of toilet bowl cleaner to the small glass. **BE CAREFUL WHILE HANDLING THE TOILET BOWL CLEANER**. If you get it on your hands, immediately rinse them with LOTS of water. The toilet bowl cleaner will burn skin.
6. Once the saucepan and its contents have cooled somewhat, fill the measuring cup with the cabbage water. **BE CAREFUL - IT COULD STILL BE VERY HOT**. If you get a few cabbage leaves in the measuring cup, use the stirring spoon to remove them.
7. Pour the cup of cabbage water in the small glass. Use the spoon to stir the contents so that the teaspoon of toilet bowl cleaner mixes with the cabbage water. The color of the contents should be pink or red. If not, the color of your toilet bowl cleaner is too strong and you need to try a different kind of toilet bowl cleaner.
8. Use the other spoon to scoop some baking soda out of the box. **SLOWLY** add the sodium bicarbonate to the mixture in the glass. Note what happens.
9. Continue to slowly add baking soda to the mixture in the glass until the color of the mixture changes from red/pink to blue/purple.
10. Clean everything up.

What happened in the experiment? Well, when you added baking soda to the mixture, you should have seen a LOT of bubbles. In fact, if you did not add the baking soda slowly enough, the bubbles probably spilled out of the glass. When sodium bicarbonate (baking soda) reacts with acids, it neutralizes the acid. The color of the mixture in the glass changed because, just as was the case in Experiment 13.2, the cabbage water acted as an indicator. Before the acid was neutralized, the indicator was red/pink. After the acid was neutralized, the indicator turned purple/blue. One of the products of the neutralization process is carbon dioxide. That's where the bubbles came from.

Essentially the same thing happens in your small intestine when sodium bicarbonate from your pancreas mixes with chyme coming from the stomach. The chyme has hydrochloric acid in it, just as the toilet bowl cleaner does. When the sodium bicarbonate from the pancreas mixes with the chyme, a reaction occurs that neutralizes the acid and produces carbon dioxide gas.

ON YOUR OWN

13.8 Some people, because of certain problems, must have their gall bladder removed. If this happens to a person, he or she is sometimes put on a special diet. What macronutrient must be reduced in the diet?

13.9 Suppose a person's liver is converting fats and amino acids into glucose. What can you conclude about the amount of glycogen that is currently available?

The Micronutrients

In the previous module, I spent considerable time discussing the macronutrients but barely touched on the micronutrients. I want to finish this module by making up for that a bit. Although we do not need micronutrients in the quantities we need macronutrients, they are incredibly important to the human body.

Most of the micronutrients your body needs are absorbed in the small intestine. They are called **vitamins** and **minerals**. You already know what a mineral is. You learned that in Module #6. You don't yet know what a vitamin is, however.

Vitamin – A chemical substance the body needs in small amounts to stay healthy

Vitamins are effective in extremely small amounts and act mainly as regulators of the chemical processes that occur in your body. They are classified as either **fat-soluble** or **water-soluble**. A fat-soluble vitamin cannot be dissolved in water. It can only be dissolved in fat. A water-soluble vitamin cannot be dissolved in fat but can be dissolved in water.

The fat-soluble vitamins are vitamin A, vitamin D, vitamin E, and vitamin K. The water-soluble vitamins are vitamin C, and the vitamin B group (B_1, B_2, B_3, B_5, B_6, B_7, B_8, B_9, and B_{12}). The body cannot make most of these vitamins, so they must be eaten with our food. There are at least two exceptions. Although your body can also absorb it from food, vitamin D is actually manufactured in the body through the skin's exposure to sunlight. In addition, vitamin K is produced by bacteria in the large intestine.

So what do these vitamins do? Well, each vitamin has its own unique support role in the human body. Vitamin A, for example, is a component of the process that allows your eyes to detect light. Without sufficient vitamin A, you would not see properly. It also maintains the cells that protect your body, such as skin cells. Because it is essential for these processes, too litle vitamin A can lead to vision problems and difficulties fighting off infections. In fact, a common symptom of too little vitamin A in your diet is triangular gray spots (called "Bitot's spots") in your eyes.

Vitamin D allows your body to more effectively absorb certain minerals, especially calcium, from your food. It also promotes good bone health. Even if you have plenty of calcium in your diet, your bones (and other parts of your body) will not get the full benefit without the proper levels of vitamin D in your system. It is also a major component of your ability to fight off infections and tumor growth.

Vitamin E is an "antioxidant," which means it helps protect certain important chemicals in your body from being destroyed through the chemical process called "oxidation." In addition, vitamin E helps to repair your DNA. Why would your DNA need repair? Well, when your cells reproduce (to replace cells that have died, for example), your DNA gets copied. Every now and then, mistakes can be made in the copying process. Those mistakes (often called "mutations") can cause damage. Not surprisingly, however, God has designed a detailed system to repair such mistakes, and vitamin E is a part of that system.

The B vitamins help your body's metabolism in different ways. Once thought to be a single vitamin, we now know that there is an entire "family" of B vitamins. For example, you might have heard about folic acid. It has been shown that a lack of folic acid during pregnancy can result in birth defects. Well, scientists now recognize that folic acid is actually one of the B vitamins, and we now call it vitamin B_9. A lack of any one B vitamin can cause specific metabolism-related problems.

Vitamin C helps your body build all sorts of molecules it needs. For example, it is an integral component in the chemical processes that build collagen in bones, teeth, and blood vessels. It also aids in the production of certain chemicals used by the nervous system. Like vitamin E, it is also an antioxidant. One of the more common problems associated with vitamin C deficiency is **scurvy**, a disease caused by the body's inability to form collagen in the proper way. If untreated, scurvy is fatal.

The last vitamin I want to discuss is vitamin K. When you cut yourself, you bleed. What keeps all your blood from leaking out of your body through the cut? Well, the answer is that your blood **clots** so it cannot leak out of the cut anymore. Vitamin K is an important part of that blood-clotting process. If you didn't have enough vitamin K in your blood, you could easily bleed to death from even a small cut. Now it turns out that there are *several* chemicals involved in the blood-clotting process, so don't get the idea that it is all the result of vitamin K. Nevertheless, vitamin K is a necessary part of the blood-clotting process. It is so important for good health that your body has two ways to get vitamin K. You can get it from your diet, but as I mentioned earlier, it is also produced for you by bacteria in your large intestine.

If a micronutrient is not a vitamin, it is a mineral. Now as I mentioned before, you have already learned a definition for minerals. Are the minerals your body needs the same as the inorganic crystalline substances found naturally in the earth? Well, your body doesn't need *all* the inorganic crystalline substances found naturally in the earth, but it does need some. Does that mean you should go eat rocks? Of course not! Remember, these are micronutrients. You need them only in small quantities, and you need only certain minerals.

The minerals you need the most are those that contain calcium, phosphorus, magnesium, potassium, sodium, chloride, sulfur, chromium, copper, fluoride, iodine, iron, selenium, and zinc. Without enough minerals containing these elements, you will have health problems. For example, too little calcium in your diet will lead to bone problems. Remember, calcium minerals are used to harden bone. Without enough, bones will not form properly. A constant lack of calcium intake can, later in life, lead to **osteoporosis** (ah' stee oh puh roh' sis). This condition weakens the bones so they become fragile and break very easily.

Iron is an important part of the system that transports oxygen throughout your body. With too little iron, your body will not be able to distribute oxygen efficiently. As a result, you will not be able to burn the macronutrients as quickly as you need to. This leads to **anemia** (ah nee' mee uh), which is characterized by shortness of breath, dizziness, feeling worn-out all the time, and a host of digestive problems.

Now although vitamins and minerals are an important part of the digestive process, you have to remember that your body is an incredibly efficient, finely tuned biological "machine." Even though vitamins and minerals are good for you, they are called micronutrients for a reason. You only need a small amount! In fact, even though too few vitamins and minerals can cause you problems, *too many* vitamins and minerals can cause you problems as well!

For example, your liver stores the fat-soluble vitamins (A, D, E, and K). If you take too many of these vitamins, your body doesn't use them and they end up building up in the liver. They can build up to such high quantities that they actually become *toxic*! Too much vitamin A, for example, will lead to liver damage, hair loss, blurred vision, and headaches. Too much vitamin D can lead to liver damage and calcium deposits. These deposits can interfere with the smooth muscles and the cardiac muscle. Now remember, vitamin D is produced by your body when your skin is exposed to the sun. However, that cannot cause you to have too much vitamin D, because your body will not make it if it doesn't need it. However, if you overdose on vitamin D, there are consequences.

The fat-soluble vitamins are the most important ones to watch, because they tend to build up in your body easily. The water-soluble vitamins can be dissolved in the urine if there are too many of them, and thus your body can get rid of them. However, even water-soluble vitamins can be dangerous in large doses. Too much vitamin B_6, for example, can cause numbness in the mouth and hands and can interfere with the muscles that control walking. You can even have problems if you have too many minerals in your body. For example, too much iron in your body can lead to liver, heart, and pancreas problems.

So should you be terrified about eating too many vitamins and minerals? No, of course not. It is very hard to overdose on vitamins from the *food you eat*. You would have to eat an incredibly unbalanced diet to overdose on a particular vitamin. However, you *can* overdose on vitamins if you take *too many* vitamin pills, herbs, or other dietary supplements. The U.S. government has issued recommended daily allowances (RDAs) for each of the vitamins. Many health professionals view the RDAs for vitamins as *minimun* requirements for good health, but they nevertheless give you some guidance as to how much of any particular vitamin you need.

One of the main things to keep in mind is that it is easier to build up too many fat-soluble vitamins in your body than it is to build up too many water-soluble vitamins in your body. After all, if you take in more vitamins than you need, your body will simply not use them. However, it will tend to *store* the fat-soluble ones away in your body's fat reserves. Over time, this can cause them to build up to toxic levels. Excess water-soluble vitamins, however, are typically ejected in your urine. Thus, while it is *very* difficult to reach toxic levels of vitamin C, it is only *somewhat* difficult to reach toxic levels of vitamins A, D, E, and K.

ON YOUR OWN

13.10 Certain nutritional companies sell pills with amino acids in them. Sometimes they are called vitamin pills. Why is that name wrong?

ANSWERS TO THE "ON YOUR OWN" PROBLEMS

13.1 Your teeth crush, tear, and grind food into little pieces. This does not change the chemical nature of the food; it just makes the food smaller. Thus, the teeth are involved in physical digestion.

13.2 Food never passes through the gall bladder, liver, salivary glands, and pancreas. Nevertheless, these are important parts of the digestive system. You will see that in a later section of the module.

13.3 The small intestine has a lot of these blood vessels. Remember, most of the micronutrients and macronutrients are absorbed by the bloodstream through the lining of the small intestine. Thus, there must be a lot of blood vessels there ready to transport what is absorbed.

13.4 Remember, the incisor teeth are sharp and are used to cut food. The canine teeth are used to tear food, while the premolars and molars are used to crush and grind food. If you think about it, an herbivore can get away without canine teeth. They need to be able to cut food (so they don't need to eat the whole plant at once), and they need to grind food to make it small, but meat is generally what needs tearing. Since herbivores eat no meat, they don't need canines. The other way to think about it is to think where the name "canine" comes from. "Canine" means "dog." Dogs eat meat. Thus, an animal without canines can't eat meat. Please note, however, that many herbivores *do* have canine teeth. Often, they are used for protection or some other purpose. Thus, you can't say that an animal with canine teeth must eat meat. However, if an animal *does not* have canines, it is mostly likely an herbivore.

13.5 You cough when you inhale smoke because, since you are inhaling, your epiglottis stays open. Thus, the smoke gets into your larynx, and the little particles in the smoke irritate the sensitive lining of the larynx, making you cough. This is much like what happens when food "goes down the wrong pipe." Your larynx has something other than just air going down it, and the lining is irritated.

13.6 Most of the absorption of nutrients occurs in the small intestine.

13.7 The acid in your stomach kills bacteria. Thus, the bacteria can't live in your stomach because of the stomach acid. This is another reason the chyme must be neutralized before it enters the small intestine. If it stayed acidic, it would kill the bacteria living in your intestines.

13.8 The gall bladder concentrates bile and injects it into the small intestine. Bile helps you digest fats. Without the gall bladder, you usually need to reduce the fat in your diet. Interestingly enough, without a gall bladder, bile is sent directly from the liver to the small intestine. If you increase your fat intake slowly enough, the constant release of bile from the liver to the small intestine becomes manageable for the body. In time, then, even someone without a gall bladder can eat a normal amount of fat.

13.9 There is probably not a lot of glycogen available to the body. Remember, fats and amino acids are converted into glucose if glycogen is not readily available.

13.10 Amino acids are not micronutrients. Remember, amino acids are the building blocks of PROTEINS. Thus, they are macronutrients, not vitamins.

STUDY GUIDE FOR MODULE #13

1. Define the following terms:

a. Digestion
b. Vitamin

2. Using the following figure, label organs (a) through (n) with the following names:

epiglottis, liver, stomach, trachea, salivary gland, pharynx, small intestine, esophagus, large intestine, gall bladder, rectum, pancreas, anus, larynx

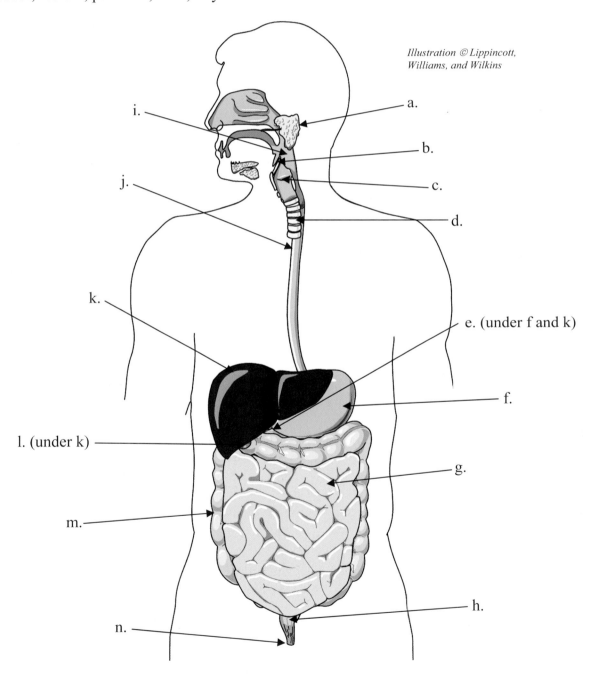

Illustration © Lippincott, Williams, and Wilkins

3. For each organ in the figure, answer the following questions:

    Is it a part of the digestive system?
    If it is a part of the digestive system, is it a part of the digestive tract?
    If it is a part of the digestive system, what is (are) its function or functions?

4. What function do we know the appendix serves?

5. What are the fat-soluble vitamins?

6. Which vitamins (fat-soluble or water-soluble) are most likely to build up to toxic levels in the body if you take too many?

7. What kind of role do most vitamins play in the body?

8. Which two vitamins can the body absorb without eating food that contains those vitamins?

MODULE #14: The Human Respiratory and Circulatory Systems

Introduction

In the previous two modules, I covered nutrition and the human digestive system. As you know, the main purpose of the digestive system is to convert the food you eat and the liquids you drink into macronutrients and micronutrients. The macronutrients are used as a source of energy, while the micronutrients play a support role in chemical processes throughout the body. As a result of studying those two modules, you should have developed a deep appreciation for the design and complexity of the human body.

Of course, the entire digestive system would be useless if the body had no way of transporting nutrients to the cells that need them. In addition, a body can have as many macronutrients as it wants, but without a good supply of oxygen, those macronutrients can never be burned for energy. Also, if there were no way to get rid of the carbon dioxide produced when the macronutrients are burned, the body would rapidly poison itself!

That's where the human circulatory and respiratory systems come in. The human circulatory system, composed primarily of the **heart** and the **blood vessels**, transports oxygen and nutrients to all the tissues in the human body. It picks up waste from the body's cells and transports them to organs that can get rid of them. The respiratory system, composed primarily of the **lungs**, allows the body to take in oxygen from the surrounding air and expel carbon dioxide. Since these two systems are intertwined, it only makes sense to talk about them together. That's what I will do in this module.

The Human Circulatory System

The human circulatory system transports nutrients and other vital chemicals around the body. It also picks up wastes to be expelled from the body. The circulatory system carries all these things in the **blood**. I will discuss the makeup of blood later. First, however, I want to concentrate on what carries the blood. Blood flows around the body in "tubes" that are generally called blood vessels. Scientists, however, have a more precise vocabulary. Blood vessels are separated into three basic categories: **veins**, **arteries**, and **capillaries**.

Veins – Blood vessels that carry blood back to the heart

Arteries – Blood vessels that carry blood away from the heart

Capillaries – Tiny, thin-walled blood vessels that allow the exchange of gases and nutrients between the blood and cells and are located between arteries and veins

Let me give you an overview of how these vessels work together to move the blood around your body so it can do its job. Then I will discuss some specifics.

If you think of the heart as a starting point, the large **pulmonary** (pull' muhn ayr' ee) **trunk** takes blood away from the heart and splits into two arteries that take the blood to the lungs. There the blood gets rid of the carbon dioxide it has picked up from the cells, and it receives oxygen from the lungs. Then large **pulmonary veins** take the blood back to the heart so it can be pumped to the rest of the body. It leaves the heart through the large artery called the **aorta** (aye or' tuh). As blood flows away from the heart, the aorta splits into smaller arteries, which in turn split into even smaller arteries. Eventually, the blood reaches the capillaries, where it gives oxygen to the cells and picks up the carbon dioxide the cells need to get rid of. After that, the blood is picked up by the veins to be brought back to the heart. As the veins get closer to the heart, they start combining to form larger and larger veins. Eventually, all the blood is returned to the heart via large veins called the **superior vena** (vee' nuh) **cava** (kay' vuh) and the **inferior vena cava**.   The figure below gives you a general idea of how all this works.

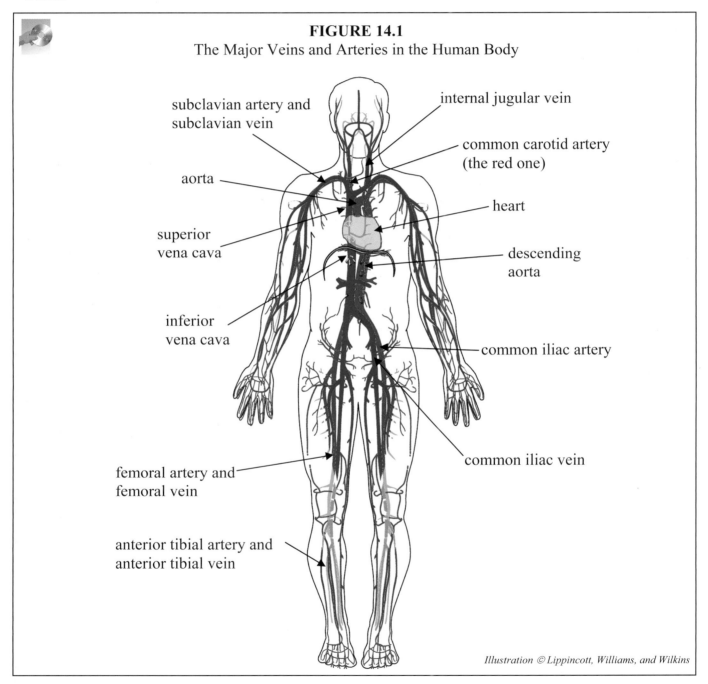

FIGURE 14.1
The Major Veins and Arteries in the Human Body

Illustration © Lippincott, Williams, and Wilkins

Now the first thing I want you to notice about the figure is the color scheme. Some of the blood vessels are blue and others are red. This is a standard color scheme in biology. Why do we use this color scheme? Well, one of the most important things about blood is the oxygen it carries. Thus, it is important for scientists to distinguish between blood that is rich in oxygen (called **oxygenated**

blood) and blood that doesn't have much oxygen (called **deoxygenated blood**). They do so with this color scheme. In the figure, red blood vessels carry oxygenated blood, and blue blood vessels carry deoxygenated blood.

How did biologists come up with this color scheme? Well, look at your wrist right below your palm. If you look closely, you should see what appear to be blue blood vessels in your skin. Those are blood vessels that contain deoxygenated blood. Although they *appear* blue when you look at them through your skin, they aren't really blue. Deoxygenated blood is dark red, while oxygenated blood is bright red. However, when you look at your blood vessels through your skin, the color gets distorted. As a result, blood vessels carrying deoxygenated blood appear to be blue, when in fact they are really dark red. Even though this is a distortion of color caused by viewing the blood vessels through the skin, the blue color is still used as a means of representing deoxygenated blood.

Okay, so now you know that some blood vessels carry oxygenated blood, and other blood vessels carry deoxygenated blood. In general, the *majority* of the veins in your body carry deoxygenated blood, while the *majority* of the arteries in your body carry oxygenated blood. Please note that this is ***not always*** the case, however. The definitions of veins and arteries have *nothing* to do with whether the blood inside them is oxygenated or deoxygenated. Instead, the definitions are based on which *way* the blood flows. If a vessel carries blood *toward* the heart, the blood vessel is a vein. If it carries blood *away from* the heart, it is an artery. However, since blood flowing away from the heart is usually being transported to the cells, it is usually rich in oxygen. Since blood flowing toward the heart is going back to the heart so it can get to the lungs, it is generally low in oxygen content.

Now that you know about veins and arteries, you need to learn a bit more about capillaries. Figure 14.2 shows you what goes on in the capillaries.

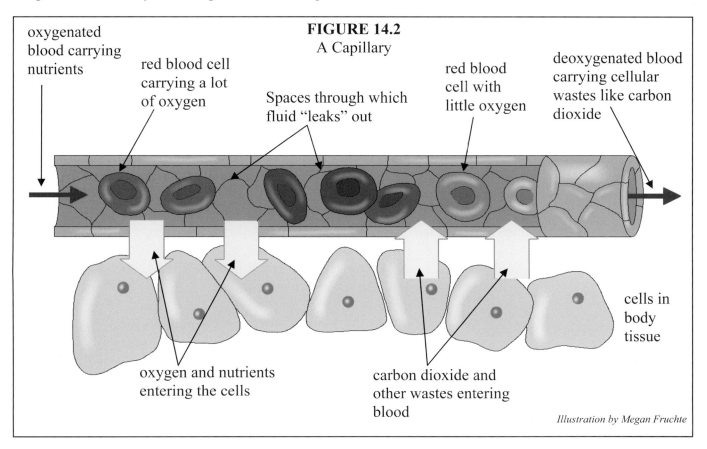

FIGURE 14.2
A Capillary

oxygenated blood carrying nutrients

red blood cell carrying a lot of oxygen

Spaces through which fluid "leaks" out

red blood cell with little oxygen

deoxygenated blood carrying cellular wastes like carbon dioxide

cells in body tissue

oxygen and nutrients entering the cells

carbon dioxide and other wastes entering blood

Illustration by Megan Fruchte

Compared to arteries and veins, capillaries are incredibly small. Their walls are also very thin. In fact, capillary walls are only one cell thick. In between these cells, there are spaces through which clear fluid can escape the capillary and bathe the cells of the surrounding tissue. That way, oxygen and other nutrients are passed from the blood to the cells that need them. Also, as the fluid bathes the cells, the cells release waste products into the fluid. The fluid is then reabsorbed by the capillaries. The fluid now has little oxygen and few nutrients, and it is full of waste products.

If you look at the entire system for a moment, then, oxygenated blood is carried away from the heart in large blood vessels called arteries. Those arteries eventually branch into smaller arteries (called "arterioles" – ar tee' ree ohlz) that branch into tiny capillaries. As the blood flows through the capillaries, clear fluid "leaks" out of the capillaries into the surrounding tissue. This fluid releases oxygen and nutrients into the surrounding cells. It also picks up waste products from the cells. That fluid is then reabsorbed by the capillaries, which eventually dump the deoxygenated blood full of waste into small veins (called "venules" – ven' yoolz). Those small veins carry the blood to larger veins that then carry the blood back to the heart.

If you were to take every artery, vein, and capillary in an adult human body and lay them end to end, the resulting "string" of blood vessels would be about *90,000 miles long*! Sit back and think about that for a minute. In the average adult, there are 90,000 miles worth of arteries, veins, and capillaries. It takes only about *1 minute* for a single drop of blood to start at the heart, travel to where it is needed in the body, and return to the heart again. In that amount of time, it supplies cells with the oxygen and nutrients they need and picks up waste products from the cells. It then travels to the lungs to get rid of those waste products and pick up oxygen so the whole process can start all over again! Isn't that amazing?

Compare this to something like the water system in a large city. The buildings in the city (houses, places of business, etc.) receive water from a central facility. That water is delivered to them through a network of large and small pipes. These pipes start from the central facility and branch out to all the buildings. After the water is used, pipes from the toilets, tubs, and sinks of the buildings dump their waste water into pipes that eventually lead to a network of tunnels. In addition, rain water and other kinds of runoff from the streets dump either directly into the tunnels or into pipes that eventually lead to tunnels. All this waste water is then dumped into a sewage treatment facility and then into a nearby river or lake.

Now, if you were to lay all of the pipes and tunnels in a city's water system end to end, would they make a 90,000-mile-long string? Probably not. Would they be nearly as complex as the blood system in the body? Not even close! After all, this water system carries only one thing: water. Blood carries a whole host of things (oxygen, nutrients, etc.). Also, the water system does not need to deliver water to all parts of each building. It delivers water only to kitchens, bathrooms, and certain other specialized rooms. The circulatory system in the body, on the other hand, supplies blood to *every living cell* of the body!

Now if you were to look at a drawing that showed the network of pipes and tunnels that make up a city's water system, you would *never* conclude that this network just appeared as the result of some random process! Nevertheless, there are people who want to convince you that the circulatory system, which is significantly more advanced and complex than a city's water system, resulted from a random process called evolution! Clearly anyone who looks at the details of the circulatory system and believes that it is the result of evolution must have an *enormous* amount of faith!

ON YOUR OWN

14.1 Blood is flowing through a vein in the leg. Is it flowing up or down the leg?

14.2 Fill in the blank below with one of the following – arteries, veins, or capillaries:

Wherever you find living cells in the body, you will find _____ very near.

The Heart and Blood Flow

The heart is a truly amazing organ! Remember from Module #11 that it has its own special muscle, called **cardiac muscle**. This muscle is controlled involuntarily (like a smooth muscle) but has many of the visible characteristics of a skeletal muscle. Thus, as you learned in Module #11, it is sort of a cross between smooth muscle and skeletal muscle. What does this muscle do? Well, it pumps blood, of course! Before I get into how the heart pumps blood, I want to spend a little bit of time on the structure of the heart. A simple sketch of a human heart is shown in the figure below. In order to match up parts in this sketch to those in Figure 14.1, notice that the superior vena cava and the aorta are in both figures.

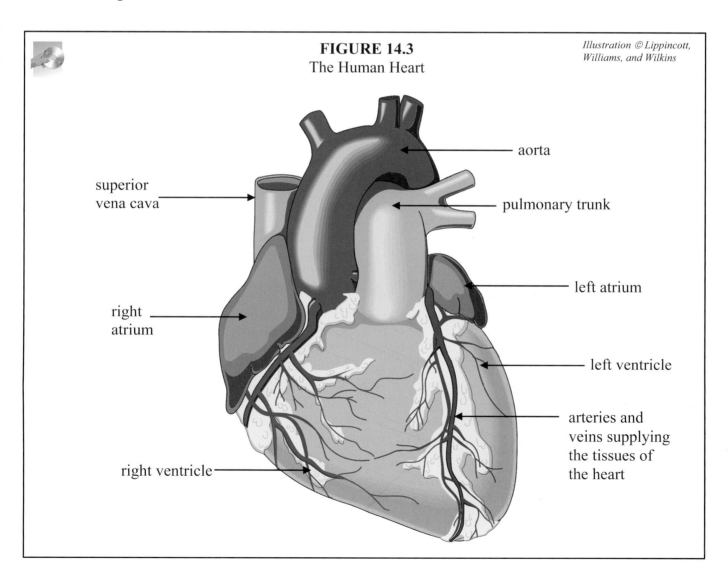

FIGURE 14.3
The Human Heart

Illustration © Lippincott, Williams, and Wilkins

The human heart is a **four-chambered heart**. It turns out that this is something all mammals have in common. Birds also have a four-chambered heart. As its name implies, it is divided into four chambers: the **left atrium** (ay' tree uhm), the **right atrium**, the **left ventricle** (ven' trih kuhl), and the **right ventricle**. This kind of heart is different from the hearts of most other animals in creation. Some animals, such as sponges (yes, sponges are animals), have no heart at all. Some animals, such as lobsters, have a heart that is made up of a single chamber. Other animals, like most fish, have a heart made of two chambers. Other animals, like frogs, have a heart with three chambers. Finally, animals like lizards have hearts that look like a cross between a three-chambered heart and a four-chambered heart.

Why do different animals have different kinds of hearts? Well, different animals require different things from their circulatory system. Remember, for example, that mammals are endothermic. This means that their internal temperature stays rather constant. As you learned in Module #12, this requires a lot of energy. Since bodies cannot get energy efficiently without oxygen, this means mammals require a lot of oxygen. Thus, mammals and other endothermic animals (like birds) must have very efficient circulatory systems. It turns out that a four-chambered heart is extremely efficient, since it pumps blood both before and after it is oxygenated, but it keeps the deoxygenated blood entirely separate from the oxygenated blood. Hearts with fewer than four chambers don't do that. Thus, mammals and birds need four-chambered hearts because they need very efficient circulatory systems. A frog doesn't need quite as efficient a circulatory system, so a three-chambered heart will do. A fish needs even less from its circulatory system, so a two-chambered heart works fine.

Notice in Figure 14.3 that there are several blood vessels running over the surface of the heart. Remember, the heart is full of living cells (cardiac muscle cells), so it must also have its own supply of blood. In fact, its cells work hard and thus require a steady supply of oxygen and nutrients. Thus, blood flows through the chambers of the heart so the heart can pump it throughout the body, but it also flows through arteries, veins, and capillaries that supply the tissues of the heart with oxygen and nutrients. So how does all this work? Well, I want to start by showing you a figure.

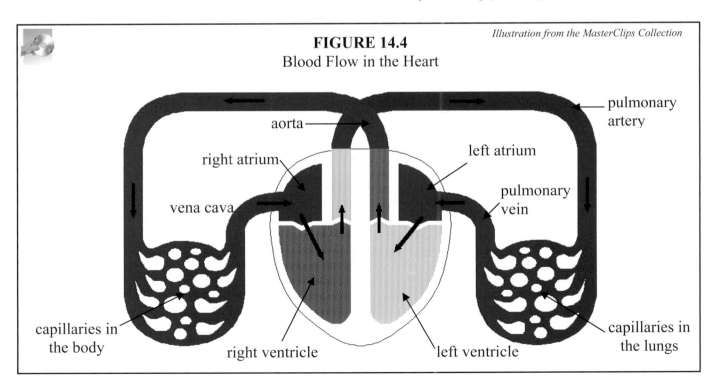

FIGURE 14.4
Blood Flow in the Heart

Illustration from the MasterClips Collection

Figure 14.4 is a simplified diagram of blood flow in the human body. It focuses (naturally) on the heart. Notice first that the same color scheme used in Figure 14.1 is employed here. Oxygenated blood is represented in red and deoxygenated blood is represented in blue. Also, notice the four chambers of the heart as pointed out in the figure. Finally, notice the terms "right" and "left" refer to the right and left sides of the *person to whom the heart belongs*, not the person looking at the heart.

Now that you know the general layout of the figure, I want to use it to explain how blood flows in your body. Let's begin with the right atrium. The main veins of the body (the superior vena cava and inferior vena cava) bring deoxygenated blood in from the various tissues of the body and dump it into the right atrium. When the right atrium receives a signal from the sinoatrial node (the pacemaker - you learned about that in Module #11), it contracts. This pushes blood out the right atrium and into the right ventricle. The atrium then relaxes to fill with blood again, and the ventricle contracts, pushing the deoxygenated blood out the right ventricle and into the pulmonary trunk, which splits into the **pulmonary arteries**.

The pulmonary arteries send the deoxygenated blood to the capillaries of both lungs. That's what the "web" of blood vessels on the right side of the figure represents. As the blood flows through the lung capillaries, it releases carbon dioxide and picks up a new supply of oxygen. Thus, after passing through the lung capillaries, the blood turns from deoxygenated blood into oxygenated blood. This newly oxygenated blood is then carried back to the heart through the **pulmonary veins**.

The pulmonary veins dump blood into the left atrium, which then contracts and sends the blood into the left ventricle. The left atrium then relaxes and the left ventricle contracts, pushing the oxygenated blood out into the **aorta**. The blood travels out the aorta to the rest of the body. If it goes to the upper parts of the body, it travels up through the arteries that branch from the aorta. If it goes to the lower parts of the body, it travels down the **descending aorta** to the various arteries that branch off from it.

In less than one minute, the blood makes it to capillaries in the various tissues of the body. That's what the web of blood vessels on the left side of the figure represents. In the capillaries, the blood gives oxygen and other nutrients to the cells and picks up waste from the cells. At that point, the blood is once again deoxygenated, and it travels back to the heart in the body's veins. Those veins all lead to the superior vena cava (if the blood is in the upper portion of the body) or the inferior vena cava (if the blood is in the lower portion of the body). These vessels take the blood back to the right atrium, where the whole process starts all over again.

Now as if that wasn't difficult enough, you need to realize something about this whole process. Although I started the story of blood flow with the right atrium and then followed the blood through the right ventricle and *then* into the left atrium, that's only what happens if you follow the same drop of blood through the circulatory system. In reality, the right and left atrium fill *at the same time* (with different blood, of course) and then contract *at the same time*, dumping blood into each ventricle *at the same time*. The ventricles then contract *at the same time*, pushing blood either into the pulmonary artery or the aorta, depending on which ventricle you look at. Each atrium, then, is either filled or emptied at the same time, as is each ventricle. The left side of the heart delivers blood to all the body except the lungs, while the right side of the heart delivers blood only to the lungs.

The entire cycle of a heartbeat – the contraction of the two atria (plural of "atrium"), the relaxation of the atria and the contraction of the ventricles, and the relaxation of the ventricles – is called the **cardiac cycle**. When the average person is at rest, his or her cardiac cycle usually takes about three quarters of a second. I want you to spend some time learning a little bit about your own cardiac cycle by performing the following experiment.

EXPERIMENT 14.1
Measuring Your Own Cardiac Cycle

Supplies:

♦ A stopwatch or a watch with a second hand
♦ A place where you can do jumping jacks

Introduction: Each person has his own cardiac cycle time that depends on his BMR and other factors. In this experiment, you will determine your own cardiac cycle time under different conditions.

Procedure:

1. You have probably been sitting down quietly (or at least reasonably quietly) reading this incredibly interesting course. Although you have, most likely, been excited about all the wonderful things you have been learning, chances are good that you are close to your "resting" cardiac cycle. Thus, I want you to measure that now. To measure your cardiac cycle, place the index finger of your right hand at the inside of your left wrist on the thumb side. Lightly push around the area until you feel a constant beat. That's your **pulse**. Count the number of times your pulse beats in 30 seconds.
2. When your heart pumps blood into your aorta, the increased pressure in your arteries causes them to expand. That expansion travels through the arteries. When you feel your pulse, you are touching an artery, and the beat that you feel is caused by the artery expanding and contracting in response to the heart pumping blood into the aorta. In the end, then, each beat you feel corresponds to a *heartbeat*. If you double the number of beats you felt in 30 seconds, you have the number of times your heart beats per minute. However, I want you to do something else. Divide 30 by the number of beats you counted. This will give you your *cardiac cycle*, which essentially tells you how long your heart takes to make one beat. The average person your age has a cardiac cycle of about 0.75, which corresponds to 80 beats per minute.
3. The cardiac cycle you just measured corresponds to your *resting* cardiac cycle. If your body starts expending lots of energy, the blood must flow more quickly so the cells in your body can get enough oxygen to make the energy they need. This changes your cardiac cycle. To measure this, do one full minute of vigorous jumping jacks right now.
4. As soon as you are done with the jumping jacks, put your finger back on your wrist and count the beats you feel for 30 seconds.
5. Wait for one full minute, sitting quietly, and count your pulse beats again for a period of 30 seconds.
6. Repeat step 5 at least 4 more times.
7. Once you are done, go back and divide 30 by each of the number of pulse beats you counted. This gives you your cardiac cycle right after the jumping jacks as well as during the time you rested after completing the jumping jacks.

What did you see in the experiment? Well, unless your heart rate is abnormal, your resting cardiac cycle was probably less than 0.9 and greater than 0.6. Most likely, it was around 0.75. However, after you did your jumping jacks, your cardiac cycle should have been smaller than your resting cardiac cycle. Why? The cells in your body (mostly your skeletal muscle cells) needed extra energy. Thus, they had to start burning more macronutrients. To do that, they needed more oxygen and perhaps more macronutrients. Thus, the blood needed to get these materials to the cells more quickly than normal. Thus, your heart started pumping *faster*. Since your heart started pumping faster, it had to take less time to make each beat, so the cardiac cycle *decreased*.

As you rested, however, your cells needed less and less energy. As a result, your heart could start slowing down, because your cells' energy demands started decreasing. This, of course, increased your cardiac cycle time, since the heart could spend more time on each beat. Thus, you should have seen your cardiac cycle increase with each subsequent measurement.

Before I leave this section, I want to point out something you might have missed. Look again at the right side of Figure 14.4. Notice that the pulmonary artery has *deoxygenated* blood in it, while the pulmonary vein has *oxygenated* blood in it. Now based on the functions of these two blood vessels, that makes sense. The pulmonary artery takes blood to the lungs to be oxygenated, and the pulmonary vein returns the oxygenated blood to the heart so it can be pumped out to the entire body. However, the general rule of thumb is *most* veins carry deoxygenated blood while *most* arteries carry oxygenated blood. The pulmonary arteries and veins represent notable exceptions to that general rule of thumb.

Now that you understand blood flow in the body, you should understand both the general rule of thumb and why these two blood vessels are exceptions. Remember, arteries carry blood away from the heart. When blood is going to parts of the body *other than the lungs*, it comes out of the left side of the heart and is oxygenated. This oxygenated blood moves away from the heart until it moves into capillaries and releases its oxygen and nutrients to the cells. At that point, it is picked up by the veins so it can be taken back to the right side of the heart, because veins carry blood toward the heart. Thus, most arteries carry oxygenated blood because while blood travels away from the heart, it has not dropped off its supply of oxygen and nutrients. Once it does that, it is picked up by veins to be carried back to the right side of the heart. Since veins are defined as those blood vessels that carry blood back to the heart, most veins carry deoxygenated blood.

A notable exception to this is the system that carries blood to the lungs. While blood is traveling away from the right side of the heart and toward the lungs, it is deoxygenated. Thus, the arteries from the heart to the lungs carry deoxygenated blood. They are arteries because they carry blood away from the heart. They carry deoxygenated blood, however, unlike most arteries. Once the blood is oxygenated in the lungs, it is carried back to the left side of the heart. At that point, then, it is traveling in veins, because only veins carry blood back to the heart. However, since the blood is oxygenated at that point, the veins that carry blood from the lungs to the heart carry oxygenated blood, unlike the majority of the veins in the body.

ON YOUR OWN

14.3 When the left atrium is mostly empty, is the right atrium mostly full or mostly empty? What about the right ventricle?

14.4 The heart of a certain full-grown animal has deoxygenated blood and oxygenated blood mixed together inside the heart. Is the animal endothermic or ectothermic?

The Components of Blood

Now that you have learned a bit about blood vessels and blood flow, you might want to learn a bit about blood itself! Blood is an incredibly complex mixture of chemicals and cells. More than half of any given sample of blood is made up of a pale yellowish liquid called **blood plasma**. It contains many chemicals, including macronutrients and micronutrients. The levels of many of these chemicals are carefully controlled by the **kidneys**, because the body is *very* sensitive to the composition of blood plasma. Even tiny changes in the concentration of many chemicals in your blood plasma could have fatal consequences! Thus, the kidneys have complex chemical sensing and regulating mechanisms, keeping many of the chemicals in blood plasma at very precise levels.

Suspended within the plasma are three main types of cells: **red blood cells, white blood cells,** and **blood platelets**. Figure 14.5 shows you an image of the cellular components of blood from an electron microscope. This is not really a picture, because an electron microscope uses electrons, not light. As a result, there is really no color in an electron microscope image; it is added artificially. As a result, such an image is often called a "colorized electron micrograph."

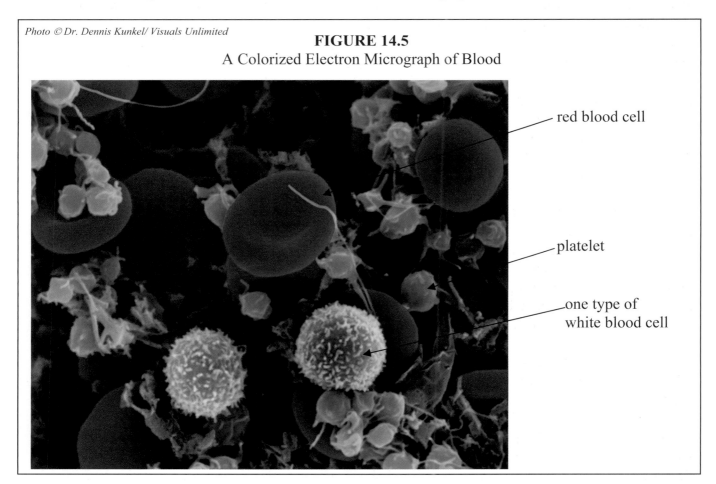

Photo © Dr. Dennis Kunkel/ Visuals Unlimited

FIGURE 14.5
A Colorized Electron Micrograph of Blood

red blood cell

platelet

one type of
white blood cell

Red blood cells transport oxygen from the lungs to the tissues. They give the blood its overall red color, because they contain a protein called **hemoglobin** (heem' uh gloh bin), which is red. This protein is inside red blood cells and receives oxygen from the lungs. It then carries the oxygen until the blood reaches cells that need it. At that point, it releases the oxygen to the cells. Without red blood cells, the blood running through your circulatory system would never be able to perform its most important function: the transport of oxygen from the lungs to the tissues of the body.

Red blood cells are short-lived, typically lasting 80 to 120 days within the circulatory system. There are so many red blood cells in our blood that roughly *2,000,000 red blood cells die every second* in a typical adult. If red blood cells are dying all the time, why don't we run out of them? Well, our bodies continue to make more in order to replace those that are dying. Where are they produced in the body? You should remember that. You learned in Module #11 that blood cells are manufactured by the **bone marrow**.

White blood cells make up only about 1 percent of blood, but they perform a vital function. They are responsible for protecting the body from agents of disease. You can think of white blood cells as little guards that continually "patrol" the body. When they recognize an organism that should not be there, they destroy it. Often, this is accomplished by engulfing the pathogen and killing it. These little guards have other "weapons" at their disposal, however. Some white blood cells tear the pathogen to pieces. Rather than directly attacking an invading organism, some white blood cells produce chemicals called **antibodies**, which are released into the blood and fight the pathogen.

Have you have ever been given an antibiotic when you were sick? An antibiotic is simply a chemical that kills pathogenic organisms. From where does this chemical come? Well, the *vast majority* of antibiotics come from bacteria and fungi! Only a few antibiotics are actually made by medical scientists. The vast majority are produced by fungi and bacteria, and scientists simply collect them for use in antibiotics. This brings up an important point. Despite the fact that medical science is amazingly advanced today, it cannot artificially produce most of the protective chemicals used to make antibiotics. Instead, it must *harvest* them from other organisms that make them *naturally*!

Think about that for a moment. Bacteria and fungi are *better* at producing chemicals than our best scientists today! If bacteria and fungi are better at making disease-fighting chemicals than are our *best* scientists, how in the world can you believe that these organisms were produced by a random process such as evolution? Indeed, evolutionists consider bacteria to be "primitive" organisms, the first step in a long, involved process in which random mutations were acted on by natural selection to produce more "advanced" creatures. Think about it, however. If you walked into a laboratory filled with scientists making disease-fighting chemicals, would you think that the laboratory was the "primitive" result of some process that depends on random chance? Of course not! A laboratory can only be made with forethought and design. Well, "primitive" organisms like bacteria and fungi are better at producing chemicals than the best laboratory that science can design! How, then, can anyone ever believe these organisms appeared by chance?

The smallest "cells" in your blood are **platelets**. They are not true cells; rather, they are pieces of a kind of white blood cell. However, they serve an important purpose: to aid in the process of **blood clotting**. This vital process keeps us from bleeding to death when we are cut. In simple terms, the blood-clotting process has three steps. In the first step, the smooth muscles in the injured blood vessel contract to make the hole as small as possible. In the second step, the platelets clump together and stick to the edges of the injury. This makes a soft clot (called a **platelet plug**) over the hole. In the third step, called **coagulation** (koh' ag you lay' shun), a host of chemicals from the blood and the injured tissue work together to transform certain proteins in the blood plasma into a threadlike protein called "fibrin," which forms a tight web that seals off the injury in the blood vessel.

The blood-clotting mechanism in which blood platelets participate is universally recognized as one of the most stunning, complex chemical processes in nature. It is a finely tuned, amazing system that has several checks and counter-checks to make sure that the blood clots *only* when a blood vessel is damaged and *only* in the area of the injury. Think about it: Blood cannot clot just anywhere at any time! Blood clotting causes blood to stop flowing! When a blood vessel is cut, blood clotting is a good thing. At any other time or place in the circulatory system, that would be a very *bad* thing. The blood-clotting process only occurs when necessary, however, due to an incredibly complex chemical mechanism. The colorized electron micrograph below shows you the end result of the blood-clotting process – a fibrin "net" holding blood cells behind the platelet plug.

FIGURE 14.6
Fibrin Forming a Blood Clot

Photo © Dr. Dennis Kunkel/ Visuals Unlimited

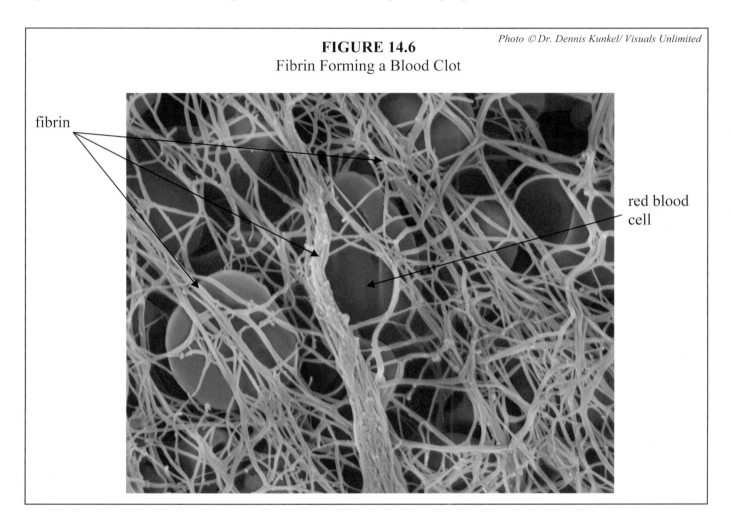

fibrin

red blood cell

Dr. Michael Behe, a prominent biochemist, says that the blood-clotting mechanism alone is very strong evidence that something is wrong with the whole idea of evolution (which he calls "Darwinian theory"). In his book, *Darwin's Black Box*, he makes this important statement:

> Blood coagulation is a paradigm of the staggering complexity that underlies even apparently simple bodily processes. Faced with such complexity beneath even simple phenomena, Darwinian theory falls silent. [Michael J. Behe, *Darwin's Black Box*, Touchstone, 1996, p. 97]

According to Behe, this statement can be made about many processes we see in nature. As I have tried to show you over and over again, there is simply no way to explain the marvels of "technology" we see in the natural world. They are so complex, so intricately pieced together, and so marvelously efficient that they cry out in testimony of their incredible Designer!

ON YOUR OWN

14.5 Sickle-cell anemia is a genetic condition that causes the body to produce an altered form of the protein hemoglobin. This affects the shape of one of the types of blood cells, causing them to have a difficult time passing through the blood vessels. This leads to "logjams" in the blood, which can have severe consequences. Which type of blood cell is affected by sickle-cell anemia?

14.6 There is a rare problem during the birth of some babies in which the baby's blood platelets are destroyed by an inconsistency between the baby's blood and the mother's blood. When this happens, the baby can die from even the slightest injury. Why?

Lungs and Blood Oxygenation

From our previous discussion, it should be clear to you that the lungs play a vital role in your body. As a result, you need to learn a few things about your lungs and how they work. A simplified sketch of human lungs is provided in Figure 14.7.

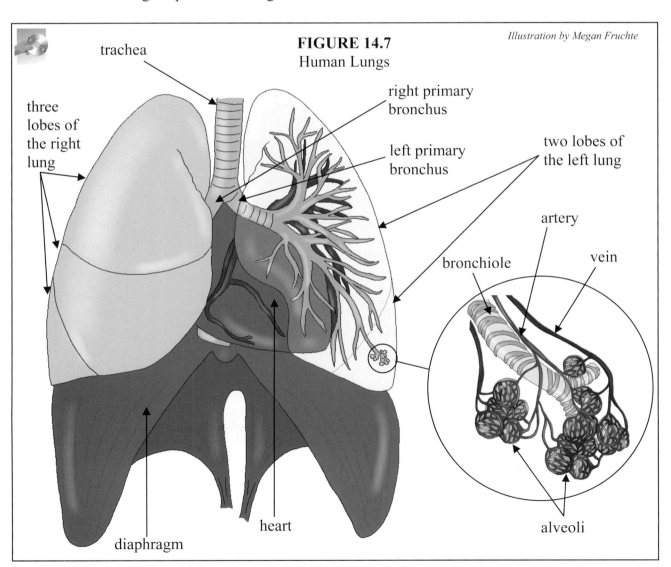

FIGURE 14.7
Human Lungs

Illustration by Megan Fruchte

trachea

right primary bronchus

left primary bronchus

three lobes of the right lung

two lobes of the left lung

artery

vein

bronchiole

alveoli

heart

diaphragm

Like all the organs in your body, your lungs are incredibly complex, efficient, and well-designed. Remember, their main job is to oxygenate the blood and allow the blood to release carbon dioxide. If you think about it, then, the lungs need to have tubes that transport air and tubes that transport blood. Well, we already know about the tubes that transport blood. Arteries carry blood to the lungs; they branch into smaller and smaller arteries until they branch into capillaries. The capillaries then allow the blood to pick up oxygen from the lungs and release carbon dioxide. Veins then carry the oxygenated blood back to the heart.

What about the air tubes? In general, the tubes in the lungs that carry air are called **bronchial** (bron' kee uhl) **tubes**. As you should remember from Module #13, air travels from the mouth or nose into the **trachea**. The air passes through the trachea, eventually reaching a branch. That branch is the end of the trachea and the beginning of the lungs' bronchial tube system. A little more than half of the air travels through the right branch into the **right lung**, and the rest travels through the left branch into the **left lung**. The right branch is called the **right primary bronchus** (bron' kus), and the left branch is called the **left primary bronchus**. These two primary tubes branch into smaller and smaller bronchial tubes. The branches become so small that there are about 30,000 of them in each lung. At the end of these tiny bronchial tubes, called **bronchioles** (bron' kee ohls), there are little sacs called **alveoli** (al vee' oh lye). There are about 300 *million* alveoli in a typical adult's lungs!

Most of the "action" in the lungs takes place in the alveoli. The alveoli are covered with capillaries. The deoxygenated blood that has come into the lung through the pulmonary arteries flows through these capillaries, getting rid of carbon dioxide and accepting oxygen from the air that has been brought into the alveoli by the bronchioles. The carbon dioxide travels back out of the alveoli, through the bronchioles, into the bronchial tube system, and out the trachea each time you exhale.

One of the diseases associated with cigarette smoking is **emphysema** (em' fuh zee' muh). In this disease, the alveoli become overlarge and merge with other alveoli. This causes the lungs to have a few large alveoli rather than many small alveoli at the end of each bronchiole. This results in significantly less efficient oxygen exchange with the blood. As a result, the blood cannot carry as much oxygen as the cells of the body need. This results in shortness of breath, wheezing, and extreme difficulty in breathing. Severe emphysema is deadly.

One interesting aspect of emphysema is that it generally *requires* smoking (or regularly breathing severely polluted air) in order to occur. Many diseases (like lung cancer) become *more likely* the more you smoke, but it is possible to get those diseases without ever smoking. Thus, there are other causes of most smoking-related diseases. Smoking just makes you more likely to get those diseases. However, it is very rare for a person who has never smoked (or never had repeated, long-term exposure to severe pollution) to get emphysema.

Interestingly enough, the left lung and right lung are different from one another. Each lung is composed of "lobes" that house the arteries, veins, and bronchial tubes. The right lung is made up of three lobes, but the left lung is made up of only two. Why the difference? Well, look at Figure 14.7 again. Notice that the heart is not exactly in the center of the two lungs. It takes up more space on the left side of the trachea than it does on the right side. The left lung is smaller to allow the heart to take up that extra room.

Since the two lungs together make up one of the largest organs in your body, you might want to know how big your lungs really are. Well, it's hard to measure the exact dimensions of your lungs, but it is relatively easy for you to measure the *vital capacity* of your lungs, which is the maximum amount you can exhale. Perform the following experiment to determine your lungs' vital capacity.

EXPERIMENT 14.2
The Vital Capacity of Your Lungs

Supplies:

♦ Flexible tubing (If you don't have some, the best place to get it is anywhere that sells aquarium accessories. It is typically called "aquarium tubing," and it is used to connect the aquarium air pump to the filter.)
♦ A plastic 1-gallon jug with a lid
♦ A sink with a plug
♦ A measuring cup

Introduction: This experiment helps you determine how much air you can exhale when you try to exhale as much as possible. This is a measure of your lungs' vital capacity.

Procedure:

1. Fill the sink about halfway full of water and plug it so the water stays in the sink.
2. Fill the jug completely with water. Try to get all of the air bubbles out.
3. Close the jug's lid and invert it so the opening of the jug is completely under water.
4. Keeping the jug completely inverted and the opening of the jug under water at all times, take the lid off of the jug. Essentially no water should escape from the jug.
5. Keeping the jug completely inverted and the opening of the jug under water at all times, insert one end of the tubing so it goes into the jug through the opening. Don't put the end of the tube too high in the jug. The opening of the tube should be just inside the jug.
6. Take the deepest breath you can and blow into the tubing. Blow in one continuous breath without pausing to breathe in again. Blow until there is no air left to blow.
7. As you blow, the air will travel into the jug, displacing water. The more you blow, the less water will be in the jug. If you are reasonably athletic or large, you might blow all the water out of the jug. Most students will not, however.
8. Put the lid back on the jug while the jug is inverted and the opening is under water.
9. Remove the jug from the water, turn it rightside up, and take off the lid.
10. Pour what water is left into the measuring cup. Try to fill the measuring cup to exactly 1 cup. If there is still water in the jug, empty the measuring cup and fill it again. Do that until the jug is empty, counting the number of cups of water in the jug.
11. The last time you fill the cup from the jug, it will probably not fill the cup exactly full. Try to estimate the amount of water to the nearest quarter. In other words, if the cup is not very full, estimate that there is ¼ cup of water there. If it's nearly half full, then estimate ½ cup. If it is more than ½ but noticeably less than 1 cup, estimate it to be ¾ cup.
12. There are 16 cups in a gallon. Subtract the number of cups of water that were in the jug from 16, and that will tell you your lung's vital capacity. Please note that this does not measure the *total* amount of air in your lungs, because even after you exhale as much as possible, there is still a significant amount of residual air left in your lungs.
13. Clean everything up.

So what was your lungs' vital capacity? Most students have a vital capacity between 12 and 16 cups. However, as I stated in the experiment, athletic people and larger individuals can have capacities greater than a gallon. Interestingly enough, when you are resting, you use only about one-fifteenth of your lungs' capacity. When you exercise, however, you start breathing more deeply, using more and more of your lungs' capacity.

ON YOUR OWN

14.7 Which would be more efficient in terms of getting oxygen into the blood: a lung with lots of little alveoli or a lung with fewer, larger alveoli?

14.8 Bronchitis (bron kye' tis) is a breathing disorder that plagues many people. Based on the name, what part of the lungs is affected by bronchitis?

<u>The Respiratory System</u>

Although I mentioned the lungs when I discussed the circulatory system, they are part of a separate system called the **respiratory** (res' per uh tor' ee) **system**. This system, as illustrated in Figure 14.8, contains all the structures that help us breathe.

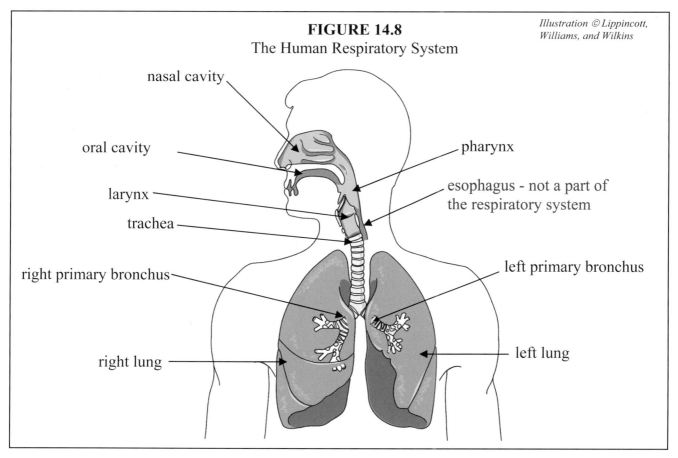

FIGURE 14.8
The Human Respiratory System

Illustration © Lippincott, Williams, and Wilkins

nasal cavity

oral cavity

pharynx

larynx

esophagus - not a part of the respiratory system

trachea

right primary bronchus

left primary bronchus

right lung

left lung

The respiratory system controls how we breathe. Air travels either through the **nasal cavity** or the **oral cavity** into the **pharynx** (which you learned about in the previous module). Most of the time, we breathe through our nose, so most of the air we breathe passes through the nasal cavity. This is actually very important. You see, the nasal cavity is lined with a sticky substance called **mucus**. Mucus is designed to trap particles. That way, any particles in the air you inhale do not make it into your lungs. When you have a cold, the cold virus stimulates your body to produce too much mucus. When that happens, the mucus leaks out your nose, and you say, "My nose is running."

When particles are trapped by the mucus in your nasal cavity, they are pushed along by tiny hairs called **cilia** (sill' ee uh). These hairs push the particles toward the front of the nose, where they will be blown out or sneezed out. If you have a "stuffy nose," you have a lot of mucus and trapped particles that have been pushed to the front of your nose, waiting for you to blow your nose and get rid of them. Sometimes, the body takes over and sneezes, essentially blowing your nose for you.

The nose doesn't just clean the air, but it also warms and moistens it. The mucus-covered lining of the nose provides moisture as the air passes over it, and the blood flowing beneath the lining warms the air. If you think about how your lungs "burn" when you exercise vigorously or breathe through your mouth on a cold day, you will appreciate what a wonderful "air conditioner" your nose really is!

When the air passes through the nasal cavity or the mouth cavity, it then travels through the pharynx. As you learned in the previous module, an automated "gatekeeper" called the epiglottis makes sure that the **larynx** is open when you breathe so air can be passed into it. Air then travels through the larynx into the **trachea** and then into one of the lungs via either the left primary bronchus or the right primary bronchus. When you swallow food, however, the epiglottis automatically closes the larynx so food travels only into the esophagus.

Now one thing I have not described is how your respiratory system actually pushes air into and out of the nasal cavity, pharynx, larynx, trachea, and lungs. That is controlled by a few skeletal muscles, the most important of which is the **diaphragm** (die' uh fram). When the diaphragm contracts, it pushes down on the nearby organs, pulling the lungs down with them. This causes the lungs to expand, which sucks air into them. That's how you inhale. When the diaphragm relaxes, those same organs push up on the lungs, making them smaller. This forces air out of your lungs, and you exhale. To give you a visual indication of how this works, perform the following experiment.

EXPERIMENT 14.3
A Model of Your Lungs

Supplies:

♦ A plastic 2-liter bottle (the kind soda pop comes in)
♦ Strong scissors
♦ A plastic sandwich bag (It needs to be large enough for the bottom of the 2-liter bottle to fit into the bag.)
♦ Tape
♦ A round balloon (12-inch is ideal, but any size greater than 6-inch will do.)
♦ Eye protection such as goggles or safety glasses

Introduction: In this experiment, you will be able to see how your diaphragm controls breathing.

Procedure:

1. Use the scissors to cut the 2-liter bottle across the middle so the bottom falls away.

2. If the sandwich bag is zippered, cut the zipper off the top.
3. Open the bag and put the top half of the bottle (bottom first) into the bag. Make it so the bag fully surrounds the bottom of the bottle but has plenty of slack in it.
4. Use tape to secure the bag to the bottle. You should put tape all the way around, making a good seal between the bottle and the plastic bag.
5. Push the bag's slack into the bottle.
6. Blow up the balloon relatively large and then let all the air out.
7. Squeeze the balloon to make sure all the air is gone. The purpose of these steps is to stretch the balloon – that's all.
8. Put the balloon in the top opening of the bottle upside down. Stretch the opening of the balloon over the opening of the bottle so the balloon hangs upside down in the bottle. Your final setup should look like this:

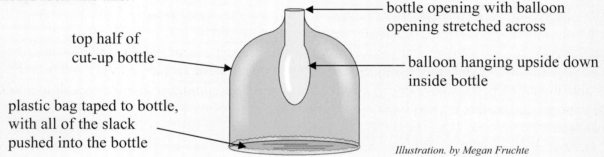

top half of
cut-up bottle

bottle opening with balloon
opening stretched across

balloon hanging upside down
inside bottle

plastic bag taped to bottle,
with all of the slack
pushed into the bottle

Illustration. by Megan Fruchte

9. You now have a reasonable model of a lung. To watch your lung "breathe," pull the slack in the plastic bag down and watch the balloon. Then, push the slack up and watch the balloon. When you pull the slack in the plastic bag down, there is suddenly more room in the system. This allows the balloon to expand, and you should see it inflate a bit with air. When you push the slack back into bottle, you get rid of the extra room, which squeezes the balloon, pushing the air out of it.
10. Clean everything up.

In your model of a lung, the plastic bag represents your diaphragm. When you push the slack of the plastic bag into the bottle, you are simulating the relaxation of your diaphragm, which allows the nearby organs to push up on your lungs. This squeezes your lungs (represented by the balloon), forcing air out of them. Just as the balloon deflates, so do your lungs. This causes you to exhale. When you pull the slack in the bag down, that simulates the diaphragm contracting and thereby pushing down on the nearby organs. This provides more room for the balloon (your lungs), allowing it to fill with air. This, then, simulates inhaling. So as your diaphragm contracts and expands, your lungs fill and empty, causing you to breathe. Your lungs never fully empty, however, no matter how forcefully you exhale. That might have happened in your model, but in your body, there is always air in the lungs, because there is always blood in need of oxygen flowing through them.

There is one other aspect of the respiratory system that I want to discuss. When you exhale, air passes through the larynx and out of your body. Your larynx is often called your **voice box**, because it contains your **vocal cords**. Your vocal cords are two thin folds of tissue that stretch across the sides of the larynx. As you exhale, air is pushed out the trachea and into the larynx, passing over these folds. When the vocal cords are relaxed, air passes through the larynx silently. When the vocal cords are tightened, however, the folds move into the airway, and the air makes them vibrate, producing sound. That sound is the basis of speech, singing, humming, etc. To get an idea of how your vocal cords work, perform the following quick experiment.

EXPERIMENT 14.4
A Model of Your Vocal Cords

<u>Supply</u>:

♦ A rubber band (It should be large enough to fit around your wrist without stretching. If the rubber band is larger, it will work fine, but a smaller one will not work.)
♦ Eye protection such as goggles or safety glasses

Introduction: Air passing over a stretched rubber band simulates how your vocal cords make noise.

<u>Procedure</u>:

1. Hold the rubber band so it loops around all your fingers (not your thumbs) on each hand.
2. Pull your hands apart a little, stretching the rubber band slightly.
3. Hold the top strand of the rubber band in front of and very near your mouth and blow on it **hard**. You might have to move your hands up and down to position the strand properly, but you should be able to get the rubber band strand to hum, because the air coming from your mouth will vibrate the rubber band, and that causes a humming noise.
4. Now you should stretch the rubber band tighter. **BE CAREFUL - DO NOT STRETCH IT HARD ENOUGH TO BREAK IT!!!!!** Repeat step 3, and try to note the difference in the hum that is produced.
5. Play a little with the strength at which you blow. See if you can find a relationship between the volume of the humming noise and the strength at which you blow.

In this experiment, the rubber band represented a vocal cord. When it was stretched tight and air passed over it, it began to vibrate, making a humming noise. Essentially the same thing happens in your larynx, producing the sound that is the basis of speech, singing, humming, etc. When you stretched the rubber band harder, the hum should have changed slightly. It probably sounded a bit higher in pitch than the previous hum. That's what controls the pitch of your voice. When you stretch your vocal cords tightly, they vibrate faster, producing a higher-pitched noise. This makes your voice sound higher. In the last step, you should have noticed that the harder you blew, the louder the hum. That's how you control the volume of your voice. The more air you use, the louder the sound you produce. In the end, then, the amount of air passing through your larynx controls the volume of your voice, while the tightness of your vocal cords controls the pitch.

ON YOUR OWN

14.9 When a person cannot breathe due to an obstruction in the nasal and mouth cavities or the pharynx, a surgical procedure called a "tracheotomy" is performed. In this procedure, an opening is cut through the neck and into the trachea. At that point, the person breathes through the hole in the trachea. People who have tracheotomies cannot speak unless they block that hole. Why?

<u>Circulation and Respiration Throughout Creation</u>

Although I have concentrated on circulation and respiration in humans, obviously *all* organisms must have some means of getting the necessary chemicals to the right place in the body.

For some organisms, the job is not as hard as others because they are smaller. Members of kingdoms Monera and Protista, for example, are typically made of only one cell. These organisms still must have systems that transport nutrients and oxygen from outside the cell to different parts within the cell and transport waste products back out. The chemical nature of such systems is *incredibly* complex. In fact, in the same book I mentioned previously, Dr. Behe uses the cell transport mechanism as another system so complex that it defies evolution. Nevertheless, even though it is *incredibly* complex, it is still not as complex as the circulatory and respiratory systems in larger creatures.

What is amazing about God's creation is the diversity among its organisms. For example, even within kingdom Animalia, there are many different means by which organisms get and transport the chemicals they need throughout their bodies. You already know that hearts vary from one-chambered to four-chambered, depending on the needs of the animal. Some animals, such as sponges, don't even *have* a heart or a circulatory system. They have mobile cells that travel freely throughout their bodies, digesting food, transporting the nutrients to where they are needed, and exchanging oxygen for cell waste products.

Other examples of the diversity of the creatures in creation include the many ways that organisms get oxygen for the combustion of macronutrients. Animals such as fish have to extract the oxygen dissolved in the water. They use **gills** instead of lungs to accomplish this feat. Other animals, such as worms, actually breathe through their skin! Then there are the insects. They have neither lungs nor gills. They have an intricate network of tubes that runs throughout the body. These tubes are connected to holes in the insects' sides. Air simply passes into the network from the holes in the insects' sides and gets distributed throughout the body through the network of tubes!

Even plants have a "circulatory" system. They must get water from the roots to the rest of the plant. In addition, photosynthesis occurs mostly in a plant's leaves. Since *all* parts of the plant need food, and since the food for a plant is made in photosynthesis, there must be a way for plants to transport food from the leaves to the rest of the plant. To see part of a plant's "circulatory" system at work, perform the following experiment.

EXPERIMENT 14.5
Xylem

Supplies:

- A reasonably fresh white carnation (Almost all big supermarkets, as well as florists, sell them.)
- Two glasses
- Blue food coloring
- Red food coloring
- A knife
- Two spoons for stirring
- Eye protection such as goggles or safety glasses

Introduction: This experiment will show you part of the "circulatory" system of a plant at work.

<u>Procedure:</u>

1. Use the knife to cut about ½ an inch from the bottom of the carnation's stem. Then, split the stem in half lengthwise using the knife. **BE CAREFUL!!! CUT THE STEM, NOT YOURSELF!!!!** You should split the stem only about halfway up the flower.
2. Fill each glass ¾ of the way with water
3. Add a few drops of red food coloring to one glass and a few drops of blue to the other.
4. Stir them with different spoons.

5. The color of each solution in the glass should be deep - not pale. If the colors are pale, add more food coloring and stir until you get deep colors.
6. Place the flower in the glasses so one half of the stem soaks in the red water and the other half soaks in the blue water. See the drawing on the right.
7. The flower should be stable and stand on its own. If not, you can tape each half of the stem to its glass.
8. Leave the flower like this overnight.
9. Note what you see the next day. You might have to wait as long as two days to see a result.
10. Clean everything up.

Illustration by Megan Fruchte

When the experiment is complete, you will see the results of part of the carnation's "circulatory" system. Most plants have tubes running throughout the entire plant. One set of tubes, called **xylem** (zy' lum), transports water up from the roots to the rest of the parts of the plant. That's what caused the results of your experiment. Some of the water in the glasses was transported from the bottom of the carnation stem all the way up to the flower's bloom through the xylem. Plants have another system of tubes called **phloem** (floh' ehm). These tubes are responsible for carrying food from the leaves to the rest of the plant.

In the end, then, all organisms have transport mechanisms that allow nutrients and essential gases (like oxygen) to be distributed throughout the organism. This is necessary for satisfying the second criterion of life. The way this happens in *all* organisms is exceedingly complex, and it defies the very foundation of the hypothesis of evolution, which essentially states that all of life has been constructed based on chance. Whether we are talking about the "simple" transport mechanisms that exist in a single-celled creature, the "moderately complex" xylem and phloem in a plant, or the incredibly complex human circulatory system, the mechanisms required to satisfy just the second criterion of life show us that life is clearly beyond the reach of chance!

ON YOUR OWN

14.10 There are certain plants (called "bryophytes") that do not have xylem and phloem. Compared to plants that do have them, would you expect bryophytes to be larger or smaller?

ANSWERS TO THE "ON YOUR OWN" PROBLEMS

14.1 It is flowing <u>up</u> the leg. Remember, veins carry blood back to the heart. Thus, the blood is traveling toward the heart, which means up the leg. If it were flowing down the leg, it would be moving away from the heart.

14.2 Wherever you find living cells in the body, you will find <u>capillaries</u> very near. Cells need oxygen and nutrients. They cannot get them from the blood unless the blood is traveling in capillaries. Thus, wherever there are living cells, there will be capillaries nearby.

14.3 Remember, both sides of the heart work simultaneously. Thus, when the left atrium fills, the right atrium will fill as well. They also empty the blood into the ventricles at the same time. This means that when the left atrium is mostly empty, <u>the right atrium will also be mostly empty, and both ventricles (including the right ventricle) will be mostly full</u>.

14.4 As stated in the section, endothermic animals must have the most efficient heart, which is a four-chambered heart. This kind of heart separates oxygenated blood and deoxygenated blood. Since the animal in question has a heart that mixes both types of blood, it is not a four-chambered heart, and the animal is not endothermic. Thus, the animal is <u>ectothermic</u>.

14.5 Only <u>red blood cells</u> contain hemoglobin, so sickle-cell anemia must affect them.

14.6 Without enough blood platelets, the child's blood cannot clot properly. <u>Even the slightest injury can cause the child to bleed to death</u>. This happens very rarely, but if not caught, the child can bleed to death even as the result of a few bruises. This problem is called "alloimmune thrombocytopenia," and it occurs in about one out of every 1,000 births in the United States.

14.7 Remember what happens in emphysema. The alveoli grow large and merge, making larger alveoli. This results in poor oxygen transfer to the blood. Thus, <u>many small alveoli are better than a few large ones</u>.

14.8 <u>The bronchial tubes are affected by bronchitis</u>. You could have said the bronchioles or the primary bronchus as well. Bronchitis is the inflammation of tissue on the inside of the bronchial tubes. This causes swelling of the tissue, which makes less room for air to travel. Typically, neither primary bronchus is affected by bronchitis. Usually the smaller bronchial tubes are affected.

14.9 The trachea is below the vocal cords. If air passes in and out of the hole, <u>the air never passes over the vocal cords</u>. Without air to vibrate the vocal cords, no sound will be produced.

14.10 <u>Bryophytes are small compared to other plants</u>. Without xylem and phloem, there is no way to transport nutrients. Thus, the plant has to be small and thin so that all cells are very near the oxygen in the air and the water that drips on the plant. Mosses, for example, are bryophytes.

STUDY GUIDE FOR MODULE #14

1. Define the following terms:

a. Veins
b. Arteries
c. Capillaries

2. What purpose do the lungs serve?

3. What purpose does the heart serve?

4. How many chambers are in a human heart? Name them.

5. What is special about a four-chambered heart as compared to a three-chambered heart or a two-chambered heart?

6. In what kind of blood vessels does the blood transfer oxygen to the cells and pick up wastes?

7. When deoxygenated blood is returning to the heart, into what chamber does it enter the heart?

8. After entering the heart, the deoxygenated blood is then transferred to a second chamber. What chamber is that?

9. When deoxygenated blood leaves the heart, where does it go?

10. When oxygenated blood comes into the heart, what chamber does it fill?

11. Once the oxygenated blood is back in the heart, it is then transferred to another chamber. What chamber is that?

12. When oxygenated blood leaves the heart, through what artery does it travel first?

13. Most veins carry what kind of blood (oxygenated or deoxygenated)? Are there any exceptions to this general rule?

14. Name the three types of blood cells and their main job in the blood.

15. What makes up more than half of your blood?

16. What is hemoglobin and where is it found?

17. Where are blood cells produced?

18. What are alveoli? What happens in the alveoli?

19. What kind of blood vessels surround the alveoli?

20. Where are bronchial tubes found, and what travels in them?

21. When you inhale, air travels through the following parts of the respiratory system:

pharynx, nasal cavity, trachea, larynx, alveoli, bronchial tubes

List these parts in the order in which inhaled air passes through them.

22. Which of the parts listed in the question above contains the vocal cords?

23. What controls the volume of the sound produced by the vocal cords? What controls the pitch of the sound produced?

24. A sample of fluid is taken from a tube within a plant. If it is mostly water, which was it taken from: a xylem or phloem tube?

Anatomy professor, Dr. Smith, doesn't quite understand the concept behind Valentine's Day.

Cartoon by Speartoons

MODULE #15: The Human Lymphatic, Endocrine, and Urinary Systems

Introduction

In this module, I want to discuss three systems in the human body that help maintain a balanced condition of health. The **lymphatic** (lim fa' tik) **system** removes excess fluid from your body's tissues and returns it to the bloodstream. At the same time, it cleans the fluid of microorganisms and other contaminants that can cause health problems. The **endocrine** (en' doh krin) **system** produces **hormones** that regulate several of the chemical processes occurring in your body. The **urinary system** controls and regulates the balance of chemicals in your blood.

Although I have lumped these three systems into one module, do not think they are less important than the other systems of the body. Without even one of these systems working properly, you would die in a very short time. Indeed, a full study of human anatomy and physiology would require many pages devoted to each of these systems. However, in this course, I want to give you just a brief overview of human anatomy without a lot of chemical details. Understanding these three systems requires a great deal of chemistry knowledge. Thus, since I cannot go into chemistry in this course, I cannot spend a lot of time on any of these systems.

There is one other reason I want to touch on these systems only briefly. The next module is the final one of the course. In that module, I want to discuss the most amazing aspect of the human body: its nervous system. Since the nervous system is so incredibly complex and interesting, I want to spend a lot of time on it. Thus, you will find that this module is a little short, which will allow me to make the final module of the course a bit longer, so as to really concentrate on the human nervous system.

The Lymphatic System

Did you know that there are vessels in your body other than those that carry blood? Indeed, there is a vast network of **lymph** (limf) **vessels** covering most of your body. What do these vessels carry? They carry the watery fluid found in between your body's cells. This clear fluid, called **interstitial** (in ter stish' uhl) **fluid**, leaks out of the capillaries and passes in and out of cells, facilitating the exchange of gases and nutrients between the cells and the blood. This fluid must ultimately be returned to the blood, but before that happens, it must be collected and cleaned. That's the job of your lymphatic system.

Interestingly enough, once the interstitial fluid is collected by the lymphatic system, it is no longer called "interstitial fluid." Instead, it is called **lymph**. What's the difference between interstitial fluid and lymph? Not much, really. When the fluid is still between your cells, it is interstitial fluid. When it enters your lymphatic system, it is called lymph. Why? Well, think about a person walking down the street. When he is walking, he is a pedestrian. However, suppose he walks to a bus stop, waits, and then gets on a bus. At that point, he is no longer a pedestrian. He is a passenger. The person has not changed, but what we call him has. It's the same thing with interstitial fluid. Once it gets in the lymphatic system, it hasn't changed substantially, but it is now called "lymph."

You can think of your lymphatic system as the "drainage system" of your body. Just as a drainage system is very important to a city, the lymphatic system is very important to your body. Without it, tissues would become waterlogged and full of toxic chemicals and pathogenic organisms. So the lymphatic system drains the interstitial fluid from your tissues, cleans it, and ultimately returns it to the blood. In addition, the lymphatic system acts as an "early warning" system, telling your body about potential disease-causing situations. Since the lymphatic system carries the fluid that has just been in and out of your body's cells, it is well-equipped to detect potential threats to your body.

A schematic illustration of the body's lymphatic system is given below. Don't worry; you will not be required to memorize its various parts. I just want to show it to you in order to give you an idea of its complexity.

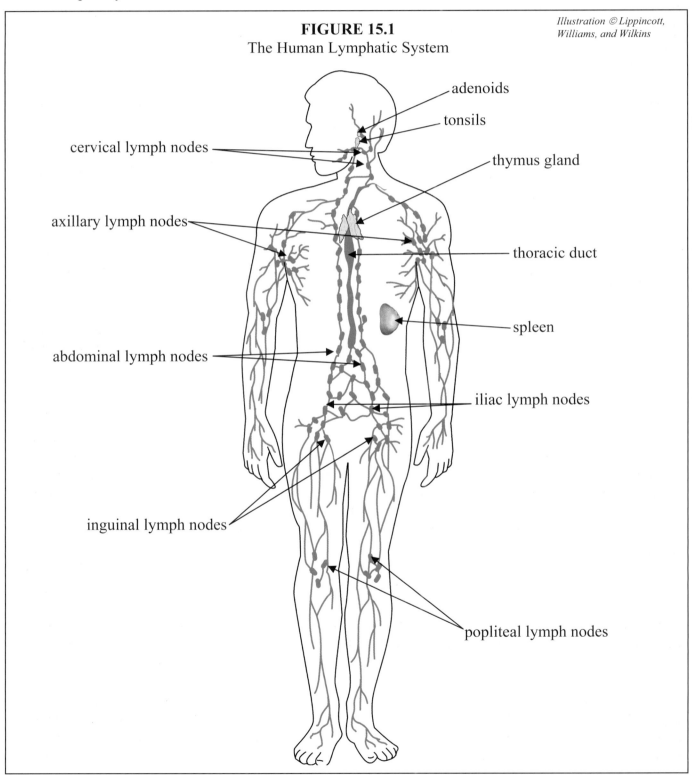

FIGURE 15.1
The Human Lymphatic System

Illustration © Lippincott, Williams, and Wilkins

adenoids

tonsils

cervical lymph nodes

thymus gland

axillary lymph nodes

thoracic duct

spleen

abdominal lymph nodes

iliac lymph nodes

inguinal lymph nodes

popliteal lymph nodes

The green lines in the figure represent the major lymph vessels in the body. There are many, many more lymph vessels than what are shown. These are simply the major ones. The network of lymph vessels is essentially the same size and scope as the network of arteries and veins in the body. After all, the lymph vessels must collect and clean the fluids surrounding all the cells in the body. In most cases, then, wherever you find capillaries, you will find lymph vessels. Unlike capillaries, however, lymph vessels begin as "dead end" vessels. Remember, in capillaries the blood comes in from an artery and goes out a vein. Thus, the capillaries provide a way in for the blood and a way out. Lymph vessels, however, are simply there to collect excess fluid. Thus, they are best described as "leaky dead ends." The end of a lymph vessel is closed, but the cells that form the vessel overlap to form "flaps" that allow interstitial fluid to leak inside. Once inside, the fluid makes its way back to where it is cleaned and put back into the blood supply. Figure 15.2 illustrates how this works.

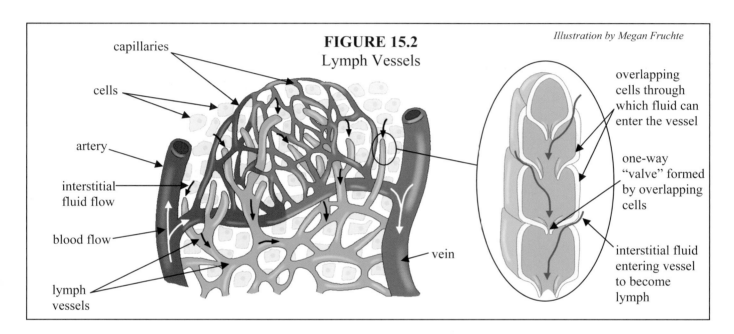

FIGURE 15.2
Lymph Vessels

Illustration by Megan Fruchte

capillaries

cells

artery

interstitial fluid flow

blood flow

lymph vessels

vein

overlapping cells through which fluid can enter the vessel

one-way "valve" formed by overlapping cells

interstitial fluid entering vessel to become lymph

Now you might wonder *how* lymph travels through the lymph vessels and back into the blood. Remember, blood travels through your blood vessels because your heart pumps it. Is there a separate pump for lymph? No, there is not. Does the heart pump it, then? No, the heart pumps only blood. How, then, is lymph able to travel throughout the lymphatic system? Well, it turns out that the lymph vessels are positioned in the body so that when certain muscles contract, the lymph vessels are squeezed. This causes a gentle flow of lymph through the lymphatic system. To keep the lymph flowing in the right direction, there are one-way "valves" that open when the lymph is flowing in the right direction and close to prevent it from flowing backward. That's pretty ingenious, isn't it? Rather than making another "heart" for the lymphatic system, God simply designed the lymph vessels to be in the right place so muscular contractions and one-way valves can govern the flow of lymph. That allows the body to use the motion of muscles (which is done for other purposes) to be used to also power the flow of lymph. What an efficient idea! Do you think some random process like evolution could come up with something so ingenious?

The green "blobs" attached to the lymph vessels in Figure 15.1 are called **lymph nodes**. These are the "filters" where the lymph is cleaned before it is returned to the blood. I will discuss the lymph nodes in greater detail in the next section of this module. For right now, just be aware that they help clean the lymph traveling through the lymphatic system. Notice that the nodes are concentrated in certain regions. There are several nodes (the "axillary nodes") near the armpits, others (the "cervical nodes") near the neck, etc. Often when a doctor is trying to determine the nature of an illness, he or she will check these areas for swollen lymph nodes. If the doctor notices swollen nodes in those areas, it indicates that those nodes are fighting an infection.

In addition to the lymph nodes and the lymph vessels, there are other lymphatic tissues to consider. The **spleen**, for example, contains many white blood cells. They grow and mature in the spleen, and as blood passes through the spleen, the white blood cells clean it of pathogens, foreign matter, and dead tissue. Remember, cells in your body and blood die all the time. This dead tissue needs to be removed from the bloodstream, and the white blood cells in the spleen are a part of that process. Interestingly enough, the spleen also acts as a "storehouse" for oxygen-rich blood. When the body is in extreme need of extra oxygen (during times of blood loss or very heavy exercise, for example), the spleen will contract and release its reserve of oxygen-rich blood.

The **tonsils** and **adenoids** form a protective ring around the throat. They work together to produce and release antibodies that attack pathogens entering your body through your mouth or nose. It turns out that the actions of your tonsils and adenoids are most important in your first year of life. As you get older, you can lose your tonsils with no increased risk of sickness. As a result, if your tonsils themselves get infected, they are often removed.

The **thymus gland** is still a bit of a puzzle to scientists. It definitely has lymphatic functions but it also has endocrine functions, which you will learn about later. First, let me define the term **gland**, which is probably new to you.

Gland – A group of cells that prepare and release a chemical for use by the body

You will hear a lot more about glands when I discuss the endocrine system. When you are young, your thymus gland is a place where certain white blood cells mature. They travel from the bone marrow to the thymus gland and actually "learn" how to do their job while they are there. As you mature, however, that function becomes less important. The thymus's endocrine function, which I will discuss in a later section, remains important throughout your life. It is interesting to note that at one time, the thymus was thought to be a useless leftover of the evolutionary process that supposedly created human beings. Of course, like most evolutionary ideas, this was abandoned as scientists learned more about the human body. We now know that far from being useless, the thymus gland is a very important part of the lymphatic system.

ON YOUR OWN

15.1 A chemist hands you two vials of a liquid. The chemist says that the liquids are identical in every way. However, the first vial contains lymph while the second vial does not. From where was the fluid in the first vial taken? From where was the fluid in the second vial taken?

15.2 The spleen can be surgically removed from a person, usually because it has been injured in a serious accident. Removing it will not kill or seriously harm the person. If this happens, what can you predict about the person's ability to fight off disease and infection?

15.3 A person's left axillary lymph nodes are swollen. Using Figure 15.1 as a guide, predict where the person is (most likely) infected.

Lymph Nodes

Scattered along the lymph vessels throughout the lymphatic system are small, bean-shaped organs called lymph nodes. As I mentioned in the previous section, the lymph that travels through the lymphatic vessels gets cleaned at these nodes. How does it get cleaned? Well, there is a complex "filtration" system in every lymph node. This system identifies the "bad" chemicals and organisms in the lymph and traps them, allowing the clean lymph to travel back to the bloodstream.

This filtration system is incredibly complex and well designed. It is so complex that there is no way I can tell you the details of how it works. You must have a lot of chemistry background before you can hope to understand how the lymph nodes really work. However, I would like to point out the general features, just so you get a feeling for what's involved. To get started, then, the following figure is a simplified illustration of a lymph node.

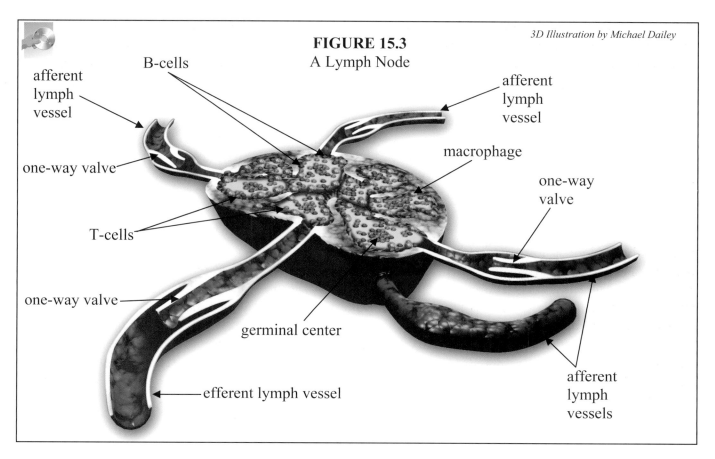

FIGURE 15.3
A Lymph Node

3D Illustration by Michael Dailey

B-cells

afferent lymph vessel

afferent lymph vessel

macrophage

one-way valve

one-way valve

T-cells

one-way valve

germinal center

afferent lymph vessels

efferent lymph vessel

The first thing you should notice about the lymph node is that several lymph vessels (called **afferent lymph vessels**) feed into it, but only one vessel (the **efferent lymph vessel**) leads out. Now if you think about it, this should make sense. After all, there are many, many tiny lymph vessels that collect interstitial fluid throughout the body. Those vessels must combine at some point into a larger vessel that will eventually dump the cleaned lymph back into the bloodstream. A lymph node, then, acts not only as a filtration system, but also a transfer station, where many vessels combine their fluid into a larger vessel. It is likely that the efferent lymph vessel leading out of one lymph node will eventually lead into another lymph node as an afferent vessel. This means that lymph usually travels through more than one lymph node (and therefore gets filtered more than once) before getting dumped back into the bloodstream.

The figure gives you another view of the one-way valves found in the lymph vessels. Notice that the valves can tell you the direction of lymph flow in the lymph vessels. Do you see that all the valves in the afferent lymph vessels are pointed toward the lymph node? That's because the lymph in those vessels travels that way. Notice that the valve in the efferent lymph vessel is pointed away from the lymph node. Once again, this ensures that the lymph travels in the proper direction. Similar one-way valves can be found in veins to ensure that blood flowing in the veins always flows toward the heart and never away from it.

The cleaning power of lymph nodes comes from the white blood cells. White blood cells found in the lymph system are called **lymphocytes** (limf' oh syts). There are several different kinds of lymphocytes, each of which performs different tasks in the lymphatic system. For example, **B-cells** produce antibodies that attack specific disease-causing microorganisms. **T-cells**, on the other hand, attack microorganisms directly. You can think about B-cells and T-cells this way: B-cells are "archers" that shoot their enemies with arrows (antibodies) from a distance, while T-cells are "swordsmen" that attack the enemy in "hand to hand" combat. Another kind of white blood cell (which is not a lymphocyte) is the **macrophage** (mak' roh fayj). Macrophage cells scavenge the lymph, eating bacteria and other debris that has been targeted by the action of the lymphocytes.

Not only do the lymph nodes serve as transfer stations and filtering centers, but they also serve as a supply station for white blood cells that can travel throughout the body. When an infection is detected by the lymph nodes, the **germinal centers** release lymphocytes. These cells mature, and some of them stay in the lymph nodes to help fight the infection. Others, however, get transferred into the bloodstream so they can travel to the source of the infection and try to destroy it there. Once a lymphocyte leaves the blood to fight an infection in the body's tissue, it is no longer called a lymphocyte. It is called a "plasma cell." Not all lymphocytes in the blood vessels come from the lymph nodes. Others come from the spleen, tonsils, and thymus gland. Thus, the lymph nodes are just one source of white blood cells.

One of the most remarkable aspects of the body's lymphatic system is that it has a "memory" of the infections it has fought. Remember, one of the weapons the lymphatic system has at its disposal is the B-cell. B-cells produce antibodies that fight specific infections. Well, when B-cells produce antibodies, they also produce **memory B-cells**. These memory cells are configured to start producing the same antibody again the moment the same infection is detected. This allows the lymphatic system to react much more quickly if the body is attacked again by the same invader.

The fact that our lymph system can "remember" a previous infection is the basis of one of the greatest achievements in medicine: the **vaccine**.

Vaccine – A weakened or inactive version of a pathogen that stimulates the body's production of antibodies that can destroy the pathogen

When a person is infected by most pathogens, the only way to rid the person of that pathogen is for the body to make a specific antibody that will aid in its destruction. In order to do this, the lymphatic system must sample the pathogen, and then its B-cells can start the process of producing an antibody that will be effective against it. The body can produce antibodies against many, many different pathogens this way, but the sampling and processing takes time. Some pathogens are so fast-acting that the body cannot produce antibodies before it is overwhelmed. As a result, the disease kills or permanently harms the person.

There are two basic types of vaccines that are intended to avoid this situation. The first type contains a weakened form of the pathogen itself. In this kind of vaccine, the pathogen has been weakened so that it cannot overtake your body's immune system. As a result, your lymph system recognizes it, makes the antibodies to kill it, and then makes the memory B-cells to "remember" the infection in case the organism attacks again. Since the pathogen is weakened, your body's immune system will destroy it before it can overtake your body. Thus, even though the vaccine actually contains a disease-causing pathogen, the vaccine is safe because the pathogen is so weak that your immune system will destroy it.

The other type of vaccine contains a human-made chemical that makes your body react the same as if a certain pathogen has entered it. This type of vaccine, then, "mimics" a real pathogen, causing your lymph system to react and produce antibodies as well as memory B-cells. Regardless of the type of vaccine, the effect is the same. The vaccine causes your body to react as if it is being infected. It then forms B-cells that produce antibodies and memory B-cells that remember how to produce those antibodies. As a result, your lymph system becomes "primed" to fight off a real infection if one should actually happen.

Think about what this means. A vaccine is *not* a cure for a disease. You can't take the vaccine *after* you have gotten sick. That's not how it works. A vaccine must be taken *before* you get sick. The vaccine then "primes" the lymphatic system for action in case the *real* pathogen ever infects your body. Thus, the act of giving someone a vaccine is often called **immunization** because it makes a person immune to the disease. This name actually gives a false notion, however. There is a small percentage of people (usually less than 2 to 5 percent, depending on the specific vaccine) that will not respond to a vaccine. As a result, their lymphatic systems never get "primed" for an attack. If these people are exposed to the real pathogen, they will, most likely, still get sick. A better way of thinking about it, then, is that a vaccine provides immunization for the vast majority of people, but not everyone. Some vaccines also require "booster shots" to maintain immunity.

The term "vaccine" was introduced by British physician Edward Jenner in 1796. There were many people in his area dying of smallpox. He noticed that cowpox, a similar sickness that struck cows, is a relatively mild disease in humans. Furthermore, people who got cowpox did not get smallpox. Thus, he injected humans with cowpox and, since smallpox and cowpox are very similar, their immune systems developed antibodies that would kill both. Thus, as long as someone was injected with cowpox *before* he or she got smallpox, the person was very likely to be immune to the effects of smallpox. Later on, a smallpox vaccine was developed, and it was so effective that currently, the only place you can find the smallpox virus is in a laboratory. The vaccine actually wiped smallpox from the face of the planet!

The concept was improved upon significantly by the great Louis Pasteur. In 1885, he developed a vaccine against rabies. In 1954, perhaps the world's most widely used vaccine was invented: the polio vaccine. Developed by the American scientist Jonas Salk, this vaccine protected children against one of the most devastating childhood diseases. This disease, also called "infantile paralysis," affects the nerves that control muscle movement. As a result, the disease slowly takes away the patient's ability to move. Albert Sabin actually improved the vaccine later (1961). Thanks to the Salk and Sabin vaccines, polio has been nearly eliminated in most parts of the world.

There is a movement afoot these days that says vaccines are bad for you. After all, proponents say, a vaccine injects a pathogen into your body! This is just like getting infected by the pathogen. In addition, the antibodies whose production it stimulates stay in your body forever. Thus, your body "remembers" the infection, and you will always have poorer health as a result. Nothing could be further from the truth! Since the pathogen in a vaccine is either weakened or a chemical mimic, it is not like getting infected by the real thing. Thus, the risk is minimal and the benefits are enormous. One of the best ways to see this is to look at the following graphs.

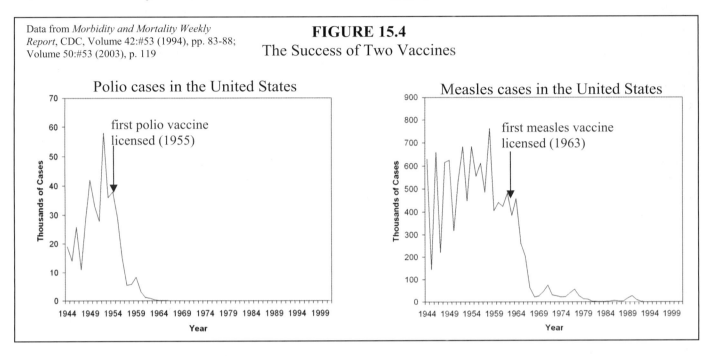

Data from *Morbidity and Mortality Weekly Report*, CDC, Volume 42:#53 (1994), pp. 83-88; Volume 50:#53 (2003), p. 119

FIGURE 15.4
The Success of Two Vaccines

These two graphs show you the number of people infected by polio and measles in the United States. Notice that for polio, the disease rate rose in a shaky but steady fashion from 1944 to 1952. Then there was a slight (34 percent) decrease in the disease rate from 1953 to 1955. Then, from 1955 to 1957, there was a *dramatic* decrease (80 percent) in the disease rate. What explains these drops in disease rate? Well, notice that the first polio vaccine was licensed in 1955. The dramatic decrease in the disease rate, then, came right after the polio vaccine was used on the general public. What about the smaller decrease from 1953 to 1955? Well, the vaccine was developed in 1952 and tested shortly thereafter. For example, in 1954, it was tested in a double-blind study of 1.8 *million* children. The slight drop in disease rates prior to 1955, then, was most likely due to the testing of the polio vaccine.

Now look at the graph for measles. The story is similar. There is a slight decrease in the disease rate just prior to the licensing of the vaccine (during the testing phase) and then a *dramatic* decrease in the disease rate after the vaccine began being used on the general public. These data dramatically illustrate the effectiveness of vaccines in preventing disease.

There are some who try to claim that the decrease in the rates of polio, measles, and other vaccine-preventable diseases is due to the fact that as time went on, cities and town developed better sanitary practices. Thus, disease rates decreased not because of vaccination, but because people were getting rid of the pathogens that cause those diseases by keeping their food and surroundings cleaner. This is certainly true of some diseases, but the data in Figure 15.4 show this is not true for measles and polio. Note that the major reduction of polio cases came *much sooner* (almost 10 years) than did the major reduction in measles cases. If both were the result of better sanitation, you would expect both disease rates to decrease over the same time interval. Thus, the decreases in both polio and measles are tied directly to the use of the vaccines made to prevent them.

The safety of the standard vaccines has been adequately demonstrated as well. While there are side effects to any medicine (indeed, some suffer side effects from certain foods), the side effects of vaccines are rare – much more rare than the chance of serious harm from the disease the vaccines prevent. Before licensing, for example, all vaccines must go through three levels of double-blind studies to show they are safe. Even after the vaccine has been licensed, its effects are constantly monitored to make sure it is safe. If a vaccine is shown to have side effects that make it riskier than the chance of getting the disease itself, the vaccine is quickly removed from the list of standard vaccines a person should be given. This is why the American Academy of Pediatrics says, "vaccines are one of the safest forms of medicine ever developed" (Samuel L. Katz, representing the American Academy of Pediatrics testimony before the Committee on Government Reform, U.S. House of Representatives, August 3, 1999).

Now if you think about it for a moment, the concept of a vaccine is, in fact, a great testament to God's power and majesty. After 3,000 years of medical science, human beings cannot fight pathogens as efficiently as God's creation (the human body) can. Thus, to protect ourselves, we simply stimulate the body to do what God designed it to do in the first place. In the case of vaccines then, human science gives the body a little push, and the body does the rest.

ON YOUR OWN

15.4 If antibodies are ineffective against a pathogen, what other defenses can the lymph nodes use against it?

15.5 For a given lymph node, which carries more lymph: an afferent lymph vessel or the efferent lymph vessel?

Tears

Before I move on to the urinary system, I want to spend a few moments talking about tears. The body produces tears in the **lacrimal** (lak' rih muhl) **glands**, which are located on the top and side of each eyeball. Tears run from the lacrimal glands through tiny tubes called **tear ducts** and then flow across the eyes. They are not a part of the lymphatic system, however. They are a part of the eye. I want to discuss them here because tears do contain infection-fighting chemicals that protect the eye, so they perform at least one function similar to the lymphatic system. In addition, when I discuss the eye, I will be concentrating on how the nervous system receives and interprets what the eye detects, so I will not have time to discuss tears then.

You already have experience with tears, because at one time or another, you have cried. The first thing you must realize, however, is that your body produces tears continuously, even when you are not crying. These tears run across your eyes, lubricating them and covering them with an infection-fighting chemical. After running across the eyes, they are collected in ducts that then drain into the nasal cavity. When you cry, you are producing *excess* tears, and they overflow the duct that normally drains them. As a result, these excess tears fall down your cheeks, which is when people say that you are crying.

Why do we produce excess tears and cry? Well, you can explore one reason by performing the following experiment.

EXPERIMENT 15.1
Working Your Lacrimal Glands Too Hard

Supplies:

♦ Three onions (any size)
♦ A cutting knife (In this experiment, a dull knife works better than a sharp one!)
♦ A freezer
♦ A cutting board
♦ A sink in which you can cut

Introduction: In this experiment, you will cut onions under three different conditions to learn why cutting onions can make you cry.

Procedure:

1. Put one of the onions in the freezer. It needs to stay in there for at least 15 minutes.
2. If you are wearing contact lenses, remove them. Contact lenses reduce experiment's effect.
3. Put a second onion on the cutting board and begin cutting it into tiny pieces. Perhaps you can use them for cooking later. **BE CAREFUL!!!!!!!! KNIVES CAN BE DANGEROUS!**
4. Hold your head so your eyes are directly over the onions.
5. Continue cutting until you start crying.
6. Get rid of the onion pieces, either by throwing them away or putting them in a container for later use.
7. Clean the cutting board.
8. Wipe away all the tears and wait until you are no longer crying.
9. Put the cutting board (or something similar that will fit) in the sink and start the water running.
10. Cut the other onion that is still out. This time, however, make sure that the onion stays under the running water while you are cutting. Cut this onion up as much as you did the first, and hold your head in the same position relative to the onion.
11. Note whether or not you cry.
12. Once again, get rid of the onion pieces and clean the cutting board.
13. Once the third onion has been in the freezer for at least 15 minutes, pull it out of the freezer and begin cutting it. Put the cutting board in the same place you put it when you cut the first onion, and cut the onion much as you did the other two. In addition, hold your head in the same position relative to the onion.
14. Note whether or not you cry.
15. Clean up everything.

Did you cry when you cut the first onion? Most likely, you did. What about when you cut the second onion? Most likely, you did not cry. What about when you cut the third onion? People with very sensitive eyes might have cried, but most people will not have. How do we explain the results of this experiment? Well, onions have sulfur-based chemicals that are contained in tiny sacs in the onion's tissues. When you cut the first onion, those sacs "exploded," releasing the chemicals as tiny droplets in the air. When those droplets reached your eyes, a chemical reaction occurred, and your eyes were irritated. This caused your lacrimal glands to produce excess tears, making you cry. Your body interpreted the chemicals reaching your eyes as a possible harm to your health and, as a result, produced excess tears designed to wash the irritant out of the eyes and kill any potential invaders.

Why didn't you cry in the second part of the experiment? Well, when you cut the second onion, the sacs still "exploded," but the tiny droplets dissolved in the water coming from the faucet and thus never reached your eyes. As a result, your body had no reason to produce excess tears. You probably didn't cry in the third part of the experiment, either. That's because the low temperature of the freezer destroyed one of the main chemicals that causes the chemical reaction that irritates your eyes. As a result, the chemical hit your eyes, but the chemical reaction could not occur, and your eyes were therefore not irritated. So, one reason you cry is to flush irritants out of your eyes.

Of course, there is another reason you cry. Human eyes also release excess tears in response to strong emotional feelings. In other words, when you are sad, you cry. Amazingly enough, the tears you cry when your eyes are irritated (like what happened in the first part of the experiment) are chemically quite different from the tears you cry when you are upset! Tears produced by strong emotions contain chemicals that do not appear (to any great extent) in tears produced by eye irritants. These chemicals include manganese (a chemical depressant), leucine-enkephalin (a chemical that helps control pain), and the adrenocorticotrophic hormone (a chemical produced by bodies under stress). When you get rid of those chemicals by crying, the net effect is to *make you feel better.* By releasing those toxins, then, the tears serve to chemically and physically make you feel less depressed! Thus, it really is true that you tend to feel better after a good, long cry.

Interestingly enough, humans are the only organisms that cry as a result of emotion. This is, in actuality, a *real* problem for evolutionists. After all, an evolutionist is forced to assume that this property of human tears evolved in only the human race over a long time period. Think about it for a minute, though. What possible survival advantage is obtained by feeling better as a result of a good cry? The answer, of course, is none whatsoever. In fact, those who bottle up their emotions are usually more aggressive, which, according to evolutionary principles, should make them more fit to battle for survival. Thus, if anything, this particular feature of human chemistry is harmful to the species' ability to survive and would be thrown out by natural selection.

According to evolutionary theory, then, this trait should *never have evolved.* If, instead, we view the human body as a marvelously designed machine, we can assume that the emotional tears we shed are a gift from the Designer. Since He built in us the capacity for emotions, He also built in us the ability to deal with those emotions. One of those is the ability to sit down and have a good, long cry.

<u>The Urinary System</u>

Although there are a lot of other infection-fighting mechanisms in your body, I need to move on, so I want to discuss the urinary system. About half of a person's weight comes from water. It is everywhere in your body. Your cells have water inside them. The interstitial fluid picked up in the lymphatic system is mostly water. Indeed, blood plasma itself is more than 90 percent water. In addition, you drink a lot of water. Even if you don't make a habit of drinking "plain old water," the liquids that you drink (juice, milk, soda pop, etc.) are mostly composed of water. As you learned in Module #11, the cells in your body also *produce* water through the burning of macronutrients.

How is all this water controlled in your body? Well, the amount of water you retain and the levels of many substances in that water are all controlled by your **urinary system**, which is illustrated in Figure 15.5. Compared to other systems you have studied so far, the urinary system might look relatively "simple." However, the tasks it performs are exceedingly complex!

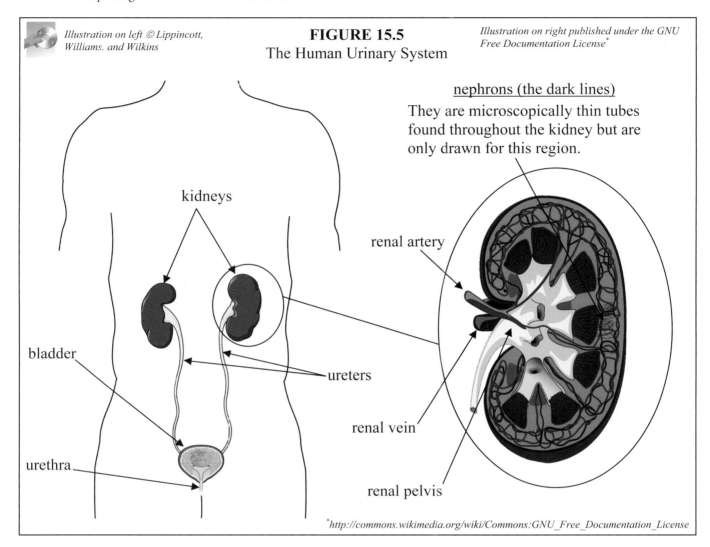

Illustration on left © Lippincott, Williams. and Wilkins

FIGURE 15.5
The Human Urinary System

*Illustration on right published under the GNU Free Documentation License**

nephrons (the dark lines)
They are microscopically thin tubes found throughout the kidney but are only drawn for this region.

kidneys

renal artery

bladder

ureters

renal vein

urethra

renal pelvis

*http://commons.wikimedia.org/wiki/Commons:GNU_Free_Documentation_License

Like the lymph nodes, the main task of the kidneys is to clean. Instead of cleaning lymph, however, the kidneys clean blood. This is important because the lymph system cannot clean the way the kidneys do. The lymph system cleans out organisms and chemicals it recognizes as disease-causing. The kidneys do something completely different. They clean out chemicals that are not dangerous to the body until they reach certain levels. Thus, the chemicals are not necessarily ones that cause disease. Instead, they are chemicals your body uses, but their levels in the blood must be monitored and maintained.

How do kidneys do their job? Each kidney is actually made up of about a million units called **nephrons** (nef' rons). Each nephron has a filter that empties into a tiny, curving tubule, and it is an individual, **urine**-making unit. Here's how it happens: The **renal artery** brings blood into the kidney. The blood supplies oxygen and nutrients to the cells of the kidneys and picks up the cells' waste products. It is important to note that the kidneys actually get much more blood than they need for their own cells. After all, they need to clean all the blood. In fact, *every twenty-five minutes,* your kidneys end up processing all the blood in your body!

In order to be cleaned, blood flows through a nephron, where it is first filtered. Most of what is in the blood plasma (all nutrients, wastes, and water, but not the blood proteins) is temporarily dumped into the nephron. Then, as this fluid flows through the tubule of the nephron, the cells that line the nephron *reabsorb* the proper amounts of nutrients and chemicals back into the blood. Excess chemicals are left behind in the nephron to become urine. Meanwhile, the proper amount of water is also reabsorbed from the nephron and put back into the blood.

The blood then leaves the kidney through the **renal vein** and travels back to the heart. Any water and chemicals that were not reabsorbed into the blood go from the nephrons into the **renal pelvis** and flow out of the kidney to the **ureter** (yur ee' ter). At this point, the mixture of water and chemicals is called urine. The urine travels through the ureter and is held in the **bladder**. Eventually, the bladder releases the urine it has stored, and the urine leaves the body through the **urethra** (yuh ree' thruh).

So if you think about how the kidneys clean the blood, they first dump *everything* (except for the proteins and cells) into a nephron, and the nephron then reabsorbs exactly what the blood needs. Everything left over is then discarded as urine. This is much like the way I clean out a messy desk drawer. Instead of picking through the drawer and determining what should stay and what should go, I typically dump *all the contents* of the drawer onto a table, and then I sift through them, putting the items I want to keep back into the desk drawer. Once I have found all the items I want to keep, I throw away any objects still left on the table.

Now if you think about it, the job the kidneys do is truly amazing. They filter the blood, and then reabsorb the water and chemicals back into the blood in just the right amounts. How in the world do they do that? Well, I can't give you all the details, because in order to understand it at even a basic level, you need at least a year of a solid high school chemistry course. However, I can give you an *idea* of how the kidneys work by having you perform the following experiment.

EXPERIMENT 15.2
A Model of Kidney Function

Supplies:

♦ A tea bag
♦ Three small glasses (like juice glasses)
♦ A paper towel
♦ A coffee filter
♦ A funnel
♦ Scissors
♦ A tea kettle or pot
♦ A stove
♦ A spoon for stirring
♦ A pile of two to three books (The pile needs to be at least ¾ as high as one of the glasses.)
♦ Eye protection such as safety glasses or goggles

Introduction: This experiment simulates how the kidney cleans your blood.

Procedure:

1. Start a pot or kettle of water boiling. You only need about a cup of water in the end.
2. Use the scissors to cut open the tea bag, spilling the contents into one of the small glasses.

3. Once the water has boiled, remove it from the heat and let it cool for 1 minute.
4. **Carefully** pour the hot water into the glass that contains the contents of the tea bag. **BE CAREFUL – THE WATER IS HOT!!!!!**
5. Use the spoon to stir the hot water with the contents of the tea bag. Do this for a while, so the water becomes a nice deep-brown color. Do not try to dissolve all of the contents of the tea bag. That would be VERY hard. Just make the water brown.
6. Place a coffee filter into the funnel so you can pour something into the filter. You may have to hold it there. Use another person to help if necessary.
7. Hold the filter/funnel combination over another one of the small glasses.
8. Pick up the glass with the water/tea leaves. **BE CAREFUL – IT IS PROBABLY STILL HOT.** You can wait for it to cool if it is too hot right now.
9. Carefully pour the solution in the glass so it fills the coffee filter. Do this slowly, so that the water filling the coffee filter never rises above either the top of the funnel or the top of the filter paper. The water will pass through the coffee filter and into the funnel. Then, it will fall down the funnel into the glass underneath.
10. Once most of the water has drained through the filter paper and funnel, put the filter paper/funnel system aside and look at the solution in the glass that was underneath. Note its appearance.
11. Now set the glass with the solution in it on the top of the pile of books.
12. Fold the paper towel in half lengthwise.
13. Repeat step #12 twice. Now you should have a long, thin paper towel.
14. Put one end of the long, thin paper towel into the solution in the glass so the end touches the bottom of the glass.
15. Bend the other end of the paper towel and position the remaining empty glass so the end of the paper towel is in that glass. DO NOT put the remaining glass on the pile of books. The glass with tea needs to be higher than the remaining glass. In the end, then, you should have two glasses: one with a brown solution in it sitting on the pile of books and one empty glass sitting on the table or counter next to the pile of books. The long, thin paper towel should have an end in both glasses, forming a "bridge" between the two.
16. Wait for an hour or so.
17. Look in the glass that was empty. Note what you see.
18. Dump the tea grounds that are in the filter into the solution that is now in the glass sitting on the table or counter.
19. Throw the paper towel in the trash.
20. Clean everything up.

What did you see in step 10? If everything went well, you should have seen that after passing through the filter paper, the tea you made was a clear brown solution with no tea leaves floating in it. Why? Well, the filter paper has tiny holes in it. The water and whatever is dissolved in it passed through those holes. The tea leaves floating in the tea, however, were too big to pass through the holes. Thus, they were stopped by the filter paper. That's the first thing that your kidneys do to your blood. They filter it, stopping any large items (such as cells and proteins) floating in it. In your experiment, then, the tea leaves floating in your tea represented the cells and proteins floating in the blood. The kidneys keep those cells from going into the nephron, while allowing everything else to pass. The clear fluid you saw in the second glass, then, represented the fluid that enters a nephron.

What did you see in step 17 of the experiment? If things worked out right, you should have seen that the empty glass ended up with a little tea in it. The tea in that glass, however, should have been a *lot* lighter than the original tea. You see, the paper towel absorbed both the water and the tea.

Because of a process a bit too difficult to explain here, the water and tea began to travel along the paper towel. The paper towel ended up allowing some of the water and some of the tea to pass to the third glass. More water than tea passed through, however, so the tea in the third glass was weaker than the tea in the second glass. What was left in the paper towel, then, was like what is left in the kidney once the fluid passes through the nephron. It was waste, which is why you threw it away. What ended up in the third glass represented the fluid that the kidney would put back into the blood – it had weaker levels of the chemicals that were initially too high.

When you mixed the tea leaves in the filter paper with the solution in the third glass, you were simulating what your kidney ultimately does to the blood that leaves by the renal vein. It takes the things held back by the filter (the cells and proteins) and adds them to the mixture of water and chemicals that were absorbed by the nephron. That mixture, then, represented the blood after it had passed all the way through the kidney. The kidney is *significantly* more complicated, but the basic process that happens is the same: The nephron filters the blood, holding back the cells and proteins. The resulting fluid flowing into the nephron contains both beneficial chemicals and wastes. The nephron processes that fluid, returning the right amounts of beneficial chemicals to the blood and leaving the wastes (and the excess beneficial chemicals) to be excreted as urine.

Now there are many differences between what the system in your experiment did and what a real kidney does. First of all, the kidneys process a *lot* more water. In the average adult, the kidneys pull about 40 gallons of water from the blood each day. They end up putting back 99 percent of that water (unlike the paper towel in your experiment), so the average amount of urine an adult produces is about one quart per day. Also, the nephrons reabsorb the chemicals from the filtered fluid in a very sophisticated way so as to separate the chemicals and decide how much of each gets back into the blood. This keeps the amount of water, as well as the level of each chemical in your blood, very constant.

Medical researchers have been able to produce an artificial kidney that can work in place of a real kidney. Like all marvels of technology, however, the abilities of an artificial kidney pale in comparison to a *real* kidney. The artificial kidney is much less efficient and does a significantly poorer job of cleaning the blood than a real kidney. It is also *much* bigger than a real kidney. As is always the case, even the best scientists and engineers alive today cannot make anything that comes close to the efficiency, compactness, and ability of the marvelous things that God designed in us!

When a sick person uses an artificial kidney, we say that the person is on **dialysis** (dye al' uh sis). In one type of dialysis, blood is taken from a vein and routed into a machine that attempts to filter and clean the blood as does a real kidney. Typically, people on dialysis use the artificial kidney for a set amount of time on a regular schedule, often three times a week for several hours. Most patients do it either while they wait for an injured kidney to heal or while they wait for a kidney transplant. In a kidney transplant, the patient's non-functioning kidney is replaced with a working kidney from someone else's body.

ON YOUR OWN

15.6 Suppose a person produces three quarts of urine each day. What can you conclude about the drinking habits of that person?

15.7 The bladder is not really an essential part of the urinary system, but you should be glad it is there. Why?

The Endocrine System

Have you ever heard the term **hormone**? If you follow professional sports, you've probably heard about problems with "steroids." Well, a steroid is an example of a hormone.

Hormone – A chemical messenger released into the bloodstream that sends signals to distant cells, causing them to change their behavior in specific ways

The word "hormone" comes from the Greek word *hormao*, which means "I excite." There is a good reason for that. Hormones excite specific cells to behave in specific ways.

Hormones are released by endocrine glands that are scattered throughout the body. Trying to get a complete picture of this complicated system is extremely difficult. There are more than 200 identified hormones in the human body, and more are being discovered. They are each very specific, targeting certain types of cells in certain ways. One author has suggested that trying to understand the endocrine system in detail is comparable to memorizing all the train, plane, and bus schedules serving New York City.

As a result, I do not want to give you a detailed view of the endocrine system. Indeed, even a rough understanding of its details requires several years of college-level chemistry. Nevertheless, I would like to discuss some of the major endocrine glands and some of what their hormones do, so you can get a basic idea of this amazing control system in your body. The figure below illustrates the placement of some of the most important endocrine glands in the body.

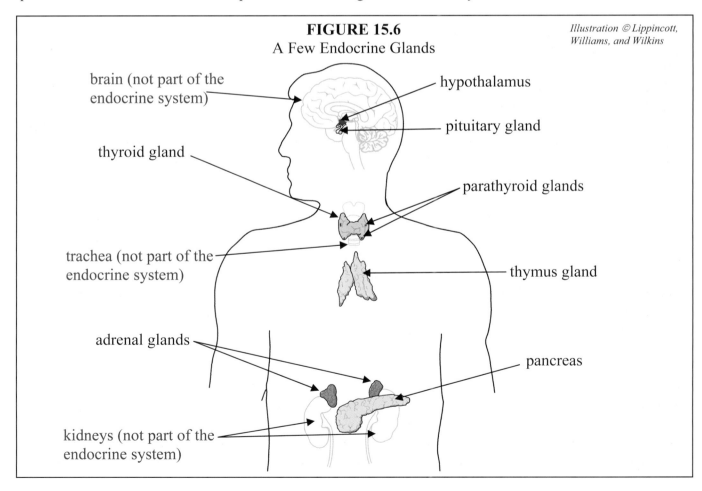

FIGURE 15.6
A Few Endocrine Glands

Illustration © Lippincott, Williams, and Wilkins

brain (not part of the endocrine system)

hypothalamus

pituitary gland

thyroid gland

parathyroid glands

trachea (not part of the endocrine system)

thymus gland

adrenal glands

pancreas

kidneys (not part of the endocrine system)

The **hypothalamus** (hi poh thal' uh mus) is one of the main regulators of the endocrine system. It is part of the lower brain and makes up less than 1 percent of the brain's total volume. Despite the fact that it is small, it influences a wide range of body functions. It regulates thirst, hunger, and body temperature. It also helps initiate the "fight or flight" responses such as the fast heart rate and increased blood flow that occur when you are frightened or angry. Its function in the endocrine system is to control the **pituitary** (pih too' uh tuh ree) **gland**, which is often referred to as the "master endocrine gland."

The pituitary gland sits right below the hypothalamus in the brain. It, too, is very small (about the size of a pea), but its effects on the body are incredible. It is referred to as the "master endocrine gland" because the hormones it makes and puts into the bloodstream control many other endocrine glands in the body. It produces and releases at least 10 separate hormones. I say "at least" because those are the ones that scientists have identified. There are probably more that just haven't been discovered yet. Some of these hormones specifically control other endocrine glands, while others directly affect bodily processes.

Here are a few examples of the pituitary hormones that directly affect processes in the body: The pituitary gland makes and releases human growth hormone (HGH), which is essential for the proper development of the skeleton. Another hormone made by the pituitary gland, endorphin, is a natural pain reliever. When the body is stressed, the pituitary gland releases endorphins to reduce the effects of pain. Another important hormone made and released by the pituitary gland is the antidiuretic (an tye dye' uh reh' tik) hormone (ADH). This hormone controls the amount of water reabsorbed by the nephrons in the kidneys, regulating the amount of water retained in the body.

Being the "master endocrine gland," the pituitary also controls other endocrine glands. For example, the pituitary gland produces the "thyroid stimulating hormone," which is often called TSH. This hormone controls the activity of the **thyroid gland**. The main thing the thyroid gland does is affect the basal metabolic rate. It does this by producing a hormone, thyroxine (thy rok' sin), that speeds up the rate at which cells burn macronutrients. The body is very sensitive to thyroid gland activity. If your thyroid produces too many hormones, you are said to have "hyperthyroidism." This results in a very high metabolism and a high heart rate. The opposite condition, "hypothyroidism," occurs when the thyroid produces too few hormones. People with this condition are lethargic, tire easily, and tend toward being overweight.

I want to stop here and illustrate the complex nature of the endocrine system and why it is so difficult to learn and understand. Remember, the hypothalamus controls the pituitary gland. But the pituitary gland controls other endocrine glands. In the end, then, the endocrine system is a multi-leveled control system. Let's look at the thyroid gland as an example. The hypothalamus receives information from the brain indicating that the body is not getting enough energy. Thus, it stimulates the pituitary gland, which releases TSH. The TSH then stimulates the thyroid into producing its hormones, which results in increased metabolism! Now *that's* complicated.

The **parathyroid glands** are tiny glands on the edges of the thyroid gland. Most people have four of them, but some have up to eight. Their main job is to regulate the level of calcium in the body. You probably know that you need calcium to build strong bones. However, you may not know that calcium is also critically important for your nerves and muscles to work properly. Thus, your body needs to constantly monitor the level of calcium in the blood. If the calcium levels get too low, the parathyroid glands release the parathyroid hormone, which stimulates certain cells to break down your bones. Why in the world would your body want to do that? Well, your bones have a lot of calcium in them, and if it is a choice between strong bones or a working nervous and muscular system, the body will sacrifice the bones in order to keep the other two systems working. This is why it is so important to get plenty of calcium from your diet. If you do not, your body will start getting it from your bones, making your bones weaker and easier to break.

The parathyroid glands allow me to illustrate something else. Often, the endocrine system has hormones that work toward opposite goals. For example, the thyroid gland also produces a hormone called calcitonin (kal sih toh' nin). Its job is to lower the calcium levels in the blood. If *too much* calcium is in the blood, the thyroid releases calcitonin, which actually reduces the amount of calcium absorbed from your food while at the same time reducing the activity of the cells that break down your bones. Because they work "against" each other, the parathyroid hormone and calcitonin are often called **antagonists**. Of course, they don't really work against each other. They just work at different times. When calcium levels are low, the parathyroid hormone is released so your body can get the calcium it needs from your bones. When calcium levels are too high, calcitonin is released to reduce the calcium levels to their proper values.

As I told you before, even though the **thymus gland** is a part of the lymphatic system, it is also a part of the endocrine system. It releases a hormone called thymosin, which stimulates the development of the white blood cells known as T-cells. Thus, even its endocrine function is related to the lymphatic system, because the T-cells being produced will help the body fight off infections.

The **adrenal glands** are another set of endocrine glands controlled by the pituitary gland. They release adrenocorticotropic (uh dree' no kort' uh cuh troh' pik) hormone (mercifully abbreviated as ACTH), which controls how the adrenal glands produce their hormone, **cortisol** (kort' uh sol). When a person gets afraid or excited, the hypothalamus stimulates the pituitary to release ACTH. This causes the adrenal glands to produce cortisol, which causes the liver to release more glucose so that there is plenty of energy available to the body. This is part of the "fight or flight" response. Essentially, the endocrine system is making sure your body has plenty of energy so you can either run from danger or defend yourself. The adrenal glands additionally produce the hormones epinephrine (eh pih nef' ruhn) and norepinephrine (nor eh pih nef' ruhn), which are also released during times of stress.

Although I have taught you to think of the **pancreas** as a digestive gland, it is also an endocrine gland. In addition to the digestive chemicals it produces, cells located within "islands" of the pancreas make **insulin**, a hormone that enables glucose to enter the cells so it can be burned. When a person has diabetes, either the cells on his pancreas do not make enough insulin, or the rest of the cells in his body don't respond to insulin the way they should. The former problem is called "insulin-dependent diabetes," while the latter is called "non-insulin-dependent diabetes." Either way, the end result is that the cells do not take in enough glucose, which causes glucose levels to be far too high in the blood.

ON YOUR OWN

15.8 Although most scientists refer to the pituitary gland as the "master endocrine gland," the hypothalamus could be considered the "master of the master." Why?

15.9 Suppose a person's thyroid begins producing too few hormones and the person gets tired and lethargic. If a doctor determines there are no problems with the thyroid itself, what should the doctor look at next?

ANSWERS TO THE "ON YOUR OWN" PROBLEMS

15.1   Remember, interstitial fluid and lymph are the same thing, but interstitial fluid becomes lymph once it goes into the lymph vessels. Thus, <u>the first vial of liquid was taken from a lymph vessel, while the second was taken from between some cells</u>. In the end, both vials contain interstitial fluid, but the first vial contains lymph because it had already entered a lymph vessel.

15.2   <u>The person will not be able to fight off disease and infection quite as well as before the spleen was removed</u>. After all, the spleen is a part of the lymphatic system, which fights infection. Take a part of that system away, and the person's ability to fight infection decreases. Remember, however, that the lymphatic system has other means by which to protect the body. Thus, losing a spleen is far from debilitating.

15.3   Remember, the lymph nodes clean lymph that is coming into them from the lymph vessels. Figure 15.1 indicates that these lymph nodes are near the armpit, on the left side. The vessels in the diagram that feed these nodes are in the left and upper left side of the body. Thus, <u>the infection is probably in the left arm or upper left part of the body</u>.

15.4   Antibodies are produced by B-cells. There are also <u>T-cells and macrophages</u> that fight infection in different ways. The lymphatic system can use them instead.

15.5   <u>The efferent lymph vessel carries more lymph</u>. Remember, several afferent lymph vessels carry lymph into a lymph node, but only one efferent lymph vessel carries lymph out. Thus, the efferent lymph vessel carries the lymph from several afferent lymph vessels.

15.6   Three quarts a day is more than the average amount. Since the amount of water in the blood stays constant, the only way this person could produce more than the average amount of urine is by <u>drinking more than the average amount of liquid</u>.

15.7   The bladder holds your urine so that you release a lot of it all at once. <u>Without the bladder, you would have a steady, slow stream of urine constantly running out of your body. That would be bad!</u>

15.8   <u>The hypothalamus controls the pituitary gland</u>.

15.9   <u>The doctor should look at the pituitary gland</u>. That's the gland producing the thyroid stimulating hormone (TSH). If the thyroid is fine but producing too few hormones of its own, perhaps the problem is that it is not getting stimulated by TSH.

STUDY GUIDE FOR MODULE #15

1. Define the following terms:

a. Gland
b. Vaccine
c. Hormone

2. Describe the main function of each of the three systems you studied in this module.

3. What two kinds of basic structures make up the lymphatic system? In which of these structures is the lymph actually cleaned?

4. How does lymph get pumped through the lymphatic system?

5. What gland produces tears? What two purposes do tears serve?

6. What three kinds of cells in the lymph nodes fight infection?

7. What kind of cell in the lymph nodes produces antibodies?

8. What kind of cell helps the lymphatic system "remember" an infection so that it can fight the infection better the next time?

9. Does it do any good to take a vaccine once you are sick with the disease the vaccine is supposed to fight?

10. Explain how a kidney functions. Start with the blood going into a kidney and end with it leaving the kidney.

11. What does a kidney do with any excess water or chemicals? Where do they go?

12. What is the purpose of dialysis?

Match the following glands with their function.

13. hypothalamus   a. Produces hormones that regulate the basal metabolic rate
14. thyroid   b. Produces cortisol, which causes the liver to release glucose into the blood
15. parathyroids   c. Produces insulin, which enables glucose to enter the cells
16. pituitary   d. Controls the pituitary gland
17. adrenal   e. Produces hormones that control many of the endocrine glands
18. pancreas   f. Produces a hormone that stimulates the production of T-cells
19. thymus   g. Produces a hormone that destroys bone to release calcium

20. Which gland is often called the "master endocrine gland"?

MODULE #16: The Human Nervous System

Introduction

Have you ever looked inside a computer? Well, if you have, you probably saw something that looked like this:

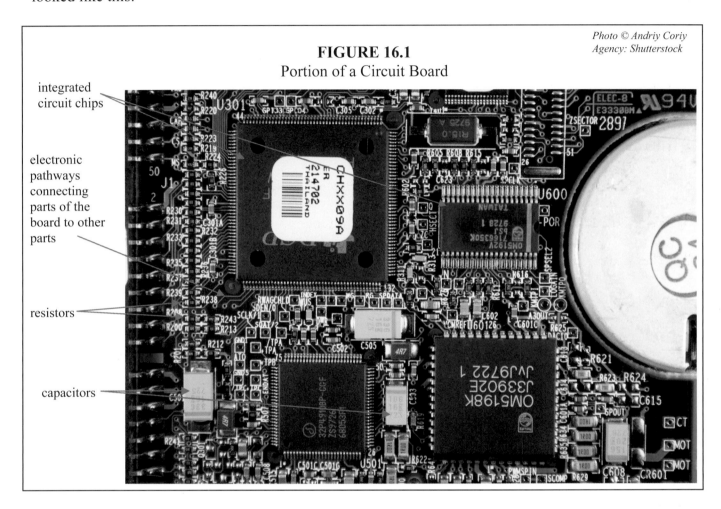

FIGURE 16.1
Portion of a Circuit Board

Photo © Andriy Coriy
Agency: Shutterstock

integrated circuit chips

electronic pathways connecting parts of the board to other parts

resistors

capacitors

Looks pretty complicated, doesn't it? There are integrated circuit chips that do a variety of different things. Most of the actual work of the circuit board occurs in those chips. However, one chip by itself cannot accomplish a lot of useful work. Thus, there are several chips that communicate with one another. They do this by sending electronic signals through pathways on the board. There are also other components like resistors and capacitors. Although the "real work" of the circuit board is done by the chips, the resistors and capacitors play a vital support role. Without them, the chips could not communicate with one another effectively.

A computer works because it is composed of several components that all work together to get a common job done. It is, of course, an amazingly complex process that only the best applied scientists really understand. Looking at the printed circuit board pictured above, you immediately understand that it must have been designed by someone smarter than you or I. After all, there is no way to explain the complex nature of the board and its resulting function (a machine that can process complicated and detailed instructions) without assuming that someone thought long and hard about how to design and build it!

Well, there are a lot of similarities between your brain and a printed circuit board. Compared to your brain, of course, the printed circuit board is *incredibly* primitive and ineffective. Nevertheless, there are some striking similarities. If you were able to magnify a section of a person's brain and then get rid of certain features, you might see something like this:

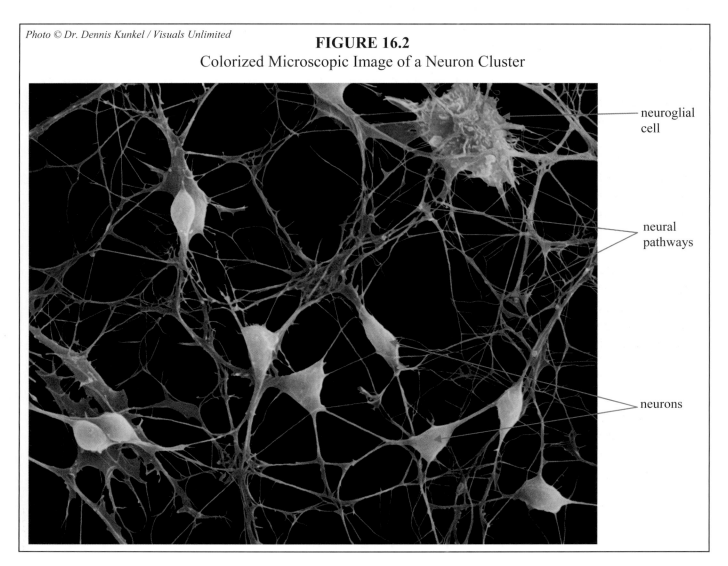

Photo © Dr. Dennis Kunkel / Visuals Unlimited

FIGURE 16.2
Colorized Microscopic Image of a Neuron Cluster

neuroglial cell

neural pathways

neurons

Looks pretty complicated, doesn't it? As I stated a moment ago, there are really a lot of similarities between the brain and a printed circuit board. For example, the "real work" of the brain occurs in cells called **neurons**. Thus, neurons can be thought of as the "chips" of the brain. Like chips, however, neurons cannot get much accomplished without communicating with other neurons. Thus, there are **neural pathways** that connect neurons to one another. They communicate by sending electrical signals down those pathways, just like the chips on the printed circuit board communicate by sending electrical signals down electronic pathways. The point at which a signal from one neuron is passed to another neuron is called a **synapse** (sin' aps), and you will learn more about that later.

What about the resistors and capacitors in a printed circuit board? Are there similar structures in the brain? Yes, there are. The neurons cannot function properly without the help of **neuroglial** (noo roh' glee uhl) **cells**, which are often called **neuroglia**. Like the resistors and capacitors on a printed circuit board, these cells support the neurons and help them communicate with one another.

There are many more neuroglial cells in the brain than there are neurons, and they account for nearly half the brain's weight.

As I mentioned previously, even though there are similarities between the two, a printed circuit board is *incredibly* primitive compared to the human brain. For example, a *really complex* computer might use a few hundred or a thousand chips. However, the average adult brain is composed of 100 **billion** neurons. Now remember, these neurons must "talk" to one another via synapses that transfer signals from one neuron to another. Most scientists who study the brain say that there are *a hundred trillion* synapses in a *single* human brain. All this communication requires a *lot* of signals. In fact, Dr. Steven Juan estimates that there are more electrical signals produced each day in a single human brain than in all the telephones in the *entire world!*

In addition, the brain processes information *significantly* more quickly than does a computer's printed circuit board. Scientists who study the brain, working with applied scientists who understand computers, have estimated that the brain can perform in 100 computational steps what it would take the most sophisticated computer nearly *1 billion* steps to accomplish! Are you beginning to see why I say that a computer's printed circuit board is primitive compared to the brain?

Why have I spent so much time discussing the complexity of the human brain? Well, your brain runs your **nervous system**, which controls many things in your body. Thus, the brain is the central focus of the human nervous system, which I want to discuss in this module. Now remember, the previous module was a little short, so this module will be a bit longer than the others. As a result, you will probably spend more time on this module than you spent on any other module of the course.

<u>Neurons: The Basic Unit of the Nervous System</u>

As I mentioned in the previous section, nerve cells are called **neurons**. As you can see from Figure 16.2, neurons are very strange-looking cells. Although the shape, size, and details of neurons vary greatly throughout both the brain and the nervous system, they all have some basic characteristics in common. These are illustrated in Figure 16.3.

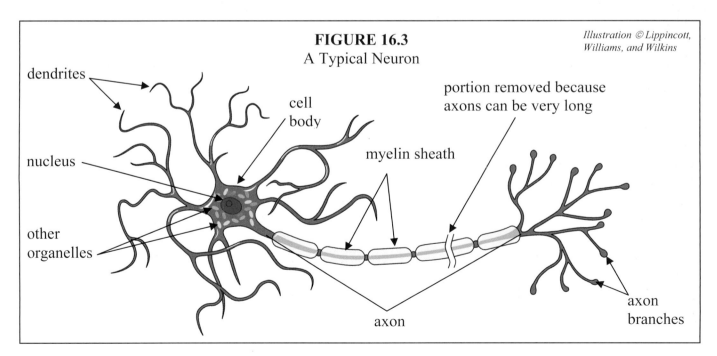

FIGURE 16.3
A Typical Neuron

Illustration © Lippincott, Williams, and Wilkins

dendrites

cell body

portion removed because axons can be very long

myelin sheath

nucleus

other organelles

axon

axon branches

Neurons, like all cells in the human body, contain many organelles that perform the functions of life. The control center, of course, is the nucleus, which is housed in the **cell body**. What make neurons look so different from other cells are the fibers that project from the cell body. They come in two types: **dendrites** (den' drytz) and **axons**. Both act a bit like wires, carrying electrical signals either toward or away from the cell body. In fact, that's how we distinguish between the two. Dendrites conduct electrical signals *toward* the cell body, while axons direct signals away from the cell body.

Neuron cell bodies have something in common with lymph nodes. Remember, several vessels carry lymph into a lymph node, but only one vessel takes lymph away. Well, neurons can have many dendrites bringing electrical signals into the cell body, but they typically have only one axon sending the signal away. As shown in the figure, that axon will almost always be branched farther down the line, but at the point where it leaves the cell body, it is always a single fiber. The axon is the longest fiber of a neuron. Some axons span over 3 feet! The axon is often covered by a fatty insulator called a **myelin** (my' uh lin) **sheath**. This sheath protects the axon and speeds up the rate at which an electrical signal can travel down it.

Okay, so that's what a neuron looks like. What, however, does a neuron do? Well, neurons have many different tasks in the body. Some neurons make up the receptors in your body. When you touch something hot, for example, you feel the warmth. That's because of neurons in your skin that sense heat. When they are stimulated by warmth, they send signals that end up in your brain, telling you that you are touching something hot. Other neurons control specific structures in your body. For example, if you want to reach out to turn a page in this book, the muscles in your arm and hand must be controlled to move so as to extend your arm, grasp the page, etc. That control is ultimately done by neurons. Of course, when you want to turn a page, the signals don't originate in the neurons that control your muscles. They originate in your brain. The neurons in your brain process information (like the fact that you are at the end of the page) and produce new signals that will lead the neurons controlling your muscles to do what is necessary to make the action (turning the page) occur.

Now if some neurons sense the outside world and generate signals meant for the brain, those signals actually need to get to the brain. In the same way, if neurons in the brain generate signals meant for neurons that control organs such as muscles, the signals must actually get to the proper controlling neurons. That's what other neurons do. Some neurons receive signals from one neuron and pass those signals on to another neuron. So some neurons receive signals from the receptor neurons and pass them on so they can get to the brain. In the same way, other neurons receive signals from the brain and pass them on so they get to the neurons that produce the desired results.

Think about these various tasks for a moment. Each of them requires that neurons communicate with other cells. Neurons either communicate with other neurons or with the cells that they control. How is that accomplished? Well, the answer to that question is surprisingly complicated. You might think that an electrical signal traveling down the axon of one neuron simply gets transferred to the next neuron. Basically, you would be right. However, the process by which this happens is *incredibly* complicated.

For reasons too complex to explore in this course, the axons and dendrites of one neuron cannot actually touch another cell. Thus, the electrical signal cannot be transferred directly from one neuron to another, or from one neuron to a target cell. Instead, there must be a tiny gap between the end of one neuron's axon and the next cell in line. This gap is called a synapse. Electrical signals cannot "jump over" the synapse. Thus, something must be done to "carry" the signal across the synapse so it can travel from the neuron that currently has the signal to the next cell in line. How is that done?

Well, an amazing thing happens when the signal reaches the end of an axon. The end of the axon is full of tiny sacs that contain chemicals we call **neurotransmitters** (noor' oh trans' mih terz). When a signal comes to the end of an axon, neurotransmitters are released out of the sacs. The neurotransmitters then travel across the synapse, chemically interacting with receptors on the cell at the other side of the tiny gap. This generates a new signal, which can then be used by the receiving cell. Figure 16.4 illustrates how this works.

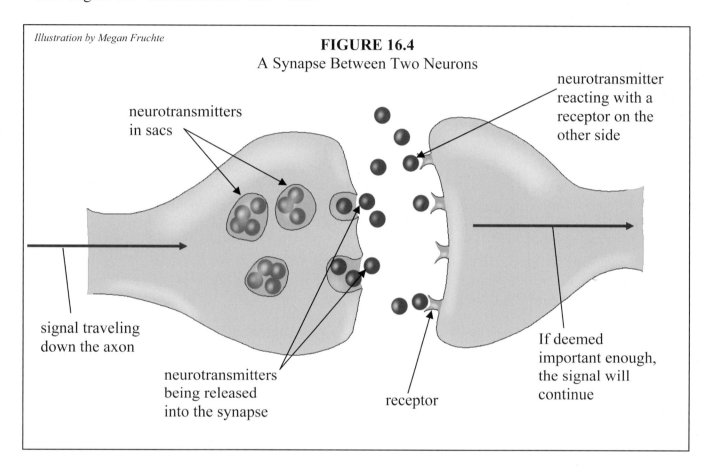

Illustration by Megan Fruchte

FIGURE 16.4
A Synapse Between Two Neurons

neurotransmitters in sacs

neurotransmitter reacting with a receptor on the other side

signal traveling down the axon

neurotransmitters being released into the synapse

receptor

If deemed important enough, the signal will continue

Interestingly enough, this process not only transfers signals from a neuron to another cell, it can actually *control* the signals that pass from one neuron to another. Consider, for example, your receptors. They are receiving an *enormous* amount of information all the time. If all that information were sent to your brain, you would constantly be distracted by useless information. Things that you regularly ignore (a tight watch band, the color of the walls, etc.) would constantly distract you. Thus, based on the "importance" of the signal being processed at the synapse, the receiving neuron might just pass the signal along, it might stop the signal altogether, or it might reduce the urgency of the signal. All this is done in a carefully controlled way so the brain gets enough information to control the body, but not *too much* information.

Pretty amazing, isn't it? I want to try to make it clear how complicated this is and how well our nervous system does its job. Suppose, for example, you are running a race against several other athletes. The beginning of the race is always the same. The runners kneel at the starting line, tense up, and wait for the starter to fire the pistol. When the runners hear the pistol fire, they take off as fast as they can. Especially for short races, the contest is often won or lost at the start. If a runner can get off the starting line faster than his competitors, he can produce a lead that simply cannot be overcome over the short duration of the race.

Now think about this process in terms of the nervous system. The runner is tensed and poised to begin. He is just waiting to hear the gun. When the gun fires, the sound is converted to an electrical signal by complex processes that occur in the ear. That signal then travels along a nerve toward the brain. This is done by each neuron receiving the signal, sending it down the axon, and releasing neurotransmitters. The neurotransmitters travel across the synapse and interact with receptors on the next neuron in the chain. If the signal is urgent enough (and thus too important to be ignored), the receiving neuron continues to transmit the signal either to the next neuron in the chain or to the brain itself.

Once the signal reaches the brain, it is then processed by many neurons. The end result is that the neurons decide whether or not this is the sound for which the runner has been waiting. The neurons in the brain then release a series of signals destined for the muscles in the arms, legs, and other parts of the body. These signals leave the brain and travel from neuron to neuron as described previously. However, this process is even more complicated, because the signals must be routed by the neurons to the proper muscle cells. The signals meant for the muscle cells in the arms, for example, must get to the muscle cells in the arms. They can't go to the legs. Thus, the neurons not only do all of the passing that I described previously, but they also analyze the signals to determine their ultimate destination, and then they route the signals to the next neuron in that direction! When the signals finally reach the last neuron in the chain, they go through the final conversion from an electrical signal to neurotransmitter, and the neurotransmitter travels across the synapse to the muscle cell. The muscle cell responds to the neurotransmitter, and the race is on!

Now think about this process for a moment. Thousands (if not millions) of neurons are involved in it. Neuron after neuron passes signals either from the ear to the brain or from the brain to the muscles. Each time the signal steps from one neuron to another, the signal must be converted from electrical energy to chemicals and then back to electrical energy. The neurons in the brain must process the signals they receive so they recognize that it is the sound the runner is waiting for, and then they determine what signals to send to the muscles. The neurons involved in passing the signals from the brain to the muscles must not only pass the signals along, but also send them along the correct route until they reach their intended destination. Now think about this: *The entire process takes a fraction of a second!* The most powerful computer designed by humankind would be *significantly* slower at accomplishing the same set of tasks!

That gives you some idea of how elegantly designed the human nervous system is, but that's not the end of the story. Remember from the introduction that the neurons make up only about half of the brain's weight. The other half of that weight comes from the neuroglia. In the entire nervous system, which includes all the nerves that run throughout the body, there are *ten to fifty times* as many neuroglia as neurons. What do these cells do? They support the neurons. What does that mean? It means they perform tasks that make it possible for the neurons to do their jobs.

Here's an example of how the neuroglia support the neurons. Have you ever noticed how a young baby's arms and legs tend to wave aimlessly and the baby has little control over them? That's because the signals are not traveling down the baby's axons as quickly as they need to for proper control. This is due to the fact that the myelin sheath is not fully formed at birth. The myelin sheath "insulates" the axon and therefore increases the speed at which signals can travel down the axon. As the baby matures, the myelin sheaths form, and the baby gains full control of his arms and legs. Well, guess what kinds of cells form the myelin sheaths? Neuroglia cells. In this case, then, the neuroglia increase the speed at which a signal can travel down an axon. This is just one of the many support functions performed by the neuroglia.

ON YOUR OWN

16.1 An electrical signal is traveling toward the cell body of a neuron. Is it traveling along a dendrite or an axon?

16.2 A neuron can stay alive even if it cannot make neurotransmitters. However, it is essentially useless without them. Why?

The Basic Layout of the Human Nervous System

The neuron is the basic unit of the **nervous system**. The brain is made up of one hundred billion of them. Of course, the brain would be essentially useless without a means of getting its signals to all parts of the body or receiving signals from all parts of the body. Thus, the axons of other neurons form "cords" that snake through the entire body. Those cords of axons are called **nerves**. Nerves are bundles of axons that carry signals to and from the brain, as discussed in the previous section.

To make it a bit more comprehensible, the nervous system is split into two components: the **central nervous system** (CNS) and the **peripheral nervous system** (PNS). The CNS is composed of both the brain and the spinal cord. This part of the nervous system does most of the information processing. Please note that this includes the spinal cord. You might not realize this, but your spinal cord does do some "thinking." For example, have you ever touched something really hot and pulled your hand away *before* you realized your skin was being burned? That action was the result of your spinal cord "thinking" for you. You see, your spinal cord received information from the receptors on your skin, telling it that your skin was touching something really hot. Since it would take time for those signals to travel to the brain, be interpreted by the brain, and produce a response, the spinal cord is designed to send a signal telling your arm to move your hand out of harm's way. That way, your skin would not be as badly burned as it would have been had your body waited for the brain to send the signals. Of course, the spinal cord still passed the information along to the brain so you could realize what happened, but it did some of the brain's job so you could save as much skin as possible. Isn't that amazing? God not only created an amazing brain, but He also created a "fast response" system to make sure you could react to certain events as quickly as possible.

Of course, all the information processing that the CNS does would be pretty useless if it weren't for the PNS. The PNS contains all the neurons involved in receiving information and sending it on to the spinal cord and brain. It also contains the neurons responsible for transmitting signals from the CNS to the various parts of your body that need to be controlled. To get an overview of your body's nervous system, study Figure 16.5.

FIGURE 16.5
The Human Nervous System

Illustration © Lippincott, Williams, and Wilkins

NOTE: The labels for the brain and spinal cord are blue to indicate they are part of the **CNS**. All other structures in the figure are part of the **PNS**.

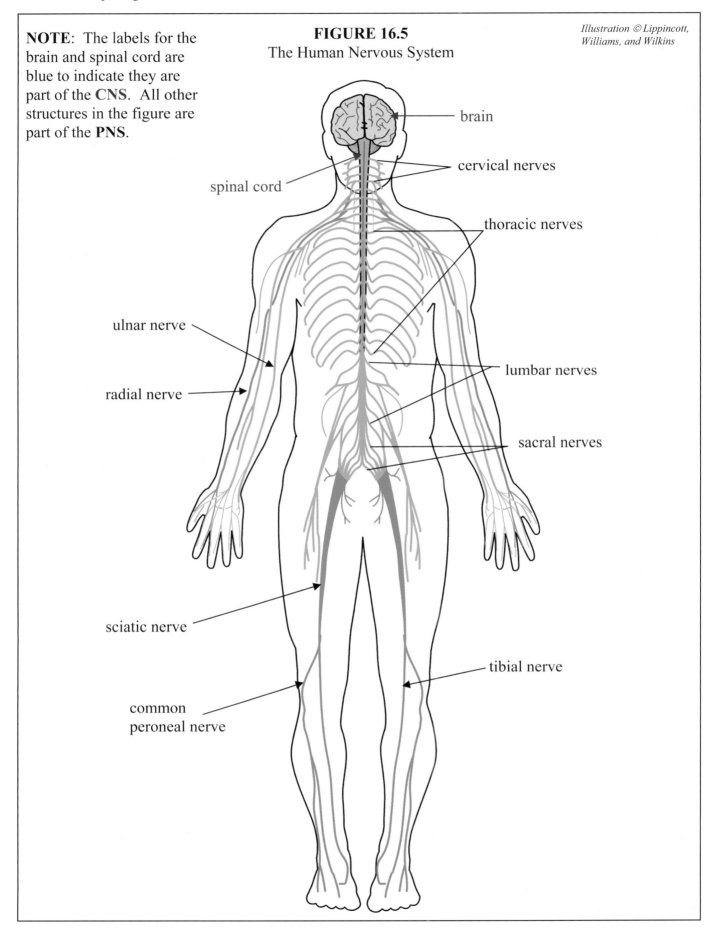

There are many more nerves in the human body than those pictured in the figure. In fact, if you were to take all the nerves in your body and lay them end to end, the resulting "string" of nerves would be roughly 93,000 miles long! The nerves pictured in the figure, then, are simply the major nerves in the body. Now don't worry: I am not going to make you memorize them! I just wanted to give you an idea of the layout.

Because nearly all the signals going to and from the brain via the PNS must pass through the spinal cord, it is of major importance to the CNS. If the spinal cord gets injured, then, the brain can lose information from and control of entire sections of the body. As a result, God has protected the spinal cord by embedding it in the backbone, which you already learned is called the vertebral column. The **vertebrae** that make up the vertebral column are stacked on top of one another. Washer joints in between the vertebrae give the backbone flexibility. Each vertebra has a hole in its center, and the hole lines up with the holes in the other vertebrae. These holes form a tunnel through which the spinal cord passes. Since the vertebrae are made of bone, the vertebral column forms a very safe, protected "shell" around the spinal cord. Now remember, animals with backbones are called "vertebrates." As you might imagine, then, all vertebrates have a spinal cord.

Although the spinal cord is an incredibly important part of the nervous system, the brain is an even more important part. It also has protection: the skull. The brain sits on close-fitting "shelves" inside the skull, and the outer bones of the skull protect it from harm. Believe it or not, however, the skull is not the only source of protection for the brain.

The brain actually floats in the skull, which contains about half a cup of a fluid. This same fluid is found surrounding the spinal cord, so it is called **cerebrospinal** (sir ee' broh spine' uhl) **fluid**. This colorless fluid is actually produced by neuroglial cells in the brain and contains several chemicals. These chemicals include glucose and proteins for many different functions.

Although the cerebrospinal fluid provides chemicals to the brain, its main function is protection. Since the brain is floating in the fluid, it serves to absorb and disperse blows that would otherwise harm the brain. Thus, the cerebrospinal fluid acts a bit like the Styrofoam® "peanuts" that people use in packaging materials. If you were to send a delicate vase to someone via mail, you would be careful to pack it in a thick layer of Styrofoam peanuts, knowing that the peanuts will absorb any bumps and blows that would otherwise break the vase. Well, the cerebrospinal fluid does the same thing for the brain!

Not only does cerebrospinal fluid provide chemicals and protection for the brain, it also serves as a way for doctors to diagnose certain problems related to the nervous system. Because the CNS is so incredibly well designed, its needs are very precise. Healthy cerebrospinal fluid, then, has specific levels of chemicals such as glucose and proteins. If there is something wrong in the nervous system, the cerebrospinal fluid's balance of chemicals will most likely not be correct, so examining the fluid can be the first step in understanding a patient's problem.

How do doctors examine the fluid? Well, they take a sample from around the spinal cord, usually in the area of the lower back. In a procedure called a **lumbar puncture**, a trained professional will stick a needle in between two vertebrae so as to reach the cerebrospinal fluid surrounding the spinal cord. Only a small amount of fluid is taken, because removal of too much will result in a lack of protection for the CNS. The fluid is then analyzed, and any abnormalities found can help diagnose what is wrong with the patient.

While the spinal cord is a very important part of the CNS, I want to concentrate on the brain. Figure 16.6 gives you two different views of a human brain.

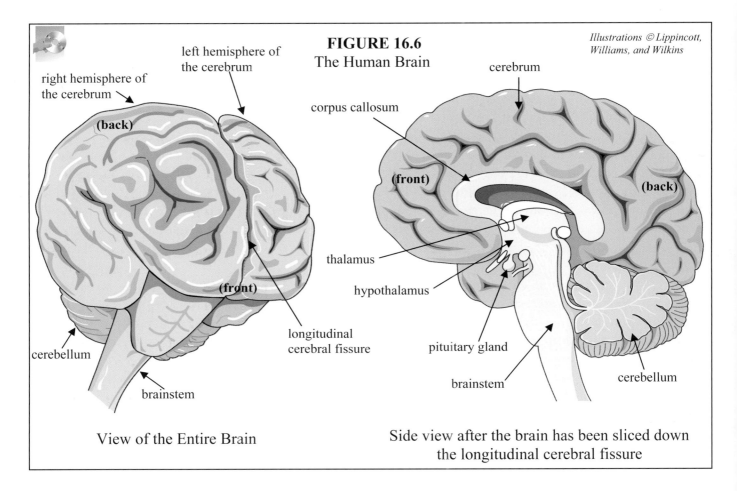

FIGURE 16.6
The Human Brain

Illustrations © Lippincott, Williams, and Wilkins

left hemisphere of the cerebrum

right hemisphere of the cerebrum

cerebrum

corpus callosum

(back)

(front)

(back)

thalamus

(front)

hypothalamus

cerebellum

longitudinal cerebral fissure

pituitary gland

brainstem

brainstem

cerebellum

View of the Entire Brain

Side view after the brain has been sliced down the longitudinal cerebral fissure

On the left side of the figure, you are looking at the brain as if you were standing in front of a person and slightly to his right. In this view, it is easy to see that the brain is divided into halves, which we call **hemispheres**. The hemispheres are separated by a "groove" called the **longitudinal** (lahn juh tood' uh nul) **cerebral** (suh ree' brul) **fissure**. Interestingly enough, each side of the brain actually controls the opposite side of the body. The right side of the brain sends signals to the PNS on the *left* side of the body, and the left side of the brain sends signals to the PNS on the *right* side of the body.

On the right side of the figure, you are looking at a "slice" of the brain from the side. We call this a **cross-section**, and it mimics what you would see if you cut the person's brain in half right between the hemispheres and then looked at it from the side. Notice that in this view, there are some easily identifiable structures. First of all, the folded tissue that surrounds the outside of the brain is called the **cerebrum** (suh ree' brum). On the left-hand side of the figure, most of what you see is the cerebrum. On the right-hand side of the figure, you can see that the cerebrum is the large outer section of the brain.

The cerebrum deals with what are often called "higher level" brain functions. These include interpreting the signals sent from the various receptors in the body, learning, reasoning, and memory. The tissue of the cerebrum is different depending on where you look. The outer layer of the cerebrum is covered in **gray matter**. Gray matter is composed almost exclusively of the cell bodies of neurons.

Underneath the cerebrum's gray matter is **white matter**. This tissue is composed mostly of the axons of the neurons in the gray matter. The lighter color of white matter comes from the myelin sheaths that cover the axons. One of the best examples of white matter in the brain is the **corpus** (kor' pus) **callosum** (kuh lah' sum). It is composed of axons running crosswise between the hemispheres that allow the two hemispheres of the brain to exchange information.

The **cerebellum** (seh ruh bel' uhm) has a lot of functions, mostly oriented around muscle movements. For example, it plays a large role in helping you to stand in one place. This is actually a difficult thing to do. Have you ever tried to get a pencil to balance on its eraser? It is not easy, is it? Why not? The pencil must be perfectly balanced. Even when you get it balanced, it might eventually tip over because air currents in the room push it out of balance. Well, it turns out that it is hard for you to stand in one place as well. It is a real balancing act! You don't think it's hard, because you do it all the time, thanks to your cerebellum. The cerebellum helps maintain the proper amount of muscle movement so that your body is constantly adjusting and maintaining its balance.

Another example of what the cerebellum does comes from **muscle preset**. What do I mean by this? Well, suppose you open your refrigerator and see a paper carton of milk. I am not talking about a clear plastic carton – I am talking about a carton you can't see through. As a result, you don't know how much milk is in there. You go to pick it up, and it almost flies away because you thought it was full. However, the carton was nearly empty, so the force you used to pick it up was far too great. Why do things like that happen? When you are about to perform a task, you often unconsciously "preset" your muscles to a certain strength. You do this because in the past, you've learned about the amount of effort needed to complete the task. For example, in the situation we just discussed, you have learned how heavy a milk carton is when it's full, and you know the amount of strength necessary to lift the full carton. As a result, you preset your muscles for that strength. If the milk carton is not full, you get surprised, because you exert way too much force in lifting the carton. That's muscle preset, and your cerebellum is a big part of that process.

The **brain stem** is right next to the cerebellum. There are actually several parts to the brain stem, but I don't want to go into that much detail. The brain stem is the general term for the area between the **thalamus** (thal' uh mus) and the spinal cord. It controls the more basic functions of the human body, such as breathing, heart rate, and the pressure at which blood is pumped through the body. The thalamus acts much like a relay station in the brain. Most of the receptors in the body send their information to the thalamus, and then the thalamus relays that information to the part of the cerebrum that is designed to receive and process it. The cerebrum also sends information back to the thalamus, which the thalamus then routes to other areas of the brain or down the spinal cord for relay to the PNS.

You learned about the **hypothalamus** in the previous module. Mostly, however, you learned that it controls the pituitary gland. That is certainly true, but it is only one function the hypothalamus performs. Typically, we refer to that as the "endocrine function" of the hypothalamus. The hypothalamus also has non-endocrine functions. It regulates thirst, hunger, and body temperature. It also helps initiate the "fight or flight" responses such as the fast heart rate and increased blood flow that occur when you are frightened or angry.

Although I have concentrated on describing the brain and the spinal cord (which make up the CNS), please remember that the PNS is a very important part of the nervous system. After all, without the nerves that run throughout your body, the signals generated in the brain and spinal cord would do little good! Interestingly enough, most nerves in the PNS transmit signals both to and from the brain, while a few transmit signals only one way. For example, the facial nerve sends information from your tongue to your brain, providing you with a sense of taste. In addition, the brain sends signals to the muscles in the face along the same nerve. These signals tell the muscles how to move so you can express yourself by "making faces." On the other hand, the olfactory nerve transmits signals only from the nose to the brain, giving you your sense of smell. No signals ever travel from the brain to the nose along the olfactory nerve.

ON YOUR OWN

16.3 An unfortunate man is in a car accident and his spinal cord is severed at the waist. Will the man be able to move his arms? What about his legs?

16.4 Although the human brain is significantly more complex than the brains of other vertebrates, the basic layout is the same. However, one part of the brain is *significantly* larger in humans than in any other vertebrates. What part of the brain would you think that is?

Our "Split" Brains

Now that you have a general idea of the basic layout of the nervous system, I want to spend a little more time on the brain itself. After all, it is the most interesting part of the entire system, so it deserves a little more attention. I want to start with the fact that the brain is composed of two hemispheres. As I mentioned in the previous section, they each control the opposite side of the PNS. Thus, the left hemisphere of the brain sends signals to and receives signals from the PNS on the right side of the body. Similarly, the right hemisphere of the brain sends signals to and receives signals from the PNS on the left side of the body. To see one consequence of our divided brain, perform the following experiment.

EXPERIMENT 16.1
Determining a Person's Dominant Side

Supplies:

♦ Scissors
♦ A pencil
♦ Paper
♦ A ball (It needs to be small enough to be thrown with one hand, like a baseball, softball, or golf ball.)
♦ A coin
♦ Some stairs or porch steps
♦ A paper towel tube or rolled-up piece of thick paper
♦ A few people to test (8 years or older)
♦ A glass

Introduction: Most people have a dominant side in their PNS. For example, most people are right-handed. We would say, then, that their dominant hand is their right hand. What you may not know is most people also have a dominant leg, eye, and ear. This experiment will help you see how this works in several people. It can be easily expanded into a science fair project.

Procedure:

(Perform this procedure on as many people as you can. **DO NOT** tell them what you are testing. Just ask them to do the things listed below and compile your results.)

1. Put the scissors, pencil, paper, ball, and paper towel tube on a table in front of the test subject. Ask your subject to cut a medium-sized circle out of the paper. Note which hand the subject uses to work the scissors.
2. After the subject has cut the circle out, ask him or her to write the word "hello" in the center of the circle. Note which hand the subject uses to write.
3. Ask your subject to pick up the ball and throw it to you. Note which hand the subject uses.
4. Put the ball on the ground and ask the subject to kick the ball gently. Note which leg is used.
5. Take your subject to a set of stairs or porch steps and ask him to climb the first step. Note which leg the subject lifts and sets on the step first. Have the subject do this a couple more times and note the first leg lifted each time.
6. Put the coin on the ground and ask the subject to step on it. Note which leg was used.
7. Point to an object a short distance away and ask your subject to look at the object through the paper towel tube. Note which eye the subject uses.
8. Take away the tube and have your subject point to the same object with both eyes open. Then ask the subject to close his right eye and say whether or not his finger is still pointing at the object.
9. Ask the subject to open his right eye and close his left eye. Once again, ask whether or not his finger is still pointing at the object. In either this or the previous step, the subject should have answered "no." Note which eye was *closed* when the subject answered "no."
10. Give the subject a glass and have him place it up against a wall. Then tell the subject to listen through the glass to see if he hears anything on the other side of the wall. Note which ear is used to press against the glass.

(This ends the tests that you do on each subject.)

11. Look at your results. Steps 1-3 test for which hand is dominant. Most likely, the subjects used the same hand in each step. If not, choose the hand they used in two of the three steps to determine which hand was dominant. How many of the subjects had their right hand dominant? How many had their left hand as dominant? In the overall population, roughly 90 percent have their right hand dominant.
12. Steps 4-6 test the dominance of the legs. Most people will use the same leg in each of the three tests. If not, choose the leg used in two of the three tests to determine which was dominant. How many people had their right leg dominant? How many had their left leg dominant? Roughly 85% of the population has their right leg dominant.
13. Steps 7-9 test which eye is dominant. In steps 8 and 9, the eye that was closed when the subject said "no" was the dominant eye. Most people will have the same eye dominant in each test. If not, call this one "not determined." How many people had their right eye dominant? Roughly 70 percent of the population has their right eye dominant.
14. The last step determines the dominant ear. How many people had their right ear dominant? How many had their left ear dominant? Roughly 60% of the population has their right ear dominant.
15. Look at the results as a whole. Were there any subjects whose dominant side changed? For example, was there any subject whose dominant hand was the right hand but whose dominant leg was the left leg? These people are in the minority. Most people have the same side dominant for the hand, ear, leg, and eye. However, I myself am one of those exceptions. My right hand, leg, and ear are all dominant, but my left eye is dominant!

The fact that the majority of people are right-handed, right-eyed, right-legged, and right-eared seems to be unique in creation. All vertebrates have two hemispheres in their brains. However, people are the only vertebrates that tend to have one side (the right side) dominant over the other throughout the entire population. An individual rat, for example, might be right-eyed, but there are roughly as many right-eyed rats as left-eyed ones. Thus, the overall population has no dominant side. Humanity as a whole, however, is mostly right-side dominant.

Quite frankly, scientists have no solid explanation as to why. In fact, scientists really have no idea why individuals have a dominant side at all, much less why most people tend to be right-side dominant. There are many theories out there, but none of them have enough experimental evidence to back them up. In the end, then, most humans clearly have one side of the CNS dominant over the other, but we really do not know why.

There is another consequence of the fact that our brain is split into two hemispheres. Have you ever heard of a person being "right-brained" or "left-brained"? These terms have arisen as a result of experiments that show some thinking skills are dominated by the left hemisphere of the cerebrum, and others are dominated by the right hemisphere of the cerebrum. For example, the right hemisphere of the cerebrum tends to govern the ability of people to think in terms of shapes, spatial relationships, and images. In addition, the right cerebrum tends to govern whether or not we recognize a face we have seen before. Also, musical abilities tend to come from the right side of the cerebrum. On the other hand, the left side of the cerebrum tends to dominate when it comes to thinking logically, using mathematical skills, and speaking. As a result, people who love science and math tend to be referred to as "left-brained people," while people who are artistic or talented at shapes and spatial relationships tend to be called "right-brained people."

Despite the fact that people tend to have a dominant side to their CNS, and despite the fact that the right brain dominates in some cerebral functions while the left brain dominates in others, it is very important to remember that these two sides of the brain are in constant communication. That's the purpose of the corpus callosum you learned about in the previous section. Thus, don't start thinking that the brain is split into two *completely separate* halves. The halves do communicate with each other; it just seems that one half tends to take more responsibility for certain functions while the other half takes responsibility for others.

ON YOUR OWN

16.5 Two accident victims are studied. The first has damage to a particular area of the right side of his brain. The second has similar damage to the same general area, but on the left side of his brain. One of the patients has had severe difficulty speaking clearly and understandably since the accident that caused the damage. The other has had no apparent speech problems after the accident. Which one (most likely) is having no speech problems?

The Brain and Blood

Although the brain makes up only 2 percent of an adult's weight, it uses 20 percent of the body's blood supply. Why? The reason is simple. It takes an enormous amount of energy to produce electrical signals, manufacture and release neurotransmitters, etc. Combine that with the fact that the brain does all this so quickly, and you are left with an organ that requires *a lot* of energy. This means that brain cells need a lot of oxygen and nutrients, which come from the blood supply. Thus, the brain needs a *lot* of blood.

However, there is a "problem" with this. The neurons of the brain are incredibly specialized cells that do their jobs very well. However, because of their precise nature, many chemicals that are necessary for other body tissues are actually toxic to the neurons of the brain. Although the brain needs lots of blood, its cells can't be exposed to many of the chemicals that are in blood. This sounds like a really difficult problem, doesn't it? The brain needs blood, but it cannot be exposed to many of the chemicals in that blood. How would you solve such a problem?

The first thing that comes to my mind is to have a *separate* circulatory system for the brain. That way, the body can provide the brain with the blood it needs without any of the chemicals it can't have. Now that's a plausible solution, but there are several problems. First of all, there would have to be a separate heart, a separate area in the lungs where the brain's blood is oxygenated, and a separate kidney system to regulate the blood. Also, you would have to figure out how to get that blood to absorb nutrients from the small intestine and be cleaned and managed by the liver without mixing with the other blood supply. That's all really complicated!

Fortunately, the Designer of the human body is a *lot* smarter than I am. God has designed an amazingly elegant solution to the problem that seems so daunting to me. He has designed the **blood-brain barrier**. To me, this is one of the most amazing aspects to the human body, yet very few people actually know about it. To best understand what the blood-brain barrier is and how elegantly it solves the problem, you need to be reminded about a few things you should have learned in Module #14.

Remember, our circulatory system is made up of veins, arteries, and capillaries. The capillaries are where blood gives up oxygen and nutrients to the cells while picking up the cells' waste products. These processes can happen because the walls of capillaries are only one cell thick, and there are gaps in between the cells. This allows fluid to "leak" out of the capillaries and bathe the cells. The exchange of gases, nutrients, and waste products is then made possible by this fluid bathing the cells.

If this were to happen in the brain, neurons would die instantly. Thus, brain capillaries are *different* from the capillaries in the rest of the body. Their walls are still only one cell thick, but there are no gaps in between the cells. In fact, the cells are sealed together by protein fibers and are covered by special neuroglial cells called "astrocytes." Have you ever heard the phrase, "He blew a gasket"? It refers to something that can happen in automobiles. Automobile engines must hold fluid inside certain chambers. These chambers are made from different metal parts joined together. Now if the makers of an engine simply put the metal pieces together and did nothing else, the fluid would leak out where the metal pieces are joined. To prevent that, a piece of rubber called a **gasket** is placed between the pieces of metal before they are joined. The rubber seals the metal junction and keeps the fluid from leaking out. When an automobile "blows a gasket," a rubber seal bursts, and fluid starts leaking out. In the blood-brain barrier, proteins form gaskets in between the cells that line the capillaries, keeping the fluid in the capillaries from leaking out.

That's all well and good. It keeps the blood from exposing the brain cells to harmful chemicals. Of course, if that were the end of the story, it would also keep the blood from giving the brain cells what they need. After all, if the brain cells are separated from the blood in the capillaries, they can't get any of the things they need from the blood, can they? Yes, they can! This is the real beauty of the blood-brain barrier. The cells that line these capillaries have special chemical processes that *transport* the things the brain needs out of the blood. Each of the cells that line the capillaries, then, can be thought of as a watchdog. When a cell "sees" things that the brain needs (water, oxygen, and glucose), it transports them through the cell. Other molecules, however, are recognized as bad for the brain and are not transported. Isn't that amazing?

Interestingly enough, not all toxins are held back by the blood-brain barrier. For example, certain drugs can pass through the blood-brain barrier and wreak havoc on the brain cells. People who use illegal drugs looking for a "high" do not realize they are getting around a system God has designed to protect very sensitive brain cells. As a result, most illegal drugs that affect the brain also kill brain cells. That's one reason the term "dope" has been used to describe illegal drugs. Many of the popular illegal drugs kill brain cells, turning habitual users into dopes! Alcohol also passes through the blood-brain barrier. It passes through as easily as water, but is not good for brain tissue. Studies have indicated that people who drink a lot of alcohol have trouble with memory functions and learning, most likely because of the adverse affect the alcohol has on neurons in the brain.

ON YOUR OWN

16.6 Would the blood-brain barrier work without the proteins in between the capillary cells? Why or why not?

The Peripheral Nervous System (PNS)

So far, I have concentrated on the brain in this module. Mostly, that's because the brain is the most important part of the nervous system. To some extent, it's also because I find the brain the most interesting part of the nervous system. However, I want to spend most of the rest of this module emphasizing several parts of the PNS. In this section, I will give you a little more general information about the PNS, and then I want to discuss specifically how the PNS works together with the brain to give us the five senses of taste, smell, vision, touch, and hearing.

As you already know, the PNS is made up of those nerves that run off the central nervous system (CNS). At this point, it is important to make a distinction that I have so far avoided. As I told you previously, the nerves in the PNS are made up of neurons. However, the term **nerve** has a very specific meaning to scientists. A nerve is made up of dendrites and axons, not the cell bodies of neurons. The cell bodies of neurons typically cluster together in groups. These groups are called **ganglia** (gan' glee uh). When several ganglia cluster together, it is called a **plexus**, which many people call a "nerve center." Interestingly enough, there are many animals (earthworms and shrimp, for example) that don't have real brains. Instead, they have ganglia and plexi (plural of plexus) that control their nervous systems.

The PNS is composed of three main divisions: **the autonomic** (aw toh nom' ik) **nervous system, the sensory nervous system,** and **the somatic motor nervous system**.

Autonomic nervous system – The system of nerves that carries instructions from the CNS to the
body's smooth muscles, cardiac muscle, and glands

Sensory nervous system – The system of nerves that carries information from the body's receptors to
the CNS

<u>Somatic motor nervous system</u> – The system of nerves that carries instructions from the CNS to the skeletal muscles

I want to discuss each one of these systems briefly so you have some idea of what's involved with each of them.

The autonomic nervous system is by far the most fascinating component of the PNS, because it regulates the automatic processes that keep the body going. The rate and strength of your heartbeat, relaxation and contraction of smooth muscles, and the functions of many glands are all controlled by your autonomic nervous system. Information about these processes is sent to the CNS and is evaluated by your hypothalamus, brain stem, and in some cases, spinal cord. Based on the results of the evaluation, instructions are then sent to your heart muscle, smooth muscles, and glands. This continuous monitoring, evaluation, and issuing of instructions happens throughout your body without any conscious thought on your part!

The autonomic nervous system is composed of two parts: the **sympathetic division** and the **parasympathetic division**. These two divisions are made up of completely different nerves and ganglia, and counterbalance each other in many ways. The sympathetic division increases the rate and strength of the heartbeat, and raises the blood pressure. It also stimulates the liver to release more glucose in the blood, producing quick energy for the "fight or flight" response we experience when we are frightened or angry. The parasympathetic system, on the other hand, slows the heart rate, which lowers the blood pressure. In addition, it takes care of certain "housekeeping" activities such as causing the stomach to churn while it is digesting a meal. To get a quick understanding of the difference between the sympathetic and parasympathetic divisions of the autonomic nervous system, perform the following experiment.

EXPERIMENT 16.2
The Pupil of the Eye

<u>Supplies</u>

♦ A mirror
♦ A room with a light switch that when closed off gets *really* dark
♦ A candle
♦ Matches

Introduction: The two divisions of the nervous system tend to counterbalance one another. You will see this effect in the following experiment.

<u>Procedure</u>:

1. Go into a room that can be closed off and gets really dark. If you have a bathroom that either has no window or has an easily covered window, that is ideal. It needs to have a mirror as well.
2. Close the door but keep the light on.
3. Use the matches to light the candle. **BE CAREFUL!!! OPEN FLAMES ALWAYS PRESENT AN ELEMENT OF RISK!!!**
4. Turn off the lights. The room should be completely dark except for the light from the candle.
5. Look at your face in the mirror, concentrating on just one eye.

6. Move the candle around so you have enough light to see one eye reasonably well, but the candle is as far away as possible. **BE CAREFUL!! IF YOU HOLD THE CANDLE TOO CLOSE, YOU CAN BURN YOURSELF OR SET YOUR HAIR ON FIRE!**
7. Concentrate on the dark circle at the center of your eye, which is called your **pupil**. Notice its size. Look at it for 15 seconds or so.
8. Without changing anything else and without looking away, turn on the lights or have someone do it for you.
9. As the lights come on, watch your pupil. You should see a change.
10. If you did not see a change, try again, really concentrating on your pupil. If you have very dark eyes, you might want to watch someone else while they do the experiment, as it might be hard for you to determine where your pupil ends and the rest of your eye begins.
11. Blow out the candle and put it away.

What did you see in the experiment? You should have seen your pupil get smaller when the light was turned on. Why did this happen? Well, your eye's main function is to collect light. Light enters your eye through the pupil. The larger the pupil, the more light it allows into your eye. When the surroundings are bright, the pupil needs to be small so only a fraction of the incoming light actually gets into your eye. Otherwise, your eye would become *overloaded* with light. However, as the surroundings get darker, your eye needs to let in more light so it can get enough information to form an image of what you are viewing. Thus, it makes the pupil bigger so more light can come in.

When the room was dark except for the candle, there wasn't much light striking your eyes. As a result, your autonomic nervous system caused your eye's pupil to open wide, allowing a large fraction of that light into your eye. When you turned on the lights, suddenly a *lot* more light started striking your eyes. The sensory nervous system sensed that suddenly too much light was entering your eye, so the pupil closed down, and you should have seen it get smaller. You know this was all a part of the autonomic nervous system's work, because you did not have to think about doing it. It happened automatically.

The reason I wanted you to do the experiment, however, was to illustrate the difference between the sympathetic and parasympathetic divisions of the autonomic nervous system. The sympathetic division of the autonomic nervous system is what caused your pupil to get large. The technical way to say it is that the sympathetic division **dilated** the pupil. When the sensory nervous system reported that too little light was getting to your eye, the sympathetic division contracted smooth muscles in the iris, which dilated the pupil. In contrast, the parasympathetic division took over when you turned the light on. When the sensory nervous system reported that too much light was getting in your eye, the parasympathetic division took over, causing the pupil to constrict (get smaller).

Of course, none of this would have happened without the actions of your sensory nervous system, which sends information to the CNS from all the receptors scattered throughout your body. These signals are absolutely necessary for you to be able to respond to the changes that occur in your surroundings (the third criterion for life). In the case of the experiment, your surroundings changed from dark to bright when you turned on the lights. Your sensory nervous system sent signals to your brain informing it of the change, and the brain responded to the change by instructing the parasympathetic division of the autonomic nervous system to constrict your pupil. Of course, this kind of thing happens all the time, because your surroundings are constantly changing.

The third division of the PNS is the somatic motor nervous system. It controls the voluntary muscles in the body. When you decide it is time to turn the page in this book, for example, your brain sends signals along the motor nervous system. These signals cause the skeletal muscles in your arm and hand to contract and relax in such a way that you move your hand, grab the page, and turn it. Now, of course, while the motor nervous system is being utilized in such a way, the autonomic and sensory nervous systems don't stop working! That's one of the amazing aspects of the human nervous system. There is no way that even the fastest computer known to man can perform as quickly as even *one part* of the human nervous system. Nevertheless, the human nervous system can handle *several parts* working simultaneously at high efficiency!

ON YOUR OWN

16.7 When you get cold and your autonomic nervous system increases your heart rate and blood pressure, which division (parasympathetic or sympathetic) is causing the change?

The Human Sense of Taste

Now that you've been given a brief overview of the PNS, I want to spend most of the rest of the module concentrating on the sensory nervous system, which gives us our senses. I want to start with my favorite sense – the sense of taste, also known as the **gustatory** (gus' tuh tor' ee) sense. When you eat food, you taste it. The foods that you like "taste good," while the foods that you don't like "taste bad." Why do we have this sense? Well, there are at least two reasons. First, God wants His people to enjoy themselves (within limits) while here on earth. Food is one source of enjoyment, so I expect that part of the reason we have a sense of taste is simply so we can enjoy eating.

There is also a biological reason for taste. When something tastes bad, we usually try to avoid eating it. Our brain has been programmed to respond to many toxic substances as "tasting bad." As a result, we avoid eating them, which helps to protect us. This biological reason is especially important in animals. Animals avoid things that are bad for them based to a large extent on taste or smell. Interestingly enough, some animals take advantage of this. For example, the monarch butterfly tastes bad to birds, because it eats milkweed, which contains chemicals that are toxic to birds. Because they taste bad, birds don't eat monarch butterflies. The North American viceroy butterfly looks a lot like a monarch, but it doesn't eat milkweed. As a result, it is not toxic to birds. Nevertheless, birds don't eat North American viceroy butterflies, because they *look like* monarch butterflies. This is called "mimicry," and several animals use it to avoid becoming another animal's dinner.

What gives you the sense of taste? The answer is simple. It comes from your tongue. If you stick out your tongue and look at it in the mirror, you will see tiny "bumps." These bumps are called **papillae** (puh pill' ee). If you have ever been licked by a cat, the rough feeling comes from the fact that a cat has very pronounced papillae on its tongue. In some of these papillae, there are tiny holes called **taste pores** that lead to microscopic clusters of cells called **taste buds**. These cells have tiny "hairs" that are sensitive to certain chemicals. When those chemicals are detected in your saliva, the taste bud cells send signals along the sensory nerves in the tongue to your cerebrum. The brain then gives you a taste sensation, which can be either bad or good, depending on many factors. The following figure illustrates the general structure of a taste bud.

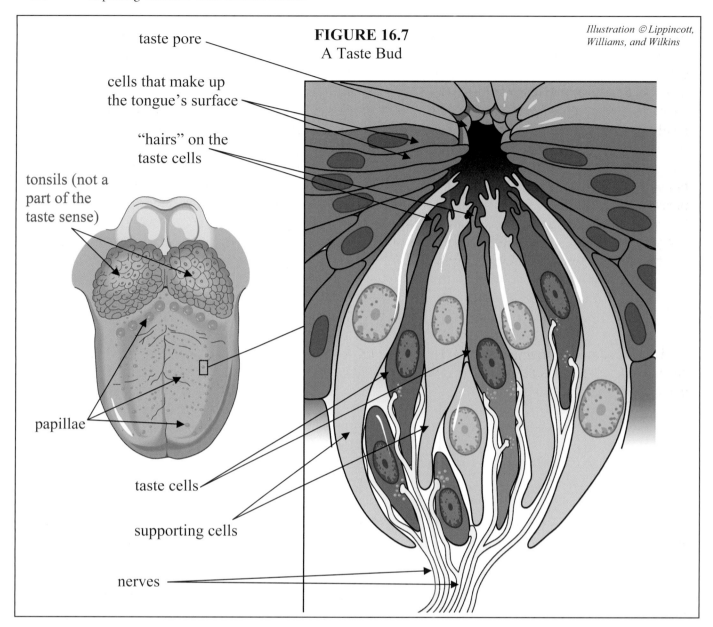

FIGURE 16.7
A Taste Bud

Illustration © Lippincott, Williams, and Wilkins

taste pore

cells that make up the tongue's surface

"hairs" on the taste cells

tonsils (not a part of the taste sense)

papillae

taste cells

supporting cells

nerves

Do you see why we call them taste buds? The taste cells and the other cells that play a supporting role form the general shape of a bud.

Interestingly enough, scientists' understanding of the human sense of taste has recently been updated. It was long thought that there were only four basic taste sensations: **sweet, salty, sour,** and **bitter**. It was always assumed that when you tasted something, you perceived a combination of those four basic tastes. While scientists still think this is essentially correct, a fifth sensation was recently added: **umami** (oo mah' me). The word for this taste sensation comes from the Japanese word for "savory" and is best explained as the taste of amino acids. Scientists' current understanding of our sense of taste, then, is that your taste buds measure the amount of sweet, salty, sour, bitter, and umami sensations in anything dissolved in your saliva. Those sensations are then blended together to form the overall taste you perceive.

The pleasantness of the five basic taste sensations changes depending on the strength. In general, the sweetness taste gets more and more pleasant the stronger the sweetness is. At some point, many people will say that a taste is "too sweet," but the general rule is that the more sweet the taste, the more pleasant it is. For the salty and sour tastes, however, the results are quite different. If something is lightly salted or just a bit sour, it is generally considered pleasant tasting. However, too much salt or too much sourness quickly turns unpleasant. Thus, most people only like the salty and sour tastes when they are relatively weak. The bitter taste is only considered pleasant at the weakest levels. When there is much bitterness at all, the overall effect is unpleasant to most people.

The basic reason for this once again is protection. One set of chemicals that tend to make things taste sour, for example, are called acids. Weak acids are good for us, so we consider their taste pleasant. Orange juice, for example, is a weak acid, providing a pleasant taste. Orange juice is good for you, so that works out fine. If something contains a strong acid, however, it tastes strongly sour, and you will avoid it because the strong sour taste is unpleasant. This is good, because strong acids can be very dangerous if they are ingested.

ON YOUR OWN

16.8 Monosodium glutamate (MSG) is a food additive that was developed in 1907. Used in a lot of Asian cooking, it tends to give food a more savory flavor. Which of the five basic taste sensations does it stimulate?

The Human Sense of Smell

I'm sure that at some point in your life, you put your nose in a flower and inhaled the flower's scent deeply. What gives us the sense of smell that allows us to enjoy such an experience? The answer at first glance is easy: the nose. But how does the nose detect smell?

An object's scent actually begins as chemicals floating in the air. A flower, for example, releases chemicals into the air in order to attract insects or birds. The insects and birds follow those chemicals to the flower and feed on the nectar it produces. In the process, they actually help the flower to reproduce. You will learn more about that in biology. When you and I inhale the chemicals that a flower releases into the air, some of them reach the roof of the nasal cavity and dissolve in the moist mucus that covers it. Millions of cells line this part of the nose, called the **olfactory** (ol fak' tor ee) **epithelium** (ep' uh theel' ee uhm). Some of these cells, called **olfactory sensory cells**, have long "hairs" that stick into the mucus.

Once the chemicals in the air dissolve in the mucus of the olfactory epithelium, they interact with the "hairs" of the olfactory sensory cells. This causes the cells to generate signals that get sent on to the brain. The brain then gives us an impression, which we call "smell." The sense of smell, then, has something in common with the sense of taste. They both rely on the interaction between chemicals that make their way into the body and the "hairs" of certain specialized cells. Not only that, the sense of smell also tends to work in tandem with the sense of taste. Perform the following experiment to see what I mean.

EXPERIMENT 16.3
The Sense of Smell and the Sense of Taste

<u>Supplies</u>:

♦ Toothpicks
♦ Apple
♦ Onion
♦ Blindfold
♦ A person to act as your subject
♦ A knife
♦ Two paper towels

Introduction: The sense of smell affects the sense of taste. This experiment will demonstrate that fact for most people.

<u>Procedure</u>:

1. Make sure your subject is not in the room when you start this experiment.
2. Cut a few bite-sized pieces from both the apple and the onion.
3. Put the pieces on a paper towel and cover them with the other paper towel.
4. Put away the rest of the apple and onion so your subject has no idea what you have been cutting up. This is very important.
5. Blindfold your subject and have your subject pinch her nose to make sure she cannot smell.
6. Use the toothpick to spear one of the pieces and feed it to your subject. Ask her to identify the food by taste. Do not give her any hints. If she cannot identify the taste, don't worry about it.
7. Do this with three more pieces of food so your subject has had two onion pieces and two apple pieces. Each time, ask the subject to identify the food by taste.
8. Now repeat steps 6 and 7, but this time allow your subject to stop pinching her nose. Let your subject smell the food before she tastes it. Once again, ask her to identify the food.
9. Clean everything up.

How did your subject do with the identification? Most people will not do well with their nose pinched, because the sense of smell really augments the sense of taste. Remember, we only taste five basic sensations: sweet, sour, bitter, salty, and umami. Most of the rest of our impressions of the "taste" of food come from our sense of smell. Think about it: Have you ever been so sick with a cold that you couldn't smell anything? When most people get that sick, they complain that their food just doesn't taste very good. Once again, this is because taste and smell work together to give you an overall impression of food, and you usually think of it as the food's taste. For some animals, this effect is even more pronounced. Cats, for example, get a large portion of their pleasure from the food's smell, not its taste. That's why they like strong-smelling things like tuna. That's also why cat food usually smells stronger than dog food. To cats, smell is almost everything when it comes to deciding whether or not they will eat their food.

There is something else in your mind that is strongly connected to your sense of smell. Have you ever noticed that smells can bring back memories? Psychology research has demonstrated that the sense of smell is the most likely sense to bring back memories. Scientists think they know why. The nerves that pass the signals from the olfactory cells to the brain are a part of the **limbic system**, the part of the brain that deals with memories and emotions. Thus, the sense of smell is very intimately connected with our memories and emotions!

ON YOUR OWN

16.9 An air purifying system claims to clean "all the chemicals" out of the air and leave behind a "pleasant scent" like that of the outdoors after a thunderstorm. What is wrong with this claim?

The Human Sense of Vision

I truly wish I could spend an entire module (perhaps even more) solely on your sense of vision. Of all the wonderfully designed organs of your body, the eye is probably eclipsed only by the brain. Since the eye and the brain must work in tandem to give you your sense of vision, together they form what I consider to be the most remarkable system in all of creation! To give you an idea of just how amazing this all is, consider a very simplified sketch of the human eye.

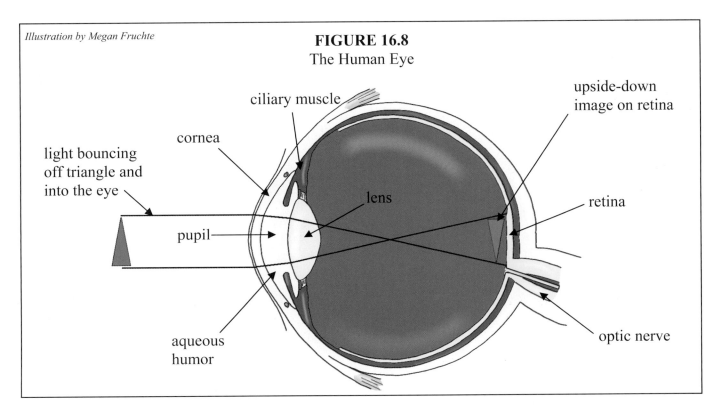

Illustration by Megan Fruchte

FIGURE 16.8
The Human Eye

As I told you in a previous section, the eye's function is to collect light. In order for us to see an object (such as the triangle in the figure), light must bounce off the object and enter the eye. When light strikes the eye, it first passes through the transparent **cornea** (kor' nee uh). The cornea is covered with a very thin layer of clear tissue that is kept moist and clean because each blink of the eye washes it in tears produced by the lacrimal glands, which you learned about in the previous module. The light then passes through a clear liquid called the "aqueous humor" and then through the **pupil**. As you already learned, the pupil is controlled by the autonomic nervous system, automatically opening wide or closing down depending on the amount of light present. The light then passes through the **lens**, which is what the eye uses to focus the image onto the **retina** (reh' tih nuh).

I want to spend at least a moment on the way the eye focuses objects onto the retina. Have you ever watched a photographer operate a camera with a manual focus? If you have, you have seen the photographer twisting the lens of the camera back and forth. Why does he do that? Well, in order to get a good picture, the image he is trying to photograph must be focused precisely onto the film in the camera. When the photographer twists the lens, he is not actually twisting it. Instead, he is *moving it back and forth*. In a camera, the photographer changes the focus by moving the lens. When the lens is close to the film, it focuses objects far from the camera onto the film. When the lens is far from the film, it focuses objects near the camera onto the film. Thus, the focus of a camera is changed by moving the position of the lens relative to the film.

That works quite well for a camera, but it would be an incredibly inefficient design for a person! Why? Well, a person needs to change the focus of his eye quickly. It takes time to move a lens back and forth. Also, if the lens moves, there must be room for it to move. In cameras, the lens moves back and forth within a tube attached to the front of the camera. The larger the range of focus you want, the larger the tube has to be. To give us the range we need for focusing by that method, human eyes would have to have their lenses mounted on long tubes that would stick out of the eye. How weird would that be?

So your eyes need to focus light from an object onto the retina, but doing so by moving the lens is simply too inefficient. How does your eye do it? It *changes the shape of the lens itself!* The lens is attached to a smooth muscle called the **ciliary** (sil' ee air ee) **muscle**. When this circular muscle is relaxed, it automatically pulls on the lens so the lens is thin. This causes the eye to focus far-away objects onto the retina. If the eye needs to focus on objects nearby, the ciliary muscle contracts, and the lens becomes fat. This mode of focusing is *significantly* more efficient than what can be achieved by the best cameras made in the world!

Think about it. You are sitting down reading this book, focusing on the words you are reading. Suddenly, your mom calls you. You look up, and she is standing at the other end of the room. You focus on her even before you realize it! As far as you are concerned, your focus changes instantaneously. Now think about how long it would take a camera (even one with automatic focus) to do this. Suppose you are trying to take a picture of this page and then suddenly decide to surprise your mom across the room by taking a picture of her. How long would it take to get the camera to change its focus? Well, at least half a second, probably more. That is *many, many times slower* than the speed at which you can change the focus of your eyes!

Notice in the figure that once the image actually does get focused on the retina, it is upside down. This is a consequence of how the light travels through the lens. The reason we don't actually see things upside down is that while we are infants, we learn to link the image on the retina to the object in the outside world. Since we spend time as infants touching everything, we learn the correct orientation of everything, so we become accustomed to flipping the image in our mind so we see right side up. The actual images on our retina, however, are upside down.

How does an image on the retina allow you to see? Well, the retina is filled with specialized cells called **rods** and **cones**. Each of them has up to 100 million molecules that are sensitive to light. The cones have molecules sensitive to three colors of light, while the rods have molecules sensitive only to light in general, not any particular color. The rods are highly sensitive to light and can react to even tiny amounts. When there is little light, your eyes rely mostly on the rods of the retina to form images. When there is a reasonable amount of light, the cones play a more important role.

When the molecules within the rods and cones are struck by light, they set off a complex chain of chemical reactions in the cell. These chemical reactions eventually form an electrical signal, which travels down a nerve fiber and eventually into the **optic nerve**. As the signal travels toward the brain, it is partly analyzed by ganglia that exist along the way. Eventually, these "preprocessed" signals reach the cerebrum, where the information is analyzed in many different parts of the brain. The brain then puts all this information together and produces an image for you. Okay, now here's the really amazing part: All this happens in less than *one thousandth of one second!*

Think about that for a minute. When light hits the retina of the eye, it causes an enormous number of cells to turn on complicated chemical machinery that sends signals down roughly 125 million nerves. As these 125 million signals travel down the nerves, each signal gets preprocessed by the neurons along the way. All 125 million signals get routed to the *different* parts of the cerebrum based on the information they carry, and the brain then analyzes each signal and adds the information together to form an image in your mind. This image is sharper, clearer, and better resolved than the image produced by the best camera in the world, and all this happens in *less than a thousandth of a second!* There is no computer today, nor any computer applied scientists can envision, that can process so many signals so accurately so quickly. In fact, it has been estimated that it would take a supercomputer *one hundred years* of computer time to simulate what takes place *each second* in the eye and brain. How in the world can anyone believe that such a system developed by chance?

There is one more thing I want you to learn about the eye before I move on to the next section. Notice that the optic nerve enters through the back of the eye. At the point where the optic nerve enters the eye, there are no rods and cones on the retina. What is the result? Perform the following experiment to find out.

EXPERIMENT 16.4
The Human Blind Spot

Supplies:

♦ Printouts from the course website, the address and password to which are given in the "Student Notes" at the beginning of the book

or

♦ Two sheets of paper
♦ A black marker or pen

Introduction: The human eye has no rods and cones at the point where the optic nerve enters the eye. This creates a minor problem, which will be demonstrated in this experiment.

Procedure:

1. If you do not have access to the course website I told you about in the "Student Notes" at the beginning of this book, you need to make a sheet like "Printout #1" given there. To do that, draw a dot about one-eighth inch in diameter on a white sheet of paper. About 4½ inches to the right of the dot, draw a plus sign that is roughly the same size. In the end, you should have a sheet of paper that you either made yourself or printed out from the website that has the following pattern on it:

●   +

2. Hold the paper away from you at arm's length.
3. Close your left eye, and look at the dot, not the plus sign. Even though you are looking at the dot, you can still see the plus sign, right? That's because your eye is accepting enough light so light bouncing off the plus sign is still getting to your retina. Thus, you are still seeing it.
4. While constantly looking at the dot, slowly pull the paper closer and closer to your face until it essentially touches your nose. What eventually happens to the plus sign? DON'T LOOK AT IT – JUST BE AWARE OF IT.
5. If you do not see an effect the first time, try again. Keep looking at the dot, but be aware of the plus sign.
6. If you want, you can reverse the procedure for the other eye. Just close your right eye and focus on the plus sign. You should now see something happen to the dot as you pull the paper closer and closer to your face.
7. If you do not have "Printout #2" from the website, draw two solid rectangles on the other piece of paper. There needs to be a noticeable space in between them. Each rectangle should be ¼ inch high and 1½ inches long. There should be about a one-eighth inch space in between. To the right of both rectangles draw a dot like the one you drew before. In the end, you should have a sheet of paper with the following pattern on it:

████████████   ████████████   ●

8. Once again, hold the paper at arm's length.
9. Close your right eye.
10. Focus on the dot.
11. Pull the paper slowly toward your face. Be aware of the rectangles. What happens?

What did you see in the experiment? In the first part, you should have seen the plus sign disappear as you moved the paper toward your face. As you kept moving, it should have re-appeared. Why did that happen? Well, as you moved the paper toward your face, you eventually reached the point at which the plus sign was being focused right where the optic nerve enters your eye. At that point, there are no rods and cones, so although the image was focused there, you did not see anything, because there were no rods and cones there to detect the light! That's the blind spot in your eye. As you moved the paper even closer, the plus sign moved to another location on the retina, and you started seeing it again.

Now realize that the blind spot is not a problem under normal circumstances, because when *both* of your eyes are open, one eye will be able to see what is in the other eye's blind spot. As a result, you can see through a whole range of vision without interruption. You can confirm this yourself by repeating the experiment. When the plus sign disappears, open your other eye and see what happens. It reappears! The blind spot, then, is only a problem when one of your eyes is shut or does not work.

The second part of the experiment gives you an idea of how the brain deals with the blind spot in each eye. As you pulled the paper closer to your face, you should have seen the space in between the rectangles actually go away. At that point, the two rectangles should have appeared as one big rectangle. Why? Well, at that point, the space in between the rectangles was being focused on your blind spot. Thus, the light from it was not generating any signals. However, on both sides of the blind spot, your brain was receiving signals indicating that there were black rectangles on the paper. Thus, the brain assumed the rectangles were actually one big rectangle and thus "filled in" what it thought "should" be in the blind spot. As a result, the two small rectangles became one larger one.

I want to give you one more fact about how your brain and your eyes work together to give you your sense of vision. Look at the figure below.

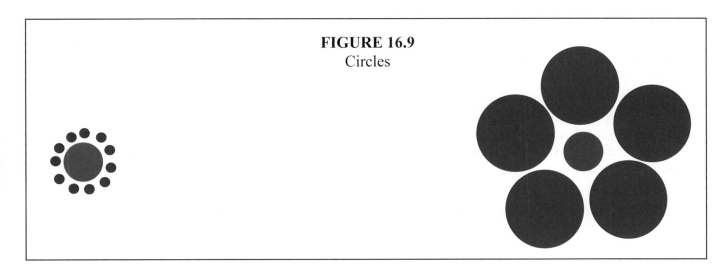

FIGURE 16.9
Circles

Which blue circle is bigger? Most people will say the one on the left is. That's not true. *They are both exactly the same size.* Get out a ruler and see for yourself! Why do you perceive the blue circle on the left to be bigger? Because it is surrounded by smaller red circles. The brain judges size (in part) by comparing the object in question to other objects. Since the blue circle on the left is so much larger than the red circles surrounding it, the brain judges it to be a large circle. Since the blue circle on the right is smaller than the red circles surrounding it, the brain judges it to be a small circle. As a result, the brain thinks the blue circle on the left is larger than the blue circle on the right, even though they are exactly the same size.

The experiment and Figure 16.9, then, show you that your sense of sight is not just dependent on your eyes. While you couldn't see anything at all without properly functioning eyes, that's not the end of the story. In order for you to actually see an image, your brain must also interpret what is coming from your eyes. That interpretation is what forms the images you actually see!

Before I leave this section on the eye, you might be wondering how in the world we see all the incredible colors we see. After all, I made the statement that your cones are sensitive to only three colors of light. How in the world do we see all the other colors? Well, I don't want to answer that question in this course. If you take physical science next year, you will learn about it then. That should give you at least one reason to study physical science!

ON YOUR OWN

16.10 Which is more relaxing: focusing on a scene far away or focusing on a picture held in your hand? Why?

16.11 Suppose a person is born with no cone cells. Will the person be able to see? If so, what will be missing?

The Human Sense of Touch

Your sense of touch is centered on your skin. Since your skin is all over your body, your sense of touch extends over your entire body, so it is called a **somatic** (soh mat' ik) **sense**. This separates it from the **special senses** like sight and smell, which are the result of the brain interacting with only one part of the body (the eye or nose, for example). Your skin is full of millions and millions of neurons that are all attached to different kinds of receptors. In order to give you all the touch sensations you need, the receptors on the skin are many and varied, so they respond to touch in different ways. Some respond quickly to even the slightest touch. Others are slow to respond and tend to give the nervous system information about alterations in the skin that last a much longer time. Others are quick to respond but only to very strong pressure, such as that caused by a crushing blow. As you learned in Module #11, an object doesn't even have to touch you in order for you to feel it. If something brushes up against the hairs on your skin, receptors at the base of the hair respond to the hair bending and send signals to the brain.

It is quite amazing how all these receptors and nerves work together. I once listened to a speech given by a medical researcher who was trying to fashion a glove for people with leprosy. If you are not aware, leprosy is a disease in which the nerve endings in the skin deteriorate. This causes the person to lose his sense of touch. Although that might not sound so bad at first, think about it. Without your sense of touch, you feel no pain. Thus, if your skin gets cut, you won't even notice it. That might sound good at first, but because you do not feel the pain, you do not know you are hurt. As a result, you do not take care of the wound. People with leprosy have terrible problems with infection for that reason. Also, since a person with leprosy cannot feel pain, he or she can destroy skin without realizing it. For example, suppose you lean on a hot stove. You will immediately jerk away because you know it is hot. A person with leprosy would not know this. Thus, he would continue to lean against the stove, burning his skin until it is completely fried. Since the skin is the body's first line of defense against disease, this can be a *real* problem.

The doctor, therefore, was trying to design a glove for people with leprosy. He wanted to be able to put it on a patient's hand so the patient would be warned if he was doing something that would normally cause pain. His idea was that when the patient did something that should cause pain, the glove would send an electric shock to some part of the body where the nerves were not yet destroyed. That way, even though the patient's hand couldn't feel pain, he would be alerted to the fact that he was doing something bad for him, which would cause him to stop whatever he was doing. Sounds simple enough, doesn't it? Well, the problem was that the doctor could not adjust the sensitivity of the sensors in the glove properly.

For example, if a patient hit his finger with a hammer, the sensor could be set to register the blow and shock the patient. However, if the sensor was set that way, the jars from simply *using* the hammer (or other normal activities) could also cause a shock! The doctor said that while his work on the glove allowed him to better appreciate the intricate design of the body's nervous system, it became incredibly frustrating, because he knew that even the state-of-the-art technology he was working with would never be able to mimic the amazingly complex human nervous system, even for something as "simple" as alerting a leprosy patient to pain!

Since I mentioned leprosy, I want to clear up some confusion you might have over this disease. The Bible mentions leprosy a lot, especially in the Old Testament (see Numbers 12:10 or 2 Kings 5:1, for example). However, the disease the Bible calls leprosy is not the disease we identify as leprosy today. In biblical times, the term leprosy covered a wide variety of skin diseases such as scaly skin, rotting skin, etc. Thus, leprosy in biblical times was a *skin disease*, while leprosy today is a *nervous system disease*. Now it is possible that in biblical times there were some people with the nervous system disease who were misdiagnosed with a skin disease. After all, if you can't feel your skin being hurt, you most likely would have a lot of wounds covering your body. As a result, a person with the nervous system disease we now call leprosy might have *looked like* he had a skin disease due to all the damage his skin suffered. Nevertheless, it is still important to understand that the term "leprosy" in the Bible means something quite different from the term "leprosy" today.

Although the sense of touch is a somatic sense, which means it covers the entire body, it is important to note that not all parts of the body are equally sensitive. Perform the following experiment to find out what I mean.

EXPERIMENT 16.5
The Variation in Touch Sensitivity

Supplies:

♦ Two well-sharpened pencils
♦ Some tape
♦ Eye protection such as goggles or safety glasses

Introduction: This experiment will help you learn what parts of the body are most sensitive to touch.

Procedure:

1. Tape the two pencils together, side by side. Make sure the pencil points are both facing the same direction and are level with one another.
2. Lightly touch the two pencil tips on your finger. Note whether or not you can tell you are being touched by two separate pencil points. In other words, ask yourself whether it feels like you are being touched by one large point or two individual small points.
3. Do the same thing on the center of the palm of your hand. Once again, note whether or not you can tell that there are two separate pencil points touching you.
4. Do the same thing on various parts of your arm. Continue to note whether or not you can tell that there are two pencil points touching you.
5. Try other parts of your body. **BE CAREFUL ABOUT THIS. YOU CLEARLY DON'T WANT TO DO THIS ON YOUR EYES OR EARS OR ANYTHING LIKE THAT!!!** Also, be gentle. Don't hurt yourself by pushing too hard. Continue to note whether or not you can tell there are two individual pencil points touching you.

What did you find out? Most likely you were able to tell that two pencil points were touching your finger and hand, but you really couldn't distinguish the two pencil points on your arm. Why? There are many more touch receptors in the skin of your hand than in the skin of your arms. As a result, your arms are less sensitive to touch. This means it is harder for you to accurately sense touch on your arms. Now if you think about that, it should make sense. Your hands need to be very sensitive to touch because they handle things all the time. Your arms are not used to give you detailed information from touch, so you do not need to have as many touch receptors in the skin of your arm. If you continued the experiment, you probably found that your lips, tongue, feet, and toes were the sensitive areas, while most of the rest of your body was not nearly as sensitive.

<u>The Human Sense of Hearing</u>

If a tree falls in the forest and no one is there to hear it, does it make a sound? Have you ever heard that question before? From a scientist's point of view, the answer is easy: YES. You see, scientists do not define sound in reference to your sense of hearing. Instead, sound is defined as a series of vibrations in the air. Indeed, that's where your hearing begins. Suppose you are listening to someone playing the violin. You hear music (hopefully good music) coming from the instrument. How is it formed?

When the violinist strokes the strings with the bow, tiny "hooks" on the bow pluck the strings. This causes them to vibrate back and forth. That vibration pushes the air surrounding the violin back and forth, setting up vibrations in the air. Those vibrations then travel to you, eventually encountering your ear. That's when you start to hear it. How do vibrations in the air turn into sounds you hear? Remember that from a scientist's viewpoint, vibrations in the air *are* sound. However, you do not perceive them as sound until your ear goes to work.

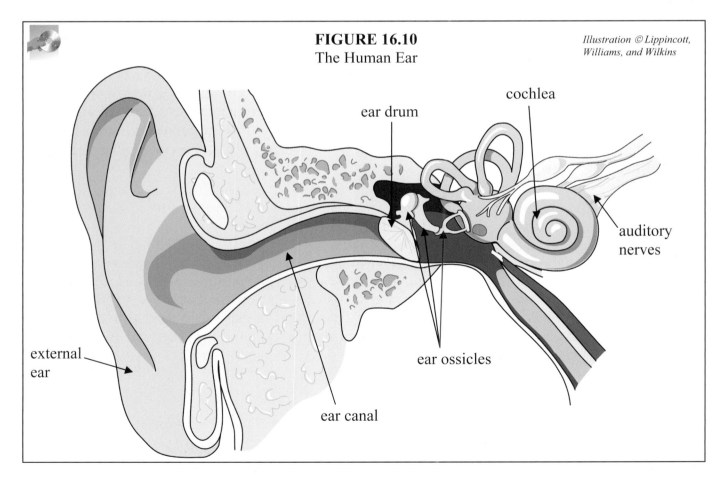

FIGURE 16.10
The Human Ear

Illustration © Lippincott, Williams, and Wilkins

cochlea

ear drum

auditory nerves

external ear

ear ossicles

ear canal

What you call "the ear" is really just the **external ear**. It acts as a "funnel" to send vibrations in the air down the **ear canal** until they reach the **ear drum**. The ear drum is, indeed, much like a drum. It is a thin sheet of tissue stretched across the ear canal. Vibrations in the air cause the ear drum to vibrate. You will learn more about how that works when you take physical science next year. The vibrations of the ear drum cause tiny bones called **ear ossicles** (ah' sik uhls) to move back and forth. This movement in turn vibrates fluid within the snail-shaped **cochlea** (ko' klee uh). There are "hair cells" in the fluid of the cochlea, which pick up the fluid's vibration and convert it into an electrical signal that is sent via the auditory nerve to the brain. The brain then interprets the signal as sound.

If you think about it then, the ear's real job is to *transform* sound. Sound hits the ear as vibrations in the air. The ear drum transforms those vibrations into vibrations in the ear drum. Those vibrations are then transformed into the rocking of the ear ossicles, which is then further transformed into the vibration of a fluid, which is then converted to electrical signals. The brain then takes those electrical signals and sends them to the auditory area of the cerebrum, and you perceive the sound.

It is useful to compare the human ear to something else that transforms sound: a microphone. When you speak into a microphone, the vibrations your vocal cords set up in the air reach a thin "drum" of material, called a diaphragm. Just like the ear drum, the diaphragm shakes in response to the air vibrations. Those shakes are then converted into electrical signals in a variety of ways. For example, one type of microphone has a quartz crystal attached to the diaphragm. When the diaphragm vibrates, it causes changes in the crystal's shape, which causes the crystal to produce electrical signals. Thus, a microphone also takes vibrations in the air and transforms them into electrical signals, somewhat like the ear.

Of course, compared to the ear, a microphone is incredibly primitive. Consider, for example, the range of volume your ears can hear compared to that of a microphone. If a microphone is set to pick up very soft sounds, it will quickly "max out" as the sound gets louder, causing distortions in the recording. Alternatively, if you want a microphone to pick up loud sounds and send them to a recording device with little or no distortion, the microphone will not be able to detect softer sounds. Your ear, however, can hear very soft and very loud sounds, with no distortion across the entire range. Like most marvels of human technology, even the best microphone cannot come close to the amazing design of the human body!

ON YOUR OWN

16.12 Infections, sudden pressure changes, or even very loud noises can cause a tear in your ear drum. When that happens, you don't hear very well, because the drum does not respond to air vibrations as well as it once did. Over time, however, a torn ear drum can heal. Suppose a person's ear drum was torn by a sudden pressure change while scuba diving. The person experiences hearing loss, but eventually, the ear drum heals almost as good as new. If the person still cannot hear very well, what else might have happened? (Look at Figure 16.10 carefully.)

Do We Really Use Only 10 Percent of our Brain?

I want to end our discussion of the human nervous system by going back to the brain for just a moment. How many times have you heard the phrase, "We use less than 10 percent of our brain." It is a very popular saying. You hear it in advertisements, in motivational seminars, and even on the news.

There is only one problem: ***it is absolutely wrong!*** There are no scientific data that lend any support to such a statement. It is simply a myth. An enormous amount of research has been done on the human brain. Doctors have found that removing even a small piece of a person's brain can have disastrous consequences. Although it is impossible for scientists to track the activity of every neuron in the brain, it is pretty apparent that all the neurons in the brain are used. In the end, then, science tells us that we really use *all* of our brain!

How did this myth get started? No one knows for sure. In the early 1900s, a scientist named Karl Spencer Lashley performed experiments on rats in which he removed large parts of their brains and demonstrated that they could still survive. This led some people to conclude that large portions of the brain go unused. Of course, the experimental data really do not justify the conclusion. After all, the rats may have survived, but Lashley didn't test to see if they could still do all the things that they could do *before* the operation. If Lashley missed the critical parts of the brain, the rats' autonomic nervous system would have remained intact, and instincts such as the need to eat could have survived. However, the rats probably could not do nearly as much as before, like running mazes, learning specific behaviors, etc.

It appears that some prominent people took those experiments and ran with them, however. American psychologist William James wrote in 1908: "We are making use of only a small part of our possible mental and physical resources" (William James, "The Energies of Men," *The Philosophical Review*, 16:1, p. 18, 1907). There are those who even attribute the very quote, "We only use 10 percent of our brain," to Albert Einstein. Regardless of its origin, this statement has been promoted by the popular media for many years. Nevertheless, as far as science can tell, it is completely false.

Summing It All Up

Well, believe it or not, you have reached the end of the course! I hope you have gotten a glimpse of why science excites me so much! Perhaps you still do not like science as much as I do. That's okay. I really hope that after taking this course, however, you can at least appreciate why some people enjoy studying science.

I also hope you have developed a deep appreciation for all that God has given you in His creation. From the majesty of rock formations to the intricacy of cells to the grand design of the human body, creation screams out in testimony to its Creator. It is up to us to recognize that and give the Creator His due.

As you finish this course, I want to remind you of a quote I gave you in the first module. Robert Boyle (the founder of modern chemistry), in his last address to the Royal Society (a group of scientists in England), said the following:

"Remember to give glory to the One who authored nature."[*]

Unfortunately, most scientists have forgotten the words of that great scientist. Do not let that happen to you!

[*]As quoted in *Scientists of Faith* by Dan Graves (Kregel Resources, Grand Rapids, 1996), p. 63

ANSWERS TO THE "ON YOUR OWN" PROBLEMS

16.1. Dendrites carry signals toward the neuron cell body, while axons carry signals away from the neuron cell body. Thus, the signal is traveling along a <u>dendrite</u>.

16.2. <u>Without neurotransmitters, the neuron cannot communicate with other cells.</u> The functions of a neuron depend on the neuron communicating with other cells, so without neurotransmitters, the neuron cannot perform any of its normal functions for the nervous system.

16.3. <u>The man will be able to move his arms but not his legs.</u> If the spinal cord is severed at the waist, CNS signals cannot reach the PNS below the waist. Since the legs are below the waist, there will be no control over the leg muscles. However, the arms are above the waist, so the CNS can still control the PNS above the waist.

16.4. Remember, "higher level" thinking such as learning and reasoning occurs in the cerebrum. Since humans are intellectually superior to other vertebrates, <u>the cerebrum is significantly larger</u>.

16.5. <u>The first patient is having no problems speaking.</u> The left side of the brain is primarily responsible for speech. Thus, the person with the left side of the brain damaged will be the one having trouble speaking. It was data like this that led to scientists first realizing that one hemisphere of the brain dominates the other in certain skills and functions.

16.6. <u>The blood-brain barrier wouldn't work without the proteins in between the cells of the capillaries. Those proteins seal the capillaries like gaskets, keeping the blood and fluid inside</u>.

16.7. <u>The sympathetic division of your autonomic nervous system is at work in this case.</u> The sympathetic division increases heart rate and blood pressure.

16.8. <u>It stimulates the umami sensation.</u> In fact, the idea of umami as a fifth basic taste sensation was accepted in Japan and China before it was accepted in the U.S.

16.9. <u>Without chemicals in the air, there can be no scent.</u> The air-purifier marketers probably wanted to say that the purifier cleans out all "foreign chemicals," or something like that. Note that some air purifiers do not live up to their claims, and certain types can be dangerous. See the course website I told you about in the "Student Notes" section for more details.

16.10. <u>Focusing on a scene far away will be more relaxing.</u> When the ciliary muscle relaxes, the lens gets thinner, and that focuses on things far from the eye. Obviously a relaxed muscle leads to a more relaxing experience.

16.11. <u>The person will be able to see, but there will be no color.</u> There will be other problems as well, but since cones detect color, the obvious problem is that he will not see color.

16.12 Notice from Figure 16.10 that the first ossicle (malleus) is attached to the ear drum, the second one (incus) is attached to it, and the third one (stapes) is attached to the incus and the cochlea. For vibrations to be transferred from the ear drum to the cochlea, the ossicles must be intact. Thus, <u>the sudden pressure change could have damaged the ear ossicles or the way they connect to one another or the other parts of the ear</u>. In fact, this is a possible complication of a torn ear drum.

STUDY GUIDE FOR MODULE #16

1. Define the following terms:

a. Autonomic nervous system
b. Sensory nervous system
c. Somatic motor nervous system

2. What are the two main types of cells in the human nervous system?

3. Identify the structures pointed out in this diagram of a neuron.

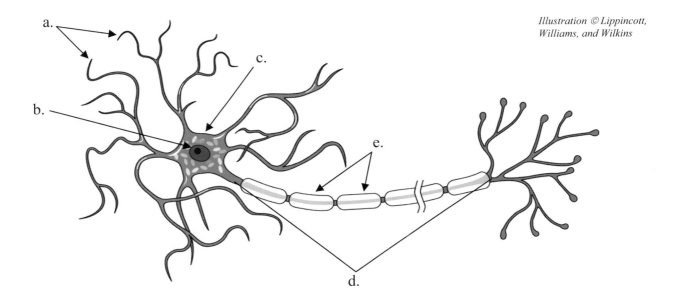

Illustration © Lippincott, Williams, and Wilkins

4. What do dendrites do?

5. What do axons do?

6. What is a synapse?

7. Explain how a signal crosses from the axon of a neuron to the receiving cell.

8. What is the function of neuroglia?

9. A nerve runs down the leg, carrying signals to and from the foot. Is it a part of the PNS or the CNS?

10. What two main structures make up the CNS?

11. What two things discussed in this module protect the brain?

12. What protects the spinal cord?

13. What is the brain's gray matter composed of?

14. What is the brain's white matter composed of?

15. What is the function of the corpus callosum?

16. What does the cerebellum primarily control?

17. What part of the brain deals mostly with higher-level thinking skills?

18. Do the two sides of the brain do exactly the same things?

19. What side of the PNS does the left side of the brain control?

20. What is the blood-brain barrier and why is it important?

21. What does the sympathetic division of the autonomic nervous system do?

22. What does the parasympathetic division of the autonomic nervous system do?

23. What are the five basic tastes we can detect?

24. When we smell something, what are we actually detecting?

25. What is the function of the eye's pupil?

26. What is the function of the eye's lens?

27. What is the function of the eye's ciliary muscle?

28. What cells of the retina detect light?

29. What causes an eye's blind spot?

30. Which part of the body has the most nerves related to touch: the fingers or the arm?

31. What is the function of the ear drum?

32. What is the function of the cochlea?

GLOSSARY

The numbers in parentheses indicate the page number where the term was first discussed.

Absolute age: The calculated age of an artifact from a specific dating method that is used to determine when the artifact was made (127)

Air resistance: The drag that air produces on objects traveling through it (37)

Alchemy: The nonscientific pursuit in which people tried to turn lead (or other inexpensive substances) into gold (or other expensive substances) (12)

Alimentary canal: The collection of organs through which food passes (322)

Altricial: A term used to describe offspring that are born without at least one of the following abilities: hear, see, move about, regulate body temperature, or eliminate waste (233)

Angular unconformity: An unconformity between strata that are tilted relative to each other (153)

Animalia: The biological kingdom containing consumers made of several eukaryotic cells (243)

Antibiotic: A substance that inhibits or destroys life, usually used to kill pathogens (70)

Appendicular skeleton: The portion of the skeleton that attaches to the axial skeleton and has the limbs attached to it (271)

Archaeology: The study of past human life as revealed by preserved relics (109)

Aristotle's dictum: The benefit of the doubt is to be given to the document itself, not assigned by the critic to himself. (111)

Arteries: Blood vessels that carry blood away from the heart (343)

Artifacts: Objects made by people, such as tools, weapons, containers, etc. (109)

Atmospheric pressure: The pressure exerted by the atmosphere on all objects within it (22)

Atom: The smallest chemical unit of matter (216)

Autonomic nervous system: The system of nerves that carries instructions from the CNS to the body's smooth muscles, cardiac muscle, and glands (402)

Axial skeleton: The portion of the skeleton that supports and protects the head, neck, and trunk (271)

Basal metabolic rate: The minimum amount of energy required by the body in a day (309)

Bibliographic test: A historical test that attempts to determine whether or not the version of the document that exists is a faithful representation of the original (110)

Blind experiments: Experiments in which the participants do not know whether or not they are a part of the control group (71)

Block and tackle: A system of multiple pulleys in which the mechanical advantage is given by the number of pulleys in the system (98)

Blood platelets: Cell fragments that help initiate the blood clotting process (352)

Capillaries: Tiny, thin-walled blood vessels that allow the exchange of gases and nutrients between the blood and cells and are located between arteries and veins (343)

Carbonization: The process by which an organism's remains are converted to a filmy residue that leaves a flattened "drawing" of the organism in rock (164)

Cardiac cycle: The entire cycle of a heartbeat, which includes the contraction of the two atria, the relaxation of the atria accompanied with the contraction of the ventricles, and the relaxation of the ventricles (350)

Cardiac muscle: Involuntary muscle that works the heart (265)

Carnivore: A consumer that eats only other consumers (295)

Cast: In paleontology, the shape formed when sediments or magma fill a mold (159)

Catastrophism: The view that most of earth's geological features are the result of large-scale catastrophes such as floods, volcanic eruptions, etc. (136)

Cell: The smallest unit of life in creation (234)

Chemical digestion: The process of breaking food down by altering its chemical nature (320)

Chemical Weathering: The process by which a rock is broken down by changing the chemical nature of the rock (144)

Circumference: The distance around a circle, equal to 3.1416 times the circle's diameter (102)

Classification: A systematic arrangement of data into groups based on set criteria (7)

Combustion: An energetic chemical reaction in which a fuel is reacted with oxygen to produce energy, carbon dioxide, and water (26)

Compact bone: Bone tissue in which the collagen and minerals are packed together tightly, forming a hard, tough structure (269)

Constellation: A recognized pattern in the stars of the night sky (14)

Consumers: Organisms that eat living producers and/or other consumers for food (294)

Control (of an experiment): The variable or part of the experiment to which all others will be compared (65)

Copernican system: The system in which the sun is at the center of the universe, and the planets and stars orbit around the sun (18)

Counter example: An example that contradicts a conclusion (38)

Decomposers: Organisms that break down the dead remains of other organisms (253)

Dehydrated food: Food in which almost all the water has been removed (249)

Delta: A typically fan-shaped area where a river deposits its sediments at its mouth (149)

Dendrochronology: The process of counting tree rings to determine the age of a tree (125)

Density: A measure of the amount of mass in an object per unit volume (6)

Dermis: The inner layer of the skin (283)

Diameter: The length of a straight line that travels from one side of a circle to another and passes through the center of the circle (93)

Digestion: The process by which an organism breaks down its food into small units that can be absorbed by the body (319)

Digestive tract: The collection of organs through which food passes (322)

Disaccharides – Carbohydrates that are made up of two monosaccharides (302)

Disconformity: An unconformity between two layers of sedimentary rock (153)

Double-blind experiments: Experiments in which neither the participants nor the people analyzing the results know who is in the control group (72)

Ectothermic: An animal that cannot regulate its internal body temperature, i.e., is "cold-blooded" (307)

Effort: In simple machines, the force being applied to the machine (88)

Electromagnetism: The union of electricity and magnetism (28)

Ellipse: The collection of points in which the sum of the distance between two points (foci) are the same (20)

Endothermic: An animal that can regulate its internal body temperature, i.e., is "warm-blooded" (307)

ENIAC: Electronic Numerical Integrator and Computer – the first electronic computer (84)

Epidermis: The outer layer of the skin (283)

Erosion: The process by which rock and soil are broken down and transported away (147)

Essential amino acids: Amino acids that cannot be produced by the body and thus must be eaten (304)

Essential fats: Fats that cannot be produced by the body and thus must be eaten (303)

Eukaryotic cell: A cell with distinct, membrane-bounded organelles (244)

Exoskeleton: A body covering, typically made of chitin, that provides support and protection (272)

Experimental variable: An aspect of an experiment that changes during the course of the experiment (59)

External test: A historical test that attempts to determine whether or not a document contradicts other established sources of history (110)

Extinct: A term applied to a species that was once living but now is not (170)

First-class lever: A lever in which the fulcrum is between the effort and the resistance (89)

Force: A push or pull exerted on an object in an effort to change that object's velocity (87)

Fossil graveyards: Deposits that contain enormous numbers of fossilized creatures, often from many different climates (199)

Fossil record: The sum total of all discovered fossils (168)

Fossil: The preserved remains of a once-living organism (159)

Fulcrum: The part of a lever that does not move (87)

Fungi: The biological kingdom containing the decomposers made of eukaryotic cells (243)

Genetics – The science that studies how characteristics get passed from parent to offspring (28)

Geocentric system: The system in which the earth is at the center of the universe, and the planets and stars orbit around the earth (10)

Geological column: A theoretical picture in which layers of rock from around the world are meshed together into a single, unbroken record of earth's past (190)

Geology: The study of earth's history as revealed in the rocks that make up the earth (110)

Glucose: A monosaccharide that is produced in photosynthesis (224)

Glycogen: A polysaccharide that animals typically use to store excess carbohydrates (334)

Gravitropism: The tendency of a plant to grow up away from the earth (282)

Groundwater: Water found underneath the surface of the earth (150)

Heliocentric system: The system in which the sun is at the center of the solar system, and the planets and orbit around the sun (18)

Hemoglobin: The protein in red blood cells that gives blood its red color (352)

Herbivore: A consumer that eats producers exclusively (295)

Hormone: A chemical messenger released into the bloodstream that sends signals to distant cells, causing them to change their behavior in specific ways (382)

Humus: The decayed remains of once-living creatures (137)

Hypodermis: The fatty tissue that connects skin to the underlying tissues (283)

Hypothesis: An educated guess that attempts to explain an observation or answer a question (40)

Igneous rock: Rock formed by the solidification of molten rock (137)

Inclined plane: A simple machine that is shaped like a ramp with the effort applied along the slope of the ramp (99)

Index fossils: Fossils that are assumed to represent a certain period in earth's past (185)

Intermediate link: A creature that is supposed to represent an evolutionary transition from one basic kind of creature to another (208)

Internal test: A historical test that attempts to determine whether or not a document contradicts itself (110)

Interstitial fluid: Fluid found between cells (367)

Keratinization: The process by which cells are hardened to make skin, nails, and hair (266)

Known age: The age of an artifact as determined by a date printed on it or a reference to the artifact in a work of history (124)

Lamination: A layer of rock less than 1 centimeter thick (143)

Lava: Molten rock on the surface of the earth (137)

Law of Mass Conservation: Matter cannot be created or destroyed. It can only change forms. (26)

Lever: A simple machine composed of a bar and a fulcrum (87)

Life science: A term that encompasses all scientific pursuits related to living organisms (109)

Ligaments: Strips of elastic tissue that hold the bones of a joint together (277)

Lymph: Fluid found in the lymphatic system (367)

Macronutrients: The nutrients animals need in large amounts for energy – carbohydrates, proteins, and fats (302)

Magma: Molten rock that is underground (137)

Mechanical advantage: The amount by which force or motion is magnified in a simple machine (89)

Messianic prophecies: Old Testament prophecies that made specific predictions about the coming Messiah (53)

Metabolism: The sum total of all processes in an organism that convert energy and matter from outside sources and use that energy and matter to sustain the organism's life functions (226)

Metamorphic rock: Sedimentary or igneous rock that has undergone substantial change, generally as the result of heat or pressure (137)

Metamorphosis: The change that occurs when an insect matures from its larval form (such as a maggot) to its adult form (such as a fly) [230]

Micronutrients: Nutrients like vitamins and minerals that are needed only in small doses (306)

Microscope: An optical device that makes enlarged images of minute objects (24)

Minerals: Inorganic crystalline substances found naturally in the earth (137)

Mold: In paleontology, the impression formed when an organism is surrounded by rock before it decomposes (159)

Molecule: Two or more atoms linked together to make a substance with unique properties (217)

Monera: The biological kingdom containing all organisms with prokaryotic cells (243)

Monosaccharides – Simple carbohydrates, also called simple sugars (302)

Morse code: A code in which ever letter of the English language is represented by a series of dots and/or dashes (219)

Nebula: A cloud of dust or gas in interstellar space (14)

Neutralization: In chemistry, the process by which acids and bases react to cancel each other's effects (328)

Nonconformity: An unconformity between sedimentary rock and either igneous or metamorphic rock (153)

Nucleus: In a eukaryotic cell, the organelle that holds most of the cell's DNA (235)

Objective data: Data whose value cannot be affected by a person's opinion (73)

Omnivore: A consumer that eats both producers and other consumers (295)

Pain threshold: The level at which a person begins to consider pain uncomfortable (71)

Paleontology: The study of life's history as revealed in the preserved remains of once-living organisms (110)

Papyrus: An ancient form of paper, made from a plant of the same name (2)

Paraconformity: An unconformity for which there is no evidence but some geologists think should exist (154)

Pasteurization: Partial sterilization of a substance that does not chemically alter the substance (27)

Pathogen: An organism that causes disease (248)

Penicillin: A mixture of chemical compounds produced by certain molds that have strong antibacterial properties (2)

Petrifaction: The conversion of organic material into rock (162)

Phloem: Tubes that carry sugar and organic substances throughout a plant (363)

Photosynthesis: The process by which green plants and some other organisms use the energy of sunlight and simple chemicals to produce their own food (224)

Phototropism: The tendency of a plant to grow toward light (282)

Physical digestion: The process of breaking food down without altering its chemical nature (320)

Physical Weathering: The process by which a rock is broken down without changing the chemical nature of the rock (144)

Plantae: The biological kingdom containing all organisms made of eukaryotic cells that make their own food and have specialized structures like roots, stems, and leaves (243)

Polysaccharides – Carbohydrates that are made up of more than two monosaccharides (302)

Precocial: A term used to describe offspring that are born able to hear, see, move about, regulate body temperature, and eliminate waste without a parent's help (233)

Producers: Organisms that produce their own food (293)

Prokaryotic cell: A cell that has no distinct, membrane-bounded organelles (244)

Protista: The biological kingdom containing all organisms made of only one eukaryotic cell as well as algae (243)

Ptolemaic system: The system in which the earth is at the center of the universe, and the planets and stars orbit around the earth (10)

Pulley: The simple machine composed of a grooved wheel that rotates freely on a frame (95)

Quantum mechanics: The modern-day view of physics, which depends on the assumption that energy comes in small packets called "quanta" (29)

Radiometric dating: Using a radioactive process to determine the age of an item (127)

Receptors: Special structures that allow living organisms to sense the conditions of their internal or external environment (227)

Red blood cells: Blood cells that carry oxygen (352)

Resin: A thick, slowly flowing liquid produced by plants that can harden into a solid (167)

Resistance: In simple machines, the weight the machine is manipulating (88)

Science: An endeavor dedicated to the accumulation and classification of observable facts in order to formulate general laws about the natural world (1)

Scientific law: A theory that has been tested by and is consistent with generations of data (40)

Scientific method: A framework in which scientists can analyze situations, explain certain phenomena, and answer certain questions (40)

Screw: A simple machine composed of a wheel and axle with an inclined plane wrapped around the axle (101)

Second-class lever: A lever in which the resistance is between the effort and the fulcrum (90)

Sedimentary rock: Rock formed by the hardening of sediments (137)

Sensory nervous system: The system of nerves that carries information from the body's receptors to the CNS (402)

Simple machine: A device that either multiplies or redirects a force (87)

Single-blind experiments: Experiments in which only the participants do not know whether or not they are a part of the control group (72)

Skeletal muscle: Voluntary muscle that moves the skeleton (265)

Smooth muscle: Involuntary muscle that causes organ and blood vessels to work (265)

Solution: The result when a substance is dissolved in another substance (74)

Somatic motor nervous system: The system of nerves that carries instructions from the CNS to the skeletal muscles (403)

Spongy bone: Bone tissue in which there are open spaces in the network of solid bone (269)

Spontaneous generation: The idea that living organisms can be spontaneously formed from non-living substances (8)

Stalactite: A sediment deposit resembling an icicle and hanging from the roof of a cave (151)

Stalagmite: A sediment deposit resembling pillar and rising from the floor of a cave (151)

Starch: A polysaccharide commonly used by plants to store extra food (224)

Stratum: In geology, a layer of rock (141)

Subjective data: Data that depend to some extent on a person's opinion (73)

Subjective data: Data that depend to some extent on a person's opinion (73)

Superconductivity: The phenomenon in which certain substances at certain temperatures conduct electricity without any resistance (46)

Supernova: The explosion of a star (15)

Surface tension: The ability of a liquid's surface to resist a force applied to it due to the attraction between the liquid's molecules (68)

Symbiosis: A close relationship between two or more species where at least one benefits (285)

Tendon: Connective tissue that attaches skeletal muscles to the skeleton (274)

The First Law of Thermodynamics: Energy cannot be created or destroyed. It can only change forms. (28)

The immutability of species: The idea that each individual species on the planet was specially created by God and could never fundamentally change (27)

The Principle of Superposition: When artifacts are found in rock or earth that is layered, the deeper layers hold the older artifacts. (128)

The Theory of Evolution: A theory stating that all life on this earth has one (or a few) common ancestor(s) that existed a long time ago (191)

Theory: A hypothesis that has been tested with a significant amount of data (40)

Third-class lever: A lever in which the effort is between the fulcrum and the resistance (90)

Transistor: An electronic device used to control the flow of electricity in an electronic circuit (85)

Turgor pressure: The pressure within a plant cell caused by the central vacuole pushing the organelles and cytoplasm against the cell wall (259)

Unconformity: A surface of erosion that separates one layer of rock from another (153)

Uniformitarianism: The view that most of earth's geological features are the result of slow, gradual processes that have been at work for millions or even billions of years (136)

Vaccine: A weakened or inactive version of a pathogen that stimulates the body's production of antibodies that can destroy the pathogen (372)

Vegetative reproduction: The process by which one part of a plant can form new roots and develop into a complete plant (257)

Veins: Blood vessels that carry blood back to the heart (343)

Vestigial organ: An organ that exists in a body but has no function (333)

Vitamin: A chemical substance the body needs in small amounts to stay healthy (337)

Weathering: The process by which rocks are broken down to form sediments (144)

Wedge: A simple machine shaped like a ramp with the effort applied at the short edge (100)

Wheel and axle: The simple machine composed of a wheel attached to a cylinder such that when one turns, the other turns as well (93)

White blood cells: Blood cells that combat disease (352)

X-axis: The horizontal axis of a graph (75)

X-rays: High-energy radiation that can be used for medical diagnosis (85)

Xylem – Tubes that carry water and dissolved minerals from the roots of a plant to its leaves (363)

Y-axis: The vertical axis of a graph (75)

APPENDIX A

The Geocentric System

In the geocentric system, the Earth sits at the center of the universe and does not move. The planets travel around the Earth in circles within circles. What this means is that the "average" path of each planet around the Earth is given by the gray lines in the figure. However, the planets themselves do not travel directly along those lines. Instead, they travel in little circles (called epicycles) centered on those lines. This makes each planet's path more of a spiral, the center of which is marked by the gray lines. The moon is closest to the Earth, followed by Mercury, Venus, the Sun, Mars, Jupiter, and Saturn. Those were the only planets known in Ptolemy's day. The stars are contained in a canopy called "the heaven." Although the stars are fixed in the heaven, the heaven rotates, which makes the stars themselves appear to move.

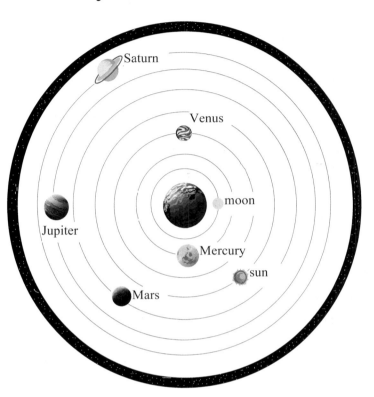

The Heliocentric System

Illustration by Sebastian Kaulitzki
Agency: www.shutterstock.com

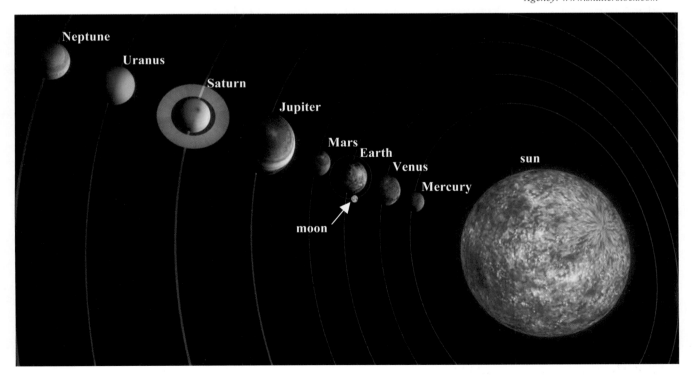

The Scientific Method

Make observations.

Form a hypothesis to explain your observations.

If the data are not consistent with the theory or the hypothesis, either adjust or discard the hypothesis or theory.

Data are consistent with the hypothesis.

Collect data that test the hypothesis.

Hypothesis becomes a theory.

Continue to test the theory with generations of data.

Theory becomes a law.

Data are consistent with the theory.

Illustrations from www.clipart.com

Simple Machine Equations

For a Lever:

Mechanical advantage = (distance from fulcrum to effort) ÷ (distance from fulcrum to resistance)

For a Wheel and Axle:

Mechanical advantage = (diameter of the wheel) ÷ (diameter of the axle)

For Pulleys in a Block and Tackle:

Mechanical advantage = number of pulleys used

For an Inclined Plane or Wedge:

Mechanical advantage = (length of the slope) ÷ (height)

For a Screw:

Mechanical advantage = (circumference) ÷ (pitch)

The Geological Column
A Uniformitarian Construct

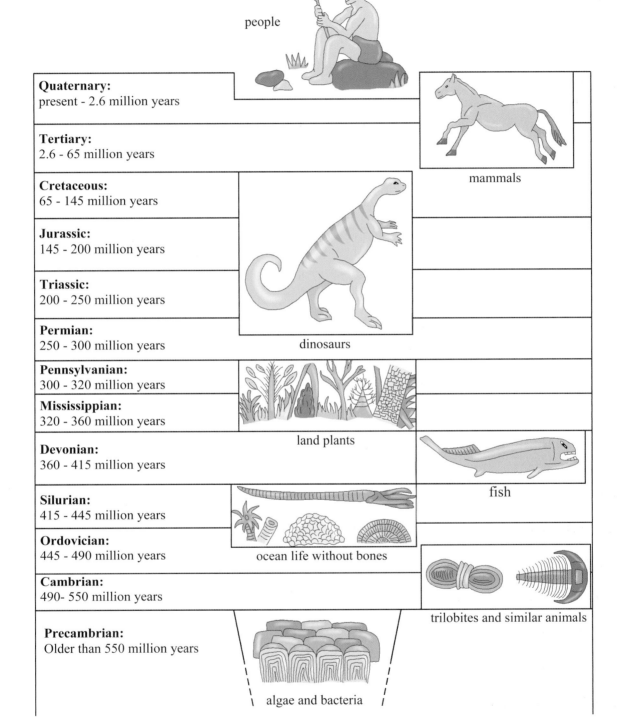

people

Quaternary:
present - 2.6 million years

Tertiary:
2.6 - 65 million years

mammals

Cretaceous:
65 - 145 million years

Jurassic:
145 - 200 million years

Triassic:
200 - 250 million years

dinosaurs

Permian:
250 - 300 million years

Pennsylvanian:
300 - 320 million years

Mississippian:
320 - 360 million years

land plants

Devonian:
360 - 415 million years

fish

Silurian:
415 - 445 million years

Ordovician:
445 - 490 million years

ocean life without bones

Cambrian:
490- 550 million years

trilobites and similar animals

Precambrian:
Older than 550 million years

algae and bacteria

Illustration by Megan Fruchte

Major Bones of the Adult Human Body

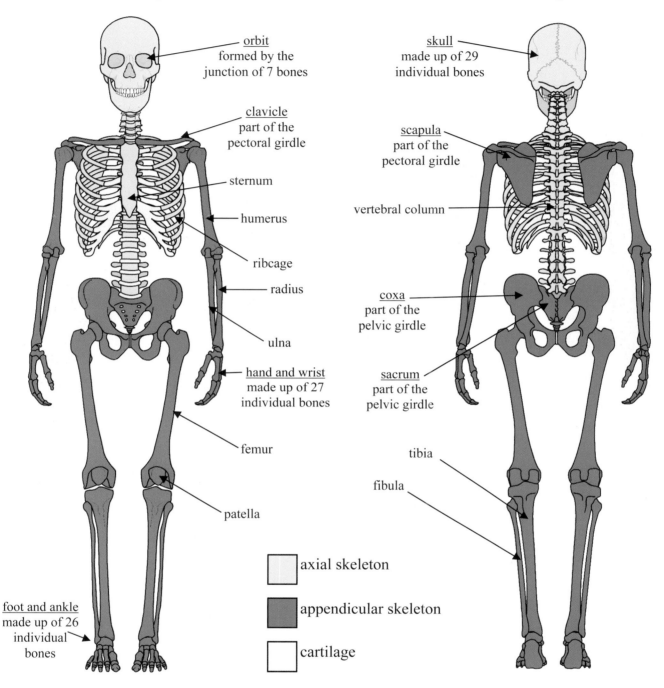

orbit
formed by the
junction of 7 bones

skull
made up of 29
individual bones

clavicle
part of the
pectoral girdle

scapula
part of the
pectoral girdle

sternum

vertebral column

humerus

ribcage

radius

coxa
part of the
pelvic girdle

ulna

hand and wrist
made up of 27
individual bones

sacrum
part of the
pelvic girdle

femur

tibia

fibula

patella

axial skeleton

appendicular skeleton

cartilage

foot and ankle
made up of 26
individual
bones

Illustration © Lippincott, Williams, and Wilkins

Selected Skeletal Muscles of the Human Body

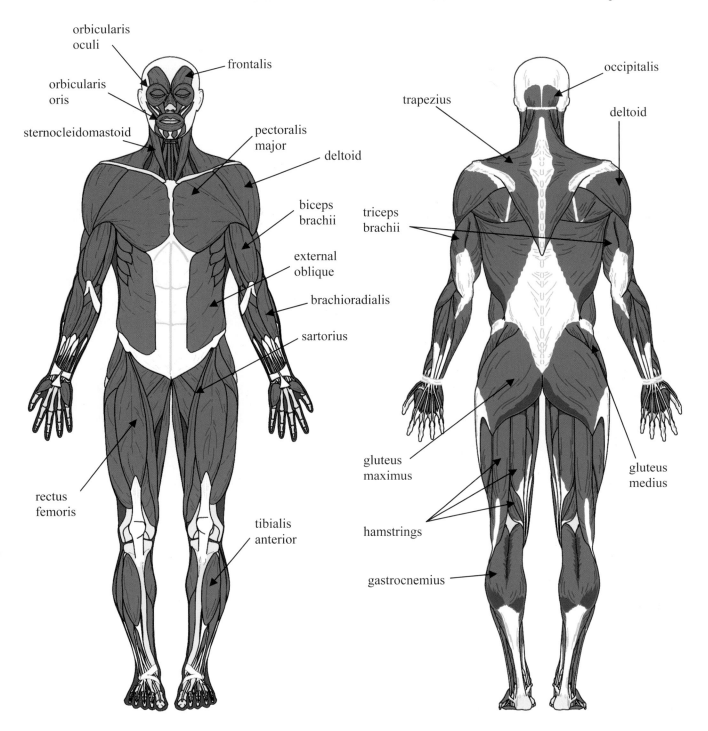

orbicularis
oculi

frontalis

orbicularis
oris

sternocleidomastoid

pectoralis
major

deltoid

biceps
brachii

external
oblique

brachioradialis

sartorius

rectus
femoris

tibialis
anterior

trapezius

occipitalis

deltoid

triceps
brachii

gluteus
maximus

gluteus
medius

hamstrings

gastrocnemius

Illustration © Lippincott, Williams, and Wilkins

The Human Digestive System

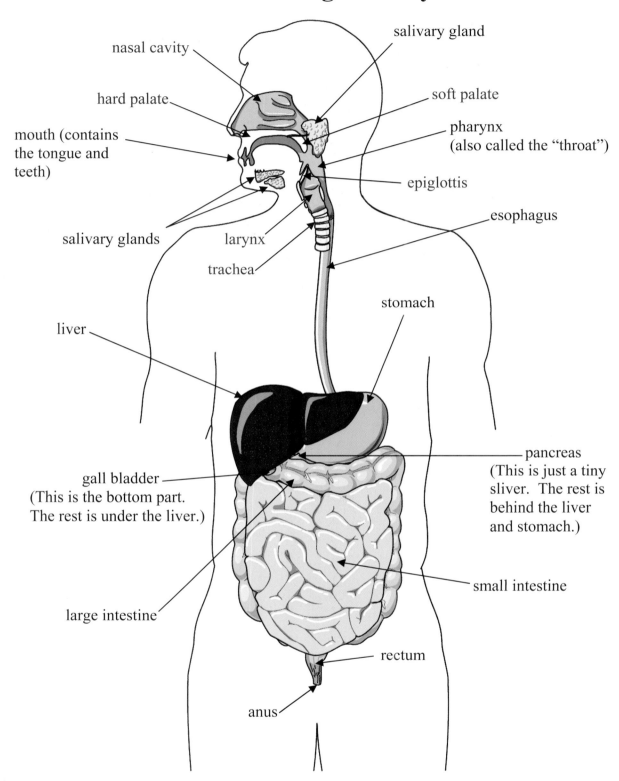

nasal cavity

salivary gland

hard palate

soft palate

mouth (contains
the tongue and
teeth)

pharynx
(also called the "throat")

epiglottis

salivary glands

larynx

trachea

esophagus

stomach

liver

pancreas
(This is just a tiny
sliver. The rest is
behind the liver
and stomach.)

gall bladder
(This is the bottom part.
The rest is under the liver.)

small intestine

large intestine

rectum

anus

Illustration © Lippincott, Williams, and Wilkins

The Major Veins and Arteries in the Human Body

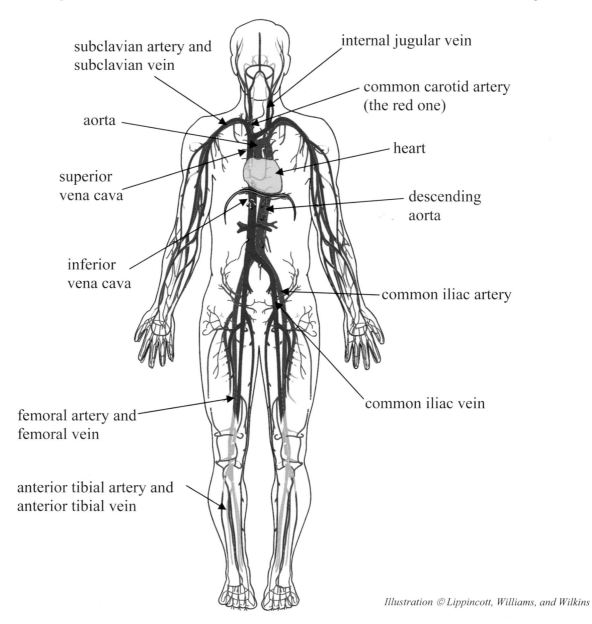

subclavian artery and
subclavian vein

internal jugular vein

common carotid artery
(the red one)

aorta

heart

superior
vena cava

descending
aorta

inferior
vena cava

common iliac artery

common iliac vein

femoral artery and
femoral vein

anterior tibial artery and
anterior tibial vein

Illustration © Lippincott, Williams, and Wilkins

Blood Flow in the Heart

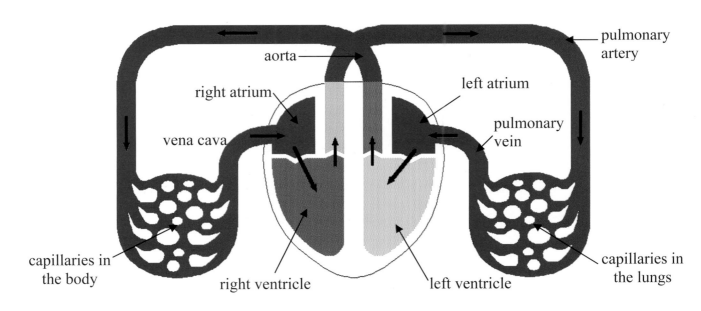

Illustration from the MasterClips Collection

Human Respiratory System

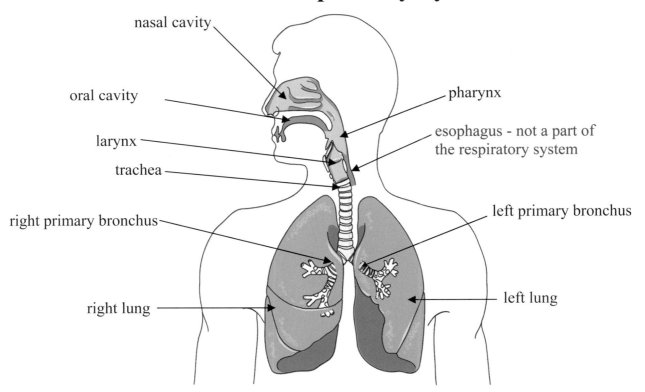

Illustration © Lippincott, Williams, and Wilkins

The Human Lymphatic System

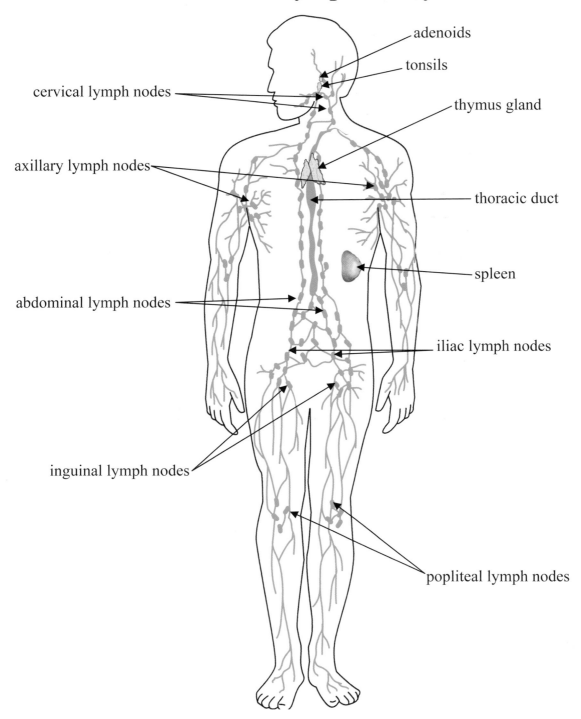

adenoids

tonsils

cervical lymph nodes

thymus gland

axillary lymph nodes

thoracic duct

spleen

abdominal lymph nodes

iliac lymph nodes

inguinal lymph nodes

popliteal lymph nodes

Illustration © Lippincott, Williams, and Wilkins

The Human Nervous System

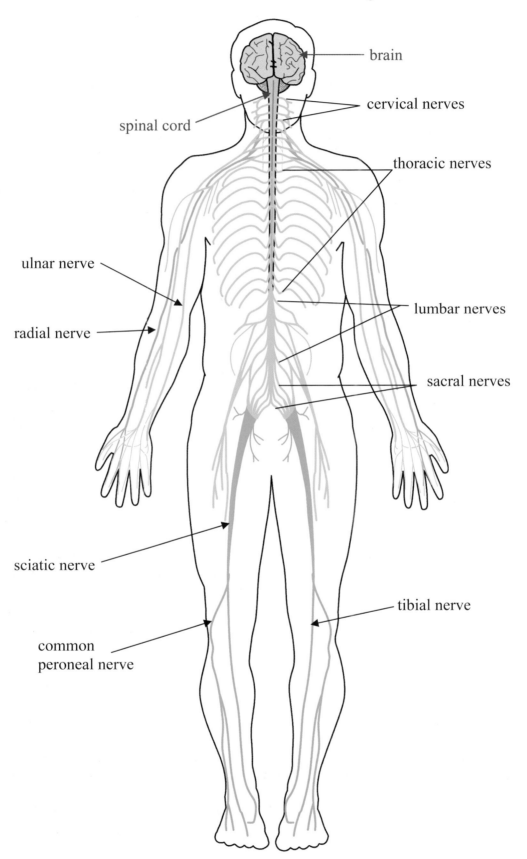

brain

cervical nerves

spinal cord

thoracic nerves

ulnar nerve

radial nerve

lumbar nerves

sacral nerves

sciatic nerve

tibial nerve

common
peroneal nerve

APPENDIX B
MODULE SUMMARIES

Summary of Module #1
Review the vocabulary words listed in Question #1 of the study guide

Fill in the blanks. Many blanks contain more than one word.
Please note: We suggest that you actually write these paragraphs out rather than just filling in the blanks in the book. The act of writing these things out is a form of studying.

1. We should support a scientific idea based on the _____, not based on the people who agree with it. Scientific progress depends not only on scientists, but also on _____ and _____. Scientific progress occurs by building on the work of _____.

2. In ancient times, people traveled for miles to visit _____ in Egypt, because he was renowned for his knowledge of medicine. Despite the fact that he could cure many ills, his medicine was based not on science, but on _____ and _____. Egyptian medicine was advanced by the invention of _____, which made recording information and passing it on from generation to generation much easier.

3. Three of the first scientists were _____, _____, and _____, who were all from ancient Greece. _____ studied the heavens and tried to develop a unifying theme that would explain the movements of the _____. His pupil, _____ mainly studied life and was probably the first to attempt an explanation for the origin of the human race without reference to a _____. _____ believed that all things were constructed of air, which led to one of the most important scientific ideas introduced by the Greeks: the concept of _____.

4. _____ was a Greek scientist who is known as the father of atomic theory, but the works of his student, _____, are much better preserved. This student built on his teacher's foundation, and although most of his ideas about atoms were wrong, he was correct that atoms are in constant _____.

5. _____ is often called the father of the life sciences. He was the first to make a large-scale attempt at the _____ of animals and plants. Although Aristotle was known for a great number of advances in the sciences, he was also responsible for nonsense that _____ science for many, many years. He believed in _____, which says that certain living organisms spontaneously formed from non-living substances. Unfortunately, his _____ caused the idea of spontaneous generation to survive for thousands of years.

6. _____ is best known for proposing the geocentric system of the heavens, where the _____ is at the center of the universe and all other heavenly bodies _____ it. It was later replaced by the more correct _____ system, in which the earth and other planets orbit the ___. Three scientists who played a huge role in giving us this system were _____, _____, and _____. _____ collected much evidence in support of this system using a _____ he built based on descriptions of a military device. He had to publicly renounce the system, however, for fear of being thrown out of his _____.

7. During the Dark ages, _____ was done in place of science. In this pursuit, people tried to turn lead or other inexpensive items into _____. These people were not scientists, because they worked strictly by _____ and _____.

8. Science began to progress towards the end of the Dark Ages because the _____ worldview began to replace the Roman worldview. _____ is generally considered the first modern scientist because he was first to use the scientific method, although his student, _____, is sometimes given that title.

9. In the Renaissance, two very important books were published. One was by _____, and it was a study of the human body. The other was by Copernicus, and it was the first serious proposal of the _____ system. In pursuit of data to confirm this system, _____ was able to develop mathematical equations that showed the planets do not orbit the sun in circles, but in _____.

10. _____ was one of the greatest scientists of all time. He laid down the laws of _____, developed a universal law of _____, invented the mathematical field of _____, wrote many commentaries on the _____, showed white light is really composed of many different _____ of light, and came up with a completely different design for _____.

11. The era of _____ produced good and bad changes for science. The good change was that science began to stop relying on the authority of past _____. The bad part of the change was that science began to move away from the authority of the _____. During this era, _____ published his classification system for life, which we still use today. In addition, _____ came up with the Law of Mass Conservation, and _____ developed the first detailed atomic theory.

12. _____ is best known for his book, *The Origin of Species*. While most of the ideas in that book have been shown incorrect, it did demonstrate that living organisms can adapt to changes in their surroundings through a process he called _____. This essentially destroyed the old, incorrect view called _____, which says that living creatures cannot change.

13. _____ was able to finally destroy the idea of spontaneous generation once and for all. He developed a process called _____, which is used to keep milk from going bad as quickly as it otherwise would. His work laid the foundation for most of today's _____, which have saved millions and millions of lives by protecting people from disease.

14. _____, an Augustinian monk, devoted much of his life to the study of _____. The entire field of modern _____, which studies how traits are passed on from parent to offspring, is based on his work. Although he loved his scientific pursuits, he gave them up in the latter years of his life because of a political struggle between the government and the _____.

15. _____ is known as the founder of modern physics, because he was able to show that _____ and _____ are really just different aspects of the same phenomenon, which is now called _____.

16. _____ determined that, like matter, energy cannot be created or destroyed. This is now known as the _____, and it is the guiding principle in the study of energy.

17. In the modern era, _____ made the assumption that energy comes in small packets called "quanta." _____ used that assumption to explain the photoelectric effect, which had puzzled scientists for quite some time. He also developed the special theory of _____ and the general theory of _____. _____ also used the assumption that energy comes in quanta to develop a mathematical description for the _____. As a result, the idea that energy comes in little packets is now a central theme in modern science, forming the basis of the theory of _____ mechanics.

Summary of Module #2

Review the vocabulary words listed in Question #1 of the study guide

1. Science can never _____ anything. However, when the correct _____ is followed, science can be used to draw _____ that are reasonably reliable, which can help us better _____ the way creation works. A scientific theory does not have to "make sense," it merely has to be consistent with the _____. A single _____ can destroy a scientific law.

2. In the absence of air, ____ objects, regardless of weight or shape, fall at the _____ rate. If one object falls slower than another in an experiment, it is most likely the result of air _____. If a penny and a feather are dropped off a cliff, the _____ will hit the ground first. If the same experiment is done in an air-free chamber, _____ will hit the ground first.

3. The scientific method starts with _____, which allows the scientist to collect data. The scientist can then form a _____ that attempts to explain some facet of the data or attempts to answer a question that the scientist asks. The scientist then collects much more data in an effort to test the _____. If the data are found to be _____, it might be discarded, or it might be modified until it is consistent with the data. If a large amount of data is collected and the _____ is consistent with all the data, it becomes a _____. If several generations of collected data are all _____ with the _____, it eventually attains the status of a scientific _____.

4. During his career, creation scientist D. Russell Humphreys had read of many observations regarding the earth's magnetic field. They all centered on the fact that ever since scientists have been measuring the earth's magnetic field, it has been weakening. He had also read of measurements of several other planets' magnetic fields. As a result, he developed a mathematical description of how planets form magnetic fields. At this point in the scientific method, his mathematical description would be considered a _____. In 1984, he wrote a paper that showed how his mathematical model could accurately reproduce the major observations regarding earth's magnetic field and the measured magnetic fields of the other planets. Even though the magnetic fields of Neptune, Uranus, and Pluto had not yet been measured, he used his mathematical description to predict what they would be if they ever were measured. He also predicted that observations should eventually show that Mars had a magnetic field at one time, but it has long since decayed away. Several years later, the magnetic fields of Neptune and Uranus were measured, and his prediction was the only one that was correct for both planets. In addition, evidence from Mars now indicates that Mars probably did have a magnetic field at one time. As a result, his mathematical description is now a _____. He is still using it to make predictions, and if those turn out to be true, eventually, it might become a scientific ___. Had his 1984 predictions not been validated by the measurements made at Neptune and Uranus, he could have either _____ his mathematical description or _____ it until it was consistent with the measurements.

5. Even though he followed the scientific method, _____ theory that there were canals on Mars was incorrect. We know now that his experiments were _____ by the lenses used in the telescopes and because of eye strain. Even though BCS theory explained all the available data regarding _____, it was shown to be at least partially incorrect when _____ were discovered, because it predicted that no such thing could exist.

6. The failures of the scientific method do not show that science is useless. It shows that science cannot _____ anything and is not _____ reliable. However, as long as you follow the _____ _____, you can use it to study anything, and it can produce reasonably _____ conclusions on how the world works.

7. Some say that science cannot be used to study anything we do not observe happening today, but that is _____. If that were the case, we could not study _____ scientifically, as they are the remains of creatures that lived long ago.

8. Based on historical records, we know the Old Testament existed in its entirety by about _____. Nevertheless, it makes accurate _____ about the fate of cities as well as about the identity and actions of the _____.

9. In the book of Ezekiel, there is a prophecy about a city called _____. Despite the fact that people during that time thought the city was _____, the prophecy says that God will destroy the city so that it becomes a _____, which will only be good for fishermen to use in order to spread their nets. It also says that the city's _____ and _____ will be thrown into the water. In fact, both of those predictions came _____. Alexander the Great threw the _____ and _____ of the mainland city into the ocean to build a bridge of debris to the island city. The once-proud city of Tyre "…is a haven today for fishing boats and a place for _____."

10. The Old Testament properly predicted that Christ would be born in _____ but would later be called out of _____. In addition, it properly predicted the _____ for which Christ would be betrayed, what Judas would do with the money, and the name of the _____ the money was used to purchase. According to Josh McDowell, there are at least 332 separate prophecies in the Old Testament that all come true in the life of _____.

11. Although I gave you _____ that it is scientifically reasonable to believe the Bible, I did *not* _____ that the Bible is something in which you should believe. Indeed, since the conclusions of science are always tentative, you should never use it as a basis for your _____.

Summary of Module #3
Review the vocabulary words listed in Question #1 of the study guide

1. An experimental variable is good when you are using it to _____ something from the experiment. An experimental variable should be reduced or eliminated when it _____ the results of the experiment but you do not _____ anything from it.

<u>Answer Questions 2 through 6, which are based on the following story:</u>

A consumer lab decides to test the germ-fighting capabilities of different brands of antibacterial soap. The scientists prepare five different dishes, each of which contain the same species of bacteria. In the first dish, no soap is added. In each of the other dishes, a different brand of soap is added and swirled around to mix it with the bacteria in the dish. After 5 minutes, the dishes are examined under a microscope, and the number of living bacteria in each dish is counted.

2. What is the control in the experiment?

3. What is the experimental variable that will be used to learn something from the experiment?

4. What experimental variables should be reduced or eliminated?

5. Are the data collected subjective or objective?

6. Should this be done as a single-blind study, a double-blind study, or neither?

7. An object that is denser than water can, under the right circumstances, float on water because of the water's _____. However, if soap is added to the water, the object may _____. In general, the stronger the _____, the more easily an object of greater density will float on its surface.

8. A student decides to test the effectiveness of an "energy bar" that has been advertised as being able to "unlock" energy reserves, allowing for a more vigorous workout. He gets ten volunteers together. The first five get a bar that looks just like the energy bar, but is really just mashed bread that has been dyed and flavored. This group is the _____. The next five get the energy bar. He has all ten do a vigorous workout, and then they each fill out a questionnaire that attempts to find out whether this workout was more vigorous than previous workouts prior to the experiment. This experiment should be done as a _____ study, since the subjects are aware that something is being tested and the data collected are _____.

<u>Answer Questions 9 through 11, which are based on the following story:</u>

A scientist tests the effectiveness of a product that claims to "reduce the severity and duration" of the common cold. He advertises for volunteers who are just starting to experience cold symptoms. To half of those who contact him, he gives a fake version of the product. To the other half, he gives the product. He has them answer a daily questionnaire that tries to determine how the person's cold is progressing. He tells each person to continue filling out the questionnaire until the cold symptoms completely go away. Once each person sends in the daily questionnaires, he uses their answers to determine the severity of the cold, and he uses the number of days they filled out their questionnaires to determine the length of the cold. He then compares the two groups to see if there are any differences.

9. Should this be a single-blind experiment, a double-blind experiment, or neither?

10. Which volunteers are in the control group?

11. Are any of the data collected objective? If so, what are the objective data?

<u>Answer the following question:</u>

12. A former Olympic athlete has just developed a new "strength-enhancing" workout that he guarantees will produce greater upper-body strength in any athlete. A scientist decides to test the workout by having a group of athletes each determine the maximum amount of weight they can lift over their head. Then, she has half do a general series of upper-body-strength workouts, and she has the other half do the workout designed by the former Olympic athlete. After a few weeks, she has them repeat the test to determine the maximum amount of weight they can lift over their head. Should this be a single-blind experiment, a double-blind experiment, or neither?

<u>Answer Questions 13 through15, which are based on the following story:</u>

A fisherman decides to determine the best time to fish on his favorite lake. He goes out and fishes on the lake from 6 AM to 9 PM. It's a tough job, but someone has to do it! He weighs the total number of pounds of fish caught during every hour and produces the following graph:

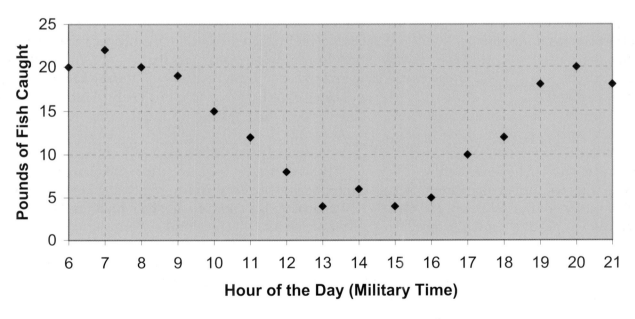

13. How many pounds of fish did the fisherman catch during the 16th hour?

14. If you could only choose one hour to fish on this lake each day, which hour would get you the most pounds of fish (based on these data)?

15. Given the fact that the x-axis is military time (0-11 means "AM" and 12-24 means "PM"), order the following in terms of the most productive fishing times, starting with the least productive and ending with the most productive: early morning, early afternoon, late evening.

Summary of Module #4
Review the vocabulary words listed in Question #1 of the study guide

1. Science is motivated by the desire to _____. In applied science, experiments are aimed at trying to find something _____. Technology is often the result of _____, _____, or _____. Experiments designed to determine why lightning bugs glow, for example, would be considered _____ experiments. Experiments designed to produce a device that glows like a lighting bug, however, would be _____ experiments. If ever produced, the actual device would be considered _____.

2. A scientist is doing experiments to determine whether or not platinum can speed up certain chemical reactions. Along the way, he discovers two things. He determines that platinum can be used to reduce the toxicity of automobile emissions. This is an example of _____, as it can be used to make people's lives better. He also learns that platinum speeds up chemical reactions by pulling the chemicals close to one another. This is an example of _____, because it explains something about how creation works.

3. There are six basic types of simple machines. The ____ consists of a bar and a fulcrum. The _____ _____ consists of a wheel that connects to a cylinder. A _____ consists of a wheel over which a rope or chain moves. An _____ is simply a ramp. It looks just like a _____, but the difference between the two is based on where the effort is exerted. The effort is exerted along the _____ of an inclined plane, but it is exerted against the _____ of a wedge. A _____ is composed of an inclined plane wrapped around the cylinder of a _____.

4. In a first-class lever, the _____ is between the effort and resistance. It _____ the direction of the effort and magnifies the _____. In a second-class lever, the _____ is between the fulcrum and the effort. It _____ the direction of the effort and magnifies the _____. In a third-class lever, the _____ is between the fulcrum and resistance. It _____ the direction of the effort and magnifies _____. You can determine the mechanical advantage of a lever with the equation:

_____

5. A single, fixed pulley offers no _____, but it does _____ the direction of the force. If several pulleys are put together in a block and tackle system, there is a _____, but you "pay" for it by needing to _____. The force with which you pull on a block and tackle system is multiplied by the _____ in the system.

6. If you turn the wheel of a wheel and axle, the mechanical advantage magnifies the _____ of the effort. If you turn the axle of a wheel and axle, the mechanical advantage magnifies the _____ of the effort. The mechanical advantage of a wheel and axle can be calculated with the equation:

_____

7. In an inclined plane, you can lift an object using less _____, but you must push it over a _____ distance. A _____ looks just like an inclined plane, but it is used to separate things. You can calculate the mechanical advantage of either with the equation:

_____

8. The mechanical advantage of a screw is calculated with the following equation:

_____

When grasping the screw's head, you use the circumference of the _____. When using a screwdriver, you use the circumference of the _____.

9. What is the mechanical advantage of a lever in which the effort is 10 inches from the fulcrum and the resistance is 2 inches from the fulcrum?

10. Five pulleys are used in a block-and-tackle system. If you pull on the rope with 50 pounds of force, how many pounds can you lift with this system? If you want to lift the load 10 feet in the air, how many feet of rope will you need to pull?

11. The wheel of a wheel and axle has a diameter of 12 inches. The axle has a diameter of 1 inch. If you turn the wheel with a force of 10 pounds, with what force will the axle turn? If you turn the axle with a speed of 1 foot per second, how fast will the edge of the wheel turn?

12. You push a box up an inclined plane so you don't have to lift it straight up in the air. If the inclined plane's slope has a length of 10 feet and a height of 2 feet, what is the mechanical advantage?

13. Two single wedges each have a slope that is 6 inches long and a height of 1 inch. What is each wedge's mechanical advantage? If they are put together as a double wedge, what is the mechanical advantage?

14. Given the screw below, what is the mechanical advantage of the screw?

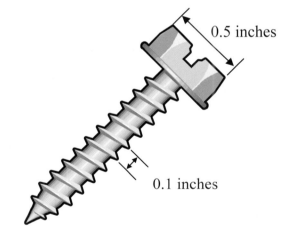

0.5 inches

0.1 inches

Illustration from www.clipart.com

15. If you used a 1-inch diameter screwdriver for the screw shown above, what would the mechanical advantage be?

Summary of Module #5
Review the vocabulary words listed in Question #1 of the study guide

1. When the history of life is studied, _____ examines all life that once existed on the planet, while _____ concentrates on human life. Studying rocks to learn the history of the earth is called _____ .

2. The three main tests used to determine whether or not a document is a valid work of history are called _____ , _____ , and _____ . The _____ makes sure that the document does not contradict itself. The _____ makes certain that the document does not contradict other known historical or archaeological facts. The _____ makes certain the documents we have today are essentially the same as the original.

3. _____ is used in the internal test. We must use it because what seems to be a contradiction in a document might not be a contradiction. It might just be the result of the fact that we cannot fully _____ the language in which the document was written.

4. In the bibliographic test, a document is considered reliable if there is a _____ time between when the original was written and the oldest copy that exists today. In addition, the _____ the number of copies made by _____ sources, the more reliable the document. This is important, because the people who could commission copies of a work might also demand that _____ be made to the original. In addition, because copying was a tedious process, copyists sometimes made _____ when they made copies.

5. The Bible _____ the internal test as well as any document of its time. Most "contradictions" that people claim exist in the Bible are not contradictions at all. For example, while the genealogies of Christ in Matthew and Luke seem contradictory, they are actually complimentary, because Luke traces _____ line, while Matthew traces _____ line. In addition, while the stories of Paul's conversion in Acts 9 and 22 appear to be contradictory, they do not contradict each other in the original language. The verb "hear" used in Acts 9:7 simply means that the men heard _____ . The verb "hear" used in Acts 22:9 requires that the hearer must actually understand _____ . The first tells us that the men heard _____ , but the second tells us that the men could not _____ those sounds as speech.

6. While there are a few difficult passages in the Bible, the same can be said of any _____ historical document. Thus, unless you can _____ demonstrate a contradiction, it is labeled a difficulty and does not cause a document to fail the _____ .

7. The Bible _____ the external test. In fact, since more archaeology has been done in relation to the Bible than any other work of history, you can say it passes the external test _____ than any other document of ancient history. In fact, the few times in which archaeology was thought to contradict the Bible, it turned out that _____ was wrong, not the Bible.

8. The New Testament _____ the bibliographic test _____ than any other ancient document of its time. The time span between when the original was written and the first copy that exists today is very _____ , and the number of independent copies of the manuscript is very _____ .

9. The Old Testament _____ the bibliographic test. One of the most important finds related to this was the discovery of the _____ . While there were several works in this group of documents, there was a complete copy of the book of _____ .

10. In archaeology, a document or relic can have a _____ age, an _____ age, or a _____ age. An object has a _____ age if the date appears on the object, or if the object is referenced in some other valid work of history. It has an _____ age if a dating method is used to calculate its age. It has a _____ age if the Principle of Superposition is used to determine whether it is older or younger than some other object. Only _____ ages are reasonably certain. The others rely on assumptions.

11. The Principle of Superposition says that the _____ you find a relic in a structure of layered rock or soil, the older the object is. Thus, if an archaeologist finds pottery in one layer of soil and bones in a layer below, he can say the bones are _____ than the pottery. This principle assumes that rock and soil layers form _____. While this is certainly true for certain situations, it has been demonstrated to be _____ for other situations, so the Principle of Superposition is not very reliable.

12. The counting of tree rings in order to determine the age of something is called _____. Typically, such ages are considered _____ limits on the true age, as some trees can grow more than one ring in a given year. In order to determine the absolute age of a log that was cut down and then preserved, the investigator looks for a _____. This pattern corresponds to a series of weather conditions for which an absolute age has already been determined.

13. In addition to dendrochronology, radiometric dating can be used to determine the _____ age of an artifact. While most forms of this dating technique are unreliable, the radiometric technique known as _____ is about as reliable as dendrochronology as long as the item being dated is less than 3,000 years old.

14. There are many seemingly unrelated cultures that all have a _____ tale. If the Flood did not really occur, you have to assume that they all _____ the tale independently, because many of the cultures had no contact with one another until well after the tales were written down. One of the more famous examples is the Epic of _____. This story details the adventures of a king who eventually seeks a wise man who _____ the worldwide flood. The man tells the king about the Flood and how to become young again. The king _____ the test needed to eat the plant that makes him young, however.

15. While there are many ways to study human history, the best place to start is the _____, because it has been shown to be an incredibly reliable source of history.

Summary of Module #6
Review the vocabulary words listed in Question #1 of the study guide

1. There are two basic viewpoints when it comes to forming hypotheses about earth's past: _____ (which assumes the majority of the geological record is the result of catastrophes that have happened during earth's past) and _____ (which assumes the majority of the geological record is the result of processes that we see happening continuously today). In general, _____ are forced to believe that the earth is billions of years old, while _____ can be more open-minded.

2. There are three basic kinds of rocks that make up the earth's crust: _____ (formed from sediments), _____ (formed from magma), and _____ (formed from either of the first two kinds of rock). Because of the changes that form _____ rock, it is typically very hard.

3. The basic building blocks of rocks are called _____, and they can often be distinguished from rocks by their nice _____ shapes.

4. Sedimentary rock often forms in layers, which are called ____. Most sedimentary strata are laid down by ____. These layers _____ greatly in thickness and appearance.

5. When molten rock is found under the surface of the earth, it is usually called ____. When it is found on the surface (because of a volcanic eruption, for example), it is called ____.

6. Rocks can experience _____ weathering, where they are broken into small pieces, or _____ weathering, where they are transformed into new substances. For example, if a rock is worn away from the constant pummeling of raindrops, it has experience _____ weathering. On the other hand, when a rock falls apart because the iron inside has been changed to rust, it has experienced _____ weathering. Either way, weathering transforms rock into _____. Generally, the process of weathering takes a long ____. Thus, it is hard to see it happening on a day-by-day basis.

7. Erosion is responsible for _____ geological structures and landscapes into what we see today. While running water (like that found in a river) is the most common agent of erosion, _____ and ____ can also be its agents. In general, the presence of _____ tends to slow erosion, because their roots hold the soil together. In addition, the _____ water erodes things faster. In general, erosion is one way creation _____ its rocks, turning rocks into sediment and then depositing the sediments somewhere, forming rocks again.

8. When a river erodes a landscape, the _____ are usually carried along and deposited wherever the river ends. As a result, a river's end is often a fan-shaped area of deposited sediments called a ____. While we normally think of rivers as the agents of erosion, _____ (water flowing beneath the earth's surface) can also erode rock. We can see the effects of this erosion by looking at a _____.

9. In a cavern, water dripping from the ceiling can deposit sediments, forming icicle-like structures called _____. When water hits the ground, it can deposit sediments there, causing a _____ to rise up from the ground. If an icicle-like structure meets a structure rising from the ground, the result is a _____, which is also called _____. While caves are the most common place to find these structures, they can form in man-made _____ as well.

10. When strata are separated by a surface that has been eroded, we call that separation an
_____. If the separation is between sedimentary rock and either igneous or metamorphic
rock, it is called a _____. If the separation is between two parallel layers of sedimentary rock,
it is called a _____. If the layers above and below the separation are tilted relative to one
another, it is called an _____. If geologists think there should be an unconformity but
there is no evidence for one, it is called a _____. Not all layers of rock are separated by
_____. If a layer of rock rests on another layer with no evidence of erosion in between, the
separation is not an _____.

11. Veins of igneous rock that shoot through layers of sedimentary rock are called _____. Veins
that run in the same direction of the strata are called ____, while veins running roughly perpendicular
to the direction of the strata are called _____.

12. In the side-on view of the Grand Canyon given below:

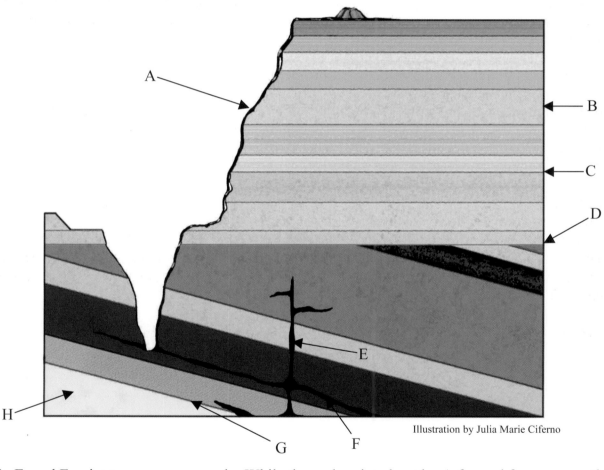

Illustration by Julia Marie Ciferno

letters A, E, and F point to _____ rock. While the rock pointed out by A formed from _____, the
rock pointed out by E and F formed from ____. Letters E and F point to an _____, and specifically,
F points to a ___ while E points to a ____. The unconformity pointed out by D is called the _____
_____, and the type of unconformity is an _____. The layers above D are all
composed of _____ rock. Letter H points to _____ rock, which makes the
unconformity pointed to by the letter G a _____. The unconformity pointed to by letter C is
a _____. If a geologist is studying the layer pointed out by B and thinks there should be an
unconformity roughly in the middle of the layer despite the fact that there is no evidence for one, it
would be called a _____.

Summary of Module #7

Review the vocabulary words listed in Question #1 of the study guide

1. In general, dead organisms _____. Only a tiny fraction of once-living organisms gets _____. As a result, the conditions under which fossils form are _____.

2. The most common means by which a dead organism can be preserved is the formation of a ____ and the making of a ____. In this process, the _____ is not actually preserved. Instead, rocks are formed in the _____ of the organism.

3. Sometimes, a mold will form without a cast. When that happens, an _____ of the organism is left in the rock, but nothing fills it.

4. _____ is the process by which the organic materials in an organism are replaced by minerals. This process requires _____ water. These fossils have more information than fossil casts and molds because the _____ fossil is preserved, which gives us more information than just the shape and outer details of the fossil.

5. When an organism is buried in sediment, the pressure can cause _____ and _____ in the organism's remains to be forced out into the surrounding sediments. This means the _____ of the organism's remains are lost. A process called _____ takes place, leaving a thin, filmy residue that often forms a detailed "drawing" of the creature in stone. _____ fossils are the most common fossils created by this process. While this process can create very detailed "drawings" of the organism, it does not preserve the details of the organism's _____, as the "drawings" are flat.

6. The fossils that contain the most information are those that _____ decomposition. This can happen, for example, when an organism is encased in ____. The cold temperatures and protection offered by the ____ slow decomposition so much that organic remains can be preserved. If an organism is encased in _____, a hardened resin, it can also be well-preserved. However, even though such a fossil appears to be intact, the _____ that make it up have been decomposing since the organism died, so the organism is not fully preserved.

7. There are four general features of the fossil record. They are as follows:

    a. _____

       _____

    b. _____

       _____

    c. _____

       _____

    d. _____

       _____

8. When paleontologists compare a fossil to its living counterpart (assuming one exists), they find that the fossil and the living counterpart are incredibly _____. Based on the fossil evidence, then, we can conclude that organisms that have survived throughout earth's history experience little _____.

This does not mean organisms experience no _____ at all. However, the _____ are minor compared to the characteristics that define the organism.

9. When an organism is found in the fossil record, but no living counterpart is found, it is assumed that the organism is _____. That assumption, however, is sometimes _____. From time to time, biologists will find a living example of an organism thought to be _____.

10. There is a lot of misinformation regarding extinction. While some claim that tens of thousands of organisms go extinct every year, scientists estimate that about _____ have gone extinct in the past 400 years.

11. Several fossils can be found in the Grand Canyon. There are fossils of _____ (mostly bottom-dwelling ocean creatures) in many of the layers above the Great Unconformity. They are assumed to be _____. In the three layers just above the Great Unconformity, there are no direct fossils of worms, but we find fossils of their _____, indicating their presence. In only one layer of the Grand Canyon, you will find fossils of _____ (fish that had bony plates covering their heads rather than the scales you see covering the heads of fish today). They are also assumed to be _____. Fish that look like the ones we see today are found only in the _____ layers of the Grand Canyon.

12. According to uniformitarians, sediments are laid down _____ over _____ of years. Eventually, conditions change and the sediments harden to form _____. The conditions during which the sediments were laid down determine the _____ of sediment, which in turn determines the _____ of rock formed. A phrase that best sums up the uniformitarian position is, "The _____ is the key to the past." According to uniformitarians, each layer of rock represents a _____ of earth's history. Thus, the different fossils found in different layers result from the fact that different plants and animals existed at _____ in any given region of the earth.

13. According to catastrophists, most of the sedimentary rocks we see today were formed during the _____. The depth, speed, and direction of the Flood waters determined what _____ of sediment was laid down, which in turn determined the _____ of rock formed. As a result, the different fossils in different layers are the result of the fact that different kinds of organisms were trapped and preserved during different _____ of the Flood.

14. Both uniformitarianism and catastrophism require speculation. Uniformitarians must speculate how _____ of time affect the processes we see working today. Catastrophists must speculate about the nature of the _____.

.

Summary of Module #8
Review the vocabulary words listed in Question #1 of the study guide

1. Uniformitarian geologists use _____ to determine what time period a layer of rock represents. If a uniformitarian geologist finds _____ for the Cambrian time period in a layer of rock, for example, the geologist says that the layer of rock was laid down during Cambrian times.

2. Uniformitarian geologists assume that not every time period of earth's history will be represented by rock in every part of the world. In a given part of the world at a give time, the conditions for _____ deposition might not have existed. Also, rock might have been laid down in a certain region, but it might have _____ before another layer of rock could form. They use geological data from all over the world to form the _____, a theoretical picture of earth's entire history. It assumes that each layer of rock represents a _____ in earth's past, and it further assumes that the index fossils found in a given layer of rock are accurate indicators of which time _____ the rock was formed. If either of these assumptions is wrong, the geological column is probably not _____.

3. In the geological column, you find trilobites and similar animals much lower than you find mammals. According to uniformitarian geologists, this is because trilobites existed _____ mammals. In the same way, you generally find the fossils of mammals higher in the geological column than dinosaurs. According to uniformitarian geologists, this is because dinosaurs existed _____ mammals.

4. Many view the geological column as evidence for _____, because it indicates that early in earth's history, there were only simple life forms. As time went on, the geological column indicates that more and more _____ life forms started to appear. This is exactly what the Theory of Evolution says. The problem with using the geological column as evidence for evolution is that the geological column is not _____. It is an abstract model based on _____ that may or may not be correct.

5. We already know that the geological column is _____ to some extent. This is because over time, paleontologists have found fossils in _____ rock that, according to the geological column, should not have existed until much ____ in earth's history. A more accurate geological column would have trilobites and similar animals, as well as ocean life without bones, all together in Cambrian, Ordovician, and Silurian rock. Unfortunately, most textbooks _____ present such an accurate picture.

6. The Theory of Evolution states that as millions of years pass and life forms reproduce, small _____ between parent and offspring appear. These small differences can "pile up" over time until there are so many differences that the offspring being produced look nothing like the life form that _____ this process. In this way, a "_____" life form can give rise to a more _____ life form. This happened over and over again as time went on, producing more and more _____ organisms over earth's history.

7. During the eruption of Mount Saint Helens, there were periods when huge volumes of _____ were released. This ground-hugging _____, mixed with volcanic ash, formed a "river" of mud that moved across the ground at speeds greater than 100 miles per hour. As _____ were deposited by this "river," they formed _____, which were laid down with varying thickness. All the _____ were deposited together, in the span of just a few hours!

8. The eruption of Mt. Saint Helens also showed how quickly fast-moving water can _____ rock. A huge canyon was carved out of solid rock as a result of the _____ that accompanied the eruption. The formation of the canyon also caused the formation of a _____ at the bottom of the canyon.

9. If the Mt. Saint Helens catastrophe can build layers of stratified sediments that are several feet high, it stands to reason that a _____ could form layers of stratified sediments that are hundreds or thousands of feet high. If the Mt. Saint Helens catastrophe can carve out canyons that are _____ _____ the scale of the Grand Canyon, a large, post-flood catastrophe could certainly carve out the Grand Canyon itself.

10. The Cumberland Bone Cave is a fossil _____ that contains many fossils from several different climates. It is excellent evidence for a _____ and is a problem for the uniformitarian view.

11. While it is commonly assumed that fossils take thousands, if not millions, of _____ to form, it is not necessarily true. Fossilized hats, legs in boots, and waterwheels tell us that fossils can form _____ under the right conditions. In addition, there are museums that carry carbonized remains of a large fish in the process of _____ a smaller fish. The best way to understand such a fossil is to realize that the fish were buried in an _____, without warning. This killed both the fish and its potential meal. Since they were buried by sediment, the process of forming a _____ fossil began.

12. A _____ is an unconformity that does not really exist in a geological formation but uniformitarians believe must exist because of the fossils found in the formation. This is one of several problems with the uniformitarian view. Another problem is that there are _____ fossils in the fossil record. In addition, fossil _____ with fossils from many different climates are hard to understand in the uniformitarian view. Another problem comes from fossils such as the *Tyrannosaurus rex* bone containing _____ tissue that should not have lasted for millions of years. Also, the entire idea of using _____ to order sedimentary strata is called into question by the many creatures we once thought were extinct but we now know are not.

13. Catastrophists have offered no good explanation for _____ between rock layers laid down by the Flood. Another problem with the catastrophism framework is the existence of fossil structures that look like they were formed under _____ living conditions, which would not exist during the Flood. In addition, catastrophists have not yet explained the enormous _____ deposits we find in terms of the Flood.

14. The fossil record contains no fossils that are undeniable _____ links. If evolution occurred, there should be _____ such fossils. If God created each kind of plant and animal individually, you would ____ expect any.

15. Evolutionists think that _____ is an intermediate link between reptiles and birds. They think this because it has _____ in its mouth. No living bird has them, but reptiles do. In addition, there are ____ on the wings. No living adult bird has them, but reptiles do. The ____ is also longer and has more bones than that of any living bird we see today. Detailed studies of the fossil, however, indicate that the animal was an excellent _____, as you would expect of a fully-developed bird. Thus it seems to be just a bird with certain _____ that no living bird has today.

16. There are _____ who are also uniformitarians. They believe in the uniformitarian view of geology, but they agree that the Theory of Evolution is not a valid explanation of life's history on earth. One such group is referred to as progressive _____. In this view, God created _____ creatures, allowed them to live, reproduce, etc., and then, after a long while, He created slightly more _____ creatures. Once again, He then paused and allowed them to "do their thing" for a long while, and then He created even more _____ creatures. After enough time, of course, this would produce all the basic kinds of organisms we see today.

Summary of Module #9
Review the vocabulary words listed in Question #1 of the study guide

1. All life forms contain deoxyribonucleic acid, which is called _____. All life forms have a method by which they extract _____ from their surroundings and convert it into _____ that sustains them. All life forms can sense _____ in their surroundings and _____ to them. All life forms _____.

2. DNA provides the _____ necessary to turn lifeless chemicals into a living organism. It is one of the _____ molecules in creation, and it is more efficient at _____ storage than the very best that human technology has to offer.

3. A DNA molecule is shaped like a double ____. It is formed by two long strands of atoms that make up the _____ of the DNA. Each strand has little units, called _____, attached to it. The units come in four varieties: _____ , _____ , _____ , and _____. The information is stored in the _____ of these little units.

4. The double helix of DNA stays together because the nucleotide bases can link together. However, only adenine and _____ can link together, and only cytosine and _____ can link together. As a result, if one strand of DNA has the following sequence of nucleotide bases:

adenine, cytosine, cytosine, thymine, guanine, guanine, thymine

The corresponding other strand must have the following sequence of nucleotide bases:

_____ , _____ , _____ , _____ , _____ , _____ , _____

5. Plants use _____ to produce food in the form of a chemical called _____. If the plant needs energy, it takes the energy from the _____ and converts it into energy it uses to survive. If the plant has plenty of energy, it converts any unused _____ into _____ (or one of a few other chemicals), which can be broken back down into _____ when the plant needs energy.

6. The process of photosynthesis uses _____, _____, and energy from the ____ to produce _____ and oxygen. Even though plants produce oxygen, they also ____ oxygen. When they want to get the _____ from the glucose, they must perform _____, which requires food (like glucose) and oxygen. However, since plants _____ more food than they ever ___, they _____ more oxygen than they ___.

7. Living organisms are equipped with some method of receiving information about their _____. Typically, they accomplish this feat with _____. This allows them to _____ to any changes that occur. People with leprosy cannot feel ___, and as a result, they tend to have real troubles when they are hurt. Their wounds get _____, and they can lose body parts because they do not know they have been hurt. The disease known as leprosy today, however, is not the disease the _____ calls leprosy. Most likely the disease called leprosy in the _____ was a variety of skin disorders that were probably caused by an infectious agent.

8. Since plants are living organisms, they can _____ to changes in their environment. One classic example of this is the fact that plants can grow _____ a light source to get as much energy as possible from the light.

9. _____ is a means by which living organisms ensure that their kind will continue. Of course, sometimes this is not enough. As we learned from geology and paleontology, some organisms go _____. This can be for a variety of reasons, but in the end, it comes down to one thing: the organisms died off faster than they could _____.

10. When flies reproduce, they make _____. Over a given time period, the _____ mature into adult flies in a process called _____.

11. While many organisms need a _____ for reproduction, many do not. A _____, for example, simply makes copies of itself. Some flatworms actually _____, and then each half regenerates so that there are two flatworms where there once was only one.

12. In general, the more _____ an animal's life, the more offspring it will have. Rabbits, for example, are _____ for all sorts of other animals. As a result, many _____ before they have a chance to reproduce. To make up for that, rabbits have _____ offspring. Most people, however, are able to stay alive and reproduce. As a result _____ don't have as many offspring as rabbits.

13. While some claim there is a problem with the population of people on the planet, it is just ____ true. The average number of babies being born to mothers throughout the world is _____. As a result, it is only a matter of time before the human population _____ growing. In fact, while predictions such as these are often unreliable, the United Nations predicts that the world's population will _____ by the year 2300.

14. _____ offspring do not need nearly as much help from their parents when they are born as do _____ offspring. Puppies, for example, are _____ because they are born unable to see. The mother must take special care of them until their eyes _____.

15. The smallest unit of life in creation is the ____. It is covered in an outer layer called a _____, and a jellylike substance called _____ fills the inside. In many of these units, small structures called _____ are suspended in the cytoplasm. They each have individual _____ they must accomplish. One of the most important structures is the _____, because it is where you will find most of the organism's DNA.

16. The three basic kinds of cells are _____ cells (like those in your body), _____ cells (found in plants), and cells with no _____ (found in bacteria). The average animal cell is about 1 to 3 ten thousandths of an ____ across. Also, it does not necessarily take a lot of them to make a living organism. Although many organisms are composed of trillions of cells, there are *billions and billions* of organisms that are composed of only ____ cell. Thus, a single cell can perform __ of the functions of life and is therefore considered alive. Cells also reproduce, so if an animal cannot have offspring, it is still _____, because its cells reproduce.

Summary of Module #10
Review the vocabulary words listed in Question #1 of the study guide

1. In the classification system we used, there are _____ kingdoms. Kingdom _____ contains all organisms that are composed of prokaryotic cells. Kingdom Protista contains those organisms that are composed of only one _____ cell as well as _____. Kingdom _____ contains mostly the organisms that feed on dead organisms. Kingdom Plantae is composed of organisms that are made of many eukaryotic cells and _____. Kingdom _____ contains organisms made of many eukaryotic cells and eat other (usually living) organisms.

2. If an organism is made of a single prokaryotic cell, it is a part of kingdom _____, because all organisms made of prokaryotic cells are a part of that kingdom. If an organism is made of _____ cells, it can be in any of the other four kingdoms. To determine which one, you have to know other details. For example, if it makes its own food, it is either a part of kingdom _____ or kingdom _____. To distinguish between these two kingdoms, you look at how many cells it is made of and its structure. If it is made of only one eukaryotic cell and makes its own food, it is in kingdom _____. If it is made of many eukaryotic cells, makes its own food, and has specialized parts like roots, stems, and leaves, it is a part of kingdom _____. If it is made of many eukaryotic cells, makes its own food, and doesn't have roots, stems, and leaves, it is a part of kingdom _____. If an organism is made of eukaryotic cells and eats dead things, it is a part of kingdom _____. If it is made of many eukaryotic cells and eats (mostly) living organisms, it is a part of kingdom _____. If it is made of only one eukaryotic cell and eats other (mostly) living things, it is part of kingdom _____.

3. The members of kingdom Monera are often called _____. Many of these organisms can survive in habitats that are _____ to other organisms, and it is impossible to see them without the aid of a _____. Some are _____, which means they cause disease. Others, however, are actually helpful, such as those that live in our intestines and provide us with vitamin __. They require _____ to survive. Thus, they cannot survive and reproduce in _____ food. In addition, as your experiment showed, the presence of _____ or _____ can reduce the amount in food, as can _____ temperatures. Since they can float on the dust particles in the air, _____ food can help reduce the amount in it.

4. Kingdom Protista is typically split into two groups: _____ and _____. In general, _____ are able to move on their own, while _____ are not. While algae use _____ to make their own food, they are not plants, because they do not have _____, ____, and _____. Algae are the _____ important source of oxygen for the planet. Like bacteria, some members of this kingdom are _____, which means they can cause disease. Like bacteria, members of kingdom Protista need _____ to live.

5. Members of kingdom _____ are called decomposers. They _____ dead matter so it can be used by the organisms in creation. While most are composed of _____ cells, there are some composed of only one cell. _____ is an example of a single-celled fungus. The main body of a fungus is called the _____. It is often unseen, existing below the surface of its habitat. As a result, when you see a mushroom growing out of the ground, you are seeing only a _____ of the actual fungus.

6. Members of kingdom _____ are made of several eukaryotic cells, use photosynthesis to produce their own food, and have specialized structures. The _____ absorb water and nutrients from the soil, while the _____ help transport the nutrients and water to the _____. You can often grow a complete plant from just a portion of another plant, in a process called _____ reproduction.

7. Plants cells are noticeably _____ from animal cells in several specific ways. They are usually more _____ than animal cells. Also, they have a _____ that surrounds the outside of the membrane. They also have a _____ that fills with water, pushing the organelles against the ___ _____. This causes pressure in the cell, called _____. This pressure helps a plant to _____ _____. A wilted plant may not be _____. It may just need water to reestablish its _____ _____.

8. Kingdom _____ contains those organisms that are made of many eukaryotic cells and eat other (mostly living) organisms. It contains _____ of the organisms with which people are familiar. While we normally think of cats, dogs, elephants, and the like as a part of this kingdom, there are _____ members of this kingdom as well, such as the cyclops shown in the book.

9. People are a part of kingdom _____. This does not mean people are animals. It just means that from the standpoint of our cells and how our bodies are made, we have many things in _____ with animals. People, however, are unique in kingdom _____, as we are made in the image of ____.

Summary of Module #11

Review the vocabulary words listed in Question #1 of the study guide

1. The body's superstructure is composed of three units: the _____, the _____, and the ____. The skeleton _____ the body, and some of its bones are specifically designed to _____ vital organs. In addition, a substance inside your bones, the _____, produces the cells that are in your blood.

2. In order to help you move, your body has about 640 different _____. In addition to those muscles, there are also _____, which control the movements necessary for your body's internal organs and blood vessels to function. Finally, there is special muscle called _____ that is found in the heart. Under the microscope, smooth muscles appear smooth and _____, while skeletal muscles appear rough and _____. Skeletal muscles are _____ (they are operated by conscious thought), while smooth muscles are _____ (they are operated unconsciously by the brain). Cardiac muscle is also _____.

3. Your skin _____ your body by preventing certain substances from getting inside. Also, it helps to _____ the outside world. Skin cells harden through a process called _____. This process forms your hair, nails, and the ____ layer of your skin.

4. Bones are as _____ as steel but as _____ as aluminum. To this day, applied scientists _____ come up with any material that has this amazing mix of characteristics. Bones are most certainly _____, because they are composed of cells. The cells are surrounded by a substance called the bone _____, which is composed principally of two things: _____ and _____.

5. Collagen is a flexible, thread-like substance that belongs to a class of chemicals known as _____. The minerals in bones are rigid, hard chemicals that contain _____. Collagen and minerals work together to make your bones both _____ and _____. There are two main types of bone tissue – _____ and _____. The main difference between the two is how the _____ and _____ are packed together. In _____ tissue, they are packed together tightly, forming a hard, tough structure that can withstand strong shocks. In _____ tissue, there are open spaces in the network of solid bone. This makes _____ lighter than _____.

6. A bone is surrounded by an outer sheath of tissue called the _____, which contains blood vessels that supply nutrients to the bones. It also contains _____ that send pain signals to your brain if the bone is damaged. Because bone is composed of _____ tissue, it continually changes to meet your body's needs. Not only do your bones change to meet your body's needs, but they also ____ as you grow.

7. The sum total of all bones in the body is called the _____. The _____ is often called the backbone, and members of kingdom Animalia that have one are called _____. Members of kingdom Animalia that do not have one are called _____.

8. The human endoskeleton can be split into two major sections: the _____ (which supports and protects the head, neck, and trunk) and the _____ (which attaches to the axial skeleton and has the limbs attached to it). In addition to bone, the human endoskeleton has _____, which is more flexible that bone.

9. Some members of kingdom Animalia have an exoskeleton, which supports and protects the creature but is on the _____ of the body. Animals with an exoskeleton are called _____.

10. Skeletal muscles are attached to the skeleton by _____. They can move the skeleton because the skeleton has joints. _____ can be found at the elbow and the knee. They allow up and down (or left and right) motion, but that is all. _____ are found at the hips and shoulders, and they allow for a wide range of motion. Your ankle is an example of a _____, which allows a range of motion more or less in between the two joints previously mentioned. _____ exist only in your backbone and allow the smallest range of motion. In general, the _____ the range of motion, the less stable the joint is.

11. The bones that make up a joint are covered in _____, which allows them to rub against each other without damage. In addition, the cartilage acts as a _____ so jarring movements do not destroy the joints. The bones in a joint are held together by strips of tissue called _____, which are like strips of stiff elastic that go from one bone to the other. Most joints are also surrounded by a "bag" called the _____. Certain cells in this "bag" produce a fluid, called _____, which lubricates the joint. If a joint has such a "bag," it is a _____ joint.

12. Skeletal muscles work in groups of _____ to move the skeleton at the joints. These groups contain muscles that _____ and _____ to produce the motion. For example, to bend your arm at the elbow, you use the biceps brachii, which _____ to move your forearm at the elbow. Its partner is the triceps brachii, which _____ and is passively stretched out while the biceps brachii _____. When you straighten your arm out again, the biceps brachii _____, and the triceps brachii _____.

13. Most members of kingdom Monera have _____, which they use to move through the water (or other liquid) they inhabit. Some protozoa use tiny hairs called _____ that beat back and forth, acting like little oars that row the organism through the water. Plants also move. When they grow towards the light, it is called _____. When they move so that they always grow upward, it is called _____.

14. Your skin is composed of two basic layers: the _____ (which is the outside layer), and the _____ (which is found underneath). Below the dermis lies the _____, which is composed mostly of fat and is not technically considered part of the skin.

15. Your epidermis is composed of a thick layer of _____ cells that have been keratinized. This layer lies on top of a thin layer of _____ cells. A good fraction of the dust you find in your home is composed of the _____ epidermal cells that have fallen from your family's (and your pets') skin.

16. Almost all of your skin produces _____, which is made from keratinized cells, but the keratin is harder in these cells than in the skin's cells. The cells that are keratinized come from a structure known as a _____ follicle, which is like a tiny "pit" of epidermis. The lowest part of this structure, called the _____, is the source of the cells that are keratinized. _____ are connected to the _____ follicle in the dermis. They produce oil that softens the _____ and the _____.

17. _____ is produced in your sweat glands, travels up through the dermis in the _____, and then pours out onto your skin through your _____. Sweating serves at least two purposes: it _____ your skin and helps _____ bacteria and fungi that live on your skin.

18. Hair has two functions: _____ and _____. Animals with hair are _____, while animals with feathers are _____. _____ and _____ have scales. _____ breathe through their skin.

19. Your skin produces _____ for certain bacteria and fungi that help fight off _____ organisms. This situation, commonly found in creation, is an example of _____.

Summary of Module #12

Review the vocabulary words listed in Question #1 of the study guide

1. The energy in most living organisms originates in the ___. Organisms that produce their own food are called _____, and most get their energy directly from the sun. Organisms that don't get energy *directly* from the sun usually get it indirectly, by eating other organisms. They are called _____. Organisms that recycle dead matter back into creation are called _____.

2. If a consumer eats only producers, it is called an _____. If it eats only other consumers, it is called a _____. If it eats both producers and consumers, it is an _____.

3. There are some living organisms that do not get their energy from the sun. For example, at the bottom of the ocean, _____ spew forth superheated water that is rich in various chemicals. Some _____ use those chemicals and the heat to make their own food, which makes them producers. These bacteria, and the _____ that eat them, do not get their energy from the sun.

4. Food is converted to energy via the process of _____, which requires _____. It produces _____, _____, and _____.

5. There are only three things that your body can burn effectively: _____, _____, and _____. Collectively, these three types of chemicals are called _____, because we must eat a lot of them every day. If given a choice, your body would rather burn _____. If it can't burn those, it will resort to burning _____. If it can't get either of those, it will burn _____.

6. Simple carbohydrates, like glucose, are called _____. When two of these simple carbohydrates link together, they form a _____, such as table sugar (sucrose). If many simple carbohydrates link together, they form a _____, such as starch.

7. There are many types of fats, but they can all be put into one of two classes: _____ or _____. Generally speaking, _____ are solid at room temperature, while _____ ___ tend to be liquid at room temperature. Fat is absolutely _____ for a healthy body. It _____ the body so the body can stay at its proper internal temperature. Many organs have a layer of fat for _____ as well. Also, much of the fat in your body serves as a great _____ of energy in case you are unable to eat for an extended amount of time. Finally, there are certain _____ that can only be stored in your body's fat reserves. Your body can produce most of the fats it needs from excess _____ and _____, but there are certain fats, called _____, that your body cannot produce. You must get those fats from your _____.

8. Your body burns proteins only if you have _____ of them, because they are essential to many other chemical processes that occur in your body. Proteins are formed when smaller chemicals, called _____, link together in long chains. Nearly every _____ that occurs in the body is affected by proteins. The information stored in _____ is used to tell the cells in your body how to make proteins. Your cells can actually _____ 11 of the 20 amino acids they need for the proteins they are required to make. However, there are nine amino acids, called _____, which your cells cannot _____. In order to get these amino acids, you must eat proteins that contain them. The best sources of these essential amino acids are _____, ____, ____, and ____.

9. People are _____, which means we use energy for the purpose of keeping our internal temperature relatively constant. In other words, we are "_____-blooded." The vast majority of

organisms are _____, which means that they do not have a means by which they can control their internal temperature. In other words, they are "_____-blooded." _____ organisms require less food than _____ organisms, because it takes *a lot* of energy to maintain a constant internal temperature.

10. A _____ is a unit used to measure energy. Since food provides you with macronutrients, and since macronutrients provide you with energy, one way to measure the macronutrient content in food is to measure the number of _____ of energy the food gives you. If you eat significantly fewer _____ than you use, you will lose weight. If you eat significantly more _____ than you use, you will gain weight.

11. The total rate at which your body uses energy is called your _____. It has two factors. The first, called the _____, is the rate at which your body burns energy just to perform the minimum functions that will keep you alive. The second is the amount of _____ you engage in every day.

12. Endothermic animals have a _____ BMR than ectothermic animals, because it takes a lot of energy to maintain a constant internal body temperature. Ectothermic animals cannot be _____ on very cold days, because the speed at which the chemical reactions occur in their bodies is reduced by the resulting cooler body temperature.

13. Two people could eat the same amount of food and engage in the same activities, but one could gain weight while the other loses weight. If this happens, you know that the one who gained weight has a _____ BMR than the one who lost weight.

14. The _____ the mammal, the larger its normalized metabolic rate. This is because small mammals have a _____ percentage of their total body exposed to the outside air. As a result, a small mammal loses _____ heat than a large mammal. This requires the smaller mammal to burn _____ food to make up for the lost heat.

15. Food is burned in most living organisms through a three-step process. The first step is called _____. In this step, the monosaccharide glucose is broken into ___ parts. This results in a small release of _____ and a little bit of _____. The two parts of the glucose and the hydrogen are then sent to a particular organelle in the cell called the _____, which is often called the "powerhouse" of the cell. In this "powerhouse," the process continues with the second step, called the _____. In this step, the two pieces of glucose react with _____ to produce _____ and _____. That results in a small release of _____ as well. The hydrogen from _____ as well as the hydrogen released in the _____ go through the third step, called the _____ _____. In this step, _____ combines with all that _____ to make _____. This results in a large release of _____.

16. The combustion process in living organisms is amazingly _____, because it must provide energy in a _____ but efficient fashion.

Summary of Module #13
Review the vocabulary words listed in Question #1 of the study guide

1. When you eat your food, your body must _____ in order to get the nutrients contained within. That process is called _____. There are two distinct parts to the process: _____ _____ (where the food is simply broken into small pieces) and _____ (where the chemical nature of the food is changed).

2. Food enters your body through your ____. It is cut, crushed, and ground into little pieces by your _____. It is also moistened by saliva, which is produced in your _____. Your _____ moves food around your mouth and provides most of the taste sensation you get when you eat. It molds the food into a soft lump called a _____. The food then goes to your _____, passes into your esophagus, and ends up in your _____. There, it is churned and mixed with juices that are made by the _____ lining. The food is gradually released it into your _____, where it is broken down chemically. Most of the micronutrients and macronutrients are absorbed by the bloodstream through the lining of your _____. The nutrient-filled blood then passes through your _____, which picks up many of those nutrients. Once the food is digested in your _____, what was not absorbed is sent to your _____. By the time food reaches this point, most of the micronutrients and macronutrients have been _____. Water is absorbed from the remains, turning them into ____, which are then sent to your _____ and expelled from your body through your _____.

3. There are parts of the digestive system that never actually come in contact with the food being digested. The sum of the parts of the digestive system through which food actually passes is often called the _____ or the _____. However, that doesn't represent the *entire* digestive system, as there are some _____ through which food never travels.

4. Your teeth are made of hard, bonelike material and are surrounded by soft, shock-absorbent _____, which most people call "gums." The _____ teeth are sharp and used to cut food; the _____ teeth are used to tear food; and the _____ and _____ are used to crush and grind food.

5. When you swallow, your _____ rises, sealing off the nasal cavity. The bolus then moves into the _____, which is a passageway for two things: ___ and _____. When you inhale, ___ passes through the pharynx to the larynx and then into the lungs. When you swallow, however, the larynx rises up. This motion causes a small flap of cartilage called the _____ to cover the larynx so food goes only into the _____.

6. In the stomach, the bolus is mixed with a liquid called _____. The most important chemical in this mixture is _____, which is sometimes called _____. This chemical is a powerful acid that activates digestive chemicals and kills _____ microscopic organisms that might have been eaten along with the food. In addition, it helps _____ the food so it is easier to digest. Smooth muscles in the stomach relax and contract, churning the bolus with the gastric juice until it is turned into a liquid mush called _____.

7. Chyme passes from the stomach to the small intestine in spurts that are controlled by a ring of muscles called the _____. In the small intestine, the chyme is mixed with several more digestive chemicals which come from the _____ and _____. Because some of these chemicals cannot work properly in the presence of acids, _____ from the pancreas, gall bladder, and small intestine are mixed with the chyme as it enters the small intestine. This _____ the stomach acid that is still in the chyme before the chyme reaches the small intestine. Unlike many

organs, the inside wall of the small intestine is not _____. Instead, it is covered with millions of projections called _____. These villi increase the amount of intestinal wall that comes in contact with the food, _____ the absorption process.

8. The large intestine is actually composed of three parts: the _____, the _____, and the _____. Chyme enters the _____ from the small intestine, and smooth muscles in the cecum push it into the _____. The main function of the _____ is to absorb water that is in the chyme. Many _____ live in your large intestine. They feed on the chyme as it travels through the large intestine and produce chemicals like _____ that are useful to your body. Anything that makes it to the _____ becomes a part of the feces, which are expelled through the _____.

9. For years, evolutionists have called the appendix a _____, which means they thought it was a useless remnant of the process of evolution. Like most evolutionary ideas, however, this has been demonstrated to be _____. We now know that the appendix is a safe haven for _____ bacteria that allows them to survive in the event of an intestine-clearing illness. That way, once the illness has passed, they can _____ the intestines quickly, helping you regain your health.

10. The liver makes _____, which is a mixture of chemicals that prepares fats for digestion. This mixture is sent to the _____ where it is concentrated to increase its strength. In addition, the liver converts glucose into _____ for storage. It also breaks down _____ when the body needs energy. It stores fats and can convert them to _____ if the body needs energy. It can also convert amino acids into _____ when the body needs energy. It is also a _____ center, recycling or transforming potentially harmful chemicals into useful or at least harmless substances. It also _____ the blood to help regulate body temperature.

11. The nutrients that your body needs in small amounts are called _____. You do not get _____ from them, but they often support your body's chemical processes, increasing your overall health. They are generally split into two categories: _____ and _____.

12. Vitamins are effective in extremely _____ amounts and act mainly as regulators of the chemical processes that occur in your body. They are classified as either _____ (A, D, E, and K) or _____ (C and the B-group). Your body can make two vitamins: _____ (made through the skin's exposure to sunlight) and _____ (produced by bacteria in the large intestine).

13. _____ is a component of the process that allows your eyes to detect light. It also maintains the cells that protect your body, such as skin cells. _____ allows your body to more effectively absorb certain minerals, especially calcium, from your food. _____ is an "antioxidant," which means it helps protect certain important chemicals in your body from being destroyed through the chemical process called "oxidation." In addition, it helps repair your DNA. The _____ help your body's metabolism. _____ helps your body build all sorts of molecules it needs. It is also an antioxidant. _____ is an important part of that blood-clotting process.

14. The _____ you need most are those that contain calcium, phosphorus, magnesium, potassium, sodium, chloride, sulfur, chromium, copper, fluoride, iodine, iron, selenium, and zinc.

15. Although the micronutrients are essential for good health, anything can become toxic if it builds to a high enough concentration. Thus, _____ vitamins and minerals can be dangerous. The vitamins that you must be most concerned about are the _____ ones, as they are stored in your body's fat reserves and can build up over time.

Summary of Module #14
Review the vocabulary words listed in Question #1 of the study guide

1. The human circulatory system is composed primarily of the _____ and the _____. It transports _____ and _____ to all the tissues. It also and picks up _____ from the tissues and transports them to organs that can get rid of them.

2. The human respiratory system, composed primarily of the _____, allows the body to take in _____ from the surrounding air and expel _____.

3. Blood vessels are separated into three basic categories: _____ (vessels that carry blood to the heart), _____ (vessels that carry blood away from the heart), and _____ (thin-walled vessels that allow for the exchange of gases and nutrients).

4. The _____ takes blood away from the heart and splits into two arteries that take the blood to the lungs. There, the blood gets rid of _____ and receives _____. Then, the _____ ____ take the blood back to the heart. It then leaves the heart through the ____. Eventually, the blood reaches the _____, where it gives _____ to the cells and picks up _____. The blood is then picked up by the _____ to be brought back to the heart. Eventually, all of the blood is returned to the heart via large veins called the _____ and the _____.

5. Like birds and all other mammals, humans have a _____ heart. Deoxygenated blood enters the heart in the _____. When the _____ receives a signal from the sinoatrial node, it contracts, pushing blood into the _____. The atrium then relaxes to fill with blood again, and the ventricle contracts, pushing the deoxygenated blood out the _____ and into the _____ _____, which sends the blood to the _____. The newly-oxygenated blood is carried back to the heart through the _____, which dump blood into the _____. The atrium then contracts, sending the blood into the _____. The atrium then relaxes and the ventricle contracts, pushing the oxygenated blood into the _____ so it can travel to the rest of the body. The entire cycle of a heartbeat – the contraction of the two atria, the relaxation of the atria and the contraction of the ventricles, and the relaxation of the ventricles – is called the _____.

6. In most veins, the blood is _____, and in most arteries, the blood is _____. The blood vessels that carry blood to the lungs and back are exceptions to this general rule. The blood in the arteries that go from the heart to the lungs is _____, while the blood in the veins that go from the lungs to the heart is _____.

7. Blood is an incredibly complex mixture of _____ and ____. The ____ are produced in the bone marrow. More than half of any given sample of blood is made up of _____. Suspended within this liquid are three main types of cells: _____, _____, and _____. _____ _____ transport oxygen from the lungs to the tissues. They give the blood its overall red color, because they contain a protein called _____, which is red. _____ are responsible for protecting the body from agents of disease. _____ are not true cells; rather, they are pieces of a kind of white blood cell. They aid in the process of _____, which keeps you from bleeding to death when you are cut.

8. The _____ system controls how you breathe. Air travels either through the _____ or the _____ into the _____. From there, it travels into the _____. The air eventually reaches a branch that marks the beginning of the lungs' _____ system. A little more than half

of the air travels through the right branch into the _____, and the rest travels through the left branch into the _____. The right branch is called the _____, and the left branch is called the _____. These two primary tubes branch into smaller and smaller _____ tubes. The tubes get smaller and smaller until they are tiny tubes called _____. At the end of these tiny tubes, there are little sacs called _____, which is where the exchange of oxygen and carbon dioxide takes place.

9. The nasal cavity is lined with a sticky substance called _____, which is designed to trap particles and keep them from reaching the lungs. When particles are trapped by the _____ of your nasal cavity, they are pushed towards the front of the nose by tiny hairs called _____, where they will be blown out or sneezed out.

10. The process of breathing is controlled by a few skeletal muscles, the most important of which is the _____. When this muscle contracts, it pushes down on the nearby organs, pulling your lungs down with them. This causes your lungs to _____, which sucks air into them. When the muscle relaxes, those same organs push up on the lungs, making them _____. This forces air ____ of your lungs, and you exhale. When you exhale, air passes through the _____, which is often called your voice box. It is called this because it contains your _____, which are two thin folds of tissue that stretch across the sides of the larynx. As you exhale, air passes over these folds. When your _____ are relaxed, air passes over them _____. When your _____ are tightened, however, the folds move into the airway, and the air makes them _____, producing sound. Small amounts of air passing over your _____ produce soft sounds, while large amounts of air passing over your _____ produce loud sounds. The _____ of the sound is determined by how tight your _____ are while the air passes over them.

11. In animals, hearts vary from _____ to _____, depending on the needs of the animal. Some animals, such as sponges, _____ have a heart or a circulatory system. They have _____ _____ that travel freely throughout their bodies, digesting food, transporting the nutrients to where they are needed, and exchanging oxygen for cell waste products. Animals such as fish have to extract the _____ that is dissolved in the water. They use _____ instead of lungs to accomplish this feat. Other animals, such as worms and amphibians, actually breathe through their ____! Insects have neither lungs nor gills. They have an intricate network of _____ that runs throughout the body, and air simply passes through them to be distributed throughout the body. Most plants have _____ (which transport water up from the roots to the rest of the plant) and _____ (which carry food from the leaves to the rest of the plant).

Summary of Module #15
Review the vocabulary words listed in Question #1 of the study guide

1. The _____ removes excess fluid from your body's tissues and returns it to the bloodstream. At the same time, it cleans the fluid of _____ and other _____ that can cause health problems. The _____ produces hormones that regulate several of the chemical processes occurring in your body. The _____ controls and regulates the balance of chemicals in your blood.

2. There is a vast network of _____ vessels that carry the watery fluid found between your body's cells. This clear fluid, called _____, leaks out of capillaries and passes in and out of cells. When it is picked up by the _____ vessels, however, it is no longer called _____. Instead, it is called _____.

3. The end of a lymph vessel is _____, but the cells that form the vessel overlap to form "flaps" that allow interstitial fluid to ____ inside. The lymph vessels are positioned in the body so that when certain _____ contract, the lymph vessels are squeezed, which causes a gentle flow of lymph through the lymphatic system. To keep the lymph flowing in the right direction, there are _____ "valves" that open when the lymph is flowing in the right direction and close to prevent it from flowing backwards.

4. _____ are the "filters" where the lymph is cleaned before it is returned to the blood. The _____ houses many white blood cells, which are there to grow and mature. These white blood cells also _____ the blood that passes through. Interestingly enough, the _____ also acts as a "storehouse" for oxygen-rich blood. The _____ and _____ form a protective ring around the throat. They work together to produce and release _____ that attack pathogens entering your body through your mouth or nose. The _____ has both lymphatic and endocrine functions. When you are young, your _____ is a place where certain white blood cells mature. They travel from the bone marrow to the thymus gland and actually "_____" how to do their job while they are there. This gland also releases a hormone called _____, which stimulates the development of the white blood cells known as T-cells.

5. A lymph node has several lymph vessels (called _____) that bring in lymph, but only one vessel (the _____) that takes lymph away. The cleaning power of lymph nodes comes from the _____, which is the name given to white blood cells found in the lymphatic system. There are several different kinds of _____, each of which performs different tasks. _____ produce antibodies that attack specific disease-causing microorganisms. _____ attack microorganisms directly. _____ scavenge the lymph, eating bacteria and other debris. When an infection is detected by the lymph nodes, the germinal centers of the lymph nodes release _____.

6. When B-cells produce antibodies, they also produce _____. These cells are configured to start producing the same antibody again the moment the same infection is detected. This gives the lymphatic system a _____, allowing it to react much more quickly if the body is attacked again.

7. The fact that the lymphatic system has a memory is the basis of a _____, which is one of medicine's greatest achievements. The overall goal of a _____ is to trick the body into thinking it is infected. That way, it will make _____ so it is ready to fight the real infection if it ever actually occurs.

8. There are two basic types of vaccines. The first type contains a _____ form of the pathogen itself. Since the pathogen is _____, your body's immune system will destroy it before it can overtake your body, and it will produce the memory B-cells that will allow it to fight a full-strength infection if one ever occurs. The other type of vaccine contains a human-made _____ that makes your body react the same as if a certain pathogen has entered it. A vaccine is not a _____ for a disease. Instead, it must be given _____ you are exposed to the disease so your body becomes ready to fight the disease if you are ever exposed to it. The act of giving someone a vaccine is often called _____, because it makes a person immune to the disease. However, a small percentage of people will not _____ to a vaccine, which means they will not become immune.

9. The body produces tears in the _____, which are located on the top and side of each eyeball. Tears run from the _____ through tiny tubes called _____ and then flow across the eyes. Your body produces tears to _____ and _____ the eye, but you can also produce tears in response to strong _____. The tears produced for the former reason are chemically quite _____ from the tears produced for the latter reason.

10. The urinary system is made up of the kidneys, ureters, bladder, and urethra. Each _____ is actually made up of about a million units called nephrons. The _____ brings blood into the kidney. In order to be cleaned, blood flows to a nephron, where it is first _____. Most of what is in the blood plasma (all nutrients, wastes, and water, but not the blood proteins) is temporarily dumped into the nephron. Then, as this fluid flows through the nephron, the cells that line the nephron _____ the proper amounts of nutrients and chemicals back into the blood. Excess chemicals are left behind in the nephron to become ____. The blood then leaves the kidney through the _____ and travels back to the heart. Any water and chemicals that were not reabsorbed into the blood go from the nephrons into the _____ and flow out of the kidney to the _____. At this point, the mixture of water and chemicals is called _____. It travels through the _____ and is held in the _____. Eventually, the bladder releases the _____ it has stored, and it leaves the body through the _____.

11. _____ are released by endocrine glands that are scattered throughout the body. The _____ is one of the main regulators of the endocrine system. It is part of the _____, and it influences a wide range of body functions. Its function in the endocrine system is to control the _____, which is often referred to as the "_____ endocrine gland." It is given this name because the hormones it makes and puts into the bloodstream control many other _____ in the body.

12. The _____ produces hormones that affect the basal metabolic rate. The _____ are tiny glands that are on the edges of the thyroid gland. Their main job is to regulate the level of _____ in the body. The _____ release cortisol, which is part of the "fight or flight" response. They also produce the hormones epinephrine and norepinephrine, which are also released during times of _____. Although the _____ has digestive functions, it is also an endocrine gland. Cells located within "islands" of the _____ make insulin, a hormone that enables glucose to enter the cells so it can be burned.

13. Often, the endocrine system has hormones that work toward opposite goals. Because they work "against" each other, such hormones are often called _____. They don't really work against each other; however, they just work at different _____.

Summary of Module #16
Review the vocabulary words listed in Question #1 of the study guide

1. The work of the nervous system occurs in _____ called neurons. They communicate with other neurons through _____. Signals pass from one neuron to another at a _____. Neurons cannot function properly without the help of _____, which are often called _____.

2. The control center of a neuron is its nucleus, which is housed in the _____. Signals are sent to the _____ along fibers called _____, and they are sent to other neurons along a single fiber called the _____. The axon is often covered by a fatty insulator called a _____, which protects the _____ and speeds up the rate at which an electrical signal can travel down it.

3. At a synapse, the end of the axon is full of tiny sacs that contain chemicals we call _____. When a signal comes to the end of an axon, these chemicals are _____ from their sacs. They travel across the synapse, chemically interacting with _____ on the cell at the other side of the tiny gap. This generates a new _____, which can then be used by the receiving cell.

4. The nervous system is split into two components: the _____ (CNS) and the _____ _____ (PNS). The CNS is composed of both the _____ and the _____. The PNS contains all the neurons that are involved in _____ information and _____ it on to the spinal cord and brain. It also contains the neurons responsible for _____ signals from the CNS to the various parts of your body that need to be controlled.

5. The spinal cord is protected by the _____. The vertebrae that make up the _____ _____ have a hole in their center, which lines up with the holes in the other vertebrae. This forms a _____ through which the spinal cord passes. The brain sits on "shelves" inside the ____, which protects it from harm. In addition, the brain floats in liquid called _____. Although this liquid provides chemicals to the brain, its main function is _____. In addition, _____ serves as a way for doctors to diagnose certain problems related to the nervous system. If there is something wrong in the nervous system, the _____ balance of chemicals will most likely not be correct, so examining the liquid can be the first step in understanding a patient's problem.

6. The brain is divided into halves called _____. The right side sends signals to the PNS on the _____ side of the body, and the left side sends signals to the PNS on the _____ side of the body. The folded tissue that surrounds the outside of the brain is called the _____, which deals with what are often called "higher-level" brain functions. The _____ is composed of axons running crosswise between the hemispheres, which allow the two hemispheres of the brain to exchange information. The _____ has a lot of functions, mostly oriented around muscle movements. The _____ is right next to the cerebellum, and it controls the more basic functions of the human body. The _____ not only controls the pituitary gland, but it also regulates thirst, hunger, and body temperature. It also helps initiate the "fight or flight" response. While some claim people use only 10% of the brain, it is _____ true.

7. Gray matter is composed almost exclusively of the _____ of neurons. White matter is composed mostly of the _____ of the neurons in the gray matter.

8. The _____ side of the cerebrum tends to be responsible for speaking, logic, and math. The _____ side is more involved with spatial relationships, recognition, and music. In addition, one side of the body tends to be _____ over the other in a given individual. For example, a person will generally

write with only one hand, because that's his _____ hand. In the majority of people, the right side of the body is _____.

9. The blood-brain barrier _____ the brain from the blood. It is important because many of the chemicals in your blood are _____ to your brain cells. The blood-brain barrier selectively _____ "good" chemicals into the brain and leaves the "bad" chemicals in the capillaries, away from the brain.

10. The _____ is made up of those nerves that run off of the CNS. A nerve is made up of _____ and _____, not the cell bodies of neurons. The cell bodies of neurons typically cluster together in groups called _____.

11. The PNS is composed of three main divisions: the _____, the _____, and the _____. The _____ carries instructions from the CNS to the body's smooth muscles, cardiac muscle, and glands. The _____ carries information from the body's receptors to the CNS. The _____ carries instructions from the CNS to the skeletal muscles.

12. The autonomic nervous system is composed of two parts: the _____ and the _____. These two divisions _____ each other in many ways. The _____ increases the rate and strength of the heartbeat and raises the blood pressure. It also stimulates the liver to release more glucose in the blood, producing quick energy for the "fight or flight" response. The _____, on the other hand, slows the heart rate, which lowers the blood pressure. In addition, it takes care of certain "housekeeping" activities such as causing the stomach to churn while it is digesting a meal.

13. The sense of taste is called the _____ sense. Your tongue has holes called _____ that lead to clusters of cells called _____. These cells have tiny "hairs" that are sensitive to certain _____. When those _____ are detected, signals are sent to the brain, generating a _____ sensation. Scientists think there are only ____ basic taste sensations: ____, ____, ____, ____, and _____. It is thought that all tastes are a _____ of these five sensations.

14. The roof of your nasal cavity houses mucus-covered tissue called the _____ epithelium. This tissue has cells, called _____, that have long "hairs" that stick into the mucus. When chemicals in the air dissolve in the mucus, they interact with the "hairs" of the _____. This causes the cells to send signals to your brain, which gives you the impression you call _____. This sense affects the _____ sense.

15. When light strikes the eye, it first passes through the _____. It then passes through a clear liquid called the aqueous humor and then through the _____. It then passes through the _____, which focuses the image onto the _____. The lens can focus light because it changes _____ based on the actions of the _____. The _____ is filled with light-sensing cells called ____ and _____.

16. Your sense of touch is all over your body, so it is called a _____. The number of touch _____ in an area of skin determines how sensitive that part of your body is to touch.

17. The _____ ear acts as a "funnel" to send vibrations in the air down the _____ until they reach the _____. Vibrations in the air cause the ear drum to vibrate, which cause tiny bones called _____ to move back and forth. This movement in turn vibrates fluid within the snail-shaped _____. Cells in the fluid of the _____ pick up the vibration and convert it into an electric signal that is sent to the brain, and the brain interprets the signals as _____.

APPENDIX C
A COMPLETE LIST OF LAB SUPPLIES

Module #1

- Eye protection such as goggles or safety glasses
- Vegetable oil
- Water
- Maple or corn syrup
- A grape
- A piece of cork
- An ice cube
- A small rock
- A tall glass
- Two glass canning jars or peanut butter jars (both the same size)
- Food coloring (any color)
- A pan and stove to boil water, and a hotpad to hold the pan
- A clear plastic 2-liter bottle
- A balloon (6-inch to 9-inch round balloons work best.)
- Clear vinegar
- Baking soda
- A funnel or butter knife
- A few leaves of red (sometimes called purple) cabbage
- A saucepan
- A stove
- Measuring cups
- A few ice cubes
- A pencil
- A sheet of paper (8 ½" by 11")
- Six thumbtacks or pushpins
- A piece of string 8 inches long
- A sheet of cardboard larger than or the same size as the sheet of paper

Module #2

- Eye protection such as goggles or safety glasses
- A reasonably heavy book
- A sheet of cardboard about the same size as the book (The cardboard that comes on the back of a pad of paper works well. You can also cut a piece out of an old cardboard box.)
- A sheet of heavy paper (like construction paper or cardstock) about the same size as the book
- A sheet of regular paper about the size of the book
- A metal paper clip
- A small rock (It needs to weigh less than the cardboard, so it should be really small.)

♦ A working flashlight
♦ A parent or helper

Module #3

♦ Eye protection such as goggles or safety glasses
♦ A tall glass
♦ Measuring cups for measuring out 1½ cups of water
♦ An egg (It is best to use one that hasn't been sitting in the refrigerator for a long time.)
♦ A teaspoon
♦ A spoon for stirring
♦ Water
♦ Salt
♦ Four sheets of reasonably thick cardboard (A cut-up cardboard box works nicely.)
♦ Scissors that will cut the cardboard
♦ A sheet of facial tissue (Make sure is it not the kind that has been treated with lotion.)
♦ A chunk of soap from a bar of soap
♦ A stick of chewing gum
♦ A bathtub or large sink (A bathtub works best.)
♦ A reasonably large bowl
♦ Black pepper
♦ Tweezers
♦ Metal paper clip (Use a standard-sized paper clip. A big one may not work.)
♦ Toilet paper

Module #4

♦ Eye protection such as goggles or safety glasses
♦ A wooden pencil
♦ A wooden ruler
♦ At least five quarters, preferably more
♦ Two brooms or a broom and a mop (You basically need two implements with long handles. The experiment works best when the handles are very smooth.)
♦ Several feet of rope (Nylon rope works best because it is slick.)
♦ Two reasonably strong people to help you

Module #5

There are no experiments in this module.

Module #6

♦ Eye protection such as goggles or safety glasses
♦ Alum (a white powder you can find in the spice section of any large supermarket)
♦ A small glass (like a juice glass)
♦ A spoon for stirring
♦ Some thin, rough string (Thread will work, but the rougher the string, the better the results.)

- Two weights (washers, nuts, fishing sinkers, etc.)
- A large plate
- A few rocks from outside (Small pebbles actually work best.)
- A sheet of dark paper (blue, black, etc.)
- A magnifying glass
- A stove
- A pot to heat water
- Gloves to protect your hands from the heat
- Sugar (optional)
- Food coloring (optional)
- A large glass jar with a lid
- Some dirt from outside (Dig straight down into the ground so you get dirt from many depths.)
- Some sand
- Some gravel composed of various sizes of rocks
- Water
- Plaster of Paris
- A medium or large margarine tub
- A few lima beans
- Paper towels
- Vinegar
- A large glass
- A limestone rock (Most gravel is limestone. You can also go to a home improvement store's garden section and ask for limestone. The rock needs to be small enough to fit in the glass.)
- Some steel wool (You can get this at any hardware store.)
- A small bowl
- A shoebox
- A gardener's spade (or something else you can use to dig)
- Scissors
- A spot in the yard in which you can dig
- A water hose and water
- A large rock

<u>Module #7</u>

- Eye protection such as goggles or safety glasses
- Modeling clay (Play-Doh® will work)
- Plaster of Paris
- A paper plate
- A shell or something else with a distinctive shape or design
- Vaseline® or another petroleum jelly
- A cup of water
- A small glass
- Table salt
- A measuring spoon that measures one-eighth of a teaspoon
- A clean glass baking pan (A large rectangular one works best)
- At least two (preferably more) leaves (They should not be dried out. You can pick them off the tree or get recently fallen ones that are not yet dried out.)

♦ Two sheets of blank, white paper per leaf
♦ Many thick books (You can use fewer books if you have some heavy weights you can put on the books.)

Module #8

♦ 18 index cards (The size is irrelevant, as is the presence or absence of lines.)
♦ A parent or someone else to write on the cards and hold the key

Module #9

♦ Eye protection such as goggles or safety glasses
♦ Long pipe cleaners (the longer the better)
♦ Four different colors of beads (They need to have holes in them large enough for the pipe cleaners to fit through. You can get beads like that at any craft store.)
♦ Scissors strong enough to cut the pipe cleaners
♦ One slice of potato (uncooked)
♦ A pale green leaf (The paler the green, the better this experiment will work.)
♦ Rubbing alcohol (available at any drugstore)
♦ Iodine (available at any drugstore)
♦ A large jar with a lid
♦ Two shallow dishes
♦ Tweezers
♦ A small potted plant that can fit inside the jar with room to spare
♦ Water
♦ An area of the house that gets sunlight almost every day
♦ A piece of masking tape or a marker
♦ A few earthworms (Get them at a live bait shop if you can't find them outside.)
♦ A container that will hold the earthworms and soil
♦ Soil
♦ A bright light
♦ Large jar (It must be large enough to fit a banana inside.)
♦ Nylon stocking large enough to stretch over the mouth of the jar
♦ Rubber band large enough to fit around the mouth of the jar
♦ A banana

Module #10

♦ Eye protection such as goggles or safety glasses
♦ One chicken bouillon cube
♦ Table salt
♦ White vinegar
♦ Four small glasses
♦ One large glass
♦ One measuring cup
♦ One teaspoon

- Masking tape
- Marker or pen
- White paper (no lines if possible)
- A brightly colored marker or crayon
- Baker's active yeast (available at any supermarket)
- Banana
- Water
- Two zippered plastic bags (like Ziploc® sandwich bags)
- A butter knife
- A houseplant (Ivy works best, but most houseplants will work. If you have a few varieties of houseplants and ivy is not among them, you might try a few instead of just one.)
- Scissors
- A stalk of wilted celery with the leaves still on it
- A reasonably sharp knife
- Some food coloring (preferably blue)

Module #11

- An uncooked chicken bone (preferably a wishbone or wing)
- A jar with a lid
- Vinegar (preferably white)
- Two houseplants. Make sure that your parents won't mind one of them looking really funny once the experiment is over.
- A few books
- A sunny window
- A plastic bandage, such as a Band-Aid®

Module #12

- Eye protection such as goggles or safety glasses
- A small candle (It needs to be in some kind of heavy holder, but the holder should not be tall. A small tealight candle in a glass holder, like the one in the figure under step 5, is ideal.)
- A glass that will cover the candle
- A deep bowl (The bowl should be deep enough so that when the candle is placed at the bottom of the bowl, the sides of the bowl are above the flame of the candle.)
- Vinegar
- Baking soda
- Matches
- A mirror (A hand-held mirror is best, but any mirror will do.)
- A paper towel
- Red (sometimes called purple) cabbage (You only need a few leaves.)
- Distilled water (You can get it at any large supermarket. You need about ½ gallon.)
- Two drinking straws
- A saucepan
- A stove
- Three small glasses (like juice glasses)

- A ¼-cup measuring cup and a 1-cup measuring cup
- A 2-liter plastic bottle (the kind soda comes in)
- A balloon (6-inch or 8-inch round balloons work best.)
- A small spoon (like a ¼ measuring teaspoon)
- An oral thermometer (The kind you use to take a person's temperature. Do not use one of those strips you put on your forehead. Use the kind of thermometer you stick in your mouth.)

Module #13

- Eye protection such as goggles or safety glasses
- A saltine cracker
- A tablespoon
- Iodine (This is available at most drugstores. You used it in Experiment 9.2.)
- Two small glasses
- Tums® antacid tablets (Try to get white ones, or at least a tub of Tums that has some white ones in it.)
- Toilet bowl cleaner (It should contain hydrochloric acid, also called hydrogen chloride, as an ingredient. The best kind to get is colorless. If you cannot get colorless, get a clear kind that has a light tint of color to it. DO NOT get the kind that clings to the bowl.)
- Red (sometimes called purple) cabbage
- A small glass (like a juice glass)
- A teaspoon
- A spoon for stirring
- A saucepan
- A measuring cup
- Distilled water (You can get it at any large supermarket. You need about ½ gallon.)
- A stove
- Baking soda
- Toilet bowl cleaner (the kind you used in the previous experiment)

Module #14

- Eye protection such as goggles or safety glasses
- A stopwatch or a watch with a second hand
- A place where you can do jumping jacks
- Flexible tubing (If you don't have some, the best place to get it is anywhere that sells aquarium accessories. It is typically called "aquarium tubing," and it is used to connect the aquarium air pump to the filter.)
- A plastic 1-gallon jug with a lid
- A sink with a plug
- A measuring cup
- A plastic 2-liter bottle (the kind soda pop comes in)
- Strong scissors
- A plastic sandwich bag (It needs to be large enough for the bottom of the 2-liter bottle to fit into the bag.)
- Tape

- A round balloon (12-inch is ideal, but any size greater than 6-inch will do.)
- A rubber band (It should be large enough to fit around your wrist without stretching. If the rubber band is larger, it will work fine, but a smaller one will not work.)
- A reasonably fresh white carnation (Almost all big supermarkets, as well as florists, sell them.)
- Two glasses
- Blue food coloring
- Red food coloring
- A knife
- Two spoons for stirring

Module #15

- Eye protection such as goggles or safety glasses
- Three onions (any size)
- A cutting knife (In this experiment, a dull knife works better than a sharp one!)
- A freezer
- A cutting board
- A sink in which you can cut
- A tea bag
- Three small glasses (like juice glasses)
- A paper towel
- A coffee filter
- A funnel
- Scissors
- A tea kettle or pot
- A stove
- A spoon for stirring
- A pile of two to three books (The pile needs to be at least ¾ as high as one of the glasses.)

Module #16

- Eye protection such as goggles or safety glasses
- Scissors
- A pencil
- Paper
- A ball (It needs to be small enough to be thrown with one hand, like a baseball, softball, or golf ball.)
- A coin
- Some stairs or porch steps
- A paper towel tube or rolled-up piece of thick paper
- A few people to test (8 years or older)
- A glass
- A mirror
- A room with a light switch that when closed off gets *really* dark
- A candle
- Matches
- Toothpicks

- Apple
- Onion
- Blindfold
- A person to act as your subject
- A knife
- Two paper towels
- Two well-sharpened pencils
- Some tape
- Printouts from the course website, the address and password to which are given in the "Student Notes" at the beginning of the book

or

- Two sheets of paper
- A black marker or pen

INDEX